Entrepreneurial Finance

ENTREPRENEURIAL FINANCE

Strategy, Valuation, and Deal Structure

Janet Kiholm Smith

Richard L. Smith

Richard T. Bliss

Stanford Economics and Finance
An Imprint of Stanford University Press
Stanford, California

Stanford University Press
Stanford, California

Special discounts for bulk quantities of Stanford Business Books are available to corporations, professional associations, and other organizations. For details and discount information, contact the special sales department of Stanford University Press. Tel: (650) 736-1782, Fax: (650) 736-1784

Printed in the United States of America on acid-free, archival-quality paper

Library of Congress Cataloging-in-Publication Data
Smith, Janet Kiholm.
Entrepreneurial finance : strategy, valuation, and deal structure / Janet Kiholm Smith, Richard L. Smith, and Richard T. Bliss.
    p. cm.
  Includes bibliographical references and index.
  ISBN 978-0-8047-7091-0 (cloth : alk. paper)
  1. Venture capital. 2. New business enterprises—Finance. 3. Entrepreneurship.
I. Smith, Richard L. (Richard Lester) II. Bliss, Richard T. (Richard Thomas), 1958– III. Title.
  HG4751.S594 2011
  658.15′224—dc22

                                                                2010026481

Original printing 2011
Last figure below indicates year of this printing:
16 15

For Kelly and Erin.
J.K.S.
R.L.S.

For my family, and especially Christine and Dylan.
R.T.B.

CONTENTS

PART 5 Information, Incentives, and Financial Contracting

ILLUSTRATIONS

ABBREVIATIONS

A	assets
A/P	accounts payable
A/R	accounts receivable
BDC	business development company
BEP	breakeven point
BRIC	Brazil, Russia, India, and China
BS	balance sheet
BV	book value
CAPM	Capital Asset Pricing Model
CEQ	certainty equivalent
CF	cash flow
CML	capital market line
COGS	cost of goods sold
D	debt or dividend per share (depending on context)
D&A	depreciation and amortization
D/E	debt to equity ratio
D/V	debt to value ratio
DCF	discounted cash flow
DPO	direct public offering
E	equity
E/V	equity to value ratio
EBIT	earnings before interest and taxes

EBITDA	earnings before interest, taxes, depreciation, and amortization
EBT	earnings before tax
ERISA	Employee Retirement Income Security Act
ESOP	employee stock ownership plan
FDA	Food and Drug Administration
FY	fiscal year
g^*	sustainable growth rate
GAAP	Generally Accepted Accounting Principles
GDP	gross domestic product
GEM	Global Entrepreneurship Monitor
GP	general partner
ICA	Investment Company Act of 1940
IFRS	International Financial Reporting Standards
INT	interest expense
IPO	initial public offering
IRR	internal rate of return
IS	income statement
IT	information technology
LBO	leveraged buyout
LP	limited partner
M&A	merger and acquisition
MBO	management buyout
MV	market value
NAICS	North American Industry Classification System
NAV	net asset value
NI	net income
NPV	net present value
NVCA	National Venture Capital Association
NWC	net working capital
NYSE	New York Stock Exchange
OCF	operating cash flow
OECD	Organization for Economic Cooperation and Development
OEM	original equipment manufacturer
OPM	Black-Scholes Option Pricing Model
OTC	over-the-counter
P	price per share
P&L	profit and loss

P/E	price to earnings ratio
PEG	price earnings to growth
PP&E	property, plant, and equipment
PV	present value
R	retention ratio (1 − dividend payout ratio)
R&D	research and development
RADR	risk-adjusted discount rate
ROA	return on assets
ROR	rate of return
ROS	return on sales
RP	risk premium
RV	relative value
SBA	Small Business Administration
SBIC	Small Business Investment Company
SBIR	Small Business Innovation Research
SEC	Securities and Exchange Commission
SEO	seasoned equity offering
SG&A	selling, general, and administrative expenses
SIC	Standard Industrial Classification
SME	small and medium-size enterprise
SML	security market line
TY	tax year
VC	venture capital/capitalist
WACC	weighted average cost of capital

PREFACE

History abounds with examples of extraordinary entrepreneurs whose new ideas and products have changed the world. Many people are enamored with the idea of creating new products and starting businesses. Accompanying the interest in venture creation, there is broad interest in venture capital, in investment banking, and in careers related to new venture financing, deal structuring, and harvesting.

Our primary motivation for writing this book is to empower students and practitioners to be more successful in developing and financing their ideas. Our overriding orientation is to apply the theory and methods of finance and economics to the rapidly evolving field of entrepreneurial finance.

This book is unique several ways. First, it builds on and significantly extends the tools and methods of corporate finance and financial economics to approach the difficult and important financial problems associated with starting and growing new ventures. Building on the foundations of financial economics makes the lessons more general and memorable and the applications easier to implement in varied settings. Mastery of the framework facilitates clearer and more defensible evaluation of different opportunities and choices than is possible on the basis of heuristics and intuition. With reliable and rigorous tools, you can be more confident that the decisions you make will be the right ones.

Second, while many books address aspects of entrepreneurship (writing business plans, leading and managing new ventures, etc.), this book has a unique and direct focus on the question of how new venture financing choices can add value and turn marginal opportunities into valuable ones. We emphasize value creation as the objective of each financial choice that an entrepreneur or investor makes—issues of strategic planning, staging, valuation, deal structure, risk and diversification, choice of financing, and exit. Understanding how each choice affects value has the potential to add tremendous value to ideas and innovations.

Third, in contrast to other books on entrepreneurial finance, we specifically address the influences of risk and uncertainty on new venture success. We use discrete scenario and simulation analysis throughout the book to evaluate alternative strategies, to assess financial needs, to assess risk and expected cash flows as elements of valuation, and to compare different deal structures and contract terms.

Fourth, because assessment of cash needs and valuation both depend on projections of cash flow, we devote significant attention to methods of forecasting the pro forma financial statements of new ventures in an integrated fashion. Integration enables the entrepreneur or investor to use financial forecasting to conduct scenario analysis and to simulate such things as how cash needs are affected by growth rates that are faster or slower than expected.

Fifth, we provide a comprehensive survey of approaches to new venture valuation with an emphasis on applications. Our approach to valuation is more comprehensive than most because we approach valuation from a contracting perspective that is affected by the different assessments of the entrepreneur and the investor. We recognize that the entrepreneur's unique circumstances can lead to value conclusions different from those of a well-diversified investor.

Why Study Entrepreneurial Finance?

Whether you are or see yourself as an entrepreneur, a corporate financial manager dealing with new projects, a venture capitalist, or a social entrepreneur, a solid understanding of entrepreneurial finance can help you make better decisions. Couple this with the estimate that over 50 percent of new businesses fail within a few years, and the value of understanding new venture finance becomes clear. Perhaps more telling is that while some businesses do survive, the entrepreneur may not. Nonfounders are appointed CEO within a few years of operation in the majority of venture capital–backed start-ups.

How can the hazards and pitfalls of forming new ventures be avoided or mitigated? We believe the answer is to understand the financial economic foundations and use the best available decision-making tools and methods. A new venture should not be undertaken unless the expected reward is high enough to compensate for the value of forgone opportunities. Investing personal resources and time in a venture that should never have been pursued is just as serious an error as failing to invest in a good venture. Throughout the book, we reiterate and demonstrate through examples that this tradeoff of risk and return is not easy to assess intuitively. Rather, this is an area where analytical rigor can add considerable value.

Even the best initial projections, however, can prove to be overly optimistic as the future unfolds. It is important to base the decision to continue or abandon a venture on the same kind of rigorous analysis that was used in making the original decision. It is all too easy to continue investing time and resources in a venture that is destined for mediocre long-run performance or to give up on a venture that has experienced a temporary setback but still offers the potential for substantial gain.

Finally, it is a rare individual who is good at both recognizing an opportunity and managing the venture to capitalize on that opportunity. Careful design of the organization and its relations at the outset helps assure that a venture does not fail just because the visionary was not well suited to manage the day-to-day operations. Careful design also can help assure that the entrepreneur does not lose control of the venture unnecessarily.

What Makes Entrepreneurial Finance Different from Corporate Finance?

It is natural to wonder why entrepreneurial finance is worthy of special study—why aren't the principles of corporate finance directly applicable in an entrepreneurial setting? After all, a basic course in corporate finance concerns investment and financing decisions of large public corporations and generally introduces valuation techniques such as discounted cash flow and cost of capital analysis. The limitation, however, is that corporate finance theory assumes away a number of issues that are of secondary importance in a large corporate setting, but are critical to decision making for new ventures. These distinctions make entrepreneurial finance an intellectually challenging area worthy of special study. The focus on entrepreneurship and early-stage ventures dramatically changes the way the finance paradigm is applied.

Moreover, certain techniques of entrepreneurial finance—such as thinking about investment opportunities as portfolios of real options—while they are particularly useful in a new venture setting, are also useful in the context of a large public corporation. They just normally do not receive much attention in corporate finance courses.

We highlight eight important differences:

1. The inseparability of new venture investment decisions from financing decisions
2. The limited role of diversification as a determinant of investment value
3. The extent of managerial involvement by investors in new ventures
4. The substantial effects of information problems on the firm's ability to undertake a project
5. The role of contracting to resolve incentive problems in entrepreneurial ventures
6. The critical importance of real options as determinants of project value
7. The importance of harvesting as an aspect of new venture valuation and the investment decision
8. The focus on maximizing value for the entrepreneur as distinct from maximizing shareholder value

Interdependence between Investment and Financing Decisions

In corporate finance, investment decisions and financing decisions are treated as independent. The manager decides in which projects the firm should invest by comparing the return on the investment to the market interest rate for projects of equivalent risk. The manager does not need to consider simultaneously how ownership of the assets will be financed or whether the firm's shareholders prefer high-dividend payouts or capital gains.

Of course, investment decisions and financing decisions are not completely independent in large public corporations. However, the interdependencies are generally simple and are usually addressed by making incremental adjustments to net present value (NPV).

For start-up businesses, however, the interdependencies between investment and financing decisions are much more complex. Among other things, the entrepreneur will probably place a very different value on the new venture than will well-diversified investors. These differences are important because the entrepreneur cannot normally sell shares of a private venture to generate funds for current consumption (analogous to receiving a dividend). Therefore, simple adjustments to NPV cannot be used to address the divergence of valuations between the entrepreneur and the investor.

More generally, some investment choices are contingent upon certain financing choices. For example, rapid growth may be possible only with substantial outside financing, whereas a large corporation might be able to finance the entire project with internally generated funds. The linkage between investment choices and financing choices creates complexity that does not arise in corporate finance.

Diversifiable Risk and Investment Value

In corporate finance, the NPV of an investment is determined by applying a discount factor to expected future cash flows. Corporate finance proposes that the discount factor depends only on nondiversifiable risk. But this proposition relies on the assumption that investors can diversify at low cost. Although the assumption holds for many investors in a new venture (e.g., venture capitalists, wealthy angel investors, or large lenders), it categorically does not hold for the entrepreneur. In fact, the entrepreneur often must invest a large fraction of his or her financial wealth and human capital in the venture. This difference between entrepreneurs and investors in their ability to diversify results in the project value for entrepreneurs being different from the project value for investors.

In corporate finance, value additivity implies that allocation of financial claims does not affect the decision to accept a project. But for new ventures, because entrepreneurs and investors view risk differently, each ascribes a different value to the same risky asset. As a result, value additivity does not hold and the allocation of financial claims becomes important.

Managerial Involvement of Investors

In public corporations, investors (stockholders and creditors) generally are passive and do not contribute managerial services. Nor do they normally have access to significant inside information. In contrast, some investors in new ventures (e.g., venture capitalists and angel investors) frequently provide managerial and other services that contribute to the venture's success. Typically, these investors will have access to inside information that they gain as a result of their continuing investment in the venture.

Information Problems and Contract Design

Separate from differences that arise even when the entrepreneur and investors agree about the expected future cash flows of a venture (and know that they agree), differences in value can arise because of the magnitude and importance of the information problem between the parties. Although information gaps also exist between insiders and outsiders of public corporations, the gaps need not materially affect the investment decisions of public corporation managers. Public corporations generally can, and often do, make investment decisions without much immediate regard to the question of how investors perceive the value of the investment.

Generally, these managers need not convince investors, lenders, or employees that a project is worth undertaking, at least in the short run. The situation is very different in the case of a start-up business that requires outside financing. In the latter case, investors look specifically to the venture to provide a return on their investments. Moreover, there is often no easy way for the entrepreneur to communicate her true beliefs about the potential for success of a new venture. From a financial perspective, this places considerable emphasis on finding ways to signal the entrepreneur's confidence in the venture.

Incentive Alignment and Contract Design

Incentive contracting clearly plays a role in the large public corporation. On the positive side, managerial stock options and performance bonuses are intended to align the interests of managers and investors. On the negative side, debt covenants and similar provisions are designed to discourage reliance on risky debt financing that can lead to inefficient investment decisions and other agency costs associated with heavy reliance on debt. The issues are similar for start-up businesses, but reliance on incentive contracts is, in some respects, more compelling. In contrast to the managers of public corporations, investors generally keep the entrepreneur on a short leash.

There are compelling reasons to find ways of investing in the projects of unproven entrepreneurs. An investor who is good at identifying the untested entrepreneurs who are likely to succeed can participate profitably in new ventures that would have been rejected by a less astute investor. The result is that investors use a variety of contractual devices to supplement their ability to identify and motivate high-quality entrepreneurs.

The Importance of Real Options

Knowledgeable students and practitioners of corporate finance know to value projects by discounting expected future cash flows back to NPV. Even in the corporate setting, this approach is oversimplified, except with respect to the most basic independent investment projects. The reality is that most investing involves a process of acquiring, retaining, exercising, and abandoning options. Nonetheless, the common practice of ignoring options in corporate investment decisions suggests that they often are of secondary importance to the decision.

The values of real options associated with an investment depend on the degree of uncertainty surrounding the investment. For projects such as investments in research and development or an investment in a new industry, uncertainty levels are likely very high. This uncertainty adds to the importance of considering embedded option values. Nowhere is the importance of option values more central to investment decision making than for a start-up business. Staging of capital infusions, abandonment of the project, growth rate acceleration, and a variety of other choices all involve real options and contribute to the need for a process of investment decision making that focuses on recognizing and valuing the real options that are associated with the project.

Harvesting the Investment

In corporate finance, investment opportunities are evaluated based on their capacity to generate free cash flow for the corporation. The investment decision does not depend on when the cash flows are distributed to investors, except that corporations generally will not retain cash that they cannot invest profitably.

In their decisions to invest in the shares of a public corporation, investors normally give little consideration to when they will sell or to valuation and costs associated with selling. Investing in new ventures is different. New venture investments normally are not liquid and often do not generate any significant free cash flow for several years. Most investors in new ventures, and many entrepreneurs, have finite investment horizons. To realize returns on their investments, a liquidity event must occur (e.g., a public offering of equity by the venture or private acquisition of the venture for cash or freely tradable shares of the acquirer). Such liquidity events are the main ways investors in new ventures realize returns on their investments. Because of the importance of liquidity events, they generally are forecasted explicitly. The forecasts are formally factored into valuation of the investment.

Value to the Entrepreneur

The final difference between start-ups and public corporations is the focus on the entrepreneur. In the public corporation, the focus of decision making is on investment returns to shareholders. In a start-up, the true residual claimant is the entrepreneur. In the corporate setting, maximum shareholder value is the most frequently espoused financial objective. In contrast, the objective of the entrepreneur in deciding whether to pursue the venture and how to structure the financing is to maximize the value of the financial claims and other benefits that the entrepreneur is able to retain as the business grows.

It is easy to envision cases where an objective of maximizing share value would not be in the entrepreneur's best interest. This is particularly true if the entrepreneur is unable to convince investors of the true value of the project and would therefore have to give up too large a fraction of ownership, or if the entrepreneur values other considerations besides share value.

What's New about This Book?

This book builds on our previous book, *Entrepreneurial Finance* (2000, 2004). Like the earlier book, it ties the applications to the underlying disciplines of finance and economics. This book, published by Stanford University Press, is reorganized and updated to reflect the latest knowledge in finance and is streamlined to stress applications in key areas: valuation, adding value through deal structure and staging, and choice of financing. The chapter on venture capital is more fully developed than in the earlier book, and decision trees and simulation are presented with more examples and step-by-step analysis. We devote additional attention to financial forecasting and the construction of integrated pro forma financial statements, as both are key to valuation, contracting, and assessment of cash needs. The analysis of new venture valuation methods is more comprehensive, whereas we have streamlined the discussion and analysis of contracting between entrepreneurs and investors.

For the most part, we draw upon recent academic literature in finance and economics as the foundation for our coverage. We break new ground in several areas by presenting material and analytical approaches that extend the frontier of academic research related to entrepreneurial finance.

The book's focus is broader than entrepreneurial finance in the context of US institutions. Instead, we have incorporated a significant international perspective by illustrating throughout the book the many similarities and the differences in analysis for US ventures versus international ventures. The book also is not limited to stand-alone entrepreneurial ventures. Rather, we have included analysis of the approaches that large corporations take, and the special challenges they face, when they seek to encourage entrepreneurship within their organizations—sometimes referred to as "intrapreneurship" or "corporate venturing."

Intended Audience

While this book can be used as a text in an advanced finance or entrepreneurship course, its intended audience is broader. The book is appropriate for students, entrepreneurs, practitioners involved with new ventures, and corporate financial managers looking for ways to encourage corporate venturing. We have designed the book for readers who are familiar with the basic concepts and tools of corporate finance, accounting, economics, and statistics and who seek a rigorous and systematic approach to adding value to new ventures through financing and deal structure. On the companion website, we provide brief reviews for those who feel the need for a refresher on some key background concepts.

This book is appropriate for MBA students, master's of finance students, advanced undergraduates in business and economics, and executive MBA students. In our own teaching, we use the book and related materials with students at all levels. Because entrepreneurial finance draws from and integrates all areas of management, a course developed around the book can serve as a capstone integrative experience to the MBA or an undergraduate business degree.

The book can be used effectively in an entrepreneurial finance course or in a course on venture capital and private equity. It is designed to be used either as a stand-alone resource or in conjunction with cases or a business planning exercise. Each chapter includes end-of-chapter review questions. The book website has end-of-chapter problems that are designed to give hands-on opportunities to apply the lessons of each chapter.

The book can be used in a variety of different course formats:

- Some users like our use of simulation throughout the book. For those, we provide our proprietary software, *Venture*.SIM™, and we also provide files on the website that contain examples and problem solutions that are prepared using Crystal Ball and @Risk.

- For those who are oriented to case method teaching, we have provided a series of our own interactive cases that correspond to the book chapters and have developed a list of commercially available cases that work well with the book.

- For those who see value in linking the coverage of entrepreneurial finance to a business planning exercise, the organization of the book follows the normal organization of the thought processes and financial contents of a business plan.

A Note about the Website and Internet Resources

The book is designed to be used most effectively in conjunction with resources we provide on the book website, www.sup.org/entrepreneurial finance. Much of the book relates to software, spreadsheets, templates, simulation applications, and interactive cases and tutorials that are available for download. For those teaching from the book, we also provide PowerPoint presentations by chapter. Instructor-specific resources are password protected. Instructors can gain access to teaching materials that accompany the book by contacting Stanford University Press at info@www.sup.org.

The website contains problems and interactive cases, along with solutions, that complement the book material. Where appropriate, we have designated the portions of the book and website resources with symbols to designate the following:

⑤ indicates that the section or problem requires simulation software. Presentations in the book are developed using Venture.SIM.

Ⓣ indicates that the figure is a template that can be downloaded from the book website and modified or adapted by the user to examine a different set of assumptions.

All Excel figures in the book, including charts, are available as downloadable files so that the user can review the spreadsheet structure and cell formulas. When we use quantitative examples in discussion, the website normally includes a file that contains the back-up spreadsheet analysis.

Simulation

As a user of this book, you have access to *Venture*.SIM, a simple simulation package that is useful for addressing the kinds of uncertainty issues that arise for new ventures. *Venture*.SIM is an Excel add-in that can be set up to launch each time you open Excel or only when you want to use it. Whenever we use simulation, we present the results as *Venture*.SIM output. Because many readers will be familiar with commercial simulation packages such as @Risk and Crystal Ball, we provide @Risk and Crystal Ball versions of the simulation analysis on the book website. When we show you the Excel syntax for a simulated cell in a spreadsheet, we will use the *Venture*.SIM syntax. If you are a user of one of the other commercial packages, you can study the parallel syntax by opening our example files.

For users who do not plan to emphasize simulation, we have marked sections of the book that are focused on applying simulation to entrepreneurial finance as well as the figures and tables that require installing the *Venture*.SIM add-in to Excel in order to open properly. The book's companion website contains suggested outlines for those who wish to emphasize simulation and those who do not.

Spreadsheets and Templates

The website contains soft copies of the figures and tables in the book, including several templates that you can use to study your own new venture valuation questions (i.e., you can easily edit the template to study and value your own cash flow projections).

ACKNOWLEDGMENTS

In preparing the book, we have benefited from numerous comments from colleagues, students, venture capitalists, business angels, entrepreneurs, and friends.

Over the years, an impressive group of reviewers and adopters have provided comments that have sharpened the presentation. Ilan Guedj (University of Texas, Austin), Frank Kerins (Montana State University), and several anonymous reviewers provided detailed comments on the current edition. We also benefited from comments on editions of the earlier book, including those of Robin Anderson (University of Nebraska), Sanjai Bhagat (University of Colorado), Carol Billingham (Central Michigan University), Carol Marie Boyer (Clarkson University), Daniel Donoghue (Discovery Group), Fernando Fabre (Endeavor and Universidad Anahuac de Sur), Samuel Gray (New Mexico State University), Thomas Hellmann (Stanford University), Glenn Hubbard (Columbia University), William C. Hudson (St. Cloud University), Steve Kaplan (University of Chicago), Jill Kickul (DePaul University), Sandy Klasa (University of Arizona), Kenji Kutsuna (Kobe University), Daniel McConaughy (California State University, Northridge), James Nelson (Florida State University), Bill Petty (Baylor University), Edward Rogoff (Baruch College), Chip Ruscher (University of Arizona), Bob Schwartz (Silver Fox Advisors), James Seward (University of Wisconsin, Madison), Jeffrey Sohl (University of New Hampshire), Howard Van Auken (Iowa State University), Nikhil Varaiya (San Diego State University), and Edward Williams (Rice University). We also thank our many colleagues at the Claremont Colleges, UC Riverside, and Babson College.

We are especially indebted to several enterprising students who helped with the development of the website, the simulation software, tutorials, and related materials: Scott Butler, Kevin Hanley, Mike Hanley, Chris Penka, and Way Yu. Thanks also to those students in our classes who read and worked through early drafts of the book and website. These include undergraduate and MBA students from UC Riverside and Chapman University, MBA, executive MBA, and undergraduate students from the Claremont Colleges. We very much appreciate their goodwill and thoughtful suggestions.

A number of practitioners, including venture capitalists, venture funds managers, entrepreneurs, and angel investors, were very generous in sharing their experiences and providing ideas for cases and other book material. Special thanks to Andy Horowitz, Russ Shields, John Sibert, Richard Sudek, Luann Bangsund, Luis Villalobos, John Jasper, John Kensey, Thomas Gephart, Kazuhiko Yamamoto, and Yoshi Bunya. In particular, their insights on valuation practices and deal negotiations and their willingness to challenge academic theory have added institutional richness to the book.

We extend special thanks to Margo Beth Crouppen, of Stanford University Press, who saw the value in developing an advanced applied book on entrepreneurial finance.

Janet Kiholm Smith
Claremont, California

Richard L. Smith
Riverside, California

Richard T. Bliss
Wellesley, Massachusetts

Janet Kiholm Smith is the Von Tobel Professor of Economics and founding dean of the Robert Day School of Economics and Finance, Claremont McKenna College. She was formerly department chair and director of the Financial Economics Institute of CMC, which supports research and teaching in financial economics and encourages interaction of theory and practice. She teaches courses on the economics of strategy, industrial organization, and finance.

She is the author of numerous journal articles on topics ranging from IPO pricing to corporate philanthropy, including publications in finance and economics journals such as the *Journal of Finance*; *Journal of Corporate Finance*; *Journal of Financial and Quantitative Analysis*; *Journal of Banking and Finance*; *Journal of Law and Economics*; and *Journal of Law, Economics, and Organization*. Current research interests include behavioral issues related to managerial turnover and the investment and spending policies of not-for-profit institutions.

Smith consults for matters related to business plan advising, working capital management, contracts, and antitrust issues. She has served as a consultant for major corporations and the Federal Trade Commission on complex business litigation.

Richard Smith is the Philip L. Boyd Chair in Finance at the A. Gary Anderson Graduate School of Management at the University of California, Riverside, where he is chair of the Department of Finance and Management Science. He regularly teaches courses on new venture finance and strategic risk management. Before joining the UC Riverside faculty, Smith held the Leatherby Chair in Entrepreneurship at Chapman University and prior to that, he was director of the Venture Finance Institute at Claremont Graduate University. He regularly teaches courses on new venture finance and strategic risk management.

Smith has authored over 35 articles appearing in the *Journal of Financial Economics, Journal of Finance, and Review of Financial Studies,* among others. His research interests include venture capital, initial public offerings, and contracting and valuation issues related to private equity and entrepreneurial firms.

He has served on the university investment committees of Arizona State University and Claremont Graduate University and is a former member of the Investment Advisory Council of the Arizona State Retirement System. He is a former member of Tech Coast Angels and has consulted extensively on valuation and deal structuring issues for venture capitalists, angel groups, and entrepreneurs. He has consulted or served as an expert witness on numerous cases involving financial contracting, securities litigation, valuation, and antitrust.

Richard T. Bliss is associate professor of finance at Babson College in Wellesley, Massachusetts, where he teaches courses on financial strategy, sustainability, and entrepreneurial finance and most recently held the Barefoot Family Chair in Finance and was division chair. He teaches in numerous executive education programs, including the Certificate in Entrepreneurial Leadership (CEL) program at the DTU Executive School of Business in Denmark. Prior to coming to Babson, Bliss was on the faculty at Indiana University and also taught extensively in central and eastern Europe, including at the Warsaw School of Economics, Warsaw University, and the University of Ljubljana in Slovenia.

With publications in the areas of corporate finance, entrepreneurship, mutual funds, and banking, Bliss has an active research agenda. His work has been published in the *Journal of Financial Economics, Derivatives Quarterly, Journal of Portfolio Management,* and *Journal of Small Business Management,* among others. He has also written numerous case studies in the areas of corporate financial strategy, risk management, socially responsible investing, and sustainability.

Bliss has been involved in corporate and entrepreneurial finance since 1987, with industry experience that includes time at Touche Ross & Company in New York as a consultant, and senior financial positions at Van Camp Seafood Company and Safety One, Inc., a specialty chemicals start-up. He has been involved with numerous start-ups as both an investor and advisor and continues to be an active consultant to new ventures.

GETTING STARTED

CHAPTER 1

INTRODUCTION

> What distinguishes the successful entrepreneur and promoter from other people is precisely the fact that he does not let himself be guided by what was and is, but arranges his affairs on the ground of his opinion about the future. He sees the past and present as other people do; but he judges the future in a different way.
>
> Ludwig von Mises, *Human Action*

Thousands of business ventures are started every year. Most fail within a short period. Of those that survive, most achieve only meager success, some achieve rates of return high enough to justify the initial investment, and a few achieve phenomenal success. What distinguishes the successes from the failures? There is not just one answer. A new venture based on a good idea can fail because of poor implementation or bad luck. One that is based on a bad idea can fail despite excellent implementation. Many that survive but do not thrive should never have been undertaken. Sometimes, even when a venture is hugely successful, early financing mistakes limit the entrepreneur's ability to share in the rewards.

This is a book on financial decision making for new ventures. In it, we provide the fundamentals for thinking analytically about whether an opportunity is worth pursuing and about how to apply the tools of financial economic theory to enhance the expected value of the undertaking. Corporate ventures and social ventures face similar challenges to those faced by stand-alone, for-profit ventures. Where there are important differences, we discuss the application of these tools to corporate venturing and social venturing.

1.1 Entrepreneurship and the Entrepreneur

The term "entrepreneur" is of French origin. Its literal translation is simply "undertaker," in the sense of one who undertakes to do something. In the early 1700s, the English banker Richard Cantillon coined the use of the word in a managerial context. He emphasized the notion of the entrepreneur as a bearer of risk, particularly with respect to provision of capital. This early usage, however, does not adequately characterize our current understanding of what it means to be an entrepreneur. Clearly, risk bearing is an aspect of entrepreneurship, but risk is also borne by capital providers who may have no involvement in managing the venture and by employees who may have no financial capital invested.

In the early 1800s, the French economist J. B. Say described the entrepreneur as a person who seeks to shift economic resources from areas of low to areas of high productivity. Although Say's notion points us in a useful direction, it is too general. Most purposeful human activity can be described as shifting economic resources to higher-valued uses (or at least attempting to do so).[1]

The contributions of Cantillon and Say gained renewed attention in the early 1900s through the writings of two other economists. Joseph Schumpeter (1912) viewed the entrepreneur as actively seeking opportunities to innovate. In his view, the entrepreneur is the driver of economic progress, continually seeking to disturb the status quo in a quest for profits from deliberate and risky efforts to combine society's resources in new and valuable ways. In contrast, Frank Knight (1921) conceived of the entrepreneur as a manager of uncertainty and the entrepreneurial function as one of directing resources in the presence of uncertainty (and realizing a reward for performing successfully). Uncertainty, in Knight's view, is an unavoidable aspect of the ordering of economic activity.[2]

Current use of the term "entrepreneurship" derives from these views and from more recent thinking by management scholars such as Peter Drucker. Drucker, who was a personal friend of Schumpeter, describes entrepreneurs as individuals who "create something new, something different; they change or transmute values" (Drucker [1985], p. 20). Today, entrepreneurship is most often described as the pursuit of opportunities to combine and redeploy resources, without regard to current ownership or control of the resources. This notion clearly draws on the definition offered by Schumpeter but adds structure by recognizing that the entrepreneur is not constrained by current control of resources.

Thinking of entrepreneurship in this way suggests a multidimensional process. The entrepreneur must do the following:

1. Perceive an opportunity to create value by redeploying society's resources

2. Devise a strategy for marshaling control of the necessary resources
3. Implement a plan of action to bring about the change
4. Harvest the rewards that accrue from the innovation

This definition is broad enough to encompass entrepreneurship that arises in the for-profit sector, including extant corporations, as well as in the not-for-profit sector, including in universities and charitable foundations.

Survival and Failure Rates of New Businesses

The sequence of actions just outlined seems to suggest that successful innovation necessarily yields a reward. This, of course, is far from true. To be successful, an entrepreneur needs to maintain a clear focus on how strategic choices and implementation decisions are likely to affect rewards.

Figure 1.1 shows the survival rates of new ventures from a US Census Bureau longitudinal study of business ventures that were launched in 1992 and tracked through 2002, as well as a subsequent study of ventures that were launched in 1997. Based on the data, 50 percent of ventures survive for at least 4 years and about 30 percent survive for at least 10. There is almost no difference in survival rates between the 1992 and 1997 samples. The figure also shows survival rates of "high-growth" ventures, where high growth is defined as at least a 50 percent increase in employees from 1992 to 1993 and a starting number of employees of at least five. The 4-year survival rates are higher for high-growth firms—about 72 percent over the 4 years following classification as high-growth.

Survival cannot be equated to success. In fact, in a Small Business Administration (SBA) study based on data compiled by the Census Bureau, one-third of the entrepreneurs of businesses that did not survive reported that they considered the venture a success.[3] Among other possibilities of successful closure, nonsurviving businesses may have been established to take advantage of transitory opportunities, may have been closed in one location and reopened in another, or may have been acquired. The dashed line in Figure 1.1 shows an adjustment of the failure rate based on the one-third estimate.

Moreover, from 2000 through 2007 an average of 904,900 new businesses were created per year. The average number of business terminations during the same period was 744,100 per year, resulting in 160,800 average annual net new business formations, about 17 percent of the

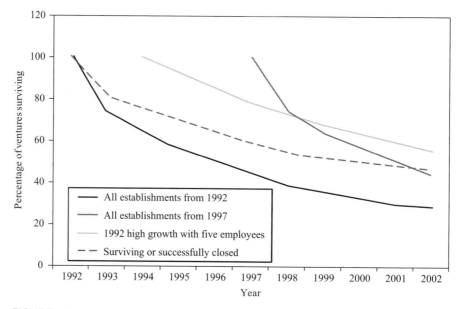

FIGURE **1.1**

Survival rates of new ventures

The figure shows survival rates of new business establishments that were initiated in 1992 or 1997, as well as survival rates for subsamples of establishments that were classified as high growth based on changes in number of employees from 1992 to 1993. The dashed line is an estimate of survivors plus nonsurvivors that were considered by the entrepreneur to have been successful.

SOURCE: 1998–2002 Business Information Tracking Series; available at http://www.census.gov/econ/sbo/ longitudinal02/longitudinal02.html. Data available in B. Headd and B. Kirchhoff, "Small Business Growth: Searching for Stylized Facts" (working paper, Small Business Administration, Washington, DC, 2007).

number of starts. As these statistics suggest, over 83 percent of new ventures eventually are terminated. The number terminated with financial loss to creditors via bankruptcy, however, is quite small—only 4.5 percent of all terminations. The remainder, "voluntary terminations," involve cases where the business was closed for inadequate profitability or where the owner simply decided to exit.[4]

Economic Downturns and Entrepreneurship

Starting a new venture or maintaining an existing small business is challenging even when product and financial markets are vibrant. The challenges can multiply when markets are stagnant. Financing can be scarce because the supply of capital to the markets is low. Moreover, providers of financing may be concerned that some prospective entrepreneurs are motivated more by necessity than by opportunity and may be concerned that the ventures they fund during recessions, if driven by necessity, will be slow to pay off. More concretely, financing can be difficult when venture capital money is not readily available, banks are not lending, and friends and family are strapped for cash.

There can, however, be positive features of starting a venture in a downturn. For an entrepreneur, the opportunity cost of starting a venture is lower when there are fewer traditional job market opportunities; competition may be less intense; it may be easier to hire qualified employees; and costs may be lower. Microsoft, Genentech, FedEx, Southwest Airlines, Gap, and The Limited were all founded during economic downturns. Hewlett-Packard, Polaroid, and Revlon were started during the Great Depression. Of the 30 companies that currently comprise the Dow Jones Industrial Average, 18 were founded during recessions or bear markets. Following the 1997 Asian financial crisis, which led to massive layoffs from South Korea's large industrial conglomerates (*chaebol*), that country saw a significant increase in entrepreneurship.[5]

Globalization of Entrepreneurship

Entrepreneurship now comes from almost everywhere, including once-closed command economies like China. Several developments have contributed to globalization. The personal computer, the wireless phone, and the Internet allow investors to reach markets that were inaccessible a few years ago. The importance of entrepreneurship in creating jobs and dynamic economies is now recognized by leading international entities like the European Union, the United Nations, and the World Bank, all of which encourage initiatives and provide financial support for entrepreneurship. Governments worldwide are enacting policies and providing financial subsidies that they hope will encourage entrepreneurs. Competition for ideas and for financing has increased dramatically in recent decades. Globalization of competition raises the stakes for everyone, particularly in the wealthier countries.

The World Bank ranks countries according to the supportiveness of their environments for starting and doing business. These rankings provide a clearer picture of international competitiveness. Figure 1.2 shows the most recent rankings of large-population countries. Ease of doing business (plotted in the figure) is based on 10 factors, including availability of financing, legal environment, and availability of employees. Ease of starting business is another of the 10 factors; we plot it separately in Figure 1.2 because it is the factor most closely related

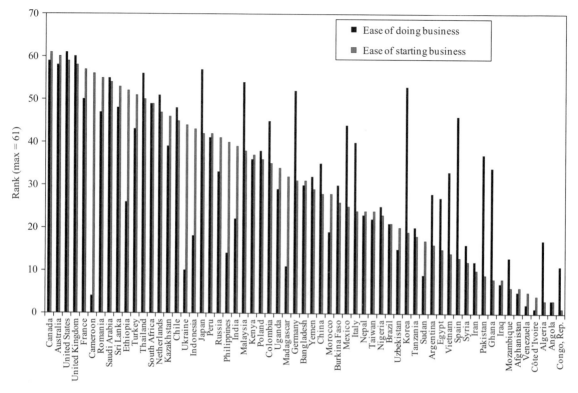

FIGURE **1.2**
Global difference in supportiveness for starting and doing business
The figure shows country ranks (highest being best) for ease of doing business and ease of starting business based on 10 equal-weighted factors that are assessed by the World Bank. Ease of starting a business is one of the 10 factors.

SOURCE: World Bank, 2009; available at http://www.doingbusiness.org/economyrankings/. Rankings are for large-population countries.

to stand-alone entrepreneurial activity. Countries that rank high on both dimensions, such as the first four in the figure, tend to be those that can support high-growth start-ups. Those that are high for ease of doing business but low for ease of starting business, such as Japan, Korea, and Mexico, tend to be countries where high-growth entrepreneurial activity is conducted mainly through established corporations and business groups. Those where ease of starting business is high but ease of doing business is low, like Cameroon, Ukraine, Indonesia, and India, tend to be relatively unregulated environments with weak infrastructures. Those where both are low, such as Iran, Iraq, Afghanistan, and Venezuela, tend to be turbulent environments with political unrest and dictatorships or militaristic factions.

Types of Entrepreneurship

Replicative versus innovative.   There is a useful distinction between "replicative" and "innovative" entrepreneurship. Schumpeter wrote extensively about innovative entrepreneurs, who "act as destabilizing influences triggering 'creative destruction'—the simultaneous creation of new industries through innovation and elimination of sectors of prior economies." Innovative entrepreneurship has the potential to add huge value to economies—the type of entrepreneurship that goes on in Silicon Valley, for example. Google, Intel, Intuit, and e-Bay were all founded by innovative entrepreneurs who challenged prevailing business models. They are what William Baumol, a leading researcher in the area, describes as "bold and imaginative deviators from established business patterns and practices" (Baumol [2002], pp. 56–57).

Replicative entrepreneurs, on the other hand, function as efficient co-ordinators of resources. They start and maintain businesses that mimic predecessors. As population grows, the economy must provide more goods and services. Economies need more grocery stores, home improvement stores, dry cleaners, and donut shops. Many of these needs are filled by replicative entrepreneurs. Replicative businesses often stay small and don't export their products or services outside the boundaries of the area they serve. Many communities and local economies try to encourage this type of entrepreneurship and do quite well, as indicated by the numbers of new businesses started and people employed by them.

In this book, we include examples of both types of entrepreneurship, but we focus primarily on innovative entrepreneurship. New ventures that involve innovations with uncertain potential pose significant challenges for strategy, forecasting, valuation, contracting, and financing choices—greater challenges than those faced by ventures that build on established business models and ventures that can be financed with small investments, traditional borrowing, and operating cash flows. By focusing on innovative entrepreneurship and high growth, we tackle the most challenging issues that entrepreneurs and investors may confront. The differences, however, are of degree rather than substance. All entrepreneurs and investors can benefit from better understanding of concepts like milestones, staging, and real options.

Opportunity-based versus necessity-based.   A related distinction is between "opportunity-based" and "necessity-based" entrepreneurship, terms coined by the Global Entrepreneurship Monitor (GEM) consor-

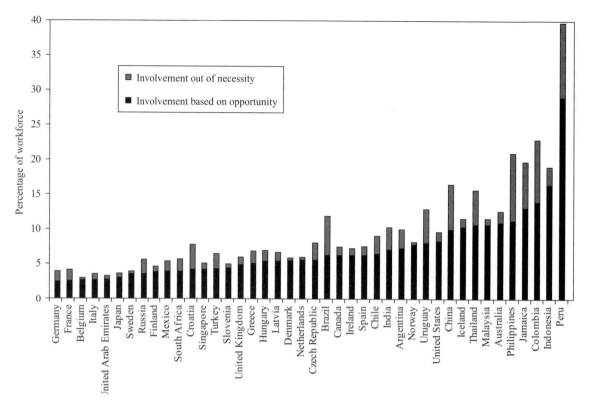

FIGURE **1.3**

Entrepreneurial involvement of workforce, 2006
The figure shows the percentage of a country's workforce that is involved in entrepreneurial ventures. The workforce is defined as the working population between ages 18 and 64. Entrepreneurial involvement is classified as opportunity based or necessity based. Data are compiled by GEM consortium members through surveys of their local economies.

SOURCE: Based on data from Global Entrepreneurship Monitor, 2006; available at http://www.gemconsortium.org/about.aspx?page=global _reports_2006.

tium.[6] Innovative entrepreneurship is virtually all opportunity based, whereas replicative entrepreneurship is divided between opportunity and necessity. Necessity-based entrepreneurship represents people driven to entrepreneurship by lack of alternatives. Necessity-based ventures may be simple businesses, including microbusinesses that require negligible capital, have no employees other than the entrepreneur, and produce near-subsistence-level earnings.

Figure 1.3 shows results of the 2006 GEM survey, ordered by the percentage of the adult workforce that is involved in opportunity-based entrepreneurship. Because opportunities vary depending on economic circumstances, perceptions of what constitutes opportunity-based entrepreneurship vary across countries. Emerging economies such as Peru, Colombia, and China show high overall entrepreneurial activity but also high percentages of necessity-based entrepreneurship. Developed countries with low barriers to business formation, such as the United States, Australia, and Malaysia, exhibit high percentages of opportunity-based but low percentages of necessity-based entrepreneurship. Countries with high barriers to new venture formation, including several Western European countries and Japan, show low percentages of both kinds of entrepreneurship. As noted above, these are countries where existing enterprises tend to carry out high-growth entrepreneurial activity.

Corporate Venturing

International evidence highlights the point that much entrepreneurial activity occurs within established businesses or in strategic partnerships among established businesses. Corporate venturing is particularly common for ventures that require large and complex research teams and use of generic testing equipment and where development times are long. For example, large pharmaceutical firms almost exclusively pursue pharmaceutical innovation. Similarly, introductions of new large commercial aircraft are normally pursued as strategic partnerships involving airframe manufacturers, engine manufacturers, and avionics manufacturers.

Corporate venturing, while easier in some respects, is more challenging in others. One obvious difficulty is that of designing appropriate incentives to motivate entrepreneurial effort in large organizations without creating perceived equity imbalances among employees. Sometimes the venturing activities are so central to the core business that they are pursued as part of the company's overall research and development (R&D) effort. Other times, corporations create separate entities that are wholly owned subsidiaries and operate much like independent venture capital firms.

Social Venturing

Social venturing involves entrepreneurial efforts where financial returns are traded off against social objectives. The distinguishing characteristic of a social venture versus a commercial one is the primacy of the objective to address social issues. Social venturing encompasses activities ranging from the pure research efforts of university faculty to any number of not-for-profit activities supported by funding sources that operate much like venture capital funds. University research is predominantly grant supported. Some universities have sought to act as incubators for research projects with the potential for commercialization, using technology transfer arrangements and ownership of intellectual property to realize returns on their support of faculty research.

Newer-style social venturing includes efforts by some not-for-profit entities to create for-profit subsidiaries. For example, the Metropolitan Museum of Art owns the Metropolitan Museum of Art Museum Store, which sells reproductions on-site, in remote locations, and on the Internet. Profits from the store go to fund activities of the museum. Not-for-profit entities, of course, cannot issue common or preferred stock, but they can design financial claims that work similarly. Innovative approaches to foster the growth of not-for-profit ventures include new structured financing instruments that are tied to realized revenues or other cash flow streams.

Recently, some venture capital funds have tapped into growing interest in environmental issues by emphasizing "green-tech" or "clean-tech" as the focus of their venture investing efforts. While the focus sounds social, these funds are not fundamentally different from other venture capital funds in that their primary objective is creating value for investors in the fund.

1.2   The Finance Paradigm

The guiding principles of financial decision making can be stated succinctly:

- More of a good is preferred to less.
- Present wealth is preferred to future wealth.
- Safe assets are preferred to risky assets.

We rely on these principles when we consider the subjects of valuation, choice of financing, and contracting.

The domain of the financial decision-making paradigm is resource allocation, including investment decisions and financing decisions. Investment decisions are those concerning acquisition of assets (the left-hand side of the balance sheet). The assets can be tangible, like a machine; intangible, like a patent; or simply an option to take some action in the future. The worth, or value, of an investment depends on its ability to generate cash flows for the investors in the future and on the riskiness of those cash flows.

Financing decisions (the right-hand side of balance sheet) concern issues such as the choice of financing (debt, equity, or some hybrid such as preferred stock), how much financing should come from investors, and how financial contracts should be structured.

The range of decisions that can be approached using the finance paradigm is much broader than may be apparent at first glance. Financial considerations are applicable, for example, to the choice of organizational form (e.g., sole proprietorship, partnership, or corporation) and to the design of financial contracts to align the incentives of investors and entrepreneurs. Similarly, issues such as the choices of scale and scope of a venture can be analyzed as financial investment decisions (i.e., larger scale requires more outside financing).

The Importance of Real Options

One theme of this book is that investing in new ventures involves a process of acquiring, retaining, exercising, and abandoning real options. A real option is a right, but not an obligation, to undertake a decision about a nonfinancial asset. Examples include the option to expand into another geographic market, to abandon a venture that is not developing as expected, or to wait to invest until additional information becomes available.

Values of real options depend importantly on the degree of uncertainty surrounding the investment. Because new ventures are started under conditions of great uncertainty, real options often are very important to the decision to engage in an entrepreneurial venture. In fact, a new venture can be viewed as a portfolio of real options. Staging of capital infusions, abandonment of the venture, and accelerating the growth rate are all choices that involve real options. As we describe below, the decision-making paradigm we use focuses on recognizing and valuing real options and exploiting real option structures to create value.

Objective: Maximum Value for the Entrepreneur

Application of a decision-making paradigm requires that we specify an objective. What, exactly, is the entrepreneur trying to accomplish? Schumpeter makes clear that creating value for society, while a result of entrepreneurial effort, is not the entrepreneur's objective. Rather, the entrepreneur's motive is to make the entrepreneur better off.

Consistent with this view, we expect that the entrepreneurial function in for-profit ventures will create value for society but that prospective entrepreneurs are driven by self-interest. Similarly, it makes sense to view the social entrepreneur's objective as maximizing value. While social ventures may be designed to create significant value for society, the venture still generates earnings for the entrepreneur and residual cash flows (which are not called profits) that the entrepreneur can use. Value maximization for the social entrepreneur comes in the forms of higher compensation and fulfillment of the entrepreneur's desire to improve some aspect of society.

Whether the venture is for-profit or not, the entrepreneur faces many choices regarding how best to develop the venture and can be expected to have a different appetite for risk and expected return than would investors. Accordingly, the entrepreneur cannot simply rely on investor recommendations concerning how best to develop the venture. Rather, she must consider the range of product market strategies and available financing choices and select the combination that offers the most attractive tradeoff of risk and expected return.

While the principles in this book are developed and presented mainly from the perspective of the entrepreneur, they are no less valuable for investors. The analysis can easily be reformulated around the objective of maximizing value for an investor, such as a venture capitalist or angel investor. Moreover, the investor can benefit from a better understanding of how the entrepreneur views the economics of the venture. With regard to valuation and contracting, because both parties can benefit from knowing how the other views the venture, we study these topics from both perspectives.

1.3   The Rocket Analogy

Practitioners draw an analogy between undertaking a venture and launching a rocket. Just as with complex rockets, the venture proceeds in stages. Each stage offers the opportunity to terminate or to make minor midcourse corrections. Because most new ventures do not generate sufficient cash to cover operating costs or provide for future growth, they must be fueled by an initial supply of cash. The normal intent is to fuel the venture with enough cash at each stage of development so that it is able to reach the next stage. At that point, it is hoped the venture will be able to raise additional cash on terms that are more favorable. Continuing the rocket analogy, the rate at which cash is consumed during one stage often is referred to as the venture's "burn rate."

The analogy is not perfect. When a rocket launches, it must carry with it sufficient fuel to propel it through all of the stages. A new venture, by contrast, does not raise all of the necessary capital up front; rather, there are stations along the way where the venture can refuel. By raising capital in stages, the entrepreneur can potentially own a more valuable share of the venture at the end.

Another difference between rockets and new ventures concerns the specificity of the objective. When a rocket is launched, the objective is clear and does not change. Midcourse corrections occur only in the event that the rocket has strayed. With a new venture it is more difficult to define the venture's objective at the time of launch, and a midcourse change of direction can result from a changed objective. Over time, as the entrepreneur and backers of the venture learn more about the market and the potential success of their efforts, it may become apparent that a change of direction would lead to higher value.

1.4 The Stages of New Venture Development

Although there is no typical life cycle for a new venture, firms do go through stages of development: they come into existence; they may undergo stages of rapid growth, slow growth, or stagnation; and they may fail. But a venture can go through these stages in any order and can go through one or more stages several times. A firm can even fail more than once.

With this caveat, Figure 1.4 depicts the stages of new venture development from inception of the opportunity through its development and eventual harvesting—the stage where the investors and maybe the entrepreneur can successfully unwind their positions.[7] To avoid overgeneralizing, the figure represents a high-tech, single-product venture for a product that gains rapid market acceptance after being introduced. The diagram shows the various stages of development, identifies the types of decisions and actions that typically are made at each stage, indicates the types of real options associated with each stage, and in the final row describes the stage in general terms.

As the diagram implies, once an opportunity is recognized some non-financial activities can begin immediately. Filing for patents, searching for personnel, assessing the size of the market, and identifying actual and potential competitors are examples of activities that need to be performed regardless of any decisions about development strategy.

From a decision-making standpoint, the entrepreneur's first action is to generate a short list of alternative potentially desirable new venture strategies. For some kinds of ventures, only one such strategy may be

Stages	Opportunity	Research and development	Start-up	Early-growth	Rapid-growth	Exit
Actions	Obtain seed financing Assess opportunity Assess strategic alternatives Determine organizational structure Determine organizational form Prepare business plan	Obtain R&D financing Build research team Conduct R&D activities, e.g.: 　Secure patent 　Develop prototype 　Build website Test market/market research Assess/update business plan	Obtain start-up financing Assess/update business plan Initiate revenue generation Initiate production Build starting inventory Build sales and marketing team Acquire facilities and equipment	Obtain early-growth financing Work toward breakeven revenue Expand team as needed Expand facilities as needed Assess/update business plan	Obtain rapid-growth financing Work toward proven viability Expand team as needed Expand facilities as needed Build track record for harvest Assess/update business plan	Obtain continuing financing: 　IPO 　Acquisition 　Buyout Early investors harvest Assess/update business plan
Real options	Continue to next stage Modify concept Abandon	Continue to next stage Extend stage/financing Modify R&D strategy Abandon	Continue to next stage Modify production/financing Modify marketing/financing Abandon	Continue to next stage Extend stage/financing Abandon	Continue to next stage Extend stage/financing	Choose form of exit
Description	All activities through preparation of business plan and before incurring significant expense	All research and development activity that must be completed before revenue generation can commence	All activities related to start of production and marketing and initiation of revenue-generating activities	All activities during the period before the venture reaches a level of sales sufficient for cash flow breakeven	All activities during the period after breakeven and before sustainable viability is established	All activities related to establishing continuing financing and enabling early investors to harvest

FIGURE **1.4**

Stages of new venture development

The figure shows the standard progression of development of a new venture from opportunity identification though stages culminating in exit. At each stage, the figure indicates the kinds of actions that normally are associated with the stage, as well as some of the real options the entrepreneur is likely to face.

feasible. For many others, it should be possible to represent the array of sensible alternatives in terms of a small number of discrete strategic scenarios.

At each stage, the entrepreneur needs to identify a limited set of real options for implementation. These real options are choices such as continue to the next stage; wait until the potential of the opportunity becomes clearer; abandon the venture altogether; or modify the R&D strategy, which typically involves revising the business plan and may affect financing as well. This analysis is done for one real option structure at a time, matched with each financing structure that could make sense for that strategy. The real option structure and financing structure are interdependent. Thus, the entrepreneur needs to search for the most valuable financing structure to complement a particular real option structure.

Performance evaluation is a continuous process, and is reflected in Figure 1.4 as "assess/update business plan." Reassessment of the venture's progress occurs throughout its development. If implementation and financing results align generally with expectations, then all that may be necessary is to periodically refine and update the business plan. If not, then the strategy is suspect and the entrepreneur should revisit the strategic plan, considering alternatives ranging from major refocusing to abandonment.

As indicated in Figure 1.4, the final stage for a successful venture is exit, which allows investors and the entrepreneur to harvest their investments.

1.5 Measuring Progress with Milestones

Rather than thinking of staging in terms of time intervals such as months or years, orienting around milestones is more useful. Although it is possible, even at an early stage, to forecast free cash flows (i.e., cash flows available to investors) and to discount them to net present value (NPV), uncertainty is extremely high. As a result, raising capital at a very early stage is difficult. Reliance on milestones enables the parties to postpone financial commitments until they are needed and to base infusions on the risk and expected return that exist at the time of investment.

Each milestone also functions as a working hypothesis about the venture. Understanding the reasons for failing to meet a milestone is important. Suppose, for example, an entrepreneur believes (or hypothesizes) that a prototype of the idea can be completed in six months. If, instead, prototype completion takes nine months, the delay is an indication that some aspects of the venture need to be reexamined. There are several possible reasons for failing to achieve a milestone on time. Perhaps the entrepreneur underestimated the technical difficulties; alternatively, the entrepreneur may have mismanaged the project. The distinction is critical to deciding how, or even if, the venture should continue. In any case, milestones enable the entrepreneur and investors to sharpen their expectations about ultimate success or failure.

Milestones also help identify ways to enhance the expected benefits of the project. Appropriate milestones differ with circumstances. For some kinds of ventures, the first significant milestone is concept testing. The objective of concept testing is to do enough fieldwork to determine whether a market opportunity exists and whether there is enough upside potential to warrant continued investment. Reaching this milestone helps resolve some of the uncertainty and contributes to convergence of expectations between the entrepreneur and investors.

A second milestone might be the completion of a prototype. Normally, a prototype is an early-stage working model of the envisioned product—a beta website for an Internet company, for example. Completing the prototype forces the entrepreneur to anticipate and encounter a variety of issues related to product development. By doing so, the entrepreneur can gain increased understanding of technological bottlenecks, manufacturing costs, and materials availability. In addition to resolving uncertainties about the product, reaching this milestone may help establish a first-mover advantage for the entrepreneur so that it is easier to control development of the idea. It also provides early tangible evidence of the entrepreneur's managerial ability.

A number of milestones may be appropriate for particular projects. The nature of the venture determines which milestones afford the most potential to assess progress and to facilitate the venture's development. The following are some examples suggested by Block and MacMillan (1985):

- *Completion of concept and product testing.* Is there a real market opportunity? What is the market? How should the product be priced, distributed, and so on?
- *Completion of a prototype.* Can the product be manufactured? What facilities are needed? How costly is manufacturing? How long does production require?
- *First financing.* Can we convince others of the value of the concept and the strength of our team? Can enough money be raised to carry the venture to the next milestone?

- *Completion of initial plant tests.* What materials are best suited to the product? What training is needed? How reliable is the production process?
- *Market testing.* Will customers buy the product? Are the early assumptions about the opportunity still supported? What level of sales can be achieved?
- *Production start-up.* Are operations working as expected? How can the manufacturing process be fine-tuned?
- *Bellwether sale.* What can be learned from the first important sale about how best to manufacture, distribute, and market the product? How will the sale affect demand from other important customers?
- *First competitive reaction.* How are competitors reacting? Is the reaction different from anticipated? What should be done to position the venture in light of competitive reaction?
- *First redesign or redirection.* In the event of such a change, has the market responded to the change in the way that was expected? If not, why not?

1.6   Financial Performance and Stages of New Venture Development

Figure 1.5 shows how financial performance can be used to delineate the stages of new venture development. The figure reflects the same stages shown in Figure 1.4 after the opportunity has been identified and a decision to proceed has been made. The horizontal axis measures time; the vertical axis, dollars. Time 0 represents initiation of sales. The three curves in the figure are sales revenue, net income, and cash flow available to investors. Sales revenue and net income are measured in the conventional ways for a firm that uses accrual-based accounting. Cash flow available to investors is defined in the figure as cash flow from operations after tax and before interest expense, less the net new investments in working capital and fixed assets that are needed to achieve the revenue levels and prepare for future growth. If cash flow available to investors is negative, the venture must finance the shortfall. If it is positive, the firm can use the surplus to pay returns to investors, including interest payments on debt, debt redemption, dividends, and share repurchase, or to pursue other investment opportunities.

Development.   During the R&D stage, the entrepreneur has not yet begun to invest in the infrastructure needed to initiate production and

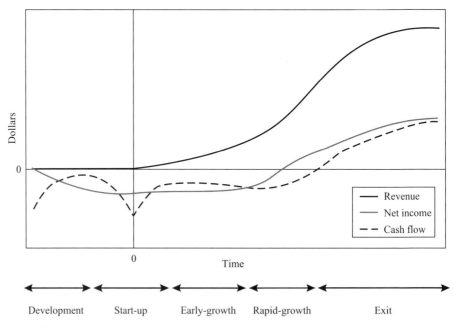

FIGURE **1.5**

Financial performance and stages of new venture development
The figure reflects five stages that are typical of new venture development. During the development stage, the venture generates no revenues and both net income and cash flow are negative. Start-up begins when the firm acquires the facilities, equipment, and employees required to produce the product. During early growth, revenue is growing, but both net income and cash flow available to investors are negative. Rapid growth is the last stage during which external financing is required. During exit, the rate of growth declines to the point where cash flow available to investors is positive.

sale of the product. The venture generates no revenues during this period. Net income is negative and may become increasingly negative as the number of people involved in product development increases. Cash flow initially is very negative as the firm invests in the capital equipment needed for development. Under existing US accounting conventions, firms must record the depreciation expense of equipment over time. As a result, net income is not as negative as cash flow.

Start-up.   The demarcation between development and start-up is when the firm begins to acquire the facilities, equipment, and employees required to produce the product.[8] The decline in cash flow preceding start-up reflects investment in production equipment, facilities, and net working capital.

Early growth.   Revenue is growing (possibly rapidly) in the third stage. Both net income and cash flow available to investors are negative. Cash flow exceeds net income, essentially because periodic depreciation expenses are larger than the increase of investment in working capital and fixed assets needed to support the growth of revenue. This is referred to as the early-growth stage because, although growth may be rapid in percentage terms, the base from which we calculate revenue growth is low. Thus, cash flow available to investors exceeds net income.

Rapid growth.   There is no clear line of demarcation between the early-growth stage and the rapid-growth stage. Many new ventures experience growth in the early stage but fizzle out before they achieve sales that are sufficient to sustain the business. Hence, entrepreneurs can benefit by being cognizant of signs that the venture has reached the rapid-growth stage. As shown in Figure 1.5, net revenues are increasing at an increasing rate (i.e., the slope of the revenue curve is increasing). More important, rapid sales growth puts heavy demands on the entrepreneur to locate the financing needed to sustain the corresponding growth of working capital and fixed assets. During the rapid-growth stage, if the venture is to survive then net income must become positive.

Exit.   During the exit stage, the venture's rate of growth declines to the point where cash flow available to investors is positive. The venture is able to provide returns to debt and equity investors without needing to increase outside financing. This is an obvious time for investors to harvest and realize the returns on their investments.

1.7   The Sequence of New Venture Financing

The stages in Figures 1.4 and 1.5 correspond roughly to measurable milestones. Correspondence also exists between the milestones and opportunities to attract outside financing.

At an early stage, the entrepreneur looks for ways to finance the venture from personal savings and from borrowing where repayment does not depend on success. Bootstrap techniques include, for example, drawing down savings accounts, taking out second mortgages, using the credit lines of multiple credit cards, and borrowing on life insurance policies.

In a sense, bootstrapping is not a form of new venture financing. Rather, the entrepreneur is financing the venture from personal resources. There is no fundamental difference between drawing down personal savings balances to finance the venture and running up credit card balances for that purpose. A provider of bootstrap financing (e.g., a credit card company) does not know that an investment is being made in the venture and is not relying on the venture's success to realize a return. Instead, willingness to lend is based on the credit history and reputation of the entrepreneur or on the entrepreneur's other assets that can serve as collateral.

Bootstrapping normally cannot be a source of permanent financing. Credit card loans carry high interest rates and eventually must be repaid. A growing venture can quickly exhaust the entrepreneur's ability to bootstrap. The more likely scenario is that the entrepreneur must turn to financing that is based on the merits or assets of the venture.

As development progresses, the entrepreneur may look to other sources of financing, including family members, friends, angel investors, banks, venture capitalists, and a variety of others. Customary venture financing terminology (to follow) reflects the correspondence between financing choices and development stages.[9]

The earliest external financing is known as seed financing. Seed financing consists of relatively small amounts of money to support exploration of a concept. It may cover such things as the cost of assessing the size of a market and preparing the business plan. The principal risk exposure of seed financing is risk of discovery. For example, the entrepreneur may discover that no significant market exists or that a competitor controls essential technology.

For high-technology ventures, seed financing may provide initial funds for R&D. In cases where R&D efforts are expensive and protracted, R&D financing could be required beyond what is typically regarded as seed financing. The critical risk exposure in such cases is that development efforts fail.

Start-up financing covers activities from later R&D to initiation of sales. Generally, start-up financing is provided when a concept appears to be worth pursuing, key members of the team are in place, and most of the risks related to development have been resolved. At this point, actual production has not yet begun, and the main risk exposure is related to whether a cost-effective manufacturing technology can be put in place.

Later-stage financing is associated with the early-growth and rapid-growth stages of development. Venture capitalists sometimes refer to rounds of financing by number, such as "round 1 financing," "round 2 financing," or by letter, such as "A-round financing," "B-round financing." These terms are somewhat arbitrary but do imply sequencing based on meeting a particular milestone and moving to the next. To avoid confusion, and to be consistent with terminology, we refer to later-stage financing as encompassing two general types of financing:

1. *Financing provided to a company that has initiated production and is generating revenues but (normally) has not yet achieved profitability.* The firm has a marketable product but substantial uncertainty remains as to achievable sales and profitability. The critical element of risk is marketing risk—the question of whether the venture can reach a level of sales sufficient to attract and compensate investors in an exit.

2. *Financing to support the continuing growth of a venture that is operating around the breakeven point of profitability.* The venture is not yet generating sufficient cash flow to support planned expansion. Uncertainty remains about ultimate market potential and profitability.

In practice, a venture may go through even more stages of growth financing. The limiting factors on the number of times the venture can "go to the well" are practicality and the desire of the investor to maintain a close monitoring relationship. The downsides of increasing the number of rounds, particularly if the investments are being made by a venture capitalist or someone else with fiduciary responsibility, are that each unplanned round reduces the entrepreneur's ownership share and that every stage requires a valuation. One venture with which we are familiar went through 16 stages of venture capital–backed financing, with a valuation at each stage!

Mezzanine financing (debt financing) supports major expansion of a profitable business. Because of continuing market uncertainty and the possible actions of competitors, the debt typically is high risk. Bridge financing is temporary financing, particularly between later-stage financing rounds and harvesting. It usually can be arranged quickly and allows the firm time to arrange permanent financing, possibly in the public market. Another use of bridge financing is to facilitate a leveraged buyout (LBO) or a management buyout (MBO) of the business.

Referring again to Figure 1.5, the exit stage is where the founders and other investors attempt to harvest their investments. Harvesting techniques include taking the company public with an initial public offering (IPO), arranging for a buyout, and other approaches we discuss in Chapter 15.

1.8   The New Venture Business Plan

Most prospective entrepreneurs regard preparing the business plan as the first step in the process of starting a new venture. They envision a process where, once an opportunity is perceived, the business plan is used to gain external validation that the entrepreneur's judgment about the opportunity is correct. But as Timmons (1999) points out, "relying on raising money as an indication that an idea is sound is a cart-before-the-horse approach, which usually results in rejection." Moreover, writing and circulating a business plan too early can be a costly mistake, even if the entrepreneur eventually is able to attract funding. Simply stated, and as reflected in Figure 1.4, the entrepreneur will benefit from planning the new venture strategy before preparing the formal plan.

Among other things, the business plan sets out the conclusions of the strategic planning exercise. It is a written document that describes the critical elements involved in starting the venture. Fundamentally, the plan is the logical implication of a set of hypotheses about a perceived opportunity in terms of what is expected to result if the opportunity is pursued in a particular way. The plan reflects expectations about such factors as when product development efforts will be completed, when the product will be ready to market, product cost and unit price, and rate of sales growth. Each of these assumptions is a hypothesis that contributes to testing the entrepreneur's perception of the value of the venture.

As the venture progresses, these hypotheses are tested. In general, meeting the expectations would lead to no revision of expectations and probably no change of direction. Failure to achieve a milestone or financial projection would signal the need to reexamine expectations and reevaluate the merits of the venture. The entrepreneur needs to understand why the projection was not achieved and, based on that new understanding, reassess the opportunity and the relative merits of going forward, redirecting effort, or abandoning the venture.

It is easier to attract investors with a business plan that sets out explicit financial projections and milestones than with a plan that is vague. By making the plan specific, the entrepreneur invites oversight and evaluation and provides a mechanism that is easy for investors to use to revalue their investments later on. Investors can easily use the milestones and financial projections to test the beliefs of the entrepreneur, for example, with contract terms that tie the entrepreneur's ownership share to attainment of revenue targets. A plan that is specific in these respects inspires more confidence among potential investors and makes contracting easier.

Business Plans of New Ventures Are Different

Although every business plan is based on a set of assumptions about the future, the bases for the assumptions are more reliable for an established business than for a start-up. For example, sales projections for an established business generally can be based on prior experience, whereas those for a new venture must be based on conjecture, economic modeling, and analogy to other ventures.

A practical implication of the lack of a track record is that the necessary investment in planning is likely to be greater for a new venture than for an established firm. An established firm may be able to project performance accurately and convincingly based on simple extrapolations and inferences drawn from experience. In contrast, the accuracy and credibility of a new venture plan depend on a number of critical assumptions: How long will it take to develop a marketable service or product? If development efforts are successful, how much will the service or product cost, and at what price can it be sold? How large is the market, and what share can the venture expect to achieve? These kinds of questions, critical to the new venture plan, must be answered using the best available data and reasoning.[10]

A carefully considered plan can contribute significantly to the value of a new venture, but it is unlikely to be the critical determinant of success or failure. That is, the entrepreneur's effort in planning contributes to success *on the margin*. A significant commitment of effort to planning can pay off in many ways. Probably the most important payoff is better and faster decision making. A solid plan can help the entrepreneur decide whether the venture is worth pursuing, and if so, how. It also can provide early warning of problems, enabling the entrepreneur to react and the venture to adapt.

Deviations from the plan mean different things for new ventures.   In businesses where the planning objectives can be specified with relative accuracy and where deviations from projections can be traced to specific factors, it is common for the plan to serve as a basis for a team member's performance evaluation and management compensation. For a new venture, use of the business plan for such a purpose is not a good idea. Actual sales may turn out to be less than projected for a variety of reasons, only one of which is the effectiveness of the person responsible for the selling efforts. Stated differently, for an established business it may be valid to reconcile actual sales with planned sales by taking the position that the assumptions in the plan are accurate and deviations reflect the amount or quality of effort to achieve the target. For a start-up or early-stage venture, it is more likely that the effort was reasonable but the assumptions in the plan were too optimistic.

New venture business plans serve different purposes.   Another difference between the plans of new and established ventures is the degree of external reliance on the plan. For an established venture, the business plan may be strictly an internal document. Decisions by outsiders, such as the decision to continue financing an established venture, are likely to be based on experience with management, track record of the business, and current financial health. They are not likely to depend significantly on review of the company's projections. For a start-up, the reverse is true. Consequently, the business plan for a start-up must be prepared with an expectation that it will be scrutinized by outsiders who may not be very familiar with the business. Many things that are unnecessary to include in the plan of an established venture are essential in a plan that outsiders rely upon heavily.

What Makes a Business Plan Convincing?

Some entrepreneurs prepare and circulate business plans in an effort to test investor interest in an idea. In such a case, the entrepreneur operates with the perception that the critical success factor for the venture is the idea and that investors, recognizing the merits of the idea, will come forth with funding. Obviously, this approach—of looking for investors before committing to the project—reduces risk for the entrepreneur. Unfortunately, it also reduces the potential for obtaining financing. Credible evidence of the entrepreneur's commitment and beliefs about the validity of projections presented in the business plan is critical to securing funding. We address these contracting issues throughout the book, but mainly in Chapters 12 and 13. Because incentive and information problems are endemic to new ventures, it is useful to introduce some of the concepts here.

Credible evidence of commitment.   Although a good idea is a necessary ingredient of a plan, investors are looking for evidence that the entrepreneur (along with key members of the team) is committed to the venture. The most convincing evidence is the investment of effort and capital that the entrepreneur has already made and is continuing to make in the venture and for which a return cannot be realized unless the project goes forward and is successful. There are many ways to demonstrate such investments. The key element for their functioning as credible commitments to the project is that they are sunk, meaning that they are not recoverable or will not generate a return for the entrepreneur unless the entrepreneur continues to commit effort to the project.[11]

It is not the action per se that matters but the irreversibility of the action. Test marketing expenses, for example, are only of value if the venture attempts to market the product. Similarly, the loss of salary that comes with resignation of current employment is credible as a signal only if the entrepreneur would have difficulty finding new employment of equal value.

Timing of resignation is also an important factor in assessing credibility. Burning bridges with an existing employer, with no clear new venture opportunity in mind, may help motivate a prospective entrepreneur to intensify the search for opportunities. However, it does very little to signal the entrepreneur's commitment to or confidence in the venture that is ultimately selected. How can the investor in such a case determine whether the entrepreneur is truly attracted to the opportunity or is merely settling on one that appears to be the best candidate from a list of not-so-attractive possibilities?[12]

Evidence of reputation and certification.   Experienced entrepreneurs sometimes attract investment without the need to make credible demonstrations of commitment to individual projects.[13] Later in the book, we explore the connection between past success and reputation, and we will see other ways in which reputation is important in entrepreneurial settings.[14]

What about the first-time entrepreneur who has yet to establish a reputation or an entrepreneur whose track record is less than perfect? We've already seen that the entrepreneur may be able to make credible commitments to the venture, but without a reputation the commitment alone may not be sufficient to attract the interest of investors. One solution for the first-time entrepreneur is to rely on the reputations of others.[15] Important suppliers or customers who have publicly committed to transact with the venture may provide the level of certification that is important for attracting investment, as can relational partners who become involved in implementing the business plan.[16]

Some pitfalls to avoid in the business plan.   Many sources offer advice on writing a convincing business plan. Most are descriptive, laying out the elements of a typical business plan in a structured way. The entrepreneur's capability and commitment to the venture are conveyed through the business plan, sometimes in subtle ways. London Business School professor John Mullins takes a different approach. He identifies five "deal killers" that entrepreneurs should avoid in the business plan:[17]

1. *Failing to identify clearly the customer problem that the venture would address.* Elegance of a new technology is not important if there is no significant market opportunity.

2. *Failing to identify clearly a narrow target market.* Casual assumptions based on getting a small share of a very large market are not convincing. Instead, the plan needs to identify specific target customer groups and support the basis for the assumption of penetration with evidence.

3. *Relying on a business model that does not make economic sense.* Elaborate financial models that show large paper profits are only as good as the validity of the underlying assumptions.

4. *Relying on a highly credentialed team that lacks the critical expertise the venture needs.* A plan that does not identify and address the critical success factors signals a lack of serious commitment and capability.

5. *Failing to recognize the threats and potential problems.* An overly optimistic plan that does not show awareness of the challenges is not likely to be credible.

Mullins also points out some common business plan phrases that can signal lack of careful thought behind the plan. Here are a few with their "translations":

- "Our market is huge." *Translation*: "We don't think it is important to get reliable data about the market potential of the venture."

- "We conservatively forecast . . ." *Translation*: "Rather than trying to get reliable information on critical factors of performance, we have made some guesses that should sound plausible."

- "Our revolutionary technology . . ." *Translation*: "Customers have yet to figure out why they might be interested in what we are doing."

- "We believe that . . ." *Translation*: "We have been too busy writing the plan to gather any actual evidence."

- "We have no competition." *Translation*: "We don't understand our market."

These common pitfalls underscore the point that no venture is likely to be able to attract funding if the entrepreneur cannot convincingly convey commitment and the capability to make the venture a success. Every portion of the business plan should contribute to delivering this message.

1.9 Organization of the Book

We address new venture finance from inception to harvesting. In Part 1, "Getting Started," we introduce key concepts for understanding entrepreneurial finance—the stages of new venture development, the concept of milestones, the sequencing of financing, and the business plan. We include a general business plan discussion early in the book because some users may want to develop a business plan as they proceed. Subsequent chapters provide the background for developing a plan more fully, including analyzing strategic alternatives for developing the opportunity, modeling uncertainty, financial modeling, identifying milestones, assessing financial needs, valuation, contracting, and so forth.

In Chapter 2, we offer an analysis of some other critical considerations for entrepreneurs—the choice of organizational form for the new venture and regulations, including features of securities law that can affect the choice of financing. The chapter also provides a menu of major sources of financing, as well as an introduction to deal structure. The question of which financing choice is best in a given situation is deferred until Chapter 14. Because venture capital financing is so important to high-growth, capital-intensive, high-impact ventures, we study it in detail in Chapter 3. We discuss the economics of the industry, including partnership agreements and contractual provisions that are common in venture capital financing.

Part 2, "Financial Aspects of Strategic Planning," makes the important connection between entrepreneurial finance and strategy. Making this connection is a unique feature of this book. A new venture can be thought of as a portfolio of real options (abandonment, expansion, and delay, among others). In this section, we introduce analytical and practical tools for examining the values of different options. We also show how to use the statistical technique of simulation to capture the uncertainty that underlies all new ventures. We illustrate how to improve financial decision making and how to add value by applying simulation to value real options.

Part 3, "Financial Forecasting and Assessing Financial Needs," contains the key components of financial modeling for a new venture. We cover methods of financial forecasting and techniques for projecting cash flows and assessing financial needs. The material in this section is practical and essential. We make the point that uncertainty about the future, rather than reducing the value of financial planning, makes good financial planning critical. We do not look at assessment of financial needs from the traditional perspective of making sure that the entrepreneur secures enough financing to avoid running out of cash. Instead, we discuss the topic from the perspective of adding value for the entrepreneur, recognizing that raising less capital now will enable the entrepreneur to retain a larger share of ownership and preserve the opportunity to attract lower-cost financing later if the venture is successful. Issues related to working capital policy are also addressed in this section.

The financial projections that are the focus of Part 3 become a key input to valuation, which is the focus of Part 4, "Valuation." The emphasis in this section is on learning to value new venture investment opportunities and on the financial claims related to those opportunities. The section contains three chapters, one that focuses on the theory and framework for valuation, one that focuses on how the concepts are applied in practice, and one that focuses on valuation from the perspective of the entrepreneur. The chapters include several templates that can be modified to fit other projections of cash flows.

A central and unique aspect of the book is recognizing that the value of a venture can be very different for an investor than for the entrepreneur. On one hand, investors typically can be better diversified, which translates into a lower cost of capital. On the other, the entrepreneur may be more optimistic about the future of the venture. We examine valuation from both perspectives and provide a series of templates to illustrate how to apply the entrepreneur's underdiversification discount in practice.

Part 5, "Information, Incentives, and Financial Contracting," demonstrates how organizational design choices and financial contracting provisions can create value for the entrepreneur and for the investor. Differences in risk tolerance between investors and entrepreneurs create opportunities for enhancing value by using contractual provisions that optimally allocate ownership and risk among the parties.

Coverage in Part 5 includes risk allocation, incentive alignment, signaling, and reputation. With the valuation methodology already established, we return to viewing projects as bundles of real options and use the methodology to study the value of different strategic alternatives for developing the venture. The material in this section has important implications for structuring ownership. We fit the earlier work on assessing financial needs into the contracting framework, beginning with a scenario in which an investor agrees with the entrepreneur about the likely development of the venture. We then extend it to the more realistic case in which the investor is concerned that the entrepreneur may be unduly optimistic or may have concealed negative information. The relation between contract structure and financial flexibility is an important aspect of Part 5. While the section is firmly grounded in financial economic theory, our objective is to develop your ability to apply the theory to real-world opportunities.

The section concludes with a chapter that is focused on matching potential financing sources to the stage of venture development and to specific financial needs considerations. The section also includes the topics of financial distress and turnaround financing.

Part 6, "Harvesting and Beyond," considers alternative ways for entrepreneurs and investors to exit the venture and realize a return. The orientation is on the choice of harvesting alternatives, including IPO, merger or acquisition, and an employee stock option plan, among others. We devote specific attention to the IPO process and the role of the investment banker.

The final chapter includes a review of major themes of the book and identifies some unresolved issues. It also contains forward-looking discussions of the future of entrepreneurial activity, including prospects for international expansion, and the effectiveness of public policy aimed at encouraging the financing of entrepreneurs.

1.10 Summary

An entrepreneur is a person who sees an opportunity to redirect resources to higher-valued uses and acts on the opportunity without being hindered by current ownership of the resources. A new venture is an enterprise organized by the entrepreneur to capitalize on the opportunity. Entrepreneurship is broader than stand-alone, for-profit venturing; it also includes corporate venturing and social venturing. While entrepreneurship is ubiquitous, there are important institutional, cultural, and infrastructure differences across countries that influence the focus of entrepreneurial effort, how entrepreneurial activity is financed, and the choice to undertake an entrepreneurial venture.

Entrepreneurial finance applies the basic tools of financial economic theory to decision making by entrepreneurs and others involved in new ventures. Although the same basic tools underlie corporate finance, there are important differences between entrepreneurial finance and corporate finance as to how the tools apply. Two key differences relate to the importance of thinking of new ventures as portfolios of real options and the distinction between value as perceived by investors and value as perceived by the entrepreneur.[18] The implications of the distinctive aspects of entrepreneurial finance are explored throughout the book.

Because new ventures are high risk, it is useful to think of their development as proceeding in stages, where the realistically available financing options change as the venture progresses from one stage to the next. Generally, new venture stages relate to milestones of progress. The milestones are working hypotheses as to what the entrepreneur believes can be achieved. Normally, the milestones also relate to real option choices. Attaining a milestone on schedule, for example, suggests that the venture is on track, whereas missing it is an indication that the entrepreneur should reconsider the strategy and may want to modify or abandon the effort.

A new venture business plan can fulfill several purposes, serving as a means of benchmarking future performance and a tool for soliciting outside financing, among others. Because new venture business plans often are used to attract funding, it is important that they be convincing about the commitment and capability of the entrepreneur.

REVIEW QUESTIONS

1. What, according to this chapter, is an "entrepreneur"?

2. What are some key differences between entrepreneurship in the United States and elsewhere?

3. How is the difference between innovative and replicative entrepreneurship related to the difference between opportunity-based and necessity-based entrepreneurship?

4. Why are real options likely to be important to the new venture development process?

5. Why is it important to have a clear objective in mind when planning an entrepreneurial venture?

6. What are the main stages of new venture development? What kinds of things go on during the different stages?

7. How are the stages of development related to the financial performance of the venture? How do the stages relate to availability of financing?

8. Explain how milestones are related to development stages and to real options.

9. What are some important differences between new venture business plans and business plans of established firms?

10. What sorts of things can entrepreneurs do to make their business plans more convincing?

NOTES

1. Kirzner (1979) discusses early views of entrepreneurship.

2. Bull and Willard (1994) survey more recent definitions of entrepreneurship and conclude that most are permutations of, or derivative of, Schumpeter's view.

3. 1998–2002 Business Information Tracking Series; available at http://www.census.gov/econ/sbo/longitudinal02/longitudinal02.html. Data available in B. Headd and B. Kirchhoff, "Small Business Growth: Searching for Stylized Facts" (working paper, Small Business Administration, Washington, DC, 2007).

4. Data are from the US Census Bureau, *Statistical Abstract of the United States* (2009), table 742.

5. See Jung (2002).

6. The Global Entrepreneurship Monitor (GEM) is a not-for-profit academic research consortium that makes international data on entrepreneurial activity publicly available.

7. Descriptions of development stages vary somewhat. We adhere generally to the taxonomy presented in Timmons (1999).

8. A venture that licenses production and sales to another firm in exchange for a fee does not directly incur the costs of acquiring these productive resources, but the license fee or royalty must be structured to compensate the other firm for doing so.

9. The terminology is derived from *Pratt's Guide to Venture Capital Sources* (see Schutt [Annual]). See also Bygrave and Zacharakis (2004) and Sahlman (1990).

10. Sykes and Dunham (1992) examine differences in the business plans of new ventures and established firms, with a focus on developing and testing assumptions.

11. See Williamson (1985) and Ghemawat (1991) for a discussion of the economics of commitment and the role of sunk costs. Besanko, Dranove, Shanley, and Schaefer (2010) provide a brief model of how sunk investments encourage a firm to stay with its existing technology.

12. Levesque and MacCrimmon (1997) report that one study (of the owners of *Inc.* magazine's list of fastest-growing companies) found that, on average, the entrepreneurs kept their existing jobs for four months beyond the founding of the new venture. They offer a theoretical model of the choice of when to resign, based on the tolerance for continuing to work and the marginal productivity of devoting effort to the venture. They indicate that timing is often affected by the entrepreneur's need for cash to defray living expenses or to help fund the venture. The evidence is generally consistent with a view that resignations tend to occur at a point when the entrepreneur perceives the specific opportunity to be more attractive than continued current employment and when resignation would lend credibility to the entrepreneur's capital-raising efforts.

13. Wright, Robbie, and Ennew (1997) study venture capital investment decisions and find a strong preference for investing in projects of entrepreneurs who have played major roles in previous successful ventures.

14. For an overview on the role of reputation, see Milgrom and Roberts (1992). Klein and Leffler (1981) provide a formal analysis of reputation formation, the role of sunk investment as a bonding mechanism, and the effect of reputational capital on product price. See also Kreps and Wilson (1982).

15. In a study of differences between venture capitalists and business angels, Fiet (1995) finds that venture capital investors are more likely to rely on information exchanges with other investors in their network as an element of the investment decision.

16. A model of certification, applied to new issue underwriting, is presented in Booth and Smith (1986).

17. J. Mullins, "Why Business Plans Don't Deliver: The Five Most Common Flaws and How to Fix Them," *Wall Street Journal*, June 22, 2009, p. R3.

18. See the Preface to this book for a review of the major differences.

REFERENCES AND ADDITIONAL READING

Basu, S. 2007. "Corporate Venture Capital: Towards Understanding Who Does It, Why and How." Working paper, University of Washington, Seattle.

Baumol, W. 2002. *The Free-Market Innovation Machine: Analyzing the Growth Miracle of Capitalism.* Princeton, NJ: Princeton University Press.

Besanko, D., D. Dranove, M. Shanley, and S. Schaefer. 2010. *Economics of Strategy.* 5th ed. New York: John Wiley & Sons.

Block, Z., and I. C. MacMillan. 1985. "Milestones for Successful Venture Planning." *Harvard Business Review* 63 (5): 184–96.

Booth, J. R., and R. L. Smith. 1986. "Capital Raising, Underwriting, and the Certification Hypothesis." *Journal of Financial Economics*1 5:261–81.

Bull, I., and G. Willard. 1994. "Towards a Theory of Entrepreneurship." *Journal of Business Venturing*9 :183–95.

Bygrave, W. D., and A. Zacharakis, eds. 2004. *The Portable MBA in Entrepreneurship*. 3rd ed. New York: John Wiley & Sons.

Drucker, P. F. 1985. *Innovation and Entrepreneurship: Practice and Principles.* New York: HarperCollins.

Fiet, J. 1995. "Reliance upon Informants in the Venture Capital Industry." *Journal of Business Venturing* 10:197–223.

Ghemawat, P. 1991. *Commitment: The Dynamics of Strategy.* New York: Free Press.

Jung, K. 2002. "An Upsurge of Entrepreneurship in Korea and Its Possible Reasons." Paper presented at the Expert Workshop on Entrepreneurship in Asia: Creating Competitive Advantage in the Global Economy, Hong Kong, July 8–11, 2002. http://www.mansfieldfdn.org/programs/program _pdfs/ent_korea.pdf.

Kirzner, I. M. 1979. *Perception, Opportunity, and Profit.* Chicago: University of Chicago Press.

Klein, B., and K. Leffler. 1981. "The Role of Market Forces in Assuring Contractual Performance." *Journal of Political Economy*8 9:615–41.

Knight, F. H. 1921. *Risk, Uncertainty, and Profit.* New York: Houghton Mifflin.

Kreps, D. M., and R. Wilson. 1982. "Reputation and Imperfect Information." *Journal of Economic Theory*2 7:253–79.

Levesque, M., and K. R. MacCrimmon. 1997. "On the Interaction of Time and Money Invested in New Ventures." *Entrepreneurship Theory and Practice* 22:89–110.

Milgrom, P., and J. Roberts. 1992. *Economics, Organization, and Management.* Englewood Cliffs, NJ: Prentice-Hall.

Phan, P. H., M. Wright, D. Ucbasaran, and W. Tan. 2009. "Corporate Entrepreneurship: Current Research and Future Directions." *Journal of Business Venturing* 24:197.

Sahlman, W. A. 1990. "The Structure and Governance of Venture Capital Organizations." *Journal of Financial Economics*2 7:473–521.

Schumpeter, J. A. 1912. *Theorie der Wirtschaftlichen Entwicklung.* Leipzig: Dunker & Humblot. Translated by Redvers Opie as *The Theory of Economic Development.* Cambridge, MA: Harvard University Press, 1934.

Schutt, D., ed. Annual. *Pratt's Guide to Venture Capital Sources.* New York: Venture Economics.

Sykes, H., and D. Dunham. 1992. "Critical Assumption Planning: A Practical Tool for Managing Business Development Risk." *Journal of Business Venturing* 7 :413–24.

Timmons, J. A. 1999. *New Venture Creation*. 5th ed. Chicago: McGraw-Hill Irwin.

US Census Bureau. 2009. *Statistical Abstract of the United States*. Washington, DC: US Government Printing Office.

Von Mises, L. 1966. *Human Action*. 3rd rev. ed. Chicago: Henry Regnery.

Williamson, O. 1985. *The Economic Institutions of Capitalism*. New York: Free Press.

Wright, M., K. Robbie, and C. Ennew. 1997. "Venture Capitalists and Serial Entrepreneurs." *Journal of Business Venturing* 1 2:227–49.

Wulf, J., and J. Lerner. 2007. "Innovation and Incentives: Evidence from Corporate R&D." *Review of Economics and Statistics* 8 9:634–44.

CHAPTER 2

NEW VENTURE FINANCING: CONSIDERATIONS AND CHOICES

Money is the seed of money, and the first guinea is sometimes more difficult to acquire than the second million.

Jean-Jacques Rousseau

The printing press, automobile, microchip, satellites, and recombinant DNA are discoveries and inventions that have transformed markets and changed the course of history. But how are such great ideas and inventions financed and brought to market? The choice of financing method is pivotal to whether an idea or product reaches the market quickly and successfully. Financing decisions during the early stages of new venture development also dramatically affect the value the entrepreneur derives from the endeavor. It takes skill and creativity to raise cash for a venture that has a limited history and an uncertain future and to do so on terms that benefit the entrepreneur.

In this chapter, we provide an overview of the new venture financing sources, choices of organizational form, and regulatory considerations that relate to financing choices. Our focus for now is on introducing the institutions and terminology. Later, in Chapter 14, we present a systematic analysis of the choice of financing. This chapter concludes with an outline of the elements of the investment agreement, or "deal," between the entrepreneur and the investor.

2.1 Sources of New Venture Financing

A menu of some of the more common venture financing sources appears in Figure 2.1. The suitability of each alternative depends on several factors, including, for example, the type of venture (expected growth, risk-

FIGURE **2.1**

Sources of new venture financing Black shading indicates primary focus of investor type; gray shading indicates secondary focus, or focus of a subset of investors.

	R&D	Start-up	Early-growth	Rapid-growth	Exit
Entrepreneur	■	▒			
Friends and family	■	▒			
Angel investors	■	■	▒	▒	
Corporate strategic partner	■	■	■	■	
Venture capital	▒	■	■	■	
Asset-based lender		■	■	■	
Venture leasing		■	■	■	
Government programs	■	▒	■	■	
Trade credit/vendor financing			■	■	
Factoring			■	■	
Franchising			■	■	
Commercial bank lending			■	■	
Mezzanine lender				■	■
Public debt				■	■
IPO				■	■
Acquisition, LBO, MBO					■

iness, etc.), extent of financial need, and duration of the need. As the figure illustrates, feasible financing sources change as the firm matures.

Self, Friends, and Family

Bootstrap financing is financing that does not depend on investor assessment of the merits of the opportunity or assets of the venture. This includes financing from personal resources, family, and friends. Family and friends generally have years of experience with the entrepreneur and probably have a sense of the entrepreneur's reliability, trustworthiness, and ability to handle adversity. Often, they are incapable of assessing the merits of the opportunity and are investing because they believe in the entrepreneur or feel compelled by family relationships.

The obvious starting point for the entrepreneur is to use personal resources to advance the project to a point where outside financing is feasible. The entrepreneur's resources include not only personal savings and assets but also debt capacity. The relevant measure of debt capacity is based on the entrepreneur's earnings in existing employment plus the market value of assets that can be liquidated to service the debt. Stories of entrepreneurs whose earliest financing was achieved by "maxing out" credit card borrowing and taking out second mortgages on their homes are common.

A study of nascent entrepreneurs indicates that personal savings is the most important early financing source. The evidence indicates that entrepreneurs turn to multiple sources, with more than 90 percent relying on personal savings as a funding source, followed by credit cards and personal loans (28 percent) and loans from friends and family (7 percent). Approximately 5 percent rely on equity investments by friends and family.[1]

In dollar terms, entrepreneur-backed bank loans and credit cards represent the primary source of financing during the first year.[2] Such sources rely on the entrepreneur's reputation and credit history and not on the merits of the venture. Accordingly, personal debt capacity gives the entrepreneur access to capital without the need to convince investors that the opportunity is worth pursuing.

Many ventures are legendary for their success in spite of getting started with bootstrap financing. Steve Jobs and his partner, Steve Wozniak, sold a Volkswagen and a programmable calculator to raise the $1,350 they used to build the first Apple computer. Bill Gates started his venture with Paul Allen from Gates's dorm room in 1975 and later relocated to a hotel room in Albuquerque.[3] They funded the start-up from savings and built a shoestring operation into Microsoft, a company with more than $58 billion in 2009 sales. But many more ventures begun by bootstrapping have failed miserably. Some undoubtedly were based on good ideas but were underfinanced.

Angel Investors

In one form or another, angel investors have been around for centuries. Queen Isabella of Spain backed Christopher Columbus's expeditions and Elizabeth I of England backed Sir Francis Drake. Two Boston-area angel investors backed the inventions of Alexander Graham Bell and, in 1877, put up money to start Bell Telephone. One of them was instrumental in creating the franchising arrangements that enabled the company to develop the telephone network that facilitated rapid diffusion of the technology. Except for a small shareholding, Bell, the entrepreneur, was out of the picture completely by 1881, four years after the company was formed.

Present-day angel investing has evolved into a quasi-institutional form. For ventures based on concepts that require lengthy development efforts, the earliest source of outside financing is often from high-net-worth individuals rather than organized financial institutions. These so-called angel investors generally are freelancers who are interested in investing relatively small amounts of money ($25,000 to $500,000) in early-stage projects.[4]

Angel investors often provide seed capital to develop an idea to the point where formal outside financing becomes feasible. Many are willing to invest over horizons of 5 to 10 years. In contrast, traditional venture capital funds usually prefer larger investments and somewhat shorter investment horizons. Angels seek to add value by identifying ventures with high potential for success and helping them progress. They usually seek to realize a return by taking equity in the venture.

Most estimates put the amount of angel capital invested in the United States in recent years at about $10 to $26 billion annually, excluding capital provided by friends and family.[5] According to the US Small Business Association, 57,000 entrepreneurial ventures received angel financing in 2007. Together, these estimates imply that the average angel investment is in the $200,000 to $400,000 range.

Many angel investors work alone; others are affiliated with angel networks. In the late 1980s, angels began to organize into informal groups that share deal flow and due diligence. Participants co-invest with each other, enabling the group to make larger commitments and bring more experience to each deal. There are several well-known groups in geographic areas known for high start-up activity: the Band of Angels (Menlo Park), Tech Coast Angels (Los Angeles, Orange County, San Diego, Santa Barbara), and New York Angels (New York City). Many groups have 50 to 100 members, and by some accounts there are over 300 such organizations in the United States.[6] There are even networking organizations to facilitate connections among angel groups. There are also angel groups, such as Investors' Circle, which focus on social venturing. The dynamics of working with each group are quite different. Some sponsor regular sessions where entrepreneurs are invited to make presentations.[7]

While angel investors may jointly investigate and discuss opportunities, US securities laws dictate that each investor must make an independent investment decision and take responsibility for his or her own due diligence. It is common for individuals in these groups to invest $25,000 to $50,000 in a company. The total investment from the members of an angel group who decide to invest typically averages around $250,000 to $750,000.[8]

Some angel investors are interested strictly in return on investment and do not want to become deeply involved with the companies in which they invest. Others are more active, often motivated by a desire to add value to the companies beyond their capital commitments. These angels typically focus on the types of companies with which they have experience. They can be good sources of information concerning financing and strategy.

Venture Capital

For financing requirements beyond seed capital, the entrepreneur can turn to organized providers of venture capital (we follow custom by using "VC" to refer to either venture capital or the venture capitalist, the meaning being clear in context). VC funds are organized as limited partnerships in which the limited partners provide almost all of the capital and the general partner is responsible for managing the fund, including investment selection, working with entrepreneurs, and harvesting the investments. VC funds have finite lives and are normally organized to last for about 10 years. Because VC funds involve small numbers of investors (the limited partners) and the investors (financial institutions or wealthy individuals) are presumed to be sophisticated enough not to require government oversight, VC funds are exempt from the key federal regulations of the securities industry. As private equity (including VC) has grown in importance and more companies have opted out of the public capital markets, private equity has increasingly attracted regulatory scrutiny in the United States and elsewhere.

VC-backed firms generally have little collateral that could provide a basis for secured lending; they also have the potential to achieve high growth with high profitability but with the commensurate high risk. Because VC is key to enabling high-growth entrepreneurship, we devote Chapter 3 to a comprehensive description of the institution. Here we focus more narrowly on identifying some of the considerations that help entrepreneurs decide when to seek VC financing.

VC investment varies considerably over time, over the business cycle, and in response to technological shocks. Annual VC investment reached a high of more than $100 billion in 2000 (the peak of the high-tech rally) but declined to $19 billion by 2003. After a fairly modest recovery, the collapse of the financial markets in 2008 and subsequent economic downturn led to a dramatic falloff in VC activity—only $17.7 billion was invested in 2009.

From the entrepreneur's perspective, a number of factors aid in determining whether VC is appropriate and which VC firm to select. First, timing is important. The venture must be developed to a point where the venture capitalist (i.e., the general partner of a VC fund) can expect to add value, not just money. The venture capitalist selects the ventures in which the fund invests, monitors the progress of portfolio companies, sits on boards of directors, and metes out infusions of financing based on attainment of milestones. The investment agreement with the entrepreneur normally gives the fund the right to force a liquidity event

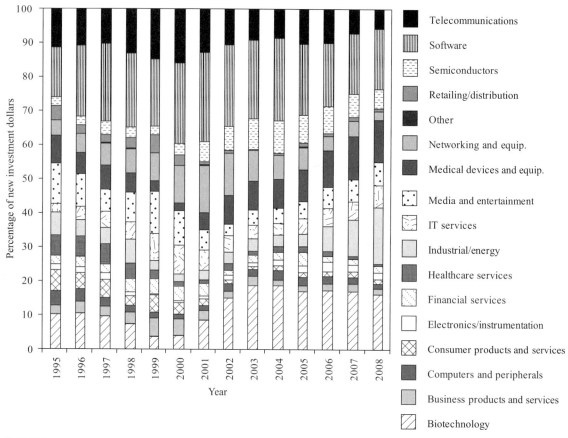

FIGURE **2.2**

New venture capital investments by sector

SOURCE: PricewaterhouseCoopers/National Venture Capital Association MoneyTree Report. Available at https://www.pwcmoneytree
.com/MTPublic/ns/nav.jsp?pge=historical; based on data from Thomson Reuters.

(such as an IPO) that can enable investors in the fund to realize returns on their investments in the fund.

Second, the venture must be in an industry sector where the venture capitalist has expertise. Figure 2.2 shows the sectors in which VC funds typically have invested. The categories are those reported by the National Venture Capital Association (NVCA). Although the majority of investments are in high-technology fields, investments occasionally are made in low-tech sectors such as health care services, consumer products, and retailing.

Third, VCs have tended to concentrate investments in particular geographic areas. The information in Figure 2.3 shows the geographic concentration of VC activity in the United States. Large fractions of the total VC investment are made in two regions—the New England (Boston) area and Silicon Valley in Northern California. Geographic concentration has changed little over time despite the efforts of many regions to foster entrepreneurial activity.

Fourth, the investment horizon and investment objectives of VC funds make VC better suited for some projects than others. VC funds seek equity or equity-like returns, and the finite life of the fund constrains the investment horizon. As a result, VCs are not likely to take an interest in projects that generate positive cash flows quickly but have limited growth potential or those that are likely to be harvested outside of a three- to eight-year window.

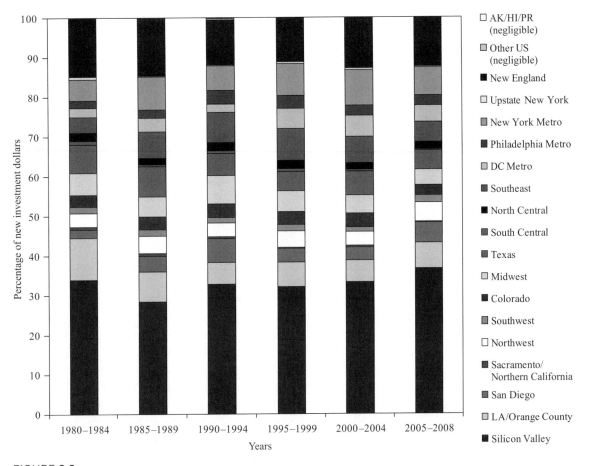

FIGURE **2.3**

New venture capital investments by region

SOURCE: PricewaterhouseCoopers/National Venture Capital Association MoneyTree Report. Available at https://www.pwcmoneytree.com/ MTPublic/ns/nav.jsp?pa.e=historical; based on data from Thomson Reuters.

While there are exceptions, there is little to be gained by seeking funding from a VC firm that does not have a presence in the geographic area. The same is true for one that does not have expertise in the entrepreneur's industry, one that is specialized in a stage of development that is different from that of the venture, or one that is not actively searching for new investments.

Asset-Based Lenders

Asset-based lenders, or "secured lenders," provide debt capital to businesses that have assets that can serve as collateral. The lender is not relying on the venture's cash flow for repayment but on the ability of the venture to liquidate business assets for debt servicing if necessary. Loans may be secured by accounts receivable, inventory, equipment, real estate, or other assets with verifiable market/liquidation values. Taking the collateral is not something the lender normally wants to do. Accordingly, asset-based lenders can also be expected to be concerned about the financial health of the venture. Total asset-based lending in the United States is estimated to have reached $590 billion in 2008.[9]

Venture Leasing

Venture leasing is a special case of leasing. Unlike most leases, leases to ventures are often subject to considerable risk. To compensate for potential loss, the lessor's return may be tied to financial performance of the venture, so that if the venture does well the lessor realizes more than the expected return, and conversely.

Venture leasing usually involves assets that are key to the operation of the venture. For example, in past years a number of ventures were launched to provide whole-body computerized tomography (CT) scans. The entrepreneurs in these ventures had to buy or lease a CT scanner, which, if purchased, was a multimillion-dollar investment. With venture leasing, the entrepreneur's initial investment is reduced, but some of the upside is shared with the lessor. Normally, the providers of leases are the companies that produce the equipment, as they are the ones who can most easily redeploy them if the venture fails.

There can also be tax advantages to leasing as compared to owning, especially for a venture that has yet to reach a profitable level of operation. Depending on its organizational form, if the venture were to purchase, it might not have sufficient income to be able to realize the tax benefit of recording depreciation expense related to the outlay for acquiring the equipment. If the venture were to buy, the tax benefit is lost to both the buyer and seller. In contrast, a profitable lessor who buys the machine and leases it to the lessee can realize the tax benefit. If lessors compete with each other to supply the equipment, some of the tax benefit should make its way to the venture in the form of more favorable lease terms.

Corporate Venturing

By some accounts, more than 100 major US corporations have, at one time or another, implemented an in-house VC program to aid in developing new business opportunities. In some ways, corporate venturing is an oxymoron, as most large, established corporations are notoriously non-entrepreneurial. They often have compelling incentives to cling to the status quo that is responsible for their profitability and could be undermined by aggressive innovation. Nonetheless, some corporations view the status quo as transitory and continuous innovation as essential to sustainability and growth. Such firms have found creative ways to supply capital to support ideas that do not "fit" with their traditional product or service line but may have market potential.

Internal corporate venture funds can help to retain creative employees and provide some assurance that great ideas will not "escape." A well-known example of an idea that escaped is the transistor idea of William Shockley and two other scientists at Bell Labs. After becoming frustrated with the research process at Bell Labs, Shockley took the idea and started his own company. Two employees of that company, Gordon Moore and Robert Noyce, later formed Intel.

Corporations provide financing to new ventures in various ways. When the innovative activity is integral to the company's business, the corporation may fund the activity through its normal research and development (R&D) budget. When the activity is more in the nature of prospecting for opportunities, a common approach is for the corporation to establish a separate, wholly owned enterprise that operates much like an independent VC firm but in which the corporation is the sole investor. The choice may reflect strategic considerations.

Internally managed venture investing.   Corporate venturing is more likely to occur in firms that depend on innovation to sustain competitive advantage. Xerox, for example, sponsors Xerox Technology Ventures, a business unit set up as a venture group. The unit has money to finance ideas from employees and by others. In exchange for bringing the idea to the company, the innovator gets a percentage stake in the venture. Another example is Bell Labs' New Ventures Group. Any Alcatel-

Lucent (Bell Labs) employee can come to the group to pitch an idea. If the idea makes the grade, the group can provide up to $100,000 of seed capital to fund work on a business plan. Larger amounts of funding are available to bring the product or idea closer to market. The researcher receives shares in the new enterprise while continuing to draw a salary from Alcatel-Lucent. The rationale is to encourage more creativity among employees and to do so with a minimum of bureaucracy.[10]

Google is an example of a company that has an explicit goal of supporting entrepreneurship within the firm. Google has sought to create a culture in which continuous innovation occurs at every level of the company. The 2005 founders' letter reinforces this idea: "We devote extraordinary resources to finding the smartest, most creative people we can and offering them the tools they need to change the world. 'Googlers' know they are expected to invest time and energy on risky projects that create new opportunities to serve users and build new markets."[11]

The company uses both formal and informal mechanisms to encourage innovation, with incentives ranging from compensation to recognition to providing in-house entrepreneurs with employees and other resources. Google engineers are encouraged to devote one day per week to working on anything they want. Some of Google's newer products (e.g., Gmail and Google News) originated during this "20 percent time."[12] Maintaining this environment, however, has become increasingly difficult as the company matures, and more than a few successful start-ups have been initiated by former Google employees.[13]

Externally managed venture investing.   Some corporations operate and provide financing to proprietary VC funds that invest in companies that are external to the corporation. In some cases, the fund acts like other VC funds, seeking investment opportunities with financial return as the sole objective. In others, the fund is a vehicle for advancing the corporation's product market strategy and selects investments based on how the ventures relate to the corporation's core business. In addition, corporations sometimes invest directly in independent ventures, acting as strategic partners.

Companies that invest directly in ventures include large pharmaceutical companies like Abbott Labs and Amgen; food giants Hormel & Co. and Nestlé; and computer-related firms like Intel, Microsoft, and Google. While these companies have significant internal R&D operations, they also set up VC divisions that act much like VC firms.

The magnitude of corporate VC investment varies widely from year to year. Figure 2.4 shows total corporate VC investment relative to total VC investment. Over the period shown, corporate VC is procyclical (as

FIGURE **2.4**
**Corporate
VC investment as a
percentage of total
VC investment**
The figure shows
total new VC invest-
ments by VC funds,
including corporate
funds. It also plots
corporate VC as a
percentage of total
investment.

SOURCE: Pricewater-
houseCoopers/National
Venture Capital Associa-
tion MoneyTree Report.
Available at https://www
.pwcmoneytree.com/
MTPublic/ns/nav.jsp?page
=historical; based on data
from Thomson Reuters.

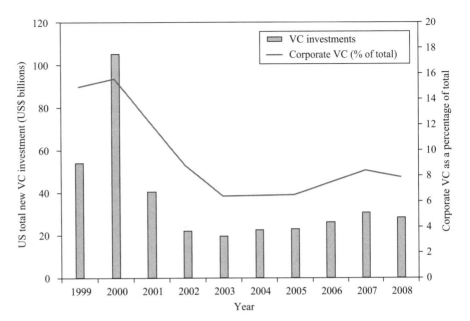

a percentage of total VC investment in the United States, corporate VC peaks when total VC investment is highest).

Government Programs

Many countries have established government-supported programs to provide loans and other financing for start-ups, small firms, and firms with growth potential and to support R&D. In the United States, Congress created the Small Business Administration (SBA) in 1953 to foster innovation and growth of small businesses.[14] The SBA is primarily a guarantor of loans made by banks and other financial institutions and does not lend directly to small businesses. The SBA provides loan guarantees through several programs; the 7(a) loan program and the 504 loan program are among the most popular.[15] In 2008, approximately $18.2 billion in new loans were guaranteed or arranged by the SBA.[16]

While the SBA does offer some grant programs, the grants generally support not-for-profit organizations, lending institutions, and state and local government entities that provide small business management or assistance to small businesses.

The SBA's Small Business Investment Companies. As an enterprise matures, the entrepreneur is able to attract financing that increasingly has the characteristics of debt. For a number of years, the SBA has sought to stimulate new ventures by providing a subsidy to encourage lenders to fund small businesses. Most of the financing is provided through Small Business Investment Companies (SBICs). SBIC financing usually takes the form of interest-bearing loans that are guaranteed by the SBA. More recently, the program has broadened to enable financing that is more like equity, such as loans that include warrants where the total return is tied to venture success. SBICs have invested in such winners as Federal Express, Cray Research (now CRAY), and Teledyne.

SBICs are privately owned and managed, for-profit organizations that are licensed by the SBA. With their own capital (raised from private sources including banks, corporations, individuals, and others) and with borrowed funds, SBICs provide capital to new and established small businesses.[17] Because of government support, the capital that the SBICs invest is obtained at below-market rates. An SBIC that is faced with competition to supply funds to a venture may be compelled to pass along some of these savings.[18]

Although SBICs are involved in financing at about the same stages as VC, the normal interest-bearing structure of the financing makes it better suited for firms that are less risky than typical VC-backed firms. SBICs prefer firms with more limited growth potential that need financing for working capital and have the ability to achieve profitable operations quickly.

The Small Business Innovation Research Program.   If the venture involves technology, several government agencies sponsor grants under the auspices of the Small Business Innovation Research (SBIR) Program. Participants include the departments of Agriculture, Commerce, Defense, Education, Energy, and Health and Human Services, as well as NASA and the National Science Foundation. SBIR Plan I research grants provide seed capital and funding up to $50,000 to determine the feasibility of a project. Plan II grants go up to $500,000 of R&D financing.

Government programs in other countries.   Most developed economies provide government-based assistance grants and other means to facilitate creation and growth of new businesses. Prominent examples include Canada's Small Business Finance Centre (SBFC) and the UK's Department of Small Business, Innovation, and Skills (BIS). Among the many programs of the BIS is a multimillion-pound equity finance program, Enterprise Capital Funds (ECFs). The program is designed to enable funding of up to £2 million for businesses that require investment that falls within what has been termed the "equity gap"—more than what angel investors generally can supply but less than VCs would consider.

Trade Credit

Trade credit, or vendor financing, is the largest source of external short-term financing for firms in the United States and is even more important in emerging economies, where risk capital is often scarce.[19] Vendor financing arises whenever a business makes a purchase from a supplier that offers trade credit. For example, a venture buys supplies on terms of "net 30," receives the supplies right away, but does not need to pay until 30 days later. In effect, the supplier is providing the venture a zero-interest loan for 30 days. Trade credit borrowing normally appears on the company's balance sheet as an account payable. The same loan appears on the supplier's balance sheet as an account receivable. The difference between a firm's accounts payable and its accounts receivable is its net trade credit. Net trade credit defines the position of the firm in terms of whether trade credit functions as a net source or net use of funds. If accounts payable exceeds accounts receivable, trade credit is a net source—that is, borrowing.

Trade credit can be very expensive. For example, terms of 2/10 net 30 are common. The buyer is offered a 2 percent discount if the invoice is paid within 10 days; otherwise the full payment is due in 30 days. If the buyer decides to use the credit and forgo the 2 percent discount, there is a sizable opportunity cost. In effect, the firm borrows the invoiced amount for 20 extra days by paying 2 percent more. The implicit interest rate on such a loan is 44 percent per annum.[20] Managers of any new venture must consider this cost when deciding whether to pay during the net period or take the discount. If the need for cash is transitory or if bank loans are not available or only available at a higher interest rate, forgoing the discount could make sense.

Entrepreneurs may not have much actual control over the decision to offer trade credit to customers. Credit terms and availability are determined by competition and tend to be uniform in a given industry. A venture that is competing against established firms may find that it must offer trade credit to get customers to try the product, whereas the venture's suppliers may insist on receiving cash until the venture has proven itself.

Factoring

When a business offers trade credit, it generates accounts receivable. In lieu of borrowing to finance the receivables, the venture may be able to sell the accounts receivable to a factor. A factor is a specialist who buys accounts receivable and manages the collection activities. Factoring comes in two basic types: with and without recourse. If factoring is without recourse and a customer of the venture does not pay its bill, the factor absorbs the loss. Factoring with recourse means that if the customer does not pay, the factor can collect from the venture directly.

The three basic parts of a factoring transaction are (1) the advance (the factor advances a percentage of the face value of the receivables to the seller), (2) the reserve (the remainder of the total invoice amount that the factor holds until it receives payment from the customer), and (3) the fees associated with the transaction, which are deducted from the reserve. The advance generally ranges from 70 to 90 percent. The fee is calculated as a percentage of the face value of the receivables. It includes a fee for handling the collection and (for a nonrecourse transaction) a fee for assuming the risk of nonpayment. Normal fees can be 2 to 6 percent and can include an additional component for explicit interest over the period during which funds are advanced. Research indicates that factoring is more common for smaller sellers and is most beneficial for sellers with geographically dispersed buyers and those with few repeat customers.[21] Although the cost of factoring may seem high, the terms are competitively determined. Factoring may be attractive to a cash-poor venture until it grows to a size that makes integrating the collections function more economical.[22]

Factoring is an international institution. Figure 2.5 shows how the use of factoring varies over time and across regions of the world. While its use in the United States has been static, factoring is a growing and significant source of financing worldwide. This trend may reflect differences in institutional constraints on bank lending that make factoring more appealing in some countries. It may also reflect differences in typical firm size and the composition of industries.

Franchising

Franchising is another way to finance growth. In business format franchising, such as a fast food restaurant franchise, the franchisor establishes a business format and offers franchising opportunities to prospective franchisees. The franchisee invests in a facility in a particular locality. The facility carries the franchisor's brand and must conform to

FIGURE **2.5**
Global growth of factoring as a source of financing

SOURCE: Factors Chain International: http://www.factors-chain.com/.

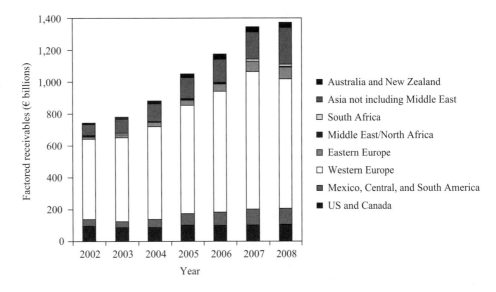

- ▪ Australia and New Zealand
- ▪ Asia not including Middle East
- ▫ South Africa
- ▪ Middle East/North Africa
- ▪ Eastern Europe
- ▫ Western Europe
- ▪ Mexico, Central, and South America
- ▪ US and Canada

the general standards of the franchise network. Franchisors provide a range of services that can include site selection, training, product supply, marketing, and assistance in arranging financing. The franchisee normally pays a franchise fee and makes periodic payments that are partly based on revenues.

The reasons for franchising are varied and not limited to financing advantages, but the arrangement does allow the franchisor to expand the size and geographic reach of the business rapidly without having to raise all the capital by itself. Among other things, the franchisee may be responsible for identifying the local market opportunity and acquiring the land and facilities, which, if the outlet were company owned, would have been costs borne by the franchisor.

Franchising is common in a number of industries such as quick-service restaurants, lodging, car rental, and table/full service restaurants. About one-third of all retail sales in the United States are made through franchised outlets (including car dealers and gas stations).[23] The practice has also increased the international reach of well-known consumer brand names (e.g., Yum! Brands, which acts as a franchisor for Kentucky Fried Chicken, Taco Bell, Pizza Hut, etc., has franchised outlets located in the United States, China, and India).

Mezzanine Capital

Mezzanine financing usually refers to capital raised after the firm has established a record of positive net income with revenues approaching

$10 million or more. Some VC firms and other types of private equity firms offer this type of financing. The financing generally is a hybrid that has characteristics of senior debt and common equity. A frequently used type of mezzanine financing is subordinated debt with an equity "sweetener" or warrants.

A warrant is a long-term call option that is issued by a firm. Warrants entitle the holder to buy shares of the firm's common stock at a stated price for a period of time. For example, each $1,000 of borrowing might provide the mezzanine lender with warrants to purchase 20 shares of stock at $5 each.

Nonpublic Debt

Debt financing may make sense for a rapidly growing venture. There are two primary reasons for using debt to finance growth. First, because interest payments are tax deductible, debt may be less expensive than equity for a firm that has consistent earnings.[24] Second, debt holders usually cannot vote. Therefore, equity owners do not lose voting control if debt is issued. However, debt is a contractual obligation, so in the event of bankruptcy bondholders have priority over equity owners.

Private debt, such as commercial bank debt, sometimes is an option for small businesses, particularly those with steady, verifiable cash flows, where the business is not expected to grow. This type of financing is more likely for replicative types of entrepreneurial ventures, such as those that employ established business models and are created to serve a growing population—for example, independently owned dry cleaners, bakeries, restaurants, health clubs, and so on. The entrepreneur should be in a position to make the interest payments and presumably to take advantage of the tax deductibility of interest payments.

Public Debt

Small and new firms do not have access to the public bond market. Investment banking firms seldom underwrite bond issues smaller than $10 million in gross proceeds. Unless a firm has a substantial asset base and steady cash flows and is in need of a significant amount of capital, it is unlikely to be able to arrange a bond issue. New ventures are more likely to borrow from commercial banks, life insurance companies, or an SBIC or other government-related entity.

Private Placements of Equity and Debt

Sometimes a firm would like to raise a specific amount of capital quickly and would prefer to avoid the cost and time required to complete a public offering. This can be accomplished by private placement of debt or equity. Prospective equity investors or lenders are identified by the company's management team, the VC, or an investment bank. The private placement market generally is more attractive than the public market for small equity or debt issues or for debt issues backed by complex security arrangements where flexibility is desired.

In a sense, angel and VC financing are equity private placements. The term "private placement," however, applies more broadly to any sale of equity or debt securities to a small number of investors by means other than a public offering.

In the United States, public offerings are regulated by the Securities and Exchange Commission (SEC). Similar regulatory bodies oversee public offerings in other countries. One advantage of placing equity privately is that the venture avoids the complex, ongoing reporting that would be required if it were to raise capital via public offering. In addition, an entrepreneur can use private placement to limit the number of people who gain access to strategic information about the venture.

While privately placed securities avoid SEC registration and reporting requirements, only certain types of offerings qualify as "private." Important factors that the SEC will consider are the number of offerees, the relationship of the offerees to the issuer, the number of units sold, the size of the offering, and the manner of offering. Often more significant than these factors, however, is the sophistication of the investors and their access to information about the issuer.

Stakeholders in the new venture, including employees, distributors, retailers, franchisees (if any), suppliers, and so on, are potential investors in equity private placements, as are insurance companies, pension funds, high-net-worth individuals, and foreign investors. Institutional investors such as insurance companies and pension funds are candidates for buying privately placed debt.

Often, private equity is structured as convertible preferred stock. The preferred stock typically converts to common at an IPO. Privately placed debt may have some advantages as compared to a public issue. As with equity, the costs of a private placement of debt tend to be lower and the placement can be quicker. Also, it is possible to negotiate greater flexibility in the terms than would be possible for a public offering.

A significant advantage of a privately placed issue is that it may facilitate monitoring. A public placement normally has many investors. The resulting diffuse ownership encourages free riding in terms of investor effort devoted to monitoring the company. In contrast, if a debt or equity issue is placed privately, ownership is concentrated and there are significant incentives to monitor company management. The small number of investors also facilitates restructuring the terms of the investment agreement if circumstances change.

Initial Public Offering

In an IPO, the issuing company raises capital by selling registered equity shares to the public via a formal offering process. An IPO is a convenient exit or harvesting mechanism for VCs and other investors. The importance of VC in the IPO market has become clear over the past few decades. For the period from 1999 to 2008 in the United States, VC-backed firms accounted for about half of all IPOs by number and 25 percent by dollars raised.[25] In industries like biotechnology, computers, and software, the fraction of VC-backed firms is even higher.[26]

The IPO market is volatile. Issuers and underwriters often try to time IPOs to reach the market after periods of marketwide price appreciation. They refrain from issuing or sometimes withdraw planned IPOs after marketwide price declines.

Going public provides a way for the venture to raise equity capital and for early investors to realize returns on their investments, achieve liquidity, and diversify.[27] An IPO also provides a market-determined valuation that can be used as a basis for negotiating merger and acquisition (M&A) transactions. In cases where the venture's track record is clear, large amounts of capital are needed, and potential synergies with other firms are absent, an IPO may bring a higher share price than a private placement. Public ownership also provides a way to create equity incentives for employees. The stock price is a barometer of market expectations and can provide useful information about how investors expect economic events and managerial decisions to affect future earnings. Finally, a publicly traded firm is able to raise additional capital more quickly and cheaply than if it were private.

On the cost side, IPOs are expensive in terms of time and costs of ongoing compliance with SEC regulations and reporting requirements. Already-scarce managerial time must be diverted from the business and devoted to the IPO process. The presence of a visible stock price may induce management to be unduly concerned with short-term stock price fluctuations.

Direct Public Offering

Between an IPO and a private placement, US securities regulations provide a variety of safe harbors whereby a firm can issue equity to small numbers of investors without going through the formal public offering process. Generally, the safe harbors relate to raising capital from small numbers of investors, employees, and sophisticated investors. SEC safe harbors operate on the premise that specialized or inside knowledge will protect these investors sufficiently even in the absence of SEC oversight.

As an example, in 1984 Ben and Jerry's, a company founded in Vermont, built its first ice cream plant by selling $750,000 of equity directly to Vermont residents in a direct public offering (DPO). The firm later raised $6.5 million in a public offering. This experience suggests that DPOs can make sense for a firm that has a loyal customer and employee base.

Later-Stage Financing Alternatives

The list of financing sources could be extended considerably. Other possibilities identified in Figure 2.1 include acquisition, leveraged buyout (LBO), and management buyout (MBO). We address these alternatives later in the text when we analyze the choice of new venture financing and the issue of how early-stage investors harvest their investments.

2.2   What's Different about Financing Social Ventures?

While social (not-for-profit) ventures have access to most of the same financing sources as for-profit ventures, they are not able to issue equity. But risky not-for-profit ventures still must be able to offer risky claims. A common solution is to structure debt instruments so that they are tied to venture performance. Thus, for example, debt that pays interest where the amount of interest is tied to financial performance can be a solution. Other alternatives include royalty-based financing or revenue rights, where the investor's return is a direct function of revenue. Such instruments are not equity, but they do give the venture a means of raising capital from investors who seek high-risk/high-return opportunities.

Some not-for-profit entities attract philanthropic funding. For example, the Calvert Foundation offers donors/investors a "Community

Investment Note," which provides a (low) fixed rate of return. The foundation uses the borrowed funds to make (risky) loans that support social enterprises such as microcredit initiatives, affordable housing, and community development—investments that they believe will have a positive social impact. Investors who provide financing for this type of social venturing are making tradeoffs between social returns and financial returns.

Not-for-profit foundations have developed other creative ways to provide funding for social ventures. One is to allow investors to make tax-deductible contributions to "giving funds," where the foundation uses the contributions to make loans and provide grants for socially responsible businesses and initiatives.[28] Increasingly, philanthropic organizations and foundations are mimicking VC funds that stage their financing and tie financing rounds to milestones. This allows social entrepreneurs to apply for grants and other aid and to receive subsequent rounds of financing, provided they meet certain performance goals.

Finally, organizations such as Investors' Circle provide a forum for attracting angel investors who are specifically interested in promoting social goals but want to do so by investing in for-profit ventures. Investors' Circle is a network of over 200 angels, professional VCs, foundations, and others who seek to invest private capital to "promote the transition to a sustainable economy." Since 1992, Investors' Circle reports that it has facilitated the flow of over $130 million into more than 200 companies and small funds that address social and environmental issues. The investments are in for-profit organizations, however, and the financial arrangements and returns are not unlike returns to angels and VC funds.[29]

2.3   Considerations When Choosing Financing: The Organizational Form

One of the early decisions an entrepreneur must make concerns the organizational form of the venture. The choice has implications for a variety of factors, including ability to attract financing, tax treatment, liability, succession, and ability to attract employees. Table 2.1 identifies some of the more common organizational forms in the United States. The choice of organizational form can be addressed most effectively by considering the growth potential of the venture and the factors that affect availability of key financing sources.

The choice of corporate form requires careful consideration of several issues. Answering a few key questions can aid the process.

TABLE **2.1** Common organizational forms in the United States

Organizational form	Ownership rules	Tax treatment	Liability	Transferability of ownership	Financial capacity
Sole proprietorship	A single owner.	Earnings pass through to owner.	Owner is liable for business debts.	Only through sale of the business.	Limited by financial capacity of owner.
Partnership	Two or more co-owners.	Earnings pass through; flexibility concerning allocation of gains and losses.	Each partner is fully liable for business debts.	Partnership interests may be transferable through sale, subject to approval of other partners.	Limited by combined financial capacity of the partners. Partners may disagree about borrowing to support the venture.
Limited liability company	One or more co-owners, referred to as members.	Earnings pass through; flexibility concerning allocation of gains and losses.	Liability of members is limited to the extent of their investments.	Membership interests may be transferable through sale, subject to approval of other members.	Limited by combined financial capacity of the members. Members may disagree about borrowing to support the venture.
Limited partnership	General partner(s) with control and limited partners who are passive investors.	Earnings pass through; flexibility concerning allocation of gains and losses.	Each general partner is fully liable for business debts. Limited partners are liable to the extent of their investments.	Partnership interests may be transferable through sale, subject to approval of other partners.	Limited by combined financial capacity of the partners. Limited partners may have substantial financial capacity.
S corporation	Up to 75 shareholders, one class of stock.	Earnings pass through to owners.	Liability of shareholders is limited to the extent of their investments.	Shares are transferable without approval of other investors as long as SEC and state rules are followed.	Limited by constraint on maximum number of shareholders.
C corporation	Unlimited numbers of shareholders and classes of stock.	Earnings taxable to corporation when earned and to shareholder when received as dividends.	Liability of shareholders is limited to the extent of their investments.	Shares are transferable without approval of other investors as long as guidelines and SEC rules are followed. Registered shares of public corporations are freely transferable.	Unlimited, since number of investors is not limited.

- Are not-for-profit status and the attendant tax exemption worthwhile?
- Should liability be limited, or should losses be passed on to the company's owners?
- Is it important to be able to switch corporate forms easily as the company evolves?
- How important is it to avoid corporate-style taxation (i.e., double taxation)?
- Who are the best monitors of the firm—owners, investors, or managers?
- How will the monitors be monitored?

All of these considerations factor into our discussion below.

The organizational forms listed in Table 2.1 are all for-profit forms. Many economic enterprises, however, such as churches, foundations, and many universities, are not intended to be profit-making ventures. In the United States many are organized under Section 501(c)(3) of the Internal Revenue Code, which allows not-for-profit entities to avoid paying tax on earnings in excess of expenses. The rationale is that the excess is not distributed to owners but rather is retained to fund the ongoing activities of the enterprise.

The organizational form choice can be subject to ongoing review. A venture at an early stage might be organized as an S corporation because operating losses are expected and the S form allows losses to be passed through to owners. Later, when the venture needs to access larger capital sources and early owners are looking to exit, it may be reorganized as a C corporation. Even a venture that starts as a 501(c)(3) corporation (not-for-profit) can be reorganized as a taxable entity.

While the tax exemption may seem like a tremendous advantage, when income is a small fraction of revenue the economic advantage can be small. A for-profit venture has advantages associated with equity financing and more effective monitoring of managers. These benefits can more than make up for the tax benefit of the 501(c)(3) corporation. For example, for-profit and not-for-profit universities currently compete for students, and for-profit and not-for-profit medical care providers compete for patients. Entities occasionally convert from not-for-profit to for-profit status, or not-for-profit entities are acquired by for-profit entities. Factors that bear on the choice of not-for-profit status are complex. They relate to the ability to attract funding from particular sources or by methods such as tax-deductible donations. Not-for-profit entities can accumulate wealth tax free. Converting them to for-profit status may enable owners to withdraw capital while avoiding substantial tax liability.

Assuming the venture under consideration is to be operated for profit, the next question might relate to long-run capital needs. C corporations and limited partnerships can raise large amounts of money from investors whose involvement with the enterprise may be passive. The other forms all restrict capital-raising ability by limiting the number of investors or limiting investment to parties who are actively involved in the venture. The important distinctions between a C corporation and a limited partnership relate to transferability of ownership and tax treatment of earnings.

A C corporation, particularly if it is publicly held, can most easily raise capital from diverse groups of investors, and organizing as a C corporation facilitates transfer of ownership. Public corporations have the additional benefit of an established and verifiable market value for their shares, which can serve as the currency in a variety of business transactions.

Limited partnership interests are less easily transferable. However, the limited partnership avoids taxation of earnings at the corporate level and facilitates structures that allocate taxable gains and losses most effectively among partners. Both forms offer limited liability to investors who are not actively involved in the venture. Limited liability is essential to large-scale fundraising from investors who wish to play passive roles in the venture.

If raising large amounts of capital is not important, a venture may be organized as a general partnership. Doing so subjects the partners to unlimited liability but enables venture earnings to flow through to the partners untaxed. Sometimes the number of partners can be so large and the activities of the enterprise so diffuse that the pure partnership form is an impediment to growth. In that case, a limited liability partnership form can preserve the tax advantages of partnership and still offer some protection against liability. Protection from liability can break down, however, if partners act negligently in monitoring the activities of the venture.

The early choice of organizational form is of strategic importance to a new venture. Sole proprietorships and small partnerships are relatively easy to convert to other forms; but as the venture grows and more parties become involved as partners or owners, ability to transition from one form to another decreases. Thus, it is important to make the decision as to organizational form in light of the overall strategic orientation of the venture.

In terms of numbers of business entities, small proprietorships dominate, especially those with annual receipts less than $1,000,000. Figure 2.6 shows that C corporations comprise less than 25 percent of business entities for each size class under $500,000, but their share grows

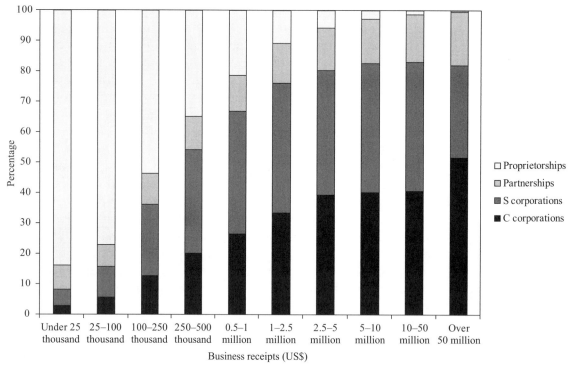

FIGURE **2.6**

Percentage of businesses by form and business receipts

SOURCE: Kelly Luttrell, Patrice Treubert, and Michael Parisi, "Integrated Business Data, 2003," *Statistics of Income Bulletin (IRS)* (Fall 2006): 47–103.

from 27 percent to almost 52 percent with increasingly larger receipt size classes. S corporations and partnerships, the flow-through entities, are more prevalent in the midsize receipt classes. S corporations account for between 34 and 43 percent of entities with receipts in the $250,000 and $50 million range, and partnerships have the largest percentage of entities in the midsize receipt classes. C corporations become more prevalent as business receipts increase, and (while not shown in the figure), within the over $50 million class, C corporations account for nearly 82 percent of total receipts.

2.4 Regulatory Considerations

Entrepreneurs and investors are confronted by a panoply of securities laws when considering how to finance a venture and whether to raise capital in the public markets. The laws governing access to the public capital markets (and to operating as a corporation with publicly tradable equity or debt) are complex and fluid. Here we identify the main legislation that affects the public capital markets. We focus on the United States, but all countries have laws that affect public market access and require regular financial disclosure. Below we identify the major components of US federal securities laws; discuss state regulations that affect security issuance, known as "blue sky laws"; describe the process involved in registering securities with the SEC; and identify some exemptions and safe harbors that may affect financing choices.

Prior to the Great Depression, US securities markets were largely unregulated. Stock exchanges were organized in a number of cities and companies could "go public" with relative ease. Not only was access easy for the issuers, it was also easy for investors. There were few controls to prevent investors from taking on very high levels of investment risk, and stock scams were prevalent. The business failures and personal bankruptcies of the Great Depression led to the enactment of the two federal laws that form the basis of regulations concerning the offering, sale, and trading of securities:

- *The Securities Act of 1933.* Regulates offering and sale of securities. It establishes the law pertaining to securities fraud and sets requirements to register securities formally with the federal government. It also delegates to the SEC the authority to enforce and interpret the 1933 Act.
- *The Securities and Exchange Act of 1934.* Regulates aftermarket trading of public securities. It also establishes the law on insider trading and buying on margin.

The 1933 Act is more relevant to start-ups, as it pertains to the primary offering of securities by a company and the ongoing disclosure of information once the securities are issued. The 1934 Act relates to exchange of publicly traded securities after they have been issued.

The drafters of the 1933 Act were reportedly guided by Justice Louis Brandeis's famous aphorism: "Sunshine is said to be the best of disinfectants; the electric light the best of policemen." The law seeks to foster transparency at the time of a company's public offering of securities and afterward. Under it, corporations desiring to issue securities to the public for the first time can only do so by filing a registration statement with the SEC (Form S-1, or, for small businesses seeking to raise $10 million or less, Form SB-1). The Act mandates dissemination of a disclosure document known as a prospectus and creates a complex liability scheme dealing with misinformation in the registration statement or the prospectus or during the distribution of the securities to public investors. The Act also places specific limitations on the timing and content of pre-issuance communications. The 1933 Act has been amended numerous times and has become expansive in its reach and vision.

The issuer's responsibilities do not end with filing a registration statement and circulating a prospectus. After the IPO or public debt offering, the company is subject to ongoing reporting requirements under the 1933 Act. Public companies must provide timely annual reports that include audited financial statements and are subject to other reporting rules that are intended to help level the playing field for investors. The cost of ongoing reporting can be a significant burden for a small company, a consideration that prevents all but the most successful ventures from going public.

Compliance costs for small companies are particularly high in the United States. Other countries, such as Canada, provide mechanisms for small companies that expect to remain small to go public. Companies that issue in the United States can avoid federal reporting requirements by restricting their offerings to a single state. Some states, such as Utah, have relatively lax ongoing reporting requirements and have become popular venues for IPOs by small companies.

The state laws that pertain to companies with publicly traded securities are known as "blue sky laws." The phrase derived from concerns that shady operators would try to sell unsuspecting investors pieces of clear blue sky. As of now, every state in the United States has securities laws. Unlike federal securities laws, which constitute a disclosure-based regulatory system, some states use merit-based regulation—they empower the state to decide whether an offering deserves the attention of investors.

The state laws do not regulate securities exchanges or interstate trading markets. Nor do they regulate disclosure by public companies in connection with shareholder trading or voting. State laws are not uniform. As Palmiter (2008) points out, this implies that issuers and investment advisors must comply with a largely uncoordinated and sometimes conflicting set of state and federal rules.

What Is a Security?

The boundaries of securities regulation are determined by the definition of a security. The federal securities acts provide a list of instruments that are considered to be securities, including stocks, bonds, investment contracts, profit-sharing agreements, puts, calls, warrants, and notes, among others. Over time, judicial interpretation of the 1933 and 1934

Acts has turned an "investment contract" into a catchall type of security. The definition of investment contract is today a broad concept.

The Supreme Court's pivotal 1946 decision in *US v. Howey* provided the foundational definition of an investment contract. *Howey* involved the sale of plots of an orange grove in Florida to primarily out-of-state investors, who technically owned the individual citrus trees. The seller, however, retained sole responsibility for cultivating, harvesting, and marketing the fruit. Profits were pooled among investors, each taking a share proportional to his investment. The Court determined that this scheme constituted an investment contract and was therefore subject to federal securities regulation.

According to *Howey* and later cases, an investment contract is any contract, transaction, or scheme that involves the investment of money in an enterprise where investors expect to derive a profit based primarily upon the managerial efforts of others. This definition brings under the purview of federal securities regulation certain time-share interests, some types of franchise arrangements, and even investments in pyramid schemes.

Whether ownership interests in an organization are securities also depends on the legal form of the organization. The level of involvement of investors in the enterprise often is a definitive indicator of whether an investment constitutes a security. For example, common shares and preferred shares of a corporation are securities. General partnership interests, however, rarely constitute securities, while limited partnership interests often do qualify.

Exemptions from Registration in the United States

Registration of securities can be very costly in terms of out-of-pocket expenses for both lawyers and underwriters and because of potential liability. The 1933 Act exempts from registration those transactions for which registration may be unduly expensive given investor sophistication, state securities regulation, or the issuer's modest financial needs. But even if a security is exempt, securities laws apply. Thus, the SEC can proceed against any issuer if there is misrepresentation.

There are two important types of exemptions from registration: exempt securities and exempt transactions. Exempt securities include government securities, commercial paper, and insurance policies, among others. Exempt transactions include purely intrastate offerings, private placements, and certain small offerings by the issuer.

In 1982, the SEC consolidated its exemptions for small and private offerings into a set of rules known as Regulation D (Reg D).[30] Reg D contains three exemptions from the federal registration requirements:

1. *An exemption for small offerings.* Companies can offer and sell up to $1 million of their securities in any 12-month period without registration.

2. *An exemption for offerings to accredited investors or limited numbers of investors.* Companies can offer and sell, without registration, up to $5 million of their securities in any 12-month period to an unlimited number of "accredited investors" and up to 35 other persons who do not need to satisfy the sophistication or wealth standards associated with other exemptions.[31] Investors receive "restricted securities," meaning that they cannot be sold for six months or longer without their being registered and companies cannot use general solicitation or advertising to sell the securities.

3. *An exemption for private placements.* Under the private offering exemption, companies can raise an unlimited amount of capital without registration, provided they do not use general solicitation or advertising to market the securities. The securities acquired through private placement cannot be sold for at least a year without registering them. Unlike the second exemption, all investors must be sophisticated—that is, they must have sufficient knowledge and experience of financial and business matters to make them capable of evaluating the merits and risks of the prospective investment.

2.5 The Deal

A central aspect of an entrepreneur's attempt to raise capital is negotiating "the deal."[32] The deal defines the allocation of risk and return as well as the rights and obligations of the entrepreneur and the investor. A well-structured deal can create value for the entrepreneur and provide the investor with a return that compensates for the risk. To understand the underlying economics of deal structure, it is useful to identify the basic types of information problems that confront entrepreneurs and investors. We will return to these concepts later in the book, when we look in more detail at financial contracting.

Information Problems Facing the Entrepreneur and Investors

Three basic information problems characterize the market for financing new ventures. First, the entrepreneur's information about the value of the opportunity may be incomplete and uncertain. Second, information about the value of the idea and the ability of the entrepreneur is held asymmetrically—the entrepreneur is likely to have more accurate information about technological merit, whereas investors are likely to have superior information about potential economic value. The entrepreneur probably knows more about her own abilities and commitment than does an outsider. Asymmetry of information leads to the third problem: risk of appropriation of intellectual property. How can an entrepreneur convince prospective investors of the merits of the project without risking appropriation? An untried entrepreneur cannot merely assert the existence of a valuable idea and expect to be believed, but disclosing the idea subjects the entrepreneur to the risk of appropriation.

Milestones.   These problems give rise to some unique features in the market for entrepreneurial finance. First, because information is highly uncertain and asymmetrically held, outside investors want to see tangible evidence that both reduces uncertainty and reveals the entrepreneur's abilities. The demand for better information gives rise to the use of milestones. Milestones, as we have discussed, are specific and verifiable performance benchmarks.

Staging.   The second feature, which we have also discussed, is staged financing. When entrepreneurs receive financing commitments, the funds are not normally invested up front. Rather, they are staged and linked to achieving milestones. The source of financing often is different at each stage. Thus, staging reflects the commonsense idea of "wait and see."

Reliance on staging tied to milestones may appear to serve only investors' interests since many entrepreneurs seek as much up-front cash as possible. But this perception is wrong. With the right investment partner and a good project, staging is in the entrepreneur's interest. Investor concerns about the project and about the entrepreneur make early investment capital expensive—a large fraction of ownership must be exchanged for a small amount of capital. The entrepreneur's willingness to condition investment on attainment of milestones makes it more likely that the entrepreneur will attract investment in the first place and that she will retain significant ownership.

Staging can benefit both parties even if the venture fails. Once failure becomes apparent, both parties are positioned to make clean breaks and to stop investing time and capital in the venture. Conditioning investment on objective measures of performance identifies the decision points of when to renegotiate the financing or to withdraw from the venture. Without milestones, the entrepreneur (and the investors) may erroneously believe things are progressing well and overinvest rather than exiting and finding a better opportunity.

Securing confidentiality.   The third information problem is the entrepreneur's concern about appropriation of intellectual property. Entrepreneurs often seek assurances that their ideas are secure with those to whom they are presented. The practice of asking investors to sign confidentiality agreements as a condition of receiving a copy of the business plan is a highly imperfect solution. Also, many VCs and angel investors refuse to sign these agreements because doing so can expose them to increased risk of litigation if the information leaks from any source. The investor's reputation for trustworthiness is far more important to the entrepreneur than is a signature on a confidentiality agreement.

Term Sheets and Investment Agreements

The term sheet.   Because every new venture is different, the arrangements between the entrepreneur and investors defy generalization. Nonetheless, certain elements and documents are common. First, it is common for the parties to reflect their mutual understanding in a term sheet. The term sheet reflects an agreed-upon valuation and sets out the amount of investment that is to be made, as well as the ownership claims the investor will receive.

In addition, the term sheet may identify some of the options, rights, and responsibilities of each party. For example, the investor may have the right to make appointments to the board of directors and, under some conditions, may have the right to withdraw from the project or to terminate the entrepreneur. The entrepreneur may have the right to call on the investor for additional funds in the event that certain milestones are achieved or to acquire additional shares through the exercise of stock options.

The term sheet is just a step on the path to an investment agreement. A term sheet may reflect mutual understandings and expectations, but it rarely constitutes a binding agreement on the terms of the investment. Moreover, it does not commit either party to the deal.

Pre-money and post-money valuation.   The valuation of the venture, though it may not be stated formally in the term sheet, is key to the negotiation. Consider a simple deal in which an investor contributes $1 million in exchange for 400,000 shares of common stock and the entrepreneur retains 600,000 shares. Effectively, the investor is acquiring the shares for a price of $2.50 per share. The term "post-money valuation" refers to the total value of the venture that is implied by multiplying $2.50 by the entire 1 million shares. In this case, the post-money valuation (sometimes referred to as capitalization) is $2.5 million. Pre-money valuation is the implied value of the venture before the investment. In this case, the pre-money valuation is $1.5 million (i.e., the post-money valuation less the $1 million investment). The post-money valuation is a measure of the value of the venture to the outside investor. The entrepreneur may have different beliefs about value and those beliefs affect the negotiation, but they do not appear in the term sheet.

When the investor's claim is something other than "plain vanilla" equity, post-money valuation is not an accurate measure of what the venture is worth. Suppose, in the above example, the investor pays $2.50 per share, but the shares are preferred stock that can be converted to common at a later date. Because the owner of preferred shares has a prior claim to common stockholders (i.e., the entrepreneur) in the event of bankruptcy, post-money value as calculated above overstates value. In fact, the more rights the entrepreneur is willing to surrender to the investor, the more the investor is willing to pay for the shares. The result is a higher valuation, both post-money and pre-money, but in reality value is not necessarily increased. Rather, it is transferred from the entrepreneur to the investor.

It is important to recognize that the ultimate concern of the entrepreneur is not the post-money valuation but the true value to the entrepreneur of the entrepreneur's ownership interest. Many entrepreneurs make the mistake of focusing on the post-money valuation and ignore the value of the "sweeteners" and other rights that were promised to the investor.

The investment agreement. Once the parties believe they have reached an understanding on the investment terms, the next step is to prepare a formal, legally binding agreement. The investment agreement is a contract between the entrepreneur and the investor. With the term sheet as a starting point, the investment agreement formally sets out the terms and conditions of the investment, including any options, rights, or contingencies retained by either party. In addition, the agreement sets out a comprehensive list of representations and warranties of the entrepreneur, as well as a list of covenants and undertakings.

Representations and warranties. Representations and warranties are contract clauses intended to protect the investor from the possibility that the entrepreneur has not disclosed some material fact that would affect valuation or willingness to invest. Obvious examples relate to ownership of the tangible and intangible assets, absence of litigation, and accuracy of the financial statements.

Covenants and undertakings.   Covenants and undertakings that are agreed to by the entrepreneur are intended to ensure that the investor's capital is used in the manner envisioned at the time of the agreement. A covenant is a promise of future action or nonaction. Affirmative covenants are actions the entrepreneur agrees to perform. For example, the entrepreneur might agree that the investor can make certain appointments to the board, approve annual budgets, be provided with regular financial statements, or expect that certain financial ratios will be maintained. Negative covenants are actions the entrepreneur agrees not to take. Among others, the entrepreneur may agree that, without the investor's consent, the entrepreneur will not change the nature of the business, issue additional securities, increase employee compensation, or enter into competition with the venture.

Of course, the agreement can also include covenants and undertakings of the investor, such as to provide additional funding if a given milestone is achieved. However, in deals involving established investors such as highly regarded venture capital firms, the entrepreneur is likely to have to rely more on the investor's reputation.

Liquidation and registration rights.   The investment agreement may define the rights of the parties that relate to liquidation of their investments or participation in future investments. It is common for investors to have some form of registration rights that may be exercised if the company makes a public offering. Shares that are formally registered with the SEC are freely tradable, whereas unregistered shares are not. Piggyback registration rights give the investors the right to have their shares included in any registration of shares by the venture. Demand registration rights give the investors the ability to force the venture to register their shares and, effectively, to force the company to go public. Registration rights may be coupled with a forced buyout provision that obligates the entrepreneur to buy out the investors if the venture does not go public or if a buyer is not found within a specified period.

Rights of first refusal and preemptive rights.   Conversely, the investment agreement may grant the investor rights to participate in future financings. Common examples include a right of prior negotiation, which means the entrepreneur must negotiate future financing with the investor before looking elsewhere; a right of first refusal, which means that the investor has the right to meet any outside offer to provide financing; and a preemptive right, which means the investor has a right to maintain its fractional ownership share by participating in subsequent sales as an investor.

Ratchets and antidilution rights.   Although many of the provisions of the investment agreement may seem innocuous, reasonable, or simply boilerplate, they should not be taken lightly. Many may give significant bargaining power to the investor in the event that the relationship sours. If the relationship ever breaks down, the investor will try to use those provisions as leverage with the entrepreneur and as a means to recover some of the investment. It is important to think through the implications of each provision and to understand what may happen if the venture performs either better or worse than expected or if there is reason to change the focus of the venture in a material way.

Some provisions that are not intended to be problematic can turn out to be so. A good case in point is a ratchet, or antidilution provision. A ratchet is designed to protect the investor from the possibility of a lower valuation in a subsequent financing round. If the valuation declines from what the investor paid, a full ratchet gives the investor enough new shares for free so that the investor's average cost per share is the same as the cost to a new investor. An investor who has a ratchet can be expected to demand a smaller fraction of ownership in exchange for a given level of investment. Inclusion of a ratchet, however, can also make raising subsequent financing more difficult.

Suppose an investor contributes $3 per share to a new venture and that in the next financing round the highest any investor is willing to pay is $2. If the original investor has a full ratchet and the next round is priced at $2 per share, then the original investor gets one new (free) share for every two shares of initial investment. The average cost for the investor is reduced to $2. But if the original investor gets more shares for free, then the new investor will not value the deal at $2. The price must be lower to compensate for dilution of the value caused by the ratchet. If the initial investment is large enough and the decline in value great enough, there may be no positive price at which new capital can be raised. Some ratchet agreements recognize this problem and limit the potential dilution effect of the ratchet.

Overarching considerations.   Although the overriding purpose of the investment agreement is to protect the investor, it is also the result of negotiation. In exchange for protecting the investor, the entrepreneur gains by attracting capital on terms that involve giving up less owner-ship. Sahlman (1988) discusses some of the characteristics of successful deals. Among the more important ones are the simplicity of the deal, robustness in the face of deviations from projections, and adaptability in response to unforeseen developments.

Well-structured deals also provide appropriate incentives for the parties and do not make raising future capital too difficult. On a more qualitative level, a good deal structure improves the chance of success, and the provisions of the deal reveal information about the capabilities, commitment, and beliefs of the parties. Because any formal agreement can be abused, trust, rather than legal formalism, is the single most im-portant contributor to success.

Deal Structures of Angel Investments

The above discussion is related primarily to investments by VC funds. Angel investors normally enter into investment agreements that are less complex. They might be as simple as providing a brief description of the venture and the parties' aspirations for it, then specifying an amount of investment in exchange for a percentage ownership interest. The agree-ment might call for periodic reporting, board participation, or other ac-cess to information. Angel deals normally do not involve formal staging commitments, preferential forms of investment, ratchets or other anti-dilution protection, or provisions designed to force a liquidity event.

It may seem, given that uncertainty is probably greatest at the stages suitable for angel investment, that the deal structures would be simi-larly complex. Ibrahim (2008) proposes three reasons for angel investor reliance on simple structures: (1) the preexistence of complex deal struc-tures that would need to be unwound before VC investment is possi-ble might discourage VC investment; (2) in contrast to VCs, angels rely on informal rather than contractual methods of screening and moni-toring; and (3) it is not cost effective to prepare elaborate contracts for small investments where time until the next investment round is needed is likely to be short. A further reason for simplicity is that each angel in-vestor acts on his own behalf rather than in a fiduciary capacity for lim-ited partners. The investors can more easily agree with each other if the terms are simple. In contrast, formal agreements between a VC fund and the entrepreneur are important because of the more complex struc-tures of the investing entities.

Ibrahim points out that, with the rise of organized angel investor groups, angel investment agreements have become somewhat more structured, moving more in the direction of VC deals. He ascribes the change to the greater professionalism of angel groups, the higher transactions costs of group investing, and the larger amounts that the groups are able to invest.

2.6   International Differences in Financing Options

Availability of capital to fund entrepreneurial ventures varies dramatically around the globe, in terms of both the extent of funds and the types of financing that are available. The reasons for these differences are varied. They include such infrastructure factors as enforceability of contracts, protection of minority interests, institutionalization of money management, and the economic wealth of the society.

Financing sources are also affected by the nature of the entrepreneurial activity that is prevalent in the country. In the United States, where a significant fraction of the activity is focused on high tech with the potential for very large returns, VC has emerged as an effective funding mechanism. Even so, total funds provided to entrepreneurs by VC funds are quite small compared, for example, to bank loans. In emerging economies, where the ability of entrepreneurs to undertake sustained high-risk projects is limited, entrepreneurial activity is more focused on launching and growing traditional enterprises that are relatively safe and can generate positive cash flow quickly.

Because the mix of entrepreneurial activity varies so much, it is difficult to generalize about availability of financing sources. A recent study, based on survey data compiled by the World Bank to examine global patterns of financing of small and medium-size enterprises, reports that external financing as a fraction of total financing does not depend on country infrastructure but that the mix of external financing does.[33] Enterprises in less developed countries are not as able to obtain external debt and equity financing and, therefore, rely more on operations-based financing such as trade credit.

Greater reliance on vendor financing in emerging economies is not surprising since such economies tend to have limited availability of financing from other sources. Figure 2.7 shows four categories of institution-based financing that are available, by country. The World Bank classifies countries into four per capita income groups. Data are sorted by income group (lowest on the left) and then by the amount of institutional loan financing as a multiple of country GDP (gross domestic product). Other institutional financing sources are added to institu-

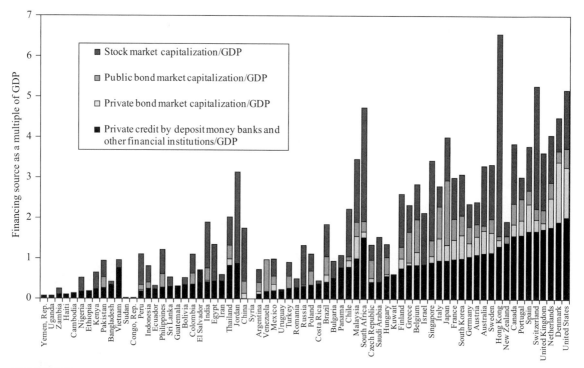

FIGURE **2.7**

Worldwide sources of business financing, 2007

The figure shows cumulative totals of various sources of financing, expressed as multiples of GDP. The countries are sorted by country wealth categories, assigned by the World Bank.

SOURCE: World Bank, Financial Structure Dataset, revised 2009. The database is downloadable from http://go.worldbank.org/ X23UD9QUX0.

tional lending to show total institutional financing. In most low-income countries, loans are the only institutional source of financing, but the amount of loan financing is small in relation to GDP, which, in low-income countries, is also quite small on a per capita basis.

For the most part, if entrepreneurs need funding in such countries, they are compelled to rely on noninstitutional sources, such as personal wealth, friends and family, and vendors and strategic partners who are willing to extend credit. But where do the companies that extend credit obtain their funds if bank lending in such countries is low? One important answer is that providers of credit are often foreign and have access to financing sources that local businesses do not.

The outlook for entrepreneurs is much better for the high-income countries. Bank lending is high compared to GDP, but in most of the countries shown it is dominated by private and public debt issues and equity offerings. Of course, these are also the countries where financing sources such as trade credit, angel investment, and VC are relatively high and where bootstrap funding and funding from friends and family are likely to be more significant.

An important and interesting question is why other countries do not simply seek to duplicate the success of the United States by imitating the infrastructure choices that seem to be associated with high income and the ability to support high-growth entrepreneurship. We address this in the policy discussion in the final chapter of the book.

2.7 Summary

Investing in new ventures is very different from investing in the shares of a public company. Because of the high degree of uncertainty about the potential for survival and success, financing commitments tend to be made in stages that are related to development of the venture. Customarily, development is described in terms of milestones that correspond to resolutions of significant uncertainty. New venture development is divided into specific stages: development, start-up, early growth, rapid growth, and exit. The boundaries between stages can be defined in terms of revenue, revenue growth, net income, and cash flow available to investors.

Appropriate forms of financing depend on the stage of new venture development. Financing typically begins with bootstrapping (tapping the resources of the entrepreneur and friends and family). Seed capital normally is external financing, such as angel investment, although angel investment can go beyond seed financing. High-tech ventures with long development stages may require specific R&D financing. Start-up financing provides funds to initiate operations. Later-stage financing options are used to finance growth before the venture is profitable or during the early- and rapid-growth stages. Mezzanine financing and other forms of debt are best suited for ventures that are generating taxable income. Exit financing, including buyout financing and public debt or equity issues, is designed to enable early-stage investors to realize the returns on their investments.

This chapter describes some of the main financing choices available to the entrepreneur, defines terms and concepts that are used frequently in the industry, and identifies considerations that bear on the choice of financing, such as securities regulations and organizational form, whether the venture is a social or a for-profit venture, and institutional differences in capital markets across countries. We return to choice of venture financing in Chapter 14, which provides an analysis of assessing financing needs and the timing of those needs.

Finally, the use of financing that involves an outside investor requires a meeting of the minds, as reflected in a deal. The entrepreneur and the investor normally describe the deal in a term sheet, which later may be set out in a formal investment agreement. The investment agreement describes the conditions under which investment will be made and is used by the entrepreneur and the investor to protect the investor and increase the ability of the entrepreneur to raise capital.

REVIEW QUESTIONS

1. Identify some types of financing that are associated with each of the following stages of new venture development: research and development, start-up, early growth, rapid growth, and exit.

2. At what stage of venture development is each of the following most likely to invest: (1) an angel investor? (2) a venture capitalist? Why?

3. How do government programs encourage new venture development? Give examples of government programs that facilitate financing of new ventures.

4. Why do small firms, especially new ones, have limited access to the public debt market? Under what conditions are ventures likely to be able to access the bond market?

5. How is the financing of social (not-for-profit) ventures different from the financing of for-profit ventures?

6. Why does organizational form affect the choice of financing?

7. What are the considerations a new venture takes into account when deciding on organizational form?

8. Identify the basic US securities laws that affect the issuance and exchange of securities. Which is more relevant for new ventures and why? What is the rationale for these laws?

9. What are the basic informational problems facing an entrepreneur when trying to raise money from an investor? How are these problems reflected in the deal between the parties?

10. Identify some common features of a term sheet or investment agreement. What problems do these provisions anticipate, and how do they help to mitigate the problems?

NOTES

1. See Stouder (2002), who analyzes data on 74 entrepreneurs. In an earlier study, Hyatt and Mamis (1997) survey founders of a sample of firms that made the Inc. 500 list in 1995–96. They find results similar to Stouder's: 70 percent rely on personal savings as a funding source, followed by credit cards (25 percent) and loans from friends and family (12 percent). Fewer than 10 percent use bank loans and equity investments by friends and family.

2. According to Robb and Robinson (2009), who base their work on a large-scale Kauffman Foundation survey.

3. See Gates (1995).

4. A few angels may commit to significantly larger amounts ($500,000 to $3 million). Angels in this category include people like Mitch Kapor, founder of Lotus; Paul Allen, cofounder of Microsoft; and Ron Conway, a Silicon Valley–based angel investor who was an early-stage investor in Google, Ask Jeeves, and PayPal.

5. See UNH Center for Venture Research, 2008 Angel Market Analysis: http://wsbe.unh.edu/cvr.

6. See the Angel Capital Association website http://www.angelcapital association.org/. The UNH Center for Venture Research reports the active number of investors in 2008 as 260,500 individuals.

7. See the Angel Capital Educational Foundation for information on angel groups, locations, and contact information: http://www.angelcapital education.org/. Also see the European Business Angel Network: http://www .eban.org/.

8. A survey by the Angel Capital Association reports that the median investment per round in 2007 was about $266,000. Many angel groups co-invest with other groups, individual angels, and early-stage VCs to make larger investments per round.

9. See Commercial Finance Association (2009).

10. See Block and MacMillan (1993), Chesbrough (2002), and Silver (1994).

11. See the 2005 annual report: investor.google.com/pdf/2005_google _annual_report.pdf.

12. See Google's 2007 Letter from the Founders at http://investor.google .com/ipo_letter.html and Groysberg, Thomas, and Wagonfeld (2009).

13. See Vascellaro (2009). Google grew from fewer than 2,000 employees in April 2004 to over 20,000 in 2009.

14. Craig, Jackson, and Thomson (2009) find evidence of a small positive impact of the SBA's guaranteed lending programs on the financial performance of companies that receive guaranteed loans.

15. The most popular type of SBA loan is the 7(a) loan, whereby a com-

mercial bank or other participating financial institution makes a loan of up to $2 million for working capital financing, equipment purchase, or purchase of real estate. The SBA guarantees up to 85 percent of the outstanding amount. SBA 504 loans are arranged by a Certified Development Company (CDC), a private, not-for-profit corporation that contributes to the economic development of the local community, Other types of loans are described on the SBA website: http://www.sba.gov/.

16. The total of $18.2 billion in loans represents 78,324 new 7(a) and 504 loans (*SBA's Citizens' Report: FY 2008 Summary of Performance and Financial Results*: http://www.sba.gov/idc/groups/public/documents/sba_homepage/serv_budget_08_citizens_report.pdf).

17. "Small" for SBIC purposes is average net income for the last two years less than $6 million and net worth below $18 million. See http://www.sba.gov/aboutsba/sbaprograms/inv/esf/INV_SBIC_FINANCING.html.

18. See Petersen and Rajan (1997). Ng, Smith, and Smith (1999) analyze trade credit terms across industries.

19. Fisman and Love (2003) find that industries in countries with poorly developed financial markets but higher rates of trade credit financing exhibit higher rates of growth.

20. The effective annual rate is calculated as $(1 + \text{discount percent})^{(365/\text{credit period})} - 1$.

21. Mian and Smith (1992) and Smith and Schnucker (1994) examine US firms' choices to factor their receivables. Factors are more likely to be used by firms when information costs about buyers and monitoring costs are high.

22. The Internet has begun to change the factoring business. Receivables Exchange LLC is an online auction site where lenders can bid on unpaid invoices posted by companies desiring immediate cash. See Simona Covel, "Getting Your Due," *Wall Street Journal*, May 11, 2009, p. R8.

23. Brickley, Smith, and Zimmerman (2009), p. 456; see also Brickley and Dark (1987).

24. Whether the tax effect is sufficient to result in a net benefit is an empirical question. Because interest payments are taxable to recipients, the benefits are less than might first appear. A firm that cannot fully exploit the debt tax shelter may actually increase its cost of capital by overreliance on debt.

25. See National Venture Capital Association (2009), p. 43.

26. See Gompers (1995), Barry et al. (1990), and Lin and Smith (1998).

27. Early-stage investors are often precluded from selling shares they own in or during the IPO. For the most part, they harvest by selling in the public market after the shares have been trading for several months.

28. See the Calvert Foundation website at http://www.calvertfoundation.org/invest/index.html.

29. In 2002, an HBS/McKinsey study found that companies invested in through Investors' Circle generated a 5–14 percent return. The study included data from 110 Investors' Circle member investments (http://www.investorscircle .net/our-impact/investment-statistics).

30. See http://www.sec.gov/answers/regd.htm.

31. Rule 501 of Reg D defines a person as an accredited investor if she has a net worth exceeding $1 million and annual income exceeding $200,000 for the last two years.

32. Discussion is drawn partly from Stevenson (1988).

33. See Beck, Demirgüç-Kunt, and Maksimovic (2008).

REFERENCES AND ADDITIONAL READING

Barry, C., C. Muscarella, J. Peavy, and M. Vetsuypens. 1990. "The Role of Venture Capital in the Creation of Public Companies: Evidence from the Going Public Process." *Journal of Financial Economics*2 7:447–72.

Beck, T., A. Demirgüç-Kunt, and V. Maksimovic. 2008. "Financing Patterns around the World: The Role of Institutions." *Journal of Financial Economics*8 9:467–87.

Berger, A. N., and G. F. Udell. 1998. "The Economics of Small Business Finance: The Roles of Private Equity and Debt Markets in the Financial Growth Cycle." *Journal of Banking and Finance*2 2:613–73.

Block, Z., and I. C. MacMillan. 1993. *Corporate Venturing: Creating New Business within the Firm*. Boston: Harvard Business School Press.

Brickley, J., and F. Dark. 1987. "The Choice of Organizational Form: The Case of Franchising." *Journal of Financial Economics*1 8:401–20.

Brickley, J., C. Smith, and J. Zimmerman. 2009. *Managerial Economics and Organizational Architecture*. 5th ed. Boston: McGraw-Hill Irwin.

Chesbrough, H. W. 2002. "Making Sense of Corporate Venture Capital." *Harvard Business Review* 80 (3): 90–99.

Commercial Finance Association. (May) 2009. *Annual Asset Based Lending and Factoring Survey, 2008*. Available at https://www.cfa.com/eweb/ Docs/2008_ABL_Factoring_Non-Member_Report.pdf.

Craig, B. R., W. E. Jackson III, and J. B. Thomson. 2009. "The Economic Impact of the Small Business Administration's Intervention in the Small Firm Credit Market: A Review of the Research Literature." *Journal of Small Business Management* 47 (2): 221–31.

Fisman, R., and I. Love. 2003. "Trade Credit, Financial Intermediary Development, and Industry Growth." *Journal of Finance* 58 (1): 353–74.

Gates, B. 1995. *The Road Ahead*. New York: Viking.

Gompers, P. 1995. "Optimal Investment, Monitoring, and the Staging of Venture Capital." *Journal of Finance*5 0:1461–89.

Gompers, P., and J. Lerner. 2001. "The Venture Capital Revolution." *Journal of Economic Perspectives*1 5:145–68.

Groysberg, B., D. Thomas, and A. B. Wagonfeld. 2009. "Keeping Google 'Googley.'" Harvard Business School Case 9-409-039. Cambridge, MA: Harvard Business Publishing.

Hyatt, J., and R. A. Mamis. 1997. "Profile of a Bootstrapper." *Inc.* (August): 61–63.

Ibrahim, D. M. 2008. "The (Not So) Puzzling Behavior of Angel Investors." *Vanderbilt Law Review* 61:1405.

Lin, T. H., and R. L. Smith. 1998. "Insider Reputation and Selling Decisions: The Unwinding of Venture Capital Investments during Equity IPOs." *Journal of Corporate Finance*4 :241–63.

Mian, S. L., and C. W. Smith. 1992. "Accounts Receivable Management Policy: Theory and Evidence." *Journal of Finance*4 7:169–200.

National Venture Capital Association. 2009. *Yearbook*. Available at http://www.nvca.org/#.

Ng, C., J. K. Smith, and R. L. Smith. 1999. "Evidence on the Determinants of Credit Terms Used in Interfirm Trade." *Journal of Finance*5 4:1109–29.

Palmiter, A. 2008. *Securities Regulation: Examples & Explanations.* 4th ed. New York: Aspen.

Petersen, M. A., and R. G. Rajan. 1997. "Trade Credit: Theories and Evidence." *Review of Financial Studies* 10 (5): 661–91.

Robb, A., and D. Robinson. 2009. "The Capital Structure Decisions of New Firms." Working paper, SSRN (Social Science Research Network). Available at http://papers.ssrn.com/sol3/papers.cfm?abstract_id=1345895.

Sahlman, W. A. 1988. "Note on Financial Contracting: Deals." Harvard Business School Note 288-014. Cambridge, MA: Harvard Business Publishing.

Silver, A. D. 1994. *The Venture Capital Sourcebook.* Chicago: Probus.

Smith, J. K., and C. Schnucker. 1994. "An Empirical Examination of Organizational Structure: The Economics of the Factoring Decision." *Journal of Corporate Finance*1 :119–38.

Stevenson, H. 1988. "Deal Structure." Harvard Business School Teaching Note 9-384-186. Boston: Harvard Business School Press.

Stouder, M. D. 2002. "The Capital Structure Decisions of Nascent Entrepreneurs." Unpublished PhD dissertation, Rutgers University.

Vascellaro, J. E. 2009. "Google Searches for Ways to Keep Big Ideas at Home." *Wall Street Journal*, June 18.

CHAPTER 3

Venture Capital

If I would have listened to my customers I would have built a faster horse and buggy.

Henry Ford

The term "venture capital" (VC) is sometimes used in a generic sense to mean capital invested in new ventures. It more accurately refers to capital supplied by a specific kind of financial institution, the VC firm. VC firms have a unique organizational structure and focus on a specific market niche of high-risk ventures with potential for rapid and significant growth. Most new ventures are not suitable for VC investing, and accordingly, most capital supplied to new ventures does not come from VC firms. On the other hand, VC has been an early source of financing for many successful high-growth companies and is an important driver of economic growth.

Understanding the nature of VC firms is important for anyone who is considering a venture that has the potential for rapid growth or anyone considering investing in a VC fund. Understanding how VC firms are organized and how they operate are aspects of a broader concern: where to search most effectively for financing. Entrepreneurs whose ventures are not well suited for VC financing can easily waste time and effort seeking funding from firms that, because of their orientation, are unlikely to find the entrepreneur's enterprise attractive.

VC firms are of interest for other reasons. First, the contract structures they use, both when they invest and when they raise capital from investors, illustrate market-based solutions to many of the information problems that surround new ventures. Second, the institutions involved in new venture financing are evolving. Innovations in institutional form and structure are continuous. The VC firm provides a useful frame of reference for examining and evaluating new organizational forms.

VC is a particular kind of private equity. Private equity refers to any investment in equity that is not traded on an organized exchange. This includes VC-style investments in early-stage companies, but may also include investments in unregistered shares of companies that have freely tradable registered shares. It is not uncommon for firms that are engaged in VC funds also to be engaged in other kinds of private equity funds such as buyout funds; similarly, it is not uncommon for private equity funds that are focused on buyouts to allocate a portion of their portfolio to VC deals.

Investments in private equity can take the form of leveraged buyouts, VC, distressed equity investments, mezzanine capital, and so forth. With a VC investment, the firm typically invests in young start-ups with growth potential and generally does not obtain majority control. In contrast, when a private equity firm undertakes an LBO transaction, the firm seeks to acquire majority control of an existing firm. Given that we are most interested in financing arrangements for new ventures, our focus is on VC as a subcategory of private equity.

3.1   Development of the Venture Capital Market

The first modern VC fund in the United States was organized in 1946 by American Research and Development (ARD). ARD's fund was organized as a closed-end mutual fund. In contrast to the VC funds of today, it was open to investment by any investor. In contrast to open-end funds, where new investors can join at any time by purchasing new shares of the fund, the total capital investment in a closed-end fund is fixed. After initial sale of the shares by the fund, a person who wishes to invest must buy existing shares from someone who owns them and wants to sell.

ARD established the practice, which persists today, of searching for high-risk deals with the potential for big wins. The fund's early-stage investment in just one of its ventures, Digital Equipment Company, accounted for roughly half of the entire return to fund investors over a period of more than two decades.[1] Several other funds that were launched during the 1950s and 1960s imitated the structure and orientation of ARD.

As documented below, early growth of the VC industry in the United States was slow, restricted by regulation, tax policy, case law, and professional investment management practices.

The Investment Company Act and the SEC

In the United States, mutual funds and other investment companies are regulated under provisions of the Investment Company Act of 1940 (ICA), enforced by the SEC. Because of SEC interpretations of some provisions of the ICA in the late 1960s, the ARD style of closed-end mutual fund for VC investment was (and still is) precluded. Specifically, the SEC required that fair value of fund investments be determined "in good faith by the fund's board of directors." Thus, reliance on consultants to determine fair value would not absolve the board of potential liability for reporting valuations later determined to be inconsistent with fair value. Particularly detrimental to VC, the SEC equated fair value with liquidation value, even with regard to assets where the acquirer has no near-term intent to liquidate, and prohibited reliance on formulaic approaches to determining the fair value.

The SEC's new emphasis on liquidation value and good faith liability of fund directors precipitated a withdrawal of closed-end funds from investing in private equity. Over most of the following decade, the VC market languished. Closed-end funds effectively were foreclosed as vehicles for investing in VC.

Consistent with the impact of the SEC's interpretations of the ICA fair value standard, Figure 3.1 shows that new capital commitments to VC generally declined from 1969 through 1977.[2] Capital commitments are reputation-enforced promises to invest a specified amount in the fund. To show percentage volatility more clearly, amounts in the figure are presented in log scale. The decline over this period is from $171 million in 1969 to $39 million in 1977.

FIGURE **3.1**
New venture capital commitments, 1969–2009

SOURCES: US Census Bureau, *Statistical Abstract of the United States* (various issues); Thomson Reuters Venture Capital data (http://thomsonreuters.com); Sahlman (1990); National Venture Capital Association (http://www.nvca.org/).

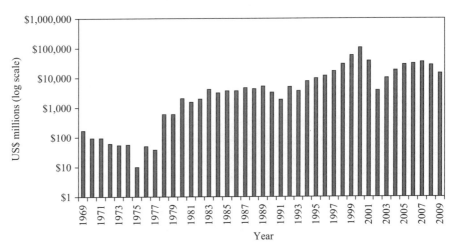

VCs could avoid being subject to SEC interpretations of the ICA by taking advantage of safe harbor provisions in the SEC acts (discussed in Chapter 2). The safe harbor provisions drove firms interested in raising capital to invest in nonpublic companies, to organize as limited partnerships, and to only raise capital from investors who are deemed by the SEC to be sophisticated investors, not requiring the protections of the SEC acts. The VC limited partnership structure that is common today is designed to fit within the safe harbors.

The Prudent Investor Standard and the Employee Retirement Income Security Act (ERISA)

An additional problem impeded the early growth of formal VC limited partnerships. To achieve their intended purpose, VC funds need access to patient capital from investors who are able to (1) accept illiquidity and high risk and (2) reliably commit to providing investment capital when called upon to do so. The natural sources of such funds are wealthy individuals and large institutional investors such as pension funds and endowments. Historically, however, professional asset managers with fiduciary liability viewed themselves as being constrained from investing in high-risk or nonmarket assets. The constraints derived from an array of old-fashioned state and federal regulations, legal precedents, and investment policies.

One specific constraint was the traditional "prudent person" standard of fiduciary responsibility. Under this constraint, responsibility to clients was based on the risk of each investment without regard to portfolio diversification. Using this standard, courts would attempt to assess whether each investment was appropriate for the manager's client (e.g., an employee participant in a retirement plan). Investment managers who were held to such standards generally avoided investing in anything but very safe securities.

Significant changes in the VC market in the United States began to occur in the late 1970s. First, in 1979 the Department of Labor reinterpreted prudence standards governing investments by pension funds. The reinterpretation enabled managers to view the risk of an individual investment in the context of its contribution to the overall risk of the pension fund portfolio. Under the new prudent investor standard, pension funds could invest in securities that traditionally had been viewed as too risky (imprudent). The result was a rapid increase in the level of pension fund investments in VC funds. Other asset managers with fiduciary responsibilities similar to those of pension fund managers, such as managers of endowment funds, have adopted the new prudent investor standard.

Second, reduction of the capital gains tax rate in the Revenue Act of 1978 spurred an increase in entrepreneurial activity. Workers had more incentive to leave salaried employment to pursue new ventures in which the principal form of compensation would be a capital gain on sale of the venture's stock. The rate reduction also increased incentives to invest in financial instruments that produce capital gains.[3]

Corresponding to the capital gains tax rate reduction, annual new commitments to VC funds increased from $39 million in 1977 to $600 million in 1978. After 1978, the level increased dramatically, reaching $106.1 billion in 2000 before dropping precipitously to $3.9 billion in 2002. New commitments grew during the mid-2000s, reaching $35.5 billion by 2007 before again starting to decline.

New VC commitments are related to what is happening in the public equity markets. The early 1980s and much of the 1990s were periods of rising stock market values, high levels of new investment in the capital markets, and high levels of IPO activity. The late 1980s was a period of lower economic growth and a generally less active capital market.[4] The decline beginning in 2000 corresponds to the collapse of the dot-com industry. The growth of new commitments during the 2000s and decline in 2008 parallel stock market performance during the period.

Despite its rapid growth, the VC market in the United States remains small relative to public equity and debt markets. In 2000, new VC commitments reached a high-water mark of $106.1 billion. This contrasts with public and private debt issues totaling $977.6 billion and public and private equity issues totaling $291.2 billion in 2000. However, VC commitments generally are large compared to SBA loans to small businesses, which in 2000 totaled $12.1 billion.[5]

VC funding can dry up quickly if the equity capital market declines. Figure 3.1 shows that new commitments dropped precipitously between 2000 and 2002, but the flow of investment capital from new commitments to new investments can be spread over several years. Figure 3.2 shows that the decline in new investments was less dramatic after 2000 than the decline in new commitments (recall that Figure 3.1 is in log scale).

Worldwide Growth of Venture Capital

Factors similar to those that slowed the early growth of organized VC in the United States have restrained growth in other parts of the world.

FIGURE **3.2**
**Venture capital
investments in the
United States,
1970–2009**

SOURCES: National Venture
Capital Association (2009);
PricewaterhouseCoopers/
National Venture Capital
Association MoneyTree
Report (https://www
.pwcmoneytree.com),
based on data from Thom-
son Reuters.

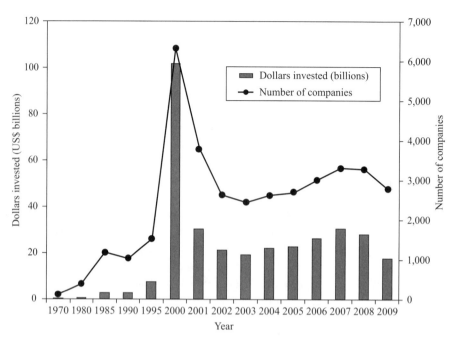

The pension funds that invest in VC in the United States, for example, are defined-benefit plans in which asset allocation choices are made by a board that acts as the agent of plan participants. In many countries, defined-benefit retirement plans do not exist or account for only a small fraction of retirement savings. Some countries rely primarily on redistribution systems similar to the US Social Security system, which is unfunded; instead, current beneficiaries receive payments from the contributions paid in by current workers. In some countries, retirement plans may have formally imposed restrictions on investment choices or may be required to invest heavily in the sovereign debt of the country or securities selected for political reasons. Similar restrictions sometimes limit the investment choices available to insurance companies, another important source of VC funding in the United States.

Figure 3.3 shows asset allocations of pension funds based in various Organization for Economic Cooperation and Development (OECD) countries. The fraction of pension fund investments in equity is highly correlated with the extent of VC investment and with the total assets of pension funds. Also, while endowments, such as those of private universities, are an important source of funding for VCs in the United States, this is not true in other parts of the world.

In general, the factors that limit availability of funding to VC are more onerous in other countries than in the United States. One re-

FIGURE **3.3**
**Pension fund assets
allocated to equity
securities, by country**

SOURCE: Organization for
Economic Cooperation
and Development, *Pension
Markets in Focus*, no. 6
(October 2009); available
at http://www.oecd.org/
dataoecd/30/40/43943964
.pdf.

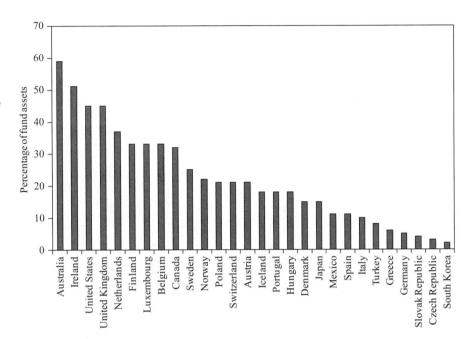

sponse has been the introduction of VC funds that raise capital from US investors for the purpose of investing in ventures in developing economies. Another has been that VC firms outside the United States tend to raise funds from traditional financial institutions, such as commercial banks. When they do, the management practices of the VC firms tend to be more conservative and based partly on the collateral or personal guarantee of the entrepreneur.

The Changing Role of Venture Capital

In Chapter 2 (Figure 2.2), we presented evidence that the sector focus of VC investment has changed over time in response to changes in the need for investment capital in high-risk ventures. The stage focus has also changed. In the early years, as shown in Figure 3.4, the commitments went predominantly to seed, start-up, and early-stage ventures. For the 1980–2000 period, later-stage investments were approximately 15 percent of the total. In more recent years, VC funds have focused increasingly on later-stage investments. For the 2001–8 period, the proportion of later-stage investments more than doubled, to 35 percent, and seed- and start-up-stage investments accounted for a very small fraction. In 2008, VC funds invested $1.5 billion in seed/start-up-stage ventures, compared to $9 billion invested by angels.[6]

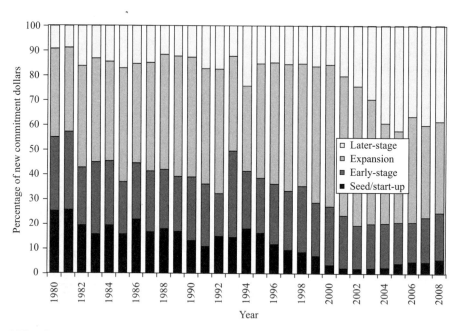

FIGURE **3.4**
Venture capital investments by stage of development

SOURCES: National Venture Capital Association, *Yearbook* (various years); PricewaterhouseCoopers/ National Venture Capital Association MoneyTree Report (https://www .pwcmoneytree.com).

Who Invests in Venture Capital Funds?

Venture capital requires investors who are able to commit substantial amounts of capital over long periods and who do not regard the illiquidity of their investments in VC as an important cost. Figure 3.5 illustrates the increasing importance of pension funds, endowments, and life insurance companies as sources of new venture funding in the United States.[7]

Earlier, we indicated that VC in countries other than the United States has been restrained by limited access to the kinds of institutions that are the primary sources of VC in the United States. Europe is second to the United States in terms of the size of the VC industry. Yet even there, we can see the impact of limited access to institutional sources of patient risk capital. According to 2008 figures prepared by the European Private Equity and Venture Capital Association (www .evca.eu/), pension funds accounted for 25.1 percent of new capital commitments, endowments and foundations accounted for 4.5 percent, and insurance companies accounted for 6.6 percent. The 36 percent total from these sources compares to 88 percent from the same sources in the United States in 2003.

The Impact of Venture Capital on the Economy

Early-stage VC investment is small compared to corporate and government R&D investments. During 2000, when new VC commitments in

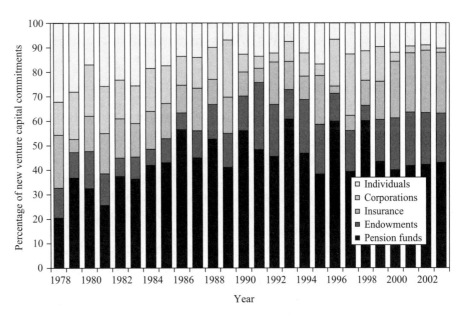

FIGURE **3.5**

Sources of new commitments of venture capital

SOURCE: National Venture Capital Association, *Yearbook* (various years); reported in US Census Bureau, *Statistical Abstract of the United States* (2004–5), table 743.

the United States reached $106.1 billion and seed and start-up investments totaled $3.1 billion, corporations invested around $133 billion in R&D activities and the US government invested $63 billion, primarily through universities.[8]

Though a small industry, VC has a large economic impact. Many of today's largest and most research active corporations received early-stage funding from VC firms. In its most recent report on the impact of VC in the United States, the National Venture Capital Association (NVCA) estimates that, as of 2008, VC-backed companies that have gone public or been acquired account for 11 percent of private sector employment and 21 percent of US GDP (gross domestic product). Over the two years ending in 2008, the NVCA estimates that VC-backed firms had materially higher rates of job growth than other firms (1.6 percent versus 0.2 percent) and materially higher rates of revenue growth (5.3 percent versus 3.5 percent). In sectors such as software, telecommunications, and semiconductors, the NVCA estimates that more than 70 percent of employees work for firms that were originally VC backed.[9]

Why is the impact of VC so great? The answer lies in the specialized market niche that VC serves. VC investors seek young companies with the potential for rapid and substantial growth that will need significant capital investments to finance that growth. VC thereby fills a niche between very early stage private investment by the entrepreneurs, their friends, and angel investors, and the market for public capital or private corporate acquisition. Firms with limited product markets and slower growth potential generally are not candidates for VC. Such firms tend to have more modest capital needs and may be better suited for debt financing.

Venture Capital and Private Equity Activity in Europe

Many factors influence the level of VC activity in a country or region. Generally, the level of formal activity is higher in developed than in emerging economies. While direct comparisons with the United States are not possible, Europe ranks a close second in the overall level of activity. In 2001, as shown in Figure 3.6, a total of €40 billion in new funds was raised by VC and private equity funds. Although the 2001 total is similar to new VC commitments in the United States, the European total includes all private equity, a much broader classification than US VC. More than half of the funds raised in Europe in 2001 were targeted for buyouts, and by 2008 more than 70 percent were targeted for buyouts. In 2001, only 25 percent of total commitments were targeted for early-stage and expansion-stage high-tech ventures.

FIGURE **3.6**

European new private equity commitments

SOURCE: European Private Equity and Venture Capital Association: http://www .evca.eu/knowledgecenter/ statistics.aspx?id=410 (fundraising tab).

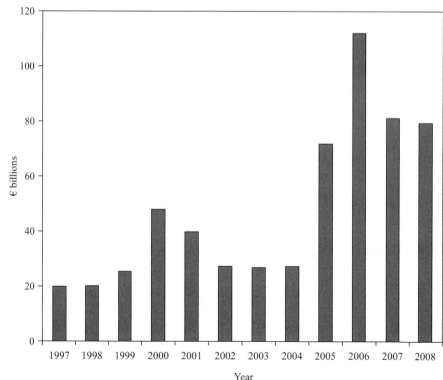

3.2   The Organization of Venture Capital Firms

Successful VC investing depends on finding solutions to an array of problems. The fund manager must sort through a plethora of business plans, each describing a venture with a negligible operating history. In addition to identifying the few ventures that have some potential for success, the investor must be able to add enough value to the deals to cover the extra costs of administering the fund's investment portfolio, including the return on the VC's commitment of effort. Beyond addressing these problems, the manager must be able to commit the fund's capital for long periods with little hard evidence that value is being created for investors. The manager must be able to expand, contract, and refocus efforts in response to changes in opportunities and new information about prospects for success, as well as be able to redeploy the VC firm's human capital when its ability to add value to a venture wanes.

The Limited Partnership Structure

To address these challenges in the context of the regulatory environment described earlier, the VC limited partnership has become the dominant organizational form for VC investing in the United States.[10] Figure 3.7 is a schematic representation of the limited partnership form of a VC fund. A VC limited partnership has a finite life span, typically 7–10 years. The general partner (GP) is the fund organizer and is responsible for raising investment capital from the limited partners (LPs) and deploying the capital by investing in portfolio companies. On the capital deployment side, the GP screens opportunities based on quality and compatibility with the GP's capabilities and with timing of the fund's capital flows. When an attractive investment prospect is identified, the GP negotiates the terms for investing.

Committing the fund's financial capital to a venture also commits some of the GP's human capital to ongoing involvement in monitoring and advising. The intensity of these efforts varies across funds. Philosophies differ, and some ventures warrant more active investor involvement than others. Finally, the GP is responsible for harvesting the investment. Harvesting enables the fund to provide a return to the LPs and allows the GP to redeploy human capital to other investments.

Raising the capital for a VC fund is a costly endeavor. The GP commits a substantial amount of time to marketing the fund to prospective investors and to managing relations with existing investors. Most institutional investors require periodic (at least annual) reporting, including valuations and status reports on the fund's portfolio companies.

FIGURE **3.7**

Organizational structure of venture capital investment VC funds are usually organized as limited partnerships. The GP manages the fund, while LPs provide most of the investment capital. The fund invests in a portfolio of new ventures.

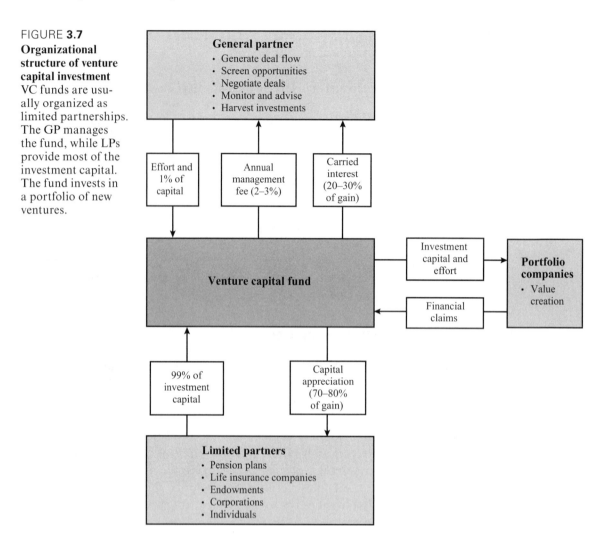

The GP's primary contribution to the fund is in the form of effort. In addition, though specifics vary, the GP normally commits 1 percent of the fund's capital; limited partners provide the other 99 percent. A small fraction of invested capital is used each year to cover costs related to managing the operation of the fund. The balance is invested in portfolio companies, in exchange for financial claims on the companies. If and when these investments are harvested, the returns are distributed to LPs, first to repay their initial investments, with the balance (the capital gain) being shared between the LPs and the GP. Normally, the LPs receive 70 to 80 percent of the gain and the GP receives the balance as a "carried interest."

Waterfalls and Clawbacks

Returns to LPs and the GP follow a progression. Commonly, the progression is as follows:

1. Payment of management fee
2. Return of LPs' principal
3. Sometimes a preferential return, such as 4 percent per year, to the LPs
4. A carried interest portion to the GP corresponding to the LPs' preferential return
5. The remaining portion of capital gain due to LPs
6. The GP's remaining carried interest

The priority in distributions is commonly referred to as a waterfall.

Challenges arise because, in a strict application of the waterfall, the GP would not realize any carried interest return until all of the assets of the fund had been liquidated through sale, acquisition, or failure of all investments. Normally, the GP does not want to wait 10 years or more until any return is realized. Accordingly, the waterfall distributions are often handled asset by asset. Thus, if the fund invests in a venture that has a successful IPO early in the life of the fund, some fraction of the proceeds may be distributed to the GP as carried interest. But what happens if the other ventures do not do well, so that the LPs do not realize the overall return that they had expected? In such cases, the GP may be subject to a "clawback" provision that requires the GP to return "excess distributions" to the partnership. A clawback represents the GP's promise that it will not receive a greater share of the distributions than was bargained for.

Returns to General Partners

Most GPs are themselves organized as partnerships. As such, they can expand or contract and deal with issues of continuity. The returns to individual partners of the GP can be sizable, even if the fund performs poorly. Consider a $100 million fund with a GP comprising five partners, a 2.5 percent fee for the operating budget, and a 20 percent carried interest.[11] Suppose the fund has a 10-year life span and a 5-year average holding period of investments, with 20 percent annual appreciation after fees. For simplicity, suppose the fund invests $20 million per year in Years 1 through 5 and realizes uniform returns of $49.8 million per year in Years 6 through 10 (a 20 percent per year return on each investment). The management fee is $2.5 million per year, or $500,000 per partner of the GP. The GP's gross return due to capital appreciation is the 20 percent carried interest [0.2 × ($49.8 million − $20 million)], or about $5.95 million annually, equivalent to about $1.2 million per partner of the GP in each of the five years.

These returns, of course, are before partnership expenses. However, even if expenses account for half of the management fee and carried interest, the return to each partner of the GP still is substantial—annual net fees of $250,000 and annual carried interest returns of $600,000 during the last five years.

Zider (1998) provides a separate estimate of the returns to individual partners of the GP. He cites annual salaries of $200,000 to $400,000 and total annual compensation, including carried interest returns, of $1.4 million. Moreover, an individual partner may manage assets for more than one VC fund. Conversely, if the first fund performs poorly, then the partner's career as a VC may be brief.

The actual returns to VCs are subject to considerable volatility over time. Figure 3.8 shows quarterly net returns to LPs. The GP's carried interest generally is equivalent to about one-fourth of the return to the LPs. In many periods the LPs' returns are small or negative; in some years, however, the return is very high.

Capital Commitments, Capital Calls, and Reputation

VC is a market where the LP's reputation is as important as the LP's money. When a new fund is created, the GP seeks capital commitments from investors at the same time that it assesses investment opportunities and negotiates deals. Each LP's commitment is formalized in a subscription agreement. Actual investments in new ventures are not made until the fund's "closing." A closing is a legal process in which the commitments are used to define an ownership group. A fund closes when sufficient commitments of capital have been made and sufficient investment opportunities have been found to warrant going forward. Each investor's commitment is conditional on the fund generating sufficient commitments from other investors to reach the minimum total for closing. When the closing occurs, the GP can make an initial "capital call" on the investors, and then the investors have a short time (such as 30 days) in which to deliver the funds.

To achieve the best performance, the GP makes capital calls only when there are immediately attractive portfolio investment opportunities. The investors may receive several capital calls during the first few years of the fund's life. Because each investor is expected to deliver cap-

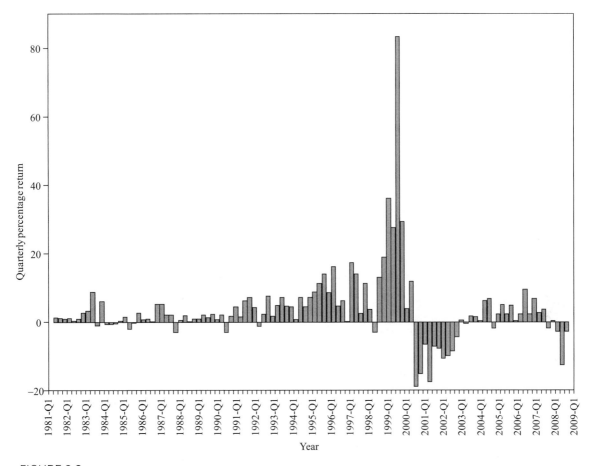

FIGURE **3.8**
Net quarterly returns to limited partners of venture capital funds
SOURCE: National Venture Capital Association: http://www.nvca.org/ (research tab).

ital when called upon, the investors' reputations are important to fund operation. Failure to respond to a capital call could cause the fund to miss investment opportunities and otherwise disrupt fund operation. Because of this, penalties for missed capital calls are substantial.

Use of closing dates and capital calls enables a VC fund to operate with very little internal liquidity. The need for liquidity does not disappear, however; it is shifted instead to the investors. Consequently, the typical investors are those whose ordinary levels of liquidity are sufficient to enable them to respond to unpredictable capital calls.

The upshot is that GPs seek investors who can reliably commit their capital for the entire life of the fund. What better place to look for such investors than institutions such as pension funds, endowments, and life

TABLE **3.1**   **Summary of terms of venture capital limited partnership agreement**

IPA Venture Capital Fund, L.P. (hereinafter "the Fund")

Terms	Description
Purpose	The "purpose" identifies the Fund's focus and investment objective, such as "to earn superior returns from early-stage investments in e-commerce ventures." Provisions may limit the amount invested in any one venture and/or restrict the types of investment vehicles the Fund can use.
General partner	Normally the general partner (GP) is a partnership of individual general partners. Investors in the Fund may seek access to the contract between the individual general partners in order to assess their incentives and perhaps seek revisions and limitations to the agreement.
Limited partnership interests	The provision specifies the total amount of the Fund that is being raised, such as $250 million, and the minimum per investor, such as $10 million.
General partner's investment	The usual contribution is 1 percent and sometimes may be in the form of a promissory note.
Minimum for closing	The provision specifies the dollar commitment, such as $100 million, that must be received before initial closing. If there is a subsequent closing, it may be required to occur within a fixed period, such as one year after the initial closing.
Payment of subscriptions	Investors must provide a specified amount of capital at the time of closing (such as 30 percent of their total commitment). Subsequent calls may be at specified times, but often are made on short notice to afford maximum flexibility for investing the funds. Penalties for late or missed calls will be enumerated.
Term	The term of the agreement is usually 10 years, with options to extend under certain conditions, which permits orderly liquidation of investments.
Allocation of profit and loss	The provision specifies allocation of profits and losses. Currently, most common allocation is 80 percent to limited partners and 20 percent to the GP, though sometimes the GP's share is higher. Other provisions are possible and are related to how gains and losses are treated. For example, an agreement may facilitate allocation of more of the taxable gain to nontaxable investors.
Distributions	The provisions ensure prompt distribution of invested capital and gains. Normally, distributions can be in the form of cash and public securities. Terms may specify that the investors receive a full return of their invested capital before the GP receives any distributions. An alternative is to distribute 20 percent of the gains to the GP, but if there are losses on some investments then the agreement would obligate the GP to make up for the overcompensation.
Service fee	Normally, the service fee is 2.5 percent of contributed and committed capital, possibly with adjustments for inflation. The fee may be linked to expenses, may specify specific offsets to be charged, and may be set in light of other funds under management.
Organizational expenses	The front-end cost of setting up the Fund is usually paid out of the capital contributions to the Fund. The agreement may specify a maximum amount and enumerate items covered.
Conflicts of interest	Provisions limit co-investing with individual general partners or with earlier funds of the venture capitalist.
Other restrictions and limitations	Other restrictions include prohibitions on borrowing, organizing follow-on funds, etc. The intent of the provisions is to control effort devoted to the Fund and to prevent risk shifting.

insurers, all of which have predictable needs for liquidity that are small relative to the overall size of their investment portfolios? By extension, the GP screens for individuals who can reliably commit to maintaining their capital investments.

The VC limited partnership agreement sets out conditions for investing, requirements for closing, distribution requirements, and the other terms. Table 3.1 contains a summary of the more important terms and provides examples for a fictional fund.

The Investment Process

Figure 3.9 illustrates the VC investment process and its relation to fund maturity. After the concept is developed, the GP makes concurrent efforts to secure commitments from investors and to generate deal flow.

FIGURE **3.9**
The venture capital investment process

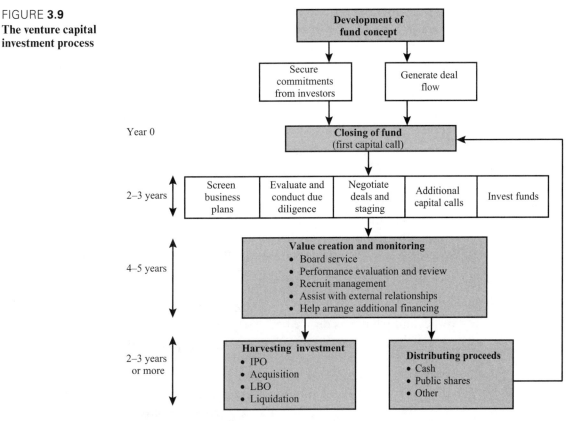

The fund closing and first capital call mark the point when the GP begins to build a portfolio of investments. Some VC statistics are based on funds grouped by "vintage year." The vintage year is the year of the first capital call or first investment, even though some activities commence months earlier.[12] Most funds are intended to last about 10 years. The role of the GP changes over the life of the fund, from activities related to investing capital to those related to managing and monitoring investments and finally to those related to harvesting.

Normally, it takes two to three years before a fund is fully invested. During this period, the GP is busy screening plans, conducting due diligence on prospective investments, and negotiating deals. Corresponding to these efforts, the GP makes additional capital calls and seeks to place the entire commitment with new ventures. While the subscription agreement makes reference to a "call-down schedule," in practice the timing can be accelerated or extended depending on how quickly appropriate deals are identified.

A fund can also have more than one closing. During the fundraising stage, the GP may bring in new investors and oversee a second or third closing. A closing defines a group of investors who are treated identically as the fund progresses. Managing a fund with multiple closings gives rise to potential opportunism as it enables investors to get into the fund at different times. Existing investors may be concerned with the potential for opportunism by new investors who might try to buy into existing successes at valuations that are too low. Conversely, new investors may be concerned that existing investors will try to exploit information advantages or get better deals for themselves. Thus, having a second closing with a different investor group elevates the importance of accurate valuations of portfolio companies and fund investments in them.

Fund managers can try to address potential opportunism by segregating existing and new investments into separate funds. Of course, an investor can also avoid opportunism by acquiring the right, *ex ante*, to participate in each closing at the same level (e.g., 5 percent of each closing). However, this may increase the investor's financial commitment beyond what was desired.

Following investment in a portfolio company, the GP's responsibility shifts to value creation and monitoring. Service on boards is routine, as is continual performance evaluation. In addition, the GP often is involved in recruiting the management team, building relations with trading partners, and helping to arrange subsequent financing.

Most GPs hope to harvest their investments about five years after the investments are made. Ideally, the GP continues to work with a portfolio company as long as the GP is able to add value and until a point when a liquidity event is possible. Harvesting enables investors to realize the gains on their involvement, through receipt of either cash or publicly tradable shares. Distributions are natural milestones for the GP in its efforts to establish another fund.

The harvesting phase is typically two to three years. The long window allows the GP to time the exits in light of market conditions and company-specific factors. Because portfolio companies progress at different rates, the periods of investment, value creation, and harvesting within a single VC fund overlap. Typically, the LPs can agree to extend the life of the fund for several years to permit orderly liquidation of investments.

The finite life of the fund limits and controls the GP's behavior. A GP that is successful in adding value will have little trouble generating commitments to a new fund, whereas one that has not been successful is unlikely to attract new investors. In practice, VC firms usually try to launch new funds more frequently than every 10 years but with enough time in between so that investors can assess whether the fund seems to be on track for success. Here again, long-term relationships and reputation are important. Compared with the public equity market, prospective investors are few and can easily communicate with each other. Concern with reputational damage disciplines the GP and protects investors from short-run opportunism.[13]

Why Limited Partnership?

The LP structure solves many of the managerial problems that arise in new venture investing. Because investors can participate in multiple funds and can diversify across a broad array of other investments, the GP is free to concentrate on opportunities in which the partner's expertise adds the most value. The finite life of a VC fund subjects the GP to ongoing market discipline. The LP structure also enables the pool of VC funds to expand or contract depending on the opportunities perceived by the GP. Finally, the structure makes efficient use of the liquidity that naturally accrues to large institutional investors. The downside, compared to the closed-end fund structure, is that most individual investors in the United States are foreclosed by SEC rules from investing directly in VC partnerships.

Reliance on the LP form, however, is not universal. JAFCO, for example, was established in 1973 as a Tokyo-based VC firm that invests in new ventures directly and manages VC funds. At the end of 2009, JAFCO was managing approximately $5.8 billion spread across

46 funds around the world.[14] In contrast to US VC firms, JAFCO is publicly traded and listed on the Tokyo Stock Exchange, with a market capitalization of $1 billion at the end of 2009. JAFCO has invested in close to 4,000 ventures globally, of which almost 900 have become publicly traded companies. JAFCO concentrates on early-stage investment, providing managerial support for portfolio companies. They emphasize the importance of deal flow at the local level and have established both buyout funds and more traditional early-stage investment funds.

Some countries, China for example, do not support the legal institution of partnership. Many have adopted the platform of a corporation and attendant limited liability. For various reasons, however, corporations are not as suitable for VC investment as are partnerships. Japan does have a US-type LP construct, known as *toushi jigyo kumiai*. JAFCO adopts this format for some of its deals but at other times acts as a merchant bank making direct investments in companies. When using the LP arrangement, JAFCO generates around 50 percent of investment capital from corporations, with the balance coming from other traditional VC sources.[15]

Attempts to establish publicly traded entities in the United States that are similar to JAFCO have not worked well. During the mid-1990s, a few new venture incubators sought to respond to public demand for the opportunity to invest in VC and to tap the public equity market by adopting structures that would enable them to go public. To avoid the problems discussed previously, these companies sought to reorganize as operating companies to circumvent direct application of the ICA. However, the SEC safe harbor provisions are quite limiting and force the companies to devote significant effort to maintaining a balance of ownership interests that enables them to be classified as operating companies instead of mutual funds. The dual objectives of finding and pursuing new venture opportunities on one hand and avoiding closed-end fund status on the other are conflicting, and it is not clear that a viable strategy exists. The companies that went public with this model in the 1990s now have lost more than 99 percent of the value they traded for at the peak of the tech rally in 2000.

Geographic Clustering of Venture Capital Activity

A notable feature of the VC industry is that firms tend to cluster in geographic areas (Figure 2.3). Currently about half the US-based VC firms, together with half the US-based companies they finance, are concentrated in just three metropolitan areas—San Francisco/San Jose, Boston, and New York.[16]

Geographic concentration suggests the presence of agglomeration economies. Such economies arise when firms' costs are reduced as a result of being proximate to their rivals and other market participants, such as suppliers and specialized labor. These characteristics fit the VC industry. Value is added through close working relationships between VCs and portfolio firms. For portfolio firms, proximity to rivals is likely to keep them competitive and better informed. When new venture activity is concentrated, VC firms can more easily monitor industry trends. In addition, VC firms and portfolio companies have specific human capital requirements. It is no accident that the two largest pockets of VC activity in the United States are located near large and talented university populations. Consistent with this, it is not uncommon for a VC that decides to fund a firm outside of its geographic area to predicate funding on relocation of the venture.

3.3 How Venture Capitalists Add Value

GPs charge substantial fees for fund management and share significantly in the success of their investments. Although GP returns may seem excessive, VC funds attract most of their financial resources from sophisticated investors. The investors, either directly or through gatekeepers, continuously monitor the actions and decisions of the GP. The sophistication of VC investors supports the inference that the compensation structures are justified. If so, it must be that the fund managers contribute significantly to performance; sophisticated investors do not reinvest with GPs in whom they do not have confidence.

VC firms, if they are to survive, must be able to add sufficient value to cover their compensation. Over and above the efforts to create value for an individual fund, the GP seeks to maximize value for the VC firm. GPs expect to realize the benefits of information economies by operating multiple funds. They also expect to maximize the value of the firm's human capital by deploying experienced partners to work with multiple portfolio companies. This means that when one fund is being liquidated, another often is being formed, so that the firm's human capital is used efficiently over the course of the investment/monitoring/harvesting cycle.

Managing a VC fund is complicated because the fund supplies a joint product consisting of investment capital and consulting services. The gross return must cover both the opportunity cost of the investment capital and the services of the GP.

Selecting Investments and Negotiating Deals

The ideal ventures to include in a portfolio are those in which the GP can add significant value without an excessive commitment of time. Other things equal, an investment is more attractive if it appears to be well managed and unlikely to require much assistance. Such a company, however, should also be able to negotiate a favorable deal with the GP. Beyond this, a venture is more attractive if its needs meld with the specific capabilities of the GP. Simple metrics of fit include industry focus, stage of development, and location.[17]

A prospective venture is more attractive if the expected time commitment for VC involvement corresponds to a time over which the market can come to recognize the value of the venture so that exit is possible. If the market takes too long to recognize value, the GP may be compelled to continue to devote time to the venture. This involvement can extend beyond the point where the GP is adding value, especially if it causes the GP to forgo work on other ventures.

Because LPs are concerned with earning returns that exceed what they can earn from other investments, the GP does not want to raise capital before it is needed. Similarly, the GP does not want to hold a portfolio company after the market recognizes its value. Market conditions affect the decision calculus. Ideally, the manager seeks to create the fund during a period when opportunities to invest in new ventures are abundant and seeks to harvest when the market is receptive to public offerings.

There is some evidence that VCs are able to time distributions to correspond with periods when market values are high. Lerner (1994c) finds that in choices between IPOs and private rounds, VC-backed biotech companies tend to select IPO after run-ups in the market values of biotech stocks and before market declines. Ball, Chiu, and Smith (2009) examine VC-backed exits by IPO or merger over a longer period and more sectors. Consistent with Lerner, they find that IPOs are selected after market or sector run-ups. However, the negative performance after IPOs appears to be idiosyncratic to the sector and period studied by Lerner. They find no evidence that VC-backed firms can spot opportunities to issue at times when investors are overly optimistic about the stock market or about the sector.

Selecting Entrepreneurs Who Are Likely to Be Successful

VC firms evaluate thousands of ventures each year. A primary component of the evaluation is assessing the entrepreneur's knowledge and skills. In a field study based on 51 VC firms (86 deals), Smart (1998) documents practices related to the methods VC firms use to value the entrepreneur's human capital.

Smart reports that venture capitalists devoted many hours to valuing the entrepreneur's human capital. They spent more than half of that time questioning the management team regarding the venture. Only 21 percent of the firms conducted a written job analysis, preferring instead to spend time in face-to-face discussions about business-related topics.

Smart also finds evidence of cognitive bias in that more VCs in his sample overestimated the value of the human capital than underestimated it. His findings support the much-quoted remark of VC Arthur Rock: "Nearly every mistake I've made has been in picking the wrong people, not the wrong idea."[18]

Changing the Management Team

A study of Silicon Valley portfolio companies indicates that professional managers replace more than half of founding entrepreneurs.[19] In about 40 percent of these cases, the founder retains a position at the company; in the remainder, the founder has no discernible tie with the company after being replaced.

In another study, based on survey data, Fiet et al. (1997) provide perspective on the types of "mistakes" that can lead to dismissal and the contractual covenants that are effective in aligning managers' incentives with the interests of the VC fund. The more important findings include:

- Limiting salaries of managers reduces the likelihood of dismissal.
- Earn-out provisions in the contract reduce the likelihood of dismissal.
- Faster revenue growth per employee reduces the likelihood of dismissal.
- The number of board seats is negatively related to the likelihood of dismissal.
- The number of VC-controlled board seats is positively related to the likelihood of dismissal.
- Explicit dismissal covenants are not related to the likelihood of dismissal.

These results do not establish causation. A VC that is concerned about the capabilities of the entrepreneur is more likely to negotiate performance-based covenants and require board representation. An entrepreneur who wants to signal confidence may be willing to accept unfavorable board composition in exchange for more funding or favorable terms.

Allocating Effort Efficiently

VC firms do best if they can continuously deploy the GP's human capital. Consequently, a VC firm usually tries to manage several funds on staggered schedules. Beyond that, the VC firm shifts resources from capital raising and prospect evaluation during the early stage of a fund to monitoring and advising in the midyears to harvesting at the later stage.

One estimate of how fund managers allocate time appears in Figure 3.10. Consulting, monitoring, and managing activities represent approximately 70 percent of time; finding investments and negotiating deals, 15 percent; and capital raising and harvesting, another 15 percent.

Estimates in the figure generally are consistent with earlier estimates of time allocations by VCs. Based on a survey from the 1980s, VCs reportedly spend about half of their time in activities related to moni-

FIGURE **3.10**

Allocation of VC time Managing and monitoring investments (medium shading) account for the largest fraction of VC time. Activities related to finding and making investments (light shading) and those related to raising and returning investment capital (dark shading) account for significantly smaller fractions of effort.

SOURCE: Zider (1998).

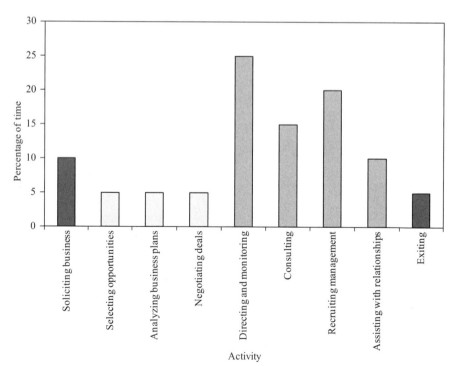

toring. Most of that effort is devoted to fundraising for portfolio companies, replacing management, and assisting the management team in other ways. An individual partner spends an average of 110 hours per year on each of nine companies.[20] Activity levels vary, however, as the very good and very bad investments normally do not warrant allocation of much effort by the VC. Board service increases during periods of CEO turnover and decreases with distance between the parties.[21]

Deal evaluation is another activity that consumes significant amounts of time. Reportedly, three full-time weeks are spent, on average, over a period of 100 days to evaluate a single deal after it gets through preliminary screening. In contrast, the initial screening may take only a few minutes.

Monitoring and Advising Portfolio Companies

VCs can add value by selecting and monitoring portfolio companies or by providing services to the companies. Evidence of the value of service to portfolio companies is mixed. One study finds that entrepreneurs do not perceive much value added through VC board service, except possibly by top-ranked VCs.[22] There is little evidence that the managers of portfolio companies value the nonfinancial advice of VCs, except when the manager is new or existing managers are moving into areas where they lack experience.[23]

On the positive side, there is evidence that VC backing is associated with job creation, higher levels of patent awards, and more citations to patents.[24] It also appears that VC backing plays a certification role in the IPO process, as VC backing is associated with less severe IPO underpricing, lower total cost of going public, and going public sooner.[25]

Consistent with the certification role of VC backing, evidence indicates that the market reacts negatively when, instead of distributing cash to the LPs, VC firms distribute shares of a portfolio company.[26] Distribution of shares may signal that the VC believes the shares are overvalued or that the VC is no longer adding value to the company. Although the evidence suggests that VC involvement does create value, it is unclear whether the benefits derive from this involvement or, more simply, from the selection of companies in which to invest.

The Quest for Home Runs Can Result in Striking Out

Not everything the VC does adds value; VCs can also make mistakes. The following is a disguised excerpt from a letter shared with us by a member of one investment group, in which he suggests that sophisticated investors sometimes encourage portfolio companies to operate in less than ideal ways.

Dear Partners:

The story of XYZ Company and ABC Investment Partners began last year with a presentation from the company. The presentation was impressive and the plan made sense. As a result, we invested a total of $1.0 million in the deal. An advisory board was formed by ABC, and descended on the company en masse and proceeded to "help" it. I am sure that everyone involved was well intentioned. I am sure that everyone thought they were helping the company succeed. I am sure some valuable contributions were made. However, the unfortunate reality is that the collective result of our involvement in the management of this company has been overwhelmingly negative. I have no doubt whatsoever that the company would not be in its present position if we had invested the money and walked away. I know that there will be arguments, denials, and rationalizations, but I am absolutely convinced that our hands-on involvement is primarily responsible for the present predicament of the company.

Lots of mistakes were made, some reasonable and some inexcusable. Most, but not all, were the result of extreme pressure from the board and the advisory group. For instance:

- The decision to do TV advertising from the outset was ridiculous and burned a huge amount of the available cash. In addition, all of the advertising was targeted at the users of the service (who use it for free) and essentially none of it reached the vendors (whom we were expecting to pay for the service).
- We changed ad agencies unnecessarily and then proceeded to get into litigation with the first agency.
- We made a number of really stupid mistakes in the development of the database system, the most notable of which was the failure to notice that the information being sent to prospective customers was incorrect.

There are lots of other notable errors, but in the end it all comes down to the one inexcusable error that makes it difficult to recover from the mistakes cited above: The board of directors completely failed to plan for the future financing requirements of the company. One board member actually told another venture capitalist that the company wouldn't need any additional investment—that it would be growing entirely from cash flow. The primary obligation of the board is the financial oversight of the company. It is their job to make sure the company does not run out of money. They did not do this. . . .

The truly sad part of this story is that the company really deserves to succeed. It is true that the entrepreneur is young and inexperienced, but he is the quintessential entrepreneur. I have no doubt whatsoever that he would have succeeded if ABC, however benevolent, had not meddled so intrusively. He simply would never have run out of money without the help of ABC, and that makes all the difference. You just can't play if you're broke. . . .

YOURS TRULY,

Frank Lee

Partner

Luck versus Skill: What Accounts for Venture Capital Success?

Kaplan and Schoar (2005) find that the returns to VC persist over funds of the same VC firm. That is, high VC returns for one fund imply that returns of subsequent funds offered by the same firm will also be high. Sorensen (2006) finds that companies funded by more experienced VCs are more likely to go public. Krishnan et al. (2011) find that VC firms with high shares of prior IPO activity tend to have higher percentages of investments that result in an IPO and better performance after the IPO. Nahata (2008) finds that new ventures backed by VCs with superior reputations are more likely to go public and tend to go public earlier. Smith, Pedace, and Sathe (2009) find that fund reputation is positively related to fund IRR (internal rate of return) and the cash-on-cash return to investors in the fund.

Sorensen (2006) poses the question of whether persistence of fund performance is due to the skill of the VC firm or luck. Conceivably, a VC firm that is lucky with an early fund can attract better deal flow and raise capital from investors with less effort than a first-time fund or one with a track record of poor performance. He finds evidence that luck plays an important role but that the direct influences of the VC firm also matter. Smith, Pedace, and Sathe (2009) find that both style persistence and sector experience are positively related to fund performance; but they also find that agility, the ability to move quickly into a new sector, contributes positively to returns.

Syndication and Venture Capital

Syndication occurs when VC funds co-invest in ventures. Typically, for any given venture, one fund is the lead investor and the others are co-investors. The lead normally is the fund with the highest level of direct involvement with the venture and is the one most likely to serve on the venture's board of directors. Syndication is a reciprocal, ongoing, informal relationship, in which VC funds tend to collaborate by taking turns serving as lead investors or co-investors. The practice enables VC firms to pool their human capital resources and to spread the investments of their funds over larger and more diverse portfolios.

In countries where VC investing is well established, syndications among reputable VCs are common. In emerging economies, the lack of both attractive investments and established VC firms is a significant impediment to syndication and industry growth.

Brander, Amit, and Antweiler (2002) identify two primary reasons for syndications: (1) syndications may add value to ventures when additional VC firms, with different skills and knowledge, are actively involved in management, and/or (2) syndications may provide reciprocal certification of investment opportunities. Using Canadian data, the authors find that syndicated investments have higher returns than investments that are not syndicated. They interpret this finding as favoring the value-added rationale. On the other hand, Hochberg, Ljungqvist, and Lu (2010) explore the networking aspects of VC, including syndications, and find that incumbent VCs may jointly impede entry of other VC firms into a local market.

There may be different reasons for later-round syndication than early-round. Based on a study of biotech investment rounds, Lerner (1994a) finds that in first-round investments, established VC firms tend to syndicate with each other and avoid less experienced firms. Later rounds are more likely to involve syndicated investments by less established VC firms. Lerner interprets the evidence as being consistent with "window dressing" in the syndication of later-round investments.

Admati and Pfleiderer (1994) develop a rationale for later-round syndication based on informational asymmetries. Because the first (lead) investor may have an informational advantage over subsequent investors, one way to avoid opportunism is for the lead to maintain a constant share of the firm's equity. If the venture needs to raise a large amount of capital in a later round, this can imply that additional investors must provide a portion of the later-round financing.

The lead investor normally is paid for assisting in the syndication. The typical fee is 2–3 percent of the money raised from co-investors. Sometimes they share the fee with the other syndicate members.

3.4 Investment Selection and Venture Capitalist Compensation

The compensation arrangement between the GP and LPs is an important determinant of investment attractiveness. The financial claim of the GP has the characteristics of a call option: a limited downside and a significant upside. If the fund does well, then the GP realizes a significant return through its carried interest. Conversely, if the investments perform poorly, most of the loss accrues to the LPs, who contribute the bulk of the financial capital; the GP continues to collect a management fee.

The structure can affect the kinds of ventures that attract the GP's interest, as well as the terms of financial contracts between the fund and its portfolio companies. A venture with an attractive expected return but limited upside potential is unlikely to be a prospect for VC, even if downside risk is small. Other things equal, such a venture does not offer the potential for the GP to benefit significantly by sharing in the appreciation.

The attractiveness of an investment to the GP also depends on the terms of the financial contract. A high-risk venture that is structured to create financial claims that offer safe but reasonable returns to investors is unlikely to attract VC funds. On the other hand, a low-risk venture can receive funding if the financial claims are structured to offer substantial upside potential by shifting downside risk to the investor.[27]

The financial claims most commonly sought by VC investors are those that align the interests of the GP with those of the LPs. Interests are aligned when both types of partners participate in new venture success but are protected against losses if the venture performs poorly. Convertible preferred stock, for example, is often used in VC financing. Convertible preferred offers some downside protection (ahead of common stock) and still preserves the potential for significant gain. Structures involving staging of investment or put options for the investor can have similar effects.

3.5 Venture Capital Contracts with Portfolio Companies

A typical VC fund portfolio results in a small number of highly successful investments, together with a much larger number that are unsuccessful. Because of the quest for high returns, the process by which GPs search for investment prospects can give rise to adverse selection.[28] Suppose the VC develops financial projections for each prospective investment and then applies the hurdle rate to select its investments. Some prospects will be screened out because the financial projections are too low, given the hurdle rate. Adverse selection arises partly because ventures that are overvalued by the VC are more likely to survive the screen.

Now, consider the decision of an entrepreneur whose venture has survived the screen. Some entrepreneurs will believe that the VC firm has overvalued their opportunity; others will believe that theirs has been undervalued. Entrepreneurs who perceive that their ventures have been overvalued are more likely to accept the VC's financing offer, giving rise to the adverse selection effect.[29]

From the investor's perspective, adverse selection is a problem only if some investors use better decision-making processes than others. Lerner (1994b) points out that syndication is one way of dealing with the problem. As discussed above, when a deal is syndicated, several VC firms contribute funds to a venture, sharing in the due diligence efforts of the lead investor and pooling the risk, including risk associated with adverse selection. Syndication, however, is no substitute for developing methods of project evaluation that deal effectively with adverse selection and other valuation issues. One way to address the adverse selection problem is to adopt contracts that limit investor reliance on *ex ante* due diligence and valuation. Staging, by forestalling part of the investment decision until the investor gains experience with the entrepreneur and until more information arrives about the prospective success of the venture, has this effect.[30] Staging also affords greater control to the investor while enabling the entrepreneur to retain a larger ownership stake.[31]

Another way to address the adverse selection problem is to employ financial contracting structures that test the beliefs of the entrepreneur, align the interests of the parties, and enable parties with different expectations to transact with each other.[32] VC investors usually hold convertible preferred stock that gives them a preferential claim in case of liquidation. This shifts more of the risk of failure to the entrepreneur. Entrepreneurs who are concerned with failure are likely to be discouraged by the risk exposure. The use of convertible shares by the investor may discourage the entrepreneur from excessive risk taking.[33] Clearly, use of contingent claims to allocate ownership, such as with performance-based rights or a ratchet, can help screen investment prospects.[34]

Staging and related contractual devices have a downside. Staging can encourage myopic behavior by the entrepreneur, because later-round investments are contingent, to some extent, on venture performance.[35] The concern is most acute when subsequent investment is guaranteed provided that a certain performance benchmark (e.g., a revenue target) is achieved or when the allocation of ownership claims depends on realizing a specific target (as in the case of a ratchet). Short-sighted behavior is discouraged if the conditions for making follow-on investments are not explicit and are subject to the investor's judgment or where the benchmarks are good proxies for actual success. Because of these concerns, some VCs avoid linking follow-on investment or allocation of ownership claims to specific benchmarks.

VCs protect themselves and their investors in other ways. For example, put options, demand registration rights, and similar provisions help ensure that the investor has an opportunity to harvest. Preemptive rights and rights of first refusal enable the investor to maintain an ownership share in the event that the venture is a success. Employment contracts, share vesting provisions, and noncompete clauses limit the entrepreneur's ability to appropriate the intellectual property and human capital of the venture. Termination rights, on the other hand, protect the investment against the entrepreneur's mismanagement and protect the investor from excessive risk taking by the entrepreneur.[36] Rights to receive information and to board representation ensure that the VC can monitor the venture effectively.

Table 3.2 (page 110) summarizes some of the standard provisions of a term sheet for an investment in preferred stock by the VC fund.

The arrangements described above are not completely one-sided. Granting protection to the VC enables the entrepreneur to retain a larger ownership stake. Some contract provisions also protect the entrepreneur.[37] For example, the VC's right to terminate the entrepreneur often is offset by a put option that gives the entrepreneur the ability to sell out of the deal if the termination option is exercised. In addition, demand registration rights may be offset by a call option that gives the entrepreneur the right to repurchase the investor's shares.

Finally, the IPO process can give a successful entrepreneur the ability to regain control of the venture from VC investors, even without achieving majority ownership. Taking a company public usually results in more disperse ownership, in which case the entrepreneur may be able to regain control, even with a limited ownership stake. Even if the venture does not go public, performance-based rights to acquire additional shares can accomplish much the same result.[38]

3.6 Venture Capital Contracts with Investors

Traditional corporate control mechanisms are not available to LPs. For example, there is no board of directors to represent the LPs' interests and no market for corporate control to discipline the GP. Thus, other mechanisms must align GP and LP incentives. Standard terms in VC

TABLE **3.2**   **Standard provisions of venture capital term sheet for convertible preferred investment**

Provision	Description and purpose
Description of financing round	
Closing date, investors, amount raised, price per share, pre-money valuation, capitalization	Describes the general parameters of the financing round. Pre-money valuation if the value implied by the price per share before including the proceeds of the round. Capitalization describes the VC structure, including preferred shares used in the funding round.
Charter provisions (establishing rights and privileges of preferred investors)	
Dividends to holders of preferred shares	Describes how dividends will accrue to preferred shareholders and timing and conditions under which dividends are paid.
Liquidation preference	Describes the order of payment of proceeds from liquidation, for example, first return the proceeds invested by preferred shareholder, then pay preferred dividends, then pay common dividends, then share the balance pro rata.
Preferred stock voting rights	Such as voting on an as-converted basis and the right to vote separately to elect a specified number of directors.
Conversion rights	Such as the right to convert to common at any time, adjusted for accrued preferred dividends.
Antidilution provisions	Such as a right to retain ownership share or a full or partial ratchet provision, and conditions under which the provision would not apply, such as a conversion of the preferred shares.
Mandatory conversion	Conditions under which a public offering of the venture would force conversion of the preferred shares.
Pay-to-play provision	Requirement for preferred investors to participate in down rounds or convert to common or lose some preferred rights.
Redemption rights	Right of preferred investors as a group to demand redemption of investment from available funds.
Stock purchase agreement	
Representations and warranties	Describing such things as ownership of intellectual property by the venture.
Conditions to closing	Due diligence requirements.
Counsel and expenses	Describes who pays for company counsel and investor counsel.
Investor rights agreement	
Registration rights	Describes rights and conditions for registration of shares issued to preferred investors, including demand registration, piggy-back, who bears cost of registration, and lock-up provisions on trading.
Management and information rights	Rights of preferred investors to be involved in management and to have access to certain information.
Right to maintain ownership share	The right to participate in subsequent rounds to avoid dilution of ownership share.
Other rights	Such as noncompete employment contracts, board meeting requirements, stock option vesting terms, and key person insurance.
Rights of first refusal and co-sale	
First refusal and co-sale	First right to purchase shares offered by the company and right to sell when other owners sell.
Voting rights	
On board of directors	Describes how preferred shareholders vote on board.
Drag-along	Right to compel common to vote with preferred on liquidation event.

SOURCE: *Based on National Venture Capital Association sample term sheet.*

TABLE **3.3** **Key covenant classes in venture capital limited partnerships**

Key covenant classes	Description and purpose
Overall fund management	
Investment in a single firm	As a way to restrict risk taking by the venture capitalist, the covenant limits the amount of the fund's investment in a single firm.
Use of debt	The covenant limits borrowing by the fund and possibly debt maturity. It may also limit borrowing by the GP (venture capitalist) or guarantees of loans by the venture capitalist. The covenant addresses concerns with leveraging the fund and creating conflicts of interest.
Co-investment by venture capitalist's other funds	To limit opportunism and avoid incentive conflicts, the covenant provides for monitoring of decisions to invest in any portfolio company that is in one of the venture capitalist's other funds. The covenant may require co-investment with the other fund.
Reinvestment of profits	The covenant restricts or prohibits reinvestment of profits from a fund and concerns possible conflict of interest regarding the venture capitalist's management fees.
Activities of general partner	
Personal investing in portfolio companies	The covenant limits the ability of the partners to invest alongside or in advance of the fund. The provision serves several purposes, including controlling incentives of the venture capitalist to overinvest efforts in those funds in which he has a personal investment and to avoiding conflicts about when to harvest. Limits on the timing of investment may prevent front running by the venture capitalist.
Sale of interest by general partner	The GP may not be permitted to sell its interest in a portfolio company separately from selling the LP's interest. This provision serves to protect the LP from self-dealing.
Fundraising	The covenant may limit the ability of the GP to raise new funds until existing funds are substantially committed (to avoid dilution of effort and prevent efforts to try to increase fees).
Outside activities	The provision ensures that the GP provides sufficient effort to portfolio companies; the provision limits its outside activities or involvement with outside companies, especially during the portfolio companies' early stages.
Addition of general partners	The covenant limits additions of partners to ensure the quality of effort to the fund remains high.
Types of investments	
Restrictions on asset classes	The provision limits the ability of the GP to invest in certain classes of assets, notably those that require less effort (such as public securities), or other venture funds, or in portfolio companies that compete in industries where partners lack expertise. The provision limits opportunistic behavior by the venture capitalist.

SOURCE: *Based on Gompers and Lerner (1996).*

partnership agreements address a series of concerns related to shirking and opportunistic behavior by the GP.

A study by Norton (1995) of VC partnership contracts classifies covenants under three headings: overall management, activities of the GP, and types of investments.[39] Table 3.3 describes some of the more common covenants, as well as also identifying common terms associated with LP agreements. With respect to overall management, investors may be concerned with the GP's incentives to take on excessive risk, to favor existing funds over new funds, and to increase management fees by delaying disbursements of investment proceeds. To address the incentive to take excessive risk, the agreement may limit the amount of investment in any single venture and restrict the ability of the GP to add leverage by borrowing.

Another concern is that the GP may make investment decisions that favor its existing funds over the new fund it is organizing. Consider a VC firm that manages several funds. Suppose an older fund has an investment in a portfolio company that is seeking second-round financing. The GP may take advantage of LPs in the new fund by using the LPs' capital to make a follow-on investment in the venture on terms that benefit the older fund. This may be a particular concern if the VC is not well established and wants to use the performance of the early fund to attract capital. To obviate this concern, a fund contract may give investors the right to review the GP's decisions to make follow-on investments in ventures held by its other funds or specify that it may do so only as a co-investor, along with another first-time investor in the venture.

To avoid fee manipulation, the agreement may restrict the GP's ability to reinvest fund assets as the fund matures. This limits the ability of the GP to increase its management fees (which usually are calculated as a percentage of the value of assets under management) by postponing distributions to keep the dollar value of assets under management as large as possible. In addition, as a means of controlling potential shirking while collecting management fees, the agreement may limit the investment the GP can make in certain types of financial instruments that offer low expected returns and do not require significant commitments of VC effort.

Additional concerns regarding the activities of GPs relate to self-dealing and dilution of effort. To address self-dealing, GPs may be precluded from buying or selling investments in a venture in advance of transactions on behalf of the fund. To control shirking, the agreement may limit the amount of outside investment a GP can make. It also may restrict the ability of the VC to raise capital for new funds. Furthermore, it may limit the outside activities of the partners, as well as the addition of new partners, and may set expectations for intensity of monitoring activity.

The LPs have ultimate control of the fund through their ability to withdraw from the partnership or to terminate the agreement. As a practical matter, however, termination is unlikely because substantial sanctions usually are contractually imposed for withdrawal and because early termination usually is not in the best interest of the partners.

3.7 The Role of Reputation in the Venture Capital Market

Reputation plays a role in the functioning of most markets; the market for VC is no exception. Reputation is an important enforcement mechanism for the explicit contract terms, such as the LPs' commitments to respond quickly to capital calls. The alternative is to insist that investors place committed funds in escrow accounts until the GP needs them. But this alternative impedes the LPs' abilities to invest the funds efficiently until they are needed. Accordingly, there can be significant advantages to working with incomplete, flexible contracts, where reputation substitutes for explicit contract terms. If the GP can depend on the LPs not to make opportunistic decisions, then elaborate provisions to limit the choices of the LPs can be avoided. If the VC can trust the entrepreneur to act in the interest of the venture, then specific provisions designed to shift risk to the entrepreneur are less important.

Contractual relationships that are based partly on the reputations of the parties can generate higher returns for the parties. Evidence of this implication is manifested in several ways. First, the preference of VCs to raise funds from institutions, whose reputations are more easily assessed, demonstrates that the cost of dealing with individual investors is expected to be higher. Second, well-established VC firms can raise larger amounts of capital more quickly, reducing the overall costs of fundraising. Third, well-established VCs are able to command higher fees and a larger carried interest, which is evidence that investors anticipate superior overall performance from those VCs. Finally, the ability of established entrepreneurs to raise capital more easily than first-time entrepreneurs indicates that investors rely on the entrepreneur's experience and demonstrated commitment as an element of the negotiation.

Several studies support the view that reputation is important for understanding the functioning of the market for VC. Barry et al. (1990) find that IPOs with VC backing are less underpriced than those without such backing. The findings suggest that VC investors perform an important monitoring function. Similarly, Megginson and Weiss (1991) find that VC involvement with companies that are going public leads to reduced underpricing and interpret the finding as evidence that VC backing works as a certification of value. Gompers and Lerner (2004) find that reputation is a positive factor in the ability to raise capital.

One economic rationale for a VC firm's investing in reputation is that, because the firm's human capital is specific to new ventures, the firm benefits by developing a reputation for not selling overpriced shares in IPOs. Evidence indicates that more established VC firms are better able to bring portfolio companies public at early stages of development than are other VCs. The data indicate that VCs with established reputations seek to maintain their reputations by selling shares in IPOs only if they expect the IPOs not to be overpriced. Established VCs are also more likely to forgo selling shares when IPO shares are overpriced or fully priced. In effect, they are more inclined than less well established VCs to sacrifice immediate return for long-run gain.[40]

Gompers (1996) provides evidence that VC funds may seek to build reputations in ways that are not necessarily in the best interest of the companies in which they invest. The study reports that VCs that are not well established tend to bring companies public too early. The study concludes that such funds are engaging in "grandstanding" in an effort to demonstrate high rates of return to attract capital. Consistent with this view, VCs that are not well established tend to raise new funds shortly after IPOs of portfolio companies.

3.8   Reputation, Returns, and Market Volatility

We noted that new commitments of VC peaked at $106.1 billion in 2000, before declining dramatically the next year. How are such large variations possible, and what are the implications for VC funds? An important source of new commitments is the proceeds from harvesting prior investments. If VC funds experience a decline in the rate at which they can harvest, then the rate at which capital is returned to LPs declines. As a significant proportion of new capital commitments is simply rolled-over capital from harvested investments in prior funds, new commitments tend to decline whenever harvest rates or harvest values decline.[41]

The 2001 decline occurred after several years of very rapid growth in the US VC market. Through the year 2000, the average time between VC investment and harvest was decreasing and harvest valuations were increasing; as a result, new capital commitments grew rapidly. Well-established VC firms could not grow rapidly enough to satisfy demand for investing in VC or to pursue all of the new venture investment opportunities. During this period, many new firms entered the VC industry and were able to generate adequate returns for investors. Established VC firms were in a relatively good position to attract the best investment opportunities and the most reliable investors. Consequently, they could generate superior returns for their investors.

With the market decline beginning in 2001, new entrants have discovered it is increasingly difficult to find attractive investments or investors. The market has tended to consolidate around the established firms with the best reputations. Consolidation has tested the efficacy of VC contracts with LPs and the reputational capital of VC firms. Well-established VC firms with good access to deal flow have adapted to the new reality by continuing to work with their existing portfolio companies and, in some cases, returning capital to investors or releasing them from their commitments because of the venture capitalist's inability to profitably invest the capital. Some of those with less well established reputations have acted more opportunistically, holding on to commitments (and the related management fees) despite their inability to find attractive investments.

3.9 Summary

The modern VC firm has its roots in the United States in the mid-twentieth century. Limited partnership is the most common structure for VC investment. The LPs provide financial capital, while the GP locates and cultivates the ventures and arranges for harvesting the investments. Harvesting usually takes the form of arranging for the venture to go public via an IPO, a private sale to another company, or a management buyout. LPs are precluded from active participation in management of the fund.

The aggregate amount of capital invested in US VC funds increased dramatically through 2000, largely as a result of institutional investors having more flexibility in their investment decisions. As commitments of capital increased, so did competition for deals, and there is some evidence that this has driven up valuations. Intensified competition has heightened incentives to improve valuation methods and to develop more sophisticated approaches to generating and structuring deals, marketing them to investors, and designing exit strategies.

Following investment of funds in portfolio companies, responsibility of the GP shifts from generating deal flow to creating value in the portfolio companies. This means that the VC may sit on the board of directors, monitor operations, recruit management team members, arrange additional financing, and generally provide expertise and industry contacts. The fund has a limited life span and at some point, usually after about five years, begins to harvest its investments.

We considered two types of contracts that characterize the industry: contracts between the LPs and the GP and contracts between the

VC fund and its portfolio companies. The terms and provisions of both types of contracts reflect fundamental issues regarding risk bearing and incentive alignment. LPs are passive investors who relinquish control of their investment to a GP that does not bear the full cost of its decisions. Among the issues that arise in this setting are sorting (selecting the portfolio companies from the deal flow) and controlling agency costs and operating costs.

Contractual compensation reflects the respective functions of the two types of partners. If the fund does well, the GP realizes a significant return through its carried interest; if the fund does poorly, almost the entire loss accrues to the LPs. Hence, GP compensation is linked to value creation.

Contracts used in the industry address incentive and risk allocation problems with a variety of provisions, including covenants restricting the VC's ability to add leverage, covenants providing oversight of subsequent investment, and covenants governing the ability to force distributions. In a similar manner, contracts between the VC fund and its portfolio companies address potential problems with adverse selection and incentive alignment. Use of convertible securities shifts more of the risk of failure to the entrepreneur.

Finally, the chapter reinforces the role of reputation in the VC market.

REVIEW QUESTIONS

1. Referring to Figure 3.1, review the major developments that have affected the growth in the VC market in the United States. Explain, for example, the impact of the Investment Company Act, ERISA's prudent investor rule, the growth of institutional investing, and general stock market activity.

2. What types of deals are most appropriate for VC and why?

3. What are some possible explanations for the variation across countries in the development of VC markets?

4. Describe the primary features of the LP structure of VC funds, including the roles of the GP and LPs, the length of the partnership, and the compensation mechanisms for the partners.

5. How do VCs add value to new ventures? When does syndication add value and why?

6. Explain the various information and incentive issues that arise in negotiations between (a) entrepreneurs and VC firms and (b) VC firms and investors.

7. How are the issues identified in your answer to Question 6 resolved with the contracts that we observe in practice?

8. Explain the risk allocation issues that arise in negotiations between (a) entrepreneurs and VC firms and (b) VC firms and investors. How are these issues resolved with the contracts that we observe in practice?

9. Why is reputation so important in the VC market?

10. Describe the steps in the VC investment process (Figure 3.9).

Notes

1. See Gompers (1994a) for more information about ARD. Huntsman and Hoban (1980) document the focus of VC investors on opportunities with the potential for great success.

2. Smith, Smith, and Williams (2001) provide a more detailed analysis of the SEC's interpretation of the ICA fair value standard.

3. See Gompers and Lerner (1998b).

4. Gompers (1994b) suggests that high rates of return and the "hot" IPO market of the early 1980s attracted a flood of investment capital to new ventures and depressed the returns in the decade. Gompers and Lerner (1998a) examine rates of return to investing in VC. They also estimate the elasticity of returns in response to changes in inflows.

5. Estimates are as reported in US Census Bureau, *Statistical Abstract of the United States* (2001).

6. Data on angel investing are from Sohl (2008).

7. Gompers (1994a) attributes the change in focus of VC funds to later-stage investment to the increased importance of pension fund investors.

8. See the National Venture Capital Association *Yearbook*s for 2002 and later years, PricewaterhouseCoopers/National Venture Capital Association MoneyTree Reports for various years (http:www.nvca.org/), and Zider (1998) for additional comparisons on the size of the VC market.

9. See National Venture Capital Association (2009).

10. The first VC limited partnership was organized in 1958; the organizational form, however, did not reach prominence until the 1980s. See Gompers and Lerner (1996).

11. In 2009, the average size of VC fund raised was $121 million; see NVCA *Yearbook* (2010), p. 9, available at http://www.nvca.org/index.php?option=com_content&view=article&id=257&Itemid=103.

12. For discussion of the organization and investment process of VC funds, see Bygrave and Timmons (1992) and Sahlman (1990). See also Timmons and Spinelli (2008).

13. Institutional investors often delegate the choice of VC funds to a professional asset manager (a "gatekeeper") who makes the investment decisions

and is responsible for monitoring performance. Gompers and Lerner (1996) note that the gatekeeper structure emerged in the mid-1980s.

14. Source: http://www.jafco.co.jp/eng/investor/pdf/factbook2009.pdf.

15. See the firm's website for additional information: http://www.jafco.co.jp/eng/home/index.html.

16. See Chen et al. (2009).

17. Gupta and Sapienza (1992) find that VC firms tend to specialize by industry. Barry et al. (1990) suggest that specialization aids in monitoring performance. Ehrlich et al. (1994) offer comparisons on sizes of positions, stages of investments, and locations of portfolio companies. Norton and Tenenbaum (1993) suggest that specialization is paradoxical, given the incentives to diversify risk.

18. See Smart (1998) and Bygrave and Timmons (1992), p. 6.

19. Hellmann and Puri (2002).

20. The survey results appear in Gorman and Sahlman (1989).

21. Evidence on board participation appears in Lerner (1995). Barry et al. (1990) find that a typical company has three VC investors, two of whom serve on the board.

22. Results are reported in Barney et al. (1996).

23. See Fried and Hisrich (1994).

24. Kortum and Lerner (2000).

25. Megginson and Weiss (1991).

26. Gompers and Lerner (1998a).

27. There is a tendency to think that, because of the desire for home runs, VC investors are only interested in high-technology investments. However, companies such as Staples, Starbucks, and FedEx have also received VC funding during rapid-growth stages of development.

28. For discussion of the adverse selection problems arising from the VC search process, see Amit, Glosten, and Muller (1990).

29. The entrepreneurs need not have any perception of the correctness of investor valuations. As long as they seek financing from more than one investor, the most optimistic investor with the lowest hurdle rate is likely to win the contest, but in doing so may end up investing too much in exchange for too small of a stake in the venture.

30. Admati and Pfleiderer (1994) demonstrate that multistage investments can result in efficient investment decision making if the VC invests in a fixed proportion over time and receives a fixed share of the total return. Lerner (1994c) finds evidence, consistent with Admati and Pfleiderer (1994), that VC investment shares tend to remain constant in subsequent rounds.

31. Gompers (1998) finds that staging intervals are shorter when more oversight is warranted.

32. For example, see Sahlman (1990).

33. See Berglöff (1994) and Gompers (1998).

34. Based on a survey of VC firms, Trester (1998) documents that convertible preferred equity dominates in early-stage financing choices. Gilson and Schizer (2003) provide a tax-based argument for using convertibles to provide incentives to management. Kaplan and Stromberg (2003) report that convertible preferred stock was used in 95 percent of a sample of 200 financing rounds.

35. See Hellmann (1998).

36. Because the investor's financial claims normally are senior to those of the entrepreneur, the entrepreneur sometimes has an incentive to increase risk, even though doing so may lower the expected return of the venture.

37. See Gompers (1994a) and Sahlman (1990).

38. See discussion in Black and Gilson (1998).

39. Norton (1995) uses agency theory to describe the structure of VC funds.

40. The Lin and Smith (1998) study reports that initial returns average 11.6 percent when venture capitalists with established reputations are among the sellers, compared to only 5.1 percent when they are not. For venture capitalists without established reputations, initial returns average 7.4 percent when they sell and 9.8 percent when they do not.

41. Gompers and Lerner (2004), p. 202, find a strong positive relation between the valuation of venture capital investments and capital inflows.

REFERENCES AND ADDITIONAL READING

Admati, A. R., and P. Pfleiderer. 1994. "Robust Financial Contracting and the Role of the Venture Capitalist." *Journal of Finance*4 9:371–402.

Amit, R., L. Glosten, and E. Muller. 1990. "Entrepreneurial Ability, Venture Investments, and Risk Sharing." *Management Science*3 6:1232–45.

Ball, E. R., H. Chiu, and R. L. Smith. 2009. "Market Timing and Exit Choices: IPO v. Acquisition." Working paper. Available at http://papers.ssrn.com/sol3/papers.cfm?abstract_id=1339426.

Barney, J. B., L. W. Busenitz, J. O. Fiet, and D. D. Moesel. 1996. "New Venture Teams' Assessment of Learning Assistance from Venture Capital Firms." *Journal of Business Venturing* 11 (4): 257–72.

Barry, C. B., C. J. Muscarella, J. W. Peavy III, and M. R. Vetsuypens. 1990. "The Role of Venture Capital in the Creation of Public Companies." *Journal of Financial Economics* 27 (2): 447–71.

Berglof, E. 1994. "A Control Theory of Venture Capital Finance." *Journal of Law, Economics and Organization* 10 (2): 247–69.

Black, B. S., and R. J. Gilson. 1998. "Venture Capital and the Structure of Capital Markets: Banks versus Stock Markets." *Journal of Financial Economics*4 7:243–77.

Brander, J. A., R. Amit, and W. Antweiler. 2002. "Venture Capital Syndication: Improved Venture Selection versus the Value-Added Hypothesis." *Journal of Economics and Management Strategy* 11 (3): 423–52.

Bygrave, W. A., and J. A. Timmons. 1992. *Venture Capital at the Crossroads.* Cambridge, MA: Harvard University Press.

Chen, H., P. Gompers, A. Kovner, and J. Lerner. 2010. "Buy Local? The Geography of Successful and Unsuccessful Venture Capital Expansion." *Journal of Urban Economics* 57: 90–102.

Ehrlich, S. R., A. F. Denoble, T. Moore, and R. R. Weaver. 1994. "After the Cash Arrives: A Comparative Study of Venture Capital and Private Investor Involvement in Entrepreneurial Firms." *Journal of Business Venturing* 9 :67–82.

Fiet, J. O., L. W. Busenitz, D. D. Moesel, and J. B. Barney. 1997. "Complementary Theoretical Perspectives on the Dismissal of New Venture Team Members." *Journal of Business Venturing* 1 2:347–66.

Fried, V. H., and R. D. Hisrich. 1994. "Toward a Model of Venture Capital Investment Decision Making." *Financial Management* 2 3:28–37.

Gilson, R. J., and D. Schizer. 2003. "Venture Capital Structure: A Tax Explanation for Convertible Preferred Stock." *Harvard Law Review* 116:875–916.

Gladstone, D., and L. Gladstone. 2002. *Venture Capital Handbook.* Upper Saddle River, NJ: Prentice-Hall.

Gompers, P. A. 1994a. "A Note on the Venture Capital Industry." Harvard Business School Case 295-065. Cambridge, MA: Harvard Business Publishing.

———. 1994b. "The Rise of Venture Capital." *Business and Economic History* 23:1–24.

———. 1995. "Optimal Investment, Monitoring, and the Staging of Venture Capital." *Journal of Finance* 5 0:1461–89.

———. 1996. "Grandstanding in the Venture Capital Industry." *Journal of Financial Economics* 4 2:133–56.

———. 1998. "An Examination of Convertible Securities in Venture Capital." Working paper, Harvard Business School, Cambridge, MA.

Gompers, P. A., and J. Lerner. 1996. "The Use of Covenants: An Empirical Analysis of Venture Partnership Agreements." *Journal of Law and Economics* 3 9:463–98.

———. 1998a. "Venture Capital Distributions: Short-Run and Long-Run Reactions." *Journal of Finance* 5 3:2161–84.

———. 1998b. "What Drives Venture Capital Fundraising?" *Brookings Papers on Economic Activity: Macroeconomics*, 149–204. Washington, DC: Brookings Institution.

———. 1999. "An Analysis of Compensation in the U.S. Venture Capital Partnership." *Journal of Financial Economics* 5 1:3–44.

———. 2001a. *The Money of Invention*. Boston: Harvard Business School Press.

———. 2001b. "The Venture Capital Revolution." *Journal of Economic Perspectives*1 5:145–68.

———. 2004. *The Venture Capital Cycle*. 2nd ed. Cambridge, MA: MIT Press.

Gorman, M., and W. A. Sahlman. 1989. "What Do Venture Capitalists Do?" *Journal of Business Venturing* 4:231–48.

Gupta, A. K., and H. J. Sapienza. 1992. "Determinants of Capital Firms' Preferences Regarding the Industry Diversity and Geographic Scope of Their Investments." *Journal of Business Venturing* 7 (5): 347–62.

Hellmann, T. 1998. "The Allocation of Control Rights in Venture Capital Contracts." *RAND Journal of Economics* 29 (1): 57–76.

Hellmann, T., and M. Puri. 2002. "Venture Capital and the Professionalization of Start-Up Firms: Empirical Evidence." *Journal of Finance* 57 (1): 169–97.

Hochberg, Y., A. Ljungqvist, and Y. Lu. 2010. "Networking as a Barrier to Entry and the Competitive Supply of Venture Capital." *Journal of Finance* 65:829–59.

Huntsman, B., and J. P. Hoban Jr. 1980. "Investment in New Enterprise: Some Empirical Observations on Risk, Return, and Market Structure." *Financial Management* 9 (Summer): 44–51.

Kaplan, S., and A. Schoar. 2005. "Private Equity Performance: Returns, Persistence and Capital Flows." *Journal of Finance*6 0:1791–1823.

Kaplan, S., and P. Stromberg. 2003. "Financial Contracting in the Real World." *Review of Economic Studies* 70 (April): 281–316.

Kortum, S., and J. Lerner. 2000. "Assessing the Contribution of Venture Capital to Innovation." *RAND Journal of Economics*3 1:674–92.

Krishnan, C. N. V., V. Ivanov, R. Masulis, and A. Singh. 2011. "Does Venture Capital Reputation Matter? Evidence from Successful IPOs." Forthcoming, *Journal of Financial and Quantitative Analysis*.

Lerner, J. 1994a. "A Note on Private Equity Partnership Agreements." Harvard Business School Case 294-084. Cambridge, MA: Harvard Business Publishing.

———. 1994b. "The Syndication of Venture Capital Investments." *Financial Management*2 3:16–27.

———. 1994c. "Venture Capitalists and the Decision to Go Public." *Journal of Financial Economics*3 5:293–316.

———. 1995. "Venture Capitalists and the Oversight of Private Firms." *Journal of Finance*5 0:301–18.

Lin, T. H., and R. L. Smith. 1998. "Insider Reputation and Selling Decisions: The Unwinding of Venture Capital Investments during Equity IPOs." *Journal of Corporate Finance*4 :241–63.

Megginson, W. L., and K. A. Weiss. 1991. "Venture Capital Certification in Initial Public Offerings." *Journal of Finance*4 6:879–903.

Nahata, R. 2008. "Venture Capital Reputation and Investment Performance." *Journal of Financial Economics*9 0:127–51.

National Venture Capital Association. 2009. *Venture Impact: The Economic Importance of VC-Backed Companies to the U.S. Economy*. 5th ed. Available at http://www.nvca.org/.

Norton, E. 1995. "Venture Capital as an Alternative Means to Allocate Capital: An Agency Theoretic View." *Entrepreneurship Theory and Practice* 20 (Winter): 19–29.

Norton, E., and B. Tenenbaum. 1993. "Specialization versus Diversification as a Venture Capital Investment Strategy." *Journal of Business Venturing* 8:431–42.

Sahlman, W. A. 1990. "The Structure and Governance of Venture Capital Organizations." *Journal of Financial Economics* 27 (2): 473–521.

Smart, G. H. 1998. "Management Assessment Methods in Venture Capital: Toward a Theory of Human Capital Valuation." Unpublished dissertation, Claremont Graduate University, Claremont, CA.

Smith, J. K., R. L. Smith, and K. Williams. 2001. "The SEC's 'Fair Value' Standard for Mutual Fund Investment in Restricted and Other Illiquid Securities." *Fordham Journal of Corporate and Financial Law*6 :421–74.

Smith, R. L., R. Pedace, and V. Sathe. 2009. "Venture Capital: Performance, Persistence, and Reputation." Working paper. Available at http://papers.ssrn.com/sol3/papers.cfm?abstract_id=1432858.

Sohl, J. 2008. "The Angel Investor Market in 2008: A Down Year in Investment Dollars but Not in Deals." Center for Venture Research, March 26, 2008. Available at http://www.wsbe.unh.edu/files/2008_Analysis_Report_Final.pdf.

Sorensen, M. 2006. "How Smart Is Smart Money? A Two-Sided Matching Model of Venture Capital." *Journal of Finance* 62 (6): 2725–62.

Timmons, J. A., and S. Spinelli. 2008. *New Venture Creation: Entrepreneurship for the 21st Century*. 8th ed. Boston: McGraw-Hill.

Trester, J. J. 1998. "Venture Capital Contracting under Asymmetric Information." *Journal of Banking and Finance*2 2:675–99.

Tyebjee, T. T., and A. V. Bruno. 1984. "A Model of Venture Capitalist Investment Activity." *Management Science* 30 (9): 1051–66.

US Census Bureau. 2001. *Statistical Abstract of the United States*. Washington, DC: US Government Printing Office.

Zider, B. 1998. "How Venture Capital Works." *Harvard Business Review* 76 (6): 131–39.

FINANCIAL ASPECTS OF STRATEGIC PLANNING

CHAPTER 4

New Venture Strategy and Real Options

If you want more, make yourself worth more.

Hong Kong Noodle Company

You may be wondering why, in a book on entrepreneurial finance, we would devote this chapter and the next to strategic planning. There are three key reasons. First, strategic planning is about choosing a course of action that is designed to achieve a particular objective. In business settings, the overarching objective is financial return, that is, the net present value (NPV). Even in not-for-profit settings where the primary objective is philanthropic, adequacy of financial return must be an intermediate goal. Second, almost any strategic plan affords opportunities to change course after the initial direction has been selected. In financial terms, these choices are described as real options. Finance provides a means of valuing real options and taking account of those values in the initial strategic choice. Third, for new ventures, the ability even to pursue a particular strategy can depend on whether financing can be found.

This chapter establishes the basics of strategic planning in an entrepreneurial setting and develops a framework for evaluating alternative strategies.[1] The framework is one that describes real options as decision trees (or game trees) and uses investment valuation to compare alternative strategies. The framework begins with identifying the objective and the strategic alternatives for achieving it. Normally, we will assume that the objective is maximum NPV for the entrepreneur. The alternatives are structures of real options that can be described and evaluated as the branches of a decision tree. We begin by highlighting the interconnected nature of product-market, financial, and organizational choices, followed by an example from business history that illustrates the importance of the financing choice in the overall design of new venture strategy. We conclude with some observations on how strategic planning is related to the business plan.

4.1 Product-Market, Financial, and Organizational Strategy

Especially for new ventures, financial strategic decisions must be determined jointly with product-market and organizational strategic decisions. The potential for success is greatest when the decisions are in harmony. Figure 4.1 provides a framework for thinking about how the three components of strategy relate. Financial strategy defines the type and timing of financing. Strategic financial decisions include the amount of outside financing, target capital structure, staging of cash infusions, and so on. Product-market strategy involves the targeted sales growth rate, product price, product quality, product differentiation, whether to produce multiple products, and the like. Organizational strategy concerns

FIGURE **4.1**
The interdependent components of strategy

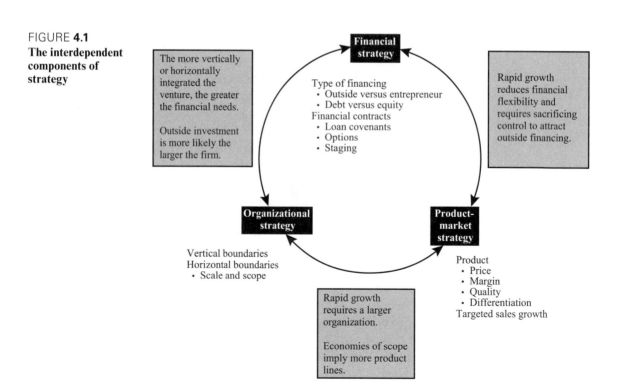

the horizontal and vertical boundaries of the firm, in whom decision-making authority resides, and so forth.

As an illustration, suppose an entrepreneur were to conclude that rapid sales growth was the preferred strategy in the product market. The strategic choice to grow rapidly commits the firm to a limited menu of financing options. Rapid growth usually requires external capital. The firm could choose to operate with high financial leverage, in which case it might sacrifice product-market and organizational flexibility, or it might turn to equity capital, in which case the entrepreneur would have to share the return.

It does not make sense to settle on a product-market strategy without considering how that choice restricts financing options. It also makes little sense to place product-market strategy ahead of financing in the decision hierarchy. While it may be possible to settle on a financing option that makes the choice of product-market strategy viable, sequencing the two decisions can lead to second-best outcomes. Even though rapid growth may appear to be attractive, the entrepreneur might be better off if the firm were to grow more slowly.

Similarly, there are interactions between financial and organizational strategy and between product-market and organizational strategy. Examples appear on the outside of Figure 4.1 and make clear that rapid growth—often the assumed goal for a new venture—has implications for the size/structure of the organization and the amount of financing that will be needed.

The interdependencies among product-market, organizational, and financial decisions can lessen in large, well-established organizations. If a large company contemplates a strategy of rapid growth in a market that accounts for a small fraction of its total activity, that decision does not necessarily commit the company to a highly leveraged capital structure or the need to raise equity capital by selling stock. Thus, investors may not be harmed if the investment decision and financing decision are treated separately.

Our point is that product-market, organizational, and financial decisions need to be viewed simultaneously. Simultaneous consideration helps guarantee that the first-best overall strategy is not overlooked. Thinking about product-market, organizational, and financial strategies as simultaneous rather than sequential choices takes us beyond the limits of intuitive decision making. Evaluating the choices simultaneously requires more formal analysis. Later in the chapter, we use decision trees and game trees as devices to capture the interplay between simultaneous and sequential decisions and to identify and evaluate alternative strategies.

4.2   The Interdependence of Strategic Choices: An Example

To illustrate the interdependencies of strategy choices, consider the case of Ford Motor Company. In the early 1900s, over 100 different firms were manufacturing and selling automobiles in the United States. At the time of this writing, only Ford Motor Company remains as a viable US automobile manufacturer.[2] Most of the attrition occurred during the early decades, offsetting the meteoric growth of Ford Motor Company.[3] From 1908 through 1921, the US market share of Ford rose steadily to 60 percent, and half of the automobiles operating in the world were Fords.[4] It looked, at the time, as if Ford would soon become the sole US manufacturer.

Many people would say that Henry Ford succeeded in the early years of the industry because he chose a strategy of mass production and his rivals did not. As he stated to one of his partners in 1903: "The way to make automobiles is to make one automobile like another, to make them all alike—just like one pin is like another pin when it comes to a pin factory."[5] But this is an incomplete explanation. Henry Ford did not invent mass production.[6] Eli Whitney, for example, began mass producing rifles with interchangeable parts in 1798. Moreover, Adam Smith recognized the economic benefits of specialization and mass production in *The Wealth of Nations* in 1776, over a century before Ford began to manufacture automobiles.

Surely, by the 1900s, it did not take a genius to recognize the cost saving that mass production could bring. A piece of the puzzle is missing. That piece is Ford's innovative marketing and financing plan. In the early stages of the industry, to limit up-front costs, Ford's rivals manufactured automobiles one by one, often to order and using generic tools and parts. Accordingly, the capital commitments of most manufacturers were negligible. The large number of early entrants was only possible because the entrants were all pursuing strategies that did not require large capital investments. Mass production, on the contrary, requires a major investment. Standardized parts must be inventoried; several automobiles must be in production at the same time by a team of employees; efficient production requires investment in customized tools and parts; and finished goods must be inventoried for future sale.

Henry Ford's true genius was in perceiving the vast market for sales of low-priced automobiles, in recognizing that low cost could be achieved through high-volume mass production, and in solving the financing problem. Without access to significant outside financing, he could never have mass produced the Model T and sold it profitably. The

1909 Model T cost $850 (about $21,000 in 2009 dollars), while competitors' cars often cost $2,000 to $3,000.

Ford financed his new venture by purchasing parts from others and performing only the assembly operation himself. He purchased on credit, assembling automobiles quickly, and selling them to Ford dealers for cash. By rapidly building a large dealer network (attracting dealers because of his ability to sell at a price well below the competition), he was able to exploit the efficiencies of large-scale mass production. The strategy soon began to generate positive cash flow, which was used to upgrade the assembly line and to integrate upstream, from assembling into manufacturing. By applying the same techniques to parts manufacturing, he was able to achieve additional efficiencies—by 1916, the retail price of a Model T had declined to $360, down 58 percent from its initial 1908 price of $850.[7]

Ford's product-market strategy emphasized high-volume, low-product-price marketing. The complementary organizational strategy focused production efforts on final assembly rather than upstream integration into manufacturing of component parts. The financial strategy overlaps both. By focusing on final assembly, Ford reduced its need for early-stage capital. It could also take advantage of vendor financing (trade credit) for the parts it purchased. By selling to dealers for cash, it shifted the burden of carrying finished goods inventory to the dealers. It is unlikely that Ford's product-market strategy could have been achieved without the complementary financial and organizational strategies.

The Model T is a compelling example of the important role that financial strategy can play in the success of a new venture. However, business strategy must be dynamic and responsive to changes in the competitive environment. Despite its domination of the automobile industry in the early 1920s, Ford Motor Company eventually faltered and fell to second place among domestic producers. This happened because Henry Ford would not depart from the strategy that had been so successful in the early years. Even though the economics of the industry had changed, Ford continued to produce the Model T from 1908 through 1927, with no substantial improvements to design or performance. Ford's strategic focus was 100 percent on cost minimization. Consumers could buy any car they wanted "as long as it is black."

Meanwhile, the few competitors who had survived the intense price competition from Ford had also moved into mass production, but with a view toward the changing tastes of consumers. Those companies made tradeoffs between cost reduction through large-scale mass production and product quality and styling. General Motors, in particular, was able to achieve most of the cost savings while offering automobiles that outperformed the Model T and catered to consumer demand for styling.[8]

Model T sales declined rapidly after 1921, as the market share of General Motors climbed. Finally, in 1927, Ford Motor Company was compelled by competitive pressure to discontinue the Model T. But still Ford failed to adjust its strategy to a market in which cost was only one dimension of competition. Ford introduced the Model A, which it attempted to sell without modification for several years. The ultimate result was the same, but the end came more quickly.

In the competitive struggle between Ford and General Motors, financing took a less important position than in the early days. Both companies were well established and could easily raise financing for whatever product-market strategy they chose to pursue. This second episode illustrates a general principle that is an important motivation for this book: the interdependencies between product-market, organizational, and financing strategies usually are more acute for entrepreneurial ventures than for established and profitable large businesses.

Interestingly, in the face of the economic downturn transpiring at the time of this writing, financing has reemerged as a key element of strategy for domestic automobile producers. Both Chrysler and General Motors have turned to government to help them survive the economic downturn. Chrysler has looked to a foreign acquirer as a means of returning to viability; General Motors has turned to the bankruptcy courts as a way to achieve financial restructuring; and Ford has resisted both, betting that the taints of government assistance and financial bankruptcy would adversely impact demand for its products. In reality, there is very little difference today between the General Motors and Chrysler reorganizations and new ventures. In some respects, the reorganizations are more challenging because the recent track records are not good and the culture has to be changed rather than just nurtured. For many years, the two companies have been unprofitable and the path to sustainable profitability, or even survival, is far from clear.

4.3   What Makes a Plan or Decision Strategic?

It is useful to distinguish strategic decisions from other decisions along three dimensions. First, strategic decisions are consequential. Unlike the decision of which way to drive home from work, strategic decisions involve substantial commitments of time and resources. They are of sufficient magnitude and importance that they are rare, and little precedent exists on which to base them.

Second, strategic decisions are both active and reactive. The decision is made in a competitive setting, with regard to the possible actions and reactions of others who have competing or complementary objectives. In selecting among alternatives, the decision maker must take into consideration the choices that may already have been made by others whose objectives overlap and must recognize that others may react to the decision. The decision of when, where, and how to locate a retail store is strategic in this sense.

Third, strategic decisions are not costless to reverse. If a decision maker selects a wrong course of action, she cannot simply retract it. Investments made to pursue the first course of action are, to some extent, sunk. Sunk investments limit flexibility because the full cost of changing direction must be compared to only the incremental cost of continuing in the same direction. Consequently, an initial wrong strategic choice is one from which the decision maker may never fully recover.

The early actions of Ford satisfy these criteria. First, the decision to appeal to the mass market was a deliberate choice to reject the prevailing view that the automobile is a luxury. Second, given the large number of small manufacturers in the early automobile industry, Ford initially did not need to be concerned that other manufacturers would react to his entry. He did, however, need to be concerned with how they would react to his unprecedented success. Manufacturers of higher-priced automobiles, acting as a group, sought to foreclose him from the industry by refusing to grant Ford licensing rights to use a patent that was argued to control the internal combustion technology.[9] Subsequently, manufacturers like General Motors imitated aspects of his success with mass production, eventually forcing the Ford Motor Company to abandon its initial strategy and move to annual model changes. Third, Ford's commitment to one model, the Model T, was costly to reverse. It required abandoning other models, investing in large-capacity facilities, and purchasing specialized inventories. These investments committed Ford to aggressive pricing and to maintaining high levels of capacity utilization.

4.4 Financial Strategy

Financial strategic choices have the same three elements. A financing choice can limit future financing options in a variety of ways. For example, contractual provisions of a debt agreement may restrict the firm's ability to redeem the debt and replace it with equity. Existing debt financing may limit the financing sources available for new projects. And debt service requirements may limit the firm's ability to undertake new projects that would generate negative cash flows in the short run.

Competitive interdependencies are also present. Financing choices that are costly to reverse or change involve sunk investments in arranging the financing. In such cases, a firm's financing choices may credibly commit the firm to a particular course of action that is observable by competitors, suppliers, customers, employees, and stockholders. Such credible commitments can influence the actions of these groups. For example, securing project financing can discourage others from moving ahead with plans of their own. Conversely, announcement of intent to develop a new product, if not backed by a credible commitment, could touch off a scramble among rivals to be first in the market. For example, when Airbus announced in 2000 that it was proceeding with the production of its super jumbo jet, the A380, Boeing immediately said that it too would introduce a new super jumbo jet to replace the aging 747. It was not until Airbus had secured financing and begun investing in A380 production capacity that Boeing abandoned its plans for a 747 replacement and pursued the 787 Dreamliner.

The scope of financial strategy is quite broad. It goes beyond the simple debt-versus-equity financing decision and includes such considerations as the connections between financing choices and growth, flexibility, and control. In addition, financial strategy includes such choices as the use of financial contracts to address or overcome informational asymmetries between entrepreneurs and investors and to better align the incentives of entrepreneurs and employees with the interests of investors.

4.5   Deciding on the Objective

For many entrepreneurs, the decisions of whether to launch a new venture or continue in current employment and how to develop the venture are made by intuition. Yet these are not decisions where intuition is likely to lead to the best outcome. There is also evidence that some entrepreneurs place weight on qualitative considerations. They may, for example, take pride in having created something new or they may value self-employment.

Our objective in this book is not to argue against the value of subjective considerations. Rather, it is to provide a framework that can help entrepreneurs make better decisions. Here, we propose a two-step process: first, select the strategy that yields the highest estimated NPV; and second, make qualitative adjustments to the NPV by assigning subjective values to the considerations that are important to the prospective entrepreneur. As we can have little to say about the qualitative considerations, our emphasis is on the first step, maximization of NPV. Generally, we examine NPV from the perspective of the entrepreneur.

More formally, the first step in developing the analytical framework for strategic planning is to clearly specify the objective. Making rational choices is a forward-looking concept. Rationality does not mean that the choice is always right *ex post*, only that it is expected to be right given the information available at the time of decision.

A prospective entrepreneur considers a variety of alternatives and selects the action that she expects will result in the highest level of satisfaction. A number of qualitative factors bear on the choice. A risk-tolerant person is more willing to abandon secure employment to pursue a venture than is a person who places a high value on security. A person who enjoys work-related challenges is more willing to start a venture than is one who values leisure time. These are the entrepreneur's personal choices, and we can do little in a formal way to assess such qualitative tradeoffs. But we can provide an analytical approach to help the entrepreneur evaluate the tradeoffs.

Strategic planning reduces the importance of intuition in the decision process so that prospective entrepreneurs can make better-informed decisions. To achieve this, we must begin with an objective that can be measured. As stated above, we assume that the entrepreneur's objective is to maximize the value of the venture to herself. Thus, in purely financial terms, 40 percent ownership of a $5 million business is more valuable to the entrepreneur than 15 percent of a $10 million business. It is the value of the entrepreneur's interest that should influence the strategic choice.[10]

This does not mean that the entrepreneur should substitute value maximization for utility maximization as the ultimate determinant of the choice. Once the quantitative value of the entrepreneur's interest is determined, it is easier for the entrepreneur to assess the qualitative tradeoffs related to such factors as control and security. To illustrate, suppose, as an entrepreneur, you are offered two choices by a prospective investor. Under one you would retain control, and under the other you would not. In exchange for relinquishing control, however, you would receive additional compensation having a present value of $100,000. You can then assess whether you would relinquish control in exchange for a $100,000 increase in the expected value of your interest.[11]

The entrepreneur is likely to be concerned with the financial return and risk is also an important consideration. Beyond this, entrepreneurial decisions are likely to be influenced by, among other things, liquidity, diversification, and flexibility; by transferability of ownership; and by the effects of the choice on the entrepreneur's control and accountability to others.

At a more fundamental level, the primary determinant of value is the tradeoff between risk and expected return. Factors such as liquidity, diversification, transferability, and flexibility are taken into consideration through their effects on expected return and risk. The value of control is an additional qualitative factor that goes beyond the objective assessment of present value.

As a final note, value maximization does not mean that an entrepreneur is greedy or that a venture is exploitative of either consumers or employees. A viable venture must offer a product or service that is attractive enough to draw consumers away from alternative purchases. Compensation packages offered to employees must be sufficient to attract them away from other positions.

4.6 Strategic Planning for New Ventures

New ventures are different from established businesses because their plans are unconstrained by previous decisions. Questions of financing, organizational design, and product-market strategy are all open. The planning process needs to reflect simultaneous consideration of all three components of the strategy.

The distinction between simultaneous and sequential consideration of strategic choices is fundamental. Suppose that on weekends while working in your current position you have perfected a technology for making calorie-free ice cream. You are trying to decide whether to resign and start a venture that will employ the technology. Should you decide to proceed, there are a number of other decisions to be made. To keep matters simple, in the product market you must choose either a high-margin, slow-growth approach or a low-margin, high-growth approach. With respect to organizational design, you must choose either to enter only at the manufacturing level and contract for distribution or to enter into both manufacturing and distribution. Let's suppose that the nonintegrated option involves selling through grocery stores

TABLE **4.1**   **Financial implications of product-market and organizational strategic choices**

		Product-market choice	
		Slow growth	Rapid growth
Organizational choice	One-level entry	Initially financed by entrepreneur; growth financed with operating cash flows. NPV = $40	Initially financed by entrepreneur; growth financed with operating cash flows and outside financing. NPV = $120
	Integrated entry	Initial financing includes outside equity; growth financed with operating cash flows. NPV = −$20	Initial financing includes outside equity; growth financed with operating cash flows and outside financing. NPV = $70

NOTE: *Product-market and organizational strategic choices are interdependent with financing choices. One-level entry combined with slow growth minimizes immediate and ongoing needs for external financing. Integrated entry and rapid growth normally require higher levels of immediate and ongoing external financing. NPV reflects the expected value to the entrepreneur.*

and the integrated approach involves creating a network of branded ice cream stores.

Table 4.1 illustrates the implications of the various product-market and organizational choices for the venture's financing needs. If you enter only manufacturing and pursue a slow-growth strategy, your own resources are sufficient to fund the initial investment. The growth rate is determined by the operating cash flows of the venture. With one-level entry and a plan of rapid growth, you must rely on outside financing to supplement the financing available through operating cash flow. If you decide to enter both manufacturing and distribution, even with slow growth the initial investment is too large for you alone, and additional start-up financing is required. With both vertical integration and rapid growth, outside financing is needed both for start-up and to sustain growth.

Table 4.1 displays the two product-market alternatives, along with the two organizational structure alternatives. These choices have direct implications for the available financing options. Each cell in the table represents a combination of a product-market and organizational choice and describes the implied financing choice. The amount shown in the cell along with the financing description is the entrepreneur's expected NPV associated with that combination of choices. The most valuable is a strategy of entering only at the manufacturing level (relying on contracting for distribution), pricing aggressively to foster rapid growth, and supporting the enterprise initially with your own resources followed by operating cash flows and outside financing. This choice provides the entrepreneur with an expected NPV of $120.

However, suppose you do not think through all of the alternatives and settle first on the integrated organizational strategy. In that case, no matter what the product-market strategy, you cannot expect to do better than $70. Moreover, if you choose a high-price/slow-growth strategy, then the expected NPV is negative. Perhaps you can go back to the investors and try to change the deal. But even if the change is possible, it will require renegotiation, and your expected value can never be as high as if you had studied the alternatives first and planned accordingly.

Even in this simple illustration, the product-market and organizational decisions limit the financing options. If entry is integrated, available outside financing is likely to be equity. You may have to sacrifice voting control or give other control rights to providers of financing. With rapid growth, financing needs to occur after the venture is established. In the early-growth stages, equity-like claims may still be required, but the fraction of ownership that must be relinquished per dollar raised is likely to be less than if funding is required at start-up. As the venture grows and begins to generate taxable income, debt financing becomes a more realistic and attractive possibility. In addition, there are alternatives such as franchising of distribution outlets and equipment leasing that may have advantages over either equity or debt financing. A well-thought-out strategic plan takes such alternatives into consideration.

Of course, any commitment of resources to a particular strategy limits flexibility. If, for example, the entrepreneur builds the ice cream factory in California, it would be costly to change and decide that New York would be a better location. But here we are concerned with something more—a loss of flexibility that arises from reliance on outside financing. Almost any outside financing that the entrepreneur can raise comes with limitations on how it can be used and even on how the other resources of the venture can be used.

Commonly, such limitations are tied to the strategy that was described in the business plan and was presented to the investors. Even if it were clear to the entrepreneur that a change of plans would be good for the venture, the change often cannot be made unless the investors are also convinced. Yet convincing them is likely to be difficult, particularly if they have not been heavily involved in the operation of the venture. The surest way to limit this problem is to methodically plan the venture before presenting a business plan to investors.

4.7   Recognizing Real Options

Strategic planning is not a one-shot exercise. With the passage of time, original targets will be exceeded or missed, and new developments will render the initial plan obsolete. Rather than planning a single immutable course of action, it is more useful to select the strategy that offers the highest expected value in light of the flexibility that the strategy affords for dealing with surprises. Opportunities to abandon a venture, expand it, or change direction are real options. You can think of the focus of strategic planning as deciding which real options to acquire, retain, and abandon at key decision points.[12]

Option Basics

An option is the right to make a decision in the future. In the stock market, for example, a call option is a right to buy a share of stock at some future date for a price that is established today.[13] The right to buy a share of Amazon.com common stock anytime during the next three months at a price of $110 is a call option with an exercise price of $110, where the underlying asset is a share of Amazon common stock.

The value of an option depends on several factors. Most basically, a call option gains value if the market price of the underlying asset rises and loses value if the price of the asset falls. Suppose that Amazon is selling at expiration for $118 per share. The $110 call option would yield an $8 payoff ($118 − $110). If the price of Amazon goes to $125, the value of the call option increases—in this example the payoff almost doubles to $15 ($125 − $110). It follows that call options with low exercise prices are more valuable than those with high exercise prices. The right to buy Amazon for $100 per share obviously is more valuable than the right to buy for $110. Figure 4.2a shows the payoffs for this call option with a $110 exercise price.

Figure 4.2 shows clearly that options limit downside risk. Since option risk is one-sided, the more volatile the underlying asset, the higher the value of an option on the asset. Suppose, over the next three months, Amazon is equally likely to increase in value to $140 or to decline in value to $100. If the price of Amazon stock increases to $140, a call option at $110 will be in the money and can be exercised to acquire the stock for a saving of $30 per share. If the price of Amazon falls to $100, the call option is out of the money and will not be exercised. Thus, buying a call option limits the downside risk of investing in Amazon but

FIGURE **4.2**
Expiration date values of call and put options on Amazon.com stock

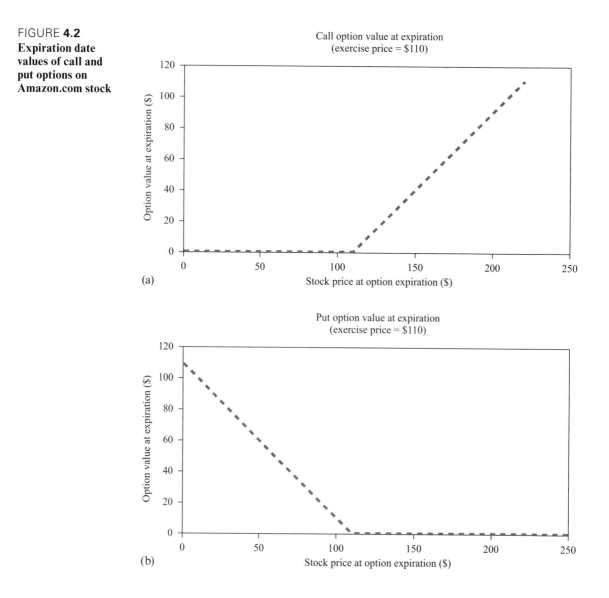

The time value of money affects option values because buying an option works like borrowing. If you buy a call, you do not have to come up with the money to exercise the option and purchase the shares until later, if and when you exercise the option. This is different from buying the stock outright, where you must pay the full price today. Accordingly, buying a call option is like borrowing the exercise price without having to pay interest. Since the value of not having to pay interest is greater the higher the interest rate for borrowing, call options increase in value with increases in the cost of money.

A put option carries the right to sell an underlying asset during a specified period at a specified exercise price. If the owner of a put decides to exercise, he receives the exercise price. In contrast to calls, puts gain value when underlying asset values are low and when exercise prices are high. As can be seen in Figure 4.2b, a put on Amazon at $110 is more valuable if Amazon is selling for $80 than $90. Like call options, put options are more valuable when the underlying asset is riskier. Because the owner of a put is effectively lending the exercise price without charging interest, a put is less valuable if the cost of money is high (i.e., more interest income is forgone).

Calls and puts can be bought or sold. The price of an option contract is called the premium. The seller (or writer) of a call option is obligated to deliver the underlying asset in exchange for the exercise price if the call is exercised. The writer of a put is obligated to buy the underlying asset at the exercise price if the put is exercised. For assuming this obligation, option sellers collect the premium.

Puts and calls can be used to allocate the risk of investing in the underlying asset. For example, an investor in Amazon common stock who buys a put option has reallocated the downside risk to the writer of the option. In this case, the stockholder is hedged against the downside risk, and the put writer is acting as an insurer.

Comparisons between Real and Financial Options

Puts and calls on stock are financial options. The underlying asset is a financial asset, and exercising or not exercising the option does not affect the value of the underlying asset. In several respects, real options are similar. As with financial options, the values of real options increase with the riskiness of the underlying asset and time to expiration. The values of real options are also affected similarly by the difference between the exercise price and the underlying asset value.[14]

Yet real options differ from financial options in important ways. First, the markets for financial options are often complete, meaning that calls and puts on a stock are available with the same exercise price and expiration date, the underlying stock is freely traded, and riskless borrowing is possible. If the market is complete, option value can be determined by appealing to the ability of investors to arbitrage risklessly any pricing disparities.[15] In contrast, real option markets are not complete.

Second, real options are often interdependent in ways that make the application of formal option pricing models inappropriate. Financial options can be bought, sold, and exercised separately, and the value of a portfolio of financial options is simply the sum of the values of the individual options. Real options, in contrast, are often interdependent, and the decision to exercise one may have implications for the values of others. Consequently, the value of a portfolio of real options often cannot be determined by simply adding up the values of the individual options.

The term "real options" is used to stress their similarity to financial options while preserving the notion that there are important differences. Returning to the calorie-free ice cream example, once you have developed the technology to manufacture the ice cream, you have options to exploit the technology in many ways. Some are reflected in Table 4.2. You also have the option to do none of those things and instead continue working in your existing position. In addition, you may have the option to delay and, for example, start the venture next year (though in a changed environment). Once you begin the venture, depending on contractual financing arrangements, you or the investor may have the option to abandon it if things do not work out as well as you hoped. We can also intentionally incorporate real options into strategic choices to create additional flexibility. For example, the ice cream venture might acquire options to lease facilities in both California and New York.

Effective strategic planning takes account of the values of important real options. Because of the importance of real options to most new ventures, it is useful to incorporate formal decision analysis techniques into the strategic planning exercise.

The Real Option Premium

The cost of acquiring an option is called the option premium. One of the important differences between real and financial options is that the real option premium bears no necessary relation to the value of the option. The value of an abandonment option, for example, depends on the highest alternative use value of the assets. But the cost of acquiring the option may have little to do with the option value. Thus, the value of a strategy can be dramatically improved by making good choices about what real options to acquire and by using them effectively.

TABLE **4.2** **Examples of real options**

Category of option	Description	Examples
Option to wait	If it is possible to postpone an action, the decision maker has an option to wait. Decisions involve comparing the value of acting now with the expected value of waiting.	The owner of a forest can cut the trees today or wait until next year when the trees will have grown larger and lumber prices may have changed.
Option to learn	Learning options are similar to waiting options except that the focus is on the resolution of uncertainty. The holder of an option to wait can either make the best choice in light of the uncertain future or wait until some important uncertainty is resolved.	A person who hopes to receive job offers from two different employers either could choose to minimize the expected commute today by buying a house located between the two or could wait for an offer and then locate near the ultimate employer.
Options to expand or contract	An entrepreneur who has the ability to increase the scale of a venture has an option to expand. One who has the ability to downsize has an option to contract.	An entrepreneur might decide to acquire an expansion option by purchasing a facility that is larger than the anticipated need. An entrepreneur might acquire an option to contract by closing down a production line if demand is less than anticipated. The option can be acquired by building a flexible production process.
Options to switch inputs or outputs	An entrepreneur has an option to switch inputs or outputs when she can alter the mix of a production process in response to market prices.	An entrepreneur who designs a facility to operate on either electricity or natural gas has the real option to switch between these two inputs. A refiner who can switch between producing heating oil and gasoline has the real option to switch outputs.
Option to abandon	An abandonment option is a right to discontinue an activity and redeploy the real assets to some other use.	Abandonment options include the options to discontinue a research project, close a store, or resign from current employment.

4.8   Strategic Planning and Decision Trees

A decision tree is a useful way to conceptualize strategic alternatives that involve real options. Constructing a decision tree imposes discipline on the evaluation process and helps the entrepreneur identify the relevant real options and the points at which critical decisions must be made. It also enables the entrepreneur to assess, in a structured way, the connections between decisions made today and the value of the venture in the future.

Building and Pruning Decision Trees

A decision tree incorporates both decisions and uncertain events that affect the value of the outcome. It identifies a sequence of decisions in which the range of available choices is limited by previous decisions, and the best decision depends on which state of the world is realized. The decision maker is uncertain about which state will be realized but knows or estimates the probabilities of the different states. In addition, the decision maker estimates the NPV of a choice conditional on which future state attains.

A few simple techniques can ensure that a decision tree accurately reflects the important choices and help to value them correctly.

- *Focus on the most important choices.* Because the number of branches expands geometrically, decision tree analyses can become intractable. Focusing on a few critical decisions and a few discrete choices is usually all that is needed (e.g., make or buy, borrow or issue equity, grow rapidly or slowly).

- *Reason forward to construct the tree.* Sequencing is chronological. The tree should illustrate how each choice limits the options for subsequent decisions. You can build the tree by first determining the important choices available today. For each of these, determine the choices that would be available at the next decision point (node), and so on. Decisions that are simultaneous (rather than sequential) can be represented as more branches emanating from the same node. For example, scale of entry (large or small) and rate of growth (rapid or slow) can be represented as four branches from the same node (large scale with rapid growth, etc.).

- *Keep track of what is known and unknown at each node.* If the decision on optimal scale of entry depends on the level of future demand (a state of the world that is uncertain today), you can only base the decision you make today on expected future demand.

- *Evaluate choices recursively.* Start with the last decision point (the terminal node) and compare the values of the alternatives that emanate from that node as if you had followed the branches up to that point. These are the payoffs conditional on having made the choices that are represented at the prior nodes.

- *Prune the tree.* Select the branch with the highest expected value, conditional on the earlier choices, and eliminate, or prune, the inferior choices. For example, if conditional on high demand, you would choose to expand, then you can eliminate the other choices. Move backward to the next earlier decision point and evaluate the choices considering only the highest-valued branch from the subsequent node—in this case, expansion.

- *Select the branch of the tree with the highest expected value.* This process of backward induction, working from the best future decision conditional on choices made previously, leads to a set of valuations that reflect the values of the embedded options in the decision process.

An Illustration

Suppose an entrepreneur is considering investing in a restaurant. For simplicity, she assumes that demand for the restaurant could turn out to be any one of three states of nature: high, moderate, or low. She is considering building a large restaurant, a small restaurant, or not entering the business at this time. The cost of the large restaurant is $750,000. The cost of the small restaurant is $600,000. The entrepreneur has $400,000 to invest and plans to bring in an investor for the balance. The investor requires 1 percent of the equity for each $10,000 invested in the venture, resulting in a 35 percent interest in the larger restaurant or a 20 percent interest in the smaller one. The entrepreneur retains the balance of ownership.

At this point, our focus is on strategic planning and our purpose is to demonstrate the use of decision trees for making strategic choices. To keep things simple, we assume (for now) that the entrepreneur has already estimated the present values (PVs) of the different restaurant sizes conditional on the different states of demand and has already estimated the probabilities of the different states. We will relax these assumptions in the next chapter.

Naturally, the large restaurant has the potential to generate more revenue, but it also necessitates a larger investment and greater fixed operating expenses. The entrepreneur's estimates of the PVs in different states of the world reflect these economies. If the high-demand state occurs, the limited capacity of the small restaurant constrains its value. In the high-demand state, we assume that the entrepreneur expects the PV of the large restaurant to be $1.5 million and the PV of the small restaurant to be $800,000. If the moderate-demand state occurs, the PV of future cash flows of both the large and the small restaurant is expected to be $800,000. In the low-demand state, the PV of the large restaurant is $300,000 and that of the small restaurant is $400,000. The difference is due to the higher fixed cost of operating the large restaurant.[16]

Evaluating the Venture as an Accept/Reject Decision

To establish a baseline for evaluating the real options, consider the project as a simple accept/reject decision with mutually exclusive alternatives—the conventional way of evaluating simple capital investment

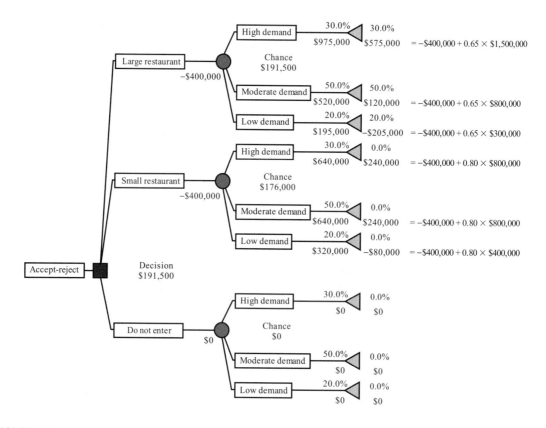

FIGURE **4.3**

Decision tree for accept/reject decision to invest in restaurant business
With a one-time accept/reject decision, the entrepreneur cannot anticipate the level of product demand that will be realized. The investment decision and choice of level of investment are made in light of existing uncertainty by maximizing expected NPV. Prepared using PrecisionTree™, Palisade Corporation.

projects. Figure 4.3 represents the choices in the form of a decision tree. The square in the figure represents the one decision point. The circles represent uncertain outcomes that are beyond the entrepreneur's control; they reflect states of the world with respect to demand. You can think of "nature" as choosing a state of the world.

Each state has an associated probability. In Figure 4.3, the entrepreneur has simplified the decision problem by thinking of it in terms of three states of demand and has estimated the probability of each. The probability of high demand is 30 percent, the probability of moderate demand is 50 percent, and the probability of low demand is 20 percent. In the accept/reject decision, the entrepreneur must decide which, if any, restaurant to open before the uncertainty about demand is resolved. Her investment is $400,000 regardless of which restaurant she chooses. Because we are examining the choice from the entrepreneur's perspective, the difference between the large and the small restaurant is shown as the fraction of the restaurant's value that accrues to the entrepreneur.

The triangles in the figure are terminal nodes. Next to each is the NPV the entrepreneur expects if she selects the corresponding branch and the specified level of demand is realized. For example, if the large restaurant is built and the high-demand state is realized, the entrepreneur will invest $400,000 in return for 65 percent of a restaurant with a total PV of $1.5 million. The figure shows that $975,000 is the entrepreneur's 65 percent share of the PV, so that the resulting NPV of the entrepreneur's investment is $575,000.

In our simple example, the entrepreneur decides how to invest by multiplying each state-contingent payoff by the probability of that state's occurrence and her fractional ownership interest (.65 or .80) and then subtracting her investment. The result of the calculation is the NPV of that choice to the entrepreneur. Thus, if the large restaurant is selected, her expected payoff is as follows:

$$\text{Expected Payoff} = .65 \,(.3 \times \$1,500,000 + .5 \times \$800,000 + .2 \times \$300,000)$$
$$= \$591,500$$

As this amount exceeds the entrepreneur's $400,000 investment by $191,500, it is better than not investing at all. The figure shows $191,500 as the NPV of selecting the large restaurant.

By a similar calculation, the entrepreneur's payoff from investing in the small restaurant is $576,000, an NPV of $176,000. Because both the large and the small restaurant have positive NPVs, either one is better than not investing. Because the large restaurant offers a higher NPV, that choice is better than investing in the small restaurant. Thus, the entrepreneur would want to prune the alternatives of investing in the small restaurant or not investing.

Ex post, it may turn out that building the large restaurant was the wrong decision. If demand turns out to be intermediate, the small restaurant would have been a better choice. If demand turns out to be low, not entering would have been better than either of the other choices. At the time of the decision, however, the entrepreneur cannot know which state of the world will occur. Given what is known and the estimated probabilities of the different states, the large restaurant is the best alternative.

In Figure 4.3, the decision facing the entrepreneur is a one-shot choice. There are no real options reflected in the figure. This is the "base case," with an NPV of $191,500. We now want to expand the range of possibilities by considering three types of real options: (1) the option to wait and learn more about market demand, (2) the option to expand if the small restaurant is selected initially, and (3) the option to abandon.

The Learning Option

By not investing immediately, the entrepreneur can learn more about which state of the world is likely to occur, but waiting increases the likelihood of entry by competitors, so that the expected payoffs in the various states are reduced. For simplicity, assume that by waiting the entrepreneur can learn market demand with certainty. Accordingly, in each case she will build the restaurant that maximizes her NPV.

Rarely does an investment opportunity involve now-or-never choices. Waiting can add value because uncertainty is reduced, or technology advances, or expenditures of resources are deferred until they are more immediately needed. The offsetting cost is that waiting to invest may encourage others to enter or market conditions may change.[17] The learning option is a call option—if a good state of nature attains, the entrepreneur can respond by investing in a restaurant that is optimally sized for demand. As with any call option, its value is higher if the level of uncertainty is high and if delay will materially reduce the uncertainty.

Because of the likelihood of competitive entry, we assume that the PV of the large restaurant declines to $1.3 million and the PV of the small restaurant declines to $700,000. To examine the value of the option to wait, we compare the NPV to the base case NPV. The difference is the value of the learning option.

Figure 4.4 modifies Figure 4.3 to reflect the learning option. Because waiting only affects the "Do not enter" branch of Figure 4.3, we have collapsed the two branches that involve investing today. For them, we show only the entrepreneur's NPV. Conditional on the high-demand state, her best course of action is to invest in the large restaurant. Her NPV of waiting and then investing in the large restaurant is $445,000 (net of the $400,000 investment). Because the "Small restaurant" and "Do not build" choices have lower NPVs ($160,000 and $0, respectively), we can prune those branches. Figure 4.4 shows that conditional on high demand, the entrepreneur chooses the large restaurant, and the resulting NPV is $445,000.

Similarly, the small restaurant is the best choice for the moderate-demand state. The NPV of investing in the small restaurant if the moderate-demand state occurs is $160,000. By waiting, the entrepreneur also avoids the potential mistake of investing only to learn that the low-demand state has been realized. If low demand is realized, not entering is the best choice.

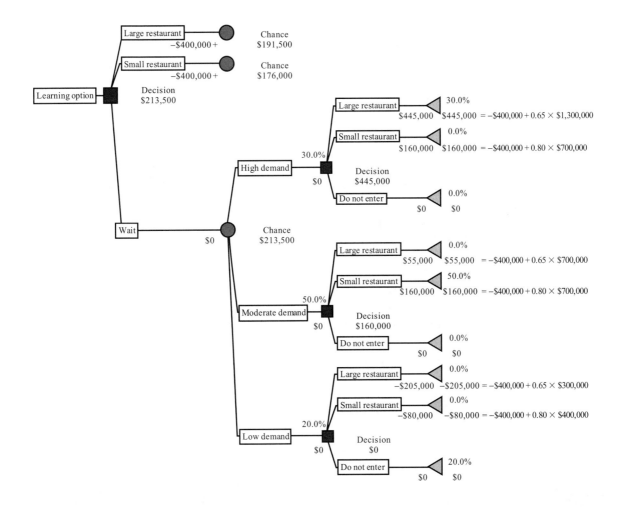

FIGURE **4.4**

Decision tree for investing in a restaurant business, with the option to delay investing until uncertainty about market demand is resolved
Not investing today may preserve an option to wait until more information is known about the true state of demand. Prepared using PrecisionTree, Palisade Corporation.

Because, at present, we do not know which of the three states will be realized, we can only compare the expected value that would result from learning against the most favorable alternative available by choosing not to wait. The expected NPV conditional on using the learning option is simply the probability-weighted average of the three possible outcomes (.3 × $445,000 + .5 × $160,000 + .2 × $0), or $213,500. Because this value is greater than the $191,500 base case expected NPV, it is better to wait. The learning option adds $22,000 to the value of the project; this is the value of the real option. The value comes from two sources: the upside gain from building the large restaurant when we know demand is high, and avoidance of the negative NPV outcome that occurs if we were to build any restaurant in the low-demand state. These two benefits outweigh the costs of waiting.

The Expansion Option

A second kind of option is the option to expand the venture after the initial investment has been made. Suppose that after an initial investment of $600,000 in the small restaurant (including $400,000 by the entrepreneur), and after learning market demand, the restaurant can be expanded to the large size by investing an additional $200,000. Assume that the $200,000 (if needed) comes from the investor, but on more favorable terms because the second investment is less risky given that uncertainty about demand is resolved. Specifically, the second $200,000 is raised in exchange for a 10 percent ownership share (1 percent of the equity for each $20,000 invested), bringing the investor's total to 30 percent in the event of expansion (rather than 35 percent in the no-waiting, large-restaurant scenario). Because the initial investment is sufficient to establish a market presence, we assume that the PV of the large restaurant is $1.4 million, higher than if no immediate investment were made but lower than if the large restaurant were built today.

What is the value of the expansion option? Figure 4.5 modifies Figure 4.3 to reflect this option. Here, we have ignored the learning option and have collapsed the branches where the expansion option does not apply. As the problem is structured, if the large restaurant is chosen initially, the expansion option is implicitly forgone. If the small restaurant is built, the entrepreneur can either expand or not. Expanding, if the high-demand state is realized, increases the entrepreneur's NPV to $580,000 ($980,000 minus the entrepreneur's original $400,000 investment). Not expanding leaves the NPV at $240,000, as in Figure 4.3. As this is below $580,000, we can prune the "High demand/Do not expand" branch.

Figure 4.5 also compares the values of expanding to not expanding in the moderate- and low-demand states of the world. Expansion is not a good idea with moderate demand because investing reduces the entrepreneur's ownership share without increasing the value of the venture. So we can ignore the "Moderate demand/Expand" branch. Not surprisingly, if demand is low, the best choice is "Do not expand."

Clearly, expansion is better if the high-demand state obtains. But is

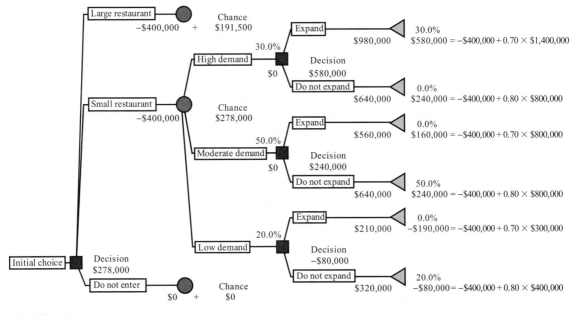

FIGURE **4.5**
Decision tree for investing in a restaurant business, with the option to expand the initial investment
The option to expand if demand turns out to be high is an example of the flexibility associated with real
options. Prepared using PrecisionTree, Palisade Corporation.

it a good idea to invest in the small restaurant first and wait to see what
happens to demand? The answer in this case is yes. As shown in Figure
4.5, the expected NPV from investing initially in the small restaurant
and expanding only if the high-demand state is realized is as follows:

$$NPV = .3 \times \$580,000 + .5 \times \$240,000 + .2 \times (\$80,000) = \$278,000$$

where the parentheses indicate a negative value. Comparing this to the
base case $191,500 expected NPV makes the expansion option worth
$86,500. This is the value of the expansion option compared to the sim-
ple accept/reject decision.

   We can also compare the expansion option with the $213,500 value
of the learning option (Figure 4.4). According to these calculations,
the NPV from investing immediately in a small restaurant (preserving the option to expand) is higher than from investing in a large restaurant ($278,000 > $191,500) and higher than from waiting to invest
($278,000 > $213,500). The incremental value of the expansion option
compared to waiting is $64,500. The key point of Figure 4.5 is that ig-
noring the option to expand would have led the entrepreneur to select

a less valuable strategy. In some cases, a project may be passed up entirely because of the failure to recognize that initial investments sometimes create valuable options that can be exercised in the future if the environment is right.

Here we see a difference between real and financial options that sometimes is important: the waiting option and the expansion option are mutually exclusive. The entrepreneur cannot acquire both. Normally, financial options are independent of each other—they can be acquired separately and decisions to exercise them can be made independently. But because real options relate to underlying real assets, they sometimes are mutually exclusive. In this case, if the entrepreneur wants to acquire the expansion option, the investment must be made today, thus forgoing the learning option.

The Abandonment Option

The final type of option we consider is the option to abandon the venture if things do not work out as well as expected. Suppose the restaurant facility has an alternative use as office space. If converted to office space (for a negligible net expenditure), the PV of the large facility would be $600,000 and the value of the small facility would be $300,000. You can see from the numbers that the option to abandon the small restaurant is worthless. This is because a small restaurant, even in the low-demand state, has a PV of $400,000, which is more than its PV as office space. But the option does have value for the large restaurant, because $600,000 is more than the $300,000 present value as a restaurant in the low-demand state.

The best strategy to this point is to build small and then expand if demand turns out to be high. Is the value of the option to abandon the large restaurant enough to tip the balance in favor of building the large restaurant immediately? The "Large restaurant/Low demand/Abandon" path would mean a $390,000 payoff to the entrepreneur (.65 × $600,000). The entrepreneur's resulting NPV from investing immediately in the large restaurant with the option to abandon is as follows:

$$NPV = -\$400,000 + .3 \times \$975,000 + .5 \times \$520,000 + .2 \times \$390,000$$
$$= \$230,500$$

This is less than the $278,000 NPV of initially investing in the small restaurant with the option to expand but higher than any other alternative. If the option to expand did not exist, then investing in the large-scale restaurant with the option to abandon would be the preferred strategy.

It would exceed the NPV of the next best alternative—waiting until the state of the world is realized—by $17,000 ($230,500 − $213,500).

The option to abandon a venture that does not work out as well as expected can be critical to value and thus to the decision to launch the venture in the first place. It can also impact the willingness of investors to fund the venture. Test pilots of new aircraft normally take along parachutes in case something goes wrong; otherwise, they would be much less interested in testing new designs.

4.9 Rival Reactions and Game Trees

Decision trees do not explicitly incorporate the reactions of rivals. For example, consider a venture that offers an innovative line of athletic shoes. Its entry strategy—of price, advertising expenditures, geographic scope, and so on—may depend critically on how it expects incumbent firms to react. The firm may decide to enter with an aggressive pricing strategy, assuming that incumbents will keep their prices constant. But if incumbents react by pricing aggressively, then the effectiveness of the new entrant's pricing strategy will be reduced.

Rival reactions are not an issue in perfectly competitive markets because other firms will not react specifically to the entry of a new rival. For a small venture entering a large market, it may make sense to think of the market as nearly perfectly competitive. Furthermore, rival reactions are not an issue for a venture that offers a unique product and anticipates no entry, and therefore has market power. But planning for rival reactions can be important in settings where there are only a few actual or potential competitors. In such situations, the decisions of the competing firms are highly interdependent.

One way to evaluate decision choices is to assign probabilities to rival reactions and use a decision tree to evaluate the choices. This approach is not likely to yield reliable results, however, because the probabilities effectively yield a weighted average reaction from among the various possibilities, whereas the actual reaction will be one choice or another. There is a better way to think about the decision when rival reactions are important. The alternative is to explicitly assess what reaction would be in the best interest of each rival. The underlying reasoning is that a firm's and its rivals' actions are interdependent. Each firm is assumed to behave rationally by trying to select the strategy that maximizes value given what it believes its rival will do.

Strategic interactions can be modeled by relying on the contributions of game theory.[18] Game theory is concerned with analysis of optimal decision making when decision makers are aware that their actions affect each other's behavior and take these interactions into account.[19] To illustrate the uses of game theory in formulating strategy, we need to introduce some new terminology. A game consists of (1) a set of players, (2) an order of play, (3) the information set available to the players, (4) the set of actions available to each player, and (5) the payoff schedule that results from the actions of the players.

The players are simply the decision makers, such as an entrepreneur, a firm manager, a VC, or a rival. The players make decisions at various points in a game (decision nodes). In a decision tree, the decisions are based on alternative states of the world, which are not strategic. In a game-theoretic setting, however, player actions are strategic and driven by rationality. The sequence in which decisions are made is the order of play. If all players make their decisions one at a time in a sequence, then the game is a sequential-move game. If all decision makers act at the same time, then the game is a simultaneous-move game. For an entrepreneur, it usually makes sense to think of the game as sequential, with the entrepreneur as the first mover.

A sequential-move game can be analyzed with a game tree.[20] A game tree is a joint decision tree for the players and is composed of nodes and branches like a decision tree. Each node represents a decision point for one of the players. Each branch represents a possible action for a player at that point.

An Illustration

Consider a common problem of a prospective entrepreneur. Kelly would like to quit her bartending job and open her own establishment, Kelly's Bar. Her options are (1) to enter with a large bar, (2) to enter with a small bar, and (3) to wait to see if the town's economy will support another bar. She has estimated the various costs and revenues associated with the two establishment sizes. Her biggest concern is a rumor that a national chain, Erin's Pub, is considering opening a bar in the same town. Erin has two options: (1) enter or (2) do not enter. Kelly's decision depends on how Erin might respond to Kelly's decision.

The decisions are illustrated as a game tree in Figure 4.6. The tree represents Kelly's perspective; both players' payoffs, shown in the two columns on the right, are expressed in terms of NPV. By acting quickly, Kelly can make the first move. Thus, the first decision node (working left to right) belongs to Kelly. The middle three decision nodes (the squares

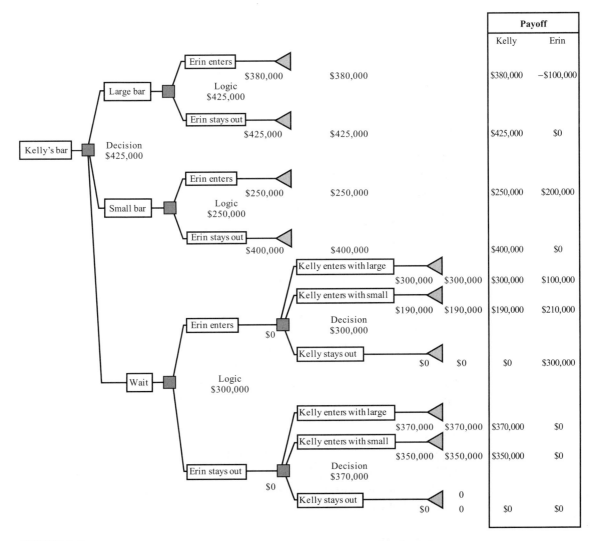

FIGURE **4.6**

Entry decision game tree

In this sequential-move game, Kelly is the first mover. Kelly assumes Erin will react rationally to Kelly's investment decision. Kelly can select the choice that maximizes value for her in light of Erin's expected reaction. Prepared using PrecisionTree, Palisade Corporation.

in the figure with darker shading) belong to Erin. If Kelly chooses large-scale entry, then Erin's Pub would make a loss of $100,000 if Erin elected to enter and $0 if Erin elected to stay out. In this case, the rational choice for Erin is to stay out. As with decision trees, we can ignore (or prune) the branches that represent inferior choices for the decision maker. Thus, we should assume that if Kelly opens a large bar, Erin will choose not to enter.

If Kelly chooses small-scale entry, then Erin's Pub would earn a $200,000 NPV if Erin were to enter and $0 if she decided to stay out. The rational decision for Erin in this case is to enter, and we can prune the tree accordingly.

Finally, if Kelly decides to wait for the market to develop further, Erin must decide between entering and staying out without knowing what Kelly is going to do. If Erin enters, she would earn $100,000, $210,000, or $300,000, depending on Kelly's decision.

If Kelly has decided to wait, then clearly Erin would prefer to enter because all the choices associated with an entry strategy generate positive payoffs for Erin's Pub. Hence, Kelly can prune the bottom branch of the game tree, "Erin stays out." If Kelly decides to wait, she knows Erin will enter. Given that, the figure shows that Kelly's best response is to open the large bar, which gives Kelly a $300,000 NPV and leaves Erin with $100,000. We can ignore the other branches, "Kelly enters small" and "Kelly stays out," of this subtree.

Examining the remaining branches, we can adopt the same technique we used with the decision tree: backward induction. Start at the terminal decision nodes that display the NPVs of the various alternatives for the two parties. Beginning at the top, if Kelly enters with a large bar, Erin will stay out (avoiding the $100,000 loss) and Kelly's payoff is $425,000. Moving down, if Kelly enters with a small bar, Erin will also enter, making Kelly's payoff $250,000. Finally, if Kelly waits, we know Erin will enter. Kelly will then respond with a large bar, giving herself a $300,000 payoff. Since Kelly has the first move, and because she knows how Erin will react, her optimal strategy is to enter immediately with a large bar.

Nash Equilibrium

The example above is a noncooperative game. In a noncooperative game, the players cannot enter into binding, enforceable agreements with each other. Any solution of the game must be a "Nash equilibrium."[21] A Nash equilibrium is a set of strategies such that each player's strategy is optimal given the strategy of the other player(s). The Nash equilibrium in our example is the pair of strategies such that (1) Kelly's strategy maximizes her payoff, given the strategy of Erin's Pub, and (2) Erin's strategy maximizes her payoff, given Kelly's strategy.

In the entry-decision game, the Nash equilibrium is (Kelly: "Enter large"; Erin: "Stay out"). That is, Kelly does not wait to see whether

Erin's Pub opens; instead, she enters first at a scale that makes it unprofitable for Erin to open. Both parties maximize their profits given the other player's action. If each expects the other to choose its Nash equilibrium strategy, then both will. In other words, in equilibrium, expected and actual behaviors converge.

Games Entrepreneurs Play

Strategic "games" include a large class of activities in which a decision maker takes into account the actions and reactions of others. Strategic games commonly played by entrepreneurs include the following:

- *The business plan.* An entrepreneur must decide how much optimism to build into the projections that are included in the plan. Overoptimism can be dangerous. The investor may counter with a proposed deal that ties the entrepreneur's return to achieving the projections.
- *Strategic partnering.* An entrepreneur must decide whether to bring in a vertically integrated company as a distributor and strategic partner or risk the possibility that, if not invited to partner, the corporation will independently develop a competing product.
- *Control.* An entrepreneur must decide how much control to forsake in exchange for securing funding. If the entrepreneur is unwilling to give up control, a prospective investor might decide to forgo the opportunity.
- *Information disclosure.* A new venture's management must decide whether to patent an idea now and risk copycat entry of rivals or maintain the idea as a trade secret.

4.10 Strategic Flexibility versus Strategic Commitment

Game theory forces the entrepreneur to think about a venture from the perspective of competitors, customers, suppliers, and investors. Decision trees and game trees are useful for assessing tradeoffs between the value of maintaining flexibility (real options) and the value of committing to a more limited course of action. As in Figure 4.6, even though the waiting option has value, committing first to a large-scale bar may have an even greater NPV. In Figure 4.6, strategic commitment is the best choice, whereas in Figure 4.5, strategic flexibility (preserving the expansion option) was the best choice.

It is important for any new venture to systematically consider the values of the important embedded real options that it may have. However, early commitment to a course of action can preempt or limit rival reactions in the best interest of the new venture.

4.11 Strategic Planning and the Business Plan

One of the risks in preparing and circulating a business plan too early is that the entrepreneur may default into a course of action that is not as valuable as a forgone alternative. Before the plan is written and circulated, the entrepreneur has a number of real options for how to develop the venture. Committing to a particular business plan necessitates giving up some of them.

In Chapter 1, we described entrepreneurship as a four-step process: recognizing an opportunity, developing a strategy for pursuing it, implementing the strategy, and harvesting the investment. A business plan is a bridge between strategy and implementation. Ideally, the entrepreneur will have settled on a strategy before preparing the business plan.

The above discussion of strategic planning does not mean that the entrepreneur can or should avoid negotiating with investors over strategic direction. Investors, if they are sophisticated, will do their own analysis and may regard a different strategy as being best. In that case, the entrepreneur will have to revisit the strategic analysis and may end up modifying the plan to better fit the investors' objective.

Plans designed for internal use can help secure the commitment of employees to critical goals and focus organizational effort on clearly articulated targets. A well-structured plan enables the entrepreneur to identify and react to problems and future developments more quickly than would otherwise be possible.

Neither strategic planning nor the business plan is a one-shot exercise. As the venture develops, some of the assumptions on which initial projections were based will prove to be incorrect. The projections will have to be modified in light of actual experience, and it may be appropriate to reassess overall strategy. Revising the plan does not imply that the original planning exercise was a failure. In fact, having the original plan as a benchmark enables the entrepreneur to diagnose the problems and opportunities that may lead to revisions. Revising the plan is important for the same reasons. The revised plan will contain a new set of projections and milestones that the entrepreneur can use to benchmark the progress of the venture.

4.12 Summary

Strategic decisions involve major commitments that limit the range of future actions. Comprehensive strategic planning involves product-market and organizational choices that are highly interrelated with financing choices. By considering all three simultaneously, the entrepreneur can be assured of identifying the alternative that yields the highest expected value.

A new venture can be thought of as a portfolio of real options, including, among others, the options to delay investing, to expand the size of the investment, and to abandon the investment. Strategic planning is a process of identifying these real options and comparing the values of alternative combinations of real options.

Decision tree analysis provides a framework for identifying and describing strategic alternatives and for identifying and managing the real options that are embedded in any new venture. The different branches of the tree describe the interplay between alternative strategic choices and uncertain states of the world. By starting at the ends of the branches, determining the highest-valued choice at each stage, and eliminating the other branches from further consideration, it is possible to identify the strategic alternative today that is expected to result in the highest overall expected value of the project.

Game tree analysis is a useful extension of decision trees when the reactions of other parties to specific strategic choices are important. Game theory forces the entrepreneur to think about a decision from the perspectives of others who will be affected by it.

Business plans for new ventures differ from those of established firms in four basic ways. First, the attainable precision of the forecast is less for a new venture. Second, entrepreneurs usually must invest more time and energy in planning, partly because the entrepreneur must develop from scratch the forecasting approach and key assumptions that underlie the projections. Third, external reliance on the plan is greater for a new venture. Fourth, for a new venture the plan must reflect simultaneous thinking about organizational, product-market, and financial strategies.

Review Questions

1. Could Henry Ford have successfully pursued his mass production strategy for automobiles if he had not simultaneously selected an innovative financing strategy? Why or why not?

2. Why did Ford's cost-oriented product-market strategy work well in the beginning but eventually fail?

3. How are product-market, organizational, and financial strategies interdependent? Why, for new ventures, is it important to consider them simultaneously rather than sequentially? Give some examples.

4. What are the three aspects of a decision that make it strategic?

5. Why is it important for strategic planning to begin with a clear sense of the objective? How might the objective for an entrepreneurial venture be different from that of a project pursued by a publicly held corporation?

6. How do embedded real options affect the values of investment opportunities? Why, when assessing investment alternatives, is it important to consider the embedded real options?

7. What are three important differences between real options and financial options?

8. Describe an investment opportunity that includes at least one real option. On what does the value of the option depend? Explain how you would construct a decision tree that includes the real option(s) and uncertainty. How would you use the tree to decide on a course of action?

9. How are game trees different from decision trees? For what kinds of decisions would you want to use game trees instead of decision trees?

10. How is the business plan related to strategic planning?

NOTES

1. Useful background on this topic is provided by Porter (1998). For specific applications to formulation of new venture strategy, see Cooper (1979) and Vesper (1989). For economic perspectives on strategy formulation, see Spulber (1992, 1994) and Williamson (1994).

2. In 2009, Chrysler was acquired out of bankruptcy by Fiat, an Italian manufacturer, and General Motors Corporation emerged from bankruptcy reorganization.

3. Rae (1965) reports that by 1927, the number of manufacturers had fallen to 44.

4. According to Rae (1965), the increase in market share coincides with Ford's decision to abandon all other models and concentrate exclusively on the Model T.

5. Ford made this remark in 1903 to one of the partners in his venture, John W. Anderson (Rae [1965], p. 59).

6. Ford implemented conveyor-belt assembly lines in 1913–14 after visit-

ing the Chicago slaughterhouses. He watched cow carcasses being dismembered as they were carried along the line. He reasoned that the technique could be applied to automobiles—except the other way around.

7. A modern-day parallel in some respects is Amazon.com, Inc. Because Amazon sells books for cash, carries little inventory of its own, and buys books on credit, it is able to exploit the traditional financing practices of a brick-and-mortar-based book distribution model to spontaneously generate the free cash flow it needs to fund its rapid growth.

8. To execute its consumer-focused strategy, General Motors had to solve a series of organizational control problems. To offer product variety efficiently, General Motors had to be able to monitor production, ordering, and inventory on a timely basis. It did so under the direction of Alfred Sloan by designing an information system that remained the operating standard of the industry for decades. Ford was unprepared to respond to these organizational improvements. For an insightful discussion, see Norton (1997).

9. Ford successfully and publicly fought the validity of the Selden patent in court (Smith [1979]).

10. Hammond, Keeney, and Raiffa (1998) offer a survey of the pitfalls of decision making that is guided by intuition or misapplication of more systematic approaches.

11. Bhide (1994) notes that a variety of factors in addition to NPV can influence the suitability of an investment.

12. Amram and Kulatilaka (1999) illustrate the application of real options approaches to new venture investing and other decisions. See Chen, Kensinger, and Conover (1998), Childs, Ott, and Triantis (1998), and Loch and Bode-Greuel (2001) for specific applications. Dixit and Pindyck (1995) provide perspective on valuing investment decisions as options. Luehrman (1998a) discusses strategic decision making in terms of real options.

13. The Options appendix, on this book's companion website, contains a more complete overview. Most corporate finance or investments texts can be used for a comprehensive introduction.

14. Luehrman (1998b) describes how simple investment opportunities can be valued as real options using financial option valuation methods.

15. See the Options appendix, on the companion website, for elaboration of this point.

16. These values are from the perspective of the entrepreneur and are not necessarily the same as values to an investor. Because the focus in this chapter is on learning to recognize and compare real options, we are abstracting from other aspects of the strategic analysis.

17. As an aspect of a theory of entrepreneurship, Baumol (1993) studies the optimal rate of innovation using the tradeoff between delaying introduction of new products as a means of improving their quality and the risk that a competitor will enter first.

18. For a more comprehensive discussion, see Bierman and Fernandez (1998).

19. See Dixit and Nalebuff (1993) for an introduction to developing strategy in a game-theoretic context.

20. Simultaneous-move games are usually analyzed using payoff matrices that display the players' outcomes for the simultaneous choices. We illustrate use of payoff matrices later in the text.

21. The Nash equilibrium concept is named in honor of John Nash, a Princeton mathematician who was a pioneer of game theory.

References and Additional Reading

Amram, M., and N. Kulatilaka. 1999. *Real Options: Managing Strategic Investment in an Uncertain World.* Boston: Harvard Business School Press.

Baumol, W. J. 1993. "Formal Entrepreneurship Theory in Economics: Existence and Bounds." *Journal of Business Venturing* 8 (3): 197–210.

Besanko, D., D. Dranove, M. Shanley, and S. Schaefer. 2010. *Economics of Strategy.* 5th ed. New York: John Wiley & Sons.

Bhide, A. 1994. "How Entrepreneurs Craft Strategies That Work." *Harvard Business Review* 72 (2): 150–61.

Bierman, H. S., and L. Fernandez. 1998. *Game Theory with Economic Applications.* 2nd ed. Reading, MA: Addison-Wesley.

Chen, A. H., J. W. Kensinger, and J. A. Conover. 1998. "Valuing Flexible Manufacturing Facilities as Options." *Quarterly Review of Economics and Finance*3 8:651–74.

Childs, P. D., S. H. Ott, and A. J. Triantis. 1998. "Capital Budgeting for Interrelated Projects: A Real Options Approach." *Journal of Financial and Quantitative Analysis* 33 (3): 305–34.

Cooper, A. 1979. "Strategic Management: New Ventures and Small Business." In *Strategic Management*, ed. D. E. Schendel and C. W. Hofer, 316–27. Boston: Little, Brown.

Dixit, A., and B. Nalebuff. 1993. *Thinking Strategically.* New York: W. W. Norton.

Dixit, A., and R. Pindyck. 1995. "The Options Approach to Capital Investment." *Harvard Business Review* 28 (4): 105–15.

Ghemawat, P. E. 2009. *Strategy and the Business Landscape.* 3rd ed. Englewood Cliffs, NJ: Prentice-Hall.

Hammond, J. S., R. L. Keeney, and H. Raiffa. 1998. "The Hidden Traps in Decision Making." *Harvard Business Review* 76 (5): 47–58.

Kim, Y. J., and G. L. Sanders. 2002. "Strategic Actions in Information Technology Investment Based on Real Option Theory." *Decision Support Systems* 33 (1): 1–11.

Klein, B., and K. B. Leffler. 1981. "The Role of Market Forces in Assuring Contractual Performance." *Journal of Political Economy* 89 (4): 615–41.

Kreps, D. M., and R. Wilson. 1982. "Reputation and Imperfect Information." *Journal of Economic Theory* 27 (2): 253–79.

Loch, C. H., and K. Bode-Greuel. 2001. "Evaluating Growth Options as Sources of Value from Pharmaceutical Research Projects." *R&D Management* 31 (2): 231–48.

Luehrman, T. A. 1998a. "Investment Opportunities as Real Options: Getting Started with the Numbers." *Harvard Business Review* 76 (4): 51–67.

———. 1998b. "Strategy as a Portfolio of Real Options." *Harvard Business Review* 76 (5): 89–99.

Magee, J. 1964. "How to Use Decision Trees in Capital Investment." *Harvard Business Review* 42 (September–October): 79–96.

Milgrom, P., and J. Roberts. 1992. *Economics, Organization, and Management.* Englewood Cliffs, NJ: Prentice-Hall.

Mintzberg, H. 1994. "The Fall and Rise of Strategic Planning." *Harvard Business Review* 72 (1): 107–14.

Norton, S. 1997. "Information and Competitive Advantage: The Rise of General Motors." *Journal of Law and Economics* 40 (1): 245–60.

Porter, M. 1998. *Competitive Strategy.* New York: Free Press.

Rae, J. 1965. *The American Automobile.* Chicago: University of Chicago Press.

Rappaport, A. 1991. "Selecting Strategies That Create Shareholder Value." In *Strategy, Seeking and Securing Competitive Advantage*, ed. C. A. Montgomery and M. E. Porter, 379–99. Cambridge, MA: Harvard University Press.

Smith, R. 1979. "The United States Automobile Industry: Three Studies of Industry Conduct and Structural Change." PhD dissertation, University of California at Los Angeles.

Spulber, D. 1992. "Economic Analysis and Management Strategy: A Survey." *Journal of Economics and Management Strategy* 1 (3): 535–74.

———. 1994. "Economic Analysis and Management Strategy: A Survey Continued." *Journal of Economics and Management Strategy* 3 (2): 355–406.

Trigeorgis, L. 1996. *Real Options: Managerial Flexibility and Strategy in Resource Allocation.* Cambridge, MA: MIT Press.

Vesper, K. 1989. *New Venture Strategies.* 2nd ed. Englewood Cliffs, NJ: Prentice-Hall.

Williamson, O. 1994. "Strategizing, Economizing, and Economic Organization." In *Fundamental Issues in Strategy*, ed. R. P. Rumelt, D. E. Schendel, and D. J. Teece, 361–401. Cambridge, MA: Harvard Business School Press.

CHAPTER 5

DEVELOPING BUSINESS STRATEGY USING SIMULATION

> To me all kinds of business decisions are options.
>
> Judy Lewent, former CFO, Merck and Co.

Decision trees are used to identify strategic alternatives and to examine the sensitivity of expected value to discrete changes in individual variables, one at a time. In Chapter 4, we simplified the analysis of strategic choice by assuming there were only a few possible states of the world. However, decision tree analysis based on discrete possibilities has limitations because the future is being described by a few discrete outcomes and related probabilities.

To deal with the limitations of decision trees with discrete scenarios, we introduce now simulation and demonstrate how it can be used to evaluate strategic choices that include real options. We begin with a few simple examples and then return to the restaurant example from Chapter 4 and use simulation to conduct a more robust analysis.

A simulation model is a representation of the behavior of a complex system through the use of another system. For our purposes, the complex system to be simulated is the future performance of a new venture. Simulation can take into consideration uncertainty about the environment, the venture itself, and possibly even the reactions of rivals.

The normal way to represent uncertainty in a simulation model is to describe each element of uncertainty as a statistical distribution, for example, a normal distribution with a given mean and standard deviation or a uniform distribution over a given range. To simulate the future of a venture, we first build a spreadsheet model of the venture and identify the key decision variables. We then introduce mathematical expressions that describe the important uncertainties that bear on the value of the venture. By using the computer to simulate the model, we can produce thousands of possible trials (outcomes), where each trial is based on making a random draw from the statistical distributions and computing the combined effect for the venture.

For example, you might wish to project the level of net income for a venture at the end of five years, given four sources of uncertainty: the economy, the market's reaction to the product, cost of production, and development lead time. If you simulate the future of the venture one time, the result is a prediction of net income in five years, given a specific outcome for each source of uncertainty.

The prediction from a single trial is not likely to be very helpful. However, with a computer it is possible to run thousands of iterations of the model and to aggregate the data from the iterations. Not only does averaging the results improve the accuracy of the prediction, but the dispersion of outcomes serves as a measure of the aggregate effect of all the various sources of uncertainty that are built into the model. Moreover, the trials data can be analyzed for the purpose of refining key decisions such as how much cash to invest in the venture at the outset or to assess the value of a particular real option.

As a management tool, simulation has been around for over three decades. David Hertz and McKinsey & Co. first advocated using simulation for investment decision making in 1968. The technique was slow to catch on for a variety of reasons. Among the early impediments were confusion about the correct way to apply simulation to investment decision making, lack of low-cost (fast) computational capacity, lack of data useful for calibrating uncertainty, and lack of user-friendly software. In spite of the difficulties, companies like Merck have been using simulation to analyze investment decisions for many years.[1]

5.1 Use of Simulation in Business Planning: An Example

Because of the nature and expense of the drug development process, simulation can be a valuable aid to decision making. Given this, it is not surprising that the pharmaceutical industry was one of the first areas of commercial application of simulation. The industry is complex and subject to uncertainty arising from many sources—health care reform, the generic drug market, tort litigation—and particularly to the uncertainty inherent in developing, testing, and marketing new drugs.

Moreover, investing in the development of new drugs has much in common with entrepreneurial investment in new ventures: uncertainty is very high; a new drug goes through several identifiable stages of development; and the firm faces many opportunities to abandon or modify its development efforts as it learns more about the drug over time.

Even during the 1990s, rather than relying on single-point estimates of the future for allocating its R&D budget, Merck was developing simulation models that incorporated probability distributions for numerous variables. Under the direction of then CFO Judy Lewent, Merck developed its Research Planning Model, an approach that integrates principles of economics, finance, statistics, and computer science to produce quantitative analyses of the specific strategic decisions that Merck faced. Using the technique of simulation, the model synthesized probability distributions for key variables such as revenues, cash flow, and NPV.

Much like the approach we will use, the output of Merck's model was a frequency distribution that showed the probability that a project's NPV would exceed a certain level. Merck could use the distribution information to compute summary statistics, such as standard deviation, which it could then use in other analyses, such as to price an option to delay investing. Merck's Research Planning Model would simulate risk and return project by project (prior to commitment of funds). Then, by allocating the research budget across the projects, it could simulate the contribution of R&D to the financial performance of the entire corporation.

Consider how the model can be used to evaluate a drug research project. Lewent describes it this way:

> We may know at the beginning of a project that there is a market for a specific treatment that includes many thousands of people, and once we reach a certain point in the process, we may know that a certain compound may be effective. But we still aren't 100% certain that the compound will prove so safe and effective that it can be turned into a drug. So we have to ask ourselves, "Do we continue to invest?" Those are the kinds of decisions we face every day. And these aren't investments that easily lend themselves to traditional financial analysis. Remember that we need to make huge investments now and may not see a profit for 10 to 15 years. In that kind of situation, a traditional analysis that factors in the time value of money may not fully capture the strategic value of an investment in research, because the positive cash flows are severely discounted when they are analyzed over a very long time frame. As a result, the volatility or risk isn't properly valued.
>
> Option analysis, like the kind used to value stock options, provides a more flexible approach to valuation of our research investments . . . be-

cause it allows us to evaluate those investments at successive stages of a project.[2]

Merck would take a systematic approach to modeling the risks associated with R&D, manufacturing, and marketing. For example, in considering a new drug's market potential, one of the constraints on development would be the expected time for FDA approval. Merck could model the range of possible time frames for approval. By drawing from the range of possibilities and simulating cash flows based on alternative assumptions, Merck could synthesize probability distributions for output variables. The output variables of interest are, of course, the standard measures of financial performance: revenue, cash flow, and NPV.[3]

5.2   Who Relies on Simulation?

Each of the early impediments to using simulation to evaluate important strategic decisions either has been or is being removed. Appropriate ways to use simulation for making investment decisions have been developed, computational capacity is inexpensive and fast, appropriate software is inexpensive and user friendly, and data are increasingly available. Furthermore, the growing recognition of the value of viewing investments as portfolios of options points to greater reliance on simulation over time.

We are advised by one provider of simulation software that currently more than 70 percent of Fortune 500 companies use at least one of the commonly available simulation packages in some parts of their business. Moreover, many universities have site licenses to standard simulation software.

Several different software packages are available for running simulations on personal computers. Some are freestanding decision analysis programs. Others function as add-ins to Excel. Some employ random sampling to generate the trial. Others use Monte Carlo techniques in an effort to generate more accurate predictions of expected outcomes and distributions of outcomes using fewer iterations. As computational speed has increased, the cost- and time-saving rationale for Monte Carlo simulation has diminished in importance.

As a user of this book, you have access to *Venture*.SIM, a simple simulation package that is sufficient for our purposes. One of the authors developed *Venture*.SIM specifically to address the uncertainty issues that arise for new ventures. *Venture*.SIM is an Excel add-in. Whenever we use simulation in this book, our modeling will use the *Venture*.SIM software and the results we present will be *Venture*.SIM output. We also provide @Risk® and Crystal Ball® versions of the simulation analyses on the companion website. When we show you the Excel syntax for a simulated cell in a spreadsheet, we use the *Venture*.SIM syntax. If you are a user of one of the commercial packages, you can study the parallel syntax by opening the appropriate files on the book website.

5.3 Simulation in New Venture Finance

Nowhere is the case for using simulation more compelling than for decision making about new ventures. Consider the following examples of where simulation can lead to better decisions.

- *Strategy formulation.* An entrepreneur is considering a risky opportunity to develop an amusement park and knows that building in options to abandon or change the nature of the venture can reduce the risk and potentially make the project more valuable. Simulation can be used to study the effects of different option structures on risk and the value of the opportunity.

- *Deal structures.* An entrepreneur and an investor are negotiating investment terms. The investor is willing to accept common stock but wants a large share of total equity in exchange. The entrepreneur would like to add sweeteners to the investor's financial claims so that the investor's fraction of ownership can be reduced. Simulation can be used to evaluate the effects of alternative deal structures on the values of both parties' positions.

- *Risk allocation.* An entrepreneur and an investor have different tolerances for bearing the risk of a new venture to build snow shovels equipped with cardiac monitors. The entrepreneur is more risk averse than the investor. Simulation can be used to design a deal structure that shifts more of the risk to the investor, raising the overall value of the opportunity.

- *Contingent claims.* An investor is not convinced by the financial projections of an entrepreneur who wants to produce and market golf balls equipped with location sensors. The entrepreneur is willing to accept financial claims that adjust the entrepreneur's ownership share contingent on success. Simulation can be used to design a deal structure that is attractive to both parties.

- *Cash needs.* An entrepreneur is trying to determine the total amount of financing that is needed for a prospective new venture to sell subscriptions to a news service. The service will email an audio file each morning containing news content that is customized to the interests and commuting time of each subscriber. If the venture performs worse than expected, the need for financing will be greater. Simulation can be used to examine the relation between attained performance and total financial need.

- *Staging investments.* A VC is interested in investing in a project but would like to stage the investment so that progress can be evaluated at critical milestones. There is uncertainty about when the next milestone can be achieved and about the cost of achieving it. Simulation can help the VC decide on an amount to invest such that the probability of reaching the milestone is reasonable and the potential for overinvesting in a project that will never succeed is limited.

- *Valuation.* An investor is trying to value an opportunity to participate in a venture and knows that the value of the investment depends not just on the expected return but also on the riskiness of the return. Simulation can be used to determine the expected return, the riskiness of the return, and the value of the investment.

In this chapter, we apply simulation to the problem of designing new venture strategy. Later in the book, we use it in some of the other ways suggested above. Among them, we apply simulation to cash needs assessment, valuation, and contract design.[4]

S 5.4   Simulation: An Illustration

Suppose you are considering starting a new parcel delivery service to capitalize on the demand created by e-commerce. As an aspect of evaluating the opportunity, you must determine the volume of warehouse space you should lease in order to handle the December activity peak. You believe the warehouse must be capable of handling 5,000 boxes per day. In addition, you know that, on average, boxes are 2.0 feet high, 1.5 feet wide, and 1.5 feet deep. Using this information, you might estimate the warehouse volume requirement as 4.5 cubic feet per box multiplied by 5,000 boxes, where 4.5 cubic feet is determined by multiplying the average of each dimension ($4.5 = 2 \times 1.5 \times 1.5$). The resulting estimate would be 22,500 cubic feet.

This would be a fine estimate if all boxes were the same size or if the different dimensions were not correlated with each other. But suppose the dimensions are correlated so that there are actually three different sizes of boxes:

1.0 foot by 1.0 foot by 1.0 foot = 1.0 cubic foot

2.0 feet by 1.5 feet by 1.5 feet = 4.5 cubic feet

3.0 feet by 2.0 feet by 2.0 feet = 12 cubic feet

Each size is equally likely to be received and stored. This makes the average size per box not 4.5 cubic feet but 5.83 cubic feet. If you need to store 5,000 boxes and there are equal numbers of each size, you will need 29,150 cubic feet of space. Even without simulation, because the dimensions are correlated, the original estimate of 22,500 is too low by almost 30 percent.

Beyond the issue of correlation, you must allow for the mix of box sizes to vary daily. You cannot assume that each day you will receive one-third of each size. Perhaps you could take a very conservative approach and contract for enough space to hold 5,000 of the 12-cubic-foot boxes. But that is certain to be wasteful—much of the resulting 60,000 cubic feet would virtually never be used.

Suppose, based on your assessment of the cost of not having enough space, you have concluded that you would like to have enough to meet the demand 90 percent of the time. How can you determine the amount of space that is adequate for the venture's needs 90 percent of the time? Simulation can be used to address this concern. In this case, the system to be simulated is quite simple. We start by modeling the volume of a single box as follows:

Volume = Height × Width × Depth

The model of the system to simulate one day's activity is simply the volume of the box multiplied by 5,000 boxes per day:

Warehouse Space Needed = Volume per Box × 5,000 boxes

Because the boxes come in three volumes (1.0, 4.5, and 12 cubic feet) that are equally likely to arrive, we can specify a function that describes the uncertainty as a discrete distribution of volumes with uniform probabilities. By making 5,000 draws from this distribution, each one simulating the arrival of a single box, we will model one day's activity. We can determine the necessary size of the warehouse by simulating the arrival of 5,000 boxes several times.

With *Venture*.SIM, we used a simulation macro to select at random

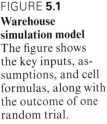

FIGURE **5.1**
Warehouse simulation model
The figure shows the key inputs, assumptions, and cell formulas, along with the outcome of one random trial.

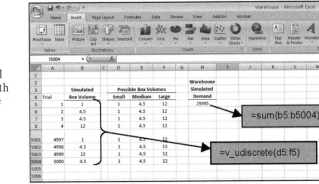

5,000 boxes such that, each time, the probability of drawing a box of any of the three sizes is one-third. To be confident of getting a good estimate of the distribution of needs, we ran this simulation 10,000 times (i.e., 10,000 trials of 5,000 box draws). Figure 5.1 is a screen shot of the Excel file that was used for the simulation. Columns D, E, and F show the possible box sizes. Cell B5 contains the result of making a random draw from the three possibilities represented in cells D5, E5, and F5. The draw is made using a *Venture*.SIM macro for sampling from a uniform discrete distribution. To simulate warehouse space demand, this draw is repeated 5,000 times (see the row numbers in the figure). Then in cell H5, we sum the results of all of the draws. The value 29,395 in the cell is the estimate of space (cubic feet) needed in the warehouse based on this single trial representing one day.

We then use *Venture*.SIM to simulate automatically 10,000 trials and keep track of the result for each trial. To run the simulation, we have to define one or more output variables. We selected the one-day volume estimate from cell H5 and labeled it "Cubic Feet Required." In Figure 5.2a, we show the standard *Venture*.SIM simulation output table. The table provides descriptive statistics and percentiles for the output variable "Cubic Feet Required" from the 10,000 trials. Based on the simulation results, a 29,171-cubic-foot warehouse would be enough for half of the trials and 29,728 would be large enough 75 percent of the time.

Figure 5.2b is a cumulative probability distribution that can be generated using the Plot feature of *Venture*.SIM. It shows that a 30,000-cubic-foot warehouse would be sufficient in 90 percent of the trials. The largest warehouse needed is 30,905 cubic feet, well below the theoretical maximum of 60,000 cubic feet we calculated earlier.

Finally, Figure 5.2c shows a histogram of the results. It turns out that the daily need for space is bimodal, a discovery that is not very intuitive

FIGURE **5.2**
Results of simulating the warehouse model
Results are based on 10,000 trials. Panel (a) shows the *Venture*.SIM output table. Panel (b) shows the cumulative distribution of warehouse capacity needed in cubic feet. Panel (c) is a histogram of the results, showing the bimodality of the outcomes.

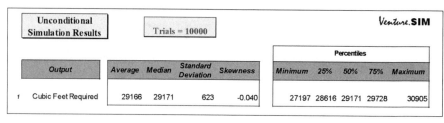

(a)

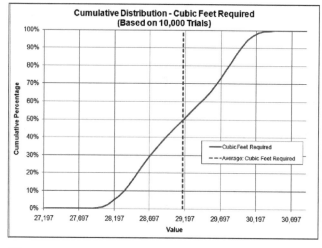

(b)

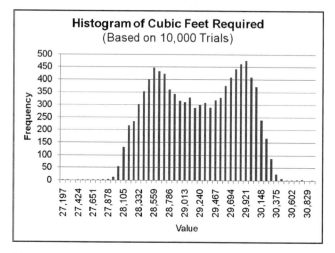

(c)

and that we probably would not have anticipated if we had not run the simulation. The existence of such irregularities in statistical distributions of complex systems is an additional reason that simulation can help improve decisions.

The example could be enriched in several ways. What if there were uncertainty about the number of boxes that would need to be stored each day? What if there were more variation in box size? What if boxes of different sizes do not stack together perfectly, so that some of the space cannot be filled? Issues such as these can be incorporated into the model to enhance the simulation.

S 5.5   Simulating the Value of an Option

Because options are important to the value of a new venture and the values of the financial claims that make up the deal structure, it is useful to see how simulation can be used to value options. To begin, consider how options can be used in financial markets. Suppose a share of stock currently sells for $118 and that calls and puts that expire in one year are available with an exercise price of $125. To keep the illustration simple, suppose that securities trade monthly. We assume, initially, that the expected return for investing in the stock is the risk-free rate of interest of 0.3 percent per month (3.66 percent per year) but that in any given month there is a 0.3 probability that the return is 4 percent lower and a 0.3 probability that it is 4 percent higher. Figure 5.3 shows the simulation model. The share price begins at $118 in cell B3. Then a *Venture*.SIM macro samples from the discrete probability-weighted returns and combines the resultant draw with the base return of 0.3 percent per month. The callout in the figure shows the syntax for cell C3, which generates the first monthly return and calculates the new share price. Similar calculations are made for the remaining 11 months. In this illustration of a single trial, the stock price does much better than expected, reaching $154.52 by year end for an annual return of 31 percent. The resulting ending value of a call with an exercise price of $125 is $29.52 ($154.52 − $125). Because the stock price ends above $125, the put is out of the money and is worth zero at expiration.

Figure 5.4 shows the results of simulating this 12-month stock price model 20 times, starting from an initial price of $118. Each line in the figure is a random draw from the possible price paths of the share of stock.[5]

We used the simulation model to estimate the expected value of the

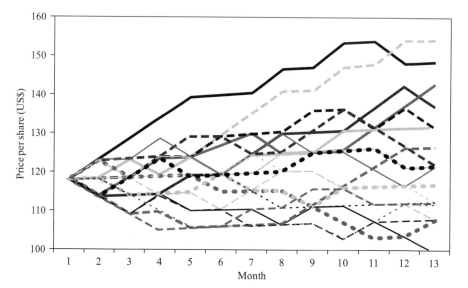

FIGURE **5.3**

Simulation model of stock price and put and call option expiration values
The figure shows the key inputs, assumptions, and cell formulas, along with the
outcome of one random trial for a 12-period model of stock price performance. The
resulting expiration-date values of puts and calls with an exercise price of $125 are
shown, as well as their Month 0 PVs.

stock at the end of 12 months and, more important, the standard deviation of annual returns for investing in the stock. Given that the risk-free
rate is 3.66 percent per year, the true (theoretically correct) expected
value of the stock at the end of one year is $122.32.[6] With 10,000 itera-
tions of the simulation model, the estimate of expected value turned out
to be $122.37, very close to the true expected value. The estimated stan-
dard deviation of ending stock prices from the simulation was $13.00,

[S] FIGURE **5.4**

**Simulation of
12 months of stock
price performance**
The figure shows the
results of 20 random
sequences of returns
for a stock that
trades monthly. The
Excel spreadsheet
that generated these
results also gener-
ates the values of
puts and calls on the
underlying stock and
can be used to simu-
late the effects of dif-
ferent assumptions.

or 11.02 percent of the initial stock price, also very close to the theoretically correct value.

A call option has value at expiration if the price of the underlying asset is above the exercise price. The value of the call, at expiration, is the excess of the stock price over the exercise price. In the simulation, the call was in the money 42.3 percent of the time. Over all 10,000 iterations, the average ending value of the call was $4.06. Discounting this by the risk-free rate of interest yields $3.91 as the estimated PV of the call option.

A put option has value at expiration if the price of the underlying asset is below the exercise price. The value of the put, at expiration, is the excess of the exercise price over the price of the stock. In the simulation, the put was in the money 57.7 percent of the time, with an average ending value of $6.68 and a PV of $6.45.

How do these simulated values compare to the values that can be derived from option theory using the Black-Scholes Option Pricing Model (OPM)? Using the true expected return and the estimated standard deviation in the OPM, the call is worth about $3.95 and the put is worth about $6.45. The simulated values are close to the theoretical values. The main reason the differences are more than trivial is that the distribution of possible stock prices in the simulation is not quite a normal distribution, which is the assumed distribution of the OPM. The normal distribution has a slightly lower standard deviation than the simulated distribution.[7]

If the OPM and simulation yield such similar values, why do we bother with simulation? In part, the answer is that often the true expected return and standard deviation of returns are not known and must be estimated by simulation. Beyond that, the other assumptions of the OPM generally are not satisfied when real options are being valued. Simulation has advantages over theoretical option pricing because financial markets related to new ventures are incomplete and because many real options are interdependent.

5.6 Describing Risk

We have already illustrated two simple ways to describe risk. In the warehouse example, we assumed that the probability distribution of outcomes was uniform and discrete. For example, six discrete outcomes are equally likely when you roll a die. In the stock option example, we modeled risk as discrete outcomes where the probabilities of different outcomes vary. Clearly, this is not very realistic, and there are better ways to describe the risk of a one-month investment in a share of stock. Perhaps a better example would be VC. Based on historical averages, about 10 percent of a VC fund's investments go public in an IPO, about 20 percent are successfully sold to an acquirer, and the rest are total losses or close to total losses. With a discrete distribution we could use these percentages and the typical number of investments made by a VC fund (approximately 20) to estimate the distribution of fund outcomes in terms of the percentages of IPOs, acquisitions, and failed investments.

Figure 5.5 provides illustrations of several other distributions that are often used in simulation models. Perhaps the most familiar way to characterize risk is as a normal distribution. Many kinds of uncertainty can be reasonably described as normal distributions. For example, a normal distribution could have been a better way to describe the evolution of stock prices over time. The discrete distribution information in Figure 5.3 yields a monthly standard deviation of 3.1 percent (not shown in the figure). Recall that we assumed a mean risk-free return of 0.3 percent monthly. We could have simulated the first month's stock price by multiplying the initial price of $118 by a draw from a normal distribution with a mean of 1.003 and a standard deviation of 0.033. The *Venture*.SIM syntax for this normal distribution is =v_normal(1.003, 0.033).

Sometimes normal distributions can be problematic. In our model and in reality, a share price can never fall below zero. Because normal distributions are unbounded, it is possible for a simulation of the share price to produce a negative value, especially after several months of repeated draws and if the monthly standard deviation is large. You can avoid this by adding a constraint that prevents the simulated share price from falling below zero; however, this may result in unintended biases in your results. A better alternative could be to choose a different distribution that does not yield negative prices or to simulate the returns from one period to the next (doing so will not result in negative prices).

Another solution to the problem of negative values is to use a lognormal distribution and apply it to a starting value that is positive. Figure 5.5b shows the result of simulating a lognormal distribution with a mean of 0.1 and a standard deviation of 0.2. The mean is an expected growth rate, so a mean of 0.1 indicates that the price is expected to increase by 10 percent; and the standard deviation of 0.2, or 20 percent, describes the uncertainty of the growth rate [entered in Excel as =v_lognormal(0.1, 0.2)]. As is evident from Figure 5.5b, the lognormal distribution never yields a negative value. Thus, a lognormal distribution could work well for simulating a stock price and for many other risky processes where values can never be negative.

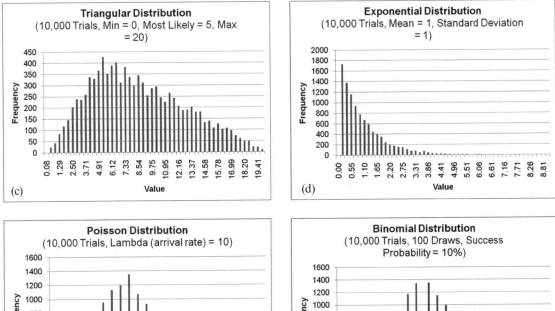

FIGURE **5.5**

Illustrations of *Venture*.SIM statistical distributions

Examples of the results of simulating some of the statistical distributions available from the *Venture*.SIM software.

A triangular distribution is a convenient way to prevent the occurrence of extreme outliers. By choosing the minimum, most likely, and maximum values to approximate what you believe is the true distribution, you can describe risk distributions that are more likely to yield low values [such as the one shown in Figure 5.5c, entered as =v_triang(0,5,20)] or high values. You can prevent negative draws with a triangular distribution by selecting the minimum to be zero or a positive value.

An exponential distribution is appropriate when outcomes at one end of the distribution are very high but unlikely to occur and those at the other end are bounded (so as not to be less than zero) and are more likely to occur. Often, time-related uncertainty is described well as an exponential distribution. For example, the length of time a product might last before breaking can be described as an exponential distribution. The example in Figure 5.5d has a mean of 1.0, such as an expected life of one year [entered as =v_exp(1)].

The last two distributions in the figure look similar to each other. Figure 5.5e is a Poisson distribution with an expected arrival rate of 10 [entered as =v_Poisson(10)] and Figure 5.5f is a binomial distribution of 100 draws with a success rate of 10 percent [entered as =v_binomial(100, 0.1)]. For large numbers of draws, the binomial distribution is approximately the same as the Poisson. In both cases, the outcomes are discrete nonnegative numbers. Poisson distributions are often used to simulate such things as how much inventory you need to have on hand if, on average, a certain number of customers per unit of time (such as 10 per day) each want to buy a unit of the product. You can see from the figure that, if your beginning inventory is 20 units, you will almost always have enough to supply the demand.

Binomial distributions are convenient for yes/no kinds of processes. For example, if you know that the probability of innovating during a given period of time is 10 percent, you can simulate how long it might take to achieve a successful innovation.

The menu of distribution functions is different in different packages, but with a little creativity, those we have discussed are sufficient to describe most risks that an entrepreneur may face.

S 5.7   Using Simulation to Evaluate a Strategy

Now that we have seen some simple illustrations of simulation and some examples of distribution functions, let's reexamine the restaurant venture from Chapter 4. Our purpose is to see how simulation can improve the evaluation of strategic alternatives that include real options.

Simulation involves six distinct steps:

1. Identify the strategies to be evaluated.
2. Establish the criteria for evaluating the alternatives.
3. Model the strategies to which simulation is applied.
4. Specify the assumptions and uncertainties that influence value.
5. Run the simulation.
6. Analyze the results.

Step 1: Identifying Strategic Alternatives

When simulation is used to evaluate strategic alternatives, the normal practice is to compare simulated results that are generated from different models of the venture, where each model incorporates a particular set of strategic choices. We might, for example, develop separate models of the large and small restaurants and compare the simulated values of the two strategies to see which is better under what circumstances.

Limiting the choices to a few discrete possibilities (e.g., a large restaurant or a small one) maintains the tractability of the analysis. Although a restaurant can be any size, it should be possible to answer the important questions by looking at only a few possibilities, such as large or small. The effects of including real options (like waiting, abandoning, and expanding) can be studied by making minor modifications to the two basic models.

Here, as we did in Chapter 4, we would like to consider:

- The large restaurant, without and with an abandonment option
- The small restaurant, without and with either the abandonment or the expansion option
- Waiting to see market demand, then deciding on the response

Step 2: Choosing Evaluation Criteria

The choice of evaluation criteria depends on the nature of the business and the focus of the simulation. For a public corporation, maximizing shareholder value is the most sensible overall objective. A marketing department that does not have responsibility for pricing might focus more narrowly on market share. For an entrepreneur, it makes sense to focus on maximizing the NPV of the entrepreneur's (or investor's) interest in the venture.

A simulation model must be designed to produce information relevant to the evaluation criteria. Accordingly, for the entrepreneur's decisions, the simulation model must generate information about the NPVs of the various alternatives so the entrepreneur can use the results to make the best decision. Later in the book, we use simulation to generate information about the cash flows the entrepreneur or investor will receive and the related risk. We use this information to compute the PV of the cash flows in a separate step that does not require simulation. In this chapter, we set aside the extra level of complexity and focus on NPV directly.

Step 3: Modeling the Problem

We use the large restaurant to illustrate the design and use of a new venture simulation model. As before, we assume that the appropriate discount rate is already determined and reflected in the results so that the values of the different outcomes are PVs. For now, we also assume that prices and costs are expressed in such a way that it is unnecessary to deal explicitly with time value.

The model must specify mathematically how the entrepreneur's decisions contribute to the PV of cash flows. We first determine the PV of the restaurant as if it were owned entirely by the entrepreneur. We then adjust that value downward to reflect the fractional ownership interest retained by the entrepreneur. The PV of the restaurant can be stated in terms of present valued streams of cash flows:

$$PV(\text{Cash Flow}) = PV[(\text{Revenues} - \text{Cash Expenses} - \text{Depreciation}) \times (1 - \text{Tax Rate})] + PV(\text{Depreciation})$$

Because the business will be privately held, the entrepreneur should be able to avoid corporate taxes. Hence, we apply a corporate tax rate of zero and simplify the above expression to:

$$PV(\text{Cash Flow}) = PV(\text{Revenues}) - PV(\text{Cash Expenses})$$

To model the restaurant venture, we need to specify the underlying determinants of revenues and cash expenses. Revenue is a function of price and unit sales. Unit sales are the lesser of the quantity demanded or restaurant capacity. The demand side of unit sales can be described as the product of market size and the restaurant's market share. On the supply side, we model unit sales to be limited by a capacity constraint based on restaurant size. If demand exceeds capacity, then the constrained quantity is what is sold. Otherwise, unit sales volume depends on market demand. Thus,

PV(Revenues) = PV(Unit Price) × Unit Sales

Unit Sales = Lesser of Demand Quantity or Capacity

Demand Quantity = Market Size × Potential Market Share

Capacity = an assumed maximum value

For simplicity, we aggregate market size and market share over the expected life of the restaurant. Unit sales is calculated based on market size and market share over the life of the restaurant. We model the PV of cash expenses in a similar fashion but include both a fixed and a variable component, where the variable component depends on unit variable cost and unit sales. Thus,

PV(Cash Expenses) = PV(Unit Cost) × Unit Sales + PV(Fixed Costs)

The above structure determines the PV of the restaurant as if it were owned entirely by the entrepreneur. But the entrepreneur is willing to commit only part of the required capital; the balance must be raised from an outside source. To determine value to the entrepreneur, we need to know what fractional share of ownership the entrepreneur retains. This depends on how much the investor contributes and how much equity the investor receives for the contribution. The PV of the entrepreneur's interest can be specified as the residual:

PV(Entrepreneur Interest) = PV(Cash Flow) − PV(Investor Interest)

where all of the PVs are expressed from the perspective of the entrepreneur. The value of the investor's interest can be expressed as:

PV(Investor Interest) = PV(Cash Flow) × (Total Investment
                        − Entrepreneur Investment)
                        × Percent Equity per Dollar Invested

Finally, the NPV of the entrepreneur's investment is:

NPV(Entrepreneur Interest) = PV(Entrepreneur Interest
                             − Entrepreneur Investment)

This completes the model of the entrepreneur's interest. Clearly, a more complex model could be developed by specifying the determinants, in equation form, of some of the terms in the above equations; however, the returns from adding complexity diminish rapidly. Although it is useful to think about the complex relationships that drive success or failure, a parsimonious model that is focused on key relationships is likely to yield results that are just as useful.

Step 4: Specifying the Assumptions and Describing the Uncertainties

For the simulation to work, each variable in the model must be specified as either an assumed value or mathematical expression, or an assumed statistical process that will generate a value. No matter how carefully you model the venture, the result will only be as good as its assumptions. Assumptions should be based on data, experience, and/or careful reasoning. If the model is to be shared with outside parties, each assumption must be defensible. As forecasting is the subject of the next two chapters, we will defer discussion of the bases for our assumptions.

Table 5.1 shows our assumptions for the model of the large restaurant.[8] These assumptions parallel the more simplified assumptions used in Chapter 4 for the decision tree analysis. For example, we allow the average price and cost of a meal to be subject to uncertainty so that the actual average price can be different from the expected value. The expected price is $10 per meal, and we assume that the uncertainty can be characterized as a normal distribution with a standard deviation of $1. Similarly, the expected cost is $5, with a standard deviation of $0.60.

For reasons that will be important later, we use a two-step process to determine market size. During the first year, the entrepreneur receives a preliminary estimate of the actual market size. To characterize market size in the simulation model, we use a triangular distribution with

TABLE **5.1**   **Assumptions and statistical processes of the large restaurant model**

Variable	Assumption
PV unit price of a meal	Normal distribution ($\mu = \$10$, $\sigma = \$1$)
PV unit cost of a meal	Normal distribution ($\mu = \$5$, $\sigma = \$0.6$)
Market size estimate (after first year)	Triangular distribution (6, 2.6, 1 million units)
Market size	Normal distribution (μ = estimate, $\sigma = 100,000$)
Market share estimate (after first year)	Normal distribution ($\mu = 10\%$, $\sigma = 1\%$)
Market share	Normal distribution (μ = estimate, $\sigma = 0.3\%$)
Capacity	500,000 meals
PV fixed costs	Normal distribution ($\mu = \$500,000$, $\sigma = \$50,000$)
Total investment	Normal distribution ($\mu = \$750,000$, $\sigma = \$25,000$)
Entrepreneur investment	$400,000
Percent equity per dollar invested	1% per $10,000 of outside investment

μ = *mean or average;* σ = *standard deviation.*

a maximum of 6.0 million meals (over the life of the restaurant), a minimum of 1.0 million, and a most likely size of 2.6 million meals.[9] The entrepreneur then receives an update of the market size estimate. Specifically, we assume that the actual size is learned and is equal to the initial estimate plus a random error. We assume the error to be normally distributed with a mean of zero and a standard deviation of 100,000 meals.

We determine market share using a similar two-step process. Demand equals the product of market size and market share. If simulated demand exceeds restaurant capacity, then sales volume is equal to capacity. Otherwise, demand determines unit sales volume. In the model for the large restaurant, capacity is 500,000 meals over the life of the restaurant.

We allow uncertainty about both the level of fixed costs and the size of the total investment that is required to construct the restaurant. Because the entrepreneur's investment is $400,000, the amount of outside investment is uncertain. The investor receives 1.0 percent of the equity for each $10,000 of capital invested.

You probably can think of other ways of setting up the model and may question some of our assumptions. For the model to be useful, it is important to give a lot of thought to the assumptions. If they are specified arbitrarily, no one will have confidence in the results. The entrepreneur can make use of a variety of information sources to improve the quality of assumptions about uncertainty. We review information sources relevant to new venture forecasting in subsequent chapters.

In addition, breaking assumptions into finer components is sometimes useful. Doing so can allow you to substitute variables that are easier to estimate for those that are difficult to estimate directly. For example, it may be easier to estimate population growth of an area and per capita restaurant meal consumption than to estimate market size directly. You can then derive expected market size, together with the uncertainty of market size, as the product of the two underlying variables.

Step 5: Running the Simulation

With the model complete and the assumptions specified, the simulation is ready to run. To illustrate the usefulness of simulation, we selected five variables in the model, which are retained by *Venture*.SIM for each trial and stored in an Excel file: market size, unit sales, PV of the venture, the entrepreneur's ownership share, and NPV to the entrepreneur. Figure 5.6 shows the simulation statistics for these five variables based

Unconditional Simulation Results

Trials = 5000

Venture.SIM

Output	Average	Median	Standard Deviation	Skewness		Percentiles			
					Minimum	25%	50%	75%	Maximum
1 Market Size	3,212,694	3,065,070	1,054,064	0.303	908,109	2,415,842	3,065,070	4,045,972	5,977,817
2 Unit Sales (Lifetime)	316,821	301,949	104,730	0.189	78,866	235,401	301,949	401,659	500,000
3 Total Present Value	1,079,180	986,546	647,450	0.557	(469,267)	577,137	986,546	1,498,539	3,415,528
4 Entrepreneur's Ownership Share	0.649	0.649	0.026	0.061	0.562	0.630	0.649	0.666	0.740
5 Entrepreneur's NPV	299,515	238,803	419,340	0.555	(710,893)	(23,065)	238,803	567,702	1,908,014

(a)

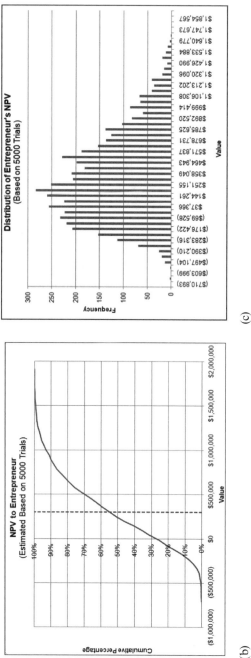

(b)

(c)

FIGURE **5.6**

Unconditional simulation results

Panel (a) shows the output generated from *Venture*.SIM, using the unconditional simulator. (Refer to the companion website for the Excel file for this figure.) Results are compiled using the model for the large restaurant. Panel (b) shows the cumulative distribution of the entrepreneur's NPV. Panel (c) is a histogram showing the dispersion of the entrepreneur's NPV estimates from the trials.

on running 5,000 iterations of the model.[10] For each iteration, the computer makes a random draw from each of the statistical distributions that describe the uncertainty in the model. Thus, simulation improves upon using discrete scenarios for sensitivity analysis by allowing us to examine the impact of changing a number of variables at the same time.

We begin by considering the total PV of the restaurant, shown in row 3 of Figure 5.6a. This is calculated for each trial as:

Total PV = PV(Cash Flow) = PV(Revenues) − PV(Cash Expenses)

The average is $1,079,180, with a standard deviation of $647,450. The minimum value is negative $469,267. As all of the cash invested in the venture went into building the restaurant, nothing is left over to fund this shortfall.

A loss of more than the initial investment is possible only if the entrepreneur makes subsequent investments or makes personal guarantees to investors or suppliers beyond the $400,000 investment. Otherwise, the loss would accrue to others who have provided resources to the venture before being paid, such as investors and creditors.

The entrepreneur's NPV is shown in row 5 of Figure 5.6a. The average value from 5,000 trials is $299,515, demonstrating that, even as an accept/reject decision (i.e., before building in real options), the venture is worth pursuing. The *Venture*.SIM summary table shows wide variability in the entrepreneur's NPV, including negative values for at least 25 percent of the trials. The cumulative distribution in Figure 5.6b shows about a 27 percent chance that the entrepreneur's NPV will be negative. Figure 5.6c shows the full distribution as a histogram. The distribution is skewed toward the right, indicating the potential for some very high valued outcomes, whereas the downside is more limited.

Figure 5.6a shows that the entrepreneur's expected ownership share is 65 percent, with a range of 56 to 74 percent. Thus, despite the uncertainty about the initial investment, the entrepreneur would always end up with a controlling (majority) interest.

Recall that we use a two-step process to simulate market size. First, we use a triangular distribution to generate a preliminary estimate. Then we add a normally distributed random error (mean = 0, standard deviation = 100,000 meals), which allows us to find the true size of the market. Figures 5.7a and 5.7b are histograms that illustrate the net effect of the two-step process. The basic shape of the distribution is still triangular and not symmetrical, so that the peak is below the mean. In panel (a), we ran only 300 iterations of the model, and the resulting shape of the sample distribution is quite irregular. Panel (b) shows the

FIGURE **5.7**

Distribution of market size estimates generated by simulation
Panel (a) shows the results of 300 iterations of the simulation of market size. Panel (b) shows the effect of increasing the number of iterations to 5,000. In both panels, the solid vertical line represents the expected value from the sampling distribution.

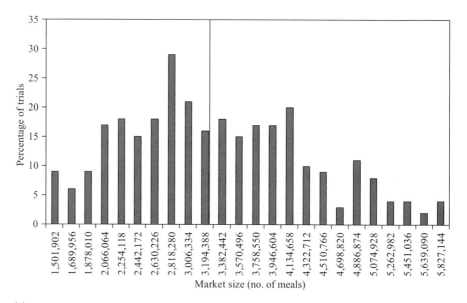

(a)

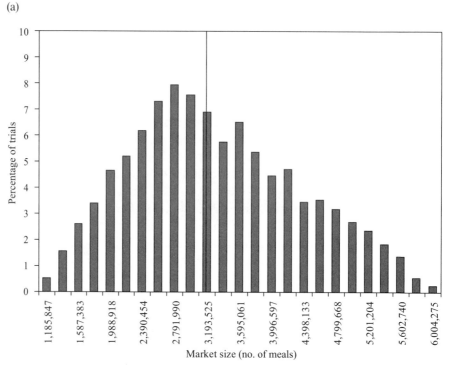

(b)

FIGURE **5.8**
Histogram of unit sales simulation results
The figure illustrates the effect of the capacity constraint at 500,000 meals on total unit sales of the larger restaurant. Results are based on a simulation of 5,000 trials.

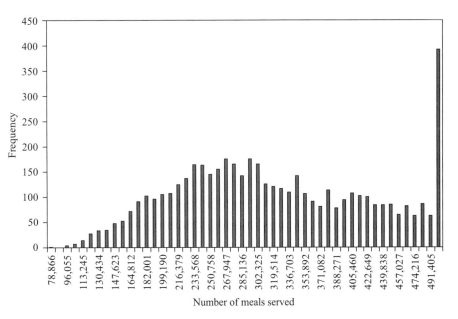

result of running 5,000 iterations. The interplay of the triangular and normal distributions is clearer in this panel.

As we discussed earlier, the realized number of meals served is the lesser of demand (market size × market share) or the capacity constraint of 500,000 meals. Figure 5.8 shows the distribution of meals served and illustrates how capacity constrains total unit sales. In about 8 percent of the trials (about 400 of 5,000), the constraint is binding and only 500,000 meals are sold.

How many iterations of the model are needed to provide a reliable basis for an investment decision? One way to find out is to look at a graph of the rate of convergence of a variable of interest. Figure 5.9 shows the convergence of estimates of the entrepreneur's NPV. Convergence is illustrated in the figure by plotting the average value of the variable for all the iterations up to a given number. The point on the far left reflects only the first trial from the model, while the point on the right reflects the average of all 5,000 trials. After about 500 iterations, the average entrepreneur's NPV does not change very much. Thus, in this instance, even a fairly small number of trials yields a reliable estimate of projected NPV.

If the entrepreneur's choice is either to invest in the large restaurant now or to do nothing, then 500 iterations are sufficient to determine that the venture is worth pursuing. But if the entrepreneur is trying to

FIGURE **5.9**

Convergence of the entrepreneur's NPV
The figure shows the rate of convergence of the entrepreneur's NPV of the large restaurant, based on 5,000 trials. After about 500 iterations, the simulated estimate of NPV is quite stable, even though individual iterations are subject to considerable uncertainty.

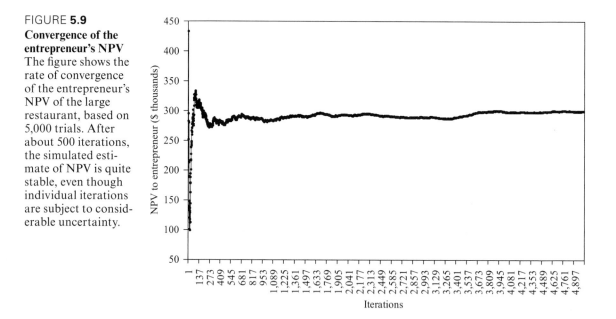

compare different alternatives, such as choosing between the large and small restaurants, more trials may be needed. Using the standard deviation and number of trials information from Figure 5.6, we compute that the standard error of the estimate for the NPV of the entrepreneur's investment is about $5,900.[11] This means there is about a 65 percent probability that the true mean NPV is between roughly $293,600 and $305,400 (i.e., $299,500 ± $5,900), and about a 95 percent probability that the true mean is in the range of $287,700 to $311,300 (i.e., $299,500 ± 2 × $5,900).[12] Adding more trials reduces the standard error of the estimate of the mean, so that better decisions can be made even when the differences between values of alternative strategies are small. Had we limited the simulation to 500 trials, the standard error would have been about $18,600 instead of $5,900.

Step 6: Analyzing the Results

The final step is to use the simulation results as a basis for making a decision. If the choice were simply between building the large restaurant and doing nothing, the positive NPV would be sufficient to conclude that the investment should be made. Most real decisions, however, are more complicated. They involve comparing several different alternatives. Many require drawing inferences about alternative scenarios that have not been formally analyzed (such as an intermediate-size restaurant). For such decisions, it may be necessary to develop several simulation models with alternative assumptions and to compare the results. This is the focus of the next section.

S 5.8 Comparing Strategic Choices

We turn now to our primary objective—use of simulation to compare strategic alternatives and to examine the values of real options. To do so, we use the same set of alternatives for establishing the restaurant venture as in Chapter 4. The branches of the decision trees from that chapter represent alternative scenarios concerning the entrepreneur's decisions. To recap, we consider the following possibilities:

- Build a large restaurant immediately.
- Build a small restaurant immediately.
- Wait for more information on demand and build whichever size is best.
- Build the small restaurant now and expand if demand is sufficient.
- Build the large restaurant now and abandon it if demand is insufficient.
- Build the small restaurant now and abandon it if demand is insufficient.

To this list, we can add more complex alternative scenarios that combine the options to wait, expand, and/or abandon.

We begin by comparing the large restaurant to the simple alternative of investing in the small restaurant. The small restaurant is modeled easily by making a few modifications to the large restaurant model.[13] Specifically, first we reduce the expected PV of fixed costs to $400,000 and the standard deviation to $40,000. Second, we reduce the capacity constraint to 260,000. Third, we reduce the expected cost of acquiring the restaurant to $600,000 and the standard deviation to $20,000.

Simulating the small restaurant, we found that the expected NPV of the entrepreneur's investment is $249,606. This is materially less than the $299,515 value of the large restaurant. Based on NPV, the entrepreneur should select the large restaurant. Anticipating the examination of real options to come, it is worth noting that for the small restaurant, the entrepreneur's NPV is negative 17.3 percent of the time and the restaurant is capacity constrained 67.5 percent of the time. The comparable numbers for the large restaurant are 27.0 percent and 8.0 percent.

Finally, the entrepreneur has a larger stake in the small restaurant, 80 percent on average versus 65 percent for the large restaurant.

Are there any considerations that would shift the balance in favor of the small restaurant? One possibility is that the entrepreneur does not want to accept the downside risk of the large project. Although the initial investment is $400,000, in the event of a loss the entrepreneur may be compelled to draw on resources beyond those originally committed. For the large restaurant, the simulation showed that additional investment would be needed to cover operating losses in about 1.0 percent of the trials; for the small restaurant, this drops slightly, to about 0.7 percent.

To gain additional insight about relative risk exposure, the standard deviations of the NPV of the two restaurants can be compared. The small restaurant has a smaller standard deviation of the entrepreneur's NPV. But as its expected return is also lower, this may not make the small project any more appealing. A desire to minimize the downside would point in favor of the small restaurant but is offset on the high end, where the large restaurant does substantially better.

Financial theory implies that the choice should be made based strictly on NPV (assuming you have correctly valued all of the cash flows and real options). So comparing the fractiles in the distributions is not defensible unless you think there is something that the NPV calculations do not take into account.

Here is where qualitative considerations may influence the decision. For example, maybe the entrepreneur cares about the potential differences in control that are implied by the two models. The expected ownership share favors the small restaurant, as does the worst case: 73 percent for the small versus 56 percent for the large. Conceivably, the difference in expected ownership share is enough to lead the entrepreneur to favor the small restaurant, despite its lower NPV.

Offsetting the smaller share of ownership, the large restaurant generates more cash for the entrepreneur. Looking back at the fractiles, however, we see that the times when control is likely to be most important to the entrepreneur are the scenarios in which the restaurant does not do as well as expected. The small restaurant tends to have a higher NPV than the large restaurant in these underperformance scenarios. Thus, the higher share and higher cash flow of the small restaurant in bad states of nature could be something the entrepreneur would want to consider as mitigating the NPV difference.

How much is the small restaurant's larger ownership stake worth to the entrepreneur? Simple NPV comparisons cannot directly address qualitative considerations such as these.

The Option to Abandon

The analysis thus far has examined two strategic scenarios: a one-time investment in either a large or a small restaurant. No real-world venture is that simple. It is usually possible, for example, to abandon a venture if results are discouraging enough.

How does the abandonment option change the values of the two restaurants? In the case of the large restaurant, we assume that the building has an alternative use value of $600,000.[14] In the terminology of finance, the owners of the restaurant have a put option with an exercise value of $600,000. As the simulation model is constructed, the exercise date is the date when true demand becomes known. The simulation model can be used to calculate the expected PV of continuing to operate the restaurant, conditional on the true state of demand. If this turns out to be less than $600,000, then an entrepreneur seeking to maximize the value of the investment will exercise the abandonment option.

To estimate the value of the abandonment option, we run 5,000 iterations of the large restaurant model, modified to include the option. For each trial we compare the restaurant's PV to the abandonment value of $600,000. If the PV is lower, we exercise the option, convert to office space, and realize $600,000, which is shared between the entrepreneur and the investor based on their ownership fractions. The resulting estimate of NPV to the entrepreneur is $331,455. Comparing this to the earlier value of $299,515 for the large restaurant, it appears that the option is worth about $31,940 to the entrepreneur.[15]

When we evaluate the abandonment option of the small restaurant, with an assumed abandonment value of $300,000, we find that it is worth about $5,738 to the entrepreneur, increasing expected entrepreneur NPV from $249,606 to $255,344. The small restaurant's abandonment option has a relatively low value for two reasons: first, the probability of a state of nature being sufficiently bad to put the option in the money is lower; second, the alternative use value of the small restaurant is low.

Based on the simulation results, the abandonment option should not alter the initial decision to invest in the large restaurant. In fact, it reinforces the relative value of the large restaurant. However, investment in either size is more attractive when it includes an abandonment option.

As the problem is structured, the abandonment option is costless to the entrepreneur. But what if it were not? Suppose some locations have high values as office space but others do not. Locations that afford valuable alternative uses are likely to sell for more because even real options are usually not costless to acquire. To see how much the entrepreneur should be willing to pay (in terms of a location premium) for the option to abandon, we would need to run the model again. The answer as to what the entrepreneur should be willing to pay is not obvious, since the entrepreneur's contribution is capped at $400,000 regardless of the location choice. Thus, the investor would contribute the full location premium and yet would have to split the increase in the venture's value with the entrepreneur based on fractional ownership. Also, because the option raises the expected value of the venture, shouldn't the entrepreneur be able to convince the investor to take a smaller equity position per dollar of capital contributed? If your intuition does not lead quickly to the answers to these questions, then you should begin to recognize the value of simulation.

The model can be used to value options that are more complex than the simple one-time option to abandon. In reality, the restaurant owner never knows demand with certainty. Each year is different from the one before. The abandonment option does not disappear just because it is not exercised at the end of the first year. With a more elaborate simulation model that explicitly covers several years, we could, in principle, estimate the value of a complex abandonment option that would give the entrepreneur the option to abandon at the end of each year.[16] If the option is exercised, the process ends; if not, the option for that year expires, but options to abandon in the future continue to contribute positively to value.

Let's look in more detail at the values of the small and large restaurants with options to abandon. Figure 5.10a plots the individual outcomes of 600 iterations of the model for the small restaurant. The horizontal axis represents the number of meals the restaurant serves over its life. You can see that the outcomes are dispersed around the upward-sloping line drawn in the figure and that there is a "floor" on the entrepreneur's NPV at around negative $175,000. This floor reflects the downside protection against losses provided by the abandonment option.

To show the option quality of the abandonment strategy more clearly, in Figure 5.10b we remove the uncertainty about prices and costs by using their expected values. The only random variable is the level of demand. In addition, we model demand so that all of the uncertainty is resolved after the first year. The pattern in the figure can be represented as a combination of three securities: (1) an underlying asset (the entrepreneur's claim on the restaurant), (2) a put option to abandon the venture for $300,000 that is exercised if demand is low, and (3) a call option the entrepreneur has "sold" by not building a restaurant large enough to handle high demand. The upward-sloping portion of the value function in Figure 5.10b shows that, by building the restaurant, the entrepreneur acquires a long position in the market demand for meals. The

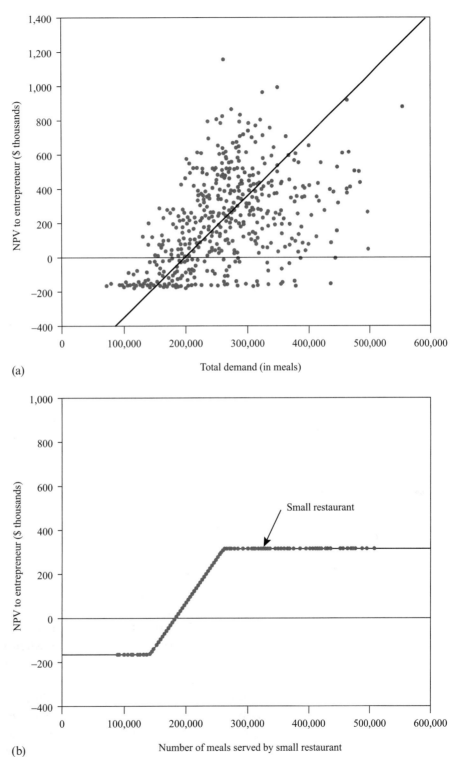

FIGURE **5.10**
Small restaurant—NPV to entrepreneur
Panel (a) shows the sample distribution of the entrepreneur's NPV from 600 iterations of the small-restaurant model with abandonment option. The effect of the option is reflected by the lower bound, or "floor," of negative NPVs. Panel (b) shows the combined effects of capacity constraints and the abandonment option for the small restaurant, leaving out the other sources of uncertainty.

(a)

Total demand (in meals)

NPV to entrepreneur ($ thousands)

Small restaurant

(b)

Number of meals served by small restaurant

NPV to entrepreneur ($ thousands)

FIGURE **5.11**

Large restaurant overlaid with small— NPV to entrepreneur
The figure shows the combined effects of capacity constraints and abandonment options for the large and small restaurants over a range of market demand. The simulation removes uncertainty by using the expected value for all variables except those related to demand quantity.

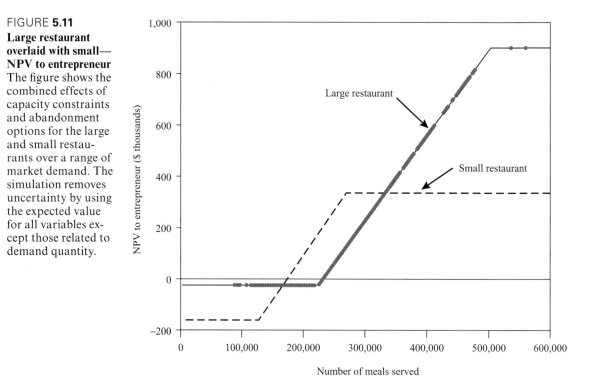

floor reflects the abandonment (put) option and the ceiling represents the call option that is implicit in the capacity constraint.

Figure 5.10 shows that the entrepreneur is effectively hedged against low demand by acquiring an abandonment (put) option, which is valuable at demand levels below about 140,000 meals. By building a restaurant that is too small to serve high levels of demand, the entrepreneur has effectively sold a call option on demand in excess of what the restaurant can serve. The implicit proceeds from the sale of the call option on high demand are reflected in the figure as a reduction in the cost of the restaurant compared with the alternative of building a much larger restaurant that can meet the highest conceivable level of demand.

To assess the differences between the small and large restaurants, in Figure 5.11 we overlay the NPV functions based only on variations in demand. It may surprise you to see that when demand is low, the large restaurant is more valuable to the entrepreneur than the small one (when demand for meals is less than about 175,000 meals). This occurs because the large restaurant requires $150,000 more in outside investment but increases abandonment value by $300,000.[17] Although the investor pays the entire incremental cost, most of the increase in abandonment value accrues to the entrepreneur, who has a majority ownership stake. Over the demand range from 175,000 to about 300,000 meals, the small restaurant is more valuable for the entrepreneur. Generally, over that range the small restaurant can meet nearly all of the demand but at lower cost than the large restaurant; this is due to its lower fixed costs. Beyond demand of 300,000 meals, the extra capacity of the large restaurant makes it more valuable than the small one.

Figure 5.11 makes the choice appear simple. As long as we know true demand and can strip away the uncertainties about other factors such as prices and costs, it is obvious which of the two restaurants should be built. Unfortunately, we cannot simply remove those uncertainties, nor can we ever be certain about the level of demand. We can, however, use the simulation to help determine which of the two restaurants has the higher expected NPV.

The Learning Option

Another choice that is available to the entrepreneur is to wait to build either size restaurant until the preliminary estimate of market size is learned. We assume that delaying investment invites competitive entry, so that the expected market share for the entrepreneur's restaurant would be reduced. Furthermore, we assume that putting off the investment for even longer—until demand is known with certainty—would result in loss of the opportunity to invest.

Because the entrepreneur invests only $400,000 but can do so in a restaurant of either size, the entrepreneur has a complex call option on an uncertain share of the value of a restaurant of uncertain size. The option is a call on the expected value to the entrepreneur of either size restaurant, whichever value is greater. The exercise price is $400,000, and the option expires shortly after the preliminary estimate of demand is revealed. If the entrepreneur decides to invest, she also acquires an option to abandon the venture once the true level of demand is clear. She will exercise the abandonment (put) option if the expected value of the restaurant is less than its value in alternative use.

The learning option is not costless. Delaying entry reduces the PV of future cash inflows. Moreover, the delay increases the chance that competitors will enter and reduce expected market share. To reflect these costs, we assume that potential demand is 10 percent less than if entry were not delayed.

Figure 5.12 is the branch of the decision tree (i.e., the subtree) that the entrepreneur faces if she decides to wait and learn before investing. With simulation, we no longer describe the states of nature (demand) as

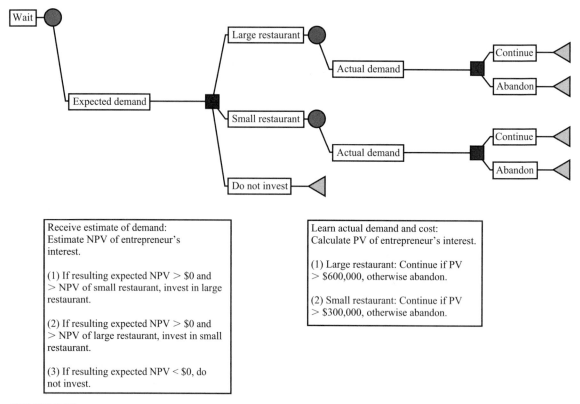

Receive estimate of demand:
Estimate NPV of entrepreneur's
interest.

(1) If resulting expected NPV > $0 and
> NPV of small restaurant, invest in large
restaurant.

(2) If resulting expected NPV > $0 and
> NPV of large restaurant, invest in small
restaurant.

(3) If resulting expected NPV < $0, do
not invest.

Learn actual demand and cost:
Calculate PV of entrepreneur's interest.

(1) Large restaurant: Continue if PV
> $600,000, otherwise abandon.

(2) Small restaurant: Continue if PV
> $300,000, otherwise abandon.

FIGURE **5.12**
Subtree for restaurant learning option with simulated uncertainty
The entrepreneur's decisions are represented by squares; information received by the entrepreneur is represented by circles. Prepared using PrecisionTree, Palisade Corporation.

a few discrete possibilities (low, moderate, high). Instead, as in the figure, we describe the decision rule the entrepreneur will use to respond to nature's choice, whatever it may be. The three-pronged choice after an estimate of demand for the restaurant is received reflects a complex call option on either a large or a small restaurant. The binary choices, once true demand is learned, reflect the abandonment (put) options.

To simulate this complex structure, we modified the restaurant model. After the estimate of demand is received, the simulation uses it to estimate the entrepreneur's NPV for both the large and small restaurants. If both NPVs are negative, the entrepreneur will not invest in a restaurant of either size; if both are positive, the entrepreneur selects whichever size has the higher expected NPV. Then the entrepreneur learns actual demand and recalculates PV. Based on the actual demand, she compares the PV of the selected restaurant against the PV of the abandonment option and decides whether to continue or abandon.

At the starting point, the entrepreneur cannot know which, if any, of the options should be exercised. The only decision is whether waiting is more valuable than the highest-NPV immediate alternative (i.e., more valuable than building the large restaurant with option to abandon). When we simulated the model represented by the decision tree in Figure 5.12, the resulting expected entrepreneur's NPV was $306,409. Thus, the learning option's expected value is $25,046 lower than the expected value of investing today in the large restaurant with an abandonment option (NPV = $331,455).

It may seem counterintuitive that one strategy containing the same and in fact more options than another strategy could have a lower NPV. The main reason the option to wait does not add value relative to the large restaurant/abandon alternative is that waiting encourages competitive entry, which reduces the entrepreneur's expected market share in the event that the large restaurant is built. As mentioned, the expected loss of market share can be thought of as the cost of acquiring the option to delay investing. For the large restaurant, the cost of acquiring the option, measured in terms of the expected loss of future business, is more than the increase in value that results from learning more about actual demand.

As it turns out, the abandonment option is not very valuable in conjunction with the option to delay. This is because most of the uncertainty about future sales is resolved when the initial estimate is received. Accordingly, the option to abandon is almost never exercised when the option to wait is employed. Generally, when combinations of real options are used, their values are not additive.

Techniques such as simulation or other numerical evaluation methods are extremely valuable for assessing such structures. Because the values of individual options diminish as more choices are added, we do not need to employ overly complicated models or to completely describe and model the strategic alternatives. A parsimonious model that captures the main strategic choices can generate a reliable estimate of the expected value of a venture.

The Expansion Option

Finally, if the small restaurant is built immediately, the entrepreneur acquires an option to expand in the event that realized demand justifies the large restaurant. The small restaurant is built, and afterward the entrepreneur receives an estimate of demand; based on the estimate, the entrepreneur decides whether to expand the restaurant. The option to expand is a call option on additional capacity, with a $200,000 exercise price (the cost to increase capacity).

As we have styled this example, the entrepreneur does not need to invest anything further to exercise the option; all of the $200,000 comes from the investor. However, the expansion does reduce the entrepreneur's ownership share. This structure, where additional financing is provided by an investor in exchange for an ownership percentage that reduces the entrepreneur's share, is typical of VC financing arrangements. Finally, the model is structured to reflect the realistic expectation that the cost of building the large restaurant in stages ($600,000 + $200,000) is higher than that of building it at once ($750,000).

When demand is allowed to vary continuously and the initial estimate of demand is uncertain, the best course of action (large or small restaurant) is not clear. Simulation can help evaluate the range of expected demand levels over which exercising the option to expand would add value.

Figure 5.13 shows the subtree facing the entrepreneur who initially invests in the small restaurant. The option to expand is evaluated by comparing the expected PV of the expanded restaurant with the expected PV of the small restaurant over a range of critical values for expected unit sales. Waiting to expand until more information about market demand is obtained reduces the risk of the outside investment that is required for expansion. Because the risk of investing at this point is lower, we assume that the investor receives relatively less equity compared to the earlier investment round: 1.0 percent of the equity for each $20,000 invested in expansion. Again, the entrepreneur also has an option to abandon once true demand becomes known.

Our purpose is to determine the value of a strategy of investing small and waiting to see the market response before a larger investment is made. When we evaluated the option to delay investing in Chapter 4, we set up the analysis to always select the choice with the highest expected value. This time we search for the best decision by examining different critical values for the decision to expand and comparing the values for this strategy to the alternative of investing immediately in the large restaurant.

Using the simulation model, we evaluated options to expand at critical values of expected demand ranging from 200,000 units to 500,000 units, in 20,000-unit increments. Exercising the option to expand benefits the entrepreneur over the entire range when compared to keeping the restaurant small. However, the benefit to the entrepreneur from expanding when expected demand is at the low end of the range comes at the expense of the investor. This is because at low levels of sales it is actually better to abandon the restaurant. Bringing in an investor under such conditions effectively subsidizes part of the entrepreneur's losses. An

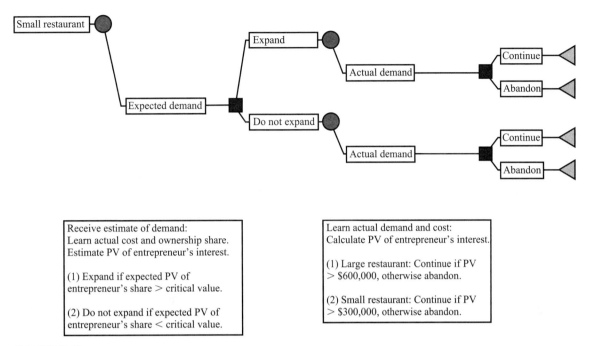

FIGURE **5.13**
Subtree for restaurant expansion option with simulated uncertainty
The entrepreneur's decisions are represented by squares; information received by the entrepreneur is represented by circles. Prepared using PrecisionTree, Palisade Corporation.

investor is unlikely to enter into such an arrangement. Accordingly, we limit the option to expand to the range of expected demand levels where the investor derives a positive expected NPV from the project.

With this constraint, the option can only be exercised if expected demand is at least 300,000 units. At this level, the option to expand increases the value of the entrepreneur's position to about $432,000, almost $100,000 higher than building the large restaurant initially. Using the model, we found that expected NPV is roughly constant up to a critical value of about 340,000 meals. Accordingly, we settled on a strategy of exercising the option only if expected demand exceeds 340,000 meals.

Why does the option to expand create so much value for the entrepreneur even though it increases the overall cost of getting a large restaurant? There are two reasons: First, the expansion option allows the entrepreneur to avoid the higher costs of having a large restaurant when demand is low. Second, it reduces the uncertainty of the second stage of outside investment, prompting the investor to accept a smaller equity stake in exchange for contributed capital.

This is an important lesson and one that will be explored in greater detail later. By staging the needs for outside capital, the entrepreneur can offer the investor a safer bet and can retain a larger share of the venture as a result.

5.9 Summary

The objective of strategic planning for a new venture is to develop a framework for maximizing value. While we examine strategic choices from the perspective of the entrepreneur, a similar analysis could be done for the investor. By the value-maximization criterion, success depends on making good assessments of the risks and uncertainties and on developing a strategy that anticipates the need to adapt to new information as it arrives. An effective framework is one that helps the entrepreneur decide whether to undertake the venture, promotes effective negotiation with providers of financing, and encourages value-maximizing decisions.

Simulation is a powerful tool for evaluating the critical decisions that a prospective entrepreneur faces. It is especially valuable for new venture strategies, which typically contain numerous real options. It can add substantial value to the venture and to the entrepreneur's ownership stake.

There are six steps to implementing a simulation for strategic purposes. First, identify the important strategic alternatives, possibly by representing them in a decision tree. Second, decide on the criteria for evaluating the choices, such as the NPV of the entrepreneur's investment. Third, develop a model of each strategy that can be used to evaluate the various options facing the entrepreneur, and specify mathematically how the decisions of the entrepreneur contribute to the evaluation criteria. Fourth, specify the assumptions of the model and describe the uncertainties. Fifth, run simulation. Sixth, interpret the results.

The best way to appreciate the value of simulation is to work through specific examples.

Review Questions

1. How did Merck use simulation in its R&D process?

2. What are four ways that simulation can foster better decision making for new ventures? In each case, explain how simulation could be beneficial.

3. What are the six steps involved in using simulation to evaluate a strategy? Explain each using a specific example of your own.

4. In the warehouse illustration in Section 5.4, identify the six steps of the simulation process used to evaluate the choice.

5. If you were trying to simulate the value of a call option, why would you first simulate the value of the underlying stock rather than simulating the option risk directly?

6. Identify each of the six steps of the simulation process used to evaluate a strategic alternative for the restaurant example.

7. Describe how you could use simulation to evaluate an expansion option. How could you determine the value of the option?

8. Describe how you could use simulation to evaluate an abandonment option. How could you determine the value of the option?

9. If you simulate distributions of NPVs for two different strategies, why would it usually be inappropriate to compare the distributions and choose the one that is less risky?

10. When evaluating risk, why is it better to simulate the distribution of possible NPVs rather than taking the expected value of each risky factor and calculating the expected NPV based on the expected values?

NOTES

1. See Nichols (1994).

2. Available at http://hbr.org/1994/01/scientific-management-at-merck-an-interview-with-cfo-judy-lewent/ar/1.

3. Drawn from Nichols (1994).

4. See Stevenson, Muzyka, and Timmons (1987) for an application of simulation techniques to changes in investment patterns of venture capital funds. They simulate a multistage investment process based on a large number of funds, all operating under a common set of assumptions. They use models to examine the impact of management and venture capital industry practices on fund results.

5. Figure 5.4 is part of an Excel file (available on the companion website) that also contains the model used for the simulation and the summary output table from *Venture*.SIM.

6. By going to the Excel file on the companion website, you can see the structure of this model.

7. Those familiar with options will recognize that in order to justify using the risk-free rate to project stock price growth, we must adjust the true probabilities to "risk-neutral probabilities." Even if the expected return is higher because, say, the stock has a positive beta, adjusting the probabilities

and compounding at the risk-free rate will produce simulated value estimates that are closer to formal option pricing valuations.

8. The companion website contains a copy of the Excel simulation model of the restaurant incorporating the assumptions described here. Separate simulation models are constructed to reflect the various real option structures for the large and small restaurants. All can be studied on the website.

9. It is up to the user to select and calibrate a distribution that provides an accurate representation of future uncertainty. We use a triangular distribution to describe market size partly because it is an easy way to provide for a high degree of uncertainty but avoid the possibility of negative simulated values.

10. The NPV estimate converges quickly to a stable value. We use a large number of trials because we also want good information on the rest of the distribution. In a model that includes real options that are likely to be exercised only infrequently, a large number of trials will give us more reliable information on the options.

11. The standard error equals the standard deviation of the entrepreneur's NPV (from Figure 5.6) divided by the square root of the number of iterations.

12. Confidence intervals are derived using the properties of a normal distribution: approximately 65 percent of the distribution is within one standard deviation of the mean and about 95 percent is within two standard deviations. A more accurate approach to estimating confidence intervals would rely directly on the trials data.

13. You can open the Excel file on the companion website to review the modifications.

14. We do not allow for any uncertainty about this value, but with simulation we easily could do so.

15. Because the option changes the riskiness of the project, it could also affect the discount rate that is appropriate for valuing cash flows. At this early stage, we have not taken account of this in the simulation assumptions.

16. This is comparable to a model for new drug development, where the pharmaceutical company has the option to abandon the effort at numerous points in the clinical testing and FDA approval stages.

17. If the investor is astute, the terms of the deal will be different for the large restaurant than for the small one, in part because the entrepreneur gets more benefit from the abandonment option of the large restaurant.

References and Additional Reading

Bell, D., and A. Schleifer Jr. 1995. *Decision Making under Uncertainty.* Cambridge, MA: Course Technology, Inc.

Hertz, D. B. 1968. "Investment Policies That Pay Off." *Harvard Business Review* 46 (1): 96–108.

————. 1979. "Risk Analysis in Capital Investment." *Harvard Business Review* 57 (5): 169–81.

Nichols, N. A. 1994. "Scientific Management at Merck: An Interview with CFO Judy Lewent." *Harvard Business Review* 72 (1): 89–99.

Stevenson, H. H., D. F. Muzyka, and J. A. Timmons. 1987. "Venture Capital in Transition: A Monte Carlo Simulation of Changes in Investment Patterns." *Journal of Business Venturing* 2 (2): 103–21.

FINANCIAL FORECASTING AND ASSESSING FINANCIAL NEEDS

CHAPTER 6

METHODS OF FINANCIAL FORECASTING: REVENUE

The more successful a new venture is, the more dangerous is lack of financial foresight.

Peter Drucker, *Innovation and Entrepreneurship*

Many entrepreneurs of profitable and rapidly growing ventures are puzzled that they never seem to have enough cash to finance their operations. Financial forecasting is a critical element of planning for a new venture. The principal benefits of a good financial forecast include the following:

- Forecasting is a disciplined way to evaluate how much cash the venture is likely to require and how much it might need if the venture develops more quickly or more slowly than expected.

- Forecasting provides a basis for estimating value so that an entrepreneur can make objective comparisons between pursuing the venture and other opportunities.

- Forecasting helps the entrepreneur and investors to compare strategic alternatives and select the one with the highest expected value.

- Forecasting helps the entrepreneur and investors to understand the strengths and weaknesses of the venture.

- A forecast provides a benchmark against which to compare actual performance, thereby providing early warning if the venture is not developing as expected.

We use this chapter to introduce the basics of financial forecasting, with an emphasis on forecasting revenue. Revenue forecasting is important for two reasons. First, revenue usually is a key driver of value. Second, forecasting revenue is important for determining how much to invest in such things as physical plant, employees, raw materials, and finished goods—all of the inputs that are essential to position the firm to respond to demand when it develops.

To develop a revenue forecast, we begin by specifying the assumptions that drive revenue and revenue growth—assumptions about such things as market size, market share, and price. Clear, explicit, and well-supported assumptions make the forecast more than just an exercise and make it credible to investors. In this chapter, we present a variety of forecasting techniques and review important information sources that can serve as foundation for assumptions. In Chapter 7, we use forecasting methods developed here to design and construct forward-looking pro forma financial statements that allow us to forecast venture performance in an integrated way. In Chapter 8, we use the integrated pro forma financial statements to assess the cash needs of the venture through time. Later in the book, we use the financial forecast as a basis for valuation.

6.1   Principles of Financial Forecasting

Before turning to the details of financial forecasting, it is useful to provide an overview of the principles that guide the forecasting process.

- *Build and support a schedule of assumptions.* The assumptions may come from fundamental analysis of the opportunity, information about the financial characteristics of comparable firms, or reliance on expert judgment. These assumptions will guide construction of a financial model of the venture.

- *Begin with a forecast of revenue.* It is usually easiest to build the financial model by starting with a revenue forecast. Most other aspects of the model are linked to revenue. For example, the targeted level of sales or rate of sales growth can determine the investment in production capacity and the necessary size of the inventory.

- *Decide whether to develop the forecast in real or nominal terms.* Nominal-term forecasts include an explicit forecast of inflation, whereas real-term forecasts are in constant dollars. If you expect selling prices and input costs to track the inflation rate, then forecasting in real terms can simplify the model. If prices and costs are unrelated to inflation, it can be better to forecast in nominal terms and make explicit adjustments for price changes. Interest rates on debt and discount rates used in discounted cash flow (DCF) valuation are usually quoted in nominal terms. It is important to recognize this and be consistent.

- *Integrate the financial statements.* Integrating, through spreadsheet formulas, the pro forma balance sheet, income statement, and cash flow statement is essential for (1) testing sensitivity to assumptions, (2) performing scenario analysis, and (3) simulating the uncertainty of future performance.

- *Choose an appropriate time span for the forecast.* The span covered by the forecast depends on the purpose of the forecast. If the forecast is to be used to determine financial needs, it should cover a period long enough that by the end of the period the venture is in a position to attract follow-on financing based on its track record. If the forecast is to be used for valuation, the period must be long enough to carry the venture to a point where opportunities for harvesting are likely.

- *Choose an appropriate forecasting interval.* The appropriate interval depends on the planning period of the venture. For assessing financial needs of an early-stage venture, intervals of one year are too long. The entrepreneur needs to project cash needs over much shorter intervals in order to arrange financing on a timely basis. If the forecast is to be used for control and assessment, the important performance milestones are unlikely to be annual. On the other hand, daily or even weekly forecasts are unlikely to be of much value. Departures from projected results for short intervals can be highly variable and are largely random. Generally, for an early-stage venture an interval of about a month provides a sensible balance of timeliness and reliability.

- *Assess the reasonableness of the model.* Think through the relations among the assumptions and line items within and across the financial statements. Do they make sense? Are they internally consistent? Try a basic "what if" analysis to see if the results are internally consistent and conduct stress tests to make sure the model is robust to extreme outcomes.

6.2 Forecasting Revenue

To anticipate financing requirements, we need to link product-market performance to financing needs. The revenue forecast is the customary link. This is because financing supports the start-up investments that are necessary before revenue generation can begin. Once the venture is producing and selling a viable product, sales growth is the primary driver of financing needs. For any given forecast of future revenue, we can work back to estimate the cash flows from operations that are expected to be available or the additional financing needed to support the growth.

Forecasting the Revenue of an Established Business

A reliable revenue forecast for an established business can sometimes be based on prior experience. For example, we might project that revenue will grow at the average rate of the previous five years. A more sophisticated approach could take into consideration the trend in the rate of revenue growth (as opposed to the average), or the forecast could be tied to changes in underlying economic and demographic factors. In this section, we illustrate simple forecasting approaches for established businesses.

Suppose that for an existing business we observe the following levels of sales and macroeconomic information for the previous six years and wish to forecast sales in Year 0 (the current year):

Year	−6	−5	−4	−3	−2	−1
Sales ($ millions)	$2.0	$2.4	$2.7	$2.6	$2.6	$2.9
Sales growth		+20.0%	+12.5%	−3.7%	0.0%	+11.5%
Inflation		+3.0%	+6.0%	+7.0%	+4.0%	+2.0%
Change in real GDP		+3.0%	+1.5%	−1.0%	−1.0%	+2.0%

For example, from Year −6 to Year −5, sales increased from $2.0 to $2.4 million, a 20 percent increase. During the same year, the inflation rate was 3.0 percent and real gross domestic product (real GDP) increased 3.0 percent.

Forecasting based on the historical nominal growth rate.
One approach to forecasting revenue is to extrapolate the average historical growth rate. The simple average of the five growth rates in the table is 8.06 percent. Multiplying the most recent sales level of $2.9 million by 1.0806 yields a Year 0 forecast of $3.13 million. However, the five-year range of growth rates varies from −3.7 percent to 20 percent. Knowing that the historical average is 8.06 is useful, but the high degree of uncertainty about the rate can be problematic. A more precise estimate would be better.

Forecasting based on the historical real growth rate.   A possible way to improve the sales forecast may be to make it in real (inflation-adjusted) rather than nominal terms. This could help especially if price increases for the venture track the inflation index well and if inflation forecasts are available publicly.[1] By subtracting the inflation rate from the sales growth rate, we can express the growth rate in real terms.

Year	−6	−5	−4	−3	−2	−1
Sales growth		+20.0%	+12.5%	−3.7%	0.0%	+11.5%
Inflation		+3.0%	+6.0%	+7.0%	+4.0%	+2.0%
Real sales growth		+17.0%	+6.5%	−10.7%	−4.0%	+9.5%

The simple average of the real rates of sales growth over the period is 3.66 percent. While this might be better as a forecast of expected sales, in this case we may not have improved the accuracy of the forecast. The range in real terms, −10.7 percent to 17 percent, is actually wider than that of the nominal data. However, the real numbers may provide a more accurate characterization of uncertainty.

Suppose that publicly available forecasts indicate that inflation next year will be around 1.0 percent. If we add this 1.0 percent rate to the historical average real growth (3.66 percent), then we forecast that sales revenue is expected to increase by 4.66 percent, making the Year 0 forecast $3.04 million.

Using the average nominal growth rate, we would forecast sales growth of 8.06 percent, no matter what the expected rate of inflation. Which forecast is better? The answer depends on how the inflation rate affects sales. If product price tends to follow the inflation rate, then a forecast based on expected inflation is likely to be better than simple trend extrapolation of nominal growth.

There is no way to avoid making an assumption about inflation. The most useful method of presenting a pro forma income statement usually is in nominal terms, where the projections reflect expected inflation explicitly. If the forecast is easier to develop in real terms, then when building the pro forma statements, it usually is better to convert the real sales numbers into nominal terms. This is helpful because some income statement items, such as depreciation and interest expense, are fixed in nominal terms.

Regardless of which approach is used—real or nominal—treatment in the pro forma statements must be consistent. Thus, if the revenue forecast is in real terms and some expense items are fixed in nominal terms, an internally consistent forecast would require that those nominal items be deflated at the expected inflation rate.

Weighting the historical growth rates.   Another way to improve forecast accuracy is to weight historical data so that the more recent experience receives greater weight. Weighting is based on the idea that the future will probably be more like the recent past than the more distant past. With enough historical data and appropriate software, one could determine the weights that yield the (statistically) best estimates of sales in later years.[2] In the context of our example, five years of data are not enough to support a formal analysis to determine appropriate weights. Accordingly, we use a judgmental approach of applying a weight factor of 5/15 to the real growth rate of sales in the most recent year, 4/15 to the prior year, and so on. The following table shows the weight factors applied to the real sales growth rates. Note that the weight factors over five years sum to one, that is, 15/15.

Year	−5	−4	−3	−2	−1
Real sales growth	+17.0%	+6.5%	−10.7%	−4.0%	+9.5%
Weight factor	1/15	2/15	3/15	4/15	5/15
Weighted growth	+1.13%	+0.87%	−2.14%	−1.07%	+3.17%

The resulting forecast of real sales growth is 1.96 percent, the sum of the numbers in the last row of the table. The weighted forecast is below the simple average forecast of 3.66 percent, in large part because the high growth in Year −5 carries much less weight in the average than the negative growth rates in Years −3 and −2.

Exponential smoothing.   In the above forecast, the weights we used are linearly related to each other. Exponential smoothing is an alternative weighting scheme that is easy to apply and can work well when historical data are limited. The simplest form of the exponential smoothing model is:

$$\text{Forecast}_{T+1} = \alpha \times \text{Actual}_T + (1 - \alpha) \times \text{Forecast}_T \tag{6.1}$$

where α is a weighting factor between zero and one. Although the equation does not refer to periods before T, they are reflected in the forecast implicitly. Because the period T forecast is estimated in the same way as the $T + 1$ forecast, actual results of earlier periods are implicit in the $T + 1$ forecast, through the previous forecast. The term "exponential smoothing" signifies that, when Eq. (6.1) is used, the weights applied to earlier results decrease exponentially.

The relative importance of each year's data to the forecast is determined by the weight factor, α. A high value of α is used if recent results are believed to be an important predictor of future results. A lower value increases the weight on older results. If α is high, the forecast adjusts quickly to new results. In the extreme, if α is equal to 1.0, then the next period's forecast is equal to this period's actual result. If α is low, the forecast adjusts gradually. These properties of speed of adjustment also apply if a linear smoothing approach is used.

If exponential smoothing is used to generate a forecast from the above data and α is set to 0.2, then Eq. (6.1) produces a Year 0 forecast of 7.5 percent real growth.

$$\text{Forecast}_0 = \alpha \times \text{Actual}_{-1} + (1 - \alpha) \times \text{Forecast}_{-1}$$
$$= 0.2 \times 9.5\% + 0.8 \times 7.0\% = 7.5\%$$

This compares to a 4.4 percent forecast when α is set to 0.6. The higher forecast arises because with $\alpha = 0.2$, the adjustment to recent results is more gradual, placing more weight on the high growth that occurred in Year -5.

Year	-5	-4	-3	-2	-1	Forecast
Real sales growth	$+17.0\%$	$+6.5\%$	-10.7%	-4.0%	$+9.5\%$	?
Forecast with $\alpha = 0.2$		$+17.0\%$	$+14.9\%$	$+9.8\%$	$+7.0\%$	$+7.5\%$
Forecast with $\alpha = 0.6$		$+17.0\%$	$+10.7\%$	-2.1%	-3.3%	$+4.4\%$

The approaches to revenue forecasting that we have discussed are examples of "naïve forecasting" methods. They extrapolate existing trends without considering underlying economic forces that drive demand and revenue. More elaborate naïve models are available to deal with factors like seasonality or with a growth rate that is expected to decline systematically over time. In some cases, it may be more reliable to forecast revenue levels instead of percentage changes.

Basing forecasts on fundamentals.   Admittedly, our focus on real rather than nominal sales is a slight departure from naïve forecasting, as it does bring the inflation rate into play in a fundamental way. Beyond that, we could consider underlying economic forces that affect the level of sales or the growth rate. These forces might be macroeconomic variables, such as the growth rate of GDP, or demographic factors, such as the population growth rate or the average age of the population. Finally, they could be industry-specific factors, such as the revenue growth rate for the industry, emergence of new competitors, or product innovations.

The table we used to initiate this discussion of forecasting methods includes information on the change in real GDP as a factor that potentially affects the sales growth of the business. Simple statistical analysis of the relationship between sales growth and real GDP shows that the sales growth rate is about five times as volatile as GDP and that the two are highly correlated.[3] More simply, using visual inspection of the relationship, the expected growth of sales generated by multiplying the change in real GDP by 5 is close to the actual growth rate.

Year	−5	−4	−3	−2	−1
Change in real GDP	+3.0%	+1.5%	−1.0%	−1.0%	+2.0%
Expected sales growth (×5)	+15.0%	+7.5%	−5.0%	−5.0%	+10.0%
Real sales growth	+17.0%	+6.5%	−10.7%	−4.0%	+9.5%
Difference	+2.0%	−1.0%	−5.7%	+1.0%	−0.5%

This table shows a strong historical relationship between GDP growth and sales growth. To use this to forecast the growth rate, we must have some confidence that the relationship will persist. This is an issue of judgment. It does not make sense to search arbitrarily for variables that, historically, have been correlated with sales growth. Instead, it is important to think critically about the factors that are likely to influence sales growth and then use historical information to test the strength of the relationship (i.e., "back-testing").

It is not helpful to identify relationships between sales and other factors that are themselves difficult to forecast. In our example, public forecasts of GDP growth are abundant. If the forecast of real GDP growth for next year is 1.5 percent, then our simple multiplier approach would imply real sales growth of 7.5 percent.

Forecasting Revenue of a New Venture

Developing a revenue forecast for a venture with no track record is more difficult, and the result is likely to be less certain. How can we forecast sales for a product that does not yet exist, where the full scope of applications and customers is not yet known, and where actions and reactions of competitors are yet to be seen? Rather than allowing these concerns to overwhelm us, it is important to search for simplicity. We consider two approaches: (1) yardsticks and (2) fundamental analysis.

Yardsticks.   An approach that is useful for some new ventures is to identify reasonable yardstick companies for which public (and possibly nonpublic) data are available. A yardstick is an established firm that is comparable to the venture on some dimensions that are important to forecasting. Actual comparability may not need to be very close. Depending on the kind of information we wish to forecast, it is not necessary that a yardstick firm even be producing the same product. Comparability can be based on factors such as the expected market for the product, distribution channels, adoption rates, uniqueness of the product, or manufacturing technology.

Data availability is one advantage of the yardstick approach. Hundreds of small companies go public every year; in the process, they supply a great deal of information about the period before the company was public. Companies that go public are ideal candidates for assessing revenue growth potential. Revenue estimates based on public companies are by nature optimistic for a new venture. The public firms are success stories and have already survived for longer than the typical new venture.[4] Moreover, issuing shares publicly suggests the firms have grown so rapidly that outside equity financing became important for growth. By studying the experiences of yardstick companies, the entrepreneur can obtain information on the various stages of new venture growth and their changing financing needs.

Sometimes the IPO prospectus of a public company contains enough historical data to measure revenue growth over a number of years during which the company was private. In some cases, there is enough historical information that it is possible to infer the length of the development period before the company was able to market a product successfully and to infer the costs involved in the process.

Financial information from yardstick companies has value beyond forecasting. The prospectus also contains information on how those companies met their financing needs before going public. Each company can serve as a case study, providing insight into the financing choices the entrepreneur faces. In addition, the companies' financial statements can aid in formulating the assumptions the entrepreneur needs for projecting the financial statements of the new venture.

Copies of IPO prospectuses are available from various sources, including the issuing company and the underwriter. The SEC maintains an electronic database of prospectuses and other corporate submissions on its EDGAR website.[5]

How can we use the sales information from yardstick companies to generate a revenue forecast for a new venture? The techniques are fundamentally the same as for an established business using its own historical revenue. For an existing business, its own historical experience is simply one yardstick that is likely to be particularly good. For a new venture, this convenient sales record is not available, but the task is the same—to use historical sales experience (in this case, of other firms) to generate a forecast.

A simple example.   To begin with a simple example, suppose you are considering opening a coffee shop, Morebucks, that would be similar to, and compete with, other retail coffee shops. As a means of estimating revenue, you have collected data from the SEC reports of four publicly held businesses that operate company-owned coffee shops. From the public filings, you have collected information on sales per company-owned shop.

Company	Year	No. of shops owned	Revenue ($ millions)	Revenue/shop ($)
Coffee People, Inc.[a]	1997	31	27.7[a]	893,500
Diedrich Coffee, Inc.	2008	5	4.4	880,000
Peet's Coffee & Tea, Inc.	2008	188	187.7	998,400
Starbucks, Inc.	2008	7,238[b]	6,997.7[b]	966,800

[a]*Coffee People, Inc. revenue adjusted to 2008 dollars using an inflation rate of 3 percent per year.*
[b]*Data are for US company-operated stores. All Peet's retail stores in the United States are company operated.*

Coffee People, Inc. was public until 1997, when it was acquired by Diedrich Coffee. Diedrich, though substantially larger, sells mainly through franchise outlets, so that the number of company-owned shops as of 2008 was quite low. Diedrich, even with its franchise outlets, has revenue materially smaller than Peet's Coffee and dramatically smaller than Starbucks. In spite of these differences, the revenue-per-shop numbers are similar across all four companies. These are averages from a large sample, mainly of established shops.

Based on the revenue-per-shop information for the yardstick companies, it seems unlikely that Morebucks, as a new coffee shop with a single store, could do better than even the smallest of the public companies. It seems reasonable to infer that $900,000 to $1 million would be an optimistic estimate of expected annual revenue for Morebucks when it becomes established as a single coffee shop.

You should be able to improve on this estimate in several ways. For example, if you were to explore franchising opportunities with the companies shown in the table above, you could probably get information on average revenues from franchise outlets and possibly get information about the range of performance for franchise outlets, as well as revenue by age of outlet. You could also contact other companies that operate privately owned coffee shops and might be able to convince the owners to share some information with you. Many industries have trade associations that provide representative financial and operating data on member firms. Finally, you could simply "observe" the stores to see how many customers visit over the course of a day and what they typically order, so that you can make your own estimate.

We do not include any information in the table about the growth rate of store revenue. This is because, except for the first year or two, there is little reason to expect that same-store revenues will grow at a rate very different from the inflation rate, or perhaps inflation plus population growth in the immediate market area. For this kind of retail venture, if you want to grow significantly, you need to add stores. The SEC reports include data on growth in numbers of shops over time.

A more challenging example. While the yardstick approach may seem simple, the reality can be quite different. Suppose you are planning a more innovative venture that will integrate the global positioning system (GPS), street maps, topographical contours, and real-time air traffic information into a navigation system for general aviation. What yardsticks could help you project revenue?

There are competitors that offer similar functionality, but there is no directly comparable firm to use as a yardstick. Table 6.1 provides revenue data for three GPS-related yardstick companies and revenue data that support inferences about the subject venture. The first, Navteq, is a highly successful company that launched in 1987 and went public in 1996. Navteq develops and licenses the street map software used in almost all land-based navigation systems. The IPO prospectus provides information on Navteq's revenues back to 1993. Revenue before 1993 is likely to have been negligible, as the company spent about six years in the development stage. Because Navteq is a supplier of proprietary mapping data, its business is related to the proposed venture, and it may be a licensor to it. While Navteq's growth experience may be relevant to the venture, its value proposition is much different.

Of the three yardstick firms, Garmin is the most comparable to the new venture in terms of offering somewhat similar products for aviation. However, Garmin's revenues come largely from simpler GPS systems than those envisioned, and its products target a number of markets besides general aviation.[6] Garmin provides aviation GPS, but sales growth in that market is erratic. This is partly because general aviation certification requirements tend to change episodically, which leads to surges in demand for navigation upgrades, followed by slow or even negative growth. Unfortunately, because Garmin did not go public until its annual revenues reached more than $200 million, the data in Table 6.1 are not very useful for benchmarking the development phase or

TABLE **6.1** **Aviation navigation yardstick companies**

Navteq Corporation

A leading developer and provider of a navigable database for use in route guidance products in the US and Europe

Founded	1987
IPO	1996
Acquired by Nokia	2007

	1993	1994	1995	1996	1997	1998	1999	2000	2001	2002
Total revenue ($ thousands)	1,855	2,486	3,673	5,268	8,678	26,844	51,088	82,195	110,431	165,849
Percent growth		34.0%	47.7%	43.4%	64.7%	209.3%	90.3%	60.9%	34.4%	50.2%

Garmin Ltd.

A leading provider of navigation communications and information devices using GPS

| Founded | 1989 |
| IPO | 2000 |

	1995	1996	1997	1998	1999	2000	2001	2002	2003	2004
Total revenue ($ thousands)	102,474	135,874	160,280	169,030	232,586	230,183	263,358	350,647	572,989	762,549
Percent growth		32.6%	18.0%	5.5%	37.6%	−1.0%	14.4%	33.1%	63.4%	33.1%
Avionics revenue ($ thousands)			38,255	33,584	63,422	115,558	105,761	114,470	120,552	171,526
Percent growth				−12.2%	88.8%	82.2%	−8.5%	8.2%	5.3%	42.3%

GPS Industries, Inc.

GPS and Wi-Fi multimedia solutions for golf facilities

| Founded | 1999 |
| Reverse merger | 2000 |

	1999	2000	2001	2002	2003	2004	2005	2006	2007	2008
Total revenue ($ thousands)	0	0	0	0	0	2,184	5,818	6,576	7,266	13,490
Percent growth						166.4%	13.0%	10.5%	85.7%	

SOURCES: *SEC filings and other public sources.*

early revenue growth. More information is available in the company's SEC filings, by searching press releases from their prepublic period, and possibly by contacting the company directly.

Finally, GPS Industries is interesting partly because it used a device called a reverse merger to go public in the development stage—well before it was generating any revenue.[7] Thus, we can see the length of the development stage and the early revenue growth of the company. GPS Industries makes navigation systems for golf courses. As such, it serves a smaller and fundamentally different market than general aviation.

Each of the three companies in Table 6.1 has bits of information that could be useful in generating a revenue forecast, and that synthesis of information from all three firms is better than relying on any one alone. It should also be clear, however, that the yardstick approach is not going to provide a reliable basis for forecasting revenues for the prospective venture. In this case, it may be more reliable and more persuasive to base the forecast on a fundamental analysis of the market.

Fundamental analysis.   Fundamental analysis is an alternative to reliance on yardsticks. Approaches to fundamental analysis can vary. For a venture such as a coffee shop that is similar to others already in operation, the fundamental approach might be mainly empirical, such as observing the traffic at other coffee shops, analyzing their product offerings and pricing, and talking to customers. For an innovative undertaking like the navigation venture, the analysis is more conceptual, such as starting with an estimate of the size of the relevant market.

Consider Morebucks. Our yardstick estimate of $900,000 to $1 million of annual revenue depends on numerous factors. Total revenue is a function of days and hours of operation, customers per hour, and average transaction size—all factors driven by product mix, advertising, competition, and location. For example, suppose you have researched two different coffee shops—one in a neighborhood that is active from early morning until late in the evening, including weekends, and one in a location such that it primarily serves employees of nearby businesses that are open standard hours. Your estimates of revenue are as follows:

Comparable type	Days per year	Hours per day	Customers per hour	Revenue per customer	Annual revenue
Business/entertainment center	360	18	25	$6.00	$972,000
Business only	300	12	30	$4.50	$486,000

As the evidence indicates, revenue is sensitive to location. While the business and entertainment location generates double the revenue, it is also likely to incur higher rent and entail longer hours of operation, resulting in higher expenses. By comparing different locations and constructing a complete financial model for each, the entrepreneur can refine the location decision. This choice may also have implications for such factors as product offering and pricing.

For the navigation venture, fundamental analysis is also more challenging than for the coffee shop. Although Garmin offers some products that would compete with the navigation venture, most of its products do not. Moreover, Garmin's early track record is not available. So, rather than relying on empirical observation of similar businesses, we must approach the analysis in more of a top-down fashion. We can start with the question of how big the potential market might be. It turns out that the General Aviation Manufacturers Association (GAMA) compiles very useful data on the aircraft market, which it publishes in annual statistical summaries. Table 6.2, which shows historical information on new shipments and the existing fleet for the US general aviation industry, is constructed using data from the 2008 GAMA summary.

Revenue forecasting for this venture is complicated because there really are two market segments—sales for use in newly manufactured aircraft (which, for convenience, we refer to as original equipment manufacturer [OEM] sales even if the equipment is purchased as an add-on), and retrofit sales for installation in existing aircraft. The GAMA statistics include data for both. Forecasting OEM sales of navigation systems is relatively easy because GAMA provides annual data on new aircraft manufactured in the United States. Forecasting retrofit sales is more difficult because those sales depend on the size of the existing aircraft fleet rather than on annual production of new aircraft. For both submarkets, we first recognize that the entrepreneur's navigation product is designed for smaller and less expensive aircraft. Thus, the feasible customers are owners of single-engine piston aircraft, single-engine turboprops, and small rotocraft.

In Table 6.2, we estimate the potential OEM and retrofit market segments by including all single-engine piston aircraft, 40 percent of turboprops, and 25 percent of rotocraft (where the percentages are reflective of the portion of each group consisting of small aircraft). In panel (c), we estimate the total OEM market from 2010 to 2015 by increasing the 2008 value each year by the average historical growth rate of 3.49 percent. We then estimate unit sales volume by assuming that over five years, the new venture will reach a 20 percent market share on new aircraft.

For retrofit sales, we start with the overall market estimates from panel (b) and assume that minimal sales will occur until the product

TABLE **6.2** Fundamental analysis of general aviation market and revenue forecast

Panel (a)—General aviation new airplane shipments by type mfd. in the US

Year	Total new	Piston single	Multi-engine	Turbo prop	Jet	Rotocraft	Estimate OEM Market[1]	Growth
			Fixed wing					
2004	2,952	1,706	52	194	403	597	1,933	
2005	3,619	2,024	71	240	522	762	2,311	19.56%
2006	4,007	2,208	79	256	604	860	2,525	9.26%
2007	4,384	2,097	77	290	815	1,105	2,489	−1.43%
2008	4,367	1,700	91	333	955	1,288	2,155	−13.42%
							Avg. growth	3.49%

[1]*Est. OEM market = all piston single + 40% of turboprop + 25% of rotocraft*

Panel (b)—US general aviation aircraft fleet by type and year

Year	Total fleet	Piston single	Multi-engine	Turbo prop	Jet	Rotocraft	Total US estimate retrofit market[1]
			Fixed Wing				
2004	190,580	146,613	18,469	8,379	9,298	7,821	151,920
2005	194,006	148,101	19,412	7,942	9,823	8,728	153,460
2006	191,345	145,036	18,708	8,063	10,379	9,159	150,551
2007	192,007	144,580	18,555	8,190	10,997	9,685	150,277
Forecast							
2008	193,120	144,220	18,385	8,300	12,000	10,215	150,094
2009	194,495	144,030	18,225	8,425	13,055	10,760	150,090
2010	196,155	144,015	18,055	8,565	14,220	11,300	150,266
2011	197,935	144,115	17,895	8,710	15,410	11,805	150,550
2012	199,765	144,325	17,725	8,855	16,590	12,270	150,935
2013	201,670	144,645	17,565	9,005	17,740	12,715	151,426
2014	203,595	145,075	17,410	9,155	18,805	13,150	152,025
2015	205,565	145,620	17,245	9,310	19,845	13,545	152,730
Forecast period CAGR:	0.14%	−0.91%	1.65%	7.45%	4.11%	0.25%	

[1]*Est. retrofit market = all piston single + 40% of turboprop + 25% of rotocraft*

Panel (c)—Unit sales and revenue forecast ($ thousands)

Year	Estimated OEM market	Estimated market share	Estimated OEM sales	Estimated retrofit market	Estimated market share	Estimated retrofit sales	Total units	Estimated revenue
2010	2,308	3%	58	150,266	1.0%	1,503	1,560	$3,901
2011	2,389	5%	119	150,550	2.0%	3,011	3,130	$7,826
2012	2,472	10%	247	150,935	3.0%	4,528	4,775	$11,938
2013	2,559	15%	384	151,426	2.0%	3,029	3,412	$8,531
2014	2,648	20%	530	152,025	1.0%	1,520	2,050	$5,125
2015	2,740	20%	548	152,730	1.0%	1,527	2,075	$5,188

SOURCE: *General Aviation Manufacturers Association,* General Aviation Statistical Databook and Industry Outlook *(2008); available at* http://www.gama.aerolfiles/GAMA_Databook_2009.pdf.

has first gained some OEM acceptance. After that, market share will follow a pattern similar to that of other durable goods, where there is increasing demand followed by eventual saturation. The estimated retrofit market share is the percentage of the potential customers who purchase each year. Totaling 2010 through 2015 gives us a cumulative retrofit share of about 10 percent. Taking account of future product improvements, we assume that the retrofit share stabilizes at around 2 percent of the fleet per year. This pattern is similar to that experienced by Garmin and is typical of products based on durable goods technological innovations, such as the DVD displacement of the VCR and digital high-definition TV replacement of analog.

Table 6.2, where we assume a $2,500 selling price per unit, shows how we can estimate overall market size and sales revenue. However, it provides no rationale for the market share estimates. Presumably we have market research data, customer feedback, and comparisons to other firms that have also introduced durable goods into an established market. The entrepreneur needs to be thinking about the combination of product features and price that will turn potential customers into buyers.

Demand and Supply Considerations

Sales estimates for a venture can be generated from either the demand side or the supply side. The demand-side approach assesses consumer willingness and ability to buy the product, assuming that the venture has adequate capacity to supply all that is demanded. The approach begins with an estimate of the venture's market share that depends on such demand-related factors as number of competitors, pricing, location, and intensity of marketing efforts. For unique products, initial market share is easy to estimate—100 percent—but the size of the market is difficult to judge, and the rate of market share erosion due to competitive entry depends on defensibility of the entrepreneur's position. For a more traditional venture, the potential market size may be easy to estimate (published estimates may even exist), but market share is more uncertain and the reactions of competitors may be important.

In contrast, the supply-side approach seeks to determine how fast the venture can grow given managerial, financial, and other resource constraints. Possible supply-side constraints include limits on access to raw materials, financing, and technology; there also may be constraints on the ability to hire and train employees. In other words, even if demand increases rapidly, the venture's growth rate may be limited on the supply side. The Nintendo Wii, introduced at the end of 2006, was in short supply until the middle of 2009. Over the period, Nintendo increased production from 1 million units per month, first to 1.8 million and then to 2.4 million, but still could not keep up with demand during the 2007 and 2008 holiday seasons. Some analysts speculated that Nintendo was hesitant to invest in increased production capacity because of the risk of competition or market saturation.[8]

Combining the supply- and demand-side approaches, the venture's expected rate of growth is whichever is lower. Slow-growth scenarios normally are constrained by the limits of market demand, whereas rapid-growth scenarios normally are constrained by the organization's ability to manage growth. One advantage of the yardstick approach is that it uses the actual experiences of other firms and therefore implicitly considers both supply- and demand-side factors.

Whether a forecast is based on yardsticks, fundamental analysis, or a combination of the two, it is important that projections be realistic and credible. Fundamental analysis is subject to the greatest potential for wild speculation. Consider the sales forecast of a proposed fast food chain, the Bunny Hutch: "Assume each person in America eats one bunny burger one night per week, at $1.00 per bunny burger. That's $10 million per week."[9] Projections made by individuals with established reputations and industry experience or by objective third parties are more likely to be realistic and credible than estimates made by an entrepreneur who is enamored of the idea in the first place. The best substitute for relying on independent expert projections is to base the analysis on solid reasoning and well-supported and well-documented assumptions.

Regardless of the approach, a useful means of validating the forecast is to consider the answers to the following questions:

Demand-side considerations
- What geographic market will the venture serve?
- How many potential customers are in the market?
- How rapidly is the market growing?
- How much, in terms of quantity, is a typical customer likely to purchase during a forecast period?
- How are purchase amounts likely to change in the future?
- What is the expected average price of the product?
- How good is the venture's product compared to those of competitors?
- How aggressively and effectively will the venture promote its product?
- How are competitors likely to react to the venture?

- Who are potential market entrants, and how likely are they to enter?
- In light of the above, what market share is the venture likely to achieve?

Supply-side considerations

- Given its existing resources, how much can the venture produce, market, and distribute?
- How rapidly can the venture add and integrate the resources needed for expansion of output?

6.3 Estimating Uncertainty

For a new or early-stage venture, efforts to forecast revenue and other results may seem to be of little value. After all, the probability that actual performance will turn out to be much like the forecast is quite low. Nonetheless, forecasting is probably more important for a business with an uncertain future than for one that has experienced steady growth and expects to continue.

For a venture with an uncertain future, the forecast of expected performance is simply an anchor for estimating uncertainty. For many purposes, the forecast of uncertainty is far more important. For example, the financial needs of a venture depend heavily on uncertainty. Failure to allow for possibilities such as development delays, lower than expected profitability, or higher than expected demand can result in critical financing errors. In addition, failure to assess the level of uncertainty can result in serious strategic errors.

In this section, we introduce some simple approaches for estimating uncertainty. We use and expand on these approaches in Chapters 7 and 8.

Assessing Risk Using Historical Data

The approaches discussed above for revenue forecasting can also be used to estimate uncertainty. One simple approach is to generate a baseline historical trend for a key variable, such as sales, and then estimate uncertainty as the historical standard deviation of differences between actual and expected values.

To illustrate, the following table shows actual and expected nominal sales growth rates from the earlier forecasting example for an established venture.

Year	−5	−4	−3	−2	−1
Sales growth	+20.0%	+12.5%	−3.7%	0.0%	+11.5%
Expected sales growth	+8.06%	+8.06%	+8.06%	+8.06%	+8.06%
Deviation from expected	+11.94%	+4.44%	−11.76%	−8.06%	+3.44%

We estimate the uncertainty of sales growth as the standard deviation of differences between historical, actual, and expected (average) growth rates. In this example, the standard deviation of differences between actual and expected growth rates is 9.71 percent (calculation not shown). Thus, we might estimate next year's forecast as expected sales growth of 8.06 percent, with a standard deviation of 9.71 percent.

For a venture without a track record, uncertainty is greater and more difficult to estimate. One approach is to base the estimate on the experiences of other companies that are similar in important respects. Another is to envision alternative realistic scenarios for the venture and develop projections consistent with each. An estimate of uncertainty can be developed by applying probability factors to the different scenarios.

Sensitivity Analysis

In sensitivity analysis, we vary the assumptions of the model and observe the impact on our forecast. Used effectively, this can clarify which parameters are most important in the forecast. Once we identify the critical input parameters, we need to develop reasonable descriptions of their uncertainty. History—from the firm's experience or the experiences of comparable firms—may provide guidance, but always with the caveat that the past may not be predictive of the future.

Another shortcoming of sensitivity analysis is that varying individual model inputs over predetermined ranges ignores possible interdependencies among variables. Finally, the forecaster's choice of maximum and minimum values for a given input may be subjective and result in a biased forecast.

Developing Alternative Scenarios

Some of the limitations of sensitivity analysis can be overcome by considering specific scenarios. Scenarios allow several assumptions to be evaluated simultaneously and can incorporate correlations between variables. Prospectuses of public companies and other public data sometimes can help you make a reasonable forecast of a success scenario. The success scenario may be the one that is most important for estimating how much financing the venture will need. For other purposes, it is important to develop a more comprehensive forecast of uncertainty. Value, for example, depends more on expected performance and uncertainty than on performance in a success scenario.

How can scenarios be developed that reasonably represent the uncertainty of a new venture? For simple businesses like retail shops and restaurants, the realistic range of performance may be narrow. For those it may be possible to rely on information from public sources, some of which we describe below. But how can scenarios be developed for a business with tremendous potential and great uncertainty?

Recently, the authors were contacted by a research professor from a leading university medical school. The professor was working on an AIDS treatment that appeared to have considerable promise but was in need of venture funding to carry out the next phase of testing. The professor asked, "How can I figure out how much my idea and the related patents are worth?" The answer depends partly on expected future cash flows and the uncertainty of the cash flows.

Defining a success scenario for the venture's revenue forecast is not difficult. Public information is sufficient to accurately forecast the number of potential candidates for treatment. Using the techniques discussed earlier, we can forecast market share and sales volumes. Data on prevailing prices for proprietary treatments for other life-threatening ailments can be used to forecast revenues. However, it is hard to imagine a project that is subject to more uncertainty. How likely is it that the development efforts will succeed and the patent holder can sell the product for a price unconstrained by government intervention? Moreover, how many other AIDS research projects are under way, and how likely is any of them to succeed either before or after the one under consideration? What effect would innovation by a competitor have on market share and selling price?

One way to come to terms with the uncertainty is to define a small number of realistic scenarios in addition to the success scenario, such as the following:

- Development efforts are successful and the product faces weak competition from other successful development efforts.
- Successful development efforts are offset by strong competing products.
- Development efforts are not successful and the project is abandoned.

The entrepreneur's challenge is to develop alternative scenarios with realistic assumptions about their effects on product price and quantity and realistic assessments of their relative probabilities. Defining a small number of realistic scenarios helps focus the research and reveals the kinds of information that will be most useful.

Incorporating Uncertainty with Simulation

Simulation is the final technique we consider for incorporating uncertainty into a revenue forecast. We first identify the assumptions behind the forecast. Then we assign a probability distribution to each key assumption and estimate correlations among the variables. These assumptions can be developed using historical data, evidence drawn from other companies, and/or fundamental evaluation of the market and potential demand for the product. We already have seen that IPO prospectuses can contain information on how long product development might take, how rapidly demand might grow, and how quickly sales might stabilize. Reports from Wall Street equity analysts often detail pharmaceutical and medical device products in the pipelines of public companies, including descriptions of target customer and estimates of market size, selling prices, and time to market. Agencies like the Food and Drug Administration (FDA) provide voluminous data on drug and device approvals, clinical trial timetables and results, and similar information. All of these sources can be used to approximate probability distributions for key variables and to establish relationships and estimate correlations among variables.

6.4 Building a New Venture Revenue Forecast: An Illustration

Consider a start-up medical device venture called NewCompany. We have done the background research described above. Based on the research, we have generated the assumptions shown in Figure 6.1. We will use these assumptions to forecast NewCompany's expected revenue and then will introduce uncertainty into the forecast. In Chapter 7, we create an integrated financial model based on this revenue forecast but extended to include a complete integrated set of forecasted financial statements.

Because NewCompany is a new venture, we decided to use a forecasting interval of one month. Based on a (hypothetical) study of similar ventures, we assume that the first 18 months will be required for prod-

> FIGURE **6.1**
>
> **NewCompany revenue assumptions**
>
> 1. Development will require 18 months, during which period no sales will be made.
>
> 2. Initial monthly sales of 100 units at a price of $200 beginning in Month 19.
>
> 3. Unit sales will grow 8 percent per month for three years and then remain constant.
>
> 4. The sales price will increase each month at the inflation rate.
>
> 5. Inflation at 6 percent per year (modeled as 0.5 percent per month).

uct development and testing. The venture will initiate sales in Month 19. Based on the study and the characteristics of the market for NewCompany's product, we expect initial monthly sales of 100 units with a selling price of $200 per unit (total revenue in Month 19 of $20,000). Following that, we expect unit volume to grow at 8 percent per month for three years. Beginning in Month 55, after three years of growth, unit sales will remain constant.

In addition to growth in volume, revenue will also increase with price inflation. We estimate that inflationary price increases will average 0.5 percent per month. This raises the question of whether it is better to forecast in real or nominal terms. In our example, by using unit volume (real growth) and inflation-adjusted selling prices, we are forecasting in nominal terms. In Chapter 7, we will add expense and other assumptions, some that are fixed in nominal terms (rent and the salary of the entrepreneur) and others fixed in real terms. Thus, we cannot escape dealing with inflation in some way. We develop the analysis in nominal terms because income taxes are based on nominal income and can be difficult to forecast in real terms.

Figure 6.2 shows the expected pattern of NewCompany's revenue for the 18-month development stage, three years of rapid growth, and two years of inflationary growth. The total forecast window is 78 months, or 6.5 years. As shown at the top of the figure, the revenue forecast in Month 19 is simply the 100-unit quantity times the $200 price, or $20,000 in total revenue. In each of the next 36 months, unit sales increases by 8 percent over the prior month and price increases by 0.5 percent over the prior month. Total revenue in the month is the product of price and quantity. The rapid-growth period ends in Month 55, after which the level of unit sales is constant but price continues to increase

Month	0	1	18	19	24	36	48	54	55	56	60	72	78
Sales (units)				100	147	373	940	1,491	1,610	1,610	1,610	1,610	1,610
Selling price/unit		$0	$0	$200.00	$205.05	$217.70	$231.12	$238.15	$239.34	$240.53	$245.38	$260.51	$268.43
Revenue		$0	$0	$20,000	$30,142	$81,201	$217,257	$355,075	$385,331	$387,258	$395,061	$419,428	$432,169
Unit growth per month					8.00%	8.00%	8.00%	8.00%	8.00%	0.00%	0.00%	0.00%	0.00%
Inflation per month					0.50%	0.50%	0.50%	0.50%	0.50%	0.50%	0.50%	0.50%	0.50%

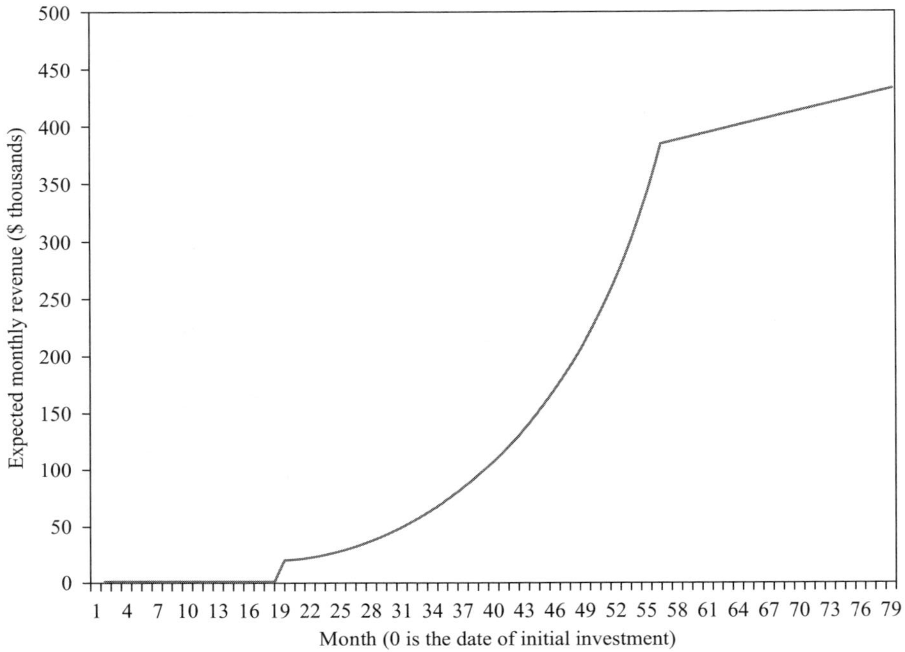

FIGURE **6.2**

NewCompany revenue forecast

The chart shows the revenue trajectory for NewCompany using the "base case" assumptions in Figure 6.1. Month 0 is date of initial investment; sales begin in Month 19 after development is completed. The rapid-growth period for sales runs for three years (until Month 55). From Month 56 to Month 78, unit sales growth is zero and the steady-growth revenue increases are due to the impact of inflation on selling price.

at the inflation rate. At the top of the figure, we have hidden the data for all but a few selected months. The bottom of the figure is a plot of monthly revenue over all 78 months.

The expected rapid-growth rate of unit sales means NewCompany must be prepared to supply about 1,600 units per month by the end of Month 55. To achieve this, the venture must quickly develop the capacity to manufacture, distribute, and support this level of sales.

6.5   Introducing Uncertainty to the Forecast: Continuing the Illustration

The forecast of *expected* sales is only the beginning of the exercise. The forecast in Figure 6.2 is only one possible outcome from a distribution that includes phenomenal success, complete failure, and many possibilities in between. At the outset, it is unclear whether NewCompany's development efforts will be successful, or if they are, when success will be achieved. It is also not clear how successful the product will be, how rapidly demand will grow, and how quickly the growth rate will slow to a steady state. The financing needs of the venture can be sensitive to outcomes that are different from expected. Factors such as development timing, rate of sales growth, and duration of the rapid-growth period are very difficult to predict with confidence but are likely to be among the most important determinants of financing need and value. They depend on unknowable factors such as competition, customer reaction, and future macroeconomic conditions.

Understanding and planning for the range of possible outcomes is essential to good decision making about the venture. Some outcomes that will require more financing than in the expected scenario will still be worth pursuing, whereas others will not. Effective financial planning requires awareness of the margins of performance where it would make sense to continue and those where it would make sense to abandon or modify the strategy. Moreover, the entrepreneur needs to have a financing plan that can accommodate outcomes where financial needs are higher than expected but the venture is still worth pursuing.

How can we incorporate uncertainty into the forecast and use the uncertainty results to assess financing needs and strategic choices? In this section, we examine ways of incorporating uncertainty into a revenue forecast. In Chapter 7, we extend the uncertainty forecast to the full financial model of the venture.

Sensitivity Analysis

In sensitivity analysis, we vary the model's key assumptions across a range of values. Impacts of uncertainty are examined by altering one variable at a time or several at the same time. The NewCompany revenue model, though simple, raises a number of issues. The key assumptions include: (1) initial unit sales, (2) initial selling price, (3) length of the development phase, (4) length of the rapid-growth phase, (5) rate of unit sales growth during the rapid-growth phase, (6) rate of unit sales growth during the mature phase, and (7) rate of price inflation.

To determine reasonable ranges to use in sensitivity analysis, we can use historical data, publicly available forecasts, data from comparable firms, and/or informed judgment. For example, inflation estimates are available from numerous sources and often include not only averages but also medians and the range of forecasts.[10] Suppose, based on such data, it appears that the inflation rate over the venture's forecast period could range from 0.25 percent to 0.75 percent per month around our base estimate of 0.5 percent. The following table shows the impact of varying the rate of inflation on Month 78 revenue, the average monthly revenue (for Months 19 through 78), and the cumulative revenue for the entire forecast period.

Inflation scenario	Annual inflation	Monthly inflation	Revenue		
			Month 78	Average/month	Cumulative
Low	3%	0.25%	$373,000	$212,000	$12,717,000
Expected	6%	0.50%	$432,000	$235,000	$14,074,000
High	9%	0.75%	$500,000	$260,000	$15,588,000

The table holds growth in unit sales and all other assumptions constant at the expected levels. By the end of the forecast period, even these modest changes in the inflation rate can result in ending revenue that is about 15 percent lower or higher than expected revenue. Such differences can be important if, for example, the venture is financed with debt at a fixed nominal interest rate.

For growth in unit sales, another key variable, we might analyze adoption rates for similar products or study the sales histories of comparable firms. Sensitivity analysis can be used to assess the impact of a more modest but realistic growth rate during the rapid-growth phase, say 4 percent per month, or a more successful scenario, such as 12 percent growth per month. The following table shows the impact of varying the growth rate of monthly unit sales while holding the other variables constant at their expected levels.

Growth scenario	Unit growth (monthly)	Units			Cumulative revenue
		Month 78	Average/month	Cumulative	
Low	4%	406	291	17,438	$4,187,000
Expected	8%	1,610	958	57,498	$13,074,000
High	12%	5,936	3,185	191,070	$47,277,000

Assuming that the ranges we selected for inflation and unit sales both reasonably reflect the true uncertainty, revenue is much more sensitive to variation in unit sales growth than to variations in the inflation rate. This is not the only difference worth noting, however. Variations associated with inflation are only important if product price increases are different from inflation rates generally or if some expenses are fixed in nominal terms. In contrast, the variations in revenue due to unit sales growth are real. If the growth rate is too slow, the venture can fail to achieve an ultimate level of sales that is sufficient for viability. Even if it does eventually begin to generate positive free cash flow, if growth is slow then the venture will need more financing to cover its operations until that point is reached. Unit sales growth is also important because it has implications for infrastructure.

In the table above, we assume that the variations in unit sales growth rates are symmetrical around the expected growth rate (8 percent $\pm$ 4 percent). However, the resulting differences in unit sales per month are not symmetrical around the expected level. Under the low-growth assumption, ultimate unit sales is 74 percent below the expected number, whereas under the high-growth assumption, ultimate unit sales is 234 percent above the expected number. Given the asymmetry, even if the venture would not be profitable at the expected growth rate, the upside might be sufficiently attractive that it would make sense to pursue the opportunity. Many VC investments are like this—the expected outcome is not sufficient to justify continuing the venture, but some possible outcomes are so attractive that accepting the high probability of failure is warranted.

Finally, we can allow both inflation and unit sales growth to vary at the same time and observe the impact on a particular variable, such as cumulative revenue. In the table below, differences in each column are due to the inflation rate assumption. Those in each row are due to the unit growth rate assumption.

Cumulative revenue over forecast period

Monthly inflation		Monthly growth in unit sales		
		Low (4%)	Expected (8%)	High (12%)
Low	0.25%	$3,857,000	$12,614,000	$42,338,000
Expected	0.50%	$4,229,000	$13,960,000	$47,104,000
High	0.75%	$4,642,000	$15,462,000	$52,432,000

Sensitivity analysis is simple to implement and can provide valuable information, but it has some shortcomings. First, there is little guidance as to what constitutes an appropriate range for any given variable. Second, it is difficult to test sensitivity to two or more variables at once. Third, even in this simple example, we have not considered the effects of changing the development period, the rapid-growth period, or growth during the harvest period. Finally, variables are often correlated, and sensitivity analysis does not readily accommodate the correlations. For example, real increases in selling prices usually reduce unit sales.

Scenario Analysis

Scenario analysis is one way to address the limitations of sensitivity analysis. With scenario analysis, the analyst develops scenarios that incorporate reasonable values for the important variables and recognize the relationships that may exist among them. For NewCompany, consider the following two scenarios:

- *Scenario 1.* Product development proceeds more quickly than expected. The venture's sales start at 100 units in Month 12 rather than Month 19. The new product does very well in the market and NewCompany is able to patent important aspects of the technology. This keeps competitors at bay, and allows NewCompany to increase the initial selling price to $220. Unit sales grow at 11 percent each month for two years and then 9 percent monthly for one year. For the balance of the forecast period, Month 49 to Month 78, monthly unit sales are assumed constant so that revenue grows at the 0.5 percent inflation rate.

- *Scenario 2.* Product development hits numerous roadblocks and a competitor beats NewCompany to the market. When NewCompany finally begins to sell (in Month 24), the market only supports a $180 price. Unit sales start at 100 and grow at 4 percent each month for two years and then 2 percent for one year before falling to zero. Expected inflation is 0.5 percent per month.

The following table shows revenue and unit sales numbers for both scenarios:

	Revenue			Unit sales		
	Month 78	Monthly average	Cumulative	Month 78	Monthly average	Cumulative
Scenario 1	$1,231,301	$693,069	$41,584,139	4,027	2,501	150,062
Scenario 2	$75,639	$47,189	$2,831,359	321	243	13,379

These two scenarios yield widely disparate forecasts, which is not surprising given their very different assumptions. They also provide a very rough picture of the uncertainty about NewCompany's future. Although scenario analysis overcomes some of the limitations of sensitivity analysis, it is not without its own shortcomings. Practical considerations limit the number of scenarios we can develop and analyze. Moreover, for scenario analysis to be valuable, we need accompanying assumptions about the probability of each scenario. Moreover, no matter how carefully we construct each scenario, the subsequent reality will inevitably differ considerably.

S Simulation

Simulation overcomes some of the difficulties of sensitivity and scenario analysis. Simulation requires that uncertainty be described in terms of probabilities or statistical distributions. When the simulation model is run, a random draw is made from each distribution and the results are used to construct a "trial." Simulation can be used to quickly generate thousands of trials based on the underlying uncertainty assumptions. In essence, each trial is a scenario, and because they are generated from statistical distributions, each trial is equally likely to occur. By analyzing the trials data, we can make inferences about the probabilities of good or bad outcomes and can evaluate choices related to the exercise of real and financial options.

In the NewCompany example, the most important risk factors are development timing, the length of the rapid-growth period, and the rate of growth during the rapid-growth period. Figure 6.3 shows how we have modified the static NewCompany assumptions to reflect uncertainty and accommodate simulation.

The first assumption in Figure 6.3 captures the uncertainty related to development timing and allows for the possibility that NewCompany never succeeds in creating a valuable product. The second assumption

---

FIGURE **6.3**

NewCompany revenue simulation assumptions

1. The earliest that successful development can occur is Month 8. After Month 8, the probability of development success is exponentially distributed with a mean of 18 months (26 months including the first 8). However, if development is not completed within 48 months, then it is clear that successful development of a valuable product is no longer feasible.

2. If development is successful, the rapid-growth stage is expected to end around Month 60, after which it is expected that unit sales growth will fall to zero. The uncertainty about when the rapid-growth stage will end is normally distributed with a mean of 60 and standard deviation of three months.

3. Sales begin the month after development is successful. The initial sales level is expected to be 100 units.

4. The initial selling price is subject to uncertainty depending on the quality of the development result and competitive factors. This uncertainty is normally distributed with a mean of $200 and a standard deviation of $10. After the first month of sales, the selling price increases at the rate of inflation each month.

5. During the rapid-growth period, monthly unit sales growth is normally distributed with a mean of 8 percent and a standard deviation of 1.5 percent.

6. Inflation is forecast to be 0.50 percent per month.

---

captures the uncertainty related to the length of the rapid-growth period. Assumptions 3 and 4 describe the starting unit sales and selling price in the month after development is successful. Assumption 5 describes the uncertainty of demand growth.

There are many ways to build timing uncertainty into a simulation model. We could assign a specific probability to each month, so that the probabilities (including the probability of failure) sum to 100 percent; then, for each trial, make one draw from the distribution to determine whether and in which month development is successful. For example, suppose that the timing for an event of interest (completion of development, FDA approval, patent approval, etc.) could occur in any of three months (Month 1, 2, or 3) and that the respective probabilities are 20, 40, and 30 percent. Because these sum to 90 percent, there is a 10 percent chance of failure. Figure 6.4 is a screen shot that illustrates use of a discrete probability distribution in *Venture*.SIM to simulate a success month.

In the NewCompany example, we model a more complex timing structure. Because we expect that development will take at least eight months

FIGURE **6.4**

Discrete probability approach to simulating development timing
The figure shows the simulation structure and a randomly generated outcome.

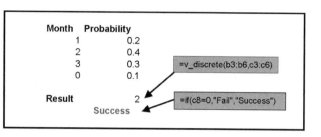

and that the probability of success will rise quickly after the eighth month and then taper off slowly, we use the exponential distribution to model development success. We also assume that if success is not achieved by Month 48, then it is not worth continuing to pursue the venture. Failure may occur because a competitor beats us to the market or because of failure of our R&D efforts to achieve a breakthrough. Based on Assumptions 1 and 2 in Figure 6.3, the cumulative probability of successful development is about 50 percent by Month 19 and about 65 percent by Month 26 (the expected mean of development timing). By Month 48, the success probability reaches about 90 percent, leaving a residual probability of failure of about 10 percent. The *Venture*.SIM cell formula to generate the development month outcome for each trial is as follows:

$$= INT(V\_Exp(18) + 8)$$

where 8 is the number of months before development success is possible and 18 is the expected development month once development is possible. The function V_Exp(μ) is the *Venture*.SIM macro for drawing from an exponential distribution with a mean of μ, and INT is an Excel function that truncates the simulation result to an integer. For example, trial outcomes of 20.1 and 20.9 both return a value of 20 months. Separately, we test to see whether the simulated development month is less than 49; if not, we replace the simulated development month with a value that is higher than the last month in the simulation model. Because the New-Company model spans 78 months, we use Month 79 to signal development failure. Figure 6.5 shows the *Venture*.SIM result summary and a histogram of the trial success months. The mean development success month is 26.6 and the median development month is 20.[11] In 989 trials, approximately 10 percent of the total, development fails.

At this point, we assume that the venture has enough cash to fund the development effort for as long as needed. Later, we will change that as-

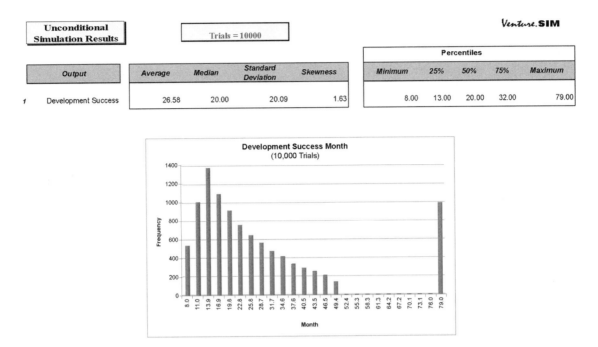

FIGURE **6.5**

NewCompany simulated distribution of development timing
The figure shows the simulated distribution of development timing based on 10,000 trials of the revenue model. The simulation is based on an exponential distribution with a mean of 18 months after the initial 8, during which development success is assumed not to be feasible. The model also reflects the assumption that development must be completed within 48 months or the venture fails.

sumption to allow for the possibility that the entrepreneur would need to raise additional capital to continue the venture.

Figure 6.6 shows plots of randomly generated revenue forecasts from five simulated trials. The figure illustrates a wide range of possible paths for NewCompany. In Trial 3, for example, development is early (Month 11) and the growth rate is very high, resulting in $2.1 million of revenue in Month 78. Trial 5 has the earliest possible start of revenue (Month 9), but the growth rate is slower than in Trial 3 and Month 78 revenue is just below $1 million. In Trial 2, development success comes late, and both the duration and rate of revenue growth are low. This results in Month 78 revenue of only about $170,000. Trial 1 shows development failure and zero revenue, an outcome that occurs about 10 percent of the time. It is apparent from the figure that, based on our starting assumptions and the uncertainty, revenue can vary widely.[12]

The results shown in Figure 6.6 represent only five of an infinite number of paths NewCompany could take based upon our starting variables

FIGURE **6.6**

NewCompany revenue forecast—sample trial results
The figure shows five iterations of the NewCompany revenue forecasting model. The model incorporates uncertainty with simulation, using the assumptions outlined in Figure 6.3. Each trial shows when/if development is successful and how long the rapid-growth period lasts. Month 0 is date of initial investment.

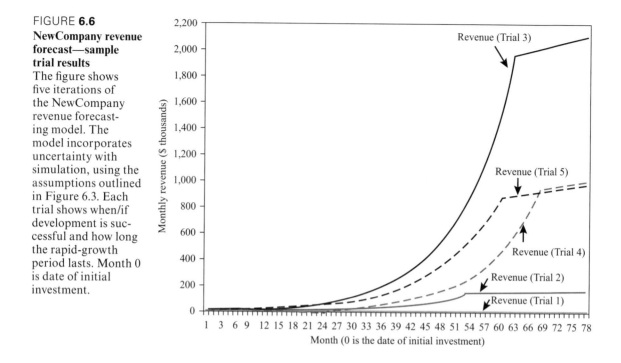

and assumptions about probabilities and statistical distributions. The simulation results incorporate many more possibilities than either sensitivity or scenario analysis and parallel more closely what a new venture's path might look like. They also dramatically reinforce the reality that the future of any new venture is highly uncertain.

6.6 Calibrating the Development Timing Assumption: An Example

When product development efforts are expensive and timing of development success is uncertain, the financial needs of a venture depend critically on development timing. A venture that runs out of cash before reaching a significant milestone in the development process (completion of a prototype, completion of preliminary testing, etc.) is likely to face great difficulty lining up additional financing.[13] The difficulty arises because failure to achieve the milestone may suggest to investors that the entrepreneur's projections are overly optimistic in other ways as well.

While there is no general rule as to how long development of a new product takes, it is possible to estimate expected time and timing uncertainty. In some cases, engineering studies or regulatory reports are helpful, as are experiences of comparable ventures. Innovation in new drugs is an example of products with protracted, variable, and unpredictable development horizons, due, in part, to technological and regulatory hurdles. New drugs make a good example because the FDA keeps records of all new drug applications. Since passage of the 1992 Prescription Drug User Fee Act, development times for new drugs (the combined time for clinical trials and regulatory approval) have fallen significantly. Figure 6.7 shows that from 1988/89 to 2000/01, the average development time fell from 122 to 82 months.

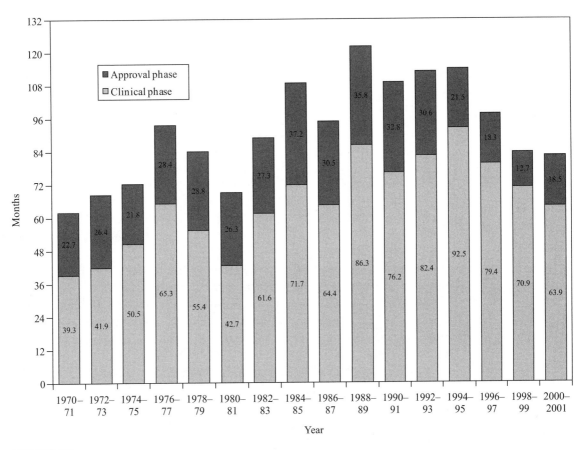

FIGURE **6.7**

New drug approval times: 1970–2001

The chart shows the average time in months it took for new drugs to be approved during the period 1970–2001. Total approval time is the combination of the clinical and FDA approval phases and is represented by the total height of each bar. The clinical and approval phase times are shown separately for each year and represented by the shaded segments of each bar.

SOURCE: Janice M. Reichert, "Trends in Development and Approval Times for New Therapeutics in the United States," *Nature Reviews: Drug Discovery* 2 (September 2003).

FIGURE **6.8**

New drug approval times in 2000
The FDA provides information for all new drug applications approved in the year 2000. Each horizontal bar represents the experience for a single, approved application. Individual approval times range from less than six months to almost five years.

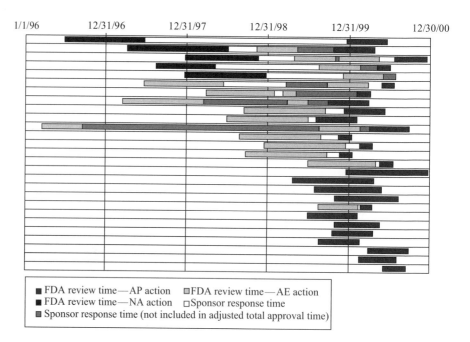

This trend is valuable information for anyone who is attempting to forecast financial information for a new pharmaceutical venture. However, the figure reveals nothing about the uncertainty of the development process, which is critical for forecasting cash flow and assessing cash needs.

Figure 6.8 provides information regarding a sample of all new drug applications approved in the year 2000. The data illustrate regulatory histories and cycles for individual products approved in 2000. Each horizontal bar represents the experience for a single approved application. As shown, two of the new drugs approved in 2000 were first submitted in 1996, a four-year process; six were submitted in 1997, six in 1998, ten in 1999, and three were submitted and approved in 2000. The figure shows the breakdown of development timing, sometimes including lengthy sponsor response times. Combining the information in Figures 6.7 and 6.8 allows us to better understand the approval process and helps us estimate the expected development time and the variation, or standard deviation, of that estimate.

One problem with the data in Figures 6.7 and 6.8 is that all of the drugs in the charts ultimately were approved. Many others were not. Sampling only successful ventures to estimate timing imparts a selection bias to the estimate. Fortunately, the FDA website (fda.gov) has data on rejected drug applications. With these additional data, we could estimate the probability that our new venture's drug makes it through the development process successfully.

6.7 Summary

Selling a product or service is at the core of any company's business model. Although estimating sales is especially challenging for a new venture, financial forecasting disciplines the way an entrepreneur thinks about the venture. Not only can forecasting be used to help determine cash needs and the timing of those needs, but it can also affect the value of the venture. A forecast can be an important fundraising tool if it convinces prospective investors of the merits of the project and provides some specific performance benchmarks.

The starting point for any financial forecast is an estimate of revenue. The venture's strategy for getting potential customers to purchase its goods or services is of critical importance for any business plan. If the forecast is for an existing business, we can use historical data as the basis for projections. There are numerous statistical techniques available to improve forecast accuracy using historical data. Selection trade-offs include data availability, model complexity, and uncertainty.

For a new venture, yardsticks and fundamental analysis can help overcome the lack of a historical track record. Yardsticks are comparable firms—either public or private—that have a product and strategy reasonably close to that of the venture. Data on yardsticks can come from IPO prospectuses, 10-K filings and annual reports, and other public sources.

Even if good yardsticks are available, it is useful to develop a sales forecast based on fundamental analysis. With fundamental analysis, the entrepreneur collects data on customer demographics, macroeconomic factors, substitute products, and so on and then uses the data to develop a set of assumptions for forecasting revenue. The forecast model is most useful if it reflects a solid understanding of the product and the industry and if the forecast links expectations for performance in the product market to implications for financial performance. The assumptions are most useful if they are defensible and backed by research and objective data.

It is important that any financial forecast reflect the uncertainty implicit in the key assumptions. Uncertainty can be analyzed using sensitivity analysis, scenarios, and simulation. With sensitivity analysis, we vary key assumptions over some reasonable range to see how revenue or some other financial metric is impacted. Sensitivity analysis is limited, as we can only vary one or two variables at a time and correlations between variables are not recognized. Scenario analysis involves developing several stories about how the venture might progress in the future and then matching assumptions to each story. Using scenarios overcomes the limitations of sensitivity analysis, but we are still limited by the number of scenarios that can reasonably be evaluated and the need to assign probabilities to each outcome. With simulation, an infinite number of possible paths can be generated and analyzed. This method allows for the most realistic assessment of the venture's future, but reliable results are dependent on the validity of the assumptions.

The new venture revenue forecast forms the basis for forecasting the rest of the financial statements, with an ultimate goal of estimating the venture's cash flows.

Review Questions

1. Why is forecasting revenue the logical starting point for preparing a new venture's financial statements?

2. What factors are important in establishing the appropriate forecast period and forecasting interval?

3. How can naïve forecasting methods be used to develop a revenue forecast for an existing business where management believes that recent historical years are more predictive of future performance?

4. What are some of the considerations when deciding whether to forecast in real or nominal terms?

5. Describe two approaches to forecasting revenue for a new venture. Describe the strengths and weaknesses of each.

6. What techniques are available to introduce uncertainty into a revenue forecast? Describe the pros and cons of each approach.

7. Why is simulation particularly suited to forecasting revenue of new ventures?

8. Why is uncertainty about development critical to many new ventures?

9. How might you use publicly available information to calibrate an assumption about the development time needed to build a new bed and breakfast, starting from when you first get the idea that the market is ripe for such a project?

10. What can you learn from a prospectus? Are the data in an IPO prospectus relevant to a new venture just getting off the ground?

NOTES

1. There is an important distinction between a forecast of revenue and a forecast of profit. Even though public forecasts of inflation may be helpful for refining the revenue forecast, profit depends on a mix of factors, some of which depend on inflation and some of which are fixed in nominal terms (e.g., depreciation expense). Whether it is better to forecast profits in real or nominal terms depends on how these factors balance. Copeland, Koller, and Murrin (1996) argue that nominal forecasts are preferred for valuation purposes. This is because most managers think in terms of nominal measures and because interest rates generally are quoted in nominal rather than in real terms. Also, historical financial statements are stated in nominal terms.

2. Using a standard statistical package, such as that available in Excel, sales levels or growth rates in one period can be regressed on several lagged values of sales levels or growth rates (the prior year, two years prior, etc.). The coefficients from the regression can then be used in conjunction with historical sales data to project future sales or sales growth.

3. Using Excel to regress sales growth on the change in GDP, the following linear model results:

Expected Growth in Sales = 3.34% + 5.24 × (% Change in GDP) $r^2 = 0.95$

4. In 1998, the median age of venture-backed IPO companies was 4.5 years. By 2008, the number was 9.6 years (Doll and Heesen 2009). By contrast, Shane (2008), p. 98, estimates only 45 percent of new firms founded in 1992 survived five years.

5. The EDGAR website can be accessed through http://sec.gov. Prospectuses of new issues normally are posted to the site within a few days of filing.

6. "General aviation" refers to all flights other than scheduled airline and military flights and includes both private and commercial aircraft (http://en.wikipedia.org/wiki/General_aviation).

7. In a reverse merger, a failed public company acquires the new venture. After the acquisition, the acquirer usually changes its name to that of the new venture and discontinues the former business. In reality, the acquirer is just a shell. The reverse merger enables the acquired venture to go public without the cost of an IPO.

8. Other analysts suggested the more strategic motive of purposely withholding inventory from the market to create shortages and generate hype and publicity for the gaming console. Nintendo was able to avoid a price reduction on the Wii until September of 2009, three full years after its release.

9. Quoted in Silver (1994), p. 20.

10. For example, in January 2010 WSJ.com reported individual inflation (CPI) forecasts from 56 economists along with an average value for the group. The Philadelphia Federal Reserve Bank conducts a quarterly survey of professional forecasters and provides mean and median economic estimates but no detail on individual forecasts (http://www.phil.frb .org/research-and-data/real-time-center/survey-of-professional-forecasters).

11. The mean is higher than 26 months (8 plus 18) because in the trials in which the venture fails, we assign a value of 79, which is included in the calculation of the mean.

12. For comparison, the average (median) Month 78 revenue for one 10,000-trial simulation was $740,000 ($430,000).

13. *Startup* (Kaplan 1995) is an insightful review of the financial difficulties encountered by a high-technology venture in the computer industry as it struggled to raise enough cash to carry it from one milestone to the next.

References and Additional Reading

Copeland, T., T. Koller, and J. Murrin. 1996. *Valuation.* 2nd ed. New York: John Wiley & Sons.

Doll, D., and M. Heesen. 2009. "NVCA 4-Pillar Plan to Restore Liquidity in the U.S. Venture Capital Industry." Presentation to National Venture Capital Association Annual Meeting. Available at http://www.slideshare .net/NVCA/nvca-4pillar-plan-to-restore-liquidity-in-the-us-venture -capital-industry-1360905.

Drucker, P. F. 1993. *Innovation and Entrepreneurship.* New York: Collins.

Kaplan, J. 1995. *Startup: A Silicon Valley Adventure.* New York: Penguin.

Shane, S. A. 2008. *The Illusions of Entrepreneurship.* New Haven, CT: Yale University Press.

Silver, D. A. 1994. *The Venture Capital Sourcebook.* Chicago: Probus.

Methods of Financial Forecasting: Integrated Financial Modeling

Prediction is very difficult, especially if it's about the future.

Niels Bohr, Nobel Laureate in Physics

Once a revenue forecast is completed, it can be used as a baseline for developing pro forma financial statements. Ultimately, we are concerned with forecasting cash flows from operations. Operating cash flow is a key factor in determining a venture's financing needs. Cash flow available to investors is central to valuation. To project cash flows, we first forecast the income statement and balance sheet and then use those statements (and period-to-period changes in the statements) to develop the pro forma statement of cash flows.

For a new venture, we confront the same issue here as we did in Chapter 6: that of estimating income statement and balance sheet relationships for a company that has no operating history. As in Chapter 6, it is useful to rely on data from comparable public and/or private companies. However, the yardsticks and dimensions of comparability that are most useful for projecting income statement and balance sheet relationships are not necessarily those that are useful for projecting revenue.

Our main objective in this chapter is to illustrate how to build and integrate the financial statements into a model that can be used in cash needs assessment and valuation. There are two aspects to this: the first is developing the key assumptions that drive the financial model; the second is the process of building and integrating the financial statements, including the interactions among them. Mastering the chapter should enable you to build your own integrated model.

If the financial statements in a model are properly integrated, the full impact of changing any assumption will be reflected automatically and consistently in all of the statements and all of the forecast periods. This makes it easier to perform sensitivity analysis and is necessary for incorporating uncertainty with simulation.

We begin with an overview of the three main financial statements and how they are linked.[1] With this as background, we develop the notion of statement integration, beginning with an overview of the cash conversion process. Next, we provide an example of how working capital policy choices act in an integrated fashion to affect cash needs. We then describe several standard sources of information and demonstrate their use for developing forecast assumptions. Finally, we work through the construction of two integrated financial models, the first for Morebucks and the second for NewCompany—both examples from Chapter 6.

7.1   An Overview of Financial Statements

Pro forma financial statements used for business forecasting can be simple, but they also require enough detail to capture the important activities of the enterprise. They are focused on the assumptions and financial statement items most important to the venture. For example, the model for a new software company might incorporate development time and cost of bringing a viable product to market. For a retailer, cost of goods sold and inventory may be the most important factors to model carefully.

The first step in building an integrated model is to identify the critical assumptions that will drive the pro forma financial statements. To a degree, this list determines the accounts and line items that need to be incorporated into the model. In an integrated model, changes to any assumption will immediately update all three financial statements—the income statement, balance sheet, and cash flow statement—through the formulas and links in the spreadsheet.

The income statement, also called a profit and loss (P&L) statement or statement of operations, describes the revenues and expenses over a period of time, such as a quarter or a fiscal year. It answers the question of whether the business is profitable. The balance sheet, also called the statement of financial position, presents a picture at a point in time of what the firm owns (its assets), how much it owes (its liabilities), and what is left for shareholders (equity, owner's equity, or net worth). Once we have created pro forma income statements and balance sheets, the cash flow statement is a simple derivation.

For the income statement, a general form sufficient for many purposes is shown in Table 7.1. The line items included in the pro forma in-

TABLE **7.1**   **Income statement**
(year ended 12/31/20XX)

Revenue
− Cost of goods sold (COGS)
Gross profit
− Operating expenses
Earnings before interest and taxes (EBIT)
+ Interest income − Interest expense
Earnings before tax (EBT)
− Income tax expense
Net income (NI)

NOTE: *COGS and operating expenses include depreciation and amortization.*

come statement depend on the type of business. In this simplified statement, COGS includes the costs of raw materials and expenses associated with manufacturing the product. A retailer or wholesaler would show COGS as the acquisition cost of the products they resell. For a service company, COGS is the labor and machinery cost associated with providing the service.

Operating expenses are other expenses related to the productive activities of the venture. These can include selling, general, and administrative (SG&A) expenses, R&D, overhead expenses, lease expenses, and similar items. Sometimes it is useful to include more detail on specific operating expenses that are central to success, especially if their inclusion makes forecasting easier, more reliable, and more convincing.

To calculate operating profit, we also deduct noncash expenses such as depreciation and amortization. Depreciation and amortization expenses depend on asset investment decisions that were made in earlier periods and are reflected in the balance sheet. Operating profit (EBIT) is a core measure of performance, as it is calculated before interest and tax expenses, two items that are usually outside the control of operating managers. For a business that is in steady state, it is also a measure of cash flow available to all investors and for taxes.

The next deduction, interest expense, is a result of the financing decision that is reflected in the balance sheet. Sometimes, in developing the pro forma forecast, it is convenient to build the model so that surplus cash is assumed to be retained in the venture. If so, it is appropriate to assume that the surplus cash is invested to earn a risk-free rate of interest. We illustrate this approach later in the chapter. Income tax expense is determined by the profitability of the venture and prevailing tax rules.

TABLE **7.2** **Balance sheet** (at 12/31/20XX)

Assets	Liabilities and equity
Current assets	Current liabilities
Cash	Accounts payable (A/P)
Accounts receivable (A/R)	Wages payable
Inventory	Notes payable
Total current assets	Total current liabilities
	Long-term debt
Fixed assets (PP&E)	Total liabilities
Gross fixed assets	Equity
Less: accumulated depreciation	Common stock
Net fixed assets	Retained earnings
Intangible assets	Total equity
Total assets	Total liabilities and equity

When developing the pro forma income statement, it is important to consider the impacts of fixed and variable costs. The notion that certain expenses will not change with increases or decreases in revenue introduces the concept of operating leverage. Operating leverage describes the relationship between percentage revenue growth and percentage profitability growth. Firms with a larger proportion of fixed expenses have higher operating leverage and will see profits increase (decrease) faster as revenue goes up (down).

However, overly simplistic classification of expenses as either fixed or variable can yield incorrect results. It is a good idea to study actual expense levels of businesses of different sizes. You may find that your intuition about fixed and variable expenses is not supported by the evidence. Few expenses are truly fixed, and others may vary more than proportionately with revenue. Consequently, assuming that variable expenses will change in proportion to revenue and that fixed expenses will not change at all can overstate the profit potential associated with revenue growth.

The balance sheet depicts the venture's financial position at a point in time. The left side reports what the company owns—its assets. The right side reflects how the ownership is financed—liabilities and equity. In the actual modeling, it will be more convenient for us to stack the balance sheet information vertically—assets first, then liabilities, then equity. This will enable us to keep all of the accounting numbers for a given period in a single spreadsheet column.

A general form of a balance sheet sufficient for many purposes is shown in Table 7.2. Asset accounts are presented in order of declining liquidity, starting with cash. Accounts receivable and inventory are both current assets and components of working capital. The fixed asset account represents the property, plant, and equipment (PP&E) of the venture and is the basis for computing depreciation expense on the income statement. For a capital-intensive manufacturing business, PP&E might be the largest balance sheet line item.

Liabilities, or what the firm owes, are shown in increasing order of maturity. Current liabilities, such as accounts payable and wages payable, are considered working capital items and are tied to the venture's day-to-day operations. Other liabilities are incurred by raising debt capital (notes payable, long-term debt). A key distinction is that financing liabilities usually carry interest payments while working capital liabilities do not. This amount of debt capital drives the interest expense calculation in the income statement.

Equity represents the shareholders' position and is made up of two main components. The first component, common stock, is the cumulative amount investors paid for the venture's stock when it was sold by the company. The second component is retained earnings; the retained earnings balance is the accumulated profit (or loss) of the venture from its inception to the date of the balance sheet, less any dividends the firm has paid. The retained earnings account does not indicate money available to shareholders. Over any given period, retained earnings will be increased by the net income for the period and reduced by dividends to shareholders paid during the period.

The result of the income statement is net income, or the "bottom line." But net income is not cash flow. To determine financing needs and as a basis for valuation, we need to calculate cash flow. The cash flow statement connects the income statement and balance sheet changes but also takes account of noncash expenses, new investments, and new financing transactions. A general format for the cash flow statement is shown in Table 7.3.

The cash flow statement is organized into three categories: operating cash flows, investing cash flows, and financing cash flows. The entry "(Increase) decrease" denotes whether the change in the balance sheet account represents a negative or positive cash flow. Increases in assets are negative cash flows (outflows), while decreases are positive cash flows (inflows). For liabilities and equity, increases are positive cash flows, while decreases are negative. For example, an increase in inventory would be a use of cash, while an increase in notes payable would be a source of cash.

The total of operating, investing, and financing cash flow is net cash flow for the period. In forecasting, when net cash flow is added to the beginning cash balance, it tells us how much cash the firm is expected to have on hand at period end. We use the "indirect" method to prepare the

TABLE **7.3**   **Cash flow statement**
(year ended 12/31/20XX)

Net income
Plus: depreciation and amortization
(Increase) decrease in accounts receivable
(Increase) decrease in inventory
Increase (decrease) in accounts/wages payable
Operating cash flow
Less: change in gross fixed assets
Investing cash flow
Increase (decrease) in notes payable
Increase (decrease) in long-term debt
Increase (decrease) in common stock
Less: dividends paid
Financing cash flow
Net cash flow
Plus: beginning cash
Ending cash

pro forma cash flow statement. This approach is mechanically straight-forward and requires only the income statement and the beginning and ending balance sheets for the period.

7.2   The Cash Conversion Cycle

Financial statements reflect the results of the venture's day-to-day operations, that is, designing, producing, selling, and delivering a product or service. The business enterprise can be thought of as part of a machine that converts cash today into cash in the future. The business assets and financial capital, as well as the services of employees, are acquired with cash and are merely inputs to the process of creating the goods or services that are sold and turned back into future cash. The entrepreneur and investors hope the venture's technology is good at converting today's cash into future cash, so that a small investment of cash today can yield a large cash payoff in the future.[2]

Across industries and firms, the processes of producing future cash display a number of features in common, which are represented diagrammatically in Figure 7.1. You can think of the venture as starting with a pool of cash, shown in the figure as "Beginning cash." Initially, because there is no revenue, the cash comes entirely from investors (the entrepreneur, VCs, and others) who either loan money to the venture or

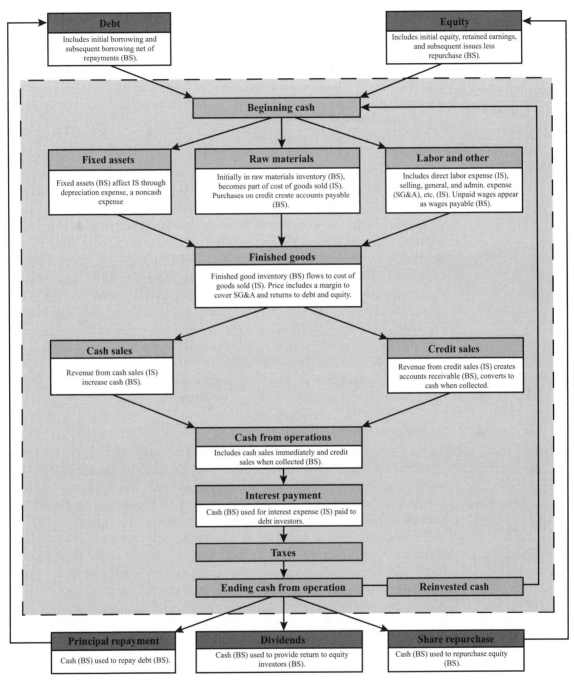

FIGURE **7.1**

The cash conversion cycle of the firm

The diagram traces the flow of cash through the venture's operations and describes the relationships between cash flow and income statement and balance sheet accounts. The box demarcated by the dashed line represents flows within the firm. Flows that cross the dashed line are between the firm and the capital markets and do not affect the income statement directly. BS = balance sheet; IS = income statement.

invest in equity. Beginning cash is converted to ending cash through the productive activities of the venture.

Figure 7.1 distinguishes those cash flows directly related to the firm's operating activities from those between the firm and its capital providers, that is, investors in the firm's debt or equity. Flows related to profit generation, shown inside the lightly shaded box, include explanatory notes that illustrate the relationships between cash flows and the income statement and balance sheet.

As the venture commences operations, it acquires resources and incurs manufacturing and operating expenses. As shown in Figure 7.1, some of these transactions impact the balance sheet, some the income statement, and some both. For example, if Morebucks purchased a new pastry oven, the cost of the oven would go onto the balance sheet as a fixed asset, but it would also impact the income statement in the form of operating expense (electricity) and depreciation expense. Depreciation expense is not a cash expense, but it does reduce taxable income and therefore reduces the firm's tax expense, which is a cash expense. This increases net income, which impacts the balance sheet when added to retained earnings. Interactions such as these between the balance sheet and the income statement are the reason we need to deal with financial forecasting in an integrated fashion.

Some transactions involve immediate payment, which reduces the cash balance. Others, for example the purchase of raw materials on 30-day credit terms, have no immediate impact on cash but result in an increase in a current liability (accounts payable). Raw materials, fixed assets, and operating expenses combine to produce an inventory of finished goods. Sales of finished goods may be carried out on a cash basis, on credit, or by some combination of the two. Credit sales generate accounts receivable, which are converted to cash over time through the venture's collection activities.

The distinctions between cash and credit sales and between buying from suppliers for cash or on credit are important factors in the difference between net income and operating cash flow. The receivables generated by credit sales and the accounts payable generated by credit purchases cause differences between profit and cash flow. This is why the cash flow statement is so valuable. It is important to distinguish between accounting income and cash flow and to recognize that a highly profitable and rapidly growing venture may have very negative cash flow for a long time. Although Figure 7.1 is static, the real process is continuous and circular, with most of the activities in the diagram occurring simultaneously.

For now, we divide financing choices broadly into equity and debt.

Cash can be distributed to equity investors (in the form of dividends or a share repurchase) and to creditors (in the form of interest payments and principal repayments). The key difference is that payments to creditors are contractual obligations of the firm, and thus failure to make debt payments has legal consequences. In contrast, distributions to stockholders are discretionary. Equity is also a "residual" claim, which means creditors must receive the interest and principal they are owed before any distribution to shareholders. Any cash not distributed to investors is retained by the venture and is available for reinvestment.

7.3 Working Capital, Growth, and Financial Needs

Among other things, Figure 7.1 graphically illustrates the impact of working capital on the income statement, balance sheet, and operating cash flow. The most important components of working capital usually are inventory, accounts receivable, accounts payable, and cash. Normally, because of the cash flow cycle, a relationship exists between sales and the levels of the various working capital accounts. A business that sells from inventory must have enough on hand to fill the orders as they arrive. Because timing of demand is not perfectly predictable and there is often an inventory "pipeline," the business normally will carry enough finished goods inventory to supply expected demand for several days, weeks, or even months.

A manufacturer also may need to carry an inventory of raw materials. Purchases of inventory, either finished goods for resale or raw materials, are often made on credit in the form of accounts payable. Purchasing on credit reduces the need for cash, since payment is deferred. Conversely, if the business sells on credit, the balance of accounts receivable will be driven by the terms it offers to credit customers, the extent of credit sales, and how quickly receivables are collected. Offering customers the option to delay payment requires additional cash; the business is deferring collection of payment but has already incurred the cost of goods. Offering credit also means facing the reality of defaults.

Some working capital transactions generate financing that is referred to as "spontaneous" in the sense that it arises naturally through the normal business practices of the venture. Since its inception, Amazon .com has taken advantage of the unique working capital characteristics inherent in its business model. Amazon sells mostly by credit card. Credit card sales are converted to cash very quickly, usually in just a few days, which keeps the company's accounts receivable balance low.

Amazon also diligently manages inventory by carrying limited stock, placing just-in-time orders, and sometimes shipping directly from the publisher to the customer. As a result, at year end 2009, Amazon's accounts receivable balance was equivalent to 14.5 days of sales and its inventory was equivalent to 41 days of cost of goods sold. The company's combined investment in those two accounts was $3.2 billion, which had to be financed in some way.

Amazon also takes advantage of the long payment terms that normally are offered by book publishers. These terms were originally offered to encourage brick-and-mortar book sellers to stock large and diverse inventories for customers to peruse and were an industry convention long before Amazon.com existed. At the end of 2009, Amazon's accounts payable balance stood at 106 days of cost of sales, or $5.6 billion. This is far more than was needed to finance the accounts receivable and inventory balances. The result is negative net working capital of $2.4 billion, which Amazon can use to fund other priorities.

The extent of spontaneous financing can be affected in deliberate ways by changing working capital policies. Usually, the most important sources of spontaneous financing are inventory (which gives rise to accounts payable) and wages (which gives rise to wages payable). A business can deliberately change its reliance on accounts payable as a financing source by changing the rate at which it pays for its inventory and wages. In a competitive industry, however, normal practices are guided by competitive pressure, and it can be difficult to gain a sustainable advantage by manipulating working capital practices.

Working Capital Financing

Net working capital is the difference between the sum of the current asset categories of working capital and the spontaneous current liabilities.[3] If the balance is positive (current assets exceed current liabilities), the resulting cash deficit must be financed. If it is negative, as in the Amazon.com example, then not only are the firm's operations self-financing but they also generate cash available for other uses. For most businesses, the net working capital balance is positive and additional financing is required. The larger and faster the firm grows, the more financing it requires for net working capital.

Figure 7.2 illustrates how working capital policy choices contribute to the funding required for net working capital. The policy choices are represented in the shaded boxes in columns 1 and 4 of the figure. The unshaded boxes in columns 2 and 3 are directly related to the income statement. The lightly shaded boxes represent the current asset (column

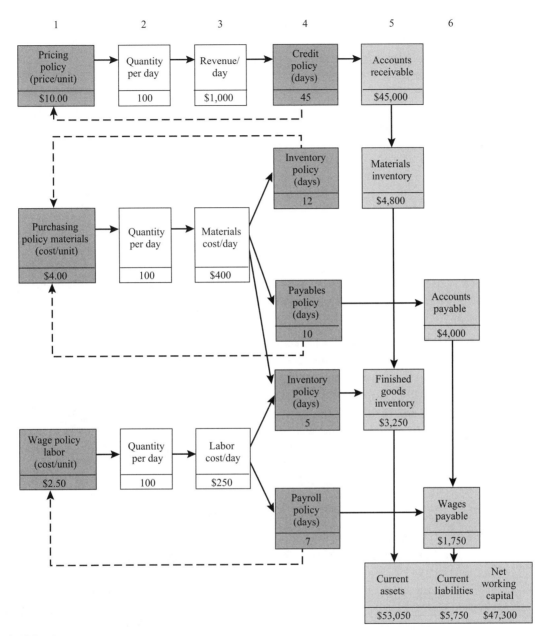

FIGURE **7.2**
Working capital policy template
This figure is a template for assessing the impact of working capital policies on financial needs. It can be used to examine how working capital policies interact to determine the balances of current asset and current liability accounts. Net working capital is the excess of current assets over current liabilities and represents a funding need (or source) for the venture.

5) and current liability (column 6) accounts from the balance sheet. Dollar amounts shown are the financial results of the working capital policy choices. The amount of net working capital (for which financing is required) is shown at the bottom of the figure. The numbers included in the figure as an illustration are representative of a manufacturing venture that carries significant inventories, offers trade credit, purchases raw material inventory on terms, and pays employees one week in arrears. The result of the specific assumptions is a positive financing need of $47,300, or approximately 47 days of sales.

Working Capital Policy

As Figure 7.2 shows, a company's working capital position is the result of several policy choices. Some are easily recognizable as aspects of working capital policy, whereas others are not. Furthermore, as we explain, the effects of individual policy choices are interdependent in ways that are not emphasized in the figure.

Pricing policy.   Pricing policy is a generic descriptor of decisions related to product positioning, pricing, and marketing. Collectively, these decisions are determinants of the expected sales volume. We emphasize pricing in the figure because the effective price (along with quantity of sales) is influenced by credit policy. If, for example, a venture sells on terms that include a discount for prompt payment, then the price used in the calculation should be the average expected price net of anticipated trade discounts and collection losses. With cash sales, the price is not discounted and there is no risk that a buyer will default. On the other hand, the quantity of sales is likely to be higher if the venture offers credit and should increase further with more generous terms.

Credit policy.   Given that credit policy influences the effective average price and quantity of sales, how does a business establish an appropriate policy? Figure 7.2 suggests that a policy of only selling on cash terms would reduce the amount required to finance net working capital. But minimizing the need for financing is usually not consistent with maximizing value. It could make sense to evaluate the effect of some alternative credit policies on profitability and value: If you were to sell only for cash, what would be the likely effect on sales? If you were to accept credit cards, how much would unit sales be expected to increase and what would be the expected effect on average net price? Credit card sales are quickly converted to cash, so the accounts receivable period would be very short. The credit provider also discounts the payments to the vendor as a fee for providing credit. As another consideration, in many cases, the acceptance of credit cards is an important convenience for the customer.

As a practical matter, new and small businesses often have limited ability to determine their own credit policies. Smaller and less well established businesses are more likely than others to offer terms that include delayed payment. Customers may demand opportunities to verify the quality of the seller's product before they pay. Also, although trade credit terms vary greatly across industries, they tend to be similar within an industry. Thus, in an industry where offering credit is common, a new or small business generally must offer terms consistent with the general practice. In an industry where cash payment is common, a new or small business still may find it important to offer credit as a means of initially attracting customers and signaling product delivery and quality.[4]

Purchasing and inventory policies. Purchasing policy relates to choices that affect cost of materials. Choices of materials and negotiations with suppliers affect the cost of materials per unit produced. Inventory policy relates to the average number of days of inventory the business seeks to maintain in raw materials and in finished goods. Inventory policy affects average cost of goods indirectly, because maintaining a large average inventory may enable the business to take advantage of purchase quantity discounts. This benefit is offset by the costs of holding inventory, including storage, spoilage, and obsolescence. Purchasing and inventory policies interact with sales quantity to determine the cost of goods and represent another link between the balance sheet and income statement.

Payables policy. Payables policy concerns the ability to defer payment for materials as a means of financing. Vendors generally require cash payment, especially for a new business with no track record of paying suppliers, or offer credit terms either with or without a discount for prompt payment. Normally, a purchaser would choose to delay payment, provided that doing so did not affect the effective price. The policy decision is whether to take advantage of discounts for prompt payment. Doing so reduces the effective cost of materials, as suggested by the feedback loop in Figure 7.2, but also reduces the accounts payable balance, giving rise to a need for additional financing. Often, discounts for prompt payment are large enough that a business with access to other sources of financing would routinely choose to pay in time to get the discount.[5]

Wage and payroll policies.   Wage policy relates to decisions such as whether to offer a higher wage rate to motivate employees and limit turnover or a lower rate that might increase turnover. Depending on the importance of experience on the job, motivation, availability of new employees, and similar considerations, average labor cost per unit of sales could be lower by either approach. The average labor and materials costs per unit of finished goods make up the direct cost of a unit. These costs interact with finished goods inventory policy to determine the value of finished goods inventory, which appears on the balance sheet.

Payroll policy relates to the frequency and timing of payroll, relative to the timing of the actual work done by the employees. The balance of wages payable as a source of spontaneous financing is increased by paying in arrears and paying less frequently (e.g., biweekly instead of weekly). Payroll policy affects wages indirectly. Wage payments that are substantially in arrears may necessitate higher wage rates. Wage and payroll policies interact with sales quantity to determine the balance of wages payable.

For many ventures, the need for working capital places a significant demand on cash. It is important to understand the working capital needs and to factor them into the pro forma financials and estimates of financial needs. As shown in Figure 7.2, the elements of working capital policy are interrelated and impact many aspects of venture operations, making even small changes important. Working capital is only one example of why the interaction of income statement, balance sheet, and cash flows is important. Other important interactions are related to fixed assets and depreciation and to debt financing and interest and debt service.

7.4   Developing Assumptions for the Financial Model

A financial model of a new venture is only as good as its underlying assumptions. Assumptions that are evidence based and well reasoned are important for reliable forecasting and for convincing investors of the validity of the projections. There are many good places to search for data useful for projecting revenue, expenses, working capital, fixed asset intensity, and cash flow. In this section, we introduce some of them and illustrate their use for making assumptions that we will use for building the Morebucks financial model.

Information Sources

One valuable source of information about small, revenue-generating, nonpublic companies is the Risk Management Association (RMA) publication *Annual Statement Studies*. RMA compiles financial statistics from information supplied by credit customers of banks. The 2008–9 data were collected from 244,000 financial statements and include income statement and balance sheet relationships for approximately 750 industries.[6] Reporting companies are classified by NAICS (North American Industry Classification System) code so that, for a given venture, it may be possible to locate one or more industry groupings as benchmarks. In addition, RMA reports within-industry groupings by firm size. An attractive aspect of the RMA data is that the sample includes many small, nonpublic companies. Although tax minimization strategies of closely held businesses can distort some of the income statement relationships, much of the information is quite useful.

Other sources with similar information include the *Almanac of Business and Industry Financial Ratios* (CCH, Inc.); *Industry Norms and Key Business Ratios* (Dun & Bradstreet, Inc.); the annual corporate income and unincorporated income publications of the Internal Revenue Service (available at http://www.irs.gov/taxstats/); and the *Quarterly Financial Report for Manufacturing, Mining, and Trade Corporations* (U.S. Department of Commerce). These sources contain a myriad of financial information summarized at the industry level and sometimes broken out by firm size. The Standard & Poor's Compustat database is a comprehensive source of financial and market information for public firms worldwide.

In addition, trade associations and investment services such as the *Value Line Investment Survey* and the *Standard & Poor's Analysts' Handbook* publish industry-level data. Moody's and Standard & Poor's report data for individual public companies. As discussed in Chapter 6, financial reports of individual companies are available on the SEC's EDGAR database and through online services such as Yahoo! Finance, Hoover's, and LexisNexis. Press releases, conference call transcripts related to periodic reports of public companies, and other information is available on the Factiva database.

Many industries have one or more specialized publications that contain valuable information and may be available online. To locate other sources, consult Gale Cengage Learning's *Encyclopedia of Business Information Sources* and the Gale Group's *F&S Business News Index*.

SEC filings of comparable firms include 10-Ks and annual reports for established companies and the prospectuses of firms making IPOs, which may include financial data from before the firm went public. If comparable firms can be identified, their income statement relationships can be used to calibrate the assumptions underlying a financial model.

For many businesses, it is likely that only a few SEC filings of comparable firms will be available. If the income statement benchmark ratios (such as gross margin) are consistent, even with only a few comparable firms, then we can be more confident when using them in a forecasting model. It is more likely that there will be substantial variation across the comparable firms, in which case it is important to try to understand why the financial ratios for apparently similar companies differ. Understanding these differences may require additional research regarding the companies and then adjusting the financial statements to make them more comparable.

Using Industry Data and SEC Filings to Develop Assumptions

How might we use industry data and information on comparable companies to develop the assumptions for Morebucks, the coffee shop venture we introduced in Chapter 6? To illustrate, we use information compiled by Dun & Bradstreet (D&B) and reported in its Key Business Ratio statistics. Table 7.4 shows the ratios reported by D&B for Drinking Establishments and Eating Establishments. The last three columns are data for the subset of Smaller Eating Establishments, those with $500,000 to $1 million in total assets. Consistent with what we would expect of a coffee shop that sells for cash or by credit card, D&B reports accounts receivable collection periods of only a few days—the medians range from 1.8 to 4.8 days' sales.[7] The financial ratio reported by D&B for measuring inventory is the ratio of sales to inventory, also known as inventory turnover. Median values range from 60.1 to 87.4.[8] These numbers imply that eating and drinking establishments typically maintain inventories sufficient for only four to six days. This is not surprising given that their inventories are highly perishable.

Table 7.4 also reports information on other ratios, including accounts payable to sales, some measures of financial solvency, and some measures of profitability. The accounts payable to sales percentage is in the 2.0–3.0 percent range, which implies an accounts payable balance between 7 and 11 days. The short payables period suggests that the

TABLE **7.4** **Key business ratios for eating and drinking establishments**

SIC code Line of business Asset size Sample size	5813 *Drinking Places* All asset ranges Statement sampling: 12			5812 *Eating Places* All asset ranges Statement sampling: 202			5812 *Eating Places* $500,000 to $1,000,000 Statement sampling: 42		
Solvency	Upper	Median	Lower	Upper	Median	Lower	Upper	Median	Lower
Quick ratio (times)	3.1	**0.9**	0.4	1.0	**0.5**	0.2	1.7	**0.7**	0.3
Current ratio (times)	6.0	**1.3**	0.7	2.0	**0.9**	0.6	2.2	**1.4**	0.7
Current liabilities/net worth (%)	6.7	**31.1**	90.3	23.0	**49.2**	103.5	19.7	**36.9**	99.7
Current liabilities/inventory (%)	86.4	**415.0**	777.3	326.9	**768.8**	999.9	263.2	**506.5**	929.6
Total liabilities/net worth (%)	40.3	**127.6**	260.9	38.5	**101.7**	275.2	24.7	**49.9**	157.8
Fixed assets/net worth (%)	80.7	**107.4**	193.2	63.4	**112.9**	194.9	29.4	**75.9**	117.2
Efficiency									
Collection period (days)	2.6	**3.5**	6.2	1.5	**4.8**	11.7	0.7	**1.8**	7.0
Sales / inventory (times)	96.8	**60.1**	46.1	128.4	**87.4**	47.0	125.9	**70.6**	36.2
Assets / sales (%)	23.5	**70.4**	112.2	24.5	**45.7**	71.4	21.2	**28.5**	46.7
Sales / net working capital (times)	144.6	**24.1**	10.4	29.4	**14.4**	7.8	28.6	**20.7**	6.8
Accounts payable / sales (%)	1.3	**1.8**	2.5	1.8	**3.0**	4.1	2.2	**3.0**	3.7
Profitability									
Return on sales (%)	8.2	**3.8**	−3.0	5.6	**2.1**	−0.6	6.8	**3.3**	0.8
Return on assets (%)	19.3	**5.1**	−4.1	13.0	**4.9**	−1.0	19.2	**10.5**	2.3
Return on net worth (%)	19.5	**11.6**	−35.9	28.3	**12.0**	−0.3	38.7	**20.6**	5.3

SOURCE: *Dun & Bradstreet, http://lkbr.dnb.com/KBR_main.asp. Data are for 2008.*

ventures are probably paying cash for some supplies and getting short credit terms for others. We do not use the profitability measures because the D&B data include private companies, where the owner may be seeking to avoid taxes by doing such things as paying unusually high salaries to family members. We do not use the solvency measures because we intend to decide separately on financing.

In addition to D&B data, the Specialty Coffee Association of America (SCAA), through its publication *The Specialty Coffee Chronicle*, has extensive information available that would be helpful for starting a coffee shop. The independent *Specialty Coffee Retailer Magazine* bills itself as providing "timely, relevant, and useful information about the profitable operation of a coffee house, coffee bar, or coffee cart." It is available—along with other information—at www.specialty-coffee.com, a website specifically targeted to specialty coffee retailers. In short, industry associations and online communities provide extensive information that can be helpful for developing the assumptions in a financial model for many new ventures.

What can you learn from a prospectus or annual report?   Prospectuses of young companies often contain historical information on early-stage financing, revenue growth, development time, margins, and relationships with suppliers and customers.

In Chapter 6, we collected data from four comparable public companies to use as yardsticks for estimating the revenue of Morebucks. After further analysis, we can eliminate Diedrich because 99 percent of its revenue is from wholesale coffee sales and Coffee People because it was acquired more than 10 years ago, making the information dated. This leaves Peet's Coffee and Starbucks as the better potential yardsticks. For simplicity, we use only information for Peet's to illustrate but note that similar data are available for other firms and that consideration of multiple yardsticks can be more informative and reliable.

The prospectus of a yardstick company such as Peet's contains both quantitative and qualitative information that can be useful. Peet's filed its prospectus (Form S-1) with the SEC in October 2000 and went public in January 2001. The prospectus describes Peet's as a coffee roaster and marketer of branded bean coffee through multiple distribution channels. At the time of the IPO, the company sold through 57 company-owned stores, as well as through specialty grocery and gourmet food stores, online and mail order, and office and restaurant accounts.

The prospectus includes the income statement and balance sheet information shown in Table 7.5, along with data on the number of stores. The statements for the most recent two years before the offering are

TABLE 7.5 Peet's Coffee and Tea, Inc. financials prior to IPO

	Fiscal year				
Income statement	1995	1996	1997	1998	1999
Total revenue	33,252	40,137	50,733	58,685	67,807
Operating expenses					
Cost of sales and related occupancy expenses	17,870	21,526	26,531	28,749	31,923
Gross profit	15,382	18,611	24,202	29,936	35,884
Operating expenses	8,545	11,247	14,768	17,969	21,902
Marketing and advertising	719	810	2,279	2,176	3,491
General and administrative expenses	3,974	2,522	3,962	5,961	6,230
Depreciation and amortization	1,586	1,790	2,211	2,711	3,404
Total operating costs and expenses	32,694	37,895	49,747	57,566	66,950
Income (loss) from operations	558	2,242	987	1,119	857
Interest expense			487	765	1,022
Other income			(90)	(56)	(37)
Interest expense, net, and other	325	244	396	709	985
Income (loss) before income taxes	233	1,998	591	410	(128)
Income tax provision (benefit)	(129)	851	250	242	16
Net income (loss)	362	1,147	342	168	(144)
Balance sheet data					
Assets					
Current assets					
Cash and cash equivalents	334	2,156	888	873	1,074
Accounts receivable				430	740
Inventories				9,007	7,211
Other current assets				963	1,168
Total current assets				11,273	10,193
Net working capital	2,402	2,230	(2,308)		
Fixed and intangible assets					
Property and equipment, net				16,385	21,780
Intangible and other assets, net				2,206	2,677
Total assets	22,293	22,637	25,724	29,864	34,650
Liabilities and shareholders' equity					
Current liabilities					
Accounts payable				4,569	4,353
Accrued compensation and benefits				1,318	1,914
Other accrued liabilities				546	996
Short-term borrowings	870	1,810	3,470	6,173	8,416
Total current liabilities				12,606	15,679
Long-term liabilities					
Long-term borrowings, less current portion	4,900	4,882	3,412	6,467	7,780
Total liabilities				19,073	23,459
Shareholders' equity					
Preferred stock	5,482	5,482	4,537	4,537	4,537
Common stock issued and outstanding				7,422	7,966
Accumulated deficit				(1,168)	(1,312)
Total shareholders' equity	10,006	11,173	10,318	10,791	11,191
Total liabilities and shareholders' equity	22,293	22,637	25,724	29,864	34,650
Number of stores in operation	1995	1996	1997	1998	1999
Beginning of year	19	25	30	39	43
Store openings	6	5	9	5	11
Stores closed				1	1
End of year	25	30	39	43	53

SOURCE: *Form S-1, filed January 23, 2001.*
NOTE: *Dollar amounts in thousands.*

provided in more detail than those for earlier years. For example, instead of a detailed breakout of current asset and liability accounts, the early-year information shows only a total for net working capital.

We use the financial data to compute the common size income statements and balance sheets shown in Table 7.6. In a common size income statement, each revenue or expense line item is stated as a percentage of revenue. In a common size balance sheet, each asset or liability account is stated as a percentage of total assets. Common size analysis allows us to compare firms of different size and also makes it easier to spot trends. For example, we can see that the gross margin of Peet's Coffee increased substantially between 1995 and 1999, which could indicate economies of scale in purchasing or production. Over the same period, operating expenses increased by about the same percentage of revenue, as do other expenses that reduce operating profit, leaving the operating profit margin almost unchanged. This suggests that profitability is not very sensitive to scale over the range of firm sizes represented by Peet's.

Table 7.7 presents some standard financial ratios calculated using the data from Peet's. In contrast to the common size statements, financial ratios often combine information from the income statement and balance sheet. For most measures in the table, we have data for only the last two years before the IPO. The asset turnover ratio in the table increases with firm size, suggesting that there are important economies of scale for businesses like Peet's. These economies may, however, have resulted from the changing nature of Peet's Coffee's business as it integrated more into retail coffee shops.

The last point above highlights an important caveat when using yardstick data. It is important to be cognizant of differences in the business models when developing assumptions. Peet's is not simply a multistore coffee shop business; rather, its business model evolved over a number of years. Peet's started with stores that sold only roasted coffee beans. By 2000, just before the IPO, approximately half of its store revenue was from beverages and pastries. About 20 percent of 1999 revenue was from online sales and through specialty grocers.

In addition to quantitative information, the Peet's prospectus contains qualitative information that could be relevant to the Morebucks financial model. For example, the risk factors described in the prospectus include:

- Inability to implement the business strategy
- Inability to identify strategic locations suitable for new stores
- Inability to manage growth
- Competitive conditions existing in the industry and local market

TABLE **7.6** Peet's Coffee and Tea, Inc. common size statements

Income statement (computed as a percentage of total revenue)	Fiscal year				
	1995	1996	1997	1998	1999
Total revenue	100.0	100.0	100.0	100.0	100.0
Operating expenses					
Cost of sales and related occupancy expenses	53.7	53.6	52.3	49.0	47.1
Gross profit	46.3	46.4	47.7	51.0	52.9
Operating expenses	25.7	28.0	29.1	30.6	32.3
Marketing and advertising	2.2	2.0	4.5	3.7	5.1
General and administrative expenses	12.0	6.3	7.8	10.2	9.2
Depreciation and amortization	4.8	4.5	4.4	4.6	5.0
Total operating costs and expenses	98.3	94.4	98.1	98.1	98.7
Income (loss) from operations	1.7	5.6	1.9	1.9	1.3
Interest expense			1.0	1.3	1.5
Other income			−0.2	−0.1	−0.1
Interest expense, net, and other	1.0	0.6	0.8	1.2	1.5
Income (loss) before income taxes	0.7	5.0	1.2	0.7	−0.2
Income tax provision (benefit)	−0.4	2.1	0.5	0.4	0.0
Net income (loss)	1.1	2.9	0.7	0.3	−0.2

Balance sheet data (computed as a percentage of total assets)					
Assets					
Current assets					
Cash and cash equivalents	1.5	9.5	3.5	2.9	3.1
Accounts receivable				1.4	2.1
Inventories				30.2	20.8
Other current assets				3.2	3.4
Total current assets				37.7	29.4
Net working capital	10.8	9.9	−8.9		
Fixed and intangible assets					
Property and equipment, net				54.9	62.9
Intangible and other assets, net				7.4	7.7
Total assets	100.0	100.0	100.0	100.0	100.0
Liabilities and shareholders' equity					
Current liabilities					
Accounts payable				15.3	12.6
Accrued compensation and benefits				4.4	5.5
Other accrued liabilities				1.8	2.9
Short-term borrowings	3.9	8.0	13.5	20.7	24.3
Total current liabilities				42.2	45.2
Long-term liabilities				0.0	0.0
Long-term borrowings, less current portion	22.0	21.6	13.3	21.7	22.5
Total liabilities				63.9	67.7
Shareholders' equity					
Preferred stock	24.6	24.2	17.6	15.2	13.1
Common stock issued and outstanding				24.9	23.0
Accumulated deficit				−3.9	−3.8
Total shareholders' equity	44.9	49.4	40.1	36.1	32.3
Total liabilities and shareholders' equity	100.0	100.0	100.0	100.0	100.0

SOURCE: *Form S-1, filed January 23, 2001.*

TABLE **7.7**   **Peet's Coffee and Tea, Inc. financial ratios**

	Fiscal year				
Financial ratio	1995	1996	1997	1998	1999
Asset turnover	1.49	1.77	1.97	1.97	1.96
Fixed asset turnover				3.58	3.11
Accounts receivable turnover				136.5	91.6
Days of sales in accounts receivable				2.64	3.93
Inventory turnover				3.19	4.43
Days of cost of sales in inventory				112.8	81.3
Sales/inventory				6.52	9.40
Accounts payable/cost of sales				15.9%	13.6%
Days of cost of sales in accounts payable				57.2	49.1
Compensation payable/cost of sales				4.6%	6.0%
Cash/revenue	1.00%	5.37%	1.75%	1.49%	1.58%
Days of revenue in cash	3.62	19.34	6.30	5.36	5.70

DEFINITIONS:
Asset turnover = sales/assets
Fixed asset turnover = sales/net fixed assets
Accounts receivable turnover = sales/accounts receivable
Days of sales in accounts receivable = accounts receivable/(sales/360)
Inventory turnover = cost of sales/inventory
Days of cost of sales in inventory = inventory/(cost of sales/360)
Days of cost of sales in accounts payable = accounts payable/(cost of sales/360)
Days of revenue in cash = cash/(revenue/360)
NOTE: *All calculations are based on data from Table 7.5.*

- Dependence on a single product, that is, specialty coffee
- Consumer tastes and preferences
- Demographic and consumer traffic trends
- Type, number, and locations of competing stores,
- Costs of employee compensation and benefits
- Fluctuations in the availability, quality, and cost of coffee
- Health concerns related to caffeine

Some of these provide important insights into specific risks facing the company.

How can we evaluate whether Peet's is a reasonable yardstick company? One test is whether the ratios of accounts receivable and inventory to sales are similar to those from the D&B data for eating and drinking establishments. From Table 7.6, we can see that the accounts receivable balance represents only three to four days of sales, which is consistent with the industry norms in Table 7.4. On the other hand, the ratio of revenue to inventory for Peet's, computed to be in the 6 to 10 range, is well below that of the D&B eating and drinking establishments. Peet's is more integrated into purchasing and roasting coffee beans than Morebucks would be. This difference in vertical integration could also distort other measures, such as the ratio of sales to assets. No matter what firms we select as yardsticks, we need to make appropriate adjustments.

Developing Assumptions Based on Fundamental Analysis

Industry data and yardsticks can be valuable, particularly when underlying business models are similar to those of the subject venture. But for in-depth planning, fundamental analysis is useful as a way to test the merits of assumptions that are based on yardsticks. Sometimes fundamental analysis is the only reasonable choice for developing a specific assumption. For example, information for estimating operating leverage or the proportions of fixed and variable expenses are rarely available from yardstick data. Because of the absence of information about closely comparable companies, heavy reliance on fundamental analysis is common for early-stage innovative ventures.

As an example of the importance of fundamental analysis, consider the assumptions used to forecast fixed asset investment. If we were to use data from Peet's, we might divide the 1999 property and equipment balance of $21.8 million by the number of stores (53 stores at the end of 1999), producing an estimate of about $410,000 in fixed assets per coffee shop. But can we really trust this to be accurate for Morebucks? The true investment in fixed assets will be a function of the store location and depends on what leasehold improvements the venture will require. Moreover, the yardstick information is for net fixed assets (which are partially depreciated), is affected by the company's decision to integrate into coffee bean roasting, and could be impacted by whether stores are purchased or leased. For reasons such as these, there is more variability in balance sheet estimates developed using yardsticks than for items on the income statement.

For a venture like Morebucks, fundamental analysis can yield a more reliable forecast of the fixed asset investment and related depreciation expenses than can a yardstick approach. When Morebucks opens, all of its furniture and equipment will be newly acquired. Suppose the space will be leased but that leasehold improvements, furniture, and equipment are estimated to cost $350,000, all of which can be depreciated. If we assume seven-year, straight-line depreciation, the annual depreciation expense will be about $50,000. Because the furniture and equipment are fully paid for at the start, there is no cash flow directly tied to depreciation. However, depreciation expense reduces pretax income and the tax the firm pays each year. At a 35 percent tax rate, the $50,000 depreciation expense would reduce income tax by $17,500 each year, which does impact cash flow.

We could, of course, do more with fundamental analysis. The data from Peet's show only a single line for operating expenses, which includes store salary and benefits. However, the operating expenses line also includes other items. We could make a better forecast by developing salary forecasts for Morebucks based on a specific staffing plan. We could collect information on local wages to help estimate the prevailing level of wages and benefits. We could develop a specific marketing plan—which we would need in any case—that would enable us to estimate how much will be spent on advertising and promotion. And we could estimate raw materials costs based on local market prices, the anticipated product mix, and volumes implicit in the revenue forecast.

Fundamental analysis is always useful when preparing pro forma financials. The questions that drive the process are a standard part of any business planning exercise. Answering these questions forces the entrepreneur to undertake significant due diligence and better understand the industry, the market, and the new venture strategy. Yardsticks can then be used to validate forecast assumptions that are developed by fundamental analysis.

7.5   Building a Financial Model of the Venture

We can now develop the integrated financial statements for Morebucks. We base the statement assumptions on the information and methods discussed in the previous section. By building the model in stages, we demonstrate how the financial statements interact and how the cash flow statement can be derived from the pro forma balance sheet and income statement.

Of course, Morebucks will not achieve full capacity instantly; for this reason the financial model needs to incorporate the anticipated growth trajectory. To reflect this reality in the dynamic relationships among the financial statements, we introduce a time dimension into the forecast. As a basis for this, we might do further research using yardstick and industry data, perform additional fundamental analysis, and meet with local coffee shop owners about their start-up experiences.

Recall from Chapter 6 that the estimate of annual revenue was approximately $900,000 for an established coffee shop. Suppose our new research and analysis supports an assumption that Morebucks revenue will reach two-thirds of the $900,000 during the first year and the full estimate in the second year. After the second year, annual revenue is expected to stay constant at $900,000.

Table 7.8 shows a partially completed template of the three financial statements we will construct. It combines elements of the basic statements discussed in Section 7.1 as well as line items from the Peet's financials. Because revenue is expected to take two years to reach steady state, we have structured the pro forma statements to cover Time 0 and three years of operation. This allows us to illustrate the impact of start-up events on the financial statements and to cover two years of steady-state operation. In the table, we have introduced only income statement data and have not yet incorporated depreciation expense.

Table 7.8 is constructed using Excel and includes the cell formulas needed to link the assumptions to the financial statements and the financial statements to each other. The columns to the right summarize the numerical assumptions and describe from where they originate. Where possible, we link the assumptions directly to the spreadsheet so the effects of changing an assumption will be automatically reflected correctly in all of the financial statements. This is standard practice for any spreadsheet model we might want to build.

The revenue forecast is taken from Chapter 6 and reflects the growth trajectory discussed above. The expense assumptions—expressed as percentages of revenue—are based on data from the Peet's prospectus. We decided to use an average of the 1995–97 data, which represents a three-year period when Peet's was relatively small and before it was approaching the point of going public. Peet's does not provide information on the breakdown between fixed and variable expenses in its income statement. In our base case model, we assume that expenses are a constant percentage of revenue. Later, however, when we add uncertainty to the model, we will relax this simplified assumption.

The final assumption required in the income statement is the effective tax rate, which we have assumed to be 35 percent if taxable income is positive, and zero otherwise. Because depreciation expense is driven by the amount invested in facilities and improvements, we defer making this assumption until we construct the balance sheet. The tax and net income totals will not be correct until the depreciation expense line is complete. Note, however, that the net income line also now appears as the first item on the cash flow statement, where it is one of the determinants of operating cash flow. This is one of many links between the financial statements.

In Table 7.9, we turn to the balance sheet, beginning with the current asset and current liability accounts. Again, the numerical assumptions and their sources are in the two right-hand columns. In some cases,

TABLE **7.8**   **Step 1 of pro forma financial model for Morebucks: Income statement assumptions**

Pro forma income statement	Time 0	Year 1	Year 2	Year 3	Assumption	Basis for assumption
Net revenue	0	600,000	900,000	900,000		From revenue forecast
Cost of sales and occupancy		319,200	478,800	478,800	53.2%	From Peet's common size statement
Gross profit	0	280,800	421,200	421,200		
Operating expenses		165,600	248,400	248,400	27.6%	From Peet's common size statement
General and administrative expenses		52,200	78,300	78,300	8.7%	From Peet's common size statement
Depreciation and amortization expenses						
Income from operations	0	63,000	94,500	94,500		
Interest income (expense), net						
Income before income taxes	0	63,000	94,500	94,500		
Income tax provision		22,050	33,075	33,075	35%	Effective rate based on statute
Net income	0	40,950	61,425	61,425		

Pro forma balance sheet	Time 0	Year 1	Year 2	Year 3	Assumption	Basis for assumption
Assets						
Current assets						
Required cash						
Surplus cash						
Accounts receivable						
Inventory						
Total current assets	0	0	0	0		
Fixed assets, gross	0	0	0	0		
Less: accumulated depreciation		0	0	0		
Net fixed assets	0	0	0	0		
Total assets	0	0	0	0		
Liabilities						
Current liabilities						
Accounts payable						
Wages payable						
Total current liabilities	0	0	0	0		
Long-term debt						
Total liabilities	0	0	0	0		
Equity						
Common stock						
Retained earnings						
Total equity	0	0	0	0		
Total liabilities and equity	0	0	0	0		

the assumptions come directly from the Peet's prospectus. Because the Peet's balance sheet data are incomplete for the period 1995–97, most of our assumptions are based on 1998–99 information. When the data from Peet's differ substantially from industry norms or the conclusions of our fundamental analysis, we have established the specific assump-

TABLE **7.8**

Pro forma cash flow statement	Year 1	Year 2	Year 3
Operating cash flow			
Net income	40,950	61,425	61,425
Plus: depreciation	0	0	0
(Increase) decrease in accounts receivable			
(Increase) decrease in inventory			
Increase (decrease) in accounts payable			
Increase (decrease) in wages payable			
Operating cash flow	40,950	61,425	61,425
Investing cash flow			
(Increase) decrease in gross fixed assets			
Investing cash flow			
Financing cash flow			
Increase (decrease) in debt			
Increase (decrease) in common stock			
Dividend paid			
Financing cash flow	0	0	0
Net cash flow	40,950	61,425	61,425
Beginning cash			
Ending cash	40,950	61,425	61,425

NOTE: *This table is derived from an Excel spreadsheet and shows partially completed financial statements for the first three years of the coffee shop venture. Revenue numbers are based on Chapter 6, and the income statement assumptions come from Peet's data.*

tion based on judgment and the evidence. For example, because of its whole bean roasting and retail activities, the Peet's inventory level is approximately 10 times higher than the industry data. Our fundamental analysis also produces a much lower inventory estimate for the coffee shop. Thus, we ignore the Peet's data and rely on the industry ratios from D&B.

With the balance sheet filled in, the changes in the various current account balances from one year to the next appear in the cash flow statement in the operating cash flow section. When the venture reaches steady state after Year 2, the net working capital balance does not change. As a result, the Year 3 cash flows from changes in current assets and liabilities are zero.

Table 7.9 also shows a $350,000 investment in fixed assets, which is based on fundamental analysis. This investment is depreciated over seven years, which means we can calculate the depreciation expense as $50,000 for each year. This completes the income statement, with

TABLE **7.9** **Step 2 of pro forma financial model for Morebucks: Working capital and fixed assets assumptions**

Pro forma income statement	Time 0	Year 1	Year 2	Year 3	Assumption	Basis for assumption
Net revenue	0	600,000	900,000	900,000		From revenue forecast
Cost of sales and						From Peet's common
occupancy		319,200	478,800	478,800	53.2%	size statement
Gross profit	0	280,800	421,200	421,200		
Operating expenses		165,600	248,400	248,400	27.6%	From Peet's common
						size statement
General and administrative						From Peet's common
expenses		52,200	78,300	78,300	8.7%	size statement
Depreciation and amortiza-						7 years, straight
tion expenses		50,000	50,000	50,000		line—on fixed
						assets, gross
Income from operations	0	13,000	44,500	44,500		
Interest income (expense),						
net						
Income before income taxes	0	13,000	44,500	44,500		
Income tax provision		4,550	15,575	15,575	35%	Effective rate based
						on statute
Net income	0	8,450	28,925	28,925		

Pro forma balance sheet	Time 0	Year 1	Year 2	Year 3	Assumption	Basis for assumption
Assets						
Current assets						
Required cash	0	9,000	13,500	13,500	1.50%	Based on Peet's cash/
						revenue ratios
Surplus cash	0	(278,494)	(193,041)	(114,116)		
Accounts receivable	0	6,000	9,000	9,000	100	Based on Peet's
						revenue/accounts
						receivable ratio
Inventory	0	7,500	11,250	11,250	80	Based on industry
						sales/inventory ratio
Total current assets	0	(255,994)	(159,291)	(80,366)		
Fixed assets, gross	0	350,000	350,000	350,000	350,000	Based on fundamen-
						tal analysis
Less: accumulated						
depreciation		(50,000)	(100,000)	(150,000)		
Net fixed assets	0	300,000	250,000	200,000		
Total assets	0	44,006	90,709	119,634		
Liabilities						
Current liabilities						
Accounts payable	0	18,000	27,000	27,000	3.00%	Based on accounts
						payable/sales ratio
Wages payable	0	17,556	26,334	26,334	5.50%	Based on Peet's
						compensation/cost
						of sales ratio
Total current liabilities	0	35,556	53,334	53,334		
Long-term debt	0	0	0	0		
Total liabilities	0	35,556	53,334	53,334		
Equity						
Common stock						
Retained earnings		8,450	37,375	66,300		
Total equity	0	8,450	37,375	66,300		
Total liabilities and equity	0	44,006	90,709	119,634		

TABLE **7.9**

Pro forma cash flow statement	Year 1	Year 2	Year 3
Operating cash flow			
Net income	8,450	28,925	28,925
Plus: depreciation	50,000	50,000	50,000
(Increase) decrease in accounts receivable	(6,000)	(3,000)	0
(Increase) decrease in inventory	(7,500)	(3,750)	0
Increase (decrease) in accounts payable	18,000	9,000	0
Increase (decrease) in wages payable	17,556	8,778	0
Operating cash flow	80,506	89,953	78,925
Investing cash flow			
(Increase) decrease in gross fixed assets	(350,000)	0	0
Investing cash flow	(350,000)	0	0
Financing cash flow			
Increase (decrease) in debt	0	0	0
Increase (decrease) in common stock			
Dividend paid	0	0	0
Financing cash flow	0	0	0
Net cash flow	(269,494)	89,953	78,925
Beginning cash	0	(269,494)	(179,541)
Ending cash	(269,494)	(179,541)	(100,616)

NOTE: *This table is derived from an Excel spreadsheet and shows financial statements for the first three years of the coffee shop venture. Revenue numbers are based on Chapter 6, and the income statement assumptions come from Peet's data. Balance sheet assumptions are a combination of Peet's data, industry data, and fundamental analysis. The balance sheet is balanced by means of the large negative "Surplus cash" line, which is used as a plug.*

the possible exception of any interest expense associated with financing. Accumulated depreciation on the balance sheet is linked to the income statement and adds the depreciation expense each year to the prior year's accumulated depreciation balance. This has the effect of reducing the net fixed assets balance over time. Because depreciation is a noncash expense, it appears in the cash flow statement, where it is added back to net income as part of the operating cash flow calculation.

Note that the balance sheet in Table 7.9 is in balance each year, that is, total assets equals total liabilities and equity. This is a modeling choice we made for this example. To force the statements to balance, we allow surplus cash to show negative balances. There are other ways to address this in an integrated financial model. One is to constrain surplus cash to be nonnegative but allow the balance sheet to be out of balance and then make subsequent adjustments. For example, suppose the model's assumptions produce assets greater than liabilities plus equity.

Balance can be achieved either by reducing assets or by increasing liabilities or equity (or some combination of the two). For example, if in the Morebucks model we were to assume an initial purchase of $350,000 of fixed assets but only $250,000 of equity investment, the balance sheet would be out of balance by $100,000. Balance could be achieved by reducing the fixed asset assumption to $250,000, increasing the equity investment to $350,000, or adjusting both accounts. While this approach works, it is cumbersome and is not helpful if the model is to be used in simulation.

Generally, it is easier to force the statement to be in balance and keep track of cash shortages or surpluses, as we have done here. In this approach, the plug becomes a line item on the asset side. In the coffee shop model, we called this surplus cash. In Table 7.9, the Year 1 balance sheet is balanced only because the surplus cash balance is extremely negative. This is attributable primarily to the assumption of a $350,000 fixed asset purchase, with no commensurate increase in liabilities or equity (i.e., financing). This funding shortfall causes surplus cash to be negative, and, as the model is structured, the negative surplus cash balance is the only way to keep the balance sheet balanced. This approach shows the financing shortage or surplus in the surplus cash line, which represents an allocation of the total cash balance or an indication of a need for additional funding.

Another good alternative is to shift the shortage or surplus to the liabilities and equity side of the statement. Were we to do this here, we would first establish a minimum cash level on the balance sheet and force the cash balance to equal the cash required. The model already has assumptions about all other asset line items, so this would effectively fix the asset (left) side of the balance sheet and produce a total assets number. We can then add a "plug" item to the right side of the balance sheet, calling it "additional funding needed" or "additional financing." The model already has assumptions about all of the liability and equity accounts except for additional financing needed. This makes the right side of the balance sheet a column of numbers, including the unknown plug, that sums to a known number (total assets). The spreadsheet would be designed so that the plug figure causes assets to equal liabilities plus equity. If the model indicates that the enterprise requires additional funding, that is, if the amount of total assets is greater than the liabilities plus equity balance, the plug will be positive; if the amount of total assets is less than liabilities plus equity, the plug will be negative. A negative balance of additional funding needed means the same thing as surplus cash being positive in the first approach.

A more elegant approach is to combine these last two alternatives. This third approach recognizes the reality that a negative balance in either the external funding or the surplus cash line items does not make sense. If, before forcing the balance, assets exceed liabilities, then the firm needs more investment capital and additional financing is the plug; and if assets are less than liabilities, then the firm has more capital than it needs and surplus cash is the plug—so there are only positive plugs. This approach provides greater flexibility than the others. For example, surplus cash might be credited with earning the risk-free rate of interest and additional financing required might be assumed, tentatively, to be in the form of debt, with a risky interest rate, or in the form of equity.

The negative cash surplus shown in Table 7.9 is addressed by adding an assumption that the venture will be entirely equity financed. Table 7.10 shows the resulting financial statements. To cover the cost of the initial investment in fixed assets and working capital, we decided to start with $375,000 of equity, which appears on the Time 0 balance sheet as $375,000 in common stock and the same amount in surplus cash.[9] The equity investment also shows up on the statement of cash flows as a positive financing cash flow. The cash flow statement shows that in Year 1, most of the invested cash is used to purchase fixed assets and acquire working capital.

Based on our initial assumptions, the coffee shop is expected to turn a small profit in Year 1 and be profitable each year thereafter. We can see the net income from each year moving to the retained earnings line in the equity section of the balance sheet. The retained earnings balance at the end of Year 3 reflects the accumulated profits from Morebucks' first three years of operation.

The balance sheet in Table 7.10 shows a significant surplus cash balance each year. Rather than assuming that the entrepreneur withdraws the cash as it accumulates, we have allowed it to remain in the venture. The surplus cash could earn a return (by being held in an interest-earning savings vehicle such as a money market fund), but to keep the model simple we ignore this for now.

The surplus cash balance at the end of Year 1 raises the question of how the assumption of a $375,000 initial investment was determined. Does the projected cash surplus in Year 1 mean that the entrepreneur put too much cash into the venture up front? The model seems to imply this possibility; if we reduce the initial investment to $275,000, there is still a surplus cash balance at the end of Year 1. However, we should not draw this conclusion without further analysis. The current model does not capture important timing issues in the first year. If $350,000 of fixed assets must be purchased before the coffee shop even opens, then clearly $275,000 of starting equity would be insufficient. To accurately estimate cash needs, we might want to prepare pro forma statements on a monthly or quarterly basis.

TABLE **7.10**   **Step 3 of pro forma financial model for Morebucks: Investment assumption**

Pro forma income statement	Time 0	Year 1	Year 2	Year 3	Assumption	Basis for assumption
Net revenue	0	600,000	900,000	900,000		From revenue forecast
Cost of sales and					53.2%	From Peet's common
occupancy		319,200	478,800	478,800		size statement
Gross profit	0	280,800	421,200	421,200		
Operating expenses		165,600	248,400	248,400	27.6%	From Peet's common size statement
General and admin-						From Peet's common
istrative expenses		52,200	78,300	78,300	8.7%	size statement
Depreciation						7 years, straight
and amortization						line—on fixed
expenses	—	50,000	50,000	50,000		assets, gross
Income from						
operations	0	13,000	44,500	44,500		
Interest income						
(expense), net						
Income before						
income taxes	0	13,000	44,500	44,500		
Income tax provision		4,550	15,575	15,575	35%	Effective rate based on statute
Net income	0	8,450	28,925	28,925		

Pro forma balance sheet	Time 0	Year 1	Year 2	Year 3	Assumption	Basis for assumption
Assets						
Current assets						
Required cash	0	9,000	13,500	13,500	1.50%	Based on Peet's cash/ revenue ratios
Surplus cash	375,000	96,506	181,959	260,884		
Accounts receivable	0	6,000	9,000	9,000	100	Based on Peet's revenue/accounts receivable ratio
Inventory	0	7,500	11,250	11,250	80	Based on industry sales/inventory ratio
Total current assets	375,000	119,006	215,709	294,634		
Fixed assets, gross		350,000	350,000	350,000	350,000	Based on fundamental analysis
Less: accumulated						
depreciation		(50,000)	(100,000)	(150,000)		
Net fixed assets	0	300,000	250,000	200,000		
Total assets	375,000	419,006	465,709	494,634		
Liabilities						
Current liabilities						
Accounts payable	0	18,000	27,000	27,000	3.00%	Based on accounts payable/sales ratio
Wages payable	0	17,556	26,334	26,334	5.50%	Based on Peet's compensation/cost of sales ratio
Total current						
liabilities	0	35,556	53,334	53,334		
Long-term debt	0	0	0	0		
Total liabilities	0	35,556	53,334	53,334		

TABLE **7.10**

Pro forma balance sheet	Time 0	Year 1	Year 2	Year 3	Assumption	Basis for assumption
Equity						
Common stock	375,000	375,000	375,000	375,000	375,000	Selected to cover start-up investments
Retained earnings		8,450	37,375	66,300		
Total equity	375,000	383,450	412,375	441,300		
Total liabilities and equity	375,000	419,006	465,709	494,634		

Pro forma cash flow statement	Time 0	Year 1	Year 2	Year 3
Operating cash flow				
Net income	0	8,450	28,925	28,925
Plus: depreciation	0	50,000	50,000	50,000
(Increase) decrease in accounts receivable	0	(6,000)	(3,000)	0
(Increase) decrease in inventory	0	(7,500)	(3,750)	0
Increase (decrease) in accounts payable	0	18,000	9,000	0
Increase (decrease) in wages payable	0	17,556	8,778	0
Operating cash flow	0	80,506	89,953	78,925
Investing cash flow				
(Increase) decrease in gross fixed assets	0	(350,000)	0	0
Investing cash flow	0	(350,000)	0	0
Financing cash flow				
Increase (decrease) in debt	0	0	0	0
Increase (decrease) in common stock				
Dividend paid	375,000	0	0	0
Financing cash flow	375,000	0	0	0
Net cash flow	375,000	(269,494)	89,953	78,925
Beginning cash	0	375,000	105,506	195,459
Ending cash	375,000	105,506	195,459	274,384

NOTE: *The table is derived from an Excel spreadsheet and shows completed financial statements for the first three years of the coffee shop venture. Revenue numbers are based on Chapter 6, and the income statement assumptions come from Peet's data. Balance sheet assumptions reflect a combination of Peet's data, industry data, and fundamental analysis. The balance sheet shows an assumed equity investment of $375,000 at Time 0.*

The Cash Flow Statement

The cash flow statement allows us to see the venture's sources and uses of cash. This information might appear to be readily available from the income statement, but that is not the case. First, income statement items such as depreciation do not translate directly to cash flow; and second, many cash transactions don't appear on the income statement.

In addition, the income statement and balance sheet provide little information about the venture's ability to generate cash to fund growth.

The cash flow statement translates the income statement and balance sheet information into cash flows and separates them into three categories: operating, investing, and financing. The coffee shop cash flow statement in Table 7.10 is straightforward. When the venture begins operation and is growing, operating cash flow reflects increases in working capital accounts. When the venture reaches steady state, between Years 2 and 3, operating cash flow includes only net income and the add-back for depreciation. Because the working capital account balances are constant, they have no impact on cash flow.

The statement next provides for changes in cash due to investing. The gross fixed assets balance represents the cumulative original cost of the firm's PP&E. The change in gross fixed assets from the balance sheet is shown as an investment cash flow on the cash flow statement. When fixed assets are purchased, the increase appears as a negative cash flow. If fixed assets are sold, the sale produces a cash inflow.

The last section of the cash flow statement covers financing activities. The only event in this example is the equity investment of $375,000 at Time 0. With all of the financing provided at Time 0, there are no changes in debt or equity for Years 1 through 3. Return of the surplus cash to the equity investor can be treated in two ways. A dividend would appear as a negative financing cash flow and would reduce retained earnings on the balance sheet. A distribution in the form of a share repurchase would be a negative financing cash flow and would reduce equity on the balance sheet.

Finally, at the foot of the cash flow statement, we use the net cash flow plus the cash balance from the prior period to compute the ending cash balance. Both beginning and ending cash balances include required and surplus cash. This information is used in the balance sheet to fill in the surplus cash amount.

An Illustration of Financial Statement Integration

Table 7.10 is a fully integrated Excel file of the Morebucks financial model. It contains all important assumptions, along with source documentation. The financial statements are linked to the assumptions, to one another, and also across time. This allows us to immediately see the impact of changing any key assumptions. For example, suppose it may be possible to acquire the needed fixed assets for $320,000 rather than the original estimate of $350,000 and that Year 1 revenue might only be $400,000. These changes can be made quickly; Table 7.11 summarizes

TABLE **7.11** **Morebucks sensitivity to key assumptions**

	Base case	New assumptions
Investment in fixed assets	$350,000	$320,000
Sales	$600,000	$400,000
Net income	$8,450	($2,414)
Operating cash flow	$80,506	$58,004
Surplus cash	$96,506	$107,004

their impact on several key Year 1 financial variables. The lower revenue causes net income to turn negative. This is partially offset by the reduction in depreciation expense arising from the smaller starting balance in gross fixed assets. Operating cash flow goes down, reflecting both the lower net income and reduced investment in working capital. However, surplus cash is actually higher, as the $30,000 reduction in fixed asset investment more than offsets the decrease in operating cash flow.

Because the model is fully integrated, the two changes to the assumptions are immediately reflected in affected line items on all three statements. This allows the entrepreneur or an investor to focus on the operational implications of the changes.

S 7.6 Adding Uncertainty to the Model

The Morebucks financial model incorporates the static assumptions shown in Table 7.10. The resultant pro forma financial statements are useful but do not reflect the uncertainty inherent in any forecast. As the model is structured, every item except the investment in fixed assets, depreciation expense, and tax rate is expressed as a fixed percentage of revenue. Because of this, varying only the Year 1 and/or Year 2 sales estimates automatically changes most of the line items in the pro forma financials.

The assumption in Table 7.10 of a constant relationship between financial statement line items and revenue is not realistic once we add uncertainty to the model and allow revenue to vary. Even if we sell nothing on a given day, there are still staffing costs, occupancy costs, and other costs that cannot be avoided. In reality, some percentage of the costs is fixed.

To introduce uncertainty, we modify the Morebucks model in two ways. Further research into the performance of new coffee shops would reveal a high variability in first-year revenue and many different three-year trajectories of revenue growth. For example, 10-K data from yardstick companies Peet's and Starbucks contain information on per-store revenue and growth based on the number of years the store has been open. Fundamental analysis and discussions with other coffee shop owners should provide additional data that can be used to estimate the variability of revenue.

To introduce uncertainty, we modify the model by replacing the static revenue assumption each year with a statistical distribution. We also introduce fixed costs and uncertainty by modifying the static assumption about operating expense. In effect, we simulate operating expense as a random percentage of revenue but with a minimum value of $120,000. The specific changes are shown below.

Variable	Distribution assumption
Year 1 sales	Triangular with minimum of $300,000, mode of $600,000, and maximum of $700,000
Year 2 sales	Triangular with minimum of $750,000, mode of $900,000, and maximum of $1,000,000
Year 3 sales	Normally distributed with mean of Year 2 sales and standard deviation of $25,000
Operating expense	Maximum of $120,000 or a percentage of sales, normally distributed with mean of 27.6 percent and standard deviation of 2 percent

Table 7.12 incorporates these elements of uncertainty into the pro forma statements and enables us to use simulation. The cells modified to reflect these uncertainty assumptions are highlighted with shading and can be reviewed in the Excel file.

Figure 7.3 (page 281) shows the results of simulating the Morebucks model. We used *Venture*.SIM to track each year's revenue, net income, and cash flow, as well as the simulated result for operating expense percentage. Based on 5,000 trials, the figure shows that expected Year 1 sales, about $532,000, is lower than the $600,000 assumed in the static model. This is because of the skewness of the assumed triangular distribution, which allows for possible outcomes to be considerably more negative but only slightly more positive. In Year 1, over 75 percent of the trials result in negative net income, and even in Years 2 and 3 there is a small chance the venture is unprofitable. Operating cash flow, however, is positive in all years for all trials, indicating that the entrepreneur would not need to invest additional cash in the venture.

Introducing uncertainty with simulation in the Morebucks example can add significant richness. We could continue to refine the assump-

TABLE **7.12**   **Pro forma financial model for Morebucks with simulation**

Pro forma income statement	Time 0	Year 1	Year 2	Year 3	Assumption	Basis for assumption
Net revenue	0	435,958	826,639	851,944		From revenue forecast
Cost of sales and occupancy		231,929	439,772	453,234	53.2%	From Peet's common size statement
Gross profit	0	204,028	386,867	398,710		
Operating expenses		124,403	235,885	243,106	28.5%	From Peet's common size statement
General and administrative expenses		37,928	71,918	74,119	8.7%	From Peet's common size statement
Depreciation and amortization expenses		50,000	50,000	50,000		7 years, straight line—on fixed assets, gross
Income from operations	0	(8,303)	29,064	31,484		
Interest income (expense), net						
Income before income taxes	0	(8,303)	29,064	31,484		
Income tax provision		0	10,172	11,020	35%	Effective rate only applies to positive income
Net income	0	(8,303)	18,892	20,465		

Pro forma balance sheet	Time 0	Year 1	Year 2	Year 3	Assumption	Basis for assumption
Assets						
Current assets						
Required cash	0	6,539	12,400	12,779	1.50%	Based on Peet's cash/ revenue ratios
Surplus cash	375,000	76,184	153,577	224,592		
Accounts receivable	0	4,360	8,266	8,519	100	Based on Peet's revenue/accounts receivable ratio
Inventory	0	5,449	10,333	10,649	80	Based on industry sales/inventory ratio
Total current assets	375,000	92,532	184,576	256,540		
Fixed assets, gross		350,000	350,000	350,000	350,000	Based on fundamental analysis
Less: accumulated depreciation		(50,000)	(100,000)	(150,000)		
Net fixed assets	0	300,000	250,000	200,000		
Total assets	375,000	392,532	434,576	456,540		
Liabilities						
Current liabilities						
Accounts payable	0	13,079	24,799	25,558	3.00%	Based on accounts payable/sales ratio
Wages payable	0	12,756	24,187	24,928	5.50%	Based on Peet's compensation/cost of sales ratio
Total current liabilities	0	25,835	48,987	50,486		
Long-term debt	0	0	0	0		
Total liabilities	0	25,835	48,987	50,486		

(continued)

TABLE **7.12**   (*continued*)

Pro forma balance sheet	Time 0	Year 1	Year 2	Year 3	Assumption	Basis for assumption
Equity						
Common stock	375,000	375,000	375,000	375,000	375,000	Selected to cover start-up investments
Retained earnings		(8,303)	10,589	31,054		
Total equity	375,000	366,697	385,589	406,054		
Total liabilities and equity	375,000	392,532	434,576	456,540		

Pro forma cash flow statement	Time 0	Year 1	Year 2	Year 3		
Operating cash flow						
Net income	0	(8,303)	18,892	20,465		
Plus: depreciation	0	50,000	50,000	50,000		
(Increase) decrease in accounts receivable	0	(4,360)	(3,907)	(253)		
(Increase) decrease in inventory	0	(5,449)	(4,884)	(316)		
Increase (decrease) in accounts payable	0	13,079	11,720	759		
Increase (decrease) in wages payable	0	12,756	11,431	740		
Operating cash flow	0	57,723	83,253	71,395		
Investing cash flow						
(Increase) decrease in gross fixed assets	0	(350,000)	0	0		
Investing cash flow	0	(350,000)	0	0		
Financing cash flow						
Increase (decrease) in debt	0	0	0	0		
Increase (decrease) in common stock						
Dividend paid	375,000	0	0	0		
Financing cash flow	375,000	0	0	0		
Net cash flow	375,000	(292,277)	83,253	71,395		
Beginning cash	0	375,000	82,723	165,976		
Ending cash	375,000	82,723	165,976	237,371		

NOTE: *This figure is taken from an Excel spreadsheet and shows completed financial statements for the first three years of the coffee shop venture. Shaded cells are the variables simulated using* Venture.SIM.

tions or consider other decision variables. There is also more we can do with simulation to understand the risks of the venture. We could, for example, use the trial results to study the relation between profitability and the operating expense result or profitability and the realized sales level.

Most new ventures would require more frequent pro formas (e.g., quarterly or monthly) and a longer forecast horizon. The current simulation

| Unconditional Simulation Results | | Trials = 5000 | | | | Venture.**SIM** | | | | |

	Output	Average	Median	Standard Deviation	Skewness	Percentiles				
						Minimum	25%	50%	75%	Maximum
1	Year 1 Sales	$532,230	$543,898	$84,897	-0.417	$302,629	$472,007	$543,898	$599,013	$699,461
2	Year 2 Sales	$883,416	$886,977	$51,483	-0.181	$750,888	$846,751	$886,977	$921,096	$997,067
3	Year 3 Sales	$883,782	$886,585	$56,238	-0.134	$730,198	$844,020	$886,585	$924,587	$1,033,112
4	Year 1 Net Income	($16,518)	($12,871)	$16,118	-0.685	($74,699)	($27,346)	($12,871)	($7,852)	$20,021
5	Year 2 Net Income	$14,508	$13,987	$12,687	-0.314	($44,566)	$5,881	$13,987	$22,924	$53,760
6	Year 3 Net Income	$14,539	$14,345	$12,737	-0.232	($45,078)	$5,963	$14,345	$23,285	$60,724
7	Operating CF Year 1	$73,047	$78,388	$18,667	-0.726	$6,426	$60,440	$78,388	$82,947	$112,907
8	Operating CF Year 2	$97,418	$97,365	$13,588	-0.243	$39,087	$88,683	$97,365	$106,589	$141,033
9	Operating CF Year 3	$84,552	$84,452	$12,848	-0.183	$24,339	$75,709	$84,452	$93,410	$133,821
10	Operating Expense %	27.6%	27.6%	2.0%	0.019	21.2%	26.2%	27.6%	28.9%	34.9%

FIGURE **7.3**
Simulation results from the Morebucks financial model
Results are shown from a 5,000-trial simulation using *Venture*.SIM. Simulated variables include revenue, profit, and operating cash flow in Years 1–3 and the operating expense percentage.

also allows ending cash to be negative (although, given our assumptions, this does not occur). Negative cash would require more initial equity or additional cash investments after start-up.

7.7 NewCompany: Building an Integrated Financial Model

We now return to our earlier example, the medical technology venture called NewCompany. In Chapter 6, we developed a static revenue forecast and then extended the revenue forecasting model to incorporate uncertainty. We follow a similar trajectory here in developing an integrated financial forecast. We begin with a static version of the NewCompany financial model. The static model is based on the assumptions that are detailed in Figure 7.4. These assumptions are intended to reflect the expected value of each assumption. After we complete the static model, we will modify the assumptions to introduce uncertainty.

You should assume that we developed the assumptions in Figure 7.4 on the basis of yardsticks, industry norms, and fundamental analysis, as we did for Morebucks. The first three assumptions were used to develop the static revenue forecast in Chapter 6. The others are the bases for individual line items in the pro forma income statement and balance sheet. The final three assumptions specify the initial investment

FIGURE **7.4**

NewCompany integrated financial model assumptions
All assumptions are expected values.

1. Development will require 18 months, during which period no sales will be made.

2. Initial volume will be 100 units with a $200 per unit selling price, beginning in Month 19.

3. Sales volume will grow 8 percent per month for three years and zero thereafter.

4. Operating expenses during the 18-month development period are projected to be $20,000 per month plus inflation (includes the entrepreneur's salary of $3,000 per month).

5. Annual inflation is projected to be 6.0 percent, or 0.5 percent per month.

6. Cost of sales is projected to be 50 percent of revenue.

7. Beginning in Month 19, the venture is expected to incur fixed selling general and administrative (SG&A) expenses of $30,000 per month, growing at the rate of inflation. This includes the entrepreneur's salary. Variable SG&A expenses are projected to be 20 percent of sales.

8. A production facility will come online at the end of Month 18 and is expected to be adequate for the ensuing five years of operation (through Month 78). Monthly lease payments for the facility and production equipment will begin in Month 19 and are included in fixed SG&A expenses.

9. The effective corporate tax rate is projected to be 35 percent on positive income with no loss carryforward; i.e., any loss in a given period gets no tax credit and cannot accumulate to offset future profits.

10. All sales are for credit. Accounts receivable (A/R) are expected to be equivalent to 45 days' sales. This means 100 percent of the current month's sales and 50 percent of the prior month's sales are in the A/R balance at the end of each month.

11. The inventory turnover rate is projected to be six times per year or 60 days' cost of sales in inventory. In each month, the inventory balance will be the forecasted cost of sales for the following two months.

12. All materials are purchased on credit. The average payables period is projected to be 20 days and is calculated based on cost of sales. This means the accounts payable balance each month will be two-thirds of the forecasted cost of sales two months later.

13. The company needs to maintain a minimum cash balance equal to either 20 percent of the prior month's sales or $15,000, whichever is greater.

14. Initial equity investment by the entrepreneur is $500,000. Additional funding, if needed, will come from a hypothetical line of credit with no limit. Interest on the credit line is 0.75 percent monthly (9 percent annually).

15. Free cash flow in any period will first be used to reduce the balance of the line of credit and then will be accumulated as surplus cash. Surplus cash earns interest income at 0.33 percent monthly (4 percent annually).

and provide a mechanism for bringing the balance sheet into balance, either by increasing financing or by building up surplus cash. We establish a minimum cash balance of the greater of $15,000 or 20 percent of the prior month's sales. We introduce a line of credit (debt) that will allow NewCompany to maintain the minimum cash balance. By adding debt to the model, we provide more flexibility in our capital structure assumptions.

Consistent with the earlier discussion, if the venture is short of cash in any period, it is assumed to draw automatically on the credit line; if it generates free cash flow, the line is paid down. If the line is fully paid off and the venture generates free cash flow, the excess is retained as surplus cash. The credit line has a 0.75 percent monthly interest rate (9 percent annually), and surplus cash earns a 0.33 percent monthly return (4 percent annually).

In contrast to the Morebucks model, we include an explicit inflation forecast in the assumptions so that we are forecasting in nominal terms. Inflation will impact the selling price and most of the expenses, because they are calculated as percentages of revenue or cost of sales. Some expenses are fixed in nominal terms.

Table 7.13 contains the pro forma financial statements on a monthly basis from the start of product development through the first five years of sales. With an expected development period of 18 months, the total forecast horizon is 78 months. The financial statements are simplified but appropriate for the venture. While only selected months are shown in Table 7.13, the Excel file upon which the table is based contains all months. We selected the months to include in the table because they correspond to major milestones: development, start of revenue, initiation of external financing, profitability, positive operating cash flow, and the end of five years of sales operation. We now work through the statements chronologically, highlighting the months shown.

Modeling the Development Stage

Under the heading for Month 0, Table 7.13 shows the beginning balance sheet. Based on the assumptions in Figure 7.4, NewCompany has only one asset at start-up—cash—all of which the entrepreneur invests in the venture as equity. For now, we assume an initial investment of $500,000. Development activity begins in Month 1 and is shown as the $20,000 of operating expenses on the income statement. The surplus cash balance earns $1,617 of interest income in Month 1, resulting in negative pretax income of $18,383. To keep the model simple, we do not consider tax-loss carryforwards or tax credits on negative net income.

			Month			
Income statement	0	1	18	19	20	21
Unit sales		—	—	100	108	117
Selling price		$—	$—	$200.00	$201.00	$202.01
Revenue	$—	$—	$—	$20,000	$21,708	$23,635
Cost of sales		$—	$—	$10,000	$10,854	$11,817
Gross profit		$—	$—	$10,000	$10,854	$11,817
Development expense		$20,000	$21,770	$—	$—	$—
SG&A expense		$—	$—	$34,000	$34,492	$35,028
Operating profit		($20,000)	($21,770)	($24,000)	($23,638)	($23,210)
Interest income (expense), net		$1,617	$488	$383	$234	$112
Profit before income tax		($18,383)	($21,281)	($23,617)	($23,404)	($23,098)
Tax expense		$—	$—	$—	$—	$—
Net income		($18,383)	($21,281)	($23,617)	($23,404)	($23,098)
Balance sheet						
Cash	$500,000	$481,617	$129,930	$85,138	$48,739	$21,526
Accounts receivable		$—	$—	$20,000	$31,708	$34,489
Inventory		$—	$20,854	$22,671	$24,607	$26,664
Total current assets		$481,617	$150,784	$127,809	$105,054	$82,679
Fixed assets, gross						
Accumulated depreciation						
Fixed assets, net						
Total assets		$481,617	$150,784	$127,809	$105,054	$82,679
Accounts payable		$—	$7,236	$7,878	$8,527	$9,249
Total current liabilities		$—	$7,236	$7,878	$8,527	$9,249
Long-term debt (credit line)	$—	$—	$—	$—	$—	$—
Total liabilities		$—	$7,236	$7,878	$8,527	$9,249
Equity	$500,000	$481,617	$143,548	$119,931	$96,527	$73,430
Total liabilities and equity	$500,000	$481,617	$150,784	$127,809	$105,054	$82,679
Statement of cash flows						
Operating cash flow						
Net income		($18,383)	($21,281)	($23,617)	($23,404)	($23,098)
Plus: depreciation expense						
Changes in:						
Less: increase in accounts receivable		$—	$—	($20,000)	($11,708)	($2,781)
Less: increase in inventory		$—	($10,854)	($1,817)	($1,936)	($2,057)
Plus: increase in accounts payable		$—	$569	$642	$648	$723
Operating cash flow		($18,383)	($31,566)	($44,792)	($36,399)	($27,213)
Investing cash flow						
Change in gross fixed assets						
Financing cash flow						
Change in long-term debt (credit line)		$—	$—	$—	$—	$—
Dividend						
Financing cash flow		$—	$—	$—	$—	$—
NET CASH FLOW		($18,383)	($31,566)	($44,792)	($36,399)	($27,213)
Beginning cash		$500,000	$161,496	$129,930	$85,138	$48,739
Ending cash	$500,000	$481,617	$129,930	$85,138	$48,739	$21,526
Financing activity						
New financing needed		$—	$—	$—	$—	$—
Debt repayment		$—	$—	$—	$—	$—

NOTE: *Based on the assumptions in Figure 7.4, this table shows the expected financial performance of NewCompany for selected months over the 78-month forecast period (the available Excel spreadsheet contains all months).*

22	23	41	42	54	55	56	77	78
126	136	549	593	1,491	1,610	1,610	1,610	1,610
$203.02	$204.03	$223.19	$224.31	$238.15	$239.34	$240.53	$267.09	$268.43
$25,580	$27,748	$122,534	$133,016	$355,075	$385,331	$387,258	$430,019	$432,169
$12,790	$13,874	$61,267	$66,508	$177,537	$192,666	$193,629	$215,009	$216,084
$12,790	$13,874	$61,267	$66,508	$177,537	$192,666	$193,629	$215,009	$216,084
$—	$—	$—	$—	$—	$—	$—	$—	$—
$35,568	$36,154	$57,986	$60,250	$106,737	$112,967	$113,531	$126,068	$126,698
($22,778)	($22,280)	$3,281	$6,258	$70,801	$79,699	$80,097	$88,942	$89,386
$22	($155)	($3,721)	($3,898)	($6,059)	($6,203)	($6,227)	$530	$707
($22,757)	($22,435)	($440)	$2,360	$64,742	$73,496	$73,870	$89,472	$90,093
$—	$—	$—	$826	$22,660	$25,724	$25,855	$31,315	$31,533
($22,757)	($22,435)	($440)	$1,534	$42,082	$47,772	$48,016	$58,157	$58,561
$15,000	$15,000	$22,564	$24,507	$65,449	$71,015	$77,066	$297,602	$351,500
$37,397	$40,538	$178,943	$194,283	$518,696	$562,869	$579,923	$643,959	$647,178
$28,945	$31,454	$138,646	$150,414	$386,294	$388,226	$390,167	$433,249	$435,416
$81,342	$86,992	$340,153	$369,204	$970,439	$1,022,109	$1,047,157	$1,374,809	$1,434,094
$81,342	$86,992	$340,153	$369,204	$970,439	$1,022,109	$1,047,157	$1,374,809	$1,434,094
$10,047	$10,922	$48,092	$52,184	$129,086	$129,731	$130,380	$144,777	$145,500
$10,047	$10,922	$48,092	$52,184	$129,086	$129,731	$130,380	$144,777	$145,500
$20,622	$47,832	$519,717	$543,142	$827,049	$830,301	$806,684	$—	$—
$30,669	$58,754	$567,810	$595,326	$956,135	$960,033	$937,064	$144,777	$145,500
$50,673	$28,238	($227,656)	($226,122)	$14,304	$62,077	$110,092	$1,230,033	$1,288,593
$81,342	$86,992	$340,153	$369,204	$970,439	$1,022,109	$1,047,157	$1,374,809	$1,434,094
($22,757)	($22,435)	($440)	$1,534	$42,082	$47,772	$48,016	$58,157	$58,561
($2,909)	($3,141)	($14,194)	($15,340)	($40,671)	($44,172)	($17,055)	($3,204)	($3,220)
($2,281)	($2,509)	($10,871)	($11,768)	($16,092)	($1,931)	($1,941)	($2,155)	($2,166)
$798	$875	$3,753	$4,092	$642	$645	$649	$720	$724
($27,148)	($27,210)	($21,753)	($21,482)	($14,038)	$2,314	$29,668	$53,518	$53,898
$20,622	$27,210	$23,544	$23,425	$19,174	$3,253	($23,617)	$—	$—
$20,622	$27,210	$23,544	$23,425	$19,174	$3,253	($23,617)	$—	$—
($6,526)	$—	$1,792	$1,943	$5,136	$5,566	$6,051	$53,518	$53,898
$21,526	$15,000	$20,772	$22,564	$60,313	$65,449	$71,015	$244,084	$297,602
$15,000	$15,000	$22,564	$24,507	$65,449	$71,015	$77,066	$297,602	$351,500
$20,622	$27,210	$23,544	$23,425	$19,174	$3,253	$—	$—	$—
$—	$—	$—	$—	$—	$—	$23,617	$—	$—

The cash flow statement reflects this loss as the first line in operating cash flow. Because the company has no depreciable assets and no activity that would create working capital, the loss is operating cash flow. The negative operating cash flow reduces the company's cash balance to $481,617, far in excess of the minimum. Except for inflationary increases in development expenses, the statements for Months 2 through 18 are similar to those for Month 1. Over this period, losses continue to erode NewCompany's cash. At the end of the development period, Month 18, there is $129,930 remaining in cash.

Modeling the Start of Sales

In Month 18, development is completed, and by the end of the month, NewCompany has 60 days (two months) of inventory on its balance sheet. The inventory balance of $20,854 represents the cost of sales for Months 19 and 20. This inventory buildup is partly funded by $7,236 of spontaneous financing, in the form of 20 days of trade credit (A/P [accounts payable]) from suppliers, calculated as two-thirds (20 days/30 days = 2/3) of the Month 20 cost of sales.

Sales commence in Month 19, and $20,000 of revenue appears on the income statement. With NewCompany granting 45-day trade credit and all sales on account, the full $20,000 goes on the balance sheet as accounts receivable. In Month 20, revenue is $21,708, again all on credit. NewCompany collects the first half of Month 19's sales, leaving the following A/R (accounts receivable) balance:

Month 20 beginning A/R	$20,000
Plus: credit sales	$21,708
Less collections	($10,000)
Month 20 ending A/R	$31,708

At this point, the venture is not profitable, with a loss in Month 20 of $23,404. Operating cash flow is even more negative, $36,399, attributable to the increase in net working capital that is needed to support the rapid growth in sales.

Modeling External Funding

At the end of Month 21, NewCompany's cash balance is down to $21,526. In Month 22, the venture is still not profitable and has a negative operating cash flow of $27,148. To maintain the minimum cash balance, NewCompany must draw on its line of credit by borrowing $20,622 in Month 22.

The credit line carries 0.75 percent monthly interest, with interest expense computed on the basis of the prior month's balance. The interest expense for the $20,622 borrowed in Month 22 ($155) appears on the Month 23 income statement. The balance sheet shows the outstanding balance of the credit line beginning in Month 22; this is the start of a period of more than two years during which NewCompany must increase its borrowing every month. Not until Month 56, after the period of rapid sales growth ends, does the credit line balance begin to decrease as cash flow is sufficient to pay down the line of credit.

By Month 23, the company has exhausted the entrepreneur's initial investment, and the balance sheet shows that, from an accounting "book value" perspective, owner's equity is almost gone. If we were to construct financial statements in terms of economic value, the statements would look very different. Assuming that the development activities are progressing, the expenditures during the first 18 months are actually capital investments in an intangible asset. The value of this asset, though not reflected in book value, is a critical element of the venture's economic value. In fact, without this economic value, NewCompany would have little ability to attract funding. We assume that perceived economic value is sufficient to convince a lender to make a long-term loan in the form of a line of credit.

In Month 25, the book value of equity turns negative, which persists until Month 53. The negative balance simply means that all of the owner's initial capital has been expended, plus part of what was borrowed from the line of credit. The equity is negative because of the long period of unprofitability. Each month's negative profit accumulates to retained earnings, and by Month 25 the aggregated losses surpass the original equity contribution. If economic value is high enough, the negative balance in the equity account should not concern us. In fact, many new ventures with negative book equity still have positive economic value.[10]

Achieving Profitability

Table 7.13 shows NewCompany reaching profitability in Month 42. As significant as this is as a milestone, operating cash flow continues to be significantly negative as a result of the continuing working capital investment. This difference between profit and cash flow is important because, even though NewCompany is profitable, it continues to need to access the line of credit to offset the negative operating cash flow.

Operating Cash Flow and Stable Growth

Unit sales grow at 8 percent per month until Month 55, when the expected growth rate drops to zero. In Month 55, NewCompany's profits exceed its working capital needs for the first time, resulting in positive operating cash flow. This is a critical milestone, because it reverses the trend of monthly borrowing.

With positive operating cash flow and reduced working capital needs due to slower growth, the company begins to repay the credit line. This continues until Month 73, when a final repayment reduces the credit line to zero. From this point until Month 78, operating cash flow accrues to each month's ending cash balance and is assumed to be retained as surplus cash.

Forecasting Financing Needs

Figure 7.5 graphically depicts NewCompany's pro forma expected financial performance over the 78-month forecast period. Surplus cash starts at $485,000, which is the entrepreneur's Time 0 equity contribution minus the $15,000 minimum cash balance. By Month 22, surplus cash reaches zero and remains there until Month 73. In Month 22, NewCompany begins to borrow on the credit line. The need for external financing continues for 24 months, with the credit line peaking at just over $830,000 in Month 55.

Under our expected assumptions, the venture is in sound financial

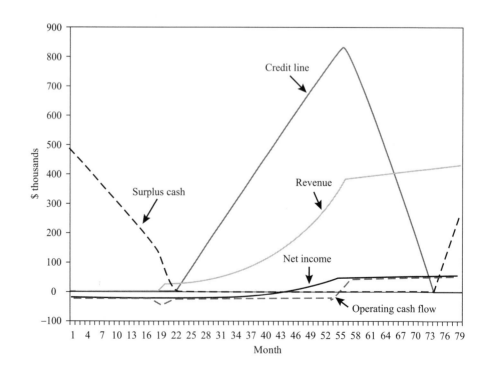

FIGURE **7.5**
NewCompany expected financial performance

shape at Month 78. It is profitable, is generating operating cash flow, has no debt, and has over $350,000 in cash. However, to reach this point the venture is expected to need to borrow over $800,000 along the way.

[S] Uncertainty in the NewCompany Model

The NewCompany financial model provokes a number of questions. For example, how might things change if some of the assumptions prove to be wrong (as they undoubtedly will)? What would change if the entrepreneur were to put more equity into the deal, or if financing were raised in the form of equity, or if it were raised in stages? Finally, how should the entrepreneur select from among the various financing options that may be available? More generally, how does uncertainty affect the financing needs of the venture and its economic value? We begin to explore these issues for NewCompany here and continue the discussion in the next chapter.

In Chapter 6, we introduced uncertainty to the NewCompany sales forecast with regard to the following assumptions:

- Development time
- Initial selling price
- Duration and magnitude of monthly sales growth

The simulation results in Chapter 6 illustrated how this uncertainty can produce very different trajectories for revenue over the 78-month projection period. This variability is shown in Figure 6.6, which presents five very different possible paths for NewCompany's sales.

We now incorporate this development timing and revenue uncertainty into the integrated financial model shown in Table 7.13 and add the following random variables to the simulation:

- Cost of sales
- Monthly development expense
- Variable SG&A expense: percent of sales

Specifically, we make the following assumptions:

Variable	Distribution assumption
Cost of sales	= uniform distribution with minimum of 45% and maximum of 55%.
Development expense	= normally distributed with mean of $20,000 and standard deviation of $200.
Variable SG&A expense	= triangular distribution with minimum of 18%, most likely of 20%, and maximum of 30%.

Again, you should assume that these distributions were developed using some combination of yardstick information, industry data, and fundamental analysis.

Linking Assumptions to the Financial Model

To facilitate use of the NewCompany model for simulation, we have specified all of the assumptions in a single worksheet that is linked directly to the financial statements. Table 7.14 shows the assumption sheet, including one random trial for the simulated variables. In this trial, it turns out that development success is achieved in Month 21, the rapid-growth period goes through Month 44, the initial selling price is $211.05, cost of sales is 48.15 percent of price, development expense begins at $19,630 per month, and SG&A is 26.42 percent. The shaded cells can be changed to test for such things as the effects of a larger initial investment and different expectations about cost percentages.

Results of the Simulation

The NewCompany simulation model is designed so the venture has an open-ended line of credit. If the venture runs short of cash in any month, borrowing is automatic and unlimited. Anytime the venture generates free cash flow, repayment of the loan is automatic. The monthly credit line balance, which reflects NewCompany's cumulative cash needs, is affected by how quickly development occurs, the growth and profitability of subsequent sales, and the amount of investment required for working capital.

Figure 7.6a provides information from five simulated trials and shows the monthly credit line balance. We can see a large variance across the trials, and the data below the chart provide clues about the sources of that variability. For example, the largest cumulative borrowing, over $1.7 million, comes in Trial 3. Trial 3 shows a development month of 79, which means development failed.[11] The credit line balance is the result of 78 months of development expense, starting at $20,000 per month and growing at the rate of inflation. Trial 1, with the second-highest cumulative borrowing, was plagued by late development success, a short rapid-growth period, and below-average growth in monthly revenue. The cumulative borrowing in Trial 2 reaches $1.1 million, but this trial is arguably the most successful of the five. Early development, a long growth period, and a very high growth rate are all indicative of success. Trial 4 is closest to the static case for NewCompany, with development in Month 19, a 38-month growth period, and monthly unit growth of 8.34 percent. The maximum loan balance for Trial 4 is about $970,000.

Revenue assumptions	
Development completion month (lognormal distribution)	
Preliminary month	21
Development completion month	21
Development failure (1 = yes)	0
Rapid-growth period (normal distribution)	
SD* of rapid-growth period	3
Realized length of rapid-growth period	44
Initial unit sales per month	
Initial units/month	100
Unit sales growth during rapid growth (normal distribution)	
Expected growth/month	8.00%
SD of growth/month	1.50%
Realized growth rate per month	9.56%
Initial selling price (normal distribution)	
Expected initial selling price	$200.00
SD of selling price	$10.00
Realized initial selling price	$211.05
Inflation rate per month	
Inflation/month	0.50%

Income statement assumptions	
Cost of sales (uniform distribution)	
Minimum cost of sales	45.00%
Maximum cost of sales	55.00%
Realized cost of sales	48.15%
Monthly development expense (normal distribution)	
Monthly development expenses (expected)	$20,000
Monthly development expenses (SD)	$200
Realized development expense	$19,630
SG&A expenses (fixed + triangular distribution)	
Monthly fixed SG&A expense	$30,000
Minimum variable SG&A	18%
(expected percentage of sales)	
Most likely SG&A expense	20%
Maximum SG&A expense	30%
Realized variable SG&A percent of sales	26.42%
Interest income and interest expense	
Interest expense per month	0.75%
Interest income on surplus cash per month	0.33%
Income tax expense	
Income tax rate (on positive income)	35%

Balance sheet assumptions	
Cash balance	
Minimum cash balance	$15,000
Continuing cash percent of prior month sales	20.0%
Accounts receivable policy (45 days)	
Percent of current month sales	100%
Percent of prior month sales	50%
Inventory policy (60 days)	
Percent of next month cost of sales	100%
Percent of two-month-hence cost of sales	100%
Accounts payable policy (20 days)	
Percent of two-month-hence cost of sales	66.67%
Initial investment	
Initial equity investment	$500,000

The table represents the assumptions page of the NewCompany integrated financial model. Shaded cells are inputs that can be changed; other cells are generated using the assumptions. Information in the assumptions page links directly to the NewCompany financial model.

*SD = standard deviation

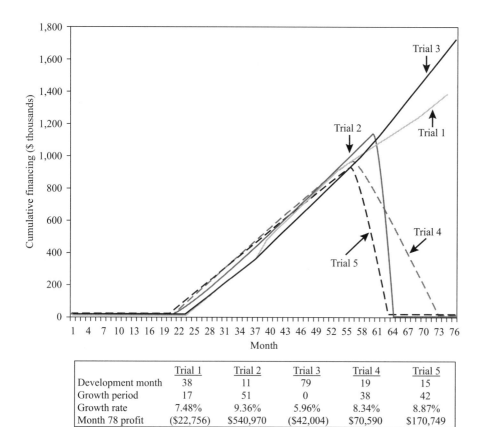

(a)

	Trial 1	Trial 2	Trial 3	Trial 4	Trial 5
Development month	38	11	79	19	15
Growth period	17	51	0	38	42
Growth rate	7.48%	9.36%	5.96%	8.34%	8.87%
Month 78 profit	($22,756)	$540,970	($42,004)	$70,590	$170,749

Unconditional Simulation Results

Trials = 10000

Venture.**SIM**

Output	Average	Median	Standard Deviation	Skewness		Minimum	25%	50%	75%	Maximum
					Percentiles					
1 Ending Revenue	$764,594	$458,514	$999,477	3.73		$0	$172,730	$458,514	$966,007	$14,519,812
2 Ending Net Income	$107,114	$51,988	$186,134	3.70		-$43,188	-$862	$51,988	$147,580	$2,458,522
3 Maximum Borrowing	$1,359,931	$1,236,377	$678,698	4.97		$376,094	$996,063	$1,236,377	$1,606,579	$11,868,962
4 Ending Cash	$1,013,584	$97,912	$2,074,395	4.14		$15,000	$34,374	$97,912	$1,118,370	$29,804,300
5 Ending Operating Cash Flow	$98,524	$47,133	$175,864	3.69		-$46,612	-$2,638	$47,133	$136,832	$2,303,521

(b)

FIGURE **7.6**

NewCompany credit line balance for five simulation trials and summary table of key variables for 10,000 trials

The top portion of the figure shows the time paths of credit balances from five trials of the NewCompany model. Data below the chart provide information on development time, duration and rate of unit growth, together with Month 78 profitability for each trial. The *Venture*.SIM summary table shows distribution information for several key variables based on 10,000 trials of the model

The point is that large credit line balances can occur for many reasons and are not necessarily evidence of NewCompany's success or failure. In the next chapter, we consider how operational performance impacts the venture's need for financing. We also consider how staging, milestones, and financing decisions can help distinguish ventures that are likely to be successful from those that are probable failures.

Figure 7.6b is a summary table of some of the important outcome variables from the NewCompany simulation. The table shows the wide range of possible outcomes with respect to each variable. Revenue in Month 78 ranges from $0 to more than $14.5 million, though half of the trials (the interquartile range) have revenue between about $172,700 and $966,000. Month 78 net income is negative in more than one-fourth of the trials but also has the potential to be very high. The maximum balance on the line of credit ranges from a low of $376,000 to almost $12 million but three-quarters of the time is less than about $1.6 million. Ending cash ranges between the minimum and almost $30 million but three-quarters of the time is less than $1.2 million. Ending operating cash flow is similar to ending net income. The similarity is because by Month 78 the assumed growth rate of unit sales has declined to zero, so that changes in working capital are slight.

Ideally, we would like to invest in the good outcomes represented in the figure but cut off investment in the bad ones as quickly as we can identify them. In Chapter 8, we explore the use of simulation to assess financing needs and opportunities to stage financing for the purpose of creating more value from investment in the venture.

7.8 Summary

Pro forma financial statements are important to any new venture and a key component in any entrepreneur's or investor's toolkit. Financial forecasting adds discipline to the way an entrepreneur or investor thinks about the venture. It provides estimates of future cash flows, which drive financing decisions and are important determinants of value. A forecast can also be important for convincing prospective investors of the merits of the project and can provide specific performance benchmarks around which financing and incentive contracts can be designed.

A well-constructed integrated financial model of a new venture accomplishes two things. First, it reflects the important aspects of the venture's business model in the three main financial statements: income statement, balance sheet, and cash flow statement. Second, it provides reliable estimates of the venture's future cash flows.

We use the venture's cash conversion cycle to better understand the important links between day-to-day operations and cash flow. The cash conversion cycle visually portrays how cash moves through the firm, as well as in and out of the firm to capital providers. Working capital policies are important determinants of a venture's operating cash flows. These include the granting of credit to customers, levels of inventory on hand, and the ability to generate spontaneous financing in the form of accounts payable.

Preparing a credible and useful financial model requires well-researched and defensible assumptions. Yardsticks based on public or private companies and industry statistics can be used to develop benchmark performance metrics and to build the new venture's financial model. Public SEC documents, primarily 10-K and prospectus filings, are one place to seek information on comparable firms. The yardstick approach is straightforward to implement and can provide robust estimates of profit margins, resource requirements, and industry practices related to working capital management.

No new venture will perform exactly like the yardstick companies, however, and financial projections should also reflect the use of fundamental analysis to develop the schedule of assumptions. An integrated financial model might use assumptions developed using yardstick data and then validated with fundamental analysis or the converse.

With a schedule of the key assumptions, spreadsheet modeling can be used to develop an integrated financial model for preparing pro forma financial forecasts. An integrated model features an income statement, a balance sheet, and a cash flow statement, all linked to one another and across time. An integrated financial model allows the entrepreneur or investor to conduct "what if" analysis and facilitates the use of simulation to assess the effects of uncertainty. Both scenario analysis and simulation analysis are valuable tools for assessing the prospects and potential future value of any new venture.

REVIEW QUESTIONS

1. What information does each of the three main financial statements convey about the venture's operations? Describe three important links across the statements.

2. Explain the cash flow cycle in Figure 7.1. Give particular attention to categorizing each cash flow shown as operating, investing, or financing. Why are these distinctions important to a new venture?

3. What are the main components of a venture's working capital policy? How does each impact the firm's operations and cash flows?

How much control does a new venture have over its working capital policies?

4. Describe several common sources of yardstick data that can be used as bases for developing forecast assumptions.

5. Under what conditions is the yardstick approach to preparing pro forma financials likely to produce accurate statements? When is fundamental analysis a preferable method?

6. What accounts are most important when forecasting a new venture's balance sheet? Which of these lend themselves to using yardsticks and which are better estimated on the basis of fundamental analysis?

7. Describe the three different approaches to making the balance sheet balance when building an integrated financial model using spreadsheets.

8. Explain the concept of depreciation as a "noncash" expense. Does this mean it has no impact at all on a venture's cash flows?

9. What can cause the retained earnings account to change from one period to the next?

10. What is the accounting impact of negative shareholders' equity? How can a venture with negative book equity continue to operate and attract capital?

NOTES

1. We assume that the reader is familiar with the basic terminology and concepts of financial accounting.

2. Elsewhere in the book we describe the entrepreneur as investing effort as well as cash, whereas here we refer only to investing cash. There is, however, no inconsistency; you can think of the entrepreneur's investment of effort in terms of its cash equivalent.

3. Net working capital is usually defined as all current assets less all current liabilities. However, some current assets, such as marketable securities, may not be central to operation of the venture, and some current liabilities, such as notes payable, which are related to financing, are not considered part of the operating activities of the business.

4. See Ng, Smith, and Smith (1999) for supporting evidence.

5. Smith (1987) interprets credit terms with significant discounts for prompt payment as a device the seller can use to gain timely information about the financial health of its customers.

6. See http://www.rmahq.org/RMA/RMAUniverse/Productsand Services/RMABookstore/StatementStudies/statementstudiesfaqs.htm for more information.

7. When developing assumptions based on comparables or industry statistics, medians are usually more meaningful than means because they are not affected by extreme outlier values.

8. Inventory turnover can also be computed as cost of sales divided by inventory. To compute days in inventory, divide 360 by the inventory turnover ratio.

9. Required cash is a function of revenue; as there is no Time 0 revenue, all of the $375,000 appears as surplus cash.

10. This is not true only for new ventures. At year end 2003, Amazon .com had stockholders' equity of *negative* $1 billion, but a market value of $21 billion.

11. We ignore the question of how long development efforts would be allowed to continue in the face of ongoing failure. This will be revisited in Chapter 8.

References and Additional Reading

Mian, S. L., and C. W. Smith Jr. 1992. "Accounts-Receivable Management Policy: Theory and Evidence." *Journal of Finance* 47:169–200.

Ng, C., J. K. Smith, and R. L. Smith. 1999. "Evidence on the Determinants of Credit Terms Used in Interfirm Trade." *Journal of Finance* 54:1109–29.

Smith, J. K. 1987. "Trade Credit and Informational Asymmetry." *Journal of Finance* 42:863–72.

CHAPTER 8

ASSESSING FINANCIAL NEEDS

Necessity never made a good bargain.

Attributed to Benjamin Franklin

The objective of this chapter is to enable the entrepreneur to answer the question, "How much money do I need and when do I need it?" For this, we build on the forecasting tools from Chapters 6 and 7 and focus on methods of assessing financial needs.

An entrepreneur must have a good sense of how much cash will be required to carry the venture to the point where it becomes self-sustaining or capable of attracting additional funding, as well as a good sense of when cash infusions are likely to be needed. An entrepreneur who does not anticipate the cash needs over the life of the venture assumes unnecessary risk. The venture may fail, not because the idea is bad but because the entrepreneur did not anticipate the cash need far enough in advance to do anything about it. Or the venture may succeed, but only after investors make such large and poorly timed cash infusions that the entrepreneur's stake is reduced unnecessarily. Even if the total cash need is large, the entrepreneur's failure to anticipate it can result in an adverse negotiating position with investors—either because the need is urgent or because the original financing agreement impedes the ability to raise cash in the future.

"Do not run out of cash" is a common admonition to entrepreneurs. But having too much cash can also be problematic. An entrepreneur who is overly cautious may find that raising "enough" cash up front is not feasible. Even if substantial early-stage financing can be arranged, it may come at a high price, and the entrepreneur may be compelled to give up more of the venture than is necessary or desirable. Although a venture cannot survive without cash, the objective is not merely survival; rather, it is to finance the venture in a way that yields the highest expected value for the entrepreneur.

As a general principle, an entrepreneur who is more confident of success than are potential investors can benefit by raising only enough cash to carry the venture to the next milestone. At that point, the lower risk of failure will be more apparent to the investors. Reduced risk can foster competition among investors and should enable the entrepreneur to raise capital on more favorable terms than in the earlier round. There is, of course, a tradeoff. Raising less cash in an early round increases the probability that the venture will run out of cash before the next milestone is achieved. Running short of cash before reaching an important milestone can suggest to investors that the venture is not on track for success.

We begin by presenting the sustainable growth model and identifying the conditions under which the growth of a venture can be sustained solely by the initial investment. We refer to this as the "sustainable growth rate."[1] If the entrepreneur anticipates that the growth may be higher than the sustainable growth rate, then additional financing may be required and the options for adding investment capital must be evaluated.

Cash flow breakeven analysis is another tool for assessing financial needs. It can be used to help identify the cash flow breakeven point (BEP), that is, the level of sales at which a venture would be able to maintain operations without additional funding (although it still could need funding for growth). Combining cash flow breakeven analysis with projections of sales growth can help the entrepreneur assess the amount of investment a venture would need in order to achieve a level of sales sufficient to maintain its operations.

Later in the chapter, we use scenario analysis and simulation to focus on how uncertainty affects the need for financing. These methods can be used to assess how cash needs may be affected by uncertainty about development timing, sales levels, fixed and variable costs, and other factors. Assessing financial need only on the basis of expected performance can expose the entrepreneur to avoidable risk of venture failure or loss of control.

Finally, when a venture's prospects are uncertain, staging the investment around milestones can be of great value; but uncertainty of performance also makes the funding need in a given financing round uncertain. We use simulation to fine-tune the funding decision in the context of staged financing.

8.1 Sustainable Growth as a Starting Point

A useful starting point for financial needs assessment is to explore the conditions under which, following an initial investment, the operating cash flow of the venture is sufficient to sustain growth. Sustainable growth starts with the assumption that as the venture grows, assets, debt, equity, sales, and net income all grow in fixed proportion to sales.[2] This means the sustainable growth rate for a venture depends on four factors:

1. Asset turnover ("turnover")—the amount of sales revenue that can be supported per dollar of assets
2. Financial leverage ("leverage")—the ratio of the venture's assets to its equity, where the difference between assets and equity represents debt financing
3. Return on sales ("ROS")—the profitability of sales in terms of after-tax net income per dollar of sales
4. Dividend policy ("retention")—the fraction of each dollar of net income that is retained in the venture as opposed to being paid out as dividends

Figure 8.1 illustrates the concept of sustainable growth, denoted as g^*, and incorporates the following assumptions:

Factor	Definition and value
Asset turnover	Sales/total assets = 3.0
Financial leverage	Total assets/equity = 1.5
Return on sales (ROS)	Net income/sales = 10%
Dividend retention (R)	Fraction of net income retained = 2/3

Suppose an entrepreneur makes an initial investment of $100 in the form of equity and wishes to calculate the rate of growth this can sustain. The leverage ratio of 1.5 (assumed to be appropriate for the venture) implies that the venture has $1.50 of assets for each $1 of equity. The difference of $50 is debt financing. These amounts are reflected in the starting balance sheet shown in Figure 8.1.

Reinforcing the notion of statement integration from Chapter 7, the turnover ratio in the figure shows that each dollar of assets is expected to support three dollars of sales. This results in sustainable sales in the first year of $450. The assumed 10 percent return on sales (shown in the income statement) implies Year 1 net income of $45. In the figure, we

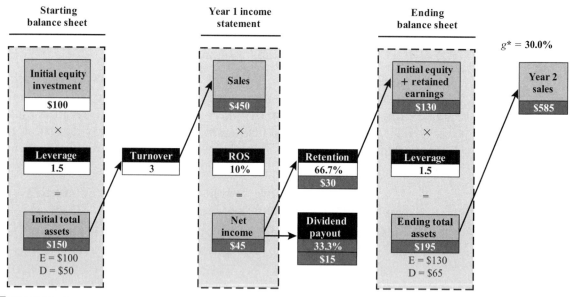

$\boxed{\text{T}}$FIGURE **8.1**

Sustainable growth model template
This figure is an Excel template that illustrates the key variables, relationships, and results in the sustainable growth model. Assumptions in the model can be changed in the template to assess their impact on g^* and the levels of assets, debt, and sales.

assume that the venture has adopted a policy of retaining two-thirds of the net income and distributing one-third as a dividend; hence, $30 goes to retained earnings in the balance sheet, increasing equity to $130. Because the leverage ratio remains constant at 1.5, $130 of equity supports $195 of assets at the beginning of the second year. This level of assets, based on the turnover ratio of 3.0, will support an increase in sales to $585. This 30 percent increase in sales is the sustainable growth rate of the venture, given its leverage and dividend policies, its profitability, and the efficiency of use of its assets.[3]

Figure 8.1 shows that the sustainable growth rate, g^*, is equal to the percentage change in equity. That is:

$$g^* = \frac{\Delta \text{Equity}}{\text{Equity}_{\text{beginning}}} \qquad (8.1)$$

where ΔEquity is the change in equity due to retaining earnings. Because the sustainable growth model excludes the possibility of issuing new equity, the change in equity comes only from net additions to retained earnings, that is:

$$\Delta\text{Equity} = \text{Net Income} - \text{Dividends} = NI \times R \qquad (8.2)$$

where R is the retention ratio. For a venture seeking the maximum sustainable growth rate, R would be 100 percent. Of course, if income is negative, as it is for many new ventures, then so is the sustainable growth rate, and the venture will depend on new investment both to sustain its current size and to grow.

Substituting Eq. (8.2) into Eq. (8.1) gives:

$$g^* = \frac{\Delta\text{Equity}}{\text{Equity}_{\text{beginning}}} = \frac{NI \times R}{\text{Equity}_{\text{beginning}}} = \frac{NI}{\text{Equity}_{\text{beginning}}} \times R = ROE \times R \qquad (8.3)$$

where ROE is return on beginning equity, a simple measure of the venture's profitability. We can decompose ROE into three components as follows:

$$ROE = \frac{NI}{E} = \frac{NI}{\text{Sales}} \times \frac{\text{Sales}}{\text{Total Assets}} \times \frac{\text{Total Assets}}{\text{Equity}}$$
$$= ROS \times \text{Turnover} \times \text{Leverage} \qquad (8.4)$$

Substituting Eq. (8.4) into Eq. (8.3) yields:

$$g^* = ROE \times R = ROS \times \text{Turnover} \times \text{Leverage} \times R \qquad (8.5)$$

Thus, the venture's sustainable growth rate is the product of (1) its profit margin or return on sales (NI/sales or ROS), (2) the asset turnover ratio (sales/total assets or turnover), (3) financial leverage (assets/equity$_{\text{beginning}}$ or leverage), and (4) the retention ratio or dividend payout policy (R). The equation reflects the assumption that sales, net income, assets, and debt all increase proportionately as the venture grows.

Equation (8.5) suggests that the sustainable growth rate of a venture can be increased in several ways. The entrepreneur can try to improve the profit margin on sales, generate more sales from its asset base, or rely more heavily on leverage. If the venture is already operating efficiently, then increasing profitability and asset turnover are not feasible. This leaves leverage and the retention ratio as the policy choices that can influence g^*.

Now it is possible to see how, given an initial investment in equity, the leverage and dividend policies affect the sustainable growth rate and achievable level of future sales. First, recognize that, because of the tax deductibility of interest payments, net income is not independent of the leverage policy. To see the interdependence, as well as the tax shelter, we restate net income as:

$$NI = EBIT - I - T = [EBIT - r(A - E)](1 - t) \qquad (8.6)$$

where *EBIT* is earnings before interest and taxes, $A - E$ is assets minus equity (the amount of debt financing), r is the interest rate on debt, and t is the corporate tax rate. The term in square brackets is simply income before taxes. Substituting Eq. (8.6) into Eq. (8.5) yields:

$$g^* = \frac{[EBIT - r(A - E)](1 - t)}{Sales} \times \text{Turnover} \times \text{Leverage} \times R \tag{8.7}$$

Equation (8.7) can be used to see how the sustainable growth rate varies in response to the policy choices facing the entrepreneur. Suppose an entrepreneur, Gill Bates, is considering a venture to develop and support an online virtual world, iFree. Bates is prepared to make an initial equity investment but prefers not to raise outside equity or debt. For strategic reasons, he believes the iFree venture must reach sales of $2.5 million by the end of the sixth year. Bates is willing to retain all earnings in the venture to reach this goal.

In the iFree business model, we assume an operating margin (*EBIT*/sales) of 10 percent, asset turnover ratio of 2.0, and corporate tax rate of 35 percent. Bates's desire to avoid debt means the leverage ratio (assets/equity) is initially 1.0. If debt is used, the interest rate will be 10 percent. His initial plan is to make a $500,000 equity investment at Time 0 to launch the venture.

Will the $500,000 investment be sufficient to achieve the Year 6 sales target? The assets funded by starting equity would generate first-year sales of $1 million based on the turnover ratio of 2.0. With no debt, assets and equity are equal. We can use Eq. (8.7) to determine whether Bates's financial policies and iFree's projected performance will enable the venture to achieve the sales target of $2.5 million by the sixth year.

Based on the assumptions and policies, the sustainable growth rate, g^*, is 13 percent:

$$g^* = \frac{[EBIT - r(A - E)](1 - t)}{Sales} \times \text{Turnover} \times \text{Leverage} \times R$$

$$= \frac{[\$100,000 - 10\%(\$0)](1 - 35\%)}{\$1,000,000} \times 2.0 \times 1.0 \times 100\%$$

$$= 13\%$$

With beginning revenue of $1 million, 13 percent annual growth compounded for five years (Years 2 to 6) will produce sales of $1.842 million by the sixth year, well below the $2.5 million sales target.[4]

Bates is considering several ways in which he can achieve his Year 6 target. First, he can increase the initial equity investment, which would not affect g^*. To reach $2.5 million of sales by Year 6, initial assets have

FIGURE **8.2**

Financial leverage and sustainable growth
The figure shows the relation between leverage and $g*$, the sustainable growth rate. The shaded bar at 26 percent is the debt-to-equity (D/E) ratio that would allow iFree to achieve the desired $2.5 million of Year 6 sales. Adding debt increases $g*$ as long as the venture's after-tax cost of debt is less than the return on assets.

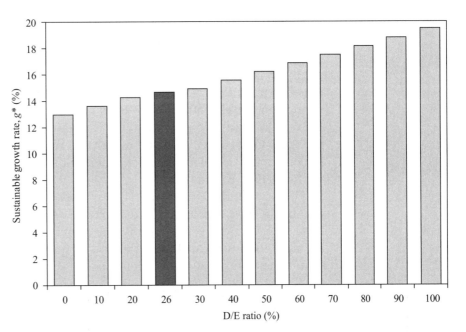

to be $678,500. However, if he contributes only $500,000, Bates would need to raise the balance of the initial equity ($178,500) from outside sources.

Another alternative is for Bates to revisit the policy of no debt financing. Unlike simply increasing initial equity, adding debt affects $g*$ in two offsetting ways. The leverage term in Eq. (8.7) will increase with greater reliance on financial leverage. In addition, return on sales will decrease as interest expense reduces net income. Bates needs to determine what financial leverage ratio would enable the venture to begin with $500,000 in equity and achieve sales of $2.5 million by the sixth year. To determine the required leverage ratio, you can again use Eq. (8.7) and experiment with various debt-to-equity (D/E) ratios (or use Goal Seek in Excel) until you find the one that makes the revenue target achievable. It turns out that a debt-to-equity ratio of 26 percent (initial borrowing of $130,000) makes the leverage ratio 1.26 and increases $g*$ to 14.7 percent.

The key to understanding the impact of leverage on $g*$ lies in the relationship between the interest rate and return on assets. As long as the after-tax cost of debt is less than the return on assets, adding leverage increases the sustainable growth rate. In Figure 8.2, we show the relationship between leverage and sustainable growth for the iFree venture.

Assuming that Bates is correct in setting a sales target of $2.5 million by the end of six years, we are still a chapter or two away from being able to answer the fundamental question of whether raising outside equity or debt would be better for him. Without knowing more, we cannot determine the fraction of equity Bates would need to give up in exchange for the $178,500 of outside equity. That will depend on the value the investor places on the venture. Nor can we determine the value of the remaining equity to the entrepreneur. We also would need to assess the feasibility of borrowing $130,000 and the impact of the debt on the venture's future cash flows.

The key points for now are (1) that the entrepreneur's financing decision can have a dramatic effect on the venture's sustainable growth rate, and (2) that rapid growth (faster than the sustainable growth rate) requires continuing new investments of equity, a higher leverage ratio, or a higher rate of earnings retention.

8.2 Assessing Financial Needs When the Desired Growth Rate Exceeds the Sustainable Growth Rate

Product-market growth that is either too rapid or too slow is problematic. Growth that is too slow threatens venture survival by encouraging competition or hastening technological obsolescence. Growth that is too rapid threatens the entrepreneur's control and the value of the entrepreneur's ownership share.

Long-run survival depends on achieving a level of sales that is sufficient for financial viability. In some product markets, survival and profitability depend on rapidly attaining a substantial market position. Computer software and some Internet ventures are good examples of markets in which long-run survival can depend on the ability to achieve a critical mass of users quickly. In the case of software, this is because many software packages benefit from important "network externalities." Demand for the product increases as more users affiliate with the network. Because of these network externalities, a software manufacturer that does not achieve substantial market share quickly may be driven from the market, even if the product is a good one. There are also significant switching costs to software users, making them more likely to adopt and continue using the market leading product. In some cases, network externalities are sufficiently important that a dominant product can hold competitors at bay, even when products that are technically superior are available at lower prices.

In other cases, rapid growth is not essential for survival but still may be an element of the entrepreneur's aspiration. Without careful analysis, it is easy to equate rapid growth with financial success. But as the sustainable growth model implies, this is not necessarily correct. There are countless examples of rapid growth ultimately destroying a venture.

Webvan was one of the companies that launched in the mid-1990s to offer home delivery of groceries ordered over the Internet. Webvan's management team pursued a "get big fast" strategy, launching distribution in many communities at the same time or in rapid succession. Webvan raised almost $800 million from private and public equity sales in 1999 and had a market capitalization of $8 billion immediately after its IPO. The company entered into a $1 billion contract with Bechtel for construction of 26 state-of-the-art distribution centers across the country.[5] The firm was betting that a significant fraction of the population in each market would switch to ordering groceries on the Internet. Unfortunately, consumer adoption was slower than Webvan had hoped, so that a profitable operation was never achieved. The company filed for bankruptcy in July 2001.

Contrast Webvan with FreshDirect, another Internet-based home-delivery grocery business. FreshDirect sells in only one market, the more densely populated and wealthier areas of New York City and surroundings, and has declined to move into other, less dense markets. FreshDirect introduced its service to NYC consumers in 2002 and has chosen to remain a privately held company. It reportedly is a highly profitable business that has succeeded on the basis of its focused no-growth strategy.

There are other examples where the venture survives but high growth results in loss of control for the entrepreneur. The housing and financial system crisis that began in 2007 provides many good examples. Developers, who hoped to capitalize on the surging demand for housing, dramatically overbuilt in a number of markets. When demand slowed, many of these developers failed even though they held valuable inventories of fully or partially constructed housing. The developers lost their equity investments and property ownership reverted to those who had provided credit for the development.

Commercial and investment banks encountered a similar problem. At the time, these companies were operating with very high financial leverage. When the market values of their assets declined, institutions such as Bear Stearns, Lehman Brothers, Merrill Lynch, Washington Mutual, and Wachovia were compelled to write down the values of their housing-related assets. In some cases the drop was sufficient to wipe out the existing stockholders.

Ironically, during this period regulations that were intended to protect those who traded with the institutions dramatically impeded the institutions' ability to raise additional capital, even though the low values of some of their housing-related assets were likely to be transitory. Institutions such as Goldman Sachs that barely managed to skirt bankruptcy or government takeover have now recovered most of their losses. From a high of $236 in October 2007, Goldman Sachs's stock price declined by 77.5 percent, to $53 in November 2008. By October 2009, the price was back up to $189; Goldman's investors had recovered most of their loss. In contrast, the shareholders of Lehman Brothers, which was slightly more aggressive than Goldman in taking on risks related to the housing market, lost everything. The point is that not providing a financing solution to cover the unexpected bad outcomes can result in a permanent loss for the stockholder (or the entrepreneur) even if the lack of adequate financing is temporary.

The challenge is to identify and implement a viable product-market strategy that fosters long-term survival and also produces value for the entrepreneur. This product-market strategy must be coupled with a financing strategy that weighs the risk of venture failure against the risk of loss of ownership and control. Careful assessment of financial needs is central to the analysis.

8.3 Planning for Product-Market Uncertainty

Financial planning prompts the entrepreneur to assess the benefits and threats of high-risk ventures. The planning process begins with tentative selection of a product-market strategy that includes a growth objective. We refer to this as a conjectural product-market strategy. The conjectural strategy is only a hypothesis as to what might be a good strategy. Financing considerations and implications for value must be assessed before committing to the strategy. Financing considerations can lead the entrepreneur to reject what may appear to be the best product-market strategy in favor of one that is less ambitious but more valuable for the entrepreneur.

For iFree, the conjectural product-market strategy implied a sales goal of $2.5 million in six years. Given the amount Gill Bates was able to invest, the strategy could not be achieved without outside financing. Whether it would be advantageous for the entrepreneur to pursue the financing or to scale back the Year 6 sales target depends on which approach would maximize value for the entrepreneur, a question we take up in the next few chapters.[6]

For now our focus is on how the uncertainty of future product-market performance affects the amount of "financial slack" the entrepreneur might want to provide. Financial slack is liquidity that would enable the venture to deal with surprises without the need to raise additional risk capital. Financial slack is available in various forms, including, for example, cash flow from operations, excess cash or other liquid assets, or an unused line of credit. Lehman Brothers failed because declining asset values wiped out its financial slack. Any entrepreneur of a risky venture faces a similar prospect of financial adversity that is short run for an otherwise healthy venture.

Planning for Success

Ironically, unexpected success in the product market can be a threat to new venture survival and control. Consider, for example, VC funds. Kaplan and Schoar (2003) find evidence that managers of successful funds are able to attract capital for the next fund more easily than are their competitors. They also find, however, that persistence of performance from one fund to the next is inversely related to the growth of funds under management. They interpret their findings as evidence that fund managers who try to grow too rapidly after an early success sacrifice performance, possibly because they are unable to grow their management teams fast enough or because they have limited ability to identify attractive investment opportunities for the funds they manage. The same can be expected for any entrepreneur who is confronted with rapidly growing demand. The entrepreneur may face such challenges as being unable to (1) grow the management team rapidly enough, (2) acquire the assets necessary for production, (3) maintain consistent quality, or (4) arrange financing to support the rate of demand growth. The last point is the focus of this chapter.

For the purpose of assessing long-run financial needs, it is important to contemplate the risk of unexpected success in the product market. If a venture is profitable and is generating cash in excess of capital replacement requirements, it can finance some growth internally. This is the lesson of the sustainable growth model. Excess operating cash flow is an important source of investment capital. For a venture that is debt-free and pays no dividends, the ability to finance growth internally is approximately equal to the venture's after-tax rate of return on beginning assets. This was demonstrated in Eq. (8.7).

If the ROA (return on assets) is, for example, 8 percent, then the venture is capable of growing assets and revenue at a rate of approximately 8 percent by relying exclusively on internally generated funds. A higher growth rate would require external funding. The larger the gap between desired and sustainable growth, the greater the need for external funding.

Conversely, if the ROA exceeds the growth rate of sales, the organization generates free cash flow. Free cash flow is cash flow above the amount needed to fund expected growth and to deal with uncertainty. Free cash flow that is retained by the venture does not contribute to its value but can be retained in an interest-bearing account so that retaining surplus cash does not diminish PV. To enable investors to make the best use of their resources, a venture that generates free cash flow and has no strategic reason for holding cash reserves should distribute the surplus funds. Dividends, share repurchase, and reducing leverage are all means of distributing free cash flow.

Unexpected product-market success compels the entrepreneur to explore alternatives for outside financing. Arranging new financing, however, takes time, and the need to devote attention to seeking financing comes at a critical point for the entrepreneur, a point when rapid growth is likely to generate a host of organizational challenges. With effective planning, the entrepreneur can prepare in advance for scenarios involving growth that is faster than expected.

Although rapid growth usually increases the need for growth-related financing, it does not increase the need for initial financing. At the start-up stage, the potential for success is uncertain. For a venture that is successful in the first stage, financing at the next stage is likely to be available on more favorable terms because of the reduced risk. Nonetheless, in structuring initial financing the entrepreneur must anticipate that growth will require additional financing and have a sense of how the necessary capital would be raised. In negotiating the investment terms for the initial rounds, the entrepreneur will want to preserve the option of raising additional funds if the growth rate justifies doing so.

Current financing decisions sometimes cause problems if the venture needs more funds at a later stage. Loan contracts, for example, sometimes contain covenants that preclude raising additional funds without the lender's approval. If that time comes, the lender's interests may conflict with the entrepreneur's. Some equity financing structures can give rise to similar difficulties. Antidilution provisions sought by equity investors can impair a venture's ability to raise capital, particularly where the venture has run into problems and needs cash to get through them. Agreeing to these constraints on future fundraising can lower the apparent cost of financing to the entrepreneur. But if the venture grows rapidly or runs into difficulties, those earlier decisions can be problematic. Before agreeing to such provisions, the entrepreneur should assess the implications if the venture grows at a rate that is different than expected. Financial modeling of the venture, including modeling of the financing terms, is a means of identifying, and designing around, these threats before they become problems.

Planning for Failure

Once a venture is established and is generating positive cash flows, unexpectedly slow growth may not pose a very serious problem. If the actual growth rate is lower than expected but still high enough to ensure viability, the venture may actually be able to reduce its reliance on external capital. If g^* is greater than actual growth, then the resulting free cash flow can be used to fund new investments or can be distributed to investors.

A more serious problem arises if unexpectedly poor performance is encountered before the organization has reached financial viability. This may occur, for example, if product development takes longer than expected or if sales growth is slower than expected and the attained level of sales is below that needed to generate funds for capital replacement. Either circumstance means the organization must depend on external financing to a greater extent than expected. This is a particularly acute problem because a venture that has not achieved financial viability and has not met growth expectations will have difficulty raising capital. A forward-looking entrepreneur can manage the risk by maintaining financial slack and preserving the ability to raise additional capital if growth is slower than expected.

High-Tech, High-Growth Innovation

Some of the most challenging financing problems are associated with a product innovation that requires a long and expensive development period, which, if successful, is followed by rapid sales growth. Negative cash flows, in such cases, can extend over many years and can last through both the development and rapid-growth stages. The venture will not begin to generate free cash flow for investors until the growth rate slows to a point where operating cash flows are more than sufficient to fund growth. NewCompany has these characteristics and we extend the model later in this chapter.

The pattern of long development lead time followed by rapid sales growth is characteristic of many high-tech innovations (pharmaceuticals, biotechnology, and some electronics, for example). It is not surprising, therefore, that large, well-established companies perform much of the development activity. Such companies can draw on their current financing capabilities without the need to convince investors of the merits of a specific project. They often also have existing infrastructure that reduces the investment required for the development process and can handle the operational demands of rapid growth.

8.4   Cash Flow Breakeven Analysis

Much is written about breakeven analysis in accounting and finance textbooks. Not all of it is flattering, primarily because the accounting approach to breakeven analysis ignores the time value of money and focuses on accounting net income rather than cash flow. In the accounting approach, the breakeven point (BEP) is the quantity of sales where the total contribution margin over all units sold equals total fixed cost. The contribution margin is the difference between price and variable cost. So, for example, if the price is $20 and variable cost is constant at $16 per unit, the contribution margin is $4. With total fixed cost of $175,000, the breakeven point is 43,750 units, or $875,000 in sales.

The accounting approach can make sense for long-run analysis if it is expected that depreciation expense will be offset by investments necessary to maintain the capital stock. This, in fact, is the same logic we invoked in the discussion of sustainable growth. But the accounting approach does not work well if one desires to assess the short-run breakeven point or if the investment needed to maintain the fixed assets is systematically different from depreciation expense. Moreover, even as a long-run concept, because the approach does not factor in the opportunity cost of capital, it is not well suited for investment decision making.

For assessing financial needs, however, cash flow breakeven analysis can provide insight. Cash flow breakeven analysis addresses the question, "What level of sales generates operating cash inflows that are sufficient to cover operating cash outflows?" The cash flow BEP is where the venture achieves a level of sales high enough to maintain its operations at the current level. At the cash flow BEP, cash inflows are sufficient to maintain and replace current assets but not to fund growth. This is the minimum level of sales the venture needs in order to survive without additional funding.

In conjunction with a forecast of sales, finding the cash flow BEP helps the entrepreneur assess initial financing needs. Once a breakeven model is constructed, the entrepreneur can use it to estimate how initial cash needs depend on sales levels, sales growth, product prices, fixed costs, variable costs, and noncash revenues and expenses. Breakeven analysis can also be used to conduct a variety of "what if" or sensitivity analyses.

An Illustration

We return to the venture under consideration by Gill Bates. His online virtual world, iFree, will generate revenue from two sources: subscriptions and advertising. Usually breakeven analysis assumes that revenues increase in proportion to unit sales and that all costs can be neatly classified as either fixed or variable. The result is that the contribution margin (the difference between unit revenue and unit variable cost) is constant. So it is easy to find the breakeven point by dividing total fixed expenses by the contribution margin per unit. You can use the same principles to find the cash flow BEP.

The problem facing Bates is more complicated. As shown in Table 8.1, the subscription price is assumed to be constant at $12 per user as the service grows, meaning subscription revenue increases linearly as the user base grows. However, advertising revenue per subscriber is a nonlinear

TABLE **8.1** **Revenue and expense assumptions of iFree at various user levels**

	Number of users (thousands)		
	up to 25	25–40	40–55
Average over all users			
Revenue per user at top of range			
Subscriptions	$12.00	$12.00	$12.00
Advertising	$9.00	$9.38	$9.89
Average total revenue	$21.00	$21.38	$21.89
Expenses per user at top of range			
Average variable expenses	$17.00	$16.06	$15.23
Average contribution to operating profit	**$4.00**	**$5.31**	**$6.66**
Average over incremental users			
Revenue per user			
Subscriptions	$12.00	$12.00	$12.00
Advertising	$9.00	$10.00	$11.25
Total	$21.00	$22.00	$23.25
Expenses per user			
Variable expenses	$17.00	$14.50	$13.00
Incremental contribution to operating profit	**$4.00**	**$7.50**	**$10.25**

NOTE: *The table shows revenue and cost assumptions for the average and incremental iFree user at various levels. Subscription revenue is constant, but advertising revenue per user increases with higher subscription levels. The incremental variable expense drops with higher user levels.*

function of the user base. As the number of users increases, advertisers are expected to perceive greater value per user from advertising. Consequently, the contribution margin per user is not constant. Variable expenses associated with attracting new customers to the site and servicing them are expected to decline as the venture achieves greater scale.

Table 8.1 shows the key revenue and expense assumptions for iFree. Because advertising revenue per user and variable expense per user both depend on the size of the subscriber base, the contribution margin is different at different levels of users. As a result, it is not simple to find the BEP.

The data on average contribution to operating profit in Table 8.1 indicate that the contribution per user increases from $4.00 to $5.31 when moving from 25,000 to 40,000 users and then to $6.66 when moving to 55,000 users. These are average data, but the change in average contribution is not the right basis for deciding whether to commit resources to expanding the user base. If an additional $2 of selling cost would be required to increase the user base from 25,000 to 40,000, the average contribution numbers suggest that this would be a bad decision—spending $2 for a $1.31 increase in the average. But this is not the correct comparison: we need to focus, instead, on the marginal effect of the expenditures.

The bottom portion of Table 8.1 shows the average contribution for each incremental increase in the user base. Each user between 25,000 and 40,000 makes a contribution of $7.50 to operating income, $3.50 more than the contribution from the first 25,000 users. Spending $2 per incremental user in this case would mean a net contribution to profit of $1.50 and would clearly be the right decision.

We can use the data in Table 8.1 along with information on fixed investment, periodic fixed cost, and (noncash) depreciation expense to prepare pro forma financial data for iFree at various user levels. We assume that Bates will need to make a one-time investment of $300,000 in site development. This nonrecurring capital expenditure can include costs of hardware infrastructure, software development, acquiring lists of potential users, and other tangible or intangible assets that do not have to be replaced once the site is launched. This investment can be depreciated over four years at $75,000 per year. There will also be recurring fixed investments of $20,000 per year, which, in steady state, will also result in depreciation expense of $20,000 per year. Recurring investments are for office equipment, computers, and other assets required for ongoing operation of the website.

Bates expects that during the first four years, the venture will incur $190,000 per year in annual fixed expenses, including all depreciation.

TABLE **8.2**   **Pro forma financial data for iFree at various user levels**

Users (thousands)	0	25	40	55
Total subscription revenue	$0	$300	$480	$660
Total advertising revenue	$0	$225	$375	$544
Total revenue	$0	$525	$855	$1,204
Variable expenses	$0	$425	$643	$838
Fixed expenses	$0	$190	$190	$190
Operating profit	**$0**	**($90)**	**$23**	**$176**
Tax @ 40%	$0	$0	$9	$71
Net income	$0	($90)	$14	$106
Plus depreciation (nonrecurring)	$0	$75	$75	$75
Plus depreciation (recurring)	$0	$20	$20	$20
Capital investment/replacement	($300)	($20)	($20)	($20)
Cash flow	**($300)**	**($15)**	**$89**	**$181**

NOTE: *The table shows simplified income statement and cash flow information for iFree at various user levels. The venture is unprofitable with 25,000 users but generates both positive net income and cash flow with 40,000 users.*

Table 8.2 shows a simplified income statement and cash flow statement for each level of users from Table 8.1. The calculations shown in the table assume a 40 percent income tax rate on positive income and zero on negative income. The table shows that with 40,000 users, iFree is slightly profitable based on net income. With 55,000 users, the venture achieves $1.2 million in revenue, a 14.6 percent EBIT, or operating profit margin, and over $100 thousand in net income.

Because we are concerned with the cash flow breakeven point, accounting net income must be adjusted to take account of noncash expenses and to provide for capital replacement. The table is based on an assumption that the assets acquired to launch the venture are still being depreciated. As noted above, because the cash flow breakeven point is examined as a steady state, we assume that depreciation expenses for such assets are exactly offset by outlays for new assets.

In Table 8.2, we compute steady-state cash flow during the period by adding back depreciation expenses and deducting the outlay for recurring investment. The table shows iFree's cash flow at various user levels. Figure 8.3 shows the breakeven analysis in graphical form. In addition, it illustrates the difference between the accounting net income BEP and the cash flow BEP in the years when the initial investment is being depreciated. The net income BEP is at about 37,000 users; this is where, in the figure, the total revenue line intersects the total expenses line. The cash flow BEP—where total revenue and total cash outflows are equal—is lower, at 27,000 users. Focusing on net income could thus lead to the wrong investment decision. If it were believed that the subscriber base

FIGURE **8.3**
iFree breakeven analysis
As the figure shows, although the growth rate of subscription revenue is linear, growth rates of total revenues, expenses, and cash flow are nonlinear. Because of the nonlinearity, incremental contribution margins are different from average contribution margins.

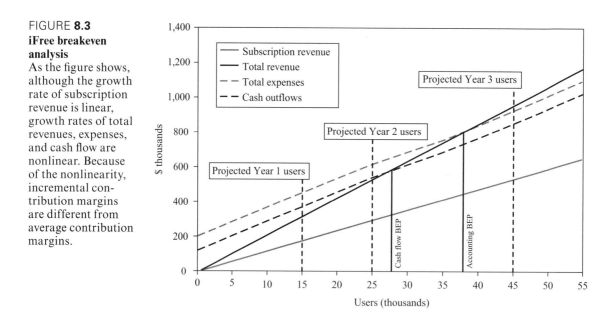

would not reach 37,000 very quickly and the decision were based on the accounting BEP, the project could be rejected incorrectly.

Using Breakeven Analysis to Project Financial Needs

Using breakeven analysis to assess financial needs requires another step. Financial need depends on two things, one being the time until breakeven is reached and the other being the amount of financing required to cover the shortfalls until that time. Thus, to estimate the amount of financing required, we can combine breakeven analysis with a sales forecast. In the case of iFree, assume Bates expects that first-year users would reach 15,000, second-year would be 25,000, and third-year would be 45,000. Figure 8.3 allows us to estimate annual cash needs. Based on the chart, the shortfalls in the first and second years, respectively, are about $55,000 and $15,000, or a total of $70,000. In the third year, the venture is expected to generate positive cash flow of more than $100,000.

The cumulative cash shortfall of $70,000 implied for the first two years by the breakeven analysis does not tell the full story. The shortfalls are steady-state shortfalls, but as the venture is expected to grow, it is not in steady state. Further, the total covers operating deficits but does not include the initial investment outlay to acquire the capital assets that are being depreciated or to provide for growth in working capital. A more comprehensive estimate would provide for investment in the capital asset base needed to produce the website, as well as for the working capital needed to support operations. Even though growth beyond the cash flow BEP may require additional investment, the fact that breakeven is achieved makes securing additional financing less difficult.

Present Value Breakeven Analysis

Cash flow breakeven analysis enables the entrepreneur to get a better feel for the venture by providing a way to assess how sales levels, prices, and fixed and variable costs affect cash needs. However, the analysis does not contribute much insight to the investment decision since it does not use the PV concept or risk assessments that are central to investment decision making.

For investment decision making, a modified form of breakeven analysis can determine the level of sales where the PV of revenues is sufficient to cover the PV of cash outflows (both cash expenses and investment outlays). Present value breakeven analysis helps answer the question, "What level of sales is needed to justify investing?" It is best suited for projects where revenue and expense streams can be described as level annuities. The PV approach is most helpful for capital budgeting and investment decisions. It is unlikely to be of much help for assessing cash needs.[7]

8.5   Assessing Financial Needs with Scenario Analysis

Because the future is uncertain, the financing decision should depend on both the expected future of the venture and uncertainty. Methods of assessing financial needs under uncertainty are particularly valuable.

Scenario analysis is a simple way to incorporate uncertainty into projections of financial need. A scenario describes one possible version of the future and specifies the key assumptions associated with the scenario. For example, an important scenario might be that overall growth of the product market is slowed by recession and that competitors react by reducing prices and advertising more aggressively. The financial model assumptions would manifest in this scenario as lower estimates of volume growth and margins. The financial information for iFree in Tables 8.1 and 8.2 and Figure 8.3 is based on the "expected" scenario.

An entrepreneur can use alternative scenarios, together with their associated assumptions, to generate alternative projections of financial needs. One might, for example, consider "expected," "best case," and "worst case" scenarios, each with its own assumptions and resultant estimate of financing need. For ventures with long product development periods, it can be helpful to consider one scenario in which product introduction is delayed and sales grow slowly and are not initially profitable, and a second scenario in which sales growth is rapid and more profitable but product development is still slow.

The key to forecasting long-run financial needs is developing a model that links product-market performance to financing requirements. We saw how this can be done in the NewCompany model in Chapter 7, as well as through the sustainable growth model and cash flow breakeven analysis in this chapter. The first step to forecasting financial needs is to specify a set of assumptions about product-market performance, for example, expected sales, costs, and resulting profitability. Incorporating the assumptions into a financial model will determine the cash flows we can anticipate the venture to generate. We can then forecast financing needs by using estimates of asset efficiency, such as the levels of fixed assets and working capital needed to support projected sales.

Our concern in this chapter is with the adequacy of financing based on a realistic "worst case" forecast, where the worst case is defined as a case that requires the heaviest reliance on external financing. This may not be the scenario with the lowest profitability. Rather, it is likely to be a case where development time is longer than expected, where development expense is higher than expected, or where sales growth is more rapid and less profitable than expected.

Scenario analysis can be developed in much the same way as decision tree analysis. For example, Table 8.3 describes 19 scenarios of sales growth, cost, and revenue for iFree. Each scenario involves different assumptions concerning sales growth, advertising revenue, and variable cost, as detailed in the notes to the table. Suppose Bates is faced with the issue of how much initial financing to secure and wants to apply scenario analysis to a cash flow breakeven study. Although there are many possible scenarios in the table, some are more realistic than others. This highlights one of the challenges of scenario analysis, namely, developing a manageable number of scenarios that accurately represent the range of possible future outcomes. As a benchmark, the top row of Table 8.3 shows projected cash flows for our "base case" assumptions, that is, that iFree would have 15,000 users in Year 1, 25,000 in Year 2, and 45,000 by Year 3. In the expected scenario, and including the initial $300,000 investment, the venture would need about $370,000 cumulatively from start-up through the second year of operation.

TABLE **8.3**   **iFree scenario analysis**

Growth rate of users[1]	Variable cost[2]	Advertising revenue[3]	Projected cash flow				Cumulative cash need	Year 3 net income
			Time 0	Year 1	Year 2	Year 3		
Expected growth	Expected cost	Expected revenue	($300,000)	($55,000)	($15,000)	$119,000	($370,000)	$44,000
High growth	High cost	High revenue						
		Low revenue						
	Expected cost	High revenue	($300,000)	$12,000	$98,000	$272,000	($300,000)	$197,000
		Low revenue						
	Low cost	High revenue						
		Low revenue						
Expected growth	High cost	High revenue						
		Low revenue						
	Expected cost	High revenue	($300,000)	($35,000)	$19,000	$158,000	($335,000)	$83,000
		Low revenue	($300,000)	($75,000)	($49,000)	$80,000	($424,000)	$5,000
	Low cost	High revenue						
		Low revenue						
Low growth	High cost	High revenue						
		Low revenue						
	Expected cost	High revenue						
		Low revenue	($300,000)	($104,000)	($96,000)	($41,000)	($541,000)	($116,000)
	Low cost	High revenue						
		Low revenue						

[1] Expected users are 15,000 in the first year, 25,000 in the second year, and 45,000 in the third. High growth is 20 percent above these expected numbers; low growth is 20 percent below.

[2] Expected variable expense and advertising are as shown in Table 8.2. High cost is variable expense 10 percent higher than expected; low cost is variable expense 10 percent lower than expected for all user levels.

[3] High advertising revenue is 15 percent above the expected levels in Table 8.2; low advertising revenue is 15 percent below expected.

Table 8.3 also shows the Year 3 net income for each scenario. Once the initial investment is fully depreciated and the venture is in steady state, annual net income and free cash flow will be equal. Thus, assuming that the venture reaches steady state by Year 3, the Year 3 net income will be the continuing annual cash flow. In the expected scenario, once the initial investment is fully depreciated, the final column of the table shows that the base case continuing cash flow is expected to be $44,000.

The remainder of this analysis focuses on 4 of the 18 other scenarios for which the outcomes are shown. The first is a success or "best case" scenario, in which Bates's new virtual world is a hit. Users sign up more rapidly than expected, and advertisers are attracted to the site. This scenario also reduces variable expenses per user, while advertising revenue per user is higher than expected. Under this outcome, iFree will have positive cash flow of $12,000 in the first year, so that the total investment would be only the initial $300,000. If the venture stabilizes at the Year 3 level of sales, based on third-year net income, once the initial investment is fully depreciated, continuing annual cash flow is expected to be $197,000.

At the other extreme is a "worst case" scenario, in which, during the first three years, iFree never catches on with users, and as a result advertisers show little interest in the site. With user growth 20 percent below expectations, variable expenses per user are higher than expected. The resulting cumulative cash shortfall for the first three years is projected to be $541,000. If the venture stabilizes at this point, it will continue to require additional infusions of cash. Based on third-year net income, continuing cash flow is expected to be negative $116,000 per year.

The other two scenarios represent a sensitivity analysis of cash flow to advertising revenues. Both scenarios use the base case assumptions for the number of users and variable expenses. In the "high revenue" scenario, advertising revenue per user is 15 percent above the base case values; in the "low revenue" scenario, it is 15 percent below the base case. The difference in cumulative impact on cash needs between the high and low advertising revenue scenarios is estimated to be $109,000, and the difference in net income is $78,000.

The information in Table 8.3 is relevant to how much financing the entrepreneur should try to secure before initiating the venture but does not fully resolve the issue. Should the entrepreneur arrange for enough financing to cover the worst-case scenario? If the venture is expected to stabilize at the Year 3 level, funding for this outcome should not be arranged. Even if the venture was slightly profitable, as in the low advertising revenue scenario, the PV of future cash flows might be too low to justify the incremental commitment of capital needed to cover that scenario. In either of these scenarios, it could make sense from an investment perspective to abandon the venture.

Also bearing on the question of how much capital to commit, keep in mind that very early stage financing is expensive because of high uncertainty. Lining up all of the financing at the outset would reduce the entrepreneur's ownership stake if the venture proved to be a success. Moreover, if it can be determined at an early point that the venture is on track for success, then the entrepreneur does not need to raise all of the capital at the outset. Gill Bates needs to think about contingency plans for raising financing or abandoning the venture if his idea for a virtual world is a failure, but he does not need to lock up all of the financing commitments at the beginning.

Even 18 scenarios plus the base case may be insufficient to capture the range of realistic uncertainty for a new venture, and computations with numerous scenarios can become burdensome. Moreover, scenario comparisons provide no information on the relative likelihoods of different outcomes.

8.6 Assessing Financial Needs with Simulation

Simulation is a more comprehensive approach for incorporating uncertainty into a decision. To see how simulation can be used to assess financial needs, we reconsider NewCompany. Refer again to Table 7.13, which contains the pro forma financial statements for the venture in selected months. The statements are generated on the basis of what is expected to occur. As we discussed in Chapter 7, if the venture is assumed to begin with $500,000 of equity and to raise additional funding as needed by drawing on a line of credit, the company's cumulative need for debt financing peaks at about $830,000 in Month 55, making the cumulative need from all sources about $1,330,000.

But what if NewCompany does not develop as expected? We demonstrated in Figure 7.6 that, given our assumptions about the uncertainty of development timing, sales growth, length of the rapid-growth period, and profitability, the actual financial needs of the venture could be much higher or lower than implied by the expected performance assumptions. It would not make sense for the entrepreneur to try to fully fund all of the possible scenarios with capital raised at the beginning. Doing so would involve raising large amounts of capital at the point where uncertainty about ultimate success is greatest and would include coverage of scenarios in which early abandonment would be a better course of action. Ultimately, we would like to approach the decision of how much initial financing to raise on the basis of NPV; that is, we want to select the level of financing that results in the greatest NPV for the entrepreneur (or the investor, depending on who is making the decision). Even without formal NPV analysis, as we illustrate in the balance of this section, a structured analysis of the results of simulating the financial model can dramatically improve the financing decision.

Figure 8.4 provides a comprehensive view of NewCompany's future cash needs based on 1,000 iterations of the simulation model. The results from the simulation present information on the distribution of the credit line balance at the end of each of NewCompany's first six years. The graph shows the cumulative distribution of financing needs as of each of the years. The horizontal axis in the graph represents the amount of external financing NewCompany needs, expressed in dollars, and the vertical axis represents the cumulative percentage of trials from the simulation. To generate the table and graph, we arbitrarily set the initial investment in NewCompany at zero so that the line of credit balance represents the full financial needs of the venture.

For example, the output table in Figure 8.4 shows that average funding required as of Year 1 (Month 12) is about $286,000. This average is closer to the bottom end of the range ($264,000) than to the top ($361,000), so the distribution is skewed, even though the range is fairly narrow. From Figure 6.5, we know the probability of development success by Month 12 is below 25 percent. This means that for most of the trials, the credit line balance represents the cost of 12 months of development and maintaining the $15,000 minimum cash balance. While the information we collected and report in Figure 8.4 does not definitively tell us why the distribution is skewed, it seems likely that many of the scenarios with relatively high Month 12 financial needs are cases in which development success occurred early and additional capital was needed to finance the growth of working capital. Such trials would appear to have a high probability of success, so later-stage financing should be available on more favorable terms.

We can examine financial needs in other years in a similar manner. The average need at the end of Year 2 is about $631,000, while the standard deviation is more than twice that of Year 1 and the range is much wider. Based on the graph of the distribution of outcomes, however, there does not seem to be very much to distinguish high-need from low-need outcomes. Perhaps the low-need outcomes are trials in which, even after 24 months, development efforts have been unsuccessful. According to Figure 6.5, however, half of the simulation trials had devel-

Unconditional Simulation Results		Trials = 1000						*Venture.***SIM**		

							Percentiles			
Output		*Average*	*Median*	*Standard Deviation*	*Skewness*	*Minimum*	*25%*	*50%*	*75%*	*Maximum*
	Year 1	285916	274730	23243	1.52	264323	272514	274730	283943	360780
	Year 2	630541	639848	55373	0.243	554544	573865	639848	676615	810917
	Year 3	1013009	1004871	78623	0.958	887204	959145	1004871	1059373	1422520
	Year 4	1433315	1401378	183739	2.75	1063220	1328476	1401378	1482589	3002670
	Year 5	1853284	1785125	560067	3.25	52575	1670415	1785125	1910229	6423074
	Year 6	1297280	1568264	829338	-0.452	0.000	482552	1568264	2007837	3329005

(a)

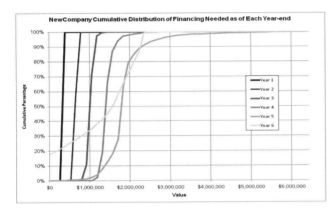

(b)

FIGURE **8.4**
NewCompany simulation: Credit line balance for Years 1–6
The graph (b) shows the cumulative distribution of financing needs as of each of the years, based on results summarized in the table (a).

opment success by Month 20. We might begin to question whether continuing to provide funding in these scenarios is still a good idea.

For those in which development has been successful, depending on whether the prospects for profitable growth appear to be good, other, less expensive financing sources may be available. The scenarios with high financial needs could be due to either rapid growth or low profitability (or both). We would like to continue to fund the profitable high-growth scenarios but maybe not the less profitable trials. So perhaps the initial investment should be small enough to enable the bad outcomes to be abandoned without wasting capital and the truly good ones to be funded on better terms with later-stage financing. Similar considerations apply to the scenarios represented in Years 3 and 4.

The cumulative distribution in Year 5 is a bit different. In some scenarios, the Year 5 needs are quite low. Apparently, these are scenarios in which development has been successful and the venture has begun to generate free cash flow that is used to pay down the line of credit. This is why some of the trials have lower financing needs in Year 5 than any of the trials in Year 4. There also are some trials in which the Year 5 need for cash is very high. In such cases, we should be trying to understand the reason for the large need: if it is due to low profitability, slow growth, or continued development failure, such scenarios should probably be abandoned; if it is due to rapid growth over earlier months and the venture is profitable, perhaps it should be maintained.

The results for financing needs at the end of Year 6 are very different from those for the other years. In about 18 percent of the trials, the credit line has been completely repaid. These are scenarios in which development efforts were successful and subsequent performance was sufficient to fully repay the borrowed funds. This could happen most easily if the venture was highly profitable and the rapid growth period ended early. To be certain, we would need to collect more information from the simulated trials. In general, financing needs in Year 6 are lower than in Year 5. There are a small fraction of trials at the upper end of the distribution, however, for which Year 6 financing needs are very high. These are probably scenarios in which development succeeded very late and was followed by slow and unprofitable growth.

Interpreting the Simulation Results

The information in Figure 8.4 can be viewed in the context of the entrepreneur's planning horizon. Suppose the entrepreneur were considering an initial investment of $275,000. The median statistics in the table show that NewCompany would require outside funding in the first year about 50 percent of the time and might need as much as $85,000. It would be a good idea for the entrepreneur to have a sense of how the financing could be raised.

In the model, we structured outside financing as an unlimited credit line that the entrepreneur can draw upon as needed and repay as free cash flow becomes available. This, of course, is not realistic; it is just a device we will use to help us assess financing needs. Loan commitments take time to arrange, and it is unlikely that any lender would make a large commitment to a venture that has yet to develop a product, has little collateral, and has no cash flow. From a planning perspective, it is important to build in several months of lead time for making financing arrangements as well as to recognize the realistic limits of the venture's ability to borrow or to raise capital by other means. Providing funding only for the first year, for which the probability of development success is less than 25 percent, is not likely to be sufficient.

The forecasts of longer-term financial needs serve a different function. There is no particular urgency for the entrepreneur to arrange financing that will not be needed for several years. The longer-term analysis, however, is relevant to consideration of how early-stage financing should be arranged. On average, NewCompany will need just over $1.4 million by the end of Year 4, including any initial investment— but it might need considerably more. Early-stage financing should not be accepted with terms that make later-stage financing for potentially valuable scenarios difficult to arrange.

It is important for the entrepreneur to examine the covenants and restrictions associated with any early-stage financing plan and to make sure they would not unnecessarily later make the venture hostage to an early investor. Conversely, there may be covenants and restrictions to which the entrepreneur can agree. Accepting restrictions that only take effect if a milestone is missed is a way in which the entrepreneur can communicate confidence in the financial projections.

In the worst case, Figure 8.4 suggests that NewCompany could need about $3.0 million of total financing by Year 4, which is assumed to be the point where successful development is no longer feasible. This is not very likely, however, and only 2 percent of the trials required more than $2 million by then. The need for high levels of financing by Year 4 is probably associated with outcomes in which product development fails or is late and is followed by high sales growth and modest profitability.

In structuring early-stage financing, it is not important or even desirable to provide for the highest conceivable level of future financial needs. Some of the high-need scenarios could be failed development scenarios, where the entrepreneur might want to abandon the venture anyway (an option we intentionally have not built into the pro forma analysis so that we could assess the full range of outcomes if the venture were fully funded). Others could be high-growth outcomes that, depending on profitability, might enable the entrepreneur to raise additional financing later.

In the best case (from a financing perspective), the venture generates sufficient cash by the end of Year 5 to repay all of its prior borrowing. This possibility has implications for structuring early-stage financing. Figure 8.4 suggests that external financing needs are sometimes transitory. When this is true, the entrepreneur should consider the choice between permanent and temporary financing. The NewCompany simulation is based on temporary debt financing in the form of a line of credit.

Permanent debt financing would enable the entrepreneur to draw more cash from the venture at an earlier stage. Alternatively, had outside equity financing been used, it might make sense for the entrepreneur to incorporate a call option to redeem the shares on pre-agreed terms. These are only a few of the possibilities. Importantly, the NewCompany model is for a single product; if the management team is able to develop other opportunities, the free cash flow from this one might be used to fund other development-stage activities.

Gauging Uncertainty and Avoiding Undue Complexity

As you can tell from the modifications we made to the static NewCompany model, a simulation that realistically incorporates uncertainty can quickly become complicated. Once the key elements of uncertainty are modeled, however, the benefits of adding complexity diminish rapidly. There are distinct advantages to a parsimonious model that is based on well-researched assumptions. The results are more tractable and convincing, and modifications are easier to make. This suggests that the decision maker should focus on only a few key sources of uncertainty and strive for accurate forecasts of their future variability.

8.7 How Much Money Does the Venture Need?

NewCompany appears to be worth pursuing but, under realistic conditions, would require outside investment. The question the entrepreneur inevitably will face from outside investors is: "How much money do you need?" A vague response would suggest that the entrepreneur has not thought seriously about the question or is trying to sidestep it because of the risks associated with development timing, market acceptance, and profitability. The entrepreneur needs to anticipate the question and may want to incorporate a response into the business plan. The entrepreneur's ability to answer concretely and directly is one test that investors use in deciding whether it is worthwhile to begin negotiating.

The question is difficult to answer partly because it has several aspects. The investor is really asking three things: "How much do you need to initiate the project? How much, ultimately, do you think you will need? And when do you expect to need it?" Financial modeling can help the entrepreneur to address all three.

To provide an overview on how much outside equity to seek, we formalize three principles/assumptions that are implied by the earlier discussion of financing needs:

- First, the entrepreneur does not need to raise capital now to cover funding needs for scenarios in which the business is thriving. If the venture is growing and is profitable, the entrepreneur should not have trouble raising additional funds later on more favorable terms.
- Second, the entrepreneur does not need to raise capital now that will only be needed if the venture is unsuccessful. There is no reason to seek financing to cover outcomes where operating losses are expected to continue, with little prospect of significant improvement.
- Third, the entrepreneur does not need to raise capital now that will not be needed until after a significant milestone is achieved. If it is achieved, financing will be less expensive; if not, perhaps the venture should be abandoned. Because of this dichotomy, attempting to raise too much capital early signals that the entrepreneur is not confident about whether the milestone can be achieved or how quickly it can be achieved.

Using Simulation to Examine Alternative Financing Arrangements

We return to the NewCompany model to apply these principles. To begin, suppose that the entrepreneur would like to raise enough cash at the outset to ensure that the venture continues to operate for the full six and one-half years of the model. To measure this, we modified the model so that all initial cash is raised as equity. We begin by increasing the initial cash investment to $4.0 million, an amount large enough to cover almost all of possible outcomes of the model, as illustrated in Figure 8.4.

When we ran the model with these assumptions, we found that an investment of $4.0 million would be sufficient to cover approximately 99 percent of the trials. The other 1 percent are all trials in which development was successful and the venture needed more money because it had experienced rapid growth and was operating profitably by the end of the simulation (Month 78). In these cases, the venture is a success and running out of cash from the initial investment would not be a problem. The continuing financing need would be for working capital to fund growth, and there are many sources to which the entrepreneur could turn.

On the other hand, an initial investment of $4.0 million funds a number of bad outcomes. In about 10 percent of the trials, the venture never successfully developed a product. The $4.0 million is sufficient to cover

R&D costs through Month 78, even though, by assumption, the probability of successful development is zero after Month 48.

Although we are not ready to delve into valuation, we can use net income in Month 78 as a simple indicator of whether, for a particular outcome, the venture has proven to be worth pursuing. The greater the net income is for Month 78, the more valuable the venture is likely to be. For 15.6 percent of the 10,000 trials, net income is still negative in Month 78. We know that about two-thirds of these trials are the result of failed development and the rest are probably the results of late development and low profitability. Another 55.1 percent of the 10,000 trials are low-growth/high-cost outcomes. These might not be worth pursuing beyond the point where the poor prospects for growth and profitability become clear.

It should be obvious that a commitment of $4.0 million in initial financing is too much. It covers a large number of bad outcomes where it would have been better to abandon the venture sooner, thereby saving some of the investment capital and freeing up the time of those involved in the venture.

Table 8.4 presents information for nine alternative levels of initial NewCompany financing. The scenarios range from the $4.0 million investment discussed above down to $500,000. Percentages shown are based on 10,000 trials, so 0.79 percent is the same as 79 trials. Panel (a) shows percentages of outcomes where the initial investment was not sufficient to fund the venture through Month 78. These are trials in which NewCompany burns through the initial equity investment and then needs to borrow on a hypothetical line of credit to meet its remaining cash needs. So, with an investment of $4.0 million, the venture needed additional capital in 0.79 percent of the trials. Panel (b) shows percentages where the initial equity investment was sufficient for the entire 78 months. With an initial investment of $4.0 million, the venture had sufficient capital in 99.21 percent of the trials. We also report the average minimum surplus cash over all 10,000 trials. For example, with $4.0 million of initial financing, the average of minimum surplus cash was $2.99 million. Moreover, with $4 million of funding, panel (a) shows that no additional funding was needed for any trial in which development failed, in which profit in Month 78 was still negative, or for low-growth/high-cost outcomes. These are clearly less desirable results, yet the initial investment is so large that the entrepreneur and investors have no structured opportunity to consider whether the venture should be abandoned or at least refocused.

Cutting initial funding to $3.0 million does no harm to the venture. The only scenarios that are not fully funded are again those in

TABLE **8.4** NewCompany simulation results for alternative initial financing decisions

Financing scenario initial equity investment	1 $4,000,000	2 $3,000,000	3 $2,000,000	4 $1,750,000	5 $1,500,000	6 $1,250,000	7 $1,000,000	8 $750,000	9 $500,000
Panel (a): Additional financing needed									
Total iterations (%)	0.79	2.07	8.72	14.08	41.94	80.61	95.22	100.00	100.00
Development before out of financing (%)	0.79	2.07	8.72	14.08	31.91	70.01	84.53	79.28	58.79
Development failed (%)	0.00	0.00	0.00	0.00	10.03	10.60	9.87	10.20	10.08
Net income still negative (%)	0.00	0.00	0.00	0.02	15.09	21.90	22.47	23.46	24.82
High growth (>9) (%)	0.79	2.03	6.89	9.84	17.33	24.80	25.05	25.08	25.22
Low variable cost (<70) (%)	0.04	0.05	0.61	0.87	6.83	13.10	21.46	25.63	26.46
High growth/low cost (%)	0.04	0.05	0.61	0.87	2.97	5.74	6.58	6.47	6.35
Low growth/high cost (%)	0.00	0.04	1.83	4.24	20.75	48.45	55.29	55.76	54.67
Panel (b): No additional financing needed									
Total iterations (%)	99.21	97.93	91.28	85.92	58.06	19.39	4.78	0.00	0.00
Development failed (%)	9.93	9.77	10.62	10.18	0.00	0.00	0.00	0.00	0.00
Net income still negative (%)	15.60	17.04	20.11	19.69	5.33	0.03	0.00	0.00	0.00
High growth (>9) (%)	24.38	23.39	19.11	15.36	8.56	1.55	0.11	0.00	0.00
Low variable cost (<70) (%)	26.08	26.57	26.04	26.72	20.42	13.54	4.78	0.00	0.00
High growth/low cost (%)	6.38	6.74	6.21	5.91	4.02	1.43	0.11	0.00	0.00
Low growth/high cost (%)	55.13	54.71	52.35	49.75	33.10	5.73	0.00	0.00	0.00
Average minimum surplus cash	$2,990,881	$1,799,846	$634,305	$370,504	$154,273	$34,054	$3,407	$0	$0
Earliest out of cash	Never	Never	Month 66	Month 58	Month 53	Month 48	Month 41	Month 33	Month 24

NOTE: *In each case, results are based on 10,000 iterations of the model. Initial investments are in the form of equity.*

which development occurs before the venture runs out of cash, and they turn out to be high-growth scenarios with positive income. Investment of $3.0 million would again fund many undesirable trials, including those in which development fails, in which income by Month 78 is still negative, and in which growth is slow and profits are low. The reduction to $3.0 million still results in very high average minimum surplus cash—$1.80 million—and still covers all of the slow-growth and no-development trials. The implication of these results is that $3 million is still too large an initial investment. It provides full financing in too many outcomes where development fails or values are likely to be low. It also is undesirable because NewCompany is using expensive early-stage financing to fund successful, rapid-growth outcomes that could have been funded later from less expensive sources.

With $2.0 million in initial financing, the venture runs out of cash in 8.7 percent of the trials. All of these are trials in which development has been successful, and most are also high-growth trials. Most should be able to attract follow-on funding. But for 1.8 percent, even though net income is positive, revenue growth is slow and variable cost is high. These might be outcomes where the venture is not sufficiently attractive to merit continuing investment. Limiting the initial investment to $2.0 million gives the entrepreneur and investors an opportunity to evaluate whether these outcomes warrant early abandonment. Based on the percentages of low-growth/high-cost trials (52.4 percent) and failed-development trials (10.6 percent) that are still fully funded, an initial investment of $2.0 million still seems to be too high. The average minimum surplus cash is still very large, at $634,000, and the earliest out-of-initial-cash point (where the venture must turn to its line of credit) is Month 66, well after the probability of successful development has reached zero.

Financing at $1.75 million still does not eliminate any outcomes where development fails (all iterations have development success before running out of initial financing). Cutting initial financing to this level gives the entrepreneur and investors an opportunity to consider and decide whether to abandon a larger fraction of low-growth/high-cost outcomes. Almost all of the Month 78 negative-income outcomes still are fully financed, as are all outcomes where development fails. It appears, based on these results, that $1.75 million in initial funding is still too much.

At $1.5 million in initial funding, there is a substantial increase in the percentage of trials in which additional funding is needed. There is an important knife-edge result at $1.5 million. Of the 41.94 percent of total iterations where initial financing was not enough to fully fund the venture, 10.03 percent are cases in which development fails; the other 31.91 percent are cases in which development success is achieved before the venture runs out of initial cash. Thus, cutting the initial investment to $1.5 million would enable the entrepreneur to avoid funding the development-failure trials and to evaluate the prospects for success of the others and possibly abandon the worst of them. Moreover, this level of financing is low enough that no development-failure trials are fully funded. However, almost one-third (33.10 percent) of the trials with low-growth/high-cost outcomes are fully funded, as are 5.3 percent where net income is still negative as of Month 78. We need to consider a smaller initial investment to see if we can further reduce the excessive investment in outcomes that may be undesirable.

It turns out that with an initial investment of $1.25 million, we preserve all of the good aspects of the higher level of investment and reduce the funding of bad outcomes. With this level of investment, 80.61 percent of the trials need follow-on funding, including all in which development fails. Initial investment of $1.25 million is also not enough for 70.01 percent of the trials, in which development is successful before the venture runs out of cash. Many of these are low-growth/high-cost outcomes where the entrepreneur and investors might decide to abandon. The percentage of fully funded scenarios is now much smaller, 19.39 percent. Most of these are low variable cost outcomes with positive incomes, where continuing funding would probably be found; only 5.73 percent are low growth/high cost. It appears that $1.25 million is a good initial funding level, but we can still check to see whether a lower level might be better. The earliest out-of-cash month is Month 48, which is also the last possible month for successful development.

At $1.0 million of initial investment, more than 95 percent of the trials need additional funding, including all in which development efforts fail. Overwhelmingly, the rest of the trials achieve development success before running out of cash. By comparing these percentages, we can determine that about 1 percent of the trials would run out of cash before development success. Were we to stop funding at this point, these trials would be abandoned even though continued funding would have resulted in development success. However, all of the low-growth/high-cost trials are now in the group that is not fully funded. Thus, for those that achieve development success before running out of cash, the entrepreneur and investors would have the opportunity to assess profitability and growth potential before deciding whether to invest more. With $1.0 million in initial funding, all of the outcomes where the initial cash is sufficient are good outcomes that appear to be worth pursuing, so it does not appear that initial capital is being wasted for these trials. The earliest out-of-cash point for any trial is Month 41, which is why some ultimately successful development efforts do not have sufficient funds.

Whether an initial investment of $1.0 million or $1.25 million is better depends on the relative value of the missed opportunities. If only $1.0 million is invested, we avoid fully funding any of the bad outcomes. But we also know that some ventures that ultimately would have been successful will run out of funding. The question is whether missing out on these is worse than the cost of fully funding the 5.73 percent of bad trials that occur. The gain, if any, must be compared to the cost of an additional $250,000 being invested.

We might be able to refine this comparison by examining some finer gradations of investment, but more fundamentally, we might want to compare the NPVs of the two different alternatives.

Investing less than $1.0 million results in increasingly large numbers of trials in which the development milestone is not achieved before the venture is out of cash. Investing less than what would be needed to reach the next milestone would not be a good strategy.

Determining the Initial Investment

Figure 8.5 summarizes the information in Table 8.4 in graphical form, along with our conclusions about the ideal range of initial investment. The figure shows that in the $1.0 to $1.25 million investment range, a high percentage of the trials will require later-stage funding if they are to continue. Almost all of these are outcomes where either development efforts would fail even if more financing were provided or development success is achieved before the venture runs out of cash.

Either eventuality gives the entrepreneur and investors an opportunity to assess whether the likely outcome warrants an additional round of investment. For those where development success occurs before the venture runs out of cash, the entrepreneur can assess the potential growth rate and profitability of the outcome. If this information can be inferred quickly after the development success, the value of staging the investment is enhanced.

In the NewCompany example, the ideal range of initial investment enables the entrepreneur to forecast growth and profitability for all trials in which there is a possibility of a weak result (those with negative income by Month 78, low-growth/high-cost trials, and trials in which development has not succeeded by the time the venture is out of cash). Conversely, at the $1.0 to $1.25 million funding level, most of the trials that do not require additional funds appear to be good outcomes.

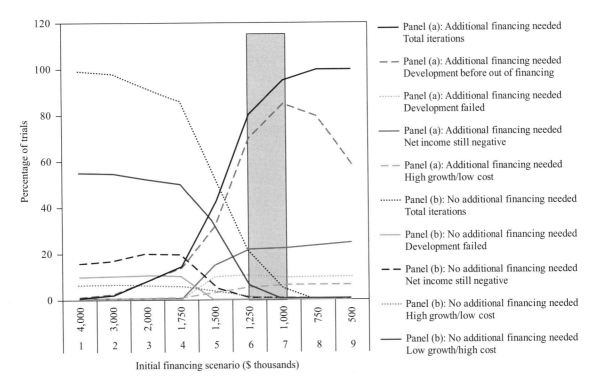

Panel (a): Additional financing needed
Total iterations

Panel (a): Additional financing needed
Development before out of financing

Panel (a): Additional financing needed
Development failed

Panel (a): Additional financing needed
Net income still negative

Panel (a): Additional financing needed
High growth/low cost

Panel (b): No additional financing needed
Total iterations

Panel (b): No additional financing needed
Development failed

Panel (b): No additional financing needed
Net income still negative

Panel (b): No additional financing needed
High growth/low cost

Panel (b): No additional financing needed
Low growth/high cost

FIGURE **8.5**

NewCompany results of initial financing choices
The figure shows the relationship between the initial financing choices shown in Table 8.4 and the
characteristics of trials that are fully funded versus those where the venture runs out of cash. The shaded
area offers the greatest ability to distinguish between good and bad outcomes before committing additional
funding.

8.8   Assessing Financial Needs with Staged Investment

Suppose the investors and/or entrepreneur commits to a first-stage investment of $1.0 million in NewCompany, with the expectation that, if
development is successful, the venture will need additional funds. How
much cash is the venture likely to need in the second round? For an answer, we again use the simulation model with $1.0 million of initial in-
vestment. From Table 8.4, we know that this amount would normally
be sufficient to carry the venture through at least Month 41. We modified the model so that additional funding is provided when the venture
runs out of cash, but only if:

1. Development has been completed.
2. The expected growth rate of sales is at least 7 percent per month during the rapid growth phase.
3. The expected total variable cost (cost of sales plus variable SG&A) is no more than 75 percent of sales.

These are conditions we can only determine after development success is achieved. If these three conditions exist, we assume that the line of credit is an appropriate source of additional financing. Now we can study the outcomes where the later-stage funding is provided versus those where it is not (because of lack of development, slow growth, or low profitability).

Figure 8.6 summarizes the simulation results. The *Venture*.SIM output table shows the results for all 10,000 trials. These results are similar to those shown in Figure 8.4. The initial investment for the simulation in Figure 8.6 is set at $1.0 million. Subsequent funding, if a later-stage investment is made, is assumed to come from a credit line. In the lower panel, we split the trial results based on whether the later-stage funding is made or not. In 53.19 percent of the trials, the conditions for making the second-stage investment are not met and the venture would be abandoned. Had these undesirable trials been allowed to continue, funded solely through the line of credit, average ending surplus cash would have been $538,000 and average ending Month 78 profit would have been $57,400. This compares to the results for the other 46.81 percent of the trials, which meet the criteria for second-stage funding. For these, the average cash surplus of $2.01 million is almost four times as high as in the abandoned trials, and the average Month 78 profit per month of $178,400 is more than three times as high.

Clearly, staging can add value by reducing the total investment in scenarios in which development does not go well. Because the model already incorporates the interest rate on borrowing, the ending surplus cash of $2.01 million is available for distribution to the entrepreneur and investors, and they also realize the future earnings. Because the venture is assumed not to grow after the rapid-growth period, ending net income is equivalent to ending free cash flow. So the entrepreneur and investors can anticipate receiving the value of a perpetuity of $178,400 per month. According to the simulation trials data, the probability of realizing these is 46.8 percent.

Is this outcome good enough to justify the initial investment? The answer depends on comparing the PV of the future cash flows with the investment amount. While we do not want to get into all of the details of PV until the next chapter, we can make a rough approximation. Sup-

*Venture.***SIM**

Unconditional Simulation Results										

Trials = 10000

						Percentiles				
Output	Average	Median	Standard Deviation	Skewness		Minimum	25%	50%	75%	Maximum
1 Ending Revenue	$788,504	$462,168	$1,055,193	4.34		$0	$175,254	$462,168	$1,013,589	$18,817,406
2 Ending Surplus	$1,228,210	$357,283	$2,018,240	3.03		$0	$0	$357,283	$1,682,656	$23,764,417
3 Ending Profit	$114,017	$56,267	$192,521	4.08		-$37,331	$3,903	$56,267	$154,800	$3,058,895
4 Maximum Loan	$689,994	$549,537	$711,818	6.35		$0	$342,200	$549,537	$889,955	$16,604,889
5 Need Loan	0.976	1.000	0.154	-6.17		0.000	1.000	1.000	1.000	1.000
6 Development Completion	26.53	20.00	20.08	1.65		8.00	13.00	20.00	32.00	79.00
7 Out of Cash	42.78	44.00	7.58	-4.32		0.000	41.00	44.00	46.00	58.00
8 Invest Next Stage	0.468	0.000	0.499	0.128		0.000	0.000	0.000	1.000	1.000

Results of Second-stage Investment/Abandonment Decision		
	Invest in Second Stage (46.8% of trials)	Do not Invest in Second Stage (53.2% of trials)
Ending Revenue	$1,071,668	$539,304
Ending Surplus	$2,012,380	$538,099
Ending Profit	$178,396	$57,360
Maximum Loan	$618,792	$752,655
Need Loan	100.0%	95.4%
Development Completion	20.8 months	31.6 months
Out of Cash	43.8 months	41.8 months
Invest if Development complete before out-of-cash, growth in unit sales > 7%, and total variable costs < 75%.		

FIGURE **8.6**

NewCompany results of second-stage investment decision rule
The figure examines the effect of a decision rule to initially invest $1.0 million and then to provide later-stage funding only for trials where the venture appears to have a promising future.

pose the entrepreneur and the investors require a return of 0.8 percent per month (10 percent per year). We can easily value the average surplus cash by weighting trials by their probability and then discounting for 78 months:

$$PV_{\text{ending surplus cash}} = \$2.01 \text{ million} \times 46.8\%/1.008^{78} = \$505,000$$

The surplus alone is not enough to justify the initial $1 million investment. We also need to estimate the value of the continuing cash flows. Suppose that ventures like NewCompany can normally be sold for 10 times annual income. We can estimate the PV of the income stream by annualizing the income, weighting it by the probability of making the second-stage investment, and discounting for 78 months at the assumed discount rate.

$$PV_{\text{continuing income stream}} = \$178,400 \times 12 \times 10 \times 46.8\%/1.008^{78} = \$5,381,000$$

Total PV = $505,000 + $5,381,000 = $5,856 million. The total PV of $5,886 million is much greater than the $1.0 million investment, which indicates that the venture would be worth pursuing on the basis of the assumed conditions for second-stage investment.

While the above analysis is sufficient for justifying the initial investment, it is possible for the entrepreneur and investors to do better. The average value of the scenarios that would be abandoned is still positive. Some of the trials that yield surplus cash and positive net income would be worth pursuing. Of the 5,319 trials that did not meet the three criteria for additional funding, 75.0 percent have development completed before the out-of-cash point, as well as a combined value of surplus cash and ending net income (annualized and multiplied by 10) that is positive. They would have positive PV after the incremental cost of the credit line (which is already built into the model). Thus, these trials are all worth pursuing. The entrepreneur can increase the value of the venture by searching for a second-stage investment decision rule that will result in funding more of these outcomes, as long as the rule does not also add negative PV outcomes.

8.9 Summary

A number of analytical techniques are available for assessing financial needs. They range from the comparatively simple sustainable growth model and cash flow breakeven analysis to more complex methods that involve scenario analysis and simulation to study how uncertainty affects financial needs.

The value of the sustainable growth model is that it links a venture's ability to finance growth from operations to a few policy decisions. For any given growth objective, the model enables the entrepreneur to understand when growth can be financed from operations and how much will need to be funded externally.

Cash flow breakeven analysis considers financial needs in a different way. On one level, the technique helps determine the level of sales a venture must achieve to finance its operations from cash flow. At that point, the venture is viable on a cash flow basis, but growth beyond the breakeven point would require additional capital. On another level, by combining cash flow breakeven analysis with a sales forecast, the entrepreneur can estimate the investment needed to sustain the venture until the breakeven point is reached.

Scenario analysis is an approach to studying the effects of uncertainty. When the technique is applied to assessing financial needs, the objective is to gain an understanding of how financial needs vary over a range of realistic scenarios. Scenario analysis can be combined easily with other methods of assessing financial needs; that is, the sustainable growth rate or cash flow breakeven point can be evaluated over a range of realistic scenarios to improve understanding of financial needs.

Simulation is by far the most powerful analytical tool for evaluating financial needs. Beginning with sound assumptions and an integrated financial model, the effects of key aspects of uncertainty can be evaluated simultaneously. Skillful application of simulation can help the entrepreneur or an investor design a financial structure that preserves the potential for success but does so with a limited amount of investment capital. At the same time, the financial structure enables the entrepreneur and investors to avoid overinvesting once it becomes apparent that success is unlikely. By using simulation, it is simple to study the effects of subtle but significant changes in financing provisions.

REVIEW QUESTIONS

1. Describe the main factors that determine a venture's sustainable growth rate. What are the key assumptions in the sustainable growth model?

2. List four ways in which managers can increase a venture's sustainable growth rate. Which do you think is easiest to implement? Which is most difficult?

3. Explain how a venture's sustainable growth rate is related to its financing needs.

4. What is the difference between accounting breakeven and cash flow breakeven analysis? Which is more important for a new venture and why?

5. Explain the difference between marginal and average contribution margins. Why is it important to distinguish between them when making operational decisions?

6. Why is it important for an entrepreneur to plan for unexpected product-market success? What are the potential consequences of failing to do so?

7. How might you determine the number of scenarios needed to analyze a new venture's uncertainty? Explain how you might estimate reasonable probabilities for each scenario.

8. What benefits does simulation bring to the analysis of venture uncertainty?

9. Explain how simulation and staging can be combined to estimate an optimal level of initial funding for a new venture.

10. Describe how you might use simulation with different assumptions about the amount of initial financing to help determine the amount that would help assure that good outcomes are not missed but bad outcomes do not receive funding beyond the point where their problems become apparent.

Notes

1. See Higgins (2009), ch. 4, and Donaldson (1991) for additional discussion of sustainable growth.

2. This is equivalent to assuming that asset turnover, financial leverage, and return on sales are constant.

3. Perhaps you are wondering why, in this model, we have not mentioned cash flow. The reason is that the sustainable growth model assumes that depreciation expense each period is equal to the investment required to replenish the assets. Thus, in order to prepare a cash flow statement, we would add back the depreciation expense. But in order to sustain operations at the same level as in the prior year, the entrepreneur would need to reinvest the same amount back in the venture. Doing so would maintain the balance sheet at its initial level.

4. A spreadsheet version of Eq. (8.7) is available on the companion website.

5. Information from Webvan Form 10K-405, year ended December 31, 1999; and "Technology Journal: *Webvan* IPO to Stir Grocery Industry," *Wall Street Journal* (Europe), November 9, 1999, p. 10.

6. The same question could be examined from the perspective of an investor, and similar issues would arise but the conclusions might be different. In later chapters, we consider how to reconcile the different perspectives of the entrepreneur and investors.

7. See Ross, Westerfield, and Jaffe (2008), pp. 233–37, for an illustration of present value breakeven analysis.

References and Additional Reading

Donaldson, G. 1991. "Financial Goals and Strategic Consequences." In *Strategy: Seeking and Securing Competitive Advantage*, ed. C. Montgomery and M. Porter, 113–34. Cambridge, MA: Harvard Business School Press.

Higgins, R. C. 2009. *Analysis for Financial Management*. 9th ed. McGraw-Hill Irwin.

Kaplan, J. 1994. *Startup*. New York: Penguin.

Kaplan, S. N., and A. Schoar. 2005. "Private Equity Performance: Returns, Persistence and Capital Flows." *Journal of Finance*, 60:1791–1823.

Ross, S. A., R. W. Westerfield, and J. Jaffe. 2008. *Corporate Finance*. 8th ed. New York: McGraw-Hill Irwin.

Sahlman, W. A. 1999. "The Financial Perspective: What Should Entrepreneurs Know?" In *The Entrepreneurial Venture*, ed. W. A. Sahlman and H. H. Stevenson, 238–61. 2nd ed. Cambridge, MA: Harvard Business School Press.

VALUATION

CHAPTER 9

FOUNDATIONS OF NEW VENTURE VALUATION

I was seldom able to see an opportunity until it ceased to be one.

Mark Twain

How do VCs and other investors select the projects in which they invest? And how do they settle on the ownership stakes, terms, and conditions they require in exchange for investing? There are no simple answers to these questions. Certainly, the perceived value of the entrepreneur's concept and capabilities are critical factors. No venture will be funded unless an investor sees the merits of the concept and regards the entrepreneur as capable of implementing it or of working with the investor to build a capable team. In addition, there are issues of fit and timing: Can the investor contribute value to the project? Does the investor have the financial and organizational capacity to take on another project? The answers to these questions depend on the particular expertise of the investor and on whether, at the time, the investor is looking for new projects.

In this chapter, we introduce the foundations of valuation and introduce the most widely used valuation methodologies, identifying the pros and cons of each. Chapter 10 concerns implementation and provides guidance on how to ensure that the valuation approach is internally consistent and how to find the information necessary to perform the valuation.

In Chapter 10, we use a single example to illustrate the use of the various valuation methods that we present in this chapter. An important lesson is that if the assumptions are all consistent, then, in a perfect world, every valuation method would produce the same estimate of value. Of course, in reality they do not. The data and assumptions in each valuation effort are estimates of the "true" underlying values.

Differences in estimated value across methods therefore reflect the effects of estimation errors. The art of valuation is in deciding how to weight the information from each of the approaches and use it to reach a conclusion about value.

9.1   Perspectives on the Valuation of New Ventures

The value of any investment depends on its ability to generate future cash flows, as well as on investor assessments of and tolerance for the riskiness of those cash flows. Two aspects of valuation make new venture investment decisions particularly difficult. First, the future cash flows of a prospective venture are volatile and difficult to forecast. Second, discount rates appropriate for new venture investments can be challenging to estimate.

In spite of the near impossibility of precision, earnings or cash flow forecasts appear in most business plans, and forecasts are made and studied by VCs and other investors who are shopping for deals. In addition, the problem of determining the appropriate discount rate is addressed routinely by VCs and other investors. We show in this chapter that financial economic theory provides considerable guidance for estimating appropriate discount rates.

In an area as competitive and complex as investing in new ventures, the importance of good decision making cannot be overemphasized. One indicator of the potential for good decision making to add value is the variation in investment performance of VC funds. Several sources compile information on the returns to investors in VC funds. In Figure 9.1, we use information reported in the Preqin Private Equity Database to produce a histogram of annualized internal rates of return (IRRs) for 1,285 funds that were launched between 1980 and 2004. The returns range from an almost total loss (−100 percent) to one fund with annual returns of more than 500 percent. To put this in perspective, a fund that returns 500 percent per year for a five-year period would return more than $1,200 for each $1.00 invested. But this is a very rare occurrence; there were only four funds in the sample with returns above 220 percent. The average IRR of funds in the sample is 13.7 percent per year, and the median is 9.6 percent. The average annual return on the S&P 500 over the same period (though not strictly comparable) was 10.3 percent, which is higher than more than half of the VC funds.

Low rates of return can result from numerous factors: unfortunate

FIGURE **9.1**
**Distribution of
VC fund average
annual IRRs**
Information is for
funds launched be-
tween 1980 and 2004.

SOURCE: Preqin Private
Equity Database; available
at http://www.preqin.com/
section/private-equity/1.

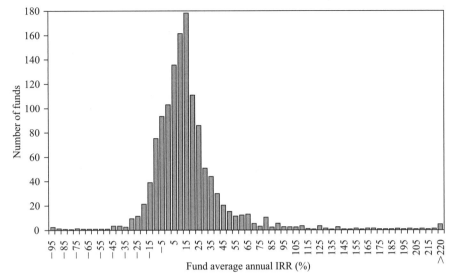

timing, bad luck, lack of skill or access to deal flow, and unforesee-able negative events. However, two important reasons for low rates of return are valuation mistakes and deal-structuring mistakes. Both of these can be avoided, or at least minimized, by using decision-making methods that give the investor a competitive advantage over its rivals in both project selection and deal structuring.

The arrival of professional investment managers to VC investing has changed the market in fundamental ways. Most important for our purpose is the changing way in which investment opportunities are valued by investors. In time, the changes will affect the ways in which entrepreneurs evaluate projects. Because the market is changing, some of the approaches and rule-of-thumb heuristics that have been used histori-cally for investing in new ventures no longer can be relied upon to iden-tify projects that are likely to yield acceptable rates of return.

9.2 Myths about New Venture Valuation

Past practices have generated four myths about new venture investing. The myths no longer serve the interest of either the entrepreneur or the investor. We begin the study of new venture valuation by examining these myths.

Myth 1: Beauty Is in the Eye of the Beholder

Over two decades ago, Gordon Baty (1990) wrote, "Pricing a new company's stock is much like pricing any other glamour item (such as perfume, paintings, rare coins) where appeal is based on emotional, as well as analytical considerations."[1] While it is reasonable to expect that the entrepreneur may care about qualitative factors, it would not be a good idea for a VC fund manager to propose to prospective investors that financial return be traded off against other factors. In fact, even investors who espouse an interest in doing something good for society often say that while they want to "do good," they also want to "do well" and would not be willing to sacrifice financial returns for social goals.

Professional investors understand that the fundamental economic tradeoff between cash flow and risk must drive valuation. We seek to present theoretically sound valuation tools while at the same time recognizing the implementation challenges.

Myth 2: The Future Is Anybody's Guess

This is a more reasonable sounding version of Myth 1. The claim is that even though cash flow is what matters, future cash flows of new ventures are so uncertain that forecasting them is of little value. Although new venture financial forecasts are subject to great uncertainty, such uncertainty—rather than making the forecast worthless—makes forecasting critical. In particular, it is important to try to understand the extent, nature, and implications of the uncertainty. It is true that a single-scenario forecast for a new venture is unlikely to be of much value. Scenario analysis and simulation are, however, of considerable practical value for understanding and dealing with the risks, for establishing strategy, for cash needs assessment, and for valuing the venture.

Myth 3: Investors Demand Very High Rates of Return to Compensate for Risk

New ventures are high-risk investments that tie up the investor's capital for several years with no easy means of exit. This has led to a broadly held perception that the required rates of return for VC investing must be very high. On this subject Michael Roberts and Howard Stevenson write, "In order to compensate for the high risk of their investments, give their own investors a handsome return, and make a profit for themselves, venture firms seek a high rate of return. Target returns of 50 percent or 60 percent are not uncommon."[2] Jeffrey Timmons and Stephen

Spinelli (2007), p. 449, provide a more comprehensive summary that echoes the same point:

Stage	Annual ROR (%)	Total expected holding period (years)
Seed and start-up	50–100% or more	More than 10
First stage	40–60	5–10
Second stage	30–40	4–7
Expansion	20–30	3–5
Bridge and mezzanine	20–30	1–3
LBOs	30–50	3–5
Turnarounds	50+	3–5

Scholars and others who remark on the high rates of return base their statements on historical practice, generally asking VC investors to identify the rates they apply when discounting the projected cash flows of proposed new ventures. Approaching the question in this way, they find that the rates are typically quite high, and so the myth endures.

These high returns, however, are not supported by historical evidence; an examination of the actual average returns for investing in new ventures tells a very different story. In addition to the information in Figure 9.1, numerous studies by academics and industry participants over more than four decades report average annual rates of return to investors in VC funds in the mid to high teens.[3] For the recent 20-year period, ending in December 2008, the average annual return from a sample of US venture capital funds was 17 percent.[4] Figure 9.2 shows two different estimates of venture capital IRRs since 1981 by vintage year: the series are similar and exhibit very high volatility.[5]

How can the common practice of using very high discount rates to value projects be reconciled with the evidence that over many years the average realized return has been much lower? Do investors suffer from chronic unfounded optimism, so that actual returns have been disappointingly low? Or is there another interpretation of the evidence, one that does not rely on biased decision making?

Surely, if rates of return in the neighborhood of 60 percent could reasonably be expected, capital would flood the new venture market, driving the returns to levels that are more consistent with those for other forms of investment. The reality is that true required rates of return are much closer to the range documented in the empirical studies than to the very high rates that are sometimes sought by investors when they evaluate individual projects. Later in this chapter, we offer a reconciliation of the above statements and evidence that places the statements in

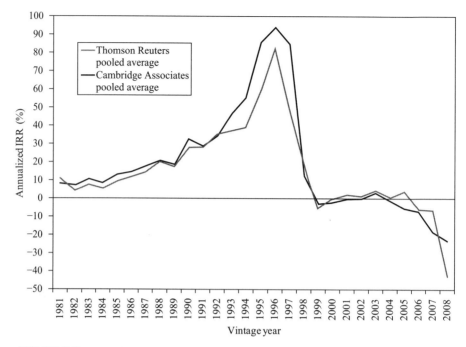

FIGURE **9.2**

VC returns to limited partners by vintage year, 1981–2008

Data are for average VC returns by vintage year, which is defined as the legal inception date as noted in a fund's financial statement. Thomson Reuters data are compiled from 1,267 US venture capital funds. Cambridge Associates data are compiled from 1,043 US venture capital funds. Returns are net of fees, expenses, and carried interest and represent the pooled average across all funds. The pooled average aggregates all cash flows and ending net asset values (NAVs) to calculate a dollar-weighted return. Vintage-year funds formed since 2005 are too young to have produced meaningful returns.

SOURCES: Thomson Reuters, Venture Economics, VentureXpert database, extracted August 2009; available at http://thomsonreuters.com/products_services/financial/financial_products/deal_making/private_equity/ private_equity_venture_capital?parentKey=586138. Cambridge Associates LLC US Venture Capital Index and Selected Benchmark Statistics, NVCA (3/31/2009); available at http://www.nvca.org/.

a more useful context and demonstrates that actual required rates are much lower. The point for now is that the contradiction is more apparent than real.

Myth 4: The Investor Determines the Value of the Venture

A common contention is that it is pointless for the entrepreneur to undertake a valuation. The argument is that investors do not accept the entrepreneur's valuation anyway, so the entrepreneur's efforts are better spent in other ways. The problem with this view is that it fails to recognize the pivotal role that valuation plays in reaching agreement between the entrepreneur and the investor, as well as the role it can play in helping the entrepreneur decide whether to undertake the venture.

VC investors report that many of their negotiations fail to result in investment. In a recent interview, Sonja Hoel, a managing director at Menlo Ventures, cited valuation issues as an important factor.

> We almost always get it right if we turned down a deal because there wasn't a market. Where we don't always get it right is valuation. If we turned it down because of valuation, we had a 10% error rate. Of all the decisions we made because of valuation, 90% were good but 10% were bad.[6]

Good working knowledge of valuation can help the entrepreneur avoid a breakdown of negotiations. It is true that investors commonly prepare valuations based on their own research and assumptions. However, there is more to new venture financing negotiations than a simple exchange of cash for a percentage of the equity. In the context of a financing negotiation, valuation is important to the entrepreneur for at least three reasons. First, the entrepreneur can better understand how the venture is likely to be valued by prospective investors. Second, the entrepreneur can better understand what the venture should be worth to her and how that differs from its value to the investor. Third, the entrepreneur needs to understand how alternative deal structures affect overall value and the values of the financial claims of investors and the entrepreneur.

The entrepreneur might expect that competition among prospective investors can eliminate the need to value complex financial claims. This expectation is incorrect. Even if several investors are vying to participate in a venture, they may have varying views of the venture's strategy and will probably seek different structures of ownership claims and financing commitments. Without studying the valuation consequences of different proposals, choosing the best alternative can be problematic for the entrepreneur. A solid understanding of basic valuation techniques can ensure that entrepreneurs better understand how investors perceive the opportunity at hand and help both sides reach a mutually beneficial agreement.

9.3   An Overview of Valuation Methods

For an investor who cares only about financial return, the value of any investment is the PV of its future cash flows. Although a variety of methods exist for estimating value, ranging from explicit discounting of future cash flows to valuation based on simple multiples to valuation based on comparable firms, they all are attempting to measure, either directly or indirectly, the PV of the right to receive future cash flows.

As discussed in Chapter 1, valuation is guided by two fundamental principles: that a dollar today is worth more than a dollar received in the future; and that a safe dollar is worth more than a risky one, that is, a safe dollar is more valuable than a gamble with an expected payoff of one dollar. Thus, the PV of any investment depends on the timing and riskiness of expected future cash flows.

In theory, if a person could correctly identify expected cash flows, risk, and cost of capital, the result of a discounted cash flow analysis would be the "true" PV. In practice, however, there is considerable judgment involved in valuation. Because we must rely on estimates, we can be sure our calculations yield only approximations of true PV. Rather than despair, we should recognize that imperfect PV estimates provide opportunity. There are potentially large rewards for doing a better job than your rivals of estimating PV. Other things being equal, the entrepreneur or investor who consistently does a good job of estimating value will outperform the one who is right on average but makes large over- and underestimation errors.

There are many theoretically sound and empirically validated valuation tools for analyzing new ventures. In this chapter, we introduce the following methods and highlight their strengths and weaknesses:

1. Discounted cash flow (DCF)
   a. The risk-adjusted discount rate (RADR) approach
   b. The certainty equivalent (CEQ) approach
2. Relative value (RV)
3. The venture capital (VC) method
4. The First Chicago method

These methods vary in their complexity and the directness of their connection to underlying economic theory, but all are used in practice and therefore are important to entrepreneurs and investors.

The Discounted Cash Flow Method

We consider two approaches for estimating PV by DCF. The first is the RADR approach and the second the CEQ approach. The difference between them lies in how the adjustment for risk is incorporated into the calculation. If the approaches are applied in a consistent manner and the underlying assumptions are consistent, they will yield identical estimates of value. However, the information needed to implement the two approaches differs. Consequently, availability and quality of information are important determinants of which to use.

The RADR approach is the more widely known and used DCF approach. In the RADR approach, an expected future cash flow is converted to PV by applying a discount rate that reflects both the time value of money and the riskiness of the future cash flow. This rate is known as the "risk-adjusted discount rate" because the effect of risk on value is built into the discount rate that is applied to the expected cash flow. The RADR approach is used most commonly in corporate finance because it is convenient and because the information requirements are easily satisfied by using data on comparable public firms.

With the CEQ approach, instead of adjusting the discount rate, the risk adjustment is made directly to the cash flow. This adjustment yields a risk-adjusted (or certainty equivalent) cash flow that is converted to PV by discounting at the risk-free rate. It turns out that for new ventures, it is often easier to estimate the CEQ cash flow than the RADR. In subsequent discussion we examine both approaches.

The Relative Value Method

Relative valuation (RV) uses market data on other companies or other transactions as bases for inferring the value of the subject venture. This method is sometimes referred to as "comparables" or "multiples valuation." It is widely used in practice, especially for established private companies, and can provide a quick and easy ballpark estimate of value. The underlying logic is that if two different companies are expected to produce identical future cash flows and are subject to identical risks, they should have the same value. If they did not, then investors should want to sell the higher-valued one and buy the lower-valued one.

Relative valuation is thus an effort to finesse questions of discount rates and explicit cash flow projections. If RV and DCF could be correctly and perfectly applied to a given venture, then they should yield identical values. Suppose, for example, that we find a perfect comparable for a venture we want to value and that the comparable has been the subject of a recent transaction that implied a value. Under RV, we could simply say that the values are the same; under DCF, we could use the expected future cash flows and implied value of the comparable to infer the discount rate that we should use to value the cash flows. We would get the same answer either way. In practice, when RV and DCF yield different estimates of value, there is something inconsistent about the assumptions. Either the assumptions need to be revised or judgment must be used to assess the significance to place on each estimate.

In RV, market prices or prices from public or private transactions are collected along with information on observable characteristics of the comparable firms. This information may include accounting ratios and operating data that can be used to estimate the value of a private firm or new venture. While the logic behind RV is straightforward, there are many challenges to valid implementation. Appropriate comparables for a new venture (with transactions at the same stage of development) can be difficult or impossible to find or to verify, and common metrics such as P/E ratios are not useful for a start-up that has not reached profitability. Because some multiples are based on accounting data, the usual caveats about quality of earnings and adjustments to ensure comparability apply.

More generally, while the idea of valuation based on comparisons to other firms sounds simple, it is not. There are many dimensions of comparability, including industry, business model, stage, size, and accounting ratios. Ideally, a comparable firm has expected cash flows and risk that are similar to those of the new venture. Certainly, no public company can be a direct comparable for an early-stage venture. Moreover, there are no readily accessible databases of transactions related to early-stage private companies that have sufficient data to be useful in a valuation.

Use of an RV approach is more common and more defensible for a company that is being valued at the time of an assumed harvesting event, such as an IPO or acquisition. At that stage, information on comparable firms and transactions is likely to be more plentiful and the necessary analogies are easier to make and defend. In fact, RV is often the approach that is used in DCF methods to estimate the harvest-date cash flow. That said, even for a mature private company there are likely to be no truly comparable public companies. Companies that are similar in some key respects but not identical to the subject company are likely to yield a wide range of value estimates. Deciding how to select the companies and how to weight the evidence are part of the art of valuation.

The Venture Capital Method

The VC method combines elements of DCF and RV and has been popular in the private equity arena. It is computationally straightforward and parallels the way some VCs approach their investments. The VC method starts with an estimate of future value conditional on success. This involves assuming a timetable for exit, typically three to five years, and then conjecturing as to the form of exit and resulting future value. The estimate of exit value conditional on success is sometimes developed using RV and applying multiples to a projection such as net income or EBIT. The success-scenario exit value is then discounted to PV, typically using a very high annual discount rate such as the "sought for" rates we presented earlier. The hurdle rate is intended to take account of (1) time value, (2) risk, (3) the bias associated with discounting only the success-scenario cash flows, and (4) the dilutive effect of subsequent financing rounds. The result is an estimate of the venture's PV.

In spite of its widespread use and intuitive appeal, the VC method has theoretical and practical shortcomings. Most important, the hurdle rate selection implicitly combines so many conditions that are difficult to specify that there is no reliable way to determine the rate that should be used; and because only a success scenario is used, the assumed timing of the harvest cash flow can impart systematic bias to value estimates. We discuss these shortcomings in greater depth below.

The First Chicago Method

The First Chicago method is also used widely by practitioners and represents an improvement upon the VC method.[7] The goals of the First Chicago method are to provide a simple way of performing DCF valuation and to mitigate the valuation biases of the VC method. Rather than limiting the analysis to a success scenario, the First Chicago method uses probability-weighted scenarios to come up with a more reliable estimate of expected (in the statistical sense) cash flows, rather than just the optimistic cash flows used in the VC method. These expected cash flows are then discounted using a more realistic cost of capital, rather than the high hurdle rates used in the VC method. If the scenario probabilities are correctly weighted, the appropriate discount rate is identical to the one that would be used in DCF valuation by the RADR approach. A benefit of the First Chicago method is that it requires the analyst to think about the range of possible outcomes for the venture and their probabilities.

The question of which valuation tool is the best for a particular situation does not have a clear answer. Like any quantitative methodology, the results of each approach are dependent on the availability and quality of the information it requires. There is a benefit to using as many of the techniques as the data will allow. Doing so will inevitably produce a range of value estimates. The final step is to compare the results, seeking to understand the reasons for material differences. On reflection, you may conclude that, in a given instance, one approach is more reliable than the others. More likely, each provides some useful information, and your task is to decide how best to weight the different estimates.

9.4   Discounted Cash Flow Valuation

We consider two approaches to DCF valuation, the RADR approach and the CEQ approach. The main difference between them is in the way we adjust for risk. Most introductory finance texts cover only RADR or only briefly describe CEQ. Because of its different information requirements, however, the CEQ method is often better suited than RADR for new venture valuation.

The Risk-Adjusted Discount Rate Approach

Under RADR, expected future cash flows are discounted to PV using a discount factor that reflects the time value of money and the riskiness of the future cash flows. The present value, PV_j, of an investment that offers a series of expected future cash flows, C_{jt}, is given as:

$$PV_j = \sum_t \frac{C_{jt}}{(1 + r_t)^t} \tag{9.1}$$

In Eq. (9.1), r_t is the risk-adjusted discount rate that is appropriate for computing the PV of an expected time t cash flow. The expression is general in that it allows for cash flows to be received at any time and for the cost of capital to be specific to the period in which the flow is expected.

Note that PV_j is the value today of all of the cash flows that are generated by the venture's operations, whether they are positive or negative. It is not the same as net present value (NPV), which is net of the investment required to receive the venture's future cash flows. To illustrate, consider a delivery business. The PV would include positive cash flows (e.g., revenue) and negative cash flows (e.g., lease payments on trucks, salaries, or fuel). Let's assume that discounting all of the cash flows using Eq. (9.1) produces a PV of $150,000. If the owner agrees to sell you the venture for $130,000, the resultant NPV is $20,000. That is, NPV is equal to PV minus the investment required to acquire the venture.

Applying Eq. (9.1) requires that we (1) identify the cash flows that are appropriate to include in the valuation model and (2) determine the appropriate discount rate for valuing each cash flow.

Identifying relevant cash flows.   Conceptually, determining the cash flows to include in an RADR valuation is straightforward. They are the cash flows the investor can expect (statistically) to receive in exchange for investing. To identify the relevant cash flow, we need to understand exactly what asset is being valued. The asset may be the entire venture or a particular financial claim on the venture, such as a portion of the common stock, preferred stock, or debt.

A share of stock, for example, yields cash flows in the form of dividends. An investor who owns the share for a finite period, of course, does not receive the entire dividend stream but receives the interim dividends and a lump-sum payment when the share is sold. The payment when the share is sold depends on the stream of dividends from that point forward. Implicitly, then, the stock price at any point reflects the value of all future dividend cash flows.[8] The expected proceeds from selling the stock at a future date can be thought of as the "continuing value" of the stock at that point, based on cash flows expected after the sale. Because we normally project dividends in simple ways, such as by assuming that they are expected to grow at a constant rate, the continuing value approach (of an actual or hypothetical sale in the future) is a shortcut approach to discounting a long stream of future cash flows.

Debt is expected to yield a stream of interest payments and the eventual repayment of principal. If the debt is risky, the interest payments and principal repayment to be valued are not those specified in the debt contract. Rather, they are the cash flows that are expected to be received, recognizing that the borrower may default on the obligation.

If the asset to be valued is a venture, the relevant cash flows are the (positive and negative) periodic free cash flows generated by the venture and available to all capital providers. Depending on your purpose, it may be advantageous to measure these cash flows net of any retention for the purpose of capital replacement or growth and (for consistency) to measure investment as only the cash infusions that investors make in the venture.

Like a share of stock, a venture can, in principle, last forever. Conceptually, we would like to know the value of all of the future cash flows, but at some point after the first few years it is more convenient (and maybe no less accurate) to assume a hypothetical sale where the selling price is based on the value (at the time of sale) of all of the free cash flows from that point forward. We refer to this value as the continuing value of the venture. The "explicit value period" is the span over which periodic cash flows are estimated explicitly and each is discounted to its PV. Total PV thus consists of two parts: (1) the PV of the expected cash flows from the explicit value period and (2) the PV of the expected continuing value.

Determining the discount rate (cost of capital). The next step in valuation by RADR is determining the discount rate for valuing each cash flow. Because in the RADR approach the discount rate takes account of both time value and cash flow risk, we can think of the discount rate used in Eq. (9.1) as having two components. The first is the return for investing in a risk-free asset that would pay off at the same time as the project cash flow. The second is a risk premium that depends on the riskiness of the expected future cash flow. For a particular project j that yields a single uncertain cash flow at time t, the appropriate discount rate can be stated as follows:

$$r_{jt} = r_{Ft} + RP_{jt} \tag{9.2}$$

where r_{Ft} is the required rate of return for investing in a risk-free asset that would pay off at time t, and RP_{jt} is a risk premium or risk adjustment. The risk adjustment depends, in some fashion, on the riskiness of the time t cash flow.

Because the cash flows being valued are expected cash flows, the appropriate discount rate for valuing them is the opportunity cost the investor could realize by investing in an alternative financial claim with the same expected return and risk. In contrast to the ad hoc determination of the hurdle rate in the VC method, the financial economic theory underlying determination of the discount rate for RADR valuation is well established.

In summary, the steps for using the RADR method are as follows: (1) forecast expected future cash flows, and (2) estimate the risky discount rate, r_{jt}, for each cash flow. Equation (9.2) is useful because it is sometimes easier to estimate r_{Ft} and RP_{jt} than to estimate r_{jt} directly. A simple way of estimating r_{Ft} is to examine currently available returns on zero-coupon government bonds of similar duration to the cash flow that is being valued. Estimating the risk premium is more difficult: first, we need a measure of risk; and second, we need a metric to determine the associated risk premium.

The measure of risk.   The measure of risk that has become the norm for investment valuation is the standard deviation of holding-period returns.[9] A holding-period return is a rate of return, expressed as a percentage, that is measured from the point of investment to the point when the return is realized. Take, for example, a common stock. Its holding-period return consists of two parts, a dividend yield and a capital gain (or loss). Uncertainty about the size of the dividend and the price at which the shares can be sold in the future are the risks faced by equity investors. Assume that a share of stock that has a market value of $20 today has the following equally likely payoffs and returns in one year:

State of the economy	Dividend (D_1)	Price (P_1)	Dividend yield	Percent appreciation	Total return
Good	$2.00	$24.00	10%	20%	30%
Average	$1.00	$22.00	5%	10%	15%
Bad	$0.00	$18.00	0%	−10%	−10%

With equally likely outcomes, the expected return over the holding period is the average of the three possible returns, or 11.67 percent, and the standard deviation of the holding-period return is 16.5.[10] Note that we calculated the holding-period returns and standard deviation based on today's market price. We can use this calculation to infer cost of capital because the stock trades in a market such that buying the stock today and holding it for one year is expected to be a zero-NPV transaction. Because new ventures are not like shares of stock that trade in a market, we cannot assume that investing is a zero-NPV choice. We will see later that this feature makes RADR difficult to apply to new venture valuation.

The price for bearing risk. How do we go from measuring risk to inferring a price for bearing risk? To answer, we must first distinguish between the entrepreneur and prospective investors in a new venture. For investors, we follow the standard corporate finance approach to estimating a risk premium, which relies on the following assumptions:

- There is active competition to invest capital in new ventures.
- Investors view new venture investing as an alternative to other investment opportunities.
- Investors assess project risk based on its contribution to the risk of a diversified portfolio.
- Illiquidity does not affect the investors' valuation of new venture investment.

These assumptions allow us to distinguish between market and nonmarket risk. The total risk, measured as the standard deviation of holding-period returns, is the sum of two categories of risk. The first—called market, systematic, or nondiversifiable risk—consists of marketwide risk factors that impact all ventures. Economic recession and boom, changes in inflation, and changes in the flow of funds into the capital markets are among the factors that tend to affect security prices marketwide. Because market risk affects all securities, it cannot be eliminated by diversifying the investor's portfolio. The second category—called firm-specific, idiosyncratic, nonmarket, or diversifiable

FIGURE **9.3**

How portfolio risk depends on the number of assets in the portfolio

The figure shows how diversification reduces total risk as the number of assets in the portfolio increases. Risk is measured by the standard deviation of holding-period returns. The risk that remains is shown as σ_M and is the market, or nondiversifiable, risk.

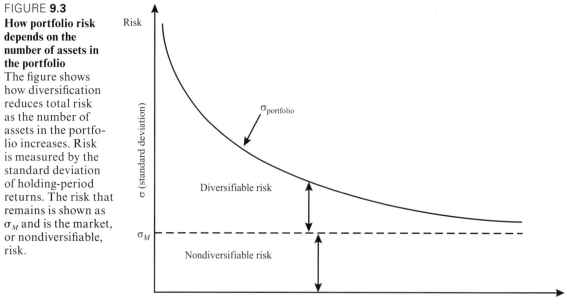

risk—includes all risk other than market risk. Examples of diversifiable risk include success or failure to achieve a technology milestone and product demand that is higher or lower than expected.

Because of diversification, the unexpected positive and negative non-market components of returns to different investments are random so that, in diversified portfolios, they tend to cancel each other out. In a portfolio with even a modest number of assets, the idiosyncratic component of risk can be substantially reduced. Diversification cannot be used, however, to reduce investor exposure to the component of risk that is due to the overall market.

Figure 9.3 demonstrates the diversification principle that the risk of a portfolio varies as a function of the number of randomly selected securities. As shown, the total risk of the portfolio is composed of diversifiable (nonsystematic) and nondiversifiable (systematic) risk. By holding more securities, diversifiable risk approaches zero and total risk approaches the risk of the market, σ_M.

Any investor can diversify by investing in an equity mutual fund that is designed to match the performance of a standard market index, such as the S&P 500. Because diversification is easy, investors cannot expect to be compensated if they choose not to take advantage of the simple opportunity to diversify. Thus, the expected return on a risky asset depends only on risk that is not diversifiable.

The nondiversifiable component of risk is known as beta (β) risk, or market risk. By convention, the beta risk of the market portfolio is defined as one unit of risk. The risk-free asset, by definition, has no risk and therefore has a beta of zero. An asset with nondiversifiable risk that is half as great as the market has a beta of 0.5, and so on.

The notion that investors care only about time value and nondiversifiable risk is reflected in the Capital Asset Pricing Model (CAPM).[11] Figure 9.4 shows the relationship between beta risk and expected return that is implied by the CAPM. The CAPM tells us that different investments with different amounts of total risk but equal amounts of beta risk will have the same expected return. Accordingly, all assets and portfolios with the same beta risk plot at the same point in the

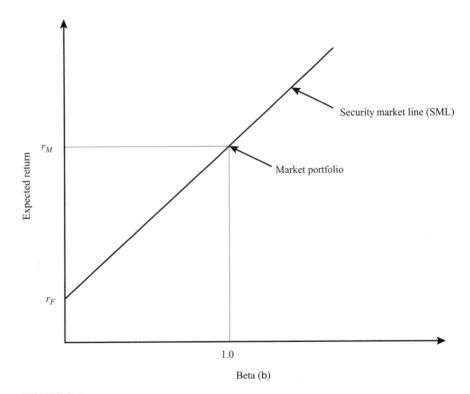

FIGURE **9.4**

The Capital Asset Pricing Model (CAPM)
The CAPM describes the required return on an asset as a function of its nondiversifiable (market) risk as measured by beta. The market portfolio by definition has a beta of 1.0 and is expected to earn r_M. The riskless asset has a beta of zero and earns r_F, the risk-free rate. The difference between r_M and r_F is called the "market risk premium." If the CAPM correctly describes investor behavior, then all market assets offer risk and expected return combinations that plot on the security market line (SML).

figure. The sloping line in Figure 9.4 is known as the security market line (SML) because all risky assets must plot on the line. The result is a single price, or expected return, for bearing a unit of nondiversifiable, or beta, risk. The difference between the expected return on the market portfolio and the return on a risk-free asset is called the market risk premium.

In algebraic form, the CAPM is:

$$r_j = r_F + \beta_j(r_M - r_F) \tag{9.3}$$

Comparing Eq. (9.2) and Eq. (9.3), we can see that the CAPM defines the risk premium for an asset as $\beta_j(r_M - r_F)$, which has two components. The term in parentheses, $(r_M - r_F)$, is the market risk premium and is computed as the difference between the expected return on the market portfolio and the return on a risk-free asset. This market risk premium is then scaled by β_j, the beta or systematic risk of asset j relative to the risk of the market portfolio. The product of the two is the risk premium for asset j.

The beta of asset j is the measure of its nondiversifiable risk. Specifically, β_j is computed as follows:

$$\beta_j = \frac{\text{Cov}_{r_j,r_M}}{\sigma_M^2} = \frac{\rho_{r_j,r_M}\sigma_j}{\sigma_M} \tag{9.4}$$

In Equation (9.4), Cov_{r_j,r_M} is the covariance of holding-period returns of asset j with the holding-period returns of the market, ρ_{r_j,r_M} is the correlation coefficient of holding-period returns between the asset and the market, σ_M^2 is the variance of market returns, and σ_M and σ_j are the standard deviations of returns of the market and of asset j.

Equation (9.3) identifies the information necessary to use the CAPM to estimate the required rate of return on an investment. Estimating the risk premium for use in the RADR model requires estimating both the beta of the asset and the market risk premium. Equation (9.4) shows two different ways to estimate beta. As an alternative to estimating beta directly, the estimate can be calculated from estimates of the standard deviations of holding-period returns for both the asset and the market and an estimate of the correlation between asset returns and market returns. In Chapter 10, we examine methods of estimating the information needed to use the CAPM in RADR valuation.

Given its focus on nondiversifiable risk, the CAPM is appropriate when investors are able to diversify at low cost. The typical investors in new ventures and in VC funds (pension plans, endowments, and insurance companies) are able to do so. The CAPM suggests that these investors should not require an increase in expected return for bearing venture-specific risk that is diversifiable. Other kinds of investors in new ventures may find diversification more difficult to achieve. In particular, private corporations and high-net-worth individuals may be compelled to hold portfolios that are not well diversified. If such investors hope to be compensated for sacrificing diversification, they must either find opportunities that well-diversified investors do not recognize or be able to contribute unique value to the venture in other ways that well-diversified investors cannot duplicate.

The Certainty Equivalent Approach

It sometimes is difficult to use the RADR form of the CAPM to value real investment opportunities with risky cash flows. The model requires that risk be measured as the standard deviation of holding-period returns. However, even if we can estimate the expected cash flows of a project and their riskiness (i.e., standard deviation), we cannot determine the expected holding-period return or the standard deviation of holding-period returns without knowing the PV of the project. When it is possible to rely on market assets to infer cost of capital, this is not a problem because market assets are zero NPV by definition (cost and present value are the same). But this does not work so simply for new ventures, where we cannot easily refer to market assets.

We can demonstrate the difficulty of using RADR by making a couple of substitutions to Eq. (9.3). Equation (9.5) makes the appropriate substitutions for r_j and β_j in Eq. (9.3), where C_j is the project j expected cash flow, σ_{C_j} is the standard deviation (risk) of this cash flow, and ρ_{C_j, r_M} is the correlation between the project j cash flow and the market return. For convenience, rates of return in the above expressions are defined over the holding period for C_j (one year, two years, etc.).

$$\frac{C_j}{PV_j} - 1 = r_F + \frac{\rho_{C_j, r_M}\left(\dfrac{\sigma_{C_j}}{PV_j}\right)}{\sigma_M}(r_M - r_F) \tag{9.5}$$

In this modified CAPM, the left-hand side of the equation is the expected return and the right-hand side is the expression for the required rate of return. In other words, we can find the required returns at the point where the expected return equals the required return. Note that PV_j appears on both sides of the equation. The two sides will only be equal at the point where PV_j is the PV of C_j. That is, Eq. (9.5) can be used to search for the PV of a future cash flow by using trial and error to find the value of PV_j that equates the two sides of the equation. Although this obviates the need to assume a standard deviation of holding-period returns (using, instead, the standard deviation of cash flows), it does not resolve the fundamental problem that the correct risky discount rate depends on the value of the cash flows.

An illustration of the difficulties of using the RADR approach. To see the nature of the problem, consider a wager that will pay either $1.00 or $2.00, with equal probability. We can easily determine that the risk of the bet (in terms of the standard deviation of the payoff cash flows) is $0.50.[12] But what about the standard deviation of holding-period returns? Suppose the wager can be acquired for $1.25. If so, the $2.00 payoff is a return of 60 percent and the $1.00 payoff is a return of −20 percent. This makes the expected return 20 percent and the standard deviation of holding-period returns 40 percent.[13]

But what if the wager costs $1.50? In this case, the $2.00 payoff yields a return of 33.3 percent and the $1.00 payoff yields −33.3 percent. At this price, the expected return is zero, and the standard deviation of holding-period returns is 33.3 percent. Thus, the standard deviation of holding-period returns depends on the cost of the wager.

To correctly find the PV of the wager, we need to know the standard deviation of holding-period returns that corresponds to investing exactly the PV of the expected payout. If the required investment is different from the PV of the expected payout, we would then correctly measure NPV as the difference between the actual investment and the investment that would yield a zero NPV.

You can see that applying the conventional RADR form of the CAPM is challenging when it is being used to value real assets. The problem is the inherent simultaneity and the lack of a zero-NPV market asset to use as a basis for inferring the correct discount rate. Valuing the expected cash flows requires knowing the discount rate, but the discount rate calculation requires a beta, which depends on the standard deviation of holding-period returns, which, in turn, depends on the PV of the project.

In corporate settings, these problems are finessed by analogizing the investment decision to an existing market asset that is publicly traded. If that is possible, a two-step approach can be used: first, estimate the beta of the market asset; second, discount project cash flows using that beta. Unfortunately, convincing analogies are unlikely to be found if the project is a new venture or a financial claim on a new venture. In Chapter 10, we seek to overcome this problem by providing some empirical estimates of betas for publicly traded corporations that are similar to entrepreneurial ventures. If those estimates are reliable, then using the RADR approach is straightforward, just as it is for public corporations. If not, the CEQ approach can be easier to use.

Advantage of the CEQ method. The certainty equivalent of a risky cash flow is the certain cash flow that, if received at the same time as the risky cash flow, would be equally valuable to the investor. For risk-averse investors, the certainty equivalent is less than the expected risky cash flow. Thus an investor might regard a risky cash flow with an expected value of $200 and a standard deviation of $50 as being equal in value to a certain $125 cash flow. See Figure 9.5 for another example.

In the CEQ approach of DCF valuation, instead of adjusting the discount rate, the risk adjustment is made to the cash flow:

$$CE(C_{jt}) = C_{jt} - RD_{jt} \tag{9.6}$$

where $CE(C_{jt})$ is the certainty equivalent of the period t expected cash flow, C_{jt}, and RD_{jt} represents the dollar-valued discount to C_{jt} that is required to convert the risky expected cash flow to its certainty equivalent. Once we have this stream of certainty equivalent cash flows, we convert them to PV using a risk-free discount rate as follows:

$$PV_j = \sum_t \frac{CE(C_{jt})}{(1 + r_{Ft})^t} \tag{9.7}$$

where r_{Ft} is the risk-free rate for period t cash flows. To apply Eq. (9.7), we need a way to compute the CEQ cash flow. Because the CEQ form of the CAPM uses the standard deviation of cash flows instead of the standard deviation of holding-period returns, it avoids the simultaneity problem of the RADR form.

The CEQ approach is general in that it does not impose any particular tradeoff between risk and return. If we assume that the CAPM is the correct asset pricing model, then Eq. (9.5), the expanded version of the RADR form of the CAPM, can be solved for PV_j to yield the CEQ form of the CAPM.

$$PV_j = \frac{C_j - \frac{\rho_{C_j r_M} \sigma_{C_j}}{\sigma_M}(r_M - r_F)}{1 + r_F} \tag{9.8}$$

The numerator in Eq. (9.8) is the CAPM-based certainty equivalent of the risky cash flow, C_j, which corresponds to Eq. (9.5). The denominator is a discount factor that is used to determine the PV of a riskless cash flow.[14] When the CEQ form of the CAPM is used, the risky cash flow is adjusted by a factor that makes the PV of the CEQ cash flow, when discounted with a risk-free rate, exactly equal to the value derived by discounting the uncertain expected cash flow at the appropriate risky rate.

To see how the CEQ approach simplifies finding PV, let's revisit the wager that will pay either $1.00 or $2.00 with equal probability. We as-

---

FIGURE **9.5**

Certainty equivalence in popular culture

An example of certainty equivalence can be found in the popular television game show *Deal or No Deal*. The show, which originated in Holland in 2002 and is now aired in over 70 countries around the world, confronts contestants with 26 sealed, numbered briefcases, each of which contains a dollar amount ranging from $0.01 up to $1 million in the following increments.*

$0.01	$1	$5	$10	$25	$50	$75	$100	$200	$300	$400	$500	$750
$1,000	$5,000	$10,000	$25,000	$50,000	$75,000	$100,000	$200,000	$300,000	$400,000	$500,000	$750,000	$1,000,000

The game begins with the contestant selecting 1 of the 26 cases as "her" case, which remains unopened until the end of the game. As the game begins, the expected payoff is a simple average of the 26 cases, or $131,478.54.

Over a series of nine rounds, the contestant is asked to choose additional cases, which are then opened to reveal their contents. The number of cases opened in each round declines, starting at six in the first round and falling to one in each of the last four. As cases are opened, the dollar amounts they represent are eliminated. At the end of each round, an off-stage "banker" offers the contestant a fixed payoff to abandon her case and give up the game.

After three rounds, 15 cases will have been chosen by the contestant, opened, and their contents removed from the game. Let's assume that, up to this point, the contestant has rejected the banker's offers and that the following amounts remain in the 11 unopened cases:

$0.01		$10	$75	$200	$500
$1,000	$10,000		$100,000	$300,000	$500,000	$1,000,000

These cases now have an expected payoff of $173,798.64. The banker offers the contestant a certain, riskless payment of $145,000 to abandon her case and the game. The contestant's certainty equivalent of the risky $173,798.64 is the amount she would accept to give up the gamble. In this situation, if the contestant's CEQ cash flow is less than $145,000, she would accept the banker's offer. If it is higher than $145,000, she would continue with the game.

---

* For a more detailed description of the game and rigorous analysis of decision making in the *Deal or No Deal* context, see Post et al. (2008).

sume that the risk-free rate is 4.0 percent; the market risk premium is 6.0 percent; the standard deviation of holding-period returns of the market portfolio is 20 percent; and the correlation between the payoff of the bet and the return you could earn by investing in the market portfolio is 0.6. Given this information, it is easy to use Eq. (9.8) to determine the PV of the wager.

$$PV_j = \frac{C_j - \frac{\rho_{C_j r_M}\sigma_{C_j}}{\sigma_M}(r_M - r_F)}{1 + r_F} = \frac{\$1.50 - \frac{0.60 \times \$0.50}{0.20}(0.06)}{1 + 0.04} = \frac{\$1.41}{1.04} = \$1.356$$

The CEQ cash flow of the expected (risky) $1.50 is $1.41, which when discounted at the riskless rate yields a PV of $1.356 for the wager. You can verify that if this value is used in Eq. (9.5), then the two sides are equal (i.e., required return equals expected return at a PV of $1.356).

Given the PV of the wager, the NPV of the opportunity to acquire it for $1.25 is $0.106 ($1.356 − $1.25 = $0.106). We also can determine that the correct risk-adjusted discount rate (the cost of capital), given the PV of $1.356, is $(C_j/PV_j) - 1$, or 10.62 percent.

Because Eq. (9.8) adjusts for risk by using the correlation between project cash flows and market returns, it circumvents the need to determine the riskiness of the holding-period returns. But it does raise another question: How can we estimate the correlation between project cash flows and market returns? A similar information requirement exists if the RADR form is used, but in that case the need is to estimate the correlation between project returns and market returns. The problem is sometimes finessed by analogizing the project to a publicly held corporation and using estimates of beta from published information.

9.5 The Relative Value Method

Relative valuation (RV) uses data from public companies and public and private market transactions to estimate value. It is widely used in the real estate industry, especially for residential real estate, for which it is particularly well suited. Owner-occupied housing does not produce observable cash flow streams that can be valued by DCF. Moreover, there are many trades of highly similar properties, where differences that affect value tend to be associated with observable factors such as square footage and number of bedrooms.

An Illustration: Valuing Residential Real Estate

We begin with a simple example to illustrate the concepts. Suppose you are in the market for a new home. You find a three-bedroom, 2,500-square-foot house that you like with an asking price of $450,000 and which the city recently assessed at $439,000. You have identified several characteristics of the house that you believe are relevant to its market value: size, number of bedrooms, and assessed value. You have also collected the following data on recent nearby transactions:

Comparable transaction	Square feet	Bedrooms	Assessed value	Selling price
House A	1,800	2	$330,000	$375,000
House B	2,100	3	$429,000	$422,000
House C	3,050	4	$500,000	$515,000

There are different ways to use the information from the comparables to estimate the value of the subject property. One simple approach, the one we illustrate here, is to consider each factor one at a time and compare the averages to the subject. A better approach, if sufficient data are available, is to fit a statistical model to the data, for example, by using multiple regression. The model can be used to assess the marginal effect of each factor in conjunction with the effects of the others.

The table below illustrates the averaging approach. We relate the market value of each comparable to the selected factor using ratios. Averaging the results across the three comparables yields the following:

Comparable	Selling price	Price/sq. ft.	Price/bedroom	Price/assessed value
House A	$375,000	$208.3	$187,500	1.14
House B	$422,000	$201.0	$140,667	0.98
House C	$515,000	$168.9	$128,750	1.03
Average		**$192.7**	**$152,306**	**1.05**

The next step is to apply each of the average values to the relevant attribute of the subject property. This yields three estimates of market value:

$$\text{MV Est.}_{\text{subject}} = \left(\frac{\text{Avg. MV}}{\text{Sq. Ft.}} \right)_{\text{comps}} \times \text{Sq. Ft.}_{\text{subject}} = \$192.7 \times 2,500 = \$481,750$$

$$\text{MV Est.}_{\text{subject}} = \left(\frac{\text{Avg. MV}}{\text{Bedroom}} \right)_{\text{comps}} \times \text{No. of Bedrooms}_{\text{subject}} = \$152,306 \times 3 = \$456,918$$

$$\text{MV Est.}_{\text{subject}} = \left(\frac{\text{Avg. MV}}{\text{Assessed Value}} \right)_{\text{comps}} \times \text{Assessed Value}_{\text{subject}} = \$1.05 \times \$439,000 = \$460,950$$

Averaging the three produces a result of $466,539, which suggests that the asking price for the house may actually be a bit low.

Relative Valuation and New Ventures

We can apply RV to new ventures by gathering information on the value drivers of comparable firms. A firm's value is driven by its profitability, expected growth, and risk. In the RV analysis, we can classify multiples into two categories: (1) multiples based on the capitalized value of equity and (2) multiples based on enterprise value, where enterprise value is defined as the market value of equity, plus the market value of interest-bearing debt, minus excess cash.[15] We can also classify multiples as either (1) accounting based or (2) non–accounting based.

Accounting-based approaches. Accounting-based multiples relate the value of venture equity or total capital to reported accounting information. The most familiar of these, the P/E ratio, is a way to estimate the value of equity on the basis of reported net income. Other accounting-based approaches to valuing equity include:

- Price to cash income, which is measured as net income plus non-cash expenses
- Price to levered free cash flow, which differs from the previous measure by subtracting increases in net working capital and fixed assets
- Price to book value of equity (more commonly referred to as market value to book value of equity)

Accounting-based approaches can also be used to estimate the combined value of equity and debt, or enterprise value. The commonly used measures are similar to those for valuing equity, except that they are usually based on cash flow measures including interest expense. Such approaches include:

- Enterprise value to EBITDA (earnings before interest, taxes, and depreciation and amortization)
- Enterprise value to unlevered free cash flow, which is EBIT minus theoretical taxes as if the company were entirely equity financed
- Enterprise value to book value of debt and equity
- Enterprise value to sales

While accounting data are readily available for public firms, accounting-based valuation multiples have two major problems. First, they are subject to accounting choices that can make comparison across firms inaccurate. Second, the data in public financial statements are based on historical results, whereas value today depends on expected future performance.

While accounting-based comparisons can work well for valuing established private businesses with simple business formats, such as dry cleaners or donut shops, they are not easily applied to early-stage ventures. Because new ventures are often unprofitable at the valuation date, may not have initiated sales, and may also have negative net worth, the commonly used accounting measures may not be meaningful. The VC method, discussed next, is designed to get around this problem while retaining the simplicity of the RV method.

Problems related to differences in accounting practices can be overcome with careful analysis. We can also overcome the backward-looking nature of accounting data by performing the RV analysis using forward projections for the comparable firms. For example, rather than calculating a P/E ratio based on the prior year's earnings, we can base the value estimate on multiples tied to earnings forecasts.

Of course, simple ratio-based comparisons are only helpful if the subject venture and the comparables have similar expected growth rates. There are more formal approaches as well to incorporating growth expectations into multiples analysis. The following are two of the most common:

- The PEG ratio (or P/E/growth), where growth is the expected growth rate of earnings
- Enterprise value to EBITDA/growth, where growth is the expected future growth rate of EBITDA

The growth-adjusted approaches are ways of dealing with differences in growth expectations between the subject venture and the comparables.

Non-accounting-based approaches. The other category of multiples we consider is industry-specific nonfinancial metrics. A magazine publishing venture could be valued on the basis of the projected number of subscribers or estimated pages of advertising. A proxy for the value of a biotechnology venture might be the number of patents, while a pharmaceutical venture's value might be estimated using the number of products in various stages of FDA approval. Internet ventures have been valued based on the number of website visits and time spent on the site.[16]

There is some evidence that industry-specific measures can be better value predictors than accounting-based multiples.[17] Industry-specific multiples may be used to estimate either equity or enterprise value. The important consideration is consistency. If the comparables used in the valuation are materially debt financed but the venture is entirely financed with equity, then the comparables ratios need to be based on enterprise value.

Private value versus market value. It is important to be cognizant of the assumptions implicit in the choice of comparables. If, for example, a private venture is valued on the basis of public company multiples, then the result is an estimate of the value as if the venture were public. If the comparables are from private transactions, such as acquisitions, then the estimate is as if the venture were to be acquired.

In principle, if everything is properly controlled, there may be no difference between the values implied by the two different kinds of comparables data. However, the choice to go public or exit via acquisition is not arbitrary. Some companies are better suited for IPO and others are better suited for acquisition. The valuation is likely to be more credible if the comparables represent the exit choice that is most appropriate for the subject venture.

The main drawback of relative value multiples is that current financial measures are linked primarily to assets in place, which may bear little relationship to likely future performance.[18] Furthermore, comparable firm and comparable transaction data can be difficult to collect.[19] That said, multiples are frequently used by practitioners, so we include them in our discussion and offer suggestions to help overcome their shortcomings.

9.6 Valuation by the Venture Capital Method

The VC method is the traditional approach for VC investment valuation. It is also the simplest approach for valuing early-stage ventures.[20] In the VC method, value is estimated on the basis of projected harvest-date cash flows under the assumption that the venture meets its performance objectives. The scenario in which the venture meets its objectives is generally referred to as a "success scenario." The procedure is as follows:

- *Step 1.* Select a terminal year for the valuation by determining a point where, if the venture is successful, harvesting by acquisition or IPO would be feasible. Estimate net income or other cash flow in that year based on the success scenario.
- *Step 2.* Use the appropriate P/E or other multiple and the harvest-date earnings or cash flow projection to compute continuing value. The multiple should reflect the expected capitalization of earnings or cash flow for a company that has achieved the level of success reflected in the scenario.

- *Step 3.* Convert the continuing value estimate to PV by discounting at a hurdle rate that is high enough to compensate for time value, risk, the probability that the success scenario will not be achieved, and dilution from anticipated future funding rounds.
- *Step 4.* Based on estimated PV, it is possible to compute the minimum fraction of ownership an investor would require in exchange for contributing a given amount of capital.

The VC method is problematic for several reasons. Most fundamentally, it is based on an optimistic forecast of the future.[21] While the hurdle rate is intended to compensate for the optimistic cash flow estimate, there is no indication of the likelihood that the success scenario will be achieved. To compensate for the optimistic forecast of continuing value, the hurdle rate must be well above cost of capital. The approach can easily be based on hurdle rates in excess of 50 percent.

In addition, the VC method does not consider cash flows in the explicit value period. This could make sense if the expected cash flows during the explicit value period are very small compared to continuing value. If they are not, the problem can be addressed by adding the PV of the cash flows from the explicit value period to the PV of continuing value. Because these cash flows are from a success scenario, the model implies that they again would be discounted at a high rate.

To illustrate, recall the stock price example from Section 9.4. If we were to value the stock using the VC method, we would consider only the good state (i.e., the success scenario) as shown here.

State of the economy	Dividend (D_1)	Price (P_1)	Dividend yield	Percent appreciation	Total return
Good	$2.00	$24.00	10%	20%	30%

We know that the actual PV is equal to today's market price of $20, and in Section 9.4 we established that the cost of capital taking account of all three possible outcomes is 11.67 percent. To get the same $20 market value by the VC method, we would need to discount the Time 1 success-scenario price of $24, plus the $2 dividend by 30 percent, well above the actual cost of capital.

The Achilles heel of the VC method is that there is nothing other than intuition and experience to tell us what hurdle rate to use. So while the method might work reasonably well for an investor who has years of experience of experimenting with different hurdle rates in different circumstances, there is no real guidance for an entrepreneur, a first-time investor, or a student who aspires to become a VC or entrepreneur. In spite of these problems and challenges, the VC method continues to be appealing because of its simplicity and intuitiveness.

9.7 Valuation by the First Chicago Method

Under the First Chicago method, a user identifies a small number of discrete scenarios and values them using a discount rate that is reflective of cost of capital. The First Chicago method is designed to be simple to use but also to address the biases of the VC method. Usually the First Chicago method is based on three scenarios: "success," "sideways," and "failure." The success scenario might be the same as in the VC method. The failure scenario is one in which investors realize essentially no return on their investment and lose the principal. The sideways scenario is one of moderate performance in which the venture languishes with no prospect of a high-value outcome; in this scenario, investors might earn a preferred dividend return and recoup the initial investment but nothing more.

If the First Chicago method is intended to correct the biases of the VC method, the scenarios and their probability weights are chosen so that opportunity cost of capital is the correct discount rate to use to value the scenario cash flows. Because the stock price example in Section 9.4 simplifies the stock price outcomes to three equally likely scenarios, we can think of it as an example of the First Chicago method. Implementation of the method involves the following steps:

- *Step 1.* Select a terminal year for the valuation based on the likely harvest date in the event of success.
- *Step 2.* Estimate the cash flows during the explicit value period based on a small number of discrete scenarios.
- *Step 3.* Compute the continuing value by applying a multiplier to the financial projection. The multiplier for the success scenario should reflect the expected capitalization for a company that has achieved the level of success reflected in the scenario. The multiplier for the sideways scenario may be different, depending on differences in expected growth rates used in the capitalization. In the failure scenario, the venture probably is not sold, but the liquidation value, if any, of the assets should be incorporated in the cash flows.
- *Step 4.* Compute the expected cash flow in each period by appropriately weighting the scenarios.

- *Step 5*. Compute PV by discounting the expected cash flows, including expected continuing value at opportunity cost of capital.
- *Step 6*. Based on PV, determine the minimum fraction of ownership the investor should require in exchange for contributing a given amount of capital.

The First Chicago method makes fundamental sense because the goal is to value expected cash flows at opportunity cost of capital. Traditional application of the First Chicago method, however, does not offer much guidance on how to determine the cost of capital. It might seem that the dispersion information reflected in the cash flow scenarios should be useful. Later, we will see that it is, but in the context of the CEQ model. In fact, if the CEQ model is applied to similar, discrete scenarios, it is the same as the First Chicago method with the CAPM being used to value the cash flows.

Ultimately, it is not possible to value cash flows by either the VC method or the First Chicago method without relying on some asset pricing model to determine the appropriate discount rates. The asset pricing model might be one that is based on experience and rules of thumb. It might be based on simple comparisons to other assets in the market. Or it might be derived from a formal asset pricing model, such as the CAPM.

9.8   Reconciliation with the Pricing of Options

The Black-Scholes Option Pricing Model (OPM) implies that the values of some kinds of claims increase with risk.[22] Because new ventures are, in effect, portfolios of options, you might ask whether the OPM would be a better valuation model for our purposes. To answer, we need to examine the principles underlying the OPM.

Risk contributes positively to the value of options because options partition risk into the risk of an increase in the price of an underlying asset and the risk of a price decrease. An investor who is optimistic about the future performance of a share of stock can buy a call option on the stock instead of the underlying share. If the stock value increases, the call option will increase as well. But unlike an investor in the stock, the call option investor is protected against price declines. If, on the date the option expires, the stock value has fallen to below the exercise price of the option, then the option is worthless. Conversely, if, on the day the call option expires, the stock price is above the exercise price, the value of the option will equal the difference between the stock price and the option exercise price. Because the exposure to risk is not symmetric (only the upside matters), the value of a call increases with anything that increases the riskiness of the underlying shares.

There is no inconsistency between using the OPM to value puts and calls and using the CAPM to value the underlying asset. The key to reconciliation is that an option is a derivative asset: its value is "derived" from the value of the underlying asset and from the risk characteristics of the underlying asset. Because the underlying asset does not partition risks into good and bad, an investor in the asset must bear the risk of loss to acquire the potential for gain. In that setting, risk aversion leads to the conclusion that investors will require compensation for bearing risk that is not diversifiable.

Although the CAPM and OPM are consistent, certain aspects of the OPM make its application to valuation of new ventures difficult. One problem is that the OPM is derived under an assumption of market completeness and continuous trading of assets. A complete market means that the underlying asset, matched pairs of puts and calls (with the same exercise price and expiration date), and riskless debt must all be continuously available, and it must be possible to take long or short positions in each. These conditions hold reasonably well for publicly traded options on stock. They also provide reasonable approximations for options on assets such as gold mines, the values of which are closely linked to the value of gold, a freely traded asset. Clearly, however, they do not hold for most new ventures. As a consequence, riskless arbitrage between options and underlying assets is not possible. The upshot is that, if risk can be estimated accurately, the OPM is likely to overvalue the real options that comprise most new ventures.

Sometimes attempts are made to finesse real option valuation by introducing a tracking portfolio of traded securities that is supposed to be a surrogate for the venture. One problem with this approach is that it is likely to understate risk substantially. Because of diversification, a tracking portfolio of biotech stocks, for example, will probably have much lower total risk than the risk of a single biotechnology venture. Because the risk is lower—and in the context of the OPM, greater risk implies greater value—this approach is likely to undervalue the real options.

Moreover, as a new venture is an amalgam of many interrelated options, some with complex exercise provisions that are controlled by different parties, use of the OPM quickly becomes impractical. In Chapter 10, we present a simulation approach to valuing new ventures and financial claims based on the CEQ form of the CAPM. The approach provides a convenient way to estimate the effects of embedded real options on the value of a new venture.[23]

9.9   Required Rates of Return for Investing in New Ventures

Early in the chapter we promised a resolution of the paradoxical difference between the rates of return sought by VC investors and those realized by the investors. The CAPM helps with the explanation and offers some supporting evidence.

Assuming that the CAPM is a reasonable way to estimate the rates of return investors in new ventures require, how high would those rates be? Clearly, a new venture is a risky proposition, which might suggest that the expected returns for investing should be very high. On the other hand, the point of the CAPM is that only nondiversifiable risk matters.

It seems likely that much of the risk associated with new ventures is diversifiable or firm specific. Consider, for example, a biotechnology venture. How much of the risk is likely to be nondiversifiable? In many respects, a biotechnology venture is like a lottery: by investing, you place a bet today, and at some future date you learn whether you have a winning ticket. The future payoff from such an investment is highly unpredictable and depends on factors such as how significant the innovation proves to be. The payoff is not likely to depend very much on economic fluctuations or similar factors that would have much greater effects on such sectors as discretionary consumer durables.

Because beta risk depends on how the venture's payoff varies with marketwide fluctuations, a biotech venture is likely to have a low beta despite its high total risk. At the same time, the cash flows from investing in a portfolio of 100 different biotech ventures might not be very risky at all. Most of the risk is specific to the individual venture and would be substantially reduced by diversifying, even within the same industry. In fact, for a large sample of public biotechnology ventures, we estimated an average beta of 0.75 but an average total risk almost five times as high.[24]

We will see in Chapter 10 that estimating the beta of an individual new venture requires judgment. But we can gain information about the betas of new ventures as a group by studying the price performance of publicly traded firms that were funded by venture capitalists. Such firms typically have betas in the range of 1.0 to 2.0.

What do betas in the range of 1.0 to 2.0 imply for the required rates of return on new venture investments? We can answer by looking back at Eq. (9.3) and filling in the other pieces of the equation with reasonable values. Suppose we use 4.0 percent as an estimate of the riskless rate of return, r_F, and 8.0 percent as the historical average market risk premium, $r_M - r_F$.[25] Beta values in the 1.0 to 2.0 range would imply required rates of return in the 12–20 percent range. Such low required rates of return seem inconsistent with the earlier-mentioned claims that, for investing in new projects, VCs use hurdle rates of return in excess of 50 percent. On the other hand, they are fully consistent with the historical evidence on VC returns cited earlier in this chapter.

To look more specifically at the rates of return required by VC firms, the discount rate for VC investing can be disaggregated into four components as follows:

$$r_{proj}^{VC} = r_F + \beta_{proj}(r_M - r_F) + \text{Effort} + \text{Illiquidity} \tag{9.9}$$

where r_{proj}^{VC} is the discount rate used by the VC to value a project, β_{proj} is the beta risk of the project, Effort is a measure of the cost of effort committed to the project by the VC and expressed in returns form, and the last term is a measure of the required return differential due to illiquidity of the investment. Note that $r_F + \beta_{proj}(r_M - r_F)$ is just the CAPM applied to the project.

With the model from Eq. (9.9) in mind, an average gross realized return as high as 25 or 30 percent on VC investing could be understandable. The gross return is different from the net return because, as discussed in Chapter 3, it includes the fees charged by the GP and the portion of capital appreciation (the carried interest) that is retained by the GP. We previously calculated that a beta of 2.0 yields a cost of capital for an entrepreneurial venture of 20 percent. This corresponds to the returns realized by LPs. VC limited partnerships segregate returns to the GP (the active investor) from returns to LPs (passive investors). The GP's return is typically 20 percent of fund returns after initial investment capital has been returned to the LPs, plus a management fee equal to about 2.5 percent of committed capital.[26] A reasonable estimate, then, is that one-fifth or more of a 25 percent gross return is actually compensation to the general partner.

This return leaves nothing to compensate for the illiquidity of the investment. However, an adjustment for illiquidity of near zero comports with recent empirical evidence on the cost of illiquidity.[27] It also makes sense given the fact that most investors in VC limited partnerships are institutions with long-term investment horizons, at least for some fraction of their portfolios. It is reasonable to expect that competition would drive them to demand a negligible return premium to compensate for illiquidity.

Why does the CAPM accurately predict average returns of VC investors? In large part, the answer appears to be that assumptions underlying the CAPM are reasonably well satisfied. Most importantly, any venture is likely to represent only a small fraction of the asset portfolio of a large pension plan or life insurance company. For such investors, a substantial component of the total risk is diversifiable.

How, then, do we account for the high sought-for rates of return? Our answer is that those returns represent hurdle rates that investors sometimes use to value cash flow projections that are developed on the presumption that the venture will be successful. VCs know that a large fraction of their deals will fail completely and others will limp along offering breakeven returns at best. These will be offset by a few home runs that will offer spectacular returns, sometimes returning 5 or 10 times the initial investment. All of the prospective ventures have rosy forecasts, and there is no way for the VC to know *ex ante* which will be home runs and which will fail. To compensate for the optimism built into the cash flow projections, the investor applies a hurdle rate that is substantially above the required return for investing in the project.[28]

9.10 Matching Cash Flows and Discount Rates

Cash Flow Definitions

The cash flow definitions used in a valuation need to be tied to the specific financial claim being valued and matched correctly with the appropriate discount rates. As an aid to identification, Table 9.1 includes specific definitions of the most important measures of expected cash flow that are appropriate for valuing debt claims and equity claims and for valuing the enterprise:

- *Cash flow to all investors* represents the amount of cash available to all capital providers, after funding net working capital and capital expenditures. Because this measure is after actual taxes in light of the venture's leveraging decision, the tax benefit of debt financing (i.e., tax deductibility of interest payments) is reflected in the cash flow measure.

- *Cash flow to creditors* is what the firm's creditors expect to receive in the form of interest and principal payments. If there is a risk of default or prepayment, then the expected cash flows to creditors are not the same as the contractual cash flows.

- *Cash flow to stockholders* represents the residual cash flow available to the equity investors in the venture. This is a measure of residual free cash flow after expected debt service (principal and interest payments to creditors), taxes, and investments in working capital and fixed assets.

- *Unlevered free cash flow* is the cash flow the venture would generate if it were unlevered, that is, financed entirely with equity (as is

TABLE **9.1** **Measures of expected cash flow**

Cash flow to all investors (both stockholders and creditors)

  Cash Flow to All Investors = EBIT − Actual Taxes + D&A − Δ NWC − Δ Fixed Assets

Cash flow to creditors

  Cash Flow to Creditors = Expected INT + Expected Δ Debt

Cash flow to stockholders (residual, in light of expected cash flows to creditors)

  Cash Flow to Stockholders = EBIT − Actual Taxes + D&A − Δ NWC − Δ Fixed Assets − Expected INT
        − Expected Δ Debt

Unlevered free cash flow (as if financed with no debt)

  Unlevered Free Cash Flow = EBIT − Theoretical Taxes without Debt + D&A − Δ NWC − Δ Fixed Assets

EBIT = earnings before interest and taxes, or operating profit
D&A = depreciation and amortization
Δ Fixed Assets = change in fixed assets = capital expenditures
Δ NWC = change in net working capital = NWC investment
INT = interest payments
Δ Debt = net change in debt financing = principal payments on outstanding debt − proceeds from new debt

typical for high-risk, early-stage ventures). By calculating tax on EBIT, we ignore the tax effect of the actual financing choice. To offset, we incorporate the tax benefits of debt financing into the discount rate.

Consistent Discount Rates

In Table 9.2, we match these cash flow measures with the appropriate discount rates. Under the RADR method, expected cash flows are discounted to PV using a discount rate that is based on the market risk of the cash flow. The tax deductibility of interest payments is a complicating factor. In a correct valuation, the tax benefit can be recognized in either the cash flow measure or the discount rate, but not in both. Therefore, it is important to make sure the cash flow definition and discount rate assumption are consistent.

- *Unlevered cost of equity.* One way to achieve consistency is to estimate expected after-tax cash flows given the target capital structure and to discount those flows at a rate that is not adjusted for the tax deductibility of interest expense. The appropriate rate is called the "unlevered cost of equity." Under this approach, the tax benefit (if any) is incorporated as an adjustment to cash flows and not to the discount factor.

- *Weighted average cost of capital (WACC).* The other way to achieve consistency is to estimate theoretical cash flows as if the

TABLE **9.2**   **Matching cash flows to discount rates for various financial claims**

Financial claim	Discount rate	Discount rate formula (CAPM)	Comment
Cash flows to all investors	Unlevered cost of equity	$r_A = r_F + \beta_A(r_M - r_F)$	The required rate of return on assets, or the unlevered cost of equity, is used to value cash flows that are expected to be received by all claimants given the target capital structure. The effect of tax deductibility of interest payments is reflected in the cash flows.
Cash flow to creditors	Cost of debt	$r_D = r_F + \beta_D(r_M - r_F)$	The cost of capital for debt depends on the extent to which debt service payments are subject to market risk.
Cash flow to stockholders	Cost of equity	$r_E = r_F + \beta_E(r_M - r_F)$	The cost of capital for equity depends not on the total risk of equity but on the market component of the risk.
Unlevered free cash flow	Weighted average cost of capital	$WACC = (D/V)(1 - t_c)r_D + (E/V)r_E$	The weighted average cost of capital (WACC) is used to value hypothetical cash flows as if the venture were financed entirely with equity. D and E are market values of debt and equity, $V = D + E$. The tax benefit of debt financing is an adjustment to the cost of debt capital.*

r_A = return on assets r_D = return on debt r_E = return on equity
$WACC$ = weighted average cost of capital
β_A = asset beta β_D = debt beta β_E = equity beta
r_F = risk-free rate r_M = expected return on the market $(r_M - r_F)$ = market risk premium
t_c = corporate tax rate
D/V = market value debt / total firm value (debt + equity) E/V = market value equity / total firm value (debt + equity)
*The correct tax adjustment should be the net advantage of debt financing, giving consideration to the offsetting effects of personal taxes. However, this number is unobservable and difficult to estimate, so in practice, t_c, the marginal corporate tax rate, is typically used. See Miller (1977) and DeAngelo and Masulis (1980).

venture were financed entirely with equity and then discount those cash flows using a discount rate that is adjusted for the benefit of the debt tax shelter at the target capital structure. Under this approach, the tax benefit (if any) of debt financing is incorporated in the discount factor and not in the cash flow.

In principle, either approach can yield a correct estimate, but the net tax advantage is difficult to determine directly. The tax advantage of debt financing depends on the aggregate supply and demand for debt and equity, the statutory corporate tax rate, the structure of personal tax rates, and the company's profitability and nondebt tax shelters. Empirical evidence suggests that the tax advantage of debt financing is usually small as a result of low effective corporate tax rates. Thus, in the calculation of WACC, the appropriate tax rate is probably well below the statutory rate. The preferred approach depends on ease of estimation and availability of information.

There are other ways to calculate cash flows beyond these definitions. Some informal valuation approaches are based on a narrower concept of operating cash flow: EBIT or EBITDA. While EBITDA is convenient to compute, it does not provide for capital replacement or expected growth. Consequently, EBITDA may not be a good measure of the cash flows investors can expect to receive. The important point is to match the cash flow of the claim being valued with a consistent discount rate.

Consistency in the Use of Continuing Value

The same issues of consistency can arise when we use continuing value in a PV calculation. Continuing value is a shortcut way of projecting future cash flows. Instead of explicitly projecting each period's cash flow, discounting it back to PV, and then summing, with continuing value a single cash flow number is capitalized using a capitalization rate that takes account of both the riskiness of the cash flow and its expected growth rate.

Consider a simple example in which, after several years of rapid growth, the cash flow available to all investors is expected to grow at a constant rate of 4 percent. Based on Table 9.2, if we are valuing cash flow to all investors, then the appropriate discount rate is the unlevered cost of equity. Suppose we have determined that the unlevered cost of equity is 10 percent. We can determine the appropriate continuing value multiple in this example as:

$$\text{Multiple} = \frac{1 \times (1 + g)}{(r_A - g)} = \frac{1.04}{(.10 - .04)} = 17.33$$

Thus, we would estimate continuing value by multiplying cash flow to all investors in the last year of the explicit value period by 17.33. To determine the PV of the continuing value, we would discount the continuing value back to Time 0 at r_A. If we assume that the D/E ratio stays constant, we can use the same approach to find the PV of debt but would use r_D to determine the multiple and to discount the continuing value.

This example demonstrates the importance of consistency. If we were to use a different cash flow measure and not adjust the cost of capital to be consistent, the result would be a different (and biased) estimate of continuing value.

Many of the cash flow measures in the earlier discussion of relative value do not have obvious discount rates and multiples that are theoretically consistent. Instead, the normal approach is to estimate the multiple based on data for comparable companies. The consistency point, however, is the same. If we are using comparables to value cash flow to all investors, then the same cash flow should be used for the comparable companies, and the comparables should either be selected to have similar leverage ratios or the cash flows should be adjusted to be based on similar leverage ratios. Our overarching point is that consistency is important to the valuation. This is true whether you are using explicit DCF or RV and whether you are using an approach based on cost of capital or a simplified approach such as the VC method.

9.11 Summary

Valuation is central for entrepreneurs and investors when they are making decisions about business planning, capital raising, and deal structuring. In the last two decades, private equity investing has become more competitive, increasing the role and importance of theoretically sound and empirically supported valuation tools. The valuation is a key contributor to a successful negotiation between the entrepreneur and investors.

We describe several valuation methodologies that fall into two basic categories: discounted cash flow and relative value. Discounted cash flow approaches start with the premise that the value is simply the PV of all future cash flows. This is a theoretically sound approach, but DCF can also be challenging to implement. To use DCF, we need estimates of future cash flows and the corresponding discount rates.

We stress the importance of matching the financial claim with the appropriate cash flow measure and discount rate and also introduce the concept of continuing value. To estimate discount rates, the notion of nondiversifiable or market risk is highlighted. Because the investors who participate in VC investing will be those best able to diversify and make illiquid investments, we are able to rely on CAPM-based measures for calculating the appropriate discount rates.

Continuing value represents a shortcut to estimating the value of the venture's long-term cash flows while avoiding the need for extensive, explicit cash flow forecasts. We review the RADR method of DCF valuation and introduce the CEQ method as a way to overcome the inherent challenges of using RADR to value new ventures.

The relative valuation method uses the values of comparable firms, relative to operating or financial multiples, to provide a basis for estimating value. The challenge in using RV is in finding comparables that are truly representative of the new venture at the point when the venture is being valued.

The venture capital method is simple and intuitively appealing but has theoretical shortcomings that raise challenges to validity and make caution in its implementation critical. Because the VC method assumes a successful outcome, the corresponding annual discount rate is typically very high (50–80 percent) to compensate for the cash flow bias.

The First Chicago approach was developed to address some of the shortcomings of the VC method. It is a scenario-based valuation methodology, which means it incorporates a range of possible outcomes and therefore uses a more reasonable, lower discount rate. The First Chicago and RADR approaches yield similar value estimates when the scenarios in the First Chicago approach are weighted to yield expected cash flows.

A key point in this chapter is to reconcile the high hurdle rates associated with use of the venture capital method with reasonable estimates of cost of capital. We demonstrate that high hurdle rates are simply a heuristic device that investors can use to compensate for optimistic cash flow projections.

The chapter concludes with a structured discussion of the importance of matching cash flow measures to discount rates and emphasizes that the tax advantage of debt financing can only be incorporated into the cash flow estimate or in the discount rate, but not in both.

REVIEW QUESTIONS

1. How might you respond to an entrepreneur who says, "There is so much risk and uncertainty associated with new ventures that forecasting future revenue and cash flows is a waste of time"?

2. Describe the recent performance of VC funds. Do the empirical results fit with your prior expectations? If not, how can you explain the discrepancy?

3. How might you respond to an entrepreneur who says, "There is no reason for me to undertake a valuation of my business. Everyone knows the investors determine what a venture is worth"?

4. Explain the theoretical basis for discounted cash flow valuation. What are the key inputs required for DCF analysis?

5. How does diversification work? What kind of risk does it reduce?

6. Explain the intuition behind the Capital Asset Pricing Model. Is the CAPM a reasonable tool for estimating the required return for an investor? for an entrepreneur? Why or why not?

7. Why is it important to match the cash flows and discount rate when using DCF valuation?

8. What are the main differences between the RADR and CEQ approaches to DCF valuation? Why is the CEQ method often preferable when valuing new ventures?

9. Explain the intuition behind each of the following valuation techniques:
   (a) relative valuation
   (b) the venture capital method
   (c) the First Chicago method

   Describe the strengths and weaknesses of each approach and the caveats regarding its implementation.

10. How would you reconcile the following?
    (a) Venture capitalists often use hurdle rates of 50–80 percent when valuing potential new investments.
    (b) The historical average return for a large sample of VC funds is around 14 percent.

NOTES

1. Baty (1990), p. 63.

2. See Roberts and Stevenson (1992).

3. For more detail on historical VC returns, see Poindexter (1976), Ibbotson and Brinson (1987), pp. 99–100, and Martin and Petty (1983), pp. 401–10.

4. The 17 percent figure is based on Thomson Reuters's US Private Equity Performance Index (PEPI) through December 31, 2008, and is net of management fees and carried interest. The PEPI includes 1,266 VC funds with a capitalization of $224 billion. See Thomson Reuters/National Venture Capital Association, "Venture Capital Performance Q4 2008" (press release), April 27, 2009.

5. All of these estimates are likely to be positively biased. Information on fund IRRs is not reported formally to any official source; rather, both Thomson Reuters and Cambridge Associates obtain the information from voluntary disclosures, from third parties such as limited partners of the fund, and through Freedom of Information Act disclosures. Funds that have not performed well are less likely to disclose performance voluntarily.

6. See Roberts and Barley (2004), p. 8.

7. The First Chicago method was developed by the VC group of First Chicago Corporation. Sahlman and Scherlis (2009) describe it as a method developed to address valuation biases inherent in the VC method.

8. See Brealey, Myers, and Allen (2008), ch. 5, for elaboration of the relation between share value and expected dividends.

9. A pioneer of modern portfolio theory, Harry Markowitz, first proposed use of the standard deviation of holding-period returns as the measure

of risk; see Markowitz (1952). Markowitz was awarded the Nobel Prize in Economics in 1990 for this contribution to the theory of decision making.

10. The expected return is computed as $[(30\% \times 1/3) + (15\% \times 1/3) + (-10\% \times 1/3)] = 11.67\%$. The standard deviation is computed as $[(30\% - 11.67\%)^2 \times 1/3 + (15\% - 11.67\%)^2 \times 1/3 + (-10\% - 11.67\%)^2 \times 1/3]^{0.5} = 16.5\%$.

11. Development of the CAPM from its roots in modern portfolio theory was the contribution of several individuals, working independently. See Sharpe (1964), Lintner (1965), and Mossin (1966). The model is based on a number of assumptions, including homogeneity of beliefs about risk and return, a one-period time horizon, availability of a risk-free asset, and quadratic utility functions for investors or normally distributed risk. Empirical testing of the CAPM is roughly consistent with the CAPM's theoretical predictions. This suggests that, in most uses, violations of the assumptions are not very important and do not impede its application as a valuation tool.

12. The expected return is computed as $[(\$1 \times 0.5) + (\$2 \times 0.5)] = \$1.50$. The standard deviation is computed as $[(\$1 - \$1.50)^2 \times 0.5 + (\$2 - \$1.50)^2 \times 0.5]^{0.5} = \$0.50$.

13. The expected holding-period return is computed as $[(60\% \times 0.5) + (-20\% \times 0.5)] = 20\%$. The standard deviation is computed as $[(60\% - 20\%)^2 \times 0.5 + (-20\% - 20\%)^2 \times 0.5]^{0.5} = 40\%$.

14. For additional discussion of the CEQ valuation approach, see Brealey, Myers, and Allen (2008), ch. 10, and Grinblatt and Titman (2001).

15. For consistency of comparison, before computing the multiples, excess cash (cash that is not needed for operation of the enterprise) should be subtracted from both the subject asset and the comparables. After the multiples are applied to estimate the enterprise value of the subject, any excess cash that is expected to be accumulated by the subject should be discounted to PV at the risk-free rate, analogous to distributing the cash as a dividend. For a firm such as Apple, which in 2010 had over $25 billion of cash, this is not a trivial adjustment.

16. See Demers and Lev (2001), Kozberg (2001), and Rajgopal, Venkatachalam, and Kotha (2003) for evidence of nonfinancial value drivers for Internet companies.

17. See Amir and Lev (1996), who explore the valuation impact of nonfinancial metrics such as population growth and market penetration in the wireless industry.

18. Black (2003) finds no value relevance of earnings in a sample of start-up and growth-phase firms. The author reports that cash flow measures are more value relevant than earnings in early stages of a firm's existence.

19. Wright and Robbie (1996) survey VC firms in the UK regarding their valuation approaches. They find that capitalization of historical or prospective earnings is the most widely relied upon approach.

20. For discussion and examples using the venture capital method, see

Lerner and Willinge (2002) and Sahlman and Scherlis (2009). Sahlman and Scherlis describe the VC method and illustrate its application. See also Timmons and Spinelli (2007).

21. The relation between net income and cash flow is not explicit. In our discussion, we assume that net income is used as an approximation of steady-state cash flow.

22. Fischer Black, Myron Scholes, and Robert Merton are the original developers of the OPM. See Black and Scholes (1973) and Merton (1973). Scholes and Merton were awarded the Nobel Prize in Economics in 1998 for their contributions. Black died in 1996, and the prize is not awarded posthumously.

23. Most proposals for valuing options that are not traded or where the market is incomplete involve some means of backing into completeness. For example, Mason and Merton (1985) and Kasanen and Trigeorgis (1994) propose that real options that are not traded can be valued by appealing to the existence of a "twin security" that is traded and has risk characteristics that are perfectly correlated with the real option. Short of that possibility, several researchers suggest that untraded options can be valued in the presence of nondiversifiable risk by replacing expected cash flows with their certainty equivalents and valuing the certainty equivalent cash flows at the risk-free rate of interest. They generally do not address how to determine the certainty equivalent. See Constantinides (1978); Cox, Ingersoll, and Ross (1985); and Harrison and Kreps (1979). For an overview and summary of the literature, see Trigeorgis (1996) and Borison (2005).

24. See Kerins, Smith, and Smith (2004).

25. These are roughly the long-run historical averages over the 1926–2007 period, as estimated in Dimson, Marsh, and Staunton (2008).

26. See Sahlman (1990) and Gompers and Lerner (1999).

27. For evidence that illiquidity premia tend to be small, see Blackwell and Kidwell (1988), Hertzel and Smith (1993), and Smith and Armstrong (1993).

28. See Bhagat (2005), who makes a similar argument.

REFERENCES AND ADDITIONAL READING

Achleitner, A., and E. Nathusius. 2005. "First Chicago Method: Alternative Approach to Valuing Innovative Start-Ups in the Context of Venture Capital Financing Rounds." *Betriebswirtschaftliche Forschung und Praxis (BFuP)* 57 (4): 333–47.

Amir, E., and B. Lev. 1996. "Value-Relevance of Nonfinancial Information: The Wireless Communications Industry." *Journal of Accounting and Economics* 22 (1–3): 3–30.

Baty, G. 1990. *Entrepreneurship in the Nineties*. Englewood Cliffs, NJ: Prentice-Hall.

Bernstein, P. 1996. *Against the Gods*. New York: John Wiley & Sons.

Bhagat, S. 2005. "Why Do Venture Capitalists Use Such High Discount Rates?" Working paper, University of Colorado, Boulder.

Black, E. 2003. "Usefulness of Financial Statement Components in Valuation: An Examination of Start-Up and Growth Firms." *Venture Capital: An International Journal of Entrepreneurial Finance* 5 (1): 47–69.

Black, F., and M. Scholes. 1973. "The Pricing of Options and Corporate Liabilities." *Journal of Political Economy* 81 (3): 637–54.

Blackwell, D. W., and D. S. Kidwell. 1988. "An Investigation of Cost Differences between Public Sales and Private Placements of Debt." *Journal of Financial Economics* 22:253–78.

Borison, A. 2005. "Real Options Analysis: Where Are the Emperor's Clothes?" *Journal of Applied Corporate Finance* 17 (2): 17–31.

Brealey, R. A., S. C. Myers, and F. Allen. 2008. *Principles of Corporate Finance*. 8th ed. New York: McGraw-Hill.

Bygrave, W. D., and J. A. Timmons. 1992. *Venture Capital at the Crossroads*. Boston: Harvard Business School Press.

Cochrane, J. H. 2005. "The Risk and Return of Venture Capital." *Journal of Financial Economics* 7 5:3–52.

Constantinides, G. 1978. "Market Risk Adjustment in Project Valuation." *Journal of Finance* 33:603–16.

Cox, J., J. Ingersoll, and S. Ross. 1985. "An Intertemporal General Equilibrium Model of Asset Prices." *Econometrica* 53 (2): 363–84.

DeAngelo, H., and R. W. Masulis. 1980. "Optimal Capital Structure under Corporate and Personal Taxation." *Journal of Financial Economics* 8:3–81.

Demers, E., and B. Lev. 2001. "A Rude Awakening: Internet Shakeout in 2000." *Review of Accounting Studies* 6 (2–3): 331–59.

Dimson, E., P. Marsh, and M. Staunton. 2008. *Global Investment Returns Yearbook 2008*. London: ABN AMRO.

Fama, E., and K. French. 1995. "Size and Book-to-Market Factors in Earnings and Returns." *Journal of Finance* 50:131–55.

Gompers, P., and J. Lerner. 1999. "An Analysis of Compensation in the U.S. Venture Capital Partnership." *Journal of Financial Economics* 51:3–44.

Grinblatt, M., and S. Titman. 2001. *Financial Markets and Corporate Strategy*. Boston: Irwin/McGraw-Hill.

Harrison, J., and D. Kreps. 1979. "Martingales and Arbitrage in Multiperiod Securities Markets." *Journal of Economic Theory* 20 (3): 381–408.

Hertzel, M., and R. L. Smith. 1993. "Market Discounts and Shareholder Gains for Placing Equity Privately." *Journal of Finance* 48:459–85.

Ibbotson, R. G., and G. P. Brinson. 1987. *Investment Markets*. New York: McGraw-Hill.

Jones, C. M., and M. Rhodes-Kropf. 2004. "The Price of Diversifiable Risk in

Venture Capital and Private Equity." Working paper, Columbia University. Available at http://papers.ssrn.com/sol3/papers.cfm?abstract_id=342841.

Kasanen, E., and L. Trigeorgis. 1994. "A Market Utility Approach to Investment Valuation." *European Journal of Operational Research* 74:294–309.

Kerins, F., J. K. Smith, and R. L. Smith. 2004. "Opportunity Cost of Capital for Venture Capital Investors and Entrepreneurs." *Journal of Financial and Quantitative Analysis*3 9:385–405.

Kozberg, A. 2001. "The Value Drivers of Internet Stocks: A Business Models Approach." SSRN Working Paper Series. Available at http://papers.ssrn .com/sol3/papers.cfm?abstract_id=256468.

Lerner, J., and J. Willinge. 2002. "A Note on Valuation in Private Equity Settings." Harvard Business School Note 9-297-050. Cambridge, MA: Harvard Business Publishing.

Lintner, J. 1965. "The Valuation of Risk Assets and the Selection of Risky Investments in Stock Portfolios and Capital Budgeting." *Review of Economics and Statistics* 47 (1): 13–37.

Markowitz, H. 1952. "Portfolio Selection." *Journal of Finance* 7 (1): 77–91.

Martin, J. D., and W. Petty. 1983. "An Analysis of the Performance of Publicly Traded Venture Capital Companies." *Journal of Financial and Quantitative Analysis* 18:401–10.

Mason, S. P., and R. C. Merton. 1985. "The Role of Contingent Claims Analysis in Corporate Finance." In *Recent Advances in Corporate Finance*, ed. E. I. Altman and M. G. Subrahmanyam, 46–51. Homewood, IL: Irwin.

Merton, R. C. 1973. "Theory of Rational Option Pricing." *Bell Journal of Economics and Management Science* 4 (Spring): 141–83.

Miller, M. 1977. "Debt and Taxes." *Journal of Finance* 32 (2): 261–75.

Mossin, J. 1966. "Equilibrium in a Capital Asset Market." *Econometrica* 34 (4): 768–83.

Poindexter, J. B. 1976. "The Efficiency of Financial Markets: The Venture Capital Case." Unpublished PhD dissertation, New York University.

Post, T., M. J. van den Assem, G. Baltussen, and R. H. Thaler. 2008. "Deal or No Deal? Decision Making under Risk in a Large-Payoff Game Show." *American Economic Review* 98 (1): 38–71.

Pratt, S. P. 2002. *Cost of Capital: Estimation and Applications*. New York: John Wiley & Sons.

Rajgopal, S., M. Venkatachalam, and S. Kotha. 2003. "The Value Relevance of Network Advantages: The Case of E-Commerce Firms." *Journal of Accounting Research* 41 (1): 135–62.

Roberts, M. J., and L. Barley. 2004. "How Venture Capitalists Evaluate Potential Venture Opportunities." Harvard Business School Case 9-805-019. Cambridge, MA: Harvard Business Publishing.

Roberts, M. J., and H. H. Stevenson. 1992. "Alternative Sources of Financing." In *The Entrepreneurial Venture*, ed. W. A. Sahlman and H. H. Stevenson, 171–78. Boston: Harvard Business School Press.

Robichek, A., and S. C. Myers. 1966. "Conceptual Problems in the Use of Risk-Adjusted Discount Rates." *Journal of Finance* 21 (4): 727–30.

Sahlman, W. A. 1990. "The Structure and Governance of Venture Capital Organizations." *Journal of Financial Economics* 27 (2): 473–521.

Sahlman, W. A., and D. Scherlis. 2009. "A Method for Valuing High-Risk Long-Term Investments: The 'Venture Capital Method.'" Harvard Business School Note 9-288-006. Cambridge, MA: Harvard Business Publishing.

Sharpe, W. F. 1964. "Capital Asset Prices: A Theory of Market Equilibrium under Conditions of Risk." *Journal of Finance* 19 (3): 425–42.

Smith, R. L., and V. Armstrong. 1993. "Misperceptions about Private Placement Discounts: Why Market Reaction to Rule 144A Has Been Lukewarm." In *Modernizing US Securities Regulation: Economic and Legal Perspectives*, ed. K. Lehn and R. Kamphuis, 175–91. Homewood, IL: Irwin.

Timmons, J. A., and S. Spinelli Jr. 2007. *New Venture Creation: Entrepreneurship for the 21st Century*. 7th ed. Chicago: McGraw-Hill Irwin.

Trigeorgis, L. 1996. *Real Options*. Cambridge, MA: MIT Press.

Venture Economics. 1997. *Investment Benchmarks Report: Venture Capital*. New York: Venture Economics.

Wright, M., and K. Robbie. 1996. "Venture Capitalists, Unquoted Equity Investment Appraisal and the Role of Accounting Information." *Accounting and Business Research*2 6:153–68.

CHAPTER 10

Valuation in Practice

In theory there is no difference between theory and practice. In practice there is.

Yogi Berra

We saw in the previous chapter that there are many tools available for valuing new ventures. Most are conceptually straightforward and intuitive; the challenges come with implementation. In this chapter, we first address use of the continuing value approach as a way to make the valuing of going concerns tractable. We then address the challenges of making the assumptions that are needed to be able to apply any CAPM-based approach to DCF valuation. In the last part of the chapter, we use a single example to illustrate all of the valuation approaches and to highlight the advantages and disadvantages of each.

The chapter can serve as a handbook for generating the information that is required to implement each valuation approach and illustrates how the approaches are related. It can aid in selecting the approaches that will be most useful for addressing a particular valuation problem.

10.1 Criteria for Selecting a New Venture Valuation Method

The primary approaches used in valuing new ventures (especially early-stage ventures with significant potential for growth) are DCF approaches. This is partly because, for early-stage ventures, application of multipliers to current income statement or balance sheet information is not very helpful and because useful comparable firm and transaction data are rare.

The main differences among the various DCF approaches concern the specific cash flows and discount rates used and the ways in which uncertainty is taken into account. Each approach has strengths and limitations.

Some methods use biased estimates of cash flows, such as expected accounting earnings or "success" scenario cash flows. Approaches that are not based on expected cash flow (i.e., the statistical mean) are often more convenient but can yield erroneous estimates of value, for two reasons. First, there is no theoretically sound way to determine the correct discount rate; second, the values of expected cash flows that will be received at different times can be biased to different degrees and in different directions. The following questions are relevant for assessing the relative merits of different approaches.

Is cost of capital used as the discount rate? Attempting to compensate for positively biased estimates of cash flow by discounting with positively biased hurdle rates tends to cause projects with more distant payoffs to be rejected incorrectly. Similarly, discount rates based on total risk rather than nondiversifiable risk can lead to rejecting projects that should be accepted by an investor who is well diversified.

How does the approach deal with cash flows that vary in risk? Different cash flow streams that occur in the same period can differ in risk. The appropriate discount rates will vary accordingly. Models that do not distinguish among cash flows that differ in risk can produce distorted estimates of value. Cash flows that occur at different times can also differ in risk. If the discount rates do not account for such differences, valuation errors can result.

Can the model be used to value embedded options and complex financial claims? Complexity affects both expected returns and risk. A financial structure that includes real or financial options can alter the overall value of a venture relative to a simple accept/reject approach. The values of the options depend on both expected cash flows and the risk of the option cash flows.

How difficult is it to estimate the information required for the valuation? There is virtue in simplicity. Valuation approaches that are complex or difficult to use are sometimes too costly to justify. This is true particularly if the project is clearly worth pursuing, alternative financial contract structures are uncomplicated, and agreements for sharing gains and losses can be reached informally.

Are there sufficient data available to have confidence in relative valuation estimates? Relative value works best if the expected future cash flows (including expected growth), total risk, and market risk of the comparables are believed to be proportional to those of the subject venture.

10.2 Implementing the Continuing Value Concept

It is not practical to value a going concern by forecasting cash flows explicitly into the indefinite future and then discounting each periodic cash flow back to PV. Instead, the normal approach is to project explicit cash flows over a period until it can be assumed that subsequent growth is likely to stabilize and then to summarize the value of cash flows beyond that point as a single "continuing value." The continuing value concept is used to convert cash flows after the explicit value period to a single estimate of value that is equivalent to valuing each subsequent cash flow. In other words, the cash flows after the first few years are valued implicitly by applying a multiplier to the last explicit cash flow, where the multiplier is intended to take account of expected growth of cash flows from that point forward and of the riskiness of those cash flows. Normally, continuing value is estimated by using a theoretically determined discount rate or is based on observed multipliers of market assets that are similar to the one being valued. For many new ventures, continuing value is an important component of total PV.[1]

The overall valuation is thus divided into two periods. For the first period, an explicit cash flow projection is made for each year, quarter, or other appropriate interval. We refer to this as the "explicit value period." We refer to the period after the explicit value period as the "continuing value period." Sometimes continuing value is referred to as "terminal value." The rationale is that it is a valuation at a point where existing investments could reasonably be "terminated" by sale to others. It does not mean that the venture is expected to be terminated or even that the financial claims are expected to be sold, only that they could be sold without unusual difficulty. We prefer "continuing value" because it suggests that the venture is ongoing.

Figure 10.1 illustrates a forecast of the future cash flows of a venture and their segregation into explicit value and continuing value periods. In the example, Year 5 is the last explicit forecast. Projections beginning in Year 6 are implicit, based on assumptions about the growth rate from that point forward. The venture's continuing value is an estimate as of the end of the explicit value period (Year 5 in the figure). To esti-

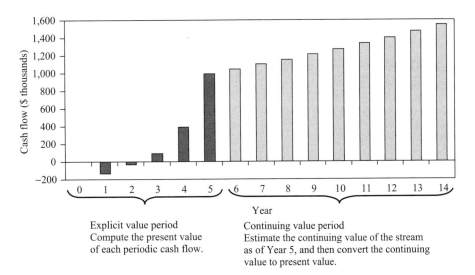

Explicit value period
Compute the present value
of each periodic cash flow.

Continuing value period
Estimate the continuing value of the stream
as of Year 5, and then convert the continuing
value to present value.

FIGURE **10.1**

Using continuing value to estimate the worth of a new venture
A common approach used in DCF valuation is to divide the forecast into two
periods. During the explicit period, cash flows are forecast individually and valued
directly. During the continuing value period, cash flows are converted to a capitalized
value at the end of the explicit value period. This capitalized value is then discounted
back to Time 0. Normally, the continuing value period begins when the venture
reaches a point of stable growth.

mate PV, continuing value must be discounted to PV, as if it were a single cash flow that was expected to be received for selling the venture or
the financial claim.

Equation (10.1) describes the value of a venture in terms of explicit
and continuing value components, based on annual data:

$$PV = \sum_{t=1}^{T} \frac{C_t}{(1 + r_t)} + \frac{CV_T}{(1 + r_T)^T} \tag{10.1}$$

where PV is the present value of the venture; C_t is the annual cash flow
for each explicit year, t; CV_T is the continuing value at the end of the
explicit value period, year T; and r_t is the discount rate for year t cash
flows.

As Figure 10.1 and Eq. (10.1) suggest, continuing value is a DCF valuation method. However, it is not one that relies entirely on explicit
forecasts of cash flows. Instead, the cash flow forecast during the continuing value period is implicit in the assumptions used to estimate continuing value. Continuing value is estimated on the basis of information from the last explicit forecast along with assumptions about the

expected growth rate and cost of capital or information on the values of comparables.

Determining the explicit value period.   The first step in using the continuing value concept is to decide where to draw the line between the explicit and continuing value periods. Continuing value estimates are most reliable if they are made for a period when a firm has established a track record and has reached a point of stable growth. Continuing value does not work well for valuing the early stages of a new venture because of the expectation of temporary high growth and the volatility of revenue and cash flows. Thus, explicit cash flows are normally estimated during development, for periods when the venture has not yet achieved a profitable level of sales, and during periods of rapid growth. In Figure 10.1, the explicit value period, Years 1 through 5, includes years when expected cash flows are negative and years when they are growing rapidly. The continuing value period begins at the point where the venture is expected to be in steady state.

Sometimes continuing value estimates are applied at earlier stages of development. Rapidly growing ventures with large capital needs sometimes seek public equity financing before establishing a stable track record. If comparable companies have gone public at similar stages, then underwriters are likely to use a combination of continuing value methods and explicit DCF methods to estimate the price at which shares will be offered to the public. In such a case, it could be appropriate to use the data from IPOs of other early-stage ventures to estimate continuing value.

Determining which multiplier to use.   Multipliers can be tied to any accounting item that can be measured at the end of the explicit value period, and they can be derived from theory or based on comparables. A free cash flow measure seems like the obvious choice for estimating the multiple, since that is the source of the investor's return. Sometimes, however, other measures, such as EBIT or sales, can yield more reliable multipliers. We showed in Chapter 9 that multipliers implicitly include an assumed growth rate and discount rate for cash flows during the continuing value period. In that example, the multiple was based on explicit assumptions about the discount rate and growth rate of cash flows. In other scenarios, we might use a multiple based on comparable transactions. For example, a firm planning to go public at the end of the explicit value period might collect multiples from the IPO valuations of comparable ventures.

Choosing the right multiplier or set of multipliers requires judgment and benefits from practical experience. Multiples of operating cash flow, net income, sales, or assets are commonly used. For example, continuing value might be capitalized at 10 times expected cash flow in the last year of the explicit value period, or 1.5 times expected sales. The relative merits of different multipliers (e.g., sales versus cash flow) are discussed in a variety of sources.[2]

Continuing value is sometimes estimated on the basis of sales or asset multiples, not because investors care specifically about sales or assets but because sales or asset levels at the end of the explicit value period bear a stronger relationship to expected future cash flows over the continuing value period than does cash flow at the end of the explicit value period.

Continuing value methodology works best when the growth rate of the accounting stream (sales, earnings, etc.) on which the valuation is based has stabilized and when the relation between the accounting stream and value is strong. The strength of the relationship can be evaluated by comparing measures of dispersion of alternative multipliers across a sample of comparable firms. In general, a multiplier with low dispersion, standardized by the mean or median value, yields a better estimate.

If you decide to use a multiple base on comparables, it is still a good idea to use the theory-based approach to test whether the multiple really makes sense for your venture. Whatever the multiple, it implies something about expected growth and cost of capital, and those implications should be assessed. Equation (10.2) below summarizes the implicit assumptions. You can easily assess whether a multiple derived from comparables implies sensible value for the expected growth rate and cost of capital for your venture.

Determining the multiplier. Equation (10.2) describes the relation between value in one period (the end of the explicit value period) and all future cash flows:

$$V_t = \frac{C_{t+1}}{r - g} = \frac{C_t(1 + g)}{r - g} \tag{10.2}$$

where V_t is value at time t, C_{t+1} is cash flow at time $t + 1$, r is the discount rate, and g is the expected growth rate of cash flows. Generally, C_t is the cash flow generated over a year, and V_t is value at the end of that same year. This is sometimes referred to as a trailing value. It does not imply that value is determined by prior earnings. Rather, it implies that prior earnings can be used in a consistent way, as shown in the equation, to predict future earnings. V_t, the value at the end of period

t, is a function of the cash flows from period $t + 1$ onward. In the equation, C_t is increased by g, which effectively means that the numerator represents the next period's cash flow.

Equation (10.2) is the standard expression for the PV of a growing perpetuity of cash flows. The equation can be rearranged to calculate the cash flow multiplier, as shown in Eq. (10.3):

$$\frac{V_t}{C_t} = \frac{(1 + g)}{r - g} \tag{10.3}$$

where V_t/C_t is the cash flow multiplier.

Equation (10.3) shows how the expected growth rate and discount rate affect the multiplier. The assumptions of a 10 percent discount rate and 4 percent annual growth rate in cash flows yield the following calculation and cash flow multiple:

$$\text{Cash Flow Multiple} = \frac{V_t}{C_t} = \frac{(1 + g)}{r - g} = \frac{1.04}{(.10 - .04)} = 17.33$$

It is easy to see that a higher rate of expected growth would increase the multiplier, as it simultaneously increases the numerator and makes the denominator smaller. A higher discount rate would reduce the multiplier by increasing the denominator. This makes intuitive sense, as cash flows growing more quickly are worth more, and riskier cash flows are worth less.

Although the connections between value and other accounting streams are indirect, the same principle applies. Higher expected growth rates imply higher multiples, and larger discount rates imply lower multiples. This suggests a way to use market data to estimate a multiplier. If, relative to comparable firms, the venture being valued has a high expected growth rate, a larger multiplier is implied. If the comparable firms are selected correctly and if the cash flow used in Eq. (10.3) is the expected cash flow, there is no reason for the discount rate to be different from that for the comparables.

The other determinant of V_t in Eq. (10.2) is C_t. There are two important issues to keep in mind about C_t. First, the cash flows of comparable public firms are based on publicly reported information. They have been prepared under US Generally Accepted Accounting Principles (GAAP) or International Financial Reporting Standards (IFRS) and have been subject to independent audit, whereas the venture's forecast has not. Second, the comparable firms have survived long enough to have gone public, whereas the venture is at an earlier stage.

How best to deal with these issues depends on the purpose of the valuation and on your comfort level with the financial projections. Suppose you believe the projections of the venture were prepared consistently with GAAP and, though not audited, are unbiased. In this case, it is reasonable to assume that the projections are comparable to the reported numbers of the public companies.

Suppose, instead, that the entrepreneur prepared the projections. Such projections are likely to reflect the entrepreneur's inherent optimism that the venture will be successful. In that case, direct application of multipliers from comparable public companies could result in an overestimate of continuing value.

One solution to this survival bias problem is to base the continuing value estimate on multipliers from private transactions. Such information can be useful, especially if the selected transactions are for companies at similar stages of development as is the subject venture. But information about private transactions is difficult to acquire and to verify.

A second solution is to adjust the public company multiplier for an estimate of the bias in the accounting projections for the venture. If, for example, you believe that the venture's probability of failure is 30 percent and is not reflected in its projected cash flows, it would be appropriate to adjust the public company multiplier down by 30 percent. The latter solution is implicit in the actual multipliers that are frequently used in private transaction valuations. Such adjustments are often characterized (incorrectly, we believe) as "illiquidity discounts." The true nature of the discount is not illiquidity but rather biased cash flow estimates. By recognizing this, you can do a better job of applying the data from comparable public firms to your own valuation questions.

This leads to the third solution. If the lack of comparability is due to positively biased projections for the venture, then one way to solve the problem is to develop a set of projections that reflect the true expectations, including the risk of failure. You would then value the asset using the comparable market data without additional adjustment.

Forecasting the multiple. A correct valuation must be based on a multiple that is expected to be accurate at the time when the continuing stream of cash flows is being capitalized. This is most obvious if it is assumed that there will be a liquidity event, such as an IPO, at the end of the explicit value period. This means that the multiples you can observe today are not necessarily the ones you would want to use in the valuation.

To illustrate, consider the data shown in Figure 10.2. In 2001, the P/E ratio of the S&P 500 Index was around 34, a historical high, and the ag-

FIGURE **10.2**

Price/earnings ratio of the S&P 500 Index, 1956–2008
The P/E ratio is calculated as the value of the S&P 500 divided by aggregate earnings over the preceding (trailing) 12 months.

SOURCE: 2009 Economic Report of the President; available at http://www.whitehouse.gov/administration/eop/cea/economic-report-of-the-president.

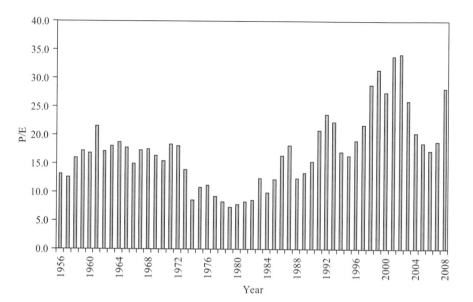

gregate dividend yield was approximately 1.3 percent, near a historical low. If the basis for equity valuation is the PV of expected future dividends, then either the expected rate of dividend growth must have been very high in 2001 or the cost of equity capital must have been very low. The true explanation probably involves a combination of both factors: optimism about future growth (and hence rising dividends) combined with a low cost of equity capital.

Imagine that you are back in 2001 and are planning to value a company based on its expected future earnings. You believe that the P/E ratio of the S&P 500 Index is appropriate to use as a benchmark for estimating continuing value. Knowing that the 2001 P/E ratio is at a historical high, you should not base the continuing value estimate on the 2001 S&P 500 P/E ratio. Because there is no plan to harvest the investment in 2001, the multiple that existed at that time is not the best one to use. A better approach is to forecast the multiple that is likely to exist at the time of a hypothetical sale of the investment.

Were you to use a 2001 multiplier, your value estimate would be biased upward relative to the actual expected future value. You would end up investing too much money in exchange for too little ownership. During periods when value multiples are high, investors will get too little for their investment. Conversely, low multiples will result in the entrepreneur giving away too much ownership. If you try to follow this strategy and are competing against investors who use more forward looking approaches, you will be outbid during low-value periods and pay too much when values are high.

P/E multiples are influenced by factors that can affect either the numerator or the denominator. In 2000 and 2001, they soared in part as a result of the high stock valuations attributable to optimism related to the Internet bubble. In contrast, the 2008 multiple of 28.2—also a historically high value—was caused by a large drop in corporate earnings brought on by the subprime and financial crises. In fact, the S&P 500 Index fell almost 40 percent in 2008, its worst annual return since 1931, but earnings fell by an even greater percentage, so the S&P 500 P/E ratio increased.

Suppose in 2008, with the S&P 500 P/E at 28.2, you want to select a multiple to use in estimating continuing value where harvesting is expected to occur in five years. Figure 10.2 shows that between 1956 and 2008 there was a great deal of variation in the annual S&P 500 P/E ratio, from a low of 7.4 in 1979 to a high of 34.2 in 2002. The simple average over the 53-year period is 17.4, but it appears that the most recent historical period has seen higher multiples, on average. Finally, from Figure 10.2 it appears that the change in P/E from one year to the next is not random; instead, a high value in one year tends to be followed by a high value in the next. So how can we best estimate an appropriate multiple for 2013?

One valid approach is to use statistical techniques—regression analysis, exponential smoothing, or the like—to estimate future P/E multiples. This level of rigor may or may not be warranted in practice. For some valuation problems it may be sufficient to recognize that historical P/E multiples appear to be mean reverting and that the current multiple of 28.2 is historically high. If we believe that recent historical multiples are more relevant than older ones for predicting the harvest-date multiple, it could make sense to overweight the recent years. Finally, in recognition of the uncertainty as to what the future exit multiple will be, we suggest using several different values of exit multiples and assessing their impact on the resultant valuation. If the accept/reject decision is not sensitive to multiples over a reasonable range, that alone may be sufficient to proceed with the venture.

Even if the appropriate multiple for your venture is not the S&P 500 Index P/E ratio, whatever multiple you do use, if it is based on comparables, is likely to be highly correlated with the S&P Index multiple. You can update Figure 10.2 and use the data to make inferences about whether other multiples are currently likely to be too high or too low.

10.3 Implementing DCF Valuation Methods

CAPM-based approaches to DCF valuation require specific assumptions about the risk-free rate, the market risk premium, and beta. In lieu of beta, they may require specific assumptions about market risk, project risk, and correlation. In the RADR form, project risk is the standard deviation of holding-period returns, and the correlation is between project returns and market returns. In the CEQ form, project risk is the standard deviation of cash flows, and the correlation is between project cash flows and market returns.

There are many subtleties and challenges involved in making good and internally consistent assumptions. In practice, it is common to use some simplifying assumptions that make implementation easier. In this section, we first outline approaches to making valid and internally consistent assumptions; we then discuss the shortcuts that are commonly used.

Estimating the Risk-Free Rate of Interest

The appropriate risk-free rate for valuing a future cash flow is one that is available in the market as of the valuation date and is for a holding period of the same duration as the cash flow being valued. Thus, for a cash flow that is expected in five years, ideally we would use the currently available risk-free rate for an instrument that would mature in five years. We normally assume that US government debt has no risk of default, so we can infer the appropriate risk-free rate directly from current interest rates of US Treasury securities of appropriate maturities.[3]

We also need to be cognizant of whether the cash flow projection is in real or nominal terms. If it is in nominal terms, then the appropriate risk-free rate is also the nominal rate, that is, the one that can be inferred directly from market data. If the forecast is in real terms, then the risk-free rate must be converted to an estimate of the real rate. Converting to real rates involves subtracting the rate of inflation that is expected in the market for the holding period—the 5-year rate in the case of a cash flow that is expected in Year 5. For this, we can search for publicly available forecasts of inflation or use historical data to infer the normal relationship between risk-free interest rates and inflation.

In most cases, the expected cash flows of the venture will have been projected in nominal terms. US Treasury yields at the time of this writing were as follows:[4]

US Treasury yields
Friday, October 29, 2010

Maturity	Yield (%)	Maturity	Yield (%)
3-month	0.12	5-year	1.24
6-month	0.17	10-year	2.95
1-year	0.21	20-year	4.19
2-year	0.28	30-year	4.45
3-year	0.54		

SOURCE: *Based on data collected from WSJ.com; available at http://online.wsj.com/mdc/
public/page/2_3020-treasury.html. Maturities of 1 year or less are from zero-coupon
securities. Maturities greater than 1 year are based on STRIP (Separate Trading of
Registered Interest and Principal) yields.*

These data suggest the use of a different risk-free rate in calculating each period's discount rate. The cash flow from Year 1 would be discounted using a rate based on the 1-year US Treasury bill. The cash flow in Year 5 would use a rate computed with the 5-year Treasury bond.

Estimating the Market Risk Premium

The market risk premium that is used in the CAPM is the expected difference between the return on the market and the risk-free rate over the period from investment until a cash flow is received. In contrast to the current risk-free rate, which is observable, the current market risk premium is not. Because it is not, there are three main approaches used to estimate the market risk premium: (1) a long-term historical average, (2) a risk premium that is implied by discounting a forecast of future dividends (i.e., the IRR that makes the PV of expected future dividends equal to today's market price), or (3) a consensus estimate.

The easiest but not necessarily most accurate way to estimate the expected market risk premium is to extrapolate from historical data. These data are readily available from numerous sources. Most introductory finance textbooks contain some version of Table 10.1, which presents historical data on stock and bond returns.

To estimate the expected market risk premium with these data, we would calculate the market risk premium as the difference between the historical average return on the S&P 500 (the market) and the historical average risk-free rate. If we are valuing a near-term cash flow (such as a year or two), we would use the historical short-term risk-free rate in the calculation. If we were valuing a longer-term cash flow, such as a return in five years, we would use the historical long-term rate, represented by US Treasury bonds.

TABLE **10.1**   **Historical stock and bond returns**

Series	1928–2009		1950–2009	
	Arithmetic average (%)	Standard deviation (%)	Arithmetic average (%)	Standard deviation (%)
S&P 500[1,2]	11.27	20.21	10.81	16.95
US Treasury bonds (LT)[2]	5.21	7.73	7.03	9.18
US Treasury bills (ST)[2]	3.74	3.01	5.33	2.75
Inflation[3]	3.21	4.16	4.11	2.96

[1] *Standard & Poor's 500 Composite Index, total return (includes dividend reinvestment).*
[2] *Sources: Stock, T-bond, and T-bill data downloaded from http://pages.stern.nyu.edu/~adamodar/New_Home _Page/datafile/histretSP.html on 10/30/2010.*
[3] *CPI (inflation) data from US Department of Labor; downloaded at ftp://ftp.bls.gov/pub/special.requests/cpi/ cpiai.txt on 10/30/2010.*

Using historical data to estimate the expected market risk premium, while simple, still requires some choices for implementation. Table 10.1 includes historical average data for two time periods, and there are other possible windows that could be used. Our computations use the arithmetic rather than the geometric averages, which is common practice among both academics and practitioners.[5] On balance, we agree with the school of thought that favors using arithmetic averages. In Figure 10.3 we explain why.

In using historical data to develop a forward-looking estimate of the market risk premium, we need to balance the relevance of older data with the statistical unreliability that comes with using fewer observations. There is also the issue of what defines the "'market." In this case, we selected the widely quoted S&P 500 Index to represent the market, even though it includes primarily large companies and is a subset of traded assets.

Note that Table 10.1 also reports historical inflation rates. Consistent with our discussion of the need to adjust the risk-free rate for inflation to derive an estimate of the real risk-free rate, we could use this information to infer the historical real rates for short- and long-term riskless debt.

For a variety of reasons, the historical average may not be the best measure of the market risk premium. Recent forward-looking estimates of the risk premium (derived by discounting forecasts of future dividends) suggest that the long-term historical average overstates the market risk premium by 2–5 percent. For example, Fama and French (2002) use dividend and earnings growth rates to estimate the equity premium over the period 1951–2000 and find equity premia of 2.6–4.3 percent. Welch (2000) surveys a large number of finance and economics profes-

FIGURE **10.3**

Using arithmetic or geometric average returns

Suppose an asset that is correctly priced is equally likely to return either 50 percent or 0 percent each year. If cost of capital for an investment is inferred by calculating the average annual return, the resulting estimate is 25 percent [i.e., (50% + 0%)/2]. If it is calculated as the geometric return, it is 22.5 percent (i.e., $[(1 + 50\%) \times (1 + 0\%)]^{0.5} - 1$). Which one is right?

Consider a one-period investment of $1.00. At the end of the period, it will be worth either $1.50 or $1.00. The average is $1.25. If you discount $1.25 at the arithmetic average rate of 25 percent, you find that the present value is $1.00. If you discount it at the geometric average rate of 22.5 percent, you find that the present value is $1.02. Apparently, the arithmetic average is right.

But consider a two-year investment. Suppose you get a 50 percent return the first year and 0 percent the second (or the reverse). The cumulative value is $1.50 for two years. If you discount the $1.50 to present value at 25 percent, you get $0.96, whereas if you discount it at 22.5 percent, you get $1.00. It appears that the geometric average is right if you are valuing long-term cash flows. This is the common argument for using the geometric average.

However, look again. The previous calculation does not consider all possible outcomes. If the probabilities remain stable over time, there is a 25 percent chance that the investment will be worth $2.25 in two years [i.e., $1.00 \times (1 + 50\%) \times (1 + 50\%)$], a 50 percent chance that it will be worth $1.50 [i.e., $1.00 \times (1 + 50\%) \times (1 + 0\%)$], and a 25 percent chance that it will be worth $1.00 [i.e., $1.00 \times (1 + 0\%) \times (1 + 0\%)$]. The expected value is $1.56 (25% × $2.25 + 50% × $1.50 + 25% × $1.00 = $1.56), not $1.50 as in the above calculation. Discounting $1.56 at 25 percent for two periods yields $1.00, the correct present value. Thus, even for a longer holding period, the arithmetic average yields the correct value. Accordingly, we favor using the arithmetic average.

sors and reports that the consensus forecast of the long-term equity risk premium is 5–5.5 percent. There is also a significant difference between the opinions of US academics and practitioners. Graham and Harvey (2007) survey 465 CFOs and find an average expected risk premium of 3.8 percent, materially lower than that suggested by most academics.

In light of the historical and recent empirical evidence, we would normally assume a market risk premium of between 5 and 7 percent. When possible, it makes sense to consult managers of asset allocation funds and similar investment vehicles to learn their current forecasts of the market risk premium. Those estimates are usually based on finding the discount rate that equates their forecast of future dividends to the current stock index value (i.e., dividend discount models of value). One should understand the range of possible estimates and remain alert to the prospect of better methods of estimating the market risk premium. As any rate is going to be an estimate of the true rate, it can also be helpful to assess the sensitivity of the decision to reasonable variations in the assumed market risk premium. If the venture looks good under both "low" and "high" assumptions, then the choice of whether to proceed is not sensitive to the assumed rate.

Estimating the New Venture Beta

The final variable we need if we are using the RADR form of the CAPM is the beta of the venture. Equation (10.4), which we saw first in Chapter 9, is the formula for computing the beta of an asset based on its returns and the returns of the market:

$$\beta_A = \frac{\text{Cov}_{r_A, r_M}}{\sigma_M^2} = \frac{\rho_{r_A, r_M} \sigma_A}{\sigma_M} \tag{10.4}$$

The expression implies several different approaches that can be used to estimate β_A. We describe each and discuss implementation in the following subsections.

Using the betas of comparable firms.   For established public companies, beta is often estimated by regressing a time series of historical stock returns on a time series of historical returns of a market index. The regression coefficient is the beta term in Eq. (10.4). For new ventures, however, there is no publicly traded stock, so the information needed to estimate the regression coefficient is not available. One common solution is to use betas estimated from comparable publicly traded firms. Beta estimates for the common stock of public companies can be calculated easily and are available from several sources.[6]

The case for using data on comparable firms is strongest when there are public companies with market risk comparable to that of the new venture. For example, if the new venture is a grocery store, it could be reasonable to use market information on public grocery store companies to infer the beta. Thus, Safeway or another grocery chain might use the company beta as an estimate of the beta for analyzing a new store.

Table 10.2 contains data on equity betas for a number of different industry groups. Ranges of equity betas reported in the table are based on averages for two-digit SIC industries as reported in a study of 3,000 firms by Kaplan and Peterson (1998). It is apparent that beta values vary in a systematic fashion across industries. For example, the betas of food companies tend to be low, whereas those of construction firms tend to be high. As beta measures the market component of total risk, these values make sense given the underlying systematic risks of the industries.

TABLE **10.2** **Equity betas by SIC code**

SIC grouping	Two-digit SIC range	Equity beta range
Agricultural Products and Services	1	1.63
Extractive	10–13	0.80–0.94
Construction	15–17	1.26–2.65
Food	20	0.66
Textile	22–23	1.00–1.02
Wood Products	24–27	1.04–1.60
Chemicals and Oil	28–29	0.63–1.30
"Plastic, Leather, Stone"	30–32	0.83–1.76
Metals	34	1.89
Manufacturing	35–39	0.78–1.75
Transportation	40–45	0.69–1.61
Utilities	46–49	0.47–0.95
Wholesale	50–51	0.95–1.38
Retail	52–59	0.64–1.34
Financial	60–67	0.96–2.23
Consumer Services	70–79	0.94–1.72
Professional Services	80–84	1.54–2.00

NOTE: *Data are pure-play equity betas, derived from a study by Kaplan and Peterson (1998) of over 3,000 public companies.*

As shown in Table 10.2, for public companies equity beta values of less than 0.5 or greater than 2.0 are rare. Keep in mind that the betas typically available from published sources are equity betas and are derived by regressing stock returns on market returns. They are affected by the financial leverage choices of the public companies. Implementation of Eq. (10.4) for a new venture, however, requires an estimate of the asset beta.

A firm's asset beta removes the effect of financial leverage and reflects only the market risk of the business; consequently, it is always less than or equal to its equity beta. To see this, consider two operationally identical businesses. One company is financed entirely with equity, while the second uses considerable debt. Since equity is a residual claim, a shareholder in the leveraged company will be behind the bondholders in the line to claim the cash flows generated by the firm's assets. The riskiness of asset cash flows is the same for both companies and is represented by β_A. The riskiness of the cash flows to shareholders, represented by the equity beta, β_E, is greater for the leveraged firm. If debt is riskless or has no market risk, equity betas can be converted to asset betas using Eq. (10.5):

$$\beta_A = \beta_E \frac{E}{V} \tag{10.5}$$

In the expression, β_E is usually estimated for a comparable firm by regression analysis (or possibly taken from a published source), E is the market value of the comparable firm's equity, and V is the market value of the comparable firm's total capital (debt plus equity). The computation in Eq. (10.5) yields only an approximation of the asset beta because it assumes that the comparable firm's debt has no market risk (i.e., the debt beta is zero). If the comparable is highly leveraged, the expression will underestimate the asset beta.[7] In practice, because market values of debt are usually not available, it is common to estimate V as the sum of the market value of equity plus the book value of debt.

Assuming comparable-firm data are available for more than one firm, we would take the following steps to estimate the new venture asset beta and to calculate the appropriate discount rate:

Step 1. Calculate or collect equity betas and data on E and V for the comparable firms.

Step 2. Use Eq. (10.5) to convert each equity beta to an asset beta.

Step 3. Use the sample of comparable firm asset betas to compute a weighted average asset beta for the new venture. The weightings should be based on judgment about comparability.

Step 4. With the definitions from Chapter 9, if we are using the cash flows to all investors to value the venture, use the weighted average β_A in the CAPM to estimate r_A, the discount rate.[8]

One significant concern with using market comparables to estimate beta is that finding true comparables for the new venture is unlikely. Many new ventures are highly specialized and involve products and market opportunities that are difficult to analogize to existing public companies. Even if a firm is in the same industry, it has survived long enough and grown large enough to have gone public.

While good public firm comparables for early-stage ventures are uncommon, the late 1990s constitutes a rare exception. During that period of several years, a large number of "new economy" ventures went public at early stages of development. Based on sample data of over 2,600 firm-years from the last half of the 1990s, Kerins, Smith, and Smith (2004) estimate the equity betas of newly public firms, including many observations of very small firms, firms that had yet to achieve profitability, and firms that had yet to begin revenue generation. Table 10.3 reports some of the findings from that study. Based on all of the observations, the average equity beta is very close to 1.0, similar to the total risk of the S&P 500 (the "market" risk). Because these firms tend not to use debt financing, their equity betas are approximately equivalent to

TABLE **10.3** Beta and correlation estimates for recently public firms

	Number of observations	Mean β	Correlation with the market	Standard deviation of returns
All observations	2,623	0.99	0.195	1.20
Industry				
Biotechnology	501	0.75	0.149	1.04
Broadcast and cable TV	105	0.80	0.237	0.87
Communication equipment	247	1.16	0.215	1.20
Communication services	407	1.02	0.241	1.04
Computer networks	130	1.02	0.208	0.93
Computer services	440	0.81	0.172	1.44
Catalog/mail order	39	1.24	0.217	1.06
Software	754	1.20	0.200	1.37
Age (years after IPO)				
0–1 year	1,263	0.93	0.162	1.35
2–3 years	957	0.96	0.212	1.04
>3 years	403	1.27	0.259	1.14
Financial condition				
No revenue	102	0.82	0.165	1.19
Revenue, but negative income	1,475	1.14	0.197	1.35
Positive income	1,033	0.82	0.200	1.00
Employees				
0–25	187	0.59	0.117	1.26
26–100	496	0.86	0.153	1.28
Over 100	1,661	1.14	0.231	1.13

SOURCE: *Kerins, Smith, and Smith (2004).*
NOTE: *Beta estimates of recently public firms that went public during the 1995–2000 period. Betas and correlations are computed using the S&P 500 index as the "market."*

asset betas. The highest reported beta in the table is 1.27, and the evidence also suggests that younger and smaller firms have lower betas. These results suggest that reasonable estimates of beta for nonpublic ventures will generally be in the range of about 0.6 to 1.25.

Estimating beta from scenarios. A second approach for estimating beta is more conceptual and involves constructing scenarios for the venture, where the scenarios are related to the overall market; the asset beta is then inferred from analysis of the scenarios. The second term in Eq. (10.4) suggests a way to use this approach to develop an estimate of beta with scenarios such as boom and bust. We use the scenarios approach to estimate the covariance between venture returns or cash flows and market returns. The covariance is the numerator of the second term in Eq. (10.4). The variance of market returns (the denominator of the second term) can be estimated directly from stock market data for the index you are using to represent the market. Because beta is a measure of market risk and not total risk, the scenarios must be related to overall economic performance.

To illustrate, suppose the developer of a product for managing the use of energy by manufacturing firms is seeking a $1 million investment from an investor. Demand is subject to an array of uncertainties, some of which are related to the overall economy. On net, the entrepreneur believes the relation between product cash flows and the economy can be described in three scenarios, as shown in the following table:

Scenario	Probability	Market return (r_M)	Project annual cash flow	Return on investment
Boom	0.3	30%	$450,000	45%
Normal growth	0.5	10%	$250,000	25%
Bust	0.2	−5%	$0	0%

The information in the table can be used to estimate the beta of the investment as follows:

Step 1. Compute the expected return on the market portfolio.

$$30\%(0.3) + 10\%(0.5) + -5\%(0.2) = 13\%$$

Step 2. Compute the variance of returns on the market portfolio.

$$(30\% - 13\%)^2(0.3) + (10\% - 13\%)^2(0.5) + (-5\% - 13\%)^2(0.2) = 1.56\%$$

Step 3. Compute the expected return on the project.

$$45\%(0.3) + 25\%(0.5) + 0\%(0.2) = 26.0\%$$

Step 4. Compute the covariance between market returns and project returns.

$$(30\% - 13\%) \times (45\% - 26.0\%) \times (0.3) + (10\% - 13\%) \times (25\% - 26.0\%)$$
$$\times (0.5) + (-5\% - 13\%) \times (0\% - 26.0\%) \times (0.3) = 1.92\%$$

Step 5. Compute beta as the ratio of the covariance to the market variance.

$$\beta_A = \frac{\text{Cov}_{r_A, r_M}}{\sigma_M^2} = \frac{1.92\%}{1.56\%} = 1.23$$

Using the beta for the proposed investment and assuming a 4 percent risk-free rate and 6.5 percent market risk premium, we can estimate the required return on the investment:

$$r_A = r_F + \beta_A(r_M - r_F) = 4\% + 1.23(6.5\%) = 12.00\%$$

If we use this rate to discount the expected cash flow of $260,000 ($450,000 × 0.30 + $250,000 × 0.50 + $0 × 0.20), we get a PV of $232,143 for one annual cash flow. The total value of the project depends, of course, on capitalizing the stream of cash flows over time.

Using scenario analysis to estimate a cash flow beta. In the CEQ form of the CAPM, instead of a beta of holding-period returns, we use a cash flow beta. Equation (10.6) is the CEQ form of the CAPM and uses notation we have already discussed:

$$PV_t = \frac{C_t - \frac{\rho_{C_t, r_M} \sigma_{C_t}}{\sigma_M} RP_M}{1 + r_F} \tag{10.6}$$

This is the expression for the PV of a single cash flow received at time t. To focus on the issues related to estimating the cash flow beta, in Eq. (10.7) we solve for the risk-adjusted discount rate that is implicit in Eq. (10.6).

$$\frac{C_t}{PV_t} - 1 = r_F + \beta_t \times RP_M = r_F + \frac{\rho_{C_t, r_M}\left(\frac{\sigma_{C_t}}{PV_t}\right)}{\sigma_M} RP_M \tag{10.7}$$

Equation (10.7) provides another way to estimate the cash flow beta, where β_t is computed using the expected cash flows rather than expected returns. Although the last term is stated in terms of cash flows, it is just an alternative way of expressing the beta of the holding-period returns.

We can use the energy management venture to illustrate how to apply scenario analysis to cash flows instead of holding-period returns. Steps 1 and 2 are the same as calculating beta based on returns.

Step 1. Compute the expected return on the market portfolio.

30%(0.3) + 10%(0.5) + (−5%)(0.2) = 13%

Step 2. Compute the variance of returns on the market portfolio.

(30% − 13%)²(0.3) + (10% − 13%)²(0.5) + (−5% − 13%)²(0.2) = 1.56%

Step 3. Compute the expected cash flow from the project.

$450,000 × 0.30 + $250,000 × 0.50 + $0 × 0.20 = $260,000

Step 4. Compute the covariance between market returns and project cash flows.

$$(30\% - 13\%) \times (\$450{,}000 - \$260{,}000) \times (0.3) + (10\% - 13\%)$$
$$\times (\$250{,}000 - \$260{,}000) \times (0.5) + (-5\% - 13\%) \times (\$0 - \$260{,}000)$$
$$\times (0.3) = \$19{,}200$$

Step 5. Compute the cash flow beta as the ratio of the covariance between market returns and project cash flows divided by the market variance.

$$\beta_{\text{cash flow}} = \frac{\text{Cov}_{C_t, r_M}}{\sigma_M^2} = \frac{\$19{,}200}{1.56\%} = \$1{,}230{,}769$$

Now that you know the cash flow beta, you can use it in the CEQ model, Eq. (10.6), to value the expected cash flow. Recall from Chapter 9 that the numerator of Eq. (10.6) is the CEQ cash flow, which is simply the expected cash flow minus a risk adjustment.

Step 1. Compute the certainty equivalent cash flow.

$$\text{CEQ Cash Flow} = C_t - \frac{\rho_{C_t, r_M} \sigma_{C_t}}{\sigma_M} RP_M$$
$$= \$260{,}000 - (\$1{,}230{,}769 \times 6.5\%) = \$260{,}000 - \$80{,}000$$
$$= \$180{,}000$$

Step 2. Discount the certainty equivalent cash flow to PV at the risk-free rate.

$$PV_t = \frac{\text{CEQ Cash Flow}}{1 + r_F} = \frac{\$180{,}000}{1 + 4\%} = \$173{,}077$$

Thus, using the previous assumptions of a 4 percent risk-free rate and 6.5 percent market risk premium, the PV of the cash flow is $173,077 and not the $232,143 value we computed using the RADR approach with an assumed investment of $1 million.[9] The CEQ estimate is unbiased, whereas the RADR estimate is not.

Estimating the Components of Beta Separately

Finally, the term on the right-hand side of Eq. (10.4) describes the beta for use in the RADR form as a function of the standard deviation of asset holding-period returns, the standard deviation of market returns, and the correlation coefficient between holding-period returns and market returns. Equation (10.6) describes the cash flow beta for use in the CEQ form as a function of the standard deviation of asset cash flows, the standard deviation of market returns, and the correlation between asset cash flows and market returns. Thus, a third approach is to derive the estimate of the returns beta or the cash flow beta from separate estimates of these three elements.

Estimating the standard deviation of cash flows or holding-period returns.   If expected cash flows are estimated by scenario analysis or simulation, the information needed to estimate the standard deviation of cash flows is generated at the same time and is easily used. We illustrate this later in the chapter.

However, as we already have stated, it is not easy to go from the standard deviation of cash flows to the standard deviation of holding-period returns. We illustrated the problem in the previous discussion of estimating beta from scenarios, where we found that the approach was not accurate when estimated holding-period returns were used to compute beta.

This may not be a serious problem. If the objective is simply to determine whether the expected cash flow is high enough to justify an investment of a certain amount that is known in advance, then an approximation of the standard deviation of holding-period returns (and beta) can be computed on the basis of the required investment. This is how we computed the variance of holding-period returns when we used scenario data to estimate beta. But if the objective is to determine how much a particular risky asset is actually worth, as we explained in Chapter 9, it is not possible to determine the correct standard deviation of holding-period returns without simultaneously determining the value of the cash flows, a trial-and-error process that can be tedious.

Our conclusion is that if you cannot derive a reliable estimate of beta from data for comparable firms, it is generally better and easier to circumvent the problem of estimating beta by using the CEQ form of the CAPM. The advantage of the CEQ approach is that it is not necessary to determine the standard deviation of holding-period returns and the PV of the cash flow simultaneously. Look back at Eq. (10.6). Instead of estimating the cash flow beta from scenarios, you can estimate the elements of the cash flow beta. The two elements we have yet to discuss are the market standard deviation and the correlation between venture cash flows and the market.

Estimating the standard deviation of market returns.   We suggest using historical data on market returns to estimate the market standard deviation. In Table 10.4, we report the standard deviation of a long-run historical average of annual holding-period returns for investing in the S&P 500.

TABLE **10.4** **Standard deviation of market return for various holding periods**

Length of holding period	Standard deviation (%)	Variance (%)
1 year	14.50	2.10
2 years	20.51	4.21
3 years	25.11	6.31
4 years	29.00	8.41
5 years	32.42	10.51
6 years	35.52	12.62
7 years	38.36	14.72
8 years	41.01	16.82
9 years	43.50	18.92
10 years	45.85	21.03

NOTE: *The 1-year standard deviation is computed from a 1950–2009 average of annual holding-period returns of the S&P 500 index. Returns for longer holding periods are calculated assuming time-series independence of annual returns.*

Our estimate is an annual standard deviation of 14.5 percent. To compute the standard deviation for a holding period other than one year, we assume that holding-period returns from one year to the next are independent of each other.[10] Under this assumption, we can compute the standard deviation for a different holding period either by multiplying the standard deviation by the square root of the time interval in years or by multiplying the annual variance by the time interval and then taking the square root. For example, the two-year standard deviation is:

$$\sigma_{2\ years} = 14.50\% \times \sqrt{2} = 20.51\%$$

or

$$\sigma_{2\ years} = \sqrt{(14.50\%)^2 \times 2} = \sqrt{2.10\% \times 2} = 20.51\%$$

For convenience, in Table 10.4 we report market standard deviations calculated for holding periods of up to 10 years.

Estimating the correlation between project cash flows and market returns. Although Eq. (10.6) circumvents the need to determine the risk of the holding-period return for a cash flow, it does raise another difficult question: How can the correlation between venture cash flows and market returns be estimated? One approach is to base the estimate on judgment, in light of the nature of the risks that the venture will face. Alternatively, it may be possible to use stock returns data for public companies to gain perspective on the range of appropriate assumptions.

Although the prospect of estimating a correlation coefficient between a new venture cash flow and the market portfolio may seem daunting, a realistic range of values can be narrowed quite easily. Assuming you can do a good job of estimating total risk, you can use data for comparable firms to generate a reasonable estimate of the correlation coefficient. Large and highly diversified corporations have returns that are more highly correlated with the market than do small and undiversified corporations. Nonetheless, even diversified corporations seldom have correlations with the market that are in excess of 0.7; a more typical level would be 0.4. For example, General Electric, widely considered one of the most diversified public companies, had a correlation coefficient of 0.65 with the S&P 500 using weekly returns data for the three-year period ended December 31, 2008. Over the same period Johnson & Johnson's correlation was 0.39. Biogen Idec Inc., an established biotechnology company with 2008 revenue of $4 billion and almost 5,000 employees, had a correlation coefficient of 0.22. For a new venture with a high degree of idiosyncratic risk and little diversification, it is unlikely that the correlation of returns with the market will exceed 0.3.

This is supported by the data in Table 10.3, where the highest reported correlation is 0.26 and most correlations are in the 0.15–0.25 range. Correlations with the market increase with firm financial maturity (measured by age and financial condition) and size (measured by the number of employees). Given the narrow range of realistic values, attempting to develop a precise estimate of the correlation between project returns and market returns is probably not worth the effort. A number near 0.5 is appropriate for a market-sensitive venture such as a financial institution or public utility. A number around 0.1 is appropriate for early-stage ventures that have characteristics more like lotteries. As with all variables, a range of estimates should be assessed for their impact on the valuation.

Shortcuts for Estimating Opportunity Cost of Capital

Sometimes it is possible to develop an estimate of the cost of capital without basing it directly on the CAPM. Suppose we can find mature public companies that are comparable to the venture that is being valued and that are expected to pay dividends at a constant rate. If we know the price of the stock, the dividend level, and the expected growth rate of dividends, we can estimate the cost of capital using the dividend discount model:

$$P_0 = \frac{D_1}{r-g} \quad \text{or} \quad r = \frac{D_1}{P_0} + g \tag{10.8}$$

where D_1 is the dividend expected next year, g is the expected rate of dividend growth, r is the unknown opportunity cost of capital, and P_0 is the current stock price. For example, if the expected dividend is $1, expected growth of dividends is 3 percent per year, and the current price is $12, then:

$$r = \frac{D_1}{P_0} + g = \frac{\$1}{\$12} + .03 = 0.083 + 0.03 = .113 = 11.3\%$$

The resulting estimate of cost of capital is 11.3 percent.

Another possible shortcut is to recognize that if a public company has no opportunity to invest retained cash flows at a rate different from its cost of capital, then the earnings/price ratio is an estimate of cost of capital. With no growth, an investor is basically purchasing a perpetual stream of risky earnings. For example, if earnings are expected to be $1 and the current price is $9, the estimated cost of capital is 11.1 percent. If the company has attractive investment opportunities, then the earnings/price ratio and cost of capital will be lower, depending on the value of the growth opportunities.

Both of these shortcuts are ways to estimate the cost of equity. To generate a cost of capital for assets, they must be unlevered or incorporated into a weighted average cost-of-capital calculation. For most new ventures, the approaches are unlikely to be of much value as stand-alone methods. Companies that are candidates for using these approaches to estimate cost of capital are very different from new ventures, where the entire value usually depends on prospective growth. Nonetheless, for some private businesses, such as retailing or service businesses, the shortcut approaches can work well. In any case, they can serve as a reality check on the cost-of-capital estimate you derive using a CAPM-based approach.

Shortcuts in the Application of DCF

The cash flows of a venture are not all the same. Some are low risk and some are highly risky. Differences in risk can arise over time as well as across activities within a single period. Ideally, we would discount each cash flow at a rate that takes account of its timing and risk characteristics; in practice, this is rarely done. Short of dealing with the unique risk characteristics of each cash flow, we might aggregate the cash flows of different risks that occur in a given period and find a weighted average discount rate that is appropriate for the aggregate. This also is rarely done, as it would imply using different discount rates for different periods.

What usually happens in the RADR approach is that a single discount rate is used to discount all of the project cash flows. In part this is because the data on comparable public firms, on which the cost-of-capital estimate is based, are for the entire firm and do not distinguish among separate cash flows based on risk or timing.

If this shortcut is used in the RADR approach, it makes sense to select parameters for the risk-free rate and market risk premium that are of approximately the same duration as the average duration of project cash flows. Thus, if continuing value is used and almost all of the value of the project is captured in the continuing value, it would make sense to use a long-term risk-free rate and a correspondingly lower market risk premium.

In the CEQ method, it is easier to take account of risk differences in cash flows over time. It could still make sense to simplify the analysis by using a single risk-free rate and market risk premium for all periods, but this does not automatically result in a single beta. Nor does it need to in the RADR approach, if the risk attributes of the project are determined by simulation rather than simply assumed to be similar to those of comparable firms.

Testing the Consistency of Assumptions

If market data for comparable firms are available, those data can be evaluated to see if the assumptions are internally consistent and reasonable. Compared to public companies, which are better established than new ventures and normally are more diversified, a new venture is likely to have higher total risk but more of the risk is likely to be idiosyncratic. Because these deviations are offsetting, Table 10.3 suggests that the asset betas of new ventures are similar to the asset betas of comparable public companies but that new ventures have higher standard deviations and lower correlations with the market.

If the factors are offsetting, then you can use your assumptions about project risk to make an *ex post* check. Do the assumptions result in an implied beta that is reasonable in light of what you know about the betas of comparable public companies? If not, you may want to reconsider your assumptions.

If comparable firm data are available, why not just estimate the asset beta from the comparables, such as those reported in Table 10.3? The answer is twofold. First, for the following reasons, it is important to assess the total risk of the venture, not only the market risk represented by beta:

- It is unlikely that you can generate a reasonable estimate of the expected cash flows without considering total risk.

- A reasonable measure of total risk is important for valuing the project from the perspective of the underdiversified entrepreneur.
- Total risk is also critical to the valuation of the complex financial claims and real options that are frequently features in new venture financing.

Second, coming at the question of beta risk from both directions—that is, by using market comparables for beta and by inferring a beta estimate from the assumptions used in the CEQ valuation—is a good way to check the reasonableness of underlying assumptions.

For an unlevered comparable firm, the estimate of correlation is given by Eq. (10.9):

$$\hat{\rho}_{C_j, r_M} = \beta_{comp} \frac{\sigma_M}{\sigma_{r_{comp}}} \tag{10.9}$$

In the above expression, the subscript "comp" stands for comparable firm assets. Because the comparable will generate cash flows in many years, the estimate in Eq. (10.9) is best interpreted as a weighted average correlation over the life of the venture.

A Caveat

The CEQ form of the CAPM works well as long as project risk (cash flow standard deviation) is not too large compared to the expected cash flow and/or as long as the correlation between project cash flows and the market is not too great. For very risky cash flows, especially if correlation with the market is high or if value is based on total risk instead of market risk only, CAPM-based valuation models tend to undervalue risky cash flows. Because this problem is more likely to arise in determining value to the entrepreneur, we defer a more complete examination of the problem. Sometimes, however, the problem can arise even for a well-diversified investor; if it does, the valuation should address it.

10.4   New Venture Valuation: An Illustration

To illustrate implementation, we introduce the example of Dylan Components, Inc. (DCI), a hypothetical start-up that will provide components to manufacturers of lithium-ion batteries. The entrepreneur, Dylan, seeks funds to increase production capacity to commercial scale. The scale-up will take one year, with revenues beginning in Year 2.

Dylan has prepared financial projections and developed three scenarios that yield the cash flow forecast shown below. He has also assigned a probability to each scenario, as shown here.

Dylan Components, Inc. (DCI) cash flow forecast ($ thousands)

| Scenario | Prob- ability | Year | | | | | | Continuing value |
		0	1	2	3	4	5	
Success	0.25	($3,000)	($1,500)	$1,000	$3,000	$5,000	$9,000	$108,000
Likely	0.50	($3,000)	($1,500)	$500	$500	$500	$500	$4,000
Failure	0.25	($3,000)	($1,500)	$0	$0	$0	$0	$0
Expected cash flow		**($3,000)**	**($1,500)**	**$500**	**$1,000**	**$1,500**	**$2,500**	**$29,000**

The expected cash flow in each period is simply a probability-weighted average of each scenario's cash flow. To simplify, we assume that DCI is entirely equity financed and that the cash flows shown are the cash flows to shareholders. This means that the appropriate discount rate is the cost of equity.[11]

The explicit value period is five years, at the end of which Dylan anticipates two possible exits for investors. If the "success" scenario is realized, DCI would go public. You have collected data on comparable IPO transactions and have estimated that if the "success" scenario is realized, the appropriate continuing value multiple will be 12 times DCI's Year 5 cash flow. Under the "likely" scenario, DCI will be sold by acquisition to a customer or supplier interested in vertical integration. You have collected information on comparable trade sale transactions and have estimated a continuing value multiple of eight times the Year 5 cash flow. The "failure" scenario results in a full loss of the investment, so that the continuing value in Year 5 is zero.

Using the RADR Form of the CAPM

Equation (10.10) is the CAPM valuation model stated in RADR form.

$$PV = \sum_{t=0}^{T} \frac{C_{jt}}{(1 + r_{jt})^t} = \sum_{t=0}^{T} \frac{C_{jt}}{[1 + r_{Ft} + \beta_{jt}(RP_{Mt})]} \tag{10.10}$$

In this expression, PV is the present value of all cash flows to investors in the venture. You can interpret the periods from Time 0 to T as the explicit value period, where the Time T cash flow includes continuing value. To allow for the possibility that different cash flows in the same period can vary in risk, C_{jt} represents a particular expected cash flow j at time t. For example, except for uncertainties about the tax status of a venture, depreciation cash flows (i.e., the tax savings in each period) are determined at the time the investment is made. Consequently, they are likely to be much less risky than net income or operating cash flow.

Each cash flow in Eq. (10.10) is discounted by a factor that is determined by the CAPM. The elements of the discount factor are the risk-free rate, r_F, the market risk premium, RP_M, and beta risk, β_{jt}. Equation (10.10) is very general. The first two variables are specific to the time period, t, while β_{jt}, which reflects the riskiness of the cash flow, is specific to both time period t and cash flow j. Thus, within a given period we may have cash flows of different risk, while across periods the risk-free rate and market risk premium may also vary. This implies that the discount rate can differ from one period to the next and for different cash flows in the same period.

The cash flows in Eq. (10.10) are expected cash flows in the statistical sense, including the risk of failure. They are not the cash flows anticipated if the venture is a success. Nor are they the "likely" cash flows, which can be seen clearly in the DCI data. The estimate of continuing value is also an expected value estimate based on the various assumptions about the venture's exit strategy. When the RADR form is used, uncertainty is addressed in the discount rate, so it is not necessary to make a direct estimate of the uncertainty of cash flows. In practice, this may not be much of an advantage: it is hard to envision good ways of estimating expected cash flows that do not involve assessing uncertainty at the same time.

When inflows and outflows within a period differ in risk, it is unlikely that you can find a single, theoretically correct discount rate that can be used to value cash flows in different periods. It is, however, possible to estimate a single (weighted average) rate that can be applied to the net cash flows in a given period. This would seem to imply that a changing (time-varying) weighted average discount rate for valuing net cash flows might be appropriate. Equation (10.10) suggests segregating the streams by riskiness and using different discount rates, both within and across time periods. In practice, it is common to simplify the RADR process by using a single rate for all cash flows.

Suppose we wish to calculate a schedule of discount rates that reflect each expected cash flow's risk and timing. We could begin by asking whether a single discount rate is appropriate. To answer, consider the venture's cash flows at Time 0 and in Year 1. Most of the cash is being used to expand capacity, and the business has not yet begun to generate revenue. Because the costs of building capacity are assumed to be certain, there is no variance in the cash flows across the three scenarios for the first two periods. Given this, these cash flows should be valued at the risk-free rate.

The important risks of the venture start in Year 2, when product sales begin. The revenue-based cash flows have much more risk than the early investment cash flows. These risks can be seen in the considerable variation across the cash flows by scenario in each of the Years 2–5. Because these cash flows are risky, the discount rates that are applied in Years 2–5 should not be the same as those applied for the Time 0 and Year 1 cash flows.

This is intuitive, yet as noted earlier it is common practice when using the RADR approach to apply a single discount rate to all cash flows. Doing so in this case would result in underestimating the PV of investment outflows, which then results in an overestimation of project NPV. Nevertheless, to be consistent with standard practice (and to illustrate an advantage of the CEQ method), we will follow the common approach.

Suppose that using the data on risk-free rates and returns, we have estimated the following CAPM parameters:

Current rate on long-term Treasury bonds	4.0 percent
Market risk premium	6.5 percent

The final variable we need before we can implement Eq. (10.10) is the estimate of beta. Dylan has identified the following three firms as being comparable, and we have collected data on their equity betas and capital structures:

Comparable	Equity β	MV equity	Debt
Genric, Inc.	1.9	$12.0	$4.0
Preces Systems	1.5	$24.0	$3.0
Visania Co.	1.2	$7.0	$0.0

NOTE: *All monetary values in $ millions.*

Because these are equity betas, the first step is to determine the asset betas using Eq. (10.5):

Comparable	Equity β	MV equity	Debt	Asset value	Equity to asset value	Asset β
Genric, Inc.	1.9	$12.0	$4.0	$16.0	0.75	1.43
Preces Systems	1.5	$24.0	$3.0	$27.0	0.89	1.33
Visania Co.	1.2	$7.0	$0.0	$7.0	1.00	1.20

NOTE: *All monetary values in $ millions.*

T TABLE **10.5**   **Valuation Template 1: RADR valuation based on a discrete scenario cash flow forecast**

				Year			
Project information	Probability	0	1	2	3	4	5
Cash flows							
Success scenario	0.25	($3,000)	($1,500)	$1,000	$3,000	$5,000	$117,000
Expected scenario	0.50	($3,000)	($1,500)	$500	$500	$500	$4,500
Failure scenario	0.25	($3,000)	($1,500)	$0	$0	$0	$0
Expected cash flow		**($3,000)**	**($1,500)**	**$500**	**$1,000**	**$1,500**	**$31,500**
Market information							
Risk-free rate			4.00%	8.16%	12.49%	16.99%	21.67%
Market rate			10.50%	22.10%	34.92%	49.09%	64.74%
Market risk premium			6.50%	13.94%	22.44%	32.10%	43.08%
Comparable firm beta			1.32	1.32	1.32	1.32	1.32
Estimated cost of capital			**12.58%**	**26.56%**	**42.10%**	**59.36%**	**78.53%**
Market value estimate							
PV of expected CF		($3,000)	($1,332)	$395	$704	$941	$17,644
Sum of PVs		**$15,352**					

NOTE: *Value is estimated using the RADR form of the CAPM. Shaded cells are inputs. All dollar values are in thousands.*

Based on a simple average of the asset betas, we arrive at an estimated β_A of 1.32 for DCI. Using our estimates of a 4.0 percent risk-free rate and a 6.5 percent market risk premium, we can now calculate the required return on assets, r_A:

$$r_A = r_F + \beta_A(r_M - r_F) = 4\% + 1.32(6.5\%) = 12.58\%$$

The cash flows, discount rate calculations, and PV computation are summarized in Table 10.5, "Valuation Template 1," which is available on the companion website as a downloadable spreadsheet. The "Project information" section is the same data we saw earlier for DCI and includes each scenario's cash flow forecast and the expected cash flow in each year. The operating cash flows in Year 5 and the continuing values have been combined.

In the "Market information" section of the template, we provide the data and calculations used to estimate the RADR each year. In this table, we use the same annual discount rate each period, ignoring the differences in risk we noted earlier. As a result, the beta is assumed to be constant, consistent with the most common use of the RADR approach. The starting values for the relevant assumptions are shown in Year 1 for a one-year holding period. The risk-free rate is 4 percent, and the market rate is 10.5 percent (based on our assumed market risk premium of 6.5 percent).

For longer holding periods, the risk-free rates and market rates shown are found by compounding the one-year rates; the market risk premium is just the difference between the two. For example, a two-year investment in the riskless asset is expected to yield a total return of 8.16 percent, and the two-year market return is estimated to be 22.10 percent. This results in the following estimated discount rate for the Year 2 cash flow:

$$r_{\text{Year 2}} = 8.16\% + 1.32(22.10\% - 8.16\%) = 26.56\%$$

Summing the PVs of each year's expected cash flow produces an estimate of $15,352 as the value of DCI.

Using the CEQ Form of the CAPM

We now use the CEQ method to estimate the value of DCI. We have already estimated RP_M and r_F (6.5 percent and 4.0 percent, respectively) and have also calculated the expected cash flows, C_t. Recall that Eq. (10.6) values a single cash flow at time t, meaning that we have to apply it to each period's cash flow. We have estimates for the standard deviation of the market from Table 10.4, so the only variables we still need are the standard deviation of DCI's cash flows and their correlation with the market. For the latter, we decided to use the overall mean correlation value of 0.195 from Table 10.3 as a reasonable estimate. The cash flows, discount rate calculations, and CEQ PV computation are summarized in Table 10.6, "Valuation Template 2," which is also available as a downloadable spreadsheet on the companion website.

First, we note the main differences between Table 10.6 and Table 10.5, the RADR valuation. Under "Project information," the cash flows and scenarios are the same, but Table 10.6 adds the "Standard deviation of CFs" line. These are computed separately for each year based on the three cash flow scenarios. Consistent with our earlier discussion, for Time 0 and Year 1, the standard deviation is zero since the cash flows are invariant across scenarios. For Year 2, the standard deviation of $354 is calculated as follows:

$$\sigma_{CF_{\text{Year 2}}} = \sqrt{(\$1,000 - \$500)^2 \times 0.25 + (\$500 - \$500)^2 \times 0.5 + (\$0 - \$500)^2 \times 0.25}$$
$$= \$354$$

In the "Market information" section of the template, we show the values for all of the relevant assumptions in Year 1. In subsequent years, the risk-free rate and market rate, both expressed in annual terms, are simply being compounded. Values for market standard deviation are taken directly from Table 10.4, and the correlation value of 0.195 is an assumption based on Table 10.3.

T TABLE **10.6** Valuation Template 2: CEQ valuation based on a discrete scenario cash flow forecast

Project information	Probability	Year					
		0	1	2	3	4	5
Cash flows							
Success scenario	0.25	($3,000)	($1,500)	$1,000	$3,000	$5,000	$117,000
Expected scenario	0.50	($3,000)	($1,500)	$500	$500	$500	$4,500
Failure scenario	0.25	($3,000)	($1,500)	$0	$0	$0	$0
Expected cash flow		**($3,000)**	**($1,500)**	**$500**	**$1,000**	**$1,500**	**$31,500**
Standard deviation of CFs		**$0**	**$0**	**$354**	**$1,173**	**$2,031**	**$49,398**
Market information							
Risk-free rate			4.00%	8.16%	12.49%	16.99%	21.67%
Market rate			10.50%	22.10%	34.92%	49.09%	64.74%
Market risk premium			6.50%	13.94%	22.44%	32.10%	43.08%
Market variance							
Market standard deviation			14.50%	20.51%	25.11%	29.00%	32.42%
Correlation			0.195	0.195	0.195	0.195	0.195
Market value estimate							
Present value of expected CF		($3,000)	($1,442)	$419	$707	$907	$15,371
Sum of PVs	**$12,963**						
Diagnostic information							
Annualized required return			4.0%	9.2%	12.2%	13.4%	15.4%
Standard deviation of returns		0.00%	0.00%	84.39%	165.76%	223.82%	321.36%
Covariance with market		0.00%	0.00%	3.37%	8.12%	12.66%	20.32%
Beta		0.00	0.00	0.80	1.29	1.51	1.93

NOTE: *Value is estimated using the CEQ form of the CAPM. Shaded cells are inputs. All dollar values are in thousands.*

In the "Market value estimate" panel, each period's value in the template is simply the application of Eq. (10.6) to the data for that year. In Year 3, for example, the calculation is as follows:

$$PV_t = \frac{C_t - \frac{\rho_{C_t, r_M}\sigma_{C_t}}{\sigma_M}RP_M}{1 + r_F} = \frac{\$1,000 - \frac{0.195 \times \$1,173}{0.2511} \times 0.2244}{1 + 0.1249} = \frac{\$796}{1.1249}$$
$$= \$707$$

The numerator in the next-to-last term of the equation, $796, is the certainty equivalent CF, which is being discounted by the three-year risk-free rate of 12.49 percent. Summing each PV gives a total (net) present value for DCI of $12,963.

Finally, the "Diagnostic information" panel in Table 10.6 contains information that can be used to help understand the valuation and to assess the reasonableness and internal consistency of the assumptions. The first line in the panel shows the annualized required rate of return for each annual cash flow. As shown, the required rates are highly variable, and each is calculated in the spreadsheet by comparing the expected cash flow in each year to its present value and converting to an annual rate. For example, the correct risk-adjusted holding-period return for the Year 2 cash flow is:

$$\frac{C_t}{PV_t} - 1 = \sqrt{\frac{\$500}{\$419}} - 1 = 0.092 \text{ or } 9.2\%$$

The "Diagnostic information" panel also shows the beta estimate for each period's cash flow. The estimate for each year is calculated based on the data in the template and the formula for the cash flow beta from Eq. (10.7). For example, the Year 4 beta estimate is computed as follows:

$$\beta_t = \frac{\rho_{C_t, r_M} \times \left(\frac{\sigma_{C_t}}{PV_t}\right)}{\sigma_M}$$

$$\beta_{\text{Year 4}} = \frac{\rho_{C_{\text{Year 4}}, r_M}\left(\frac{\sigma_{C_{\text{Year 4}}}}{PV_{\text{Year 4}}}\right)}{\sigma_{M_{\text{Year 4}}}} = \frac{0.195\left(\frac{\$2,031}{\$907}\right)}{0.2900} = 1.51$$

The estimated betas vary substantially from year to year and are also different from the assumed beta of 1.32 used in the RADR method.

Comparing the CEQ and RADR Approaches

We now can examine the differences between our CEQ and RADR results. The CEQ method produced a value estimate of $12,963, while the RADR result is $15,352. The most important factor in the difference is that the RADR method as applied in Table 10.5, by assuming a single beta, uses the wrong discount rate to value each annual cash flow. This can be seen by comparing the PV estimates for the annual cash flows computed by the RADR method with the estimates computed by the CEQ method.

The Year 1 cash flow is a good place to start. DCI will spend the first year building capacity, so there is little uncertainty about the required investment. In fact, the standard deviation of the cash flows is zero, which implies no risk. But in Table 10.5, the riskless Year 1 expected cash flow of −$1,500 is being discounted at the RADR of 12.58 percent. In Table 10.6, the expected cash flow and the CEQ cash flow are identical, and the discount rate applied is the riskless rate of 4 percent. Rather than the correct PV of −$1,442, the RADR PV of the Year 1 cash flow is −$1,332, which contributes to overvaluation of the venture.

In fact, in every year the RADR discount rate is incorrect. The biggest discrepancy is in Year 5, when the CEQ model estimates the required risk-adjusted return at 108 percent, but the rate used in the RADR calculation is only 78.5 percent. By using a discount rate that is too low, the RADR estimate is overvalued by $2,507 in Year 5 and by $2,635 in aggregate across all years.

With the RADR method, the discount rate each period is based on the assumption that the beta stays constant at 1.32. However, when we compare the two templates, we can see that an assumption of constant risk is not correct. The betas implicit in Table 10.6, the CEQ model, are different every year.

Our simple example exposes the limitations of the RADR approach when compared to the CEQ method and highlights some of the challenges of implementing both. We do not, however, want you to lose track of its advantages. The principal strengths of the RADR approach are:

- Valuation is based on expected cash flows.
- The discount rate is intended to be opportunity cost of capital.
- Market data can be used to estimate cost of capital.
- It is unnecessary to estimate the total risk or the correlation with the market.

The main disadvantages of the RADR method are:

- If separate information is unavailable on cost of capital, then holding-period returns and cost of capital must be determined simultaneously.
- Truly comparable firms are unlikely to be available for most new ventures.
- The model works best if it is applied to cash flows that are segregated according to market risk; but in that case, the appropriate discount rate for valuing a single cash flow cannot normally be determined based on data from comparable firms.
- If information on total risk is not generated, it is difficult to value complex financial claims on the underlying asset.

The benefits of the CEQ form of the CAPM are:

- Valuation is based on expected cash flows.
- Cost of capital is used to value each annual cash flow.
- Cash flows that differ in terms of total risk are handled easily by the CEQ method.
- Cash flows at different times can easily be valued separately.

- Any financial claim can be valued, as long as the CAPM assumptions hold.
- A measure of the total risk of cash flows is generated and will be particularly useful when we address valuation by the entrepreneur.

The main disadvantages of the CEQ approach are:

- An estimate of the full distribution of cash flow possibilities is required, instead of a single estimate.
- The correlation coefficient between venture cash flows and the market can be difficult to estimate, even if data on the betas of comparable firms are available.

Using the Relative Value Method

Because DCI is an early-stage venture with no revenue, it would be very difficult to find comparable public companies to apply relative valuation to the venture at an early stage. However, we can use the relative value approach to estimate the company's continuing value at the end of the explicit value period, when it is expected to look more like established firms. Under the "success" scenario, we assumed that DCI will go public at the end of Year 5 and under the "likely" scenario that the venture would be sold to a customer in a trade sale.

To estimate the value at the end of Year 5 under the "success" scenario, we have collected the data shown below on recent IPO transactions. Like DCI, all of the comparable firms are financed entirely with equity, so we do not need to adjust for capital structure.

Recent IPOs

Company	Market capitalization @ IPO	Financial data (last 12 months)			CF to all investors
		Revenue	EBIT	Earnings	
Greyport Networks	$134,125	$89,420	$14,420	$5,590	$8,770
Spectria Labs	$10,500	$6,180	$1,460	$330	$880
Indeve Inc.	$97,350	$44,250	$7,490	$5,120	$11,095

NOTE: *All data in $ thousands.*

Market capitalization in the table above is the total value of each firm calculated as the IPO price times total post-IPO shares outstanding, including IPO shares. It represents the value the entrepreneur or pre-IPO investors would receive by selling their shares as part of the IPO.

Dylan's forecast is of cash flow to all investors, so we focus our comparables analysis on the last column of data. In practice, we would also use Dylan's forecast data on revenue, EBIT, and earnings, as well as multiples of the additional data for the comparables; for this example, we use only cash flows to all investors. As discussed earlier, we would also want to consider the current market conditions and determine whether today's multiples represent reasonable estimates of transactions five years in the future.

For each IPO transaction, we calculate the ratio of market capitalization to CF to all investors. This tells us approximately how much IPO investors were willing to pay per dollar of each comparable firm's cash flow.

Recent IPOs

Company	Market capitalization @ IPO	CF to all investors	Market capitalization/CF to all investors
Greyport Networks	$134,125	$8,770	15.3
Spectria Labs	$10,500	$880	11.9
Indeve Inc.	$97,350	$11,095	8.8
			Average = 12.0

NOTE: *All monetary values in $ thousands.*

Because we consider the comparables to be equally informative about the value of DCI, we average the market cap ratio across the three comparables. The resulting market capitalization/cash flow ratio is 12.0. Based on this, we infer that 12 times cash flow to all investors is a reasonable estimate for the continuing value of DCI at the end of five years, if the venture achieves the "success" scenario.

If DCI develops according to the "likely" scenario, the exit at the end of Year 5 will be by trade sale to a strategic partner (i.e., acquisition). Relative valuation can be used to estimate the continuing value at this point, and we have collected the data below on comparable M&A transactions.

Recent M&A transactions

Target	Purchaser	Price paid	Target financial data (last 12 months)			CF to all investors
			Revenue	EBIT	Earnings	
Biros Inc.	Kinerion Inc.	$75,650	$58,190	$9,460	$3,960	$7,200
Viage Ent.	Bantic Networks	$32,500	$32,500	$5,000	$2,560	$4,710
Mecent Labs	Mercuron Co.	$145,950	$153,630	$12,160	$5,770	$17,388
Protoscan Inc.	Neurovage, L.V.	$88,275	$73,560	$9,100	$4,700	$14,240

NOTE: *All monetary values in $ thousands.*

In these transactions, price paid is what the purchaser paid for the target firm's assets and their associated cash flows. For each comparable, we compute the ratio of price paid to CF to all investors, which is shown in the right-hand column below. Considering the transactions to be equally informative, we then average the four ratios to get 8.0.

Recent M&A transactions

Target	Purchaser	Price paid	CF to all investors	Price/CF to all investors
Biros Inc.	Kinerion Inc.	$75,650	$7,200	10.5
Viage Ent.	Bantic Networks	$32,500	$4,710	6.9
Mecent Labs	Mercuron Co.	$145,950	$17,388	8.4
Protoscan Inc.	Neurovage, L.V.	$88,275	$14,240	6.2
				Average = 8.0

NOTE: *All monetary values in $ thousands.*

Based on this analysis, we use an estimate of eight times CF to all investors for the continuing value of DCI if it develops according to the expected scenario.

For consistency, we have used the multipliers derived by application of the RV method as continuing value throughout this comparison of valuation methods.

Using the Venture Capital Method

We now consider valuing DCI by the VC method. In our example, the final year is Year 5, and under the "success" scenario we assume that DCI will go public with a continuing value of 12 times cash flow to shareholders. We know from the CEQ model that the correct PV is $12,963.

The VC method includes the following steps:

Step 1. Select a year for the start of the continuing value period of the valuation by determining a point where, if the venture is successful, harvesting by acquisition or IPO or other means would be feasible. Estimate net income or other cash flow in that year based on the "success" scenario.

Step 2. Use the appropriate P/E ratio or other multiple and the harvest-date earnings or cash flow projection to compute continuing value. The multiple should reflect the expected capitalization of earnings or cash flow for a company that has achieved the level of success reflected in the scenario.

TABLE **10.7**   **Valuation by the VC method using various discount rates**

Cash flows	Total	Year					
		0	1	2	3	4	5
Success scenario		($3,000)	($1,500)	$1,000	$3,000	$5,000	$117,000
Discount rate = 40.00%							
Present value	$23,588	($3,000)	($1,071)	$510	$1,093	$1,302	$21,754
Discount rate = 60.00%							
Present value	$12,106	($3,000)	($938)	$391	$732	$763	$11,158
Implied single rate = 57.84%							
Present value	$12,963	($3,000)	($950)	$401	$763	$806	$11,943

Step 3. Convert the continuing value estimate to PV by discounting at a hurdle rate that you believe is high enough to compensate for time value, risk, and the probability that the "success" scenario will not be achieved.

Step 4. Based on estimated PV, it is possible to compute the minimum fraction of ownership an investor would require in exchange for contributing a given amount of capital.

In the VC method, we focus only on the cash flows of the "success" scenario, valuing them at a hurdle rate appropriate for the stage of development of the project. Unfortunately, this approach does not provide much guidance. If the project is considered to be in first-stage development, then the table of hurdle rates presented in Chapter 9 suggests a discount rate of 40–60 percent.

In Table 10.7, we compute the present values of DCI's "success" scenario cash flows at hurdle rates of both 40 and 60 percent. At 40 percent the value is $23,588, and at 60 percent it is $12,106, slightly lower than the CEQ valuation of $12,963. Such a broad range is not very helpful, especially if the valuation is to be used as the basis for an investment decision, such as to assess whether it would be a good idea to invest $18,000 today to acquire the venture. In Table 10.7, we also solve for the single hurdle rate that generates the true PV, which works out to be 57.84 percent.

One problem with the VC method should now be obvious: there is little basis for selecting the hurdle rate. Furthermore, small errors in the rate can dramatically affect the estimated PV. A second problem can be detected by comparing the PVs of the individual annual cash flows that are shown in Table 10.7 with the PVs of the same cash flows in Table 10.6. Using a 57.84 percent discount rate produces the same overall project value as the CEQ method, but the value of each annual cash flow provided by the VC method is wrong, usually by an amount larger than when the RADR method is used. There is no good way to generalize about the nature of these errors except to say that they are certain to occur and that the magnitudes of the errors will increase with increases in the variability of cash flows in different years. Perhaps with enough experience with using hurdle rates that eventually proved to be too high or too low, an entrepreneur or investor could find the VC method to be a useful heuristic approach.

It is easy to criticize the VC method on quantitative grounds. But the more qualitative advantages are also worth noting:

- The valuation can be driven by the financial projections for a "success" scenario that may be reported in the business plan.
- The negotiation process may be facilitated by centering the negotiations on the entrepreneur's projections.
- The investor's experience may be easiest to apply without formal analysis when comparisons of ventures are made on the basis of "success" scenarios.
- The method is easy to use and may be adequate for simple investment decisions.

The disadvantages include:

- Lack of precision due to reliance on unnecessarily limited information and rules of thumb.
- Biases resulting from discounting optimistic cash flow projections at a hurdle rate that is above cost of capital.
- Lack of information about uncertainty, which would be useful for valuing complex financial claims.

Before you decide not to use the VC method, you should give some thought to the negotiation process. Consider the following scenario: An entrepreneur who is enthusiastic about an idea comes to you with a business plan. You, as an investor, like the concept and believe the team is the right one to undertake the project. Like many entrepreneurs, however, this one seems overly optimistic; in particular, the entrepreneur's financial projections are based on a scenario in which the venture develops according to plan, with no major obstacles or setbacks.

You would like to go forward, but you believe that the entrepreneur's projections seriously overstate the likely success. What do you do? Do you engage in a debate with the entrepreneur about the projections, or do you simply try to counter optimism with pessimism by applying a discount rate that is biased upward to compensate for the entrepreneur's inflated projections? In the past, at least, the answer has often been the latter. It sometimes is easier to build the valuation on a structure of compensating errors than to work toward unbiased value projections on which both parties agree. Although the negotiation might be centered on the VC method valuation, you can protect yourself from mistakes by backing up your internal analysis with a method that does not suffer from the biases.

Using the First Chicago Method

In the way we applied the RADR method to value expected cash flows generated from discrete scenarios, we already illustrated the First Chicago method, with the specific added assumption that the CAPM is the correct asset pricing model. As such, there is no reason to repeat. Although the First Chicago method proposes to discount expected cash flows at their opportunity cost of capital, it does not provide guidance on how to determine cost of capital. A natural approach would be to use comparable ventures, but the method provides no guidance on how to assess comparability. With simple modifications to the "Market information" panel of Table 10.5, you can, if you wish, apply the First Chicago method without the constraint that the discount rate be determined by the CAPM.

The strengths of the First Chicago method include:

- Discrete scenarios provide a simple and easy method of determining both risk and expected return.
- The intent is to value expected cash flows.
- The intent is to discount the cash flows at an estimate of opportunity cost of capital.
- Because information about total risk is derived, the method provides a basis for valuing complex financial claims.

The disadvantages are:

- Discrete scenarios discard information about the risk that could be useful, especially for valuing complex claims.
- No guidance is provided about how to determine the discount rate(s) to be used in the valuation.
- No basis is provided for assigning probabilities to the different scenarios used in the valuation.

Although any valuation model has limitations, it generally makes sense to use the best one you can. The best model is one that values expected cash flows based on the opportunity cost of alternative investments, giving reasonable consideration to the cost of conducting the valuation and the importance of making a decision quickly. Generally, this points to either the First Chicago method or the CEQ model. The latter has the advantage of building on the discipline of the CAPM as a basis for selecting the discount rate and can deal with a comprehensive description of venture uncertainty.

10.5 The Cost of Capital for Non–US Investors

Perhaps the investor lives in a country other than the United States, possibly a developed country such as the UK or Japan or maybe an emerging economy such as Mexico or China. If so, you may be wondering about the relevance of diversification and the CAPM as drivers of opportunity cost of capital. While there are differences, the differences are not as great as they appear. Whether the investor is in a developed country or an emerging economy, opportunity cost is always the guiding principle of new venture investing, and the ability to invest in a diversified portfolio that includes an investment in the venture is a determinant of opportunity cost.

In all developed and many other countries, investors retain the opportunity to invest in a diversified market portfolio. However, because of currency exchange rates, doing so could subject the investor to somewhat different risks. In countries such as the UK and Japan, an investor can also invest in highly diversified domestic portfolios. So while the market index may be different, the economic principle that only non-diversifiable risk matters still applies, although estimating opportunity cost may be more difficult because of data limitations. Except for differences in expected inflation, however, the opportunity cost of capital implied by the CAPM for US investors is likely to be similar to the cost of capital implied by well-diversified portfolios throughout the world.

The practical challenge of estimating opportunity cost may be greater in emerging economies. Prohibitions may exist against investments in foreign diversified portfolios; exchange rates may be subject to dramatic swings or may be artificially constrained; investors may have limited opportunities to diversify domestically; and they may face other risks of long-term investing, such as a potential for expropriation.

Nevertheless, the investment principles are still the same. Projections of expected cash flows should include scenarios that incorporate such factors as the risk of expropriation, and the opportunity cost of capital should reflect the ability to diversify. An estimate of the opportunity cost of capital should therefore consider how the risk of investing in the venture would limit the investor's ability to diversify or would contribute to diversification.

As a first approximation, the investor could still use the CAPM model but with different assumptions for the risk-free rate, the risk premium on a portfolio that was diversified as much as possible, the total risk of the venture, and the correlation between the venture and the diversified portfolio.

10.6 Summary

Given the growth in the VC industry and the intensity of competition among investors, methods of valuation reflect increasing sophistication. The focus of the valuation effort is on the PV of future cash flows the investor would receive. Much of this chapter is devoted to methods for determining the information needed to carry out a valuation. Although we are careful and systematic in coverage of these methods, we also identify shortcuts that can sometimes be used.

The valuation approaches we apply in this chapter differ in several dimensions. The more traditional approaches are easy to use, in a computational sense, and potentially can facilitate negotiation between investor and entrepreneur in simple transactions. On the other hand, they are more prone to result in valuation errors than are approaches based on financial economic theory. Although all valuation models have limitations, it generally makes sense to use as many approaches as the data allow.

The best model from a theoretical perspective is one that values expected cash flows based on the opportunity cost of alternative investments, giving reasonable consideration to the cost of the valuation and the importance of making a decision quickly. Generally, this points to either the First Chicago method or the CEQ model. The latter has the advantage of building on the discipline of the CAPM as a basis for discount rate selection and can deal with a more comprehensive description of venture uncertainty. That said, relative valuation and multiples that incorporate current market data on comparable ventures and transactions can be used to assess continuing value and to test the DCF results.

REVIEW QUESTIONS

1. What are some of the key criteria for choosing a valuation method?

2. Explain the theory behind continuing value. What are the important factors to consider when calculating continuing value?

3. What are some of the ways to estimate the beta for a new venture? Describe some of the challenges to developing an accurate estimate. How does financial leverage impact your beta estimate?

4. Is the dividend discount model a good shortcut for estimating the cost of equity for a new venture? Why or why not?

5. Describe the process of estimating the appropriate risk-free rate for estimating a DCF discount rate. Where can data be found for estimating the risk-free rate?

6. Describe the process of estimating the appropriate market risk premium. Where can data be found for estimating the market risk premium?

7. Describe the various methods of computing beta in the CEQ approach.

8. Is relative valuation a useful approach for estimating the value of new ventures? Why or why not? Under what circumstances would you be confident using relative valuation?

9. What are the quantitative criticisms of the VC method? In spite of its shortcomings, why is this valuation approach still popular?

10. Can the approaches discussed in this chapter be used in emerging economies? What adjustments, if any, would you recommend?

NOTES

1. Application of multiplier-based approaches to valuation is more defensible when the venture is well established than when it is at an early stage of development. At later stages, inference of value from income or balance sheet information is more reasonable and accurate.

2. See Damodaran (1994), chs. 8–12, and Copeland, Koller, and Murrin (2000), ch. 12.

3. Historical information on risk-free yields and real rates beginning in

January 2003 is provided by the US Treasury at http://www.ustreas.gov/offices/domestic-finance/debt-management/interest-rate/real_yield_historical.shtml.

4. The preferred rate is from a zero-coupon security. However, only the three-month, six-month, and one-year Treasury bills are sold as zero-coupon securities. For longer-term risk-free rates, Treasury "STRIPS" (Separate Trading of Registered Interest and Principal of Securities) are used to proxy for zero-coupon bonds. Information on current US government bond interest rates is readily available from free services such as Yahoo! Finance, the Federal Reserve Bank of St. Louis (http://research.stlouisfed.org/fred2/), WSJ .com, and Bloomberg.com. Yields on STRIPS are available at WSJ.com.

5. See, for example, Brealey, Myers, and Allen (2008); Titman and Martin (2007), pp. 144–45; or Ross, Westerfield, and Jaffe (2008), pp. 271–73.

6. These include Bloomberg, Yahoo! Finance, and Value Line, among others.

7. For a more detailed exposition, including the possibility of risky debt, see Koller, Goedhart, and Wessels (2005), Appendix D.

8. We could also value the equity directly using the cash flows to stockholders. The correct discount rate is the cost of equity, r_E, which can be computed using the CAPM and β_E for the new venture. We can estimate β_E using the weighted average β_A and values for E and V in Eq. (10.5) specific to the new venture.

9. You can use the RADR approach to verify that this is the correct value. Suppose you are offered the right to acquire the expected $260,000 cash flow for $173,077 and calculate the holding-period return on that basis; you will get the same PV. If you try it using $232,143, you will get a different answer. You can also use Eq. (10.7) to ascertain that the true required rate for the project is 50 percent instead of the 12 percent we computed earlier and that the returns beta is 7.15 instead of the 1.23 we computed earlier.

10. There is both empirical and theoretical support for assuming independence of the time series.

11. Under these assumptions, the cost of equity will be the same as the required return on assets, since without leverage, β_E and β_A are the same.

References and Additional Reading

Black, E. 2003. "Usefulness of Financial Statement Components in Valuation: An Examination of Start-Up and Growth Firms." *Venture Capital: An International Journal of Entrepreneurial Finance*5 :47–69.

Brealey, R., S. Myers, and F. Allen. 2008. *Principles of Corporate Finance.* 8th ed. New York: McGraw-Hill Irwin.

Copeland, T., T. Koller, and J. Murrin. 2000. *Valuation: Measuring and Managing the Value of Companies.* 3rd ed. New York: John Wiley & Sons.

Damodaran, A. 1994. *Damodaran on Valuation: Security Analysis for Investment and Corporate Finance*. New York: John Wiley & Sons.

DeAngelo, H., and R. Masulis. 1980. "Optimal Capital Structure under Corporate Taxation." *Journal of Financial Economics*8 :5–29.

Fama, E., and K. French. 2002. "The Equity Premium." *Journal of Finance* 47: 637–59.

Fernandez, P. 2009. "Market Risk Premium Used in 2008 by Professors: A Survey with 1,400 Answers." SSRN working paper. Available at http://papers.ssrn.com/sol3/papers.cfm?abstract_id=1344209.

Graham, J. R., and C. R. Harvey. 2007. "The Equity Risk Premium in January 2007: Evidence from the Global CFO Outlook Survey." *ICFAI Journal of Financial Risk Management* 9:46–61.

Kaplan, P. D., and J. D. Peterson. 1998. "Full Information Industry Betas." *Financial Management* 27:85–93.

Kerins, F., J. K. Smith, and R. L. Smith. 2004. "Opportunity Cost of Capital for Venture Capital Investors and Entrepreneurs." *Journal of Financial and Quantitative Analysis*3 9:385–405.

Koller, T., M. Goedhart, and D. Wessels. 2005. *Valuation: Measuring and Managing the Value of Companies*. New York: John Wiley & Sons.

Miller, M. H. 1977. "Debt and Taxes." *Journal of Finance*3 2:261–76.

Robichek, A. A., and S. C. Myers. 1966. "Conceptual Problems in the Use of Risk-Adjusted Discount Rates." *Journal of Finance* 21:727–30.

Ross, S. A., R. Westerfield, and J. Jaffe. 2008. *Corporate Finance*. 8th ed. New York: McGraw-Hill Irwin.

Scherlis, D., and W. Sahlman. 1987. "Method of Valuing High-Risk, Long-Term Investments." Harvard Business School Note 9-288-006. Boston: Harvard Business Publishing.

Sick, G. 1986. "A Certainty-Equivalent Approach to Capital Budgeting." *Financial Management* 15 (4): 23–32.

Titman, S., and J. D. Martin. 2007. *Valuation: The Art and Science of Corporate Investment Decisions*. London: Pearson/Addison-Wesley.

Welch, I. 2000. "Views of Financial Economists on the Equity Premium and Other Issues." *Journal of Business* 73 (4): 501–37, with 2009 update (http://www.ivo-welch.info/academics/equpdate-results2009.html).

CHAPTER 11

THE ENTREPRENEUR'S PERSPECTIVE ON VALUE

There are only two types of people in the world, the efficient and the inefficient.

George Bernard Shaw

In this chapter, we make the transition from valuation to contracting. In Chapters 9 and 10, we considered valuation from the perspective of well-diversified investors. We now examine valuation from the perspective of the entrepreneur. The difference in perspectives is an important aspect of the contracting challenges we address in the next two chapters. A unique challenge to new venture contracting is that in many cases the entrepreneur necessarily invests a large fraction of her financial wealth and human capital in the venture. The resulting underdiversification implies that the entrepreneur faces a different risk-return tradeoff than does a well-diversified investor. The difference in perspectives that arises from underdiversification is the focus of this chapter. We begin by estimating the magnitude of the entrepreneur's underdiversification and then assess its impact on the required return for and valuation of investment in a new venture.

The entrepreneur's decision to pursue (and invest in) a new venture is among the most difficult decisions to make correctly. Yet research and books on entrepreneurial finance take the entrepreneur's investment decision as a forgone conclusion. A common perception is that the entrepreneur's investment problem is less a quantitative decision than a qualitative one, having to do with wanting to be one's own boss, one's lifestyle preferences, and one's tolerance for risk. This focus is too narrow.

The entrepreneur's investment decision problem is fundamentally different from the investor's. Even though the underlying financial economic theory is the same, the opportunity cost of capital that is appropriate for the entrepreneur is different from that of the investor. Accordingly, underdiversification is an important reason why the value of the venture is different for the entrepreneur than for an investor. This is true even if the parties hold identical financial claims.

The entrepreneur should take a separate look at value for three compelling reasons:

1. *Underdiversification causes differences in required rates of return.* A competitive capital market determines the opportunity cost of capital for well-diversified investors. In that market, investors vie to participate in ventures based on their assessments of risk and expected return. Because many investors in the venture financing market are well diversified, investors must base their valuations on nondiversifiable risk. Because an entrepreneur is necessarily sacrificing some ability to diversify, the entrepreneur's opportunity cost of capital is higher than that of investors. Thus, if the entrepreneur and investors agree about a venture's expected cash flows and risk and hold identical claims, the entrepreneur's underdiversification means that the investor will arrive at a higher valuation.

2. *Ownership claims of investors and entrepreneurs are not identical.* Investors often receive "sweeteners" such as options and preferences that make the deal more attractive. Sweeteners raise the value of an investor's ownership claims and therefore reduce the value of the entrepreneur's claim. For example, many investor claims are in the form of convertible preferred stock. Convertibility enables the investor to share in venture success, while preferred stock places the investor ahead of the entrepreneur if the venture fails and is liquidated.

   Because of sweeteners, an investor will accept a smaller fraction of ownership in exchange for a given level of investment. Other things equal, provisions that sweeten the deal for the investor make it less attractive for the entrepreneur. However, because of differences in diversification, a dollar's worth of benefit for the investor costs the entrepreneur less than a dollar's worth of value. Because the costs and benefits of different sweeteners vary, the entrepreneur needs to understand how sweetening affects the value of the deal.

3. *The parties may have different beliefs about expected performance and risk.* The entrepreneur and the investor are unlikely to agree about the risk and expected return of the venture. Often the entrepreneur is more optimistic. Differences in expectations about such things as development timing, achievable sales, and profit-

ability make contracting with investors more difficult. Clear understanding of the differences facilitates designing financing arrangements that both parties can accept, even if their expectations differ.

In this chapter, we focus on why the entrepreneur's underdiversification implies a higher required rate of return than that of the investor. Building on financial economic theory from Chapter 9 and the implementation principles of Chapter 10, we provide a valuation framework that addresses the entrepreneur's underdiversified risk. We rely on this framework in subsequent chapters that deal with financial contracting.

11.1   Opportunity Cost and Choosing Entrepreneurship

What drives the decision to become an entrepreneur? Opportunity cost is key to answering this question, along with related questions such as: Why, compared to in the United States, do greater percentages of the populations in Mexico and Korea, for example, engage in entrepreneurial activities?[1] Why do students drop out of college to start businesses, and why is interest in entrepreneurship relatively low for MBA students compared to undergraduates? Why is the probability of starting a new business in the United States positively related to wealth, especially for the top 10 percent of the wealth distribution? And why do entrepreneurs tend to be wealthier than employed workers over the entire range of incomes?

Research indicates that, in general (but not in every case), the decision to become an entrepreneur rests on rational assessments that individuals make based on two components of opportunity cost—the opportunity cost of their committed effort (their human capital) and the opportunity cost of their invested wealth (financial capital). At least intuitively, individuals try to compare the expected value of starting their own businesses with the value of the next best alternative, which for many is staying on the employment track.

The patterns of entrepreneurial activity described above are explained by two factors, both reflective of opportunity cost. First, in countries with fewer good employment opportunities, individuals are more likely to turn to self-employment out of necessity. In countries such as the United States, where numerous attractive career opportunities are usually available, there are fewer entrepreneurs as a percentage of the population than in countries with chronically limited employment opportunities. However, the opportunity cost of pursuing an entrepreneurial opportunity is not very high for a student, who can easily return to student status if the venture fails, or for an employee, who can quickly return to similar employment if the venture fails. Second, the ability to diversify financial assets can significantly reduce the entrepreneur's opportunity cost of capital and make entrepreneurship more attractive. This suggests that wealthy individuals are able to commit smaller fractions of total wealth to an entrepreneurial venture and thus are able to be better diversified. We demonstrate below that, other things being equal, greater wealth lowers the opportunity cost of becoming an entrepreneur.

Of course, factors other than opportunity cost of human capital and wealth also affect the decision to become an entrepreneur, such as a desire to be one's own boss or to pursue a particular lifestyle, as well as differences in risk tolerance. In this chapter, we set these other considerations aside in order to focus on opportunity cost.

Assessing opportunity cost is key to making value-maximizing decisions about starting and investing in new ventures. One way in which entrepreneurs can err in assessing the value of an opportunity is by not thinking clearly about the implications of underdiversification. Our goal in the first part of this chapter is to move beyond intuition and to analyze, at a conceptual level, how the risk of the venture and the opportunity costs associated with alternative scales of operation and financing structures affect the decision.

Adapting standard valuation methods to deal with the entrepreneur's underdiversification is challenging. To make the implications of the decision to become an entrepreneur clear, we need to make some simplifying assumptions that, while they may seem heroic, still produce good estimates of value.

As a means of assuring clear understanding, we provide formal analysis of the underlying foundations and derivations. To make application more practical, the chapter includes discussion of several shortcut approaches as well as a series of valuation templates that make the entrepreneur's valuation problem more tractable and intuitive. The templates integrate all of the underlying mathematics so that simply by specifying some fairly straightforward and standard assumptions, it is possible to value financial claims from the perspective of an underdiversified entrepreneur. The discussions of shortcuts are intended to provide broad guidance for thinking about the consequences of underdiversification and to do so in the framework of contracting between the entrepreneur and a prospective investor.

FIGURE **11.1**

Attributes of entrepreneurs: Evidence concerning their wealth, savings, and diversification

Researchers have examined the wealth attributes of entrepreneurs, along with their savings behavior and propensity to hold underdiversified portfolios. The research supports two propositions central to this chapter: (1) wealthy individuals can more easily justify becoming entrepreneurs because they are better able to diversify, and (2) entrepreneurs tend to invest little in riskless assets. In these studies, entrepreneurs generally are defined as those who report that they own one or more active businesses or those who report self-employment income. Hence, the numbers reflect both replicative and innovative entrepreneurs—ranging from someone who partners with a college friend to open an insurance agency to an inventor who holds a patent to a long-lasting battery and is seeking VC. Below, we report some "stylized facts" that have emerged from this literature. All findings are relative to nonentrepreneurs and are based on assets other than human capital.

Wealth

- Concentration of wealth (underdiversification) increases at higher levels of wealth and income (Gentry and Hubbard [2004]).

- Inheritance increases the probability of becoming an entrepreneur and remaining one (Holtz-Eakin, Joulfaian, and Rosen [1994a, b]; Hurst and Lusardi [2004]).

- Inability to attract outside funding creates a positive relationship between personal wealth and the choice to be an entrepreneur (Heaton and Lucas [2000]).

Savings and investment behavior

- Entrepreneurs have higher savings rates across age, income, and wealth groups (Gentry and Hubbard [2004]).

- Wealth-to-income ratios and savings-to-income ratios are higher for entrepreneurs (Gentry and Hubbard [2004]).

- Saving and investment decisions are interdependent (Evans and Javonovic [1989]; Gentry and Hubbard [2004]; Holtz-Eakin, Joulfaian, and Rosen [1994a, b]).

- The reasons for reliance on the entrepreneur's own wealth include asymmetric information about the value of the venture and moral hazard problems in financing (Evans and Javonovic [1989]).

Portfolio diversification

- Entrepreneurs' portfolios are less well diversified than those of nonentrepreneurs. They hold less wealth in liquid assets, bonds, public equity, and housing; they hold more wealth in business assets and nonresidential real estate (Gentry and Hubbard [2004]; Heaton and Lucas [2000]).

- Entrepreneurial investment is extremely concentrated. About 75 percent of all private equity is owned by households for whom it constitutes at least half of their net worth excluding human capital (Moskowitz and Vissing-Jorgensen [2002]).

- Portfolios of entrepreneurs become less diversified over time (Gentry and Hubbard [2004]).

- Wealthy entrepreneurs choose to hold portfolios that are undiversified, with the bulk of their assets held within active businesses. Entrepreneurs borrow more heavily than nonentrepreneurs (Gentry and Hubbard [2004]).

- Entrepreneurs can benefit "by issuing risky debt and using the proceeds to reduce their equity stake in the firm" (Heaton and Lucas [2000]).

11.2   The Entrepreneur as an Underdiversified Investor

Often, an entrepreneur must commit most of her time, at least for a few years, as well as a substantial fraction of her financial capital to the venture. As a result, the entrepreneur necessarily bears not only the non-diversifiable risk of the venture but also the total risk. In a competitive capital market, investors cannot expect compensation for bearing diversifiable risk. But this proposition assumes that the asset under consideration is a market asset that is equally available to all investors and that the investor is free to diversify broadly to mitigate unique, asset-specific risk.

A new venture, in contrast, is a private asset, and the entrepreneur can only capture the value of the opportunity by investing a significant portion of her own financial and/or human capital. This is different from investment by a public company, where financing is raised in a capital market from investors who can diversify easily. It is different, as well, from investment in the venture by a third party, such as a VC fund. The fund manager is acting on behalf of its LPs, who normally are well-diversified institutions or individuals wealthy enough to be well diversified even with their investments in a given VC fund.

The focus on total risk as a determinant of the entrepreneur's required rate of return is appropriate in part because entrepreneurial ventures are not market assets. We assume throughout that the venture under consideration is specific to the entrepreneur and cannot be duplicated easily by others.

To illustrate the differences between a well-diversified investor and the entrepreneur, we begin with an example. Consider an individual who has total wealth of $300,000, which includes both financial and human capital. For now, we set aside the question of how to value human capital and make the simplifying assumption that any portion of total wealth that is not invested in the venture can be invested in a diversified market portfolio.[2]

The entrepreneur is considering whether to invest one-third of her total wealth ($100,000) in a venture that will pay off in one year. Excluding the entrepreneur's salary, there are three equally likely payoffs on her $100,000 investment, as shown:

Scenario	Probability	Year 1 payoff	Return
Success	1/3	$200,000	100%
Likely	1/3	$125,000	25%
Failure	1/3	$53,000	−47%

Using the methodology from Chapter 10 and the required investment of $100,000, we can estimate the expected return and standard deviation of returns on the actual investment as 26 percent and 60 percent, respectively. The 60 percent standard deviation represents the total risk of the new venture. We assume a 4 percent risk-free rate, an expected return on the market of 12 percent, a standard deviation of market returns of 15 percent, and a correlation coefficient of the venture's returns with the market of 0.5. We can now estimate the venture's beta:

$$\beta_j = \frac{\rho_{r_j,r_M}\sigma_j}{\sigma_M} = \frac{0.5 \times 0.60}{0.15} = 2.0$$

With this beta, the CAPM return that a well-diversified investor would require in exchange for investing in the new venture is 20 percent:

$$r_j = r_F + \beta_j(r_M - r_F) = 4\% + 2.0(12\% - 4\%) = 20\%$$

However, based on the opportunity cost of bearing risk, considering her inability to fully diversify, the entrepreneur should not settle for a 20 percent return. With one-third of her total wealth in the venture, the entrepreneur is less diversified than the investor and therefore faces more risk.

Suppose the entrepreneur were to use leverage to achieve the same level of risk by investing only in the market portfolio. Her expected return would be higher than the 20 percent required by a diversified investor who held an unlevered position in the market.

We can use opportunity cost reasoning to compute the entrepreneur's required rate of return for investing in the new venture. We start by considering the standard deviation of the entrepreneur's portfolio, which (we assume) is divided between the new venture and the market. The standard deviation of a portfolio of two risky assets is calculated as:

$$\sigma_{\text{port}} = \sqrt{x_M^2\sigma_M^2 + x_P^2\sigma_P^2 + 2x_Mx_P\rho_{M,P}\sigma_M\sigma_P} \qquad (11.1)$$

The variables x_M and x_P are the value weights of total risky investments in the market and the project, respectively, where the weights sum to 100 percent. The variable $\rho_{M,P}$ is the correlation coefficient between the market and the project. In our example, the weights in the market and the venture are 2/3 and 1/3, respectively, which yields a portfolio standard deviation of 26.5 percent:

$$\sigma_{\text{port}} = \sqrt{(2/3)^20.15^2 + (1/3)^20.60^2 + 2(2/3)(1/3)(0.5)(0.15)(0.60)}$$
$$= 0.265 \quad \text{or} \quad 26.5\%$$

The following formula allows us to calculate a portfolio's required return, using the total risk of the portfolio as compared to the market:

$$r_{Port} = r_F + (\sigma_{Port}/\sigma_M)RP_M \qquad (11.2)$$

Using the CAPM-based approach, the entrepreneur's required return on her risky portfolio is

$$r_{Port} = r_F + (\sigma_{Port}/\sigma_M)(r_M - r_F) = 4\% + (26.5\%/15\%)(12\% - 4\%) = 18.1\%$$

Now that we have the required return on the portfolio, we can use the fact that the required return on the portfolio is equal to the weighted average of the required return on the project and the required return on the market. That is,

$$r_{port} = x_P r_P + x_M r_M \qquad (11.3)$$

Because we know everything except the required return on the project, we can rearrange to solve for r_P, the project required return:

$$r_P = \frac{r_{port} - x_M r_M}{x_{port}} = \frac{18.1\% - (2/3)(12\%)}{(1/3)} = 30.3\%$$

So the opportunity cost of investing one-third of total wealth in the new venture is a 30.3 percent return. This is the return the entrepreneur would need in order to forgo an investment in the market portfolio that was leveraged to achieve the same total risk as the entrepreneur's portfolio. The entrepreneur's required return for the project is significantly higher than the 20 percent required by a diversified investor, and also higher than the expected project return of 26 percent. We can conclude that if the entrepreneur would have to invest one-third of total wealth in the venture, the NPV of the investment would be negative.

This example makes clear that the entrepreneur's required return, even with less than a full commitment of wealth to the new venture, is substantially higher than the return required by a diversified investor.

To gain further perspective, the "Base case" curve in Figure 11.2a illustrates how the entrepreneur's cost of capital increases as the fraction of wealth invested in the venture increases. As the fraction approaches zero, the entrepreneur's cost of capital approaches 20 percent, the same as the cost of capital for a well-diversified investor. At 100 percent invested in the venture, it is 36 percent.

The uppermost curve in Figure 11.2a illustrates how the relation shifts if total risk changes. For "High total risk," the standard deviation of venture returns is increased from 60 percent to 80 percent, with the beta unchanged (implying that the correlation coefficient has declined to offset the increase in total risk). The "Low correlation with market"

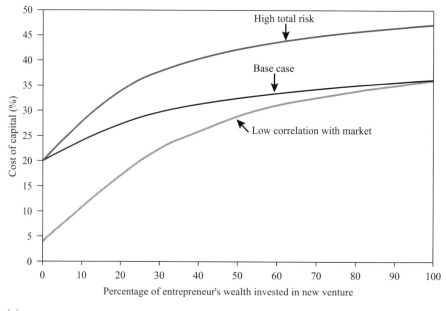

(a)

Underdiversification premium of cost of capital

Weight (%)	Base case	High total risk	Low correlation
0	0.0	0.0	0.0
10	4.3	8.5	6.8
20	7.4	14.2	13.3
30	9.7	17.9	18.4
40	11.4	20.5	22.2
50	12.7	22.3	25.0
60	13.6	23.6	27.1
70	14.4	24.6	28.8
80	15.0	25.5	30.1
90	15.6	26.1	31.1
100	16.0	26.7	32.0

(b)

FIGURE **11.2**

How venture risk and diversification affect the entrepreneur's cost of capital

Panel (a) shows how diversification and risk affect required return. If a venture is undertaken as a full commitment (100 percent of risk capital invested), required return is determined by total risk. If a trivial fraction of risk capital is invested, required return depends only on the systematic risk. The higher the total risk, the higher the required return, and the lower the correlation with the market, the lower the required return. The "Base case" venture has total risk that is four times as high as the market and a beta of 2.0. The risk-free rate is 4 percent, and the market risk premium is 8 percent. The "High total risk" venture has total risk that is more than five times as high as the market but a beta the same as the base case. The "Low correlation with market" venture has the same total risk as the base case but a beta of 0.0. Panel (b) shows underdiversification premia for ventures with risk characteristics similar to each case.

curve illustrates how the relation shifts if the correlation between the venture and the market is reduced to zero but total risk is not changed. In the CAPM framework, this zero-beta project would result in the required return for a fully diversified investor being equal to the risk-free rate.

Figure 11.2b describes the effect of underdiversification on cost of capital in terms of an underdiversification premium that can be added to the standard cost of capital that is estimated based on the CAPM. At 30 percent of risk capital in the venture, the underdiversification premium for the base case (beta = 2.0 and standard deviation = 60 percent) is 9.7 percent, based on the annual numbers; so the entrepreneur would require a 29.7 percent return, versus 20 percent for the investor. The premium is higher if beta is lower or if the standard deviation of returns is higher. Thus, if beta and the standard deviation of the venture can be estimated using public data, such as the stock price history for a comparable public company, the entrepreneur's underdiversification premium can be estimated as a simple adjustment to cost of capital. We return to this point later in the chapter.[3]

In summary, by controlling the fraction of wealth invested in the venture, the entrepreneur has a degree of control over her cost of capital. An entrepreneur who acts as the sole investor effectively chooses the required rate of return along with venture scale. The larger the scale, the larger is the fraction of the entrepreneur's capital that must be invested, and therefore the higher is the required rate of return. In Chapter 12, we explore how the decision to bring in investors can affect the entrepreneur's required rate of return.

How Ability to Diversify Affects Cost of Capital

Figure 11.3 makes use of the above example to illustrate how differences in abilities to diversify between entrepreneurs and well-diversified investors result in different required rates of return and different investment decisions. Given the venture's standard deviation of 60 percent, an entrepreneur who must make a full commitment requires a return of 36 percent. This is what the capital market line (CML) in the figure implies. However, given that the venture beta is 2.0, a diversified investor requires only 20 percent. The horizontal line at 20 percent represents the investor's required return for any venture having a beta of 2.0.

Now consider three ventures that differ in expected return but have total risk with a standard deviation of 60 percent and beta risk of 2.0. Project A in the figure has an expected return of 18 percent. Both the entrepreneur and a diversified investor would reject it because the ex-

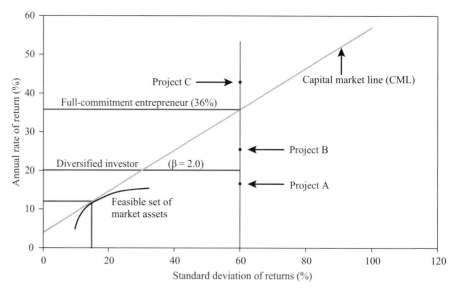

FIGURE **11.3**

The capital market line and required rates of return for diversified and undiversified investors

The capital market line (CML) represents the opportunities available by investing in the market portfolio and the risk-free asset. The risk-free rate is 4 percent, and the market risk premium is 8 percent. Consider a project with a standard deviation of returns of 60 percent and a beta of 2.0. A diversified investor values the project according to its beta and requires a return of 20 percent. An undiversified investor values the project based on its total risk, which is four times that of the market, and requires a return of 36 percent.

pected return is not sufficient to compensate for either market risk or total risk. Project B has a 24 percent expected return. A diversified investor would accept the project, since it is above his 20 percent required return, but the entrepreneur would not. Finally, Project C has a 42 percent expected return. Either party would accept this project, but it would have a higher NPV for the diversified investor.

More generally, Eq. (11.4) is the expression for the entrepreneur's RADR valuation based on the discount rate in Eq. (11.2):

$$PV_t = \frac{C_t}{1 + r_F + (\sigma_P^E/\sigma_M)RP_M} \qquad (11.4)$$

where PV_t is the PV of the time t cash flow. All variables are measured over the holding period.

Suppose it is possible to invest $1 million in a computer-aided learning venture with risk characteristics as described above. The venture would pay off at the end of five years. An entrepreneur who commits all of her wealth to the venture and requires an expected 36 percent rate of return per year needs an expected cash return of at least $4.653 million in Year 5 (i.e., $1 million $\times$ 1.36^5). A diversified investor requires an expected cash return of only $2.488 million (i.e., $1 million $\times$ 1.20^5).

The following table shows the terminal cash flows of the three ventures in Figure 11.3, assuming an initial investment of $1 million and five years to harvest. It also compares the PVs and NPVs by discounting the cash flows at the entrepreneur's and the investor's costs of capital. Neither party would want to invest in projects like A since NPV is always negative. Projects like B are attractive to the investor but not to the entrepreneur. Projects like C are attractive to both but are more valuable to the investor.

Comparisons of estimated project values for entrepreneurs making full commitments and for well-diversified investors

	Project A	Project B	Project C
Project returns			
Annualized rate of return	16%	24%	42%
Terminal value (Year 5)	$2,100,342	$2,931,625	$5,773,534
Entrepreneur making a full commitment (required rate = 36%)			
Present value	$451,435	$630,106	$1,240,930
Net present value	($548,565)	($369,894)	$240,930
Well-diversified investor (required rate = 20%)			
Present value	$844,080	$1,178,154	$2,320,254
Net present value	($155,920)	$178,154	$1,320,254

NOTE: *Beta = 2.0; σ = 60%; initial investment of $1 million.*

Factors That Offset the Entrepreneur's Cost-of-Capital Disadvantage

Based on the preceding discussion, the entrepreneur's cost-of-capital disadvantage may seem hopeless. In a competitive market for launching new ventures, we should find that, because of their lower cost of capital, public corporations can spend more resources searching for viable ventures than can entrepreneurs and that corporations can legitimately undertake ventures before they reach the threshold of economic profitability for underdiversified entrepreneurs.

Offsetting their cost-of-capital advantage, however, corporations face unique challenges when they seek to engage in entrepreneurship. As discussed earlier in the book, because of internal equity concerns, the maximum reward a corporation can offer to an employee for perceiving and pursuing entrepreneurial opportunities is likely to be less than what an individual can realize acting alone. Consequently, corporate employees with good new venture opportunities frequently jump ship to pursue them on their own. As a result, the venture cash flows that are available to entrepreneurs may not be equally available to large corporations. Hence, a tradeoff exists between some of the organizational efficiencies and expediencies of stand-alone entrepreneurial ventures and the cost-of-capital advantage of a public corporation.

This tradeoff gives insight into the kinds of ventures that are likely to be pursued by corporations rather than individuals.

- The larger the scale of the venture and the more complex the organization that is required to undertake it, the more likely the venture is to be pursued by a corporation.
- The higher the level of total risk, as compared to beta risk, the greater the cost-of-capital advantage of the diversified investor, and hence the more likely the venture is to be pursued by a public corporation.
- With a longer expected holding period between investment and harvesting, the diversified investor's cost-of-capital advantage compounds, making corporate entrepreneurship more likely.

There are additional reasons why, in the market for new venture investing, large public corporations and diversified investors do not entirely displace entrepreneurs. As one example, for any given venture investors may not perceive the opportunity or may be less optimistic than the entrepreneur. In such cases, the entrepreneur may need to invest more personal resources because money from diversified investors is not available, or the entrepreneur may need to make a larger initial investment to help convince prospective investors of the merits of the venture.

Defining the Entrepreneur's Commitment to a Venture

While the previous example illustrates how the entrepreneur's underdiversification affects required returns, we intentionally glossed over issues related to human capital. We now need a more comprehensive measure of the entrepreneur's wealth that includes the value of human capital. Much of the entrepreneur's investment is likely to be in the form of effort (i.e., human capital) devoted to the venture. Effort has an opportunity cost; the entrepreneur could have devoted the effort to a different occupation than the venture. Accordingly, the entrepreneur's wealth includes both present financial capital and the PV of the entrepreneur's human capital in its highest-valued alternative use.

Three issues are of concern:

1. How can we estimate the value of the entrepreneur's human capital?
2. How can we estimate the value of the human capital that the entrepreneur commits to the venture?
3. What should we assume about the risk and return to human capital that is not invested in the venture?

We address the first two questions in this subsection and offer some suggestions for making reasonable assumptions about risk and return.

As to the first, we use a conventional approach to valuing the prospective entrepreneur's human capital: it is the PV of expected future earnings in the highest-valued use other than the venture under consideration. Often we can derive a reasonable estimate of the value of human capital by using the expression for a growing annuity:

$$PV_{comp} = \frac{C_1}{r - g}\left(1 - \frac{(1 + g)^t}{(1 + r)^t}\right) \tag{11.5}$$

where PV_{comp} is the PV of future compensation over the entrepreneur's work life if the venture is not undertaken, C_1 is first-year annual compensation in the best alternative employment to the venture, g is the expected growth rate of compensation in that employment over the entrepreneur's work life, t is the expected number of years of work life remaining, and r is an estimate of the cost of capital for compensation given its riskiness.

Suppose we wish to value the human capital of a prospective entrepreneur whose expected salary next year is $150,000. If the individual decides not to pursue the venture, his salary is expected to grow at a rate of 5 percent per year for his remaining 15-year career. These assumptions are sufficient to enable us to project future earnings—but what about the discount rate? The correct rate depends on the risk of the individual's employment. For our purposes, it is sufficient to use a low rate if employment is very secure and a significantly higher rate if employment is very risky. For this example, we assume that employment is about as risky as investing in the market and therefore use a 12 percent rate. The resulting estimate of the PV of human capital, using the formula for a growing annuity, is $1.329 million.

$$PV_{comp} = \frac{C_1}{r - g}\left(1 - \frac{(1 + g)^t}{(1 + r)^t}\right) = \frac{\$150,000}{0.12 - 0.05}\left(1 - \frac{(1 + 0.05)^{15}}{(1 + 0.12)^{15}}\right) = \$1,328,973$$

The value of the entrepreneur's investment in the venture can be approached in a similar way. For example, if the individual commits one year to the venture and works without compensation, then the entrepreneur loses the first year of income in the above calculation. Its PV is an investment of human capital in the venture. The commitment may be offset partly by a salary paid by the venture, which would reduce the effective investment. Consistently, there is empirical evidence that company founders are paid less than nonfounder peers.[4] In addition, forsaking one's current career for a new venture would probably reduce prospects for starting salary and subsequent raises upon returning to the workforce. Finally, in our example, the commitment to the new venture is for only one year, which is likely shorter than the commitment most entrepreneurs make.

Given that total wealth includes both financial and human capital, we define the entrepreneur's commitment to a venture in terms of the fraction of total wealth committed. A full commitment would mean that the entrepreneur devotes all financial and human capital to the venture. In practice, no entrepreneur can make a full commitment. Doing so would require the entrepreneur to irrevocably commit to work on the venture for the rest of his work life, no matter how unsuccessful the venture might prove to be. It also would require, for example, that all existing retirement savings be invested in the venture, something that normally is not possible. Thus, we are more concerned with investment decisions involving substantial partial commitments (i.e., neither a full commitment nor the commitment of a well-diversified investor).

Scenario 1. We start by considering the commitment of the "typical" entrepreneur. If we define entrepreneurship broadly as self-employed individuals, the population includes small businesses with negligible potential for growth, as well as service professionals such as many accountants and lawyers. Numerous studies and surveys based on this definition have shown the typical entrepreneur to be a married male in his 40s with a college degree or some college experience.[5]

With this picture in mind, we can make some reasonable assumptions about the potential entrepreneur and his level of commitment to a new venture. Assume he is 45 years old with a current salary (including benefits) of $150,000 and net worth of $2.0 million, including $800,000 of liquid assets and $1.2 million in retirement savings. He is planning to retire at age 60, which means that he has 15 years left to work. He is considering resigning to pursue a new venture that would require a five-year commitment at two-thirds of his current salary ($100,000) plus a financial investment of $400,000.

To measure the entrepreneur's commitment, we need to estimate what percentage of his total current wealth will be invested in the venture. This investment is composed of two parts: the direct financial investment of $400,000 plus the opportunity cost of accepting a reduced salary for five years. Earlier we estimated the human capital wealth of this individual if he continues in his current job to be $1.329 million. Adding this to his financial net worth of $2.0 million yields estimated total current wealth of $3.3 million.

Undertaking the new venture means a $100,000 salary for the next five years. We will assume that after five years, if the venture fails or if he exits, he can return to employment in his prior field but at a starting salary equal to his current pay of $150,000. And after he reenters the workforce, his salary will only grow at 4 percent annually for the remaining 10 years. Thus, if he decides to pursue the venture and it fails, the PV of his future earnings is:

$$PV_{comp} = \frac{\$100,000}{0.12 - 0.0}\left(1 - \frac{(1 + 0.00)^5}{(1 + 0.12)^5}\right) + \frac{\left[\frac{\$150,000}{0.12 - 0.04}\left(1 - \frac{(1 + 0.04)^{10}}{(1 + 0.12)^{10}}\right)\right]}{(1 + 0.12)^5}$$
$$= \$917,337$$

The first term represents the PV of the five-year, $100,000 new venture salary, and the second term is the PV of $150,000 starting in Year 6 and then growing 4 percent annually for 10 years discounted to today. The difference of $411,636 ($1,328,973 − $917,337) represents the implicit investment in the form of reduced compensation if the venture is undertaken. We add to this the $400,000 cash investment, making the potential entrepreneur's total investment $811,636, or approximately 24 percent of his total wealth of $3.3 million. For a lower salary differential, a smaller investment in the venture, or higher retirement savings, the percentage committed to the venture would be lower. With more information about the risk and return of the venture, we could use Figures 11.2 and 11.3 to estimate the entrepreneur's required return based on his 24 percent commitment.

Scenario 2. An entrepreneur has just completed college and has an opportunity to begin working in a corporate position with a starting salary (including benefits) of $50,000. Her salary is expected to grow at a rate of 5 percent per year on average, and her expected work life is 40 years. The rate of future salary growth is subject to the same degree of risk as in the previous example. The entrepreneur has no savings or other financial assets of any consequence. The venture would require a five-year commitment during which her expected salary would only be $25,000 per year. Should the venture fail, the entrepreneur could take on other employment, with a starting salary of $50,000 in Year 6, with the same average annual growth of 5 percent for the remaining 35 years of her work life.

The entrepreneur's commitment is measured against the opportunity cost of accepting employment immediately. Using Eq. (11.5), we can find the PV of her employment opportunity, using $50,000 as the Time 1 salary, 12 percent as the required rate of return, 5 percent as the growth rate, and 40 years as the horizon:

$$PV_{comp} = \frac{\$50,000}{0.12 - 0.05}\left(1 - \frac{(1 + 0.05)^{40}}{(1 + 0.12)^{40}}\right) = \$660,245$$

This is also her total wealth, since all she has is human capital. Should the entrepreneur decide to undertake the venture, the calculation becomes:

$$PV_{comp} = \frac{\$25,000}{0.12 - 0.0}\left(1 - \frac{(1 + 0.0)^5}{(1 + 0.12)^5}\right) + \frac{\left[\frac{\$50,000}{0.12 - 0.05}\left(1 - \frac{(1 + 0.05)^{35}}{(1 + 0.12)^{35}}\right)\right]}{(1 + 0.12)^5}$$
$$= \$453,082$$

The PV of the entrepreneur's current commitment to the venture is the difference of $207,163 ($660,245 − $453,082), or 31 percent of the total PV of the entrepreneur's human capital. The assumptions in this example are very different from those in Scenario 1, where the salary and tangible wealth were higher, the work life shorter, and a significant cash investment was required of the entrepreneur. Yet the commitments in both cases yield reasonably similar percentages of investment. The percentage in Scenario 2 would be lower with a shorter commitment to the venture or if the entrepreneur had financial assets that were not being committed.

Generalizations. The previous scenarios represent two very different situations but yield similar results in terms of the fraction of present-valued wealth invested by the entrepreneur. Given the specifics of the examples, they also represent reasonable upper bounds on how high the entrepreneur's fractional commitment of wealth is likely to be, and they shed light on the kinds of factors that can be expected to affect the required rate of return.

The examples highlight the factors that affect the fraction of risk capital committed to a new venture. Generally, the fraction decreases as time to retirement increases; it decreases as the shortfall in compensation for involvement with the venture decreases compared to compensation in alternative employment; it increases with increases in the duration of commitment; and it decreases with the entrepreneur's long-run ability to maintain his or her level of earnings in alternative employment. The fraction of risk capital committed increases with commitment of financial capital to the venture and decreases as more financial capital is allocated to other investments.

A Shortcut for Estimating Wealth and Investment

Because the fraction of wealth committed to the venture is important to the entrepreneur's valuation and because calculating the human capital commitment can be tedious, we provide a template, Table 11.1, to streamline the calculation. In the table, "Valuation Template 3," we have assumed that an entrepreneur with a 40-year remaining work life is considering giving up current employment that pays a salary of $100,000 per year to commit three years to a venture that will pay only $40,000 each year. His salary, if he forgoes the venture, is expected to grow at a rate of about 5 percent per year, but the position is moderately risky, so that expected future earnings in that employment are discounted at 12 percent per year (similar to the prevailing market rate).

T|TABLE **11.1**   Valuation Template 3: Present value of the entrepreneur's wealth and commitment

Present value of total wealth	Inputs	Value
Years until expected retirement	40	
Current annual compensation	$100,000	
Expected growth rate of compensation	5.00%	
Cost of capital for compensation (based on risk)	12.00%	
Present value of earnings in alternative employment		**$1,320,490**
Other assets (savings, retirement savings, house, etc.)	$2,500,000	
Other liabilities (mortgage, etc.)	$1,000,000	
Net other assets		**$1,500,000**
Total wealth		**$2,820,490**
Commitment to venture		
Years committed to venture	3	
Starting annual compensation in venture	$40,000	
Growth in annual compensation in venture	0%	
Present value of annual compensation while in venture		$96,073
Starting compensation if venture is abandoned	$90,000	
Growth in compensation if venture is abandoned	5%	
Present value of compensation if venture is abandoned		$831,117
Present value of human capital if venture is pursued and abandoned		**$927,191**
Present value of human capital investment in venture		**$393,299**
Present value of other assets invested in venture	$200,000	
Entrepreneur's total investment in venture		**$593,299**
Total investment as a percentage of total wealth		**21.0%**

NOTE: *Shaded cells are inputs. See book website version of table for guidance on using this template.*

If the entrepreneur undertakes the venture and it fails, the entrepreneur will return to his alternative employment but at a starting salary of $90,000, about 10 percent lower than his current salary. He will get the expected 5 percent annual increases after returning to the workforce. The entrepreneur has also estimated the PVs of his other assets ($2.5 million) and liabilities ($1.0 million) and has estimated the value of assets other than human capital that he will commit to the venture ($200,000) if it is undertaken.

Based on the inputs that the entrepreneur has supplied, the table shows his human capital to be currently worth about $1.32 million and his total current wealth to be $2.82 million. Undertaking the venture would involve a human capital investment of $393,000. Combining this with his financial investment of $200,000, the entrepreneur would be committing $593,000 in total to the venture, or about 21 percent of his total wealth.

In case you are concerned about the discount rate assumption, it turns out that the estimate is not very sensitive to the assumption. Rates from 6 percent to 20 percent all yield about the same estimate of the entrepreneur's percentage commitment.

11.3   Valuing Partial-Commitment Investments

The entrepreneur's valuation problem is significantly more difficult than the investor's. However, we have already done much of the spadework in Chapters 9 and 10 to show you how to address it. Here we take up the remaining difficulties and demonstrate how to use the RADR and CEQ methods to value partial-commitment investments by underdiversified entrepreneurs. Every DCF approach requires an estimate of expected future cash flows. The CEQ method also requires an estimate of the standard deviation of cash flows. The discrete scenario and simulation approaches discussed earlier in the book can be used to estimate both the expected cash flow and cash flow uncertainty.

Using RADR to Estimate Value

To simplify the entrepreneur's valuation problem, we assume that a partially diversified entrepreneur can allocate wealth between only two investment opportunities: the new venture and a market index. Of course, the restriction to two risky assets does not square with reality; while the entrepreneur's human capital can be invested in the venture, it cannot be converted to a financial investment in the market index. However, the additional complexity of treating human capital as a third risky asset does not qualitatively affect any of our conclusions and is unlikely to have an important effect on the estimated value of the venture to the entrepreneur. Hence, we limit the presentation to the two-asset assumption.

As shown in Figure 11.2, the entrepreneur's cost of capital for the venture should reflect attained diversification. To summarize the approach presented earlier in the chapter, the required return for a partial commitment can be estimated by the RADR method as follows:

Step 1. Estimate the standard deviation of holding-period returns of the entrepreneur's total portfolio of risky assets (i.e., the venture and the market portfolio) (Eq. 11.1).

Step 2. Use the CML to estimate the required return on the portfolio (Eq. 11.2).

Step 3. Set the portfolio required return equal to the weighted average of the required returns on the market and the venture (Eq. 11.3) and solve for the venture required return.

As always, the RADR method is problematic because it requires that you search simultaneously for PV and the equilibrium standard deviation of holding-period returns. However, because the entrepreneur can partially diversify, the focus of the search is on the entrepreneur's portfolio rather than just on the venture.

The RADR approach works well as long as it is possible to specify *ex ante* assumptions about correlation and equilibrium standard deviation of holding-period returns for a well-diversified investor. The standard finance approach for *ex ante* specification is to rely on public market data for comparable firms for this type of information.

Using CEQ to Estimate Value

For new ventures, there often is no good public market analogy. In such cases, the CEQ method is easier and likely to yield more reliable results.[6]

Valuation of the venture by the CEQ method involves two steps:

Step 1. Use the CEQ method to value the entrepreneur's portfolio.

Step 2. Find the value of the venture by deducting the investment in the market portfolio from total portfolio value.

The first step is accomplished by using Eq. (11.6), the CEQ form of the DCF valuation model, applied to valuing the entrepreneur's portfolio of risky investments.

$$PV_{\text{port}} = \frac{C_{\text{port}} - \dfrac{\sigma_{C_{\text{port}}}}{\sigma_M} RP_M}{1 + r_F} \tag{11.6}$$

In Eq. (11.6), for convenience, we drop the time subscripts. The expression requires an estimate of the expected harvest-date cash return of the portfolio, C_{port}, and the standard deviation of the portfolio cash flow, $\sigma_{C_{\text{port}}}$. Given that you already have developed an estimate of the expected harvest-date cash flow and cash flow standard deviation of the venture, Eq. (11.7) gives the expected harvest-date cash flow of the portfolio, and Eq. (11.8) gives the standard deviation of the portfolio's cash flow.

$$C_{\text{port}} = C_P + w_M(1 + r_M) \tag{11.7}$$

$$\sigma_{C_{\text{port}}} = \sqrt{\sigma_{C_P}^2 + (\sigma_M w_M)^2 + 2\rho_{P,M}\sigma_{C_P}(\sigma_M w_M)} \tag{11.8}$$

The expected cash return of the entrepreneur's portfolio is the sum of the expected cash return from investing in the venture and the expected cash return from the investment in the market. In Eq. (11.7), we compute the expected cash return for investing in the market index as 1 plus the expected rate of return, r_M, times the dollar value of the investment, w_M. The dollar investment in the market is the PV of the entrepreneur's total wealth (including human capital) minus the PV of financial wealth and human capital investment in the venture. The standard deviation of the entrepreneur's portfolio cash flows is computed in Eq. (11.8) similarly to the approach in Eq. (11.1) but based on dollar-valued investments instead of percentages of invested wealth.

For the second step, we use the CEQ value of the portfolio from Eq. (11.6). In Eq. (11.9), project value is found by deducting the investment in the market.

$$PV_P = PV_{\text{port}} - w_M \tag{11.9}$$

11.4   Implementation: Partial Commitment

Using Simulation to Forecast Expected Cash Flow and Risk✳

To focus on the essential issues of valuation, we abstract from the details of modeling the pro forma financial statements. They were covered fully in Chapters 6 and 7. Table 11.2 portrays a simple venture in which the entrepreneur makes an initial investment and receives an uncertain cash return in Year 6, when the investment is assumed to be sold. The

S|TABLE **11.2**   **New venture simulation model**

Forecast of market demand	Year						
	0	1	2	3	4	5	6
Potential sales	0.0	928.9	984.9	1,486.6	1,838.5	2,706.9	3,833.5

Forecast of revenue, profit, free cash flow, and cash flow to investor/entrepreneur at harvest

Sales	$0.0	$928.9	$984.9	$1,486.6	$1,838.5	$2,706.9	$3,833.5
Profit		($74.9)	($55.3)	$120.3	$243.5	$547.4	$941.7
Cash needed	$100.0	$464.4	$492.5	$743.3	$919.2	$1,353.5	$1,916.8
Initial investment	$2,000.0						
Free cash	$1,900.0	$1,536.7	$1,514.8	$1,444.9	$1,570.2	$1,746.2	$2,194.5
Out of cash test		0	0	0	0	0	0
Invest	$2,000.0						
Ending value	$8,600.8						
Ending cash	$2,194.5						
Total to investor/entrepreneur	**$10,795.3**						

NOTE: *All monetary values in $ thousands.*
ASSUMPTIONS:
Potential sales is a simulated series including a random starting value in Year 1, a random growth rate to Year 2.
Profit is 35 percent of sales, less a fixed cost of $400.
Cash needed is 50 percent of sales.
Free cash is prior year free cash, plus interest at 4 percent, plus prior year cash needed, plus profit minus current year cash needed.
If free cash is negative, the venture is terminated the next year.
Ending value is a multiple of Year 6 profit. The multiple is an increasing function of sales growth in the last two years.
Ending cash is Year 6 free cash and is assumed to be distributed to the entrepreneur.
Total to investor/entrepreneur is ending value plus ending cash.

spreadsheet is constructed so that the Year 6 cash flow includes continuing value as well as any accumulated free cash from the first six years of operation.

The table sets out the simulation model of pro forma cash flows of the venture. The values actually shown are from a single random iteration of the model.[7] The relatedness of cash flows over time is built into the model by making potential sales in each year depend on prior-year potential sales, plus a random growth component. Other assumptions are detailed in the table. We further simplify by assuming that operating cash flow and profit are equivalent.

In the table, the entrepreneur makes an initial investment of $2 million. Free cash is a balance that is computed each year as the balance from the previous year, plus interest computed at 4 percent (the risk-free rate), plus profit, and minus the year-to-year increase in cash needed. We simplify the valuation problem by assuming that cash is not distributed until Year 6. The six-year investment horizon is assumed to be long enough to enable the entrepreneur to harvest by selling or liquidating the venture.

We estimate value to the entrepreneur by assuming a hypothetical sale at the end of the explicit value period. At that point, the entrepreneur withdraws any free cash and sells the venture for an estimate of the Year 6 value based on its ability to generate cash flows after Year 6. The assumption that cash cannot be distributed early approximates reality, as early distributions of cash by new ventures are usually limited, and many ventures do not generate much free cash flow during the early stages. We assume that the entrepreneur sells the venture for a multiple of Year 6 profit; the specific multiple reflects the level of sales in Year 6 and the growth rate in the prior year. Thus, we have built into the multiplier the realistic assumption that ventures with high expected growth rates sell for higher multiples. The potential for failure and early liquidation is also incorporated in Table 11.2. This is done by assuming that if cash is not sufficient to meet interim financing needs, the residual cash balance is invested at the riskless rate until Year 6. Retaining the cash until Year 6 even in the event of failure is a convenient way to treat the venture as a one-period valuation problem (cash in at Time 0 and cash out at Year 6). By simulating the model, we were able to estimate that, for the $2 million investment at Time 0, the expected cash flow in Year 6 is $10,743, with a standard deviation of $5,527.

Valuing the Venture as a Partial Commitment

Suppose that undertaking the venture described in Table 11.2 does not require the entrepreneur's entire wealth; rather, the entrepreneur invests effort for the next few years and some financial capital in the venture. Specifically, to undertake the venture the entrepreneur would have to invest $2 million of financial capital from $6 million of total wealth.[8] Doing so would leave $4 million of financial and human capital to invest in a market index and result in 33 percent of her total wealth in the venture. As discussed earlier, we make the simplifying assumption that the remainder of the entrepreneur's capital (both financial and human) is invested in a market portfolio. To estimate the value of the venture as a partial commitment, we use the approach described in the previous section.

The analysis is summarized in Table 11.3, "Valuation Template 4," which can be modified to evaluate other choices of input variables.[9] The "Market information" panel contains details on market returns and risk. The Year 1 risk-free rate is 4 percent. Rates for longer holding periods are derived by compounding, so that the cumulative six-year risk-free rate is 26.53 percent. The annual market rate of 12.0 percent is compounded in the same manner. The market risk premium for the holding

TABLE **11.3**   Valuation Template 4: Valuation—Partial commitment of the entrepreneur

Market information	Annual	Holding period
Risk-free rate	4.00%	26.53%
Market rate	12.00%	97.38%
Market risk premium	8.00%	70.85%
Market variance	2.25%	13.50%
Market standard deviation	15.00%	36.74%
Correlation		0.2

Cash flows	Invest date	Harvest date
Years until harvest		6
Investment in project	$2,000	
Expected project cash flow		$10,743
Project standard deviation of cash flows		$5,527
Investment in market	$4,000	
Percentage of entrepreneur's total wealth invested in project	33.3%	
Expected market cash flow		$7,895
Market standard deviation of cash flows		$1,470
Expected portfolio cash flow	$6,000	$18,638
Portfolio standard deviation		$5,996

CAPM market value estimate (diversified investor)		
Portfolio present value		$10,806
Market investment		$4,000
Present value—project		**$6,806**
Net present value—project		**$4,806**
Project required return for diversified investor	7.90%	57.85%
Project equilibrium standard deviation of returns		81.21%
Project implied beta		0.44

CAPM private value estimate—partial-commitment entrepreneur		
Present value—portfolio		$5,592
Market investment		$4,000
Present value—project		**$1,592**
Net present value—project		**($408)**
Project required return for underdiversified investor	37.47%	574.90%
Equilibrium standard deviation of returns		347.22%

NOTE: *All monetary values in $ thousands.*

period is computed as the difference between the market rate and the risk-free rate. Market variance and market standard deviation are computed from the initial assumption that the market has a 15 percent standard deviation of annual returns and the assumption that market returns are uncorrelated over time. We also assume that the correlation between the venture and the market is 0.2.

The "Cash flows" panel includes not only the venture-specific information but also the expected cash flow and standard deviation of cash flows for investing in the market and for the portfolio that combines the two investments. The expected market cash flow is computed by applying the market rate of return to the $4 million investment in the market. The standard deviation of cash flows for the investment in the market is computed by multiplying the market standard deviation in percentage terms by the $4 million investment in the market. The project expected cash flow and standard deviation are determined by simulating the model in Table 11.2, as discussed above. The expected portfolio cash flow and portfolio standard deviation values are computed using Eqs. (11.7) and (11.8). In the "CAPM market value estimate" panel, we show the PV of the project cash flows as $6.806 million, which yields an NPV of $4.806 million after subtracting the $2 million investment. For a diversified investor in the venture, the annual required return is 7.9 percent.

In the "CAPM private value estimate—partial-commitment entrepreneur" panel, we value the entrepreneur's investment in the new venture using the CEQ form of the CAPM-based model, Eq. (11.6). Under that approach, the entrepreneur's total portfolio is worth $5.592 million in PV. To find the value of the venture, we subtract the $4 million value of the market index. The resulting estimate of venture PV is $1.592 million, or a negative NPV of $0.408 million based on the entrepreneur's $2 million investment. With this level of partial diversification, the entrepreneur's cost of capital is 37.5 percent, and the project is worth much less to the entrepreneur than to a well-diversified investor.

Wealth, Diversification, and Venture Value

Calculations aside, the entrepreneur's required return declines as the fraction of risk capital invested in the venture declines. If the entrepreneur were to invest a trivial fraction of total wealth in the venture, the required return would drop to 7.9 percent, the same as for a well-diversified investor. Using the spreadsheet in Table 11.3, with some trial and error you could determine that the venture would have a zero NPV at a 32.3 percent discount rate, which corresponds to 27.2 percent of wealth being invested, somewhat less than the current level. If the cost of the venture remains $2 million, then the entrepreneur needs to be a bit wealthier and to have $5.355 million to invest in the market index to yield a zero NPV for the venture.

More generally, Figure 11.4 illustrates the relation between the NPV of the venture and the fraction of the entrepreneur's risk capital invested in it. The breakeven NPV occurs at the point where the $2 mil-

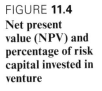

FIGURE **11.4**

Net present value (NPV) and percentage of risk capital invested in venture

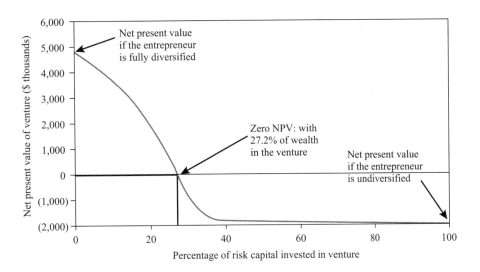

lion investment accounts for 27.2 percent of risk capital. Venture NPV continues to increase as the entrepreneur's total capital (and investment in the market index) increases, as this reduces her exposure to the risk of the new venture. In the limit, venture value is the same as for a well-diversified investor.

11.5 Shortcuts and Extensions

Shortcuts to Valuing Partial-Commitment Investments

"Valuation Template 4" (Table 11.3) requires only a few inputs:

1. *The annualized risk-free rate.* As discussed earlier in the book, it makes sense for an investor in a US venture to choose a currently available US Treasury borrowing rate for a term that is approximately the same as the anticipated holding period.

2. *The annualized expected return on the market portfolio.* In Chapter 10, we saw that the expected market return and market risk premium are difficult to estimate with precision. Values in the 5–8 percent range for the market risk premium can all be justified. Our calculations in this chapter are based on 8 percent.

3. *The annualized standard deviation of market returns.* Using the S&P 500 as a proxy for the market portfolio, over the 60 years

from 1950 through 2009 the standard deviation of market returns has averaged 14.5 percent. The long-term historical average is normally a reasonable estimate of expected forward-looking volatility. We use estimates of 15–20 percent in our calculations.

4. *The estimated correlation between the venture and the market.* While it might be best to generate this estimate from a financial model, in Table 10.3 we present estimates of correlation generated by Kerins, Smith, and Smith (2004). The overall average correlation is 0.195; the table also shows estimates by industry sector, stage of development of the venture, and venture size.

5. *The expected holding period for the venture.* For a venture that does not have staged investments, this is normally the time until the entrepreneur believes an exit would be possible, meaning that the venture will have established a track record that is sufficient to enable a third party to make a reasonable assessment of value.

6. *The entrepreneur's investment in the venture.* This includes the financial investment and the PV of time invested, based on the opportunity cost of forgone employment. The investment amount is only used to find NPV; PV is calculated before the investment amount is specified.

7. *Expected cash return.* This is an estimate of the expected cash flow to the entrepreneur when the venture is harvested.

8. *Standard deviation of harvest cash return.* This is an estimate of the standard deviation of the cash return. The estimate can be derived from scenario analysis, simulation, or by other means. If the entrepreneur is comfortable assuming that the total risk is similar to that of other firms in the same industry or of the same maturity, the cash flow standard deviation question can be finessed by choosing a standard deviation that makes the implied beta in the template equal to the beta in Table 10.3 for firms in the same industry or with similar maturity characteristics.

Using Data for Public Firms to Estimate the Entrepreneur's Cost of Capital

It is possible to use market data to infer C_{port} and $\sigma_{C_{port}}$, the two parameters we need for the CEQ method in Eq. (11.6), to determine the PV of an underdiversified entrepreneur's portfolio. We can then solve for the entrepreneur's cost of capital, which in turn can be used to value the expected cash flow to the entrepreneur. Suppose an entrepreneur who has total wealth of $1.0 million is considering investing $150,000 of financial and human capital in a venture. The investment is expected to return $350,000 in two years. The entrepreneur would like to know if the return is high enough to justify the investment. One difficulty with trying to use public data is that not much data are available for early-stage ventures. Using post-IPO data for early-stage high-technology ventures, however, Kerins, Smith, and Smith (2004) report an average beta of 0.99 and average correlation of 0.195, suggesting that total risk is a little more than five times as high as market risk (because correlation is about one-fifth of market risk). Their evidence, which is elaborated in Table 10.3, can be used to estimate cost of capital for entrepreneurial investments in a representative early-stage venture.

How can we use the above information to find the entrepreneur's cost of capital and value the investment? First, we assume (counterfactually) that the entrepreneur uses the required rate for a well-diversified investor to find the zero-NPV cash flow for a portfolio that is invested partly in the market and partly in the venture. We can use the beta of the venture to compute the zero-NPV portfolio cash return for any given arbitrary allocation of wealth between the market and the venture. Because the entrepreneur and the diversified investor value the venture differently, they will not have the same value weights.[10] To find the entrepreneur's required rate of return, we will need to experiment with these weights later on, but for now we can start with the entrepreneur's weights of 15 percent in the venture and 85 percent in the market. For an investor who values the opportunity using the required returns for diversified investors, we can use Eq. (11.10) to compute the expected cash flow:

$$C_{\text{port}} = w_M(1 + r_M) + w_P^I[1 + r_F + \beta_P(r_M - r_F)] \tag{11.10}$$

where w_P^I is based on the diversified investor's valuation. For convenience, we assume that Eq. (11.10) is standardized so that w_M and w_P^I sum to $1. The result is that C_{port} is the required cash return per dollar invested in the portfolio by a diversified investor. With a risk-free rate of 4 percent per year, a market return of 12 percent per year, a beta of 0.99, and 15 percent of wealth allocated to the venture, the required portfolio cash flow per dollar invested is calculated as follows:

$$
\begin{aligned}
C_{\text{port}} &= w_M(1 + r_M) + w_P^I[1 + r_F + \beta_P(r_M - r_F)] \\
&= \$0.85(1 + .254) + \$0.15[1 + .082 + .99(.254 - .082)] = \$1.254
\end{aligned}
$$

The market and risk-free rates have been compounded to reflect the two-year investment. We then can use the same weights to compute the equilibrium portfolio cash flow risk, $\sigma_{C_{\text{port}}}$, for an investor who uses only market risk to value the project:

$$\sigma_{C_{\text{port}}} = \sqrt{(w_M \sigma_M)^2 + (w_P^I \sigma_P)^2 + 2\rho_{P,M} w_M w_P^I \sigma_M \sigma_P} \tag{11.11}$$

With the already stated assumptions, annualized market risk of 15.0 percent, and a correlation of 0.195, the portfolio cash flow standard deviation for an investor who considers only market risk is $0.265 per dollar invested in the portfolio.

Given the portfolio expected cash flow and standard deviation, we can use Eq. (11.6) to solve for the value of the portfolio to an entrepreneur who takes account of underdiversification. Also, because we know that in the framework we are using the investment in the market is valued the same by the entrepreneur as by the investor, we can determine the value of the project to the entrepreneur by subtracting w_M from the entrepreneur's value of the portfolio. Because the entrepreneur cares about diversification, her valuation will be less than that of an investor who is diversified. In the example we have been developing, the entrepreneur's valuation of the portfolio turns out to be $0.96 (relative to the $1 value determined by the investor), which means that the entrepreneur's realized weight of investment in the venture would be 11.5 percent [i.e., ($0.96 − $0.85)/$0.96].

Recall that we are searching for the required rate of return for an entrepreneur who invests 15 percent of wealth in the venture. So the 15 percent weight we have been using for an investor who ignores non-market risk is too low. We need to find an allocation to that investor that would result in our target weights for the underdiversified entrepreneur. To find this, we need to adjust the weights for the investor who only cares about market risk until we find the point where they produce a valuation where the entrepreneur would have 15 percent in the venture. This is the point where the entrepreneur realizes a zero NPV on the investment of 15 percent of total wealth. Once we find this zero-NPV point, we can use Eq. (11.12) to solve for the entrepreneur's required rate of return on the project.

$$r_P^E = \frac{C_P}{PV_P^E} - 1 \tag{11.12}$$

In this example, increasing the weight in the project for the investor who ignores underdiversification to 21.1 percent results in a value of the entrepreneur's portfolio ($0.928) that yields a 15 percent weight for the entrepreneur [i.e., ($0.928 − $0.789)/$0.928]. Using Eq. (11.12), we find that the entrepreneur's required return is 38.0 percent per year. Discounting the expected $350,000 payoff by 38.0 percent per year yields a present value of $183,785, or a positive NPV of $33,785.

Shortcuts for Estimating the Entrepreneur's Cost of Capital from Market Data

The process for valuing the entrepreneur's investment, as described above, is complicated. To simplify the calculations, Table 11.4, "Valuation Template 5," can be used to find the entrepreneur's cost of capital by using risk and expected return data for a comparable public firm or data from Table 10.3. Because it is based on the CEQ method, required-

TABLE **11.4**   Valuation Template 5: Entrepreneur's cost of capital

Inputs	Per year	Partial commitment
Years until expected harvest		2.0
Hypothetical fraction of wealth invested in market portfolio by diversified investor	(Adjustment)	78.8%
Hypothetical fraction of wealth invested in venture by diversified investor		21.2%
Market data		
Risk-free rate of interest	4.0%	8.2%
Expected return on market	12.0%	25.4%
Standard deviation of market returns	15.0%	21.2%
Comparable public firm data		
Correlation of comparable public firm with market	0.195	0.195
Beta of comparable public firm	0.990	0.990
Standard deviation of comparable public firm returns		107.7%
Portfolio cash flow results		
Expected harvest cash flow of entrepreneur's portfolio		$1.254
Cash flow standard deviation of portfolio		$0.308
Value of entrepreneur's portfolio		$0.928
Venture valuation results		
Value of entrepreneur's investment in venture		$0.139
Expected cash flow from investment in venture		$0.265
Venture cost-of-capital estimates		
Entrepreneur's holding-period cost of capital for venture		90.4%
Entrepreneur's annualized cost of capital for venture		38.0%
Diversified investor's annualized cost of capital for venture		11.9%
Entrepreneur's annualized underdiversification premium		26.1%
Standard deviation of entrepreneur's return from venture		163.7%
Entrepreneur's wealth allocation		
Fraction of entrepreneur's wealth invested in venture	(Target)	15.0%
Fraction of entrepreneur's wealth invested in market		85.0%

NOTE: *Shaded cells are inputs that can be changed. See book website version for guidance on using this template.*

rate-of-return estimates derived from the template correctly reflect the effect of underdiversification and yield a cost of capital that can be used to value project cash flows.

In the table, we illustrate the solution discussed above. The highlighted cells are assumptions you will need to supply. One of them, the weight invested in the market by the diversified investor, is labeled "Adjustment" because it is the cell that you would need to adjust until the cell at the bottom of the figure labeled "Target" reaches the entrepreneur's planned weight of investment in the venture.

Other than the assumptions, most of the information in the table is diagnostic. The important result is the entrepreneur's cost of capital. We used the Goal Seek feature of Excel to find the value of the diversified investor's investment in the market that would make the entrepreneur's fraction of present-valued wealth in the venture equal to 15 percent.

Another way to think of this approach to estimating the entrepreneur's required rate of return is to focus on the underdiversification premium to the standard CAPM:

$$r_P^E = r_P^I + UP_P^E = r_F + \beta_P(r_M - r_F) + UP_P^E \tag{11.13}$$

where UP_P^E is the underdiversification premium that is specific to the risk properties of the venture and the fraction of wealth invested by the entrepreneur. In the example in Table 11.4, a well-diversified investor would have an annualized cost of capital for this venture of 11.9 percent; the entrepreneur, who requires 38.0 percent, therefore expects an annualized underdiversification premium of 26.1 percent. Recall that we introduced the idea of an underdiversification premium early in the chapter. The approach we illustrated at that point produced negatively biased estimates of the entrepreneur's required rate of return. This example is a bit more complex, but yields estimates that are unbiased in the CAPM context.

Another shortcut approach is to simply look up an estimate of the underdiversification premium in a table. Table 11.5 shows various estimates of the entrepreneur's underdiversification premium as a function of the percent of the diversified investor's wealth in the venture and the holding period. As in Table 11.4, calculations are based on the CEQ method, with an assumed beta of 1.0, a correlation of 0.20, a risk-free rate of 4 percent per year, an annual market return rate of 12 percent, and standard deviation of the market rate of 15 percent per year. Reasonable changes in assumptions about the risk-free rate and market risk premium have little effect on the estimated underdiversification premium. The assumed correlation and standard deviation are comparable to those in Table 10.3. Table 11.5 shows that the underdiversification

TABLE **11.5**   **Underdiversification premium**

Holding period (years)	Percentage of diversified investor's wealth in the venture								
	40.0	35.0	30.0	25.0	20.0	15.0	10.0	5.0	0.0
1	33.6	30.9	27.9	24.4	20.4	15.8	10.7	5.3	0.0
2	43.2	39.0	34.3	29.3	23.8	17.9	11.8	5.7	0.0
3	65.1	55.4	46.2	37.4	28.9	20.8	13.1	6.1	0.0
4	NM	159.4	84.5	55.9	38.1	25.1	14.8	6.6	0.0
5	NM	NM	NM	NM	64.5	32.5	17.1	7.1	0.0

NM = not meaningful
NOTE: *Values are percentages based on estimates of beta, total risk, and correlation for a representative early-stage venture as reported by Kerins, Smith, and Smith (2004) and summarized in Chapter 10.*

premium is higher the larger the fraction of the entrepreneur's wealth that is invested and the longer the holding period. This makes sense because investing a large fraction of wealth for a very short period does not expose the entrepreneur to much nonmarket risk; neither does investing a small fraction of wealth for a long period. As most of the estimates of risk in Table 10.3 are similar, Table 11.5 provides reasonable estimates of the underdiversification premium for most ventures.

Valuing Ventures That Have Cash Flows in Multiple Periods

The spreadsheet in Table 11.3 is designed to accommodate valuation of ventures with harvest cash flows that occur in a single period. For many ventures, this is a reasonable approximation, especially for ventures in which the main return is realized at the exit. However, many entrepreneurs are involved in ventures they do not plan to harvest or where they can realize cash flow returns over a number of years. For such entrepreneurs, it is useful to be able to value projects with cash flows in multiple periods. Though valuing multiperiod investments is easy for well-diversified investors, it is tricky for an entrepreneur who is not well diversified. Ventures that generate cash flows in multiple periods can offer a degree of intertemporal diversification that might be important to the entrepreneur.

In Table 11.3, although different cash flow streams within a period are merged in a way that takes their correlation into consideration, there is no obvious consideration of how to value cash flows that are correlated over time. This is not a problem if the investor is well diversified, because required rates of return are only affected by market risk. But it is a problem for an underdiversified investor, such as an entrepreneur. Were we to calculate the values of cash flows separately for each period, we would in effect be assuming that the benefits of intertemporal diversification are negligible.

In Table 11.2, we demonstrated a simple way to deal with the problem. When the venture generated free cash flow in different periods, we effectively transferred all of those cash flows to the last period by assuming that the venture retained the free cash and invested it at the risk-free rate until the time of exit. At that point, we assumed that the entrepreneur's return would consist of two parts: a distribution of the accumulated free cash and the return from selling the ownership interest. Interestingly, none of this needs to be true for the valuation approach to work well. The entrepreneur might in reality take the free cash out of the venture as it becomes available and at the time of the exit may not actually liquidate his investment. But as long as the free cash flows are shifted to the assumed exit year at the risk-free rate, these nuances do not have much effect on estimated PV. The same is true if the entrepreneur's investment is actually made over several years. If future investments are shifted back to their PVs by discounting at the risk-free rate, then the PV of the investment will be accurate.

If you are concerned about the effects of diversification on value, you can take account of diversification by constructing a hypothetical one-period venture that should have a value similar to that of the multiperiod venture. This can be done by first simulating the expected cash flows in each period and then compounding or discounting the periodic returns to a single date, such as a point that is a few years in the future. The time-shifted cumulated cash flow can then be used in the RADR or CEQ valuation models to estimate present value. Shifting the cash flows to a single period implicitly considers intertemporal diversification. The idea is that instead of valuing the business that generates cash flows in many periods, you can substitute a hypothetical venture that pays off in one period and should have approximately the same value.

11.6 Benefits of Diversification

In the preceding examples, it was possible to lower the required rate of return on the venture by diversifying the entrepreneur's risk capital between the venture and the market portfolio. Doing so raises the PV of the venture. Figure 11.5 illustrates more generally how diversification can yield an expected portfolio return that is higher than the required return.

FIGURE **11.5**
Why diversification adds value

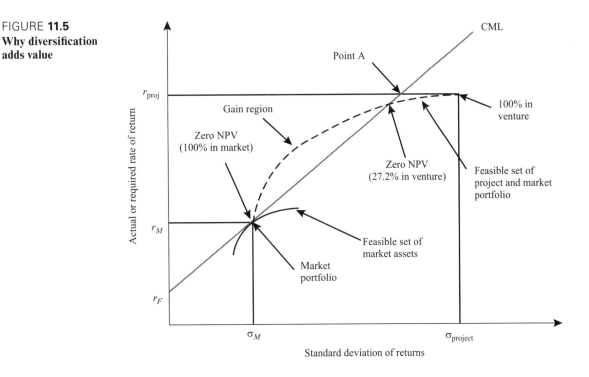

Points on the feasible set, represented by the dashed arc in Figure 11.5, are attainable by varying the allocation of the entrepreneur's total investment between the venture and the market. At one extreme, the entrepreneur invests all her wealth in the market portfolio; at the other, she invests all her wealth in the venture. Alternatively, the entrepreneur could use financial leverage to achieve points along the CML. The CML reflects the entrepreneur's opportunity cost of investing in the venture. As the figure shows, the expected return for investing only in the venture, r_{proj}, can also be achieved by leveraging the market but at much lower risk (Point A on the CML). Accordingly, the NPV of investing exclusively in the venture is negative.

The figure also shows the two points where the CML and the entrepreneur's feasible set intersect. Those intersections are where the entrepreneur's portfolio has a zero NPV. Between the two zero-NPV points, the entrepreneur's expected return is above the CML. Over this gain region, investing in the portfolio of the venture and the market has a positive NPV. The gain arises because diversification reduces the required return on the venture. The range of portfolio risk levels where the expected portfolio return is greater than the required return reflects weights between the venture and the market where the NPV of the venture would be positive.

Although the primary focus of this discussion is on not investing too much in the venture, Figure 11.5 also shows that it is possible for the entrepreneur to invest too little. Beyond a certain point, underweighting a good venture reduces the net benefit of diversification. In the extreme, investing nothing (or a trivial amount) in the venture results in a zero (or near-zero) NPV for the entrepreneur.

Achieving the Right Balance

You can see that it is much more challenging to value a venture from the perspective of the entrepreneur than to assess value to a well-diversified investor. We simplify the task by providing some shortcuts and spreadsheet templates that incorporate the necessary calculations, but the critical factors in making the valuation are the assumptions about the venture and the entrepreneur. We offer guidance for thinking about the important assumptions, but ultimately the quality of the valuation estimate is left to the entrepreneur or investor. In some cases, a formal estimate is not critical for deciding whether to go forward. But it still makes sense to try to structure the deal to add as much value as possible.

An essential point to take away from this discussion is that an entrepreneur who is able to select the amount to invest in the venture can reduce the required rate of return by choosing a venture scale that makes diversification feasible. Because the entrepreneur's investment involves both human and financial capital, one way to reduce scale is to shorten the time committed to the venture as much as is practicable. Financial and human capital commitment can also be limited by initially pursuing the venture on a small scale and by using milestones that can help decide whether to abandon early, thereby shortening the time committed to the venture.

11.7 A Sanity Check—The Art and Science of Investment Decisions

Any formal analysis of value layers assumptions on assumptions. Such a framework may compound the effects of valuation errors—differences between assumed parameters and true parameters. For example, we know that as a theoretical construct, for any given risky cash flow there is a true cost of capital that yields a correct (value-maximizing) decision to accept or reject the investment. But in practice we are estimating both the expected cash flow and risk. We are also assuming that the CAPM is the correct model of cost of capital, and we are using estimates of the risk-free rate, market risk premium, and correlation. For investment by the entrepreneur, we are also estimating the fraction of risk capital committed to the venture. With so many assumptions, the estimate of value can be very different from the true PV. Best practice involves making sure that the expected valuation error is as small as possible and is not biased, as well as testing sensitivity of the valuation to variations in key assumptions.

Assessing Sensitivity to Assumptions

The valuation models and templates we have introduced can be used to gain perspective on the magnitude of valuation errors. One simple approach is to examine sensitivity to individual changes in assumptions about cash flows, risk, and required rates of return. Evaluating sensitivity in this way can help to identify the more critical assumptions. Understanding how uncertainty about assumptions affects PV is an additional benefit of sensitivity analysis.

Sensitivity analysis is not convenient for testing sensitivity to the key assumptions collectively, which is important because input variables are rarely uncorrelated. By applying simulation to the valuation model, we see how value changes when all key assumptions are permitted to vary at the same time. There are three principal benefits of simulating the valuation: First, you can determine the combined effect of uncertainty about assumptions on the PV estimate. Second, you can assess the value of trying to get better information about the assumptions. Third, you gain perspective to use in negotiating funding.

Using and Misusing Simulation

It is easy to use simulation incorrectly for valuation. Sometimes decision makers try to value projects by simulating cash flows and converting them to PV by discounting at the risk-free rate. This generally overstates value. The error is that if the venture is risky, then the risk-free rate is usually not the opportunity cost of capital. Conversely, if total risk is used to determine cost of capital, then the ability to diversify is ignored and the project will be undervalued.

One common mistake is to effectively discount the future cash flows twice. Suppose you are comparing two projects. You simulate their expected cash flows and value them using the approach in Table 11.3. The analysis shows that Project A is slightly more valuable than Project B. However, you notice that A is much riskier than B, and therefore you decide to pursue B instead. Doing so is the wrong decision. Your analysis should have ended with the comparison of NPVs, which indicated that A is more valuable. You had already taken account of the risk differences in the PV calculations. So if you look back at risk again and select B because it is less risky, you have, in effect, discounted twice for the risk of Project A.

Our approach avoids these pitfalls. First, for the diversified investor, we use simulation to determine the uncertainty of cash flows. But to determine the cost of capital we use the CEQ version of the CAPM, because it is usually difficult to infer appropriate discount rates for entrepreneurial ventures simply by looking for public firm data. Second, for entrepreneurs who are unable to diversify fully, we allow value to depend on what else the entrepreneur could do with assets that are not invested in the venture. Finally, we avoid the error of discounting twice.

Treatment of Sunk Costs in the Valuation

Sunk costs are costs that have already been incurred and cannot be recovered. Not all historical costs are sunk: for example, if you buy lab equipment to pursue a venture, the cost is only sunk to the extent that the equipment cannot be diverted to other uses or sold. If you need to learn some accounting to do the bookkeeping for a venture, that investment is only sunk to the extent that you cannot apply the same skills to another project. If your alternative activity is to become a professional athlete, then perhaps your accounting knowledge would be worthless; in that case, the cost of learning accounting is indeed sunk.

The decision to invest or to continue investing in a venture should not depend on sunk costs. In the example from Table 11.3, we computed NPV by subtracting $2 million from the PV of cash flows. For that comparison to be valid, the $2 million must be net of costs that are already sunk. It is appropriate to reflect tangible and intangible assets but at their alternative use values rather than at their historical costs. The relevant distinction is not between historical and future outlays but between nonrecoverable historical outlays and those that are recoverable.

Entrepreneurs often err by measuring project value against the entrepreneur's total investment, including any sunk outlays the entrepreneur has already made. We occasionally hear of investment offers being turned down because the entrepreneur does not believe the deal would provide enough return to compensate for investments already made. But it does not make sense for the entrepreneur to pass up a venture because the expected return is not sufficient to compensate for sunk investments. Even as a negotiating ploy, seeking a return on sunk investments may not be a good tactic: to pull it off, you would have to send the message that you do not understand the irrelevance of sunk costs. Why would an investor want to work with an entrepreneur who is confused about the appropriate criteria to be used in trying to decide whether to commit to the next milestone?

11.8 Summary

In this chapter we develop a framework for evaluating the underdiversified investments of entrepreneurs. This framework recognizes that entrepreneurs, as undiversified investors, should value projects at discount rates that can be substantially higher than the rates appropriate for well-diversified investors. Because the entrepreneur's required rate depends on total risk and not just market risk, a significant opportunity exists to select value-enhancing strategies for undertaking new ventures and to design value-enhancing contracts between entrepreneurs and outside investors.

This chapter explores the benefits that can derive from regarding entrepreneurial investment in this way. Among other factors, the entrepreneur's required return declines as the fraction of wealth that must be invested in the venture declines. This gives rise to a significant opportunity to create value by selecting the size of the investment or bringing in an outside investor to share in the risk of the venture. Doing so can reduce the overall required rate of return.

Given the complexity of the entrepreneur's valuation problem, it is useful to consider some ways to shortcut the decision process. To that end, we offer the following generalizations:

- The entrepreneur's required rate of return depends on the total risk the entrepreneur must bear.
- Because their attitudes toward risk are different, entrepreneurs cannot rely on valuations of well-diversified outside investors.
- Except for differences in beliefs about expected future cash flows and risk, together with subjective considerations, there is no way a venture can be more valuable to the entrepreneur than to a diversified investor.
- The main factor that can bring the entrepreneur's value closer to that of the outside investor is when the entrepreneur does not have to commit a very large fraction of total wealth to the venture.

- Investments that are recoverable reduce the size of the entrepreneur's commitment and increase venture acceptability, as does shortening the length of the commitment.
- Because the entrepreneur cares about total risk but the investor cares only about market risk, the disparity between their valuations is greater the higher the total risk of the venture compared with its market risk.
- Relative values also differ if the financial claims differ. Sweeteners that increase value for the outside investor do so by reducing the value of the entrepreneur's residual claim.

It is intuitive that underdiversification should motivate the entrepreneur to seek a higher return than a well-diversified investor would require. However, the appropriate magnitude of the return premium that should be required to compensate for underdiversification is not intuitive. In fact, it is not uncommon for advisors to suggest arbitrary "haircuts" to value in order to compensate for such things as illiquidity and underdiversification. The approaches presented in this chapter are more systematic and are solidly grounded in financial economic theory. We devote significant attention to presentation and discussion of the analytics to help make clear that (1) the premiums to required rates of return that arise from underdiversification can be substantial, and (2) there is no single, arbitrary haircut that can do a good job of helping you to make good decisions in light of opportunity cost. Beyond the analytics, however, the chapter provides several shortcut approaches to estimating discount rates that take account of underdiversification.

REVIEW QUESTIONS

1. Why might it not be a good idea for the entrepreneur to rely on the investor's valuation in deciding whether to pursue a potential venture?

2. How does underdiversification affect the entrepreneur's opportunity cost of capital for investing time and money in a new venture?

3. Why, all else equal, would you expect a wealthier entrepreneur to value a new venture opportunity more highly than an entrepreneur who is less wealthy?

4. Why, all else equal, are new venture opportunities worth less to entrepreneurs than to well-diversified investors?

5. While underdiversification implies lower valuation, entrepreneurs often see ventures as being more valuable than do investors. Why might the entrepreneur value an opportunity more highly?

6. What is meant by "human capital"? How might you estimate the value of an individual's human capital?

7. What is meant by the human capital investment in a venture? How do salary in alternative employment, salary in the venture, and the ability to resume alternative employment if the venture fails affect the size of the human capital investment?

8. How, all else equal, does the difference between the total risk and the market risk of a new venture opportunity affect the relative values of the opportunity to an underdiversified entrepreneur and to a diversified investor? Explain.

9. What factors increase the likelihood of corporate venturing as opposed to a stand-alone pursuit of an opportunity by an entrepreneur? Why?

10. What, in the context of this chapter, is meant by the entrepreneur's "commitment to the venture"?

NOTES

1. See Shane (2008), who studies patterns of self-employment and entrepreneurship around the world.

2. Alternatively, we could model a three-asset portfolio that includes human capital as the third asset. Adding this complexity, while analytically more correct, does not change the results over reasonable ranges of assumptions.

3. The underdiversification premium estimated by this approach is a negatively biased estimate. We explain why later in the chapter and provide an approach that corrects the bias.

4. Wasserman (2006) reports annual salaries that are $25,000 (approximately 14 percent) lower for founder CEOs compared to nonfounders.

5. Data are from the "Kauffman Firm Survey: Results from the Baseline and First Follow-Up Surveys," March 2008, Ewing Marion Kauffman Foundation, Kansas City, MO; downloaded September 30, 2009 at http://sites.kauffman.org/kfs/.

6. See Kerins, Smith, and Smith (2004) for more complete development of using the CEQ method to value ventures when the entrepreneur is underdiversified.

7. The spreadsheet for Table 11.2 is accessible on the book's companion website. By uncovering some of the hidden rows in the spreadsheet of Table 11.2, you can also see the simulation model run using staged investment.

8. To keep the example simple, we assume that the entrepreneur's salary from the venture is the same as her next best alternative and that pursuing the venture would not affect subsequent earnings if the venture were to fail. Thus,

the entrepreneur, though working for the venture, is not committing human capital to it.

9. The spreadsheet in Table 11.3 is a valuation template that is available on the book's companion website.

10. We can either start with the investor's value weights (such as 80 percent in the market and 20 percent in the venture) or solve by trial and error for the investor weights that yield the target weights for the entrepreneur (such as 85 percent of wealth in the market and 15 percent in the venture).

REFERENCES AND ADDITIONAL READING

Chen, H., J. Miao, and N. Wang. 2010. "Entrepreneurial Finance and Non-Diversifiable Risk." *Review of Financial Studies* 23 (12): 4348–88.

Evans, D., and B. Javanovic. 1989. "An Estimated Model of Entrepreneurial Choice under Liquidity Constraints." *Journal of Political Economy* 97:808–27.

Gentry, W. M., and G. Hubbard. 2004. "Entrepreneurship and Household Saving." *Advances in Economic Analysis and Policy* 4. Available at http://www.bepress.com/bejeap/advances/vol4/iss1/art8/.

Golder, S. C. 1986. "Structuring and Pricing the Financing." In *Pratt's Guide to Venture Capital Sources*, ed. Stanley E. Pratt and Jane K. Morris, 79–88. 10th ed. Wellesley, MA: Venture Economics.

Hall, R., and S. Woodward. 2010. "The Burden of Nondiversifiable Risk of Entrepreneurship." *American Economic Review* 100:1163–1194.

Heaton, J., and D. Lucas. 2000. "Portfolio Choices and Asset Prices: The Importance of Entrepreneurial Risk." *Journal of Finance* 55:1163–98.

———. 2004. "Capital Structure, Hurdle Rates, and Portfolio Choice: Interactions in an Entrepreneurial Firm." University of Chicago working paper. Available at http://fisher.osu.edu/fin/dice/seminars/Lucas.pdf.

Holtz-Eakin, D., D. Joulfaian, and H. S. Rosen. 1994a. "Entrepreneurial Decisions and Liquidity Constraints." *RAND Journal of Economics* 23:334–47.

———. 1994b. "Sticking It Out: Entrepreneurial Survival and Liquidity Constraints." *Journal of Political Economy* 102:53–75.

Hurst, E., and A. Lusardi. 2004. "Liquidity Constraints, Household Wealth, and Entrepreneurship." *Journal of Political Economy* 112:319–47.

Inderst, R., and H. Müller. 2004. "The Effect of Capital Market Characteristics on the Value of Start-Up Firms." *Journal of Financial Economics* 72:319–56.

Kerins, F., J. K. Smith, and R. L. Smith. 2004. "Opportunity Cost of Capital for Venture Capital Investors and Entrepreneurs." *Journal of Financial and Quantitative Analysis* 39:385–405.

Kraus, A., and R. H. Litzenberger. 1976. "Skewness Preference and the Valuation of Risk Assets." *Journal of Finance* 31:1085–1100.

Moskowitz, T., and A. Vissing-Jorgensen. 2002. "The Returns to Entrepreneurial Investment: A Private Equity Premium Puzzle." *American Economic Review* 92:745–78.

Shane, S. A. 2008. *The Illusions of Entrepreneurship*. New Haven, CT: Yale University Press.

Wasserman, N. 2006. "Stewards, Agents, and the Founder Discount: Executive Compensation in New Ventures." *Academy of Management Journal* 49:960–76.

INFORMATION, INCENTIVES, AND FINANCIAL CONTRACTING

CHAPTER 12

DEAL STRUCTURE: ADDRESSING INFORMATION AND INCENTIVE PROBLEMS

> A reputation, once broken, may possibly be repaired, but the world will always keep their eyes on the spot where the crack was.
>
> Joseph Hall

In this chapter and the next, we turn to the contractual relationship between the entrepreneur and investor and explore how financial contracting can be used to benefit both parties. We emphasize the considerations that bear on the choice of contract terms: diversification differences, information differences, differences in expectations, and incentive effects. In Chapter 13, we apply the ideas developed here to the design of value-enhancing deal structures.

Entrepreneurs often think of investors as a necessary evil—better done without, if possible. Although dealing with investors can be inconvenient and sometimes even harmful, investors can also benefit the entrepreneur. Potential benefits derive from three sources:

- Outside investment enables the entrepreneur to invest less and increase diversification.
- Because well-diversified investors have lower required rates of return, increasing outside investment can increase the PV of the venture.
- An investor may contribute advice and information that enhance value.

Of course, there are also potential problems—disagreements over direction, more time devoted to maintenance of the relationship, and conflicts of interest, among others. While we recognize the potential problems, our focus here is on how investors can add value.

We begin by using a financial contracting framework to study the benefits of outside investment. In financial terms, contracts with investors have three effects: they allocate risk; they allocate expected returns; and they change expected returns. Debt financing, for example, allocates most of the risk to the equity investor/entrepreneur, allocates expected returns differently between the equity holder and creditors, and changes overall returns due to the tax effect and incentive effect.

To sharpen understanding of how financial contracting affects value, we focus separately on each effect. We begin with a pure risk-allocation provision, one that transfers risk from one party to another but does not change the allocation of expected returns and does not alter the overall level of expected returns. Next, we consider a pure return-allocation provision. Finally, we consider the ability to affect value by contracting with investors who participate actively in the venture. In this analysis, we build upon the lessons from Chapter 11, related to the effects of underdiversification on the entrepreneur's required rate of return.

We focus on a project in which all investment by both the entrepreneur and an investor is made at the beginning, both parties have identical expectations about future performance and risk, and both parties know that they share the same expectations. Thus, any contracting gains derive entirely from the parties' differing attitudes toward risk. Later in the chapter, we relax the assumption of symmetric information to focus on incentive and information effects related to financial contracts.

12.1 Some Preliminaries

In any negotiation, you can assess the effects of a proposed contracting provision by examining how the provision affects the allocation of risk, the allocation of expected returns, and the overall expected return. To benchmark the effects, we start with the assumption that the entrepreneur and the investor share proportionally in risk and expected returns, based on the relative magnitudes of their investments. This arbitrary starting point provides an easy transition from Chapter 11 and enables us to examine the three separate effects of contract provisions.

Because the parties have different required rates of return, the clearest picture is achieved by assuming that one party or the other captures the entire gain. We have adopted the convention of allocating the gain to the entrepreneur. This allocation is consistent with assuming that the market for new venture financing is highly competitive, so that investors compete to participate in the venture and the entrepreneur realizes the full gain. In reality, the parties are likely to share the gains based on the intensity of competition and the negotiating leverage of the parties.

12.2   **Proportional Sharing of Risk and Return**

We saw in Chapter 11 that the entrepreneur's required rate of return increases with the fraction of her wealth that is invested in the venture. We introduced the idea that if a project is perfectly scalable, the entrepreneur, acting without outside funding, can choose how much to invest, and in doing so will also determine the scale of the venture. With no outside investor, the optimal scale depends only on the entrepreneur's wealth.

Choosing the Scale of the Venture

Consider a venture with constant returns to scale. We expect that the entrepreneur, as the sole investor, would choose the scale to maximize net present value (NPV). It might seem that the venture should be run on the largest scale possible. That would be correct for a diversified investor but not for a wealth-constrained entrepreneur. Because under-diversification increases the entrepreneur's required rate of return, the largest feasible scale is not the one with the highest NPV.

We can use the example from Table 11.2 to study the effect of project scale on value. Recall that the entrepreneur was considering an investment of $2 million, which was assumed to be the cost of the project. Using the template in Table 11.3, we saw that if her total wealth were $6 million, so that she would be committing one-third of her wealth to the venture, the entrepreneur would require a return of 37.5 percent per year over the six-year holding period. As shown in the table, however, with this level of commitment the NPV is −$408,000. To examine the choice of scale, we assume that the entrepreneur's wealth is fixed at $6 million; thus, the entrepreneur can invest up to her full $6 million in the project.

At one extreme, if the entrepreneur were to invest 100 percent of total wealth in the venture, based on opportunity cost, we can modify Table 11.3 to verify that the entrepreneur's required rate of return would be far higher than what the venture described in Table 11.2 is expected to deliver. At the other extreme, investing 100 percent in the market would yield the expected return on the market portfolio. Because the market portfolio is a point on the capital market line (CML), it is a zero-NPV investment opportunity, as shown in Figure 11.5.

By experimenting with other amounts of investment, scaling the returns and risk proportionately, and maintaining the entrepreneur's total wealth at $6 million, you can verify that the NPV of the portfolio reaches a maximum when the entrepreneur invests about $636,000 in the project and the balance in a market portfolio. That portfolio—with about 10.6 percent of wealth invested in the project—yields the maximum project NPV of approximately $661,000 for the entrepreneur. Of course, perfect scalability is not realistic, but we are only using this as a way to launch our discussion of contracting.

The table below displays the results of using this approach to compute the PVs and NPVs of project cash flows. The calculations are shown for points corresponding to 0 percent of wealth invested in the project, 10.6 percent invested, 27.2 percent invested, and 33.3 percent invested. NPV is positive at investment levels between zero and 27.2 percent ($1.631 million). Maximum NPV of about $1.252 million is reached when 10.6 percent of wealth ($636,000) is invested in the venture.

How the fraction of wealth invested in a venture affects NPV

Percentage of wealth invested in venture	Dollars invested in venture	Dollars invested in market index*	PV of investment in venture	NPV of entrepreneur's portfolio
0.0%	$0	$6,000,000	$0	$0
10.6%	$636,000	$5,364,000	$1,297,000	$661,000
27.2%	$1,631,000	$4,369,000	$1,631,000	$0
33.3%	$2,000,000	$4,000,000	$1,592,000	($408,000)

The market index is a zero-NPV investment.

Sharing Ownership in Proportion to Investment

The entrepreneur can affect the size of the investment in either of two ways: by selecting scale as we have been discussing or by keeping scale fixed and bringing in an investor. You can reinterpret the preceding analysis by assuming that project scale is given. In that case, the entrepreneur's decision of how much to invest also determines how much capital to raise from investors. This view implies that the entrepreneur and the investor share risks and rewards proportionally. If the project requires a total investment of $2 million, and the entrepreneur invests $636,000, then, with proportional sharing, the entrepreneur is entitled to 31.8 percent of the equity. An investor provides the other $1.364 million in exchange for 68.2 percent of the equity.

With proportional sharing, the entrepreneur's investment decision looks exactly like it did for the choice of scale. The only difference is that scale is fixed and the entrepreneur's share of the investment is allowed to vary. The entrepreneur maximizes NPV by choosing ownership share. So, for example, in the above table, if the entrepreneur wants to maximize NPV by investing \$636,000 in a venture that requires a total of \$2 million, then an investor will need to be found to provide the additional \$1.364 million. If ownership is shared in proportion to investment, then the entrepreneur's NPV will be \$661,000, the same as shown in the table.

12.3 Asymmetric Sharing of Risk and Return

Proportional sharing is not a likely contract structure. Investors generally seek a variety of "me-first" provisions and other sweeteners. The contract may specify, for example, that the investor receives warrants to acquire additional shares if performance targets are not met, or that the outsider's investment will not be diluted if additional capital must be raised. Conversely, the entrepreneur is likely to draw a salary and may receive supplemental compensation if performance is better than expected.

Here we offer a structured way of analyzing how risk allocation affects value. There is a double benefit to bringing in a well-diversified investor. First, reducing the entrepreneur's investment enables her to realize some of the benefits of diversification. Second, if the parties agree about expected future cash flows and risk, the investor values the venture more highly than does the entrepreneur. Thus, other things equal, the investor will accept a lower ownership interest per dollar of investment.

Generally, each party seeks to increase the NPV of his or her investment by shifting as much risk as possible to the other while retaining as much of the expected return as possible. However, as new ventures are often collaborations between investors and an underdiversified entrepreneur, risk allocation is not a zero-sum game. Because the parties view risk differently, contract provisions that shift nonmarket risk to the investor can increase value.

How Shifting Risk Affects the Entrepreneur

Contract provisions that shift nonmarket risk to well-diversified investors yield pure gains in NPV. The entrepreneur is better off and the investor is not worse off. To illustrate, we extend the previous example by adding a contract provision that shifts diversifiable risk. Because we shift only diversifiable risk, the beta risk of each party is unchanged. With her investment reduced but expected return unaltered, the entrepreneur's feasible set improves. The entrepreneur's gain does not affect the value of the investor's claim. To model this new contract using the valuation template in Table 11.3, we first reduce the standard deviation of project cash flows by 10 percent (from $5.527 million to $4.974 million) to reflect the reduction in the entrepreneur's risk. To keep the market risk (beta) unchanged and to have no impact on the diversified investor's required return, we increase the correlation to exactly offset the lower total risk.

The table below shows how shifting nonmarket risk affects the NPV of the entrepreneur's investment. We continue with the same example. Consider the zero-NPV investment of 27.2 percent of wealth from the previous table. Shifting 10 percent of the total risk to the investor increases the entrepreneur's NPV to $603,000. With proportional allocation, the maximum achievable NPV is $661,000, which occurs when 10.6 percent of the entrepreneur's wealth is invested in the venture. In contrast, with risk shifted the maximum is $865,000 and is attained when about 14.7 percent of the entrepreneur's wealth is invested in the venture. Thus, in this example, reducing the entrepreneur's nonmarket risk increases the optimal fraction of wealth for the entrepreneur to invest in the venture. The venture now has a positive NPV up to the full investment of $2 million.

How shifting nonmarket risk to the outside investor affects NPV

Percentage of wealth invested in venture	Dollars invested in venture	Dollars invested in market index	NPV of entrepreneur's portfolio	
			Proportional sharing contract	Risk-shifting contract*
0%	$0	$6,000,000	$0	$0
10.6%	$636,000	$5,364,000	$661,000	$818,000
14.7%	$880,000	$5,120,000	$604,000	$865,000
27.2%	$1,631,000	$4,369,000	$0	$603,000
33.3%	$2,000,000	$4,000,000	($408,000)	$362,000

Contract has 10 percent of total risk shifted to the outside investor. All shifted risk is diversifiable.

The Investor's Perspective

Why does risk allocation increase the entrepreneur's ability to invest risk capital in the project? And why would an investor agree to such a contract? As shown in the preceding table, shifting some risk to the investor enables the entrepreneur to devote a larger fraction of wealth to the venture, reducing the need for outside investment. With a larger investment, the entrepreneur can actually bear greater project risk under the risk-allocation contract than under proportional sharing. The investor is bearing more nonmarket risk but has a smaller total investment in the project. Such a contract should be acceptable given that the investor can eliminate nonmarket risk through diversification.

Risk-Allocation Contracting in Practice

This discussion may not seem to comport with conventional wisdom or practice. VCs, after all, generally try to shift risk toward the entrepreneur, and the investor usually holds financial claims that are less risky than those held by the entrepreneur (convertible preferred stock instead of common). There are three responses to this observation. First, remember that the starting point for measuring the effects of changes in contract provisions is arbitrary. We could have compared an initial proposed contract that shifted considerable nonmarket risk to the entrepreneur with an alternative contract that shifted less.

Second, the common wisdom underlying the observation arises from thinking about the negotiation one element at a time. Generally, the amount the entrepreneur wants to raise from outside sources is predetermined, and negotiations focus on the terms for providing that amount of funding. In our analysis, by contrast, both risk allocation and the amount of outside funding vary at the same time. The entrepreneur is negotiating to reduce nonmarket risk in exchange for taking on more of the investment. Such negotiations can be explicit or implicit.

Third, conventional wisdom is based on observations where the entrepreneur has already made sunk investments in the project. The investor is contributing financial capital in exchange for equity. The entrepreneur's interest is a residual. But if we view the project before any investment has been made, then the negotiation is conducted on the basis of whether the entrepreneur's risk is low enough to justify undertaking the project at all. If the return is not high enough to compensate for opportunity cost, then the investor must either take on more of the risk or forgo the project.

12.4 Contract Choices That Allocate Expected Returns

Proportional sharing, while it clarifies how bringing in an investor can benefit the entrepreneur, is not a good deal for the entrepreneur. Why, after all, would the entrepreneur want to leave so much money on the table? If investors compete to participate in the venture, then the entrepreneur should be able to do better.

When investors provide capital, they usually start by assessing value. Recognizing that well-diversified investors provide most venture capital and assuming that the market for outside funding is competitive, we refer to value as determined by such investors as the venture's market value.

In a competitive capital market, the ownership claim the investor receives in exchange for contributing capital depends on the venture's market value. Consider a venture that requires $2 million of total capital and has a market value of $6 million (roughly the market value in the example we have been using). Suppose a well-diversified investor contributes $1.5 million, with the entrepreneur contributing the balance. If there is competition to invest, then the investor can expect to receive 25 percent of the equity (i.e., $1.5 million/$6 million makes 25 percent a zero-NPV investment).

With proportional sharing, the investor would receive 75 percent of the equity ($1.5 million/$2.0 million). The investor's return would be higher than needed. In fact, in a competitive market, the investor would have been willing to pay the entrepreneur just to gain the right to purchase the fractional ownership interest on such terms. In a competitive setting, the investor is compelled to make such a payment implicitly and effectively does so by contributing more capital than the investor's share of ownership.

Consider the project we have been discussing. From Table 11.3, we can see that the implied beta of the project is 0.44. However, that beta is calculated as if the venture NPV were zero, which it would be only if the investor were providing $5.103 million (75 percent of the $6.806 million PV as measured by the investor) in exchange for the 75 percent interest. With only $2 million invested in total, the standard deviation of holding-period returns on the actual investment is increased by a factor of 3.4 (i.e., 6,806/2,000), which results in a beta of 1.50. Using the 26.5 percent risk-free rate and the market rate of 97.4 percent, both for a six-year holding period, we can use the CAPM to compute an investor's zero-NPV required return:

$$r_j = r_F + \beta_j(r_M - r_F) = 26.5\% + 1.50(97.4\% - 26.5\%) = 133.1\%$$

From Table 11.3, the anticipated ($6,806/2,000 - 1 = 240.3\%$) return over the holding period is much higher than the investor's required return. Because the venture has a positive NPV, the investor would be willing to pay the entrepreneur for the right to share proportionally in it. You can think of the payment actually coming in the form of accepting a less-than-proportional share of the equity in exchange for the investment.

The practical interpretation is demonstrated in Table 12.1.[1] Begin with the actual capital requirement of $2 million and assume that the investor contributes 75 percent, or $1.5 million. In a competitive market, this should be a zero-NPV investment, which means that the investor gets 22.0 percent of the venture. This makes the PV of his ownership stake (22.0% × $6.806 million = $1.5 million) exactly equal to his investment. Of the total $1.5 million investment by the investor, you can think of $440,800 (i.e., 22.0 percent of the $2 million total cost of the project) as a proportional investment by the investor and the remaining $1,059,200 as, effectively, a side payment to the entrepreneur. The side payment reduces the entrepreneur's capital contribution for the remaining 78.0 percent interest to $500,000 and enables the entrepreneur to invest more in the market. As a result, the PV of the entrepreneur's investment in the venture increases to $1.908 million, an NPV of more than $1.4 million.

In other words, the investor's capital contribution in excess of proportional sharing works like free leverage for the entrepreneur. Table 12.1 is a valuation template for valuing the financial claims of the investor and the entrepreneur and uses the assumptions discussed earlier. The "Investor allocation" panel is used to determine the fraction of the equity that must be allocated to the investor to compensate for the $1.5 million investment. That allocation is based on the CAPM. The "Cash flow to entrepreneur" panel shows the residual project cash flow that goes to the entrepreneur. By structuring the deal in this way, we effectively assume that the entrepreneur captures all of the venture's positive NPV.

The Entrepreneur's Gain from Contracting with a Well-Diversified Investor

Consider three entrepreneurs, X, Y, and Z, with different amounts of wealth and a venture requiring $2 million of capital. (We continue to use the same example.) Each contributes $500,000 to a venture and invests the balance of his or her wealth in a market portfolio. An investor contributes the remaining $1.5 million required by each entrepreneur. The last two columns in the table on page 487 show the NPV of each entrepreneur's investment for two types of contracts. The first illustrates proportional sharing; in the second, the parties allocate ownership claims so that the investor earns a zero-NPV return.

TABLE 12.1 Valuation Template 6: Valuation—Investor and entrepreneur's partial commitment

Market information	Annual	Holding period
Risk-free rate	4.00%	26.53%
Market rate	12.00%	97.38%
Market risk premium	8.00%	70.85%
Market variance	2.25%	13.50%
Market standard deviation	15.00%	36.74%
Correlation		0.2

Project cash flows	Invest date	Harvest date
Years until harvest		6
Investment in project	$2,000	
Expected project cash flow		$10,743
Project standard deviation of cash flows		$5,527

Investor allocation		
Project beta (based on cost of project)		1.504
Fraction of investment that is notionally in project		0.294
Outside investment	$1,500	
Required percent of equity		22.04%
Cash flow to investor		
Expected cash flow		$2,368
Standard deviation of cash flow		$1,218
Outside investor value		**$1,500**

Cash flow to entrepreneur		
Entrepreneur's investment	$500	
Expected project cash flow		$8,375
Project standard deviation		$4,309
Investment in market	$5,500	
Expected market cash flow		$10,856
Market standard deviation of cash flows		$2,021
Expected portfolio cash flow	$6,000	$19,231
Portfolio standard deviation		$5,112

CAPM market value estimate		
Portfolio present value		$10,806
Market investment		$5,500
Present value—project		**$5,306**

CAPM private value estimate—partial commitment		
Present value—portfolio		$7,408
Market investment		$5,500
Present value—project		**$1,908**

NPV—project to entrepreneur		**$1,408**

NOTE: *All monetary values in $ thousands. Shaded cells are inputs that can be changed.*

The entrepreneur's gain from contracting to provide the investor a CAPM-based allocation of ownership

Entrepreneur	Total wealth of entrepreneur	Percentage of wealth invested in venture	NPV of entrepreneur's investment in venture*	
			Proportional sharing contract	CAPM-based contract*
X	$500,000	100.0%	($483,000)	($447,000)
Y	$2,000,000	25.0%	$44,000	$174,000
Z	$6,000,000	8.3%	$639,000	$1,408,000

*Under CAPM-based allocation, the NPV of the investor's interest is zero.

Any entrepreneur, regardless of wealth, will find the project more valuable under CAPM-based allocation than under proportional allocation. The shift also enables the entrepreneur to justify investing a larger fraction of total wealth in the project.

How Much of the Entrepreneur's Wealth Should Be Invested in the Venture?

Now consider the entrepreneur's allocation of wealth between the venture and a market portfolio. The change from proportional sharing to CAPM-based allocation for the investor can have a surprising effect on the entrepreneur's wealth allocation decision. To demonstrate, we continue to assume that the venture requires a total investment of $2 million and that the entrepreneur has total wealth of $6 million. We can use the template in Table 12.1 to examine CAPM-based allocation.

It turns out that the entrepreneur's PV and NPV are highest when outside investors provide all $2 million of the needed capital. When this is the case, the investor's zero-NPV stake is 29.4 percent, with the entrepreneur retaining 70.6 percent.

One natural question is: If the entrepreneur is devoting human capital to the venture, how can her contribution be zero? The answer is that the $2 million from the investor is sufficient to "purchase" the entrepreneur's human capital, in much the same way that any employee is compensated.

Perhaps you are concerned that with an investment of zero, the entrepreneur will have little incentive to commit effort. This is not the case. The entrepreneur owns 70.6 percent of the equity. Thus, even though the entrepreneur's investment is zero, she still has a strong incentive to make the venture a success.

In fact, the entrepreneur may be able to do even better. Because the entrepreneur cares about total risk, whereas a diversified investor cares only about nondiversifiable risk, if the parties agree about the expected future cash flows, the investor should buy almost all of the equity from the entrepreneur. Under these conditions, the entrepreneur would realize the highest possible NPV by selling out to a diversified investor.

Reconciling Theory and Practice

The conclusions above may not seem to be consistent with the normal ownership structures of new ventures. Entrepreneurs usually do not sell out entirely, or, if they do and the value is material and subject to significant uncertainty, the transactions can involve complex structures in which the entrepreneur continues to bear significant risk. Such transactions, in reality, tend to occur once the entrepreneur's continuing contribution of effort is not critical to the venture.

If the preceding analysis is correct, why does the entrepreneur ever own any of the risky claims? We can now provide some answers:

- Entrepreneurs often are (rightly or wrongly) more optimistic about success than are investors. If so, an investor may not offer enough to buy out the entrepreneur.
- If the market for investment capital is not competitive, then the investor will be able to capture some of the NPV by making a below-market offer, in which case selling out might not be the entrepreneur's most valuable choice.
- If the entrepreneur's effort is important to success, then maintaining significant entrepreneurial ownership is a way of aligning the incentives of the entrepreneur with the interests of the investor.
- The entrepreneur may place subjective value on ownership or control of the venture, beyond the financial calculation.

One other reason why our theory-based value conclusions could diverge from practice is that the CAPM makes very specific assumptions about the risk/return tradeoff of investors. Our valuation model for an underdiversified investor also is specific. However, as long as diversifiable risk is more important to an underdiversified entrepreneur than to a well-diversified investor, venture cash flows will be more valuable to the investor. So, although different assumptions would result in different estimates of value, they would not alter the conclusion that the entrepreneur would achieve maximum NPV by selling the venture to a diversified investor.

12.5 Contract Choices That Alter Venture Returns

Given that an entrepreneur requires outside capital, how should she select an investor, and how does the investor's involvement affect value to the entrepreneur? New venture funding can come from either passive or active investors. Some prospective investors may not be well diversified, while others may be subsidized and accept below-market rates of return. Active investors are likely to demand higher expected returns and may insist on mechanisms for directly influencing venture development. But they may also contribute substantial value. How can the entrepreneur select the best investor from the array of prospects?

Until now, we have focused on a well-diversified, passive investor. In this section, we discuss two other cases: first, a passive investor who is willing to subsidize the project by accepting an expected return that is below the market rate, and second, an active VC who both adds value and demands a larger share of the business. For convenience, we assume that the contracts involve financial claims that are identical to those of the entrepreneur and that both investors are well diversified.

Evaluating Investment by Subsidized Investors

Small business investment companies (SBICs) and certain other kinds of investors in new ventures receive subsidies that are intended to encourage new venture formation or to support small businesses. The forms of the subsidies vary. Some investors receive direct access to low-cost funds, whereas others can use loan guarantees to reduce the cost of borrowing. The extent to which a subsidy is passed through to a venture can also vary. As discussed below, the effects of a specific subsidy program can be evaluated in much the same way that we evaluated the effects of passive outside investment.

How subsidized financing affects the entrepreneur's NPV. Except for the subsidy, a subsidized investor who is well diversified must earn the same return on investment as a well-diversified passive investor who is not subsidized. The only substantive difference is that part of the capital supplied to the subsidized investor comes at a below-market rate. We can represent this subsidy by reducing the investor's fractional ownership claim to reflect the subsidy. The investor's required ownership share is determined by how the subsidy affects the required rate of return.

Implications for the choice of financing sources.   Other things being equal, raising capital from a subsidized investor is preferable to raising capital from one that is not. But other things are unlikely to be equal. Subsidized investors often seek lower-risk financial claims than do other investors in new ventures. They frequently prefer debt (or debt with equity sweeteners) to common or preferred stock. Accordingly, they are better suited to invest in small businesses with positive income and cash flow, and they tend to shift more of the total risk to the entrepreneur. Compared to raising an equivalent amount of capital from a diversified investor who receives equity, this could reduce the entrepreneur's NPV.

Furthermore, it is not always clear that the entrepreneur can realize the benefit of the subsidy. If subsidized investors do not need to compete aggressively with each other, then the investor is competing against investors whose opportunity cost of capital is determined by the market. If so, then the subsidized investor should be able to capture the benefits of the subsidy instead of passing them on to the entrepreneur.

Evaluating Investment by Active Investors

Active investors contribute both financial capital and expertise. Typically, they realize the returns on investment of effort through their financial claims. Thus, an active investor demands a larger, more valuable ownership interest to compensate for effort. If the involvement is constructive, it can increase the overall expected return and possibly reduce risk.

We assume that the objective of an entrepreneur who is deciding among active, passive, and subsidized investors is to maximize her own NPV. With respect to VC or angel investor financing, the critical issue is whether the investor is expected to add enough value (by increasing expected returns, reducing risk, or both) to offset the higher claim on ownership. The issue can be examined by modifying the project valuation assumptions to reflect the expected effect of active involvement.

12.6   Implementation and Negotiation

In this section, we adapt spreadsheet "Valuation Template 6" (Table 12.1) to examine how specific financing proposals affect value. We continue with the example where the opportunity requires $2 million of total funding, including $1.5 million from an investor. We now drop the assumption that investor claims have NPVs of zero; rather, the proposals are generated by investors who seek positive NPVs. The entrepreneur knows the proposed terms and has a sense of how the required return of each investor is determined.

The entrepreneur is considering the following four alternatives:

1. *Proportional sharing.* A passive investor will provide $1.5 million in exchange for 75 percent of the common stock.

2. *Ownership shifted.* A well-diversified passive investor will provide $1.5 million in exchange for 40 percent of the common stock.

3. *Subsidized investor.* A subsidized passive investor will provide $1.5 million in exchange for 30 percent of the common stock. The investor's annual cost of funds is 2 percent below the CAPM opportunity cost measure.

4. *Active investor.* An active investor will provide $1.5 million in exchange for 45 percent of common stock. The entrepreneur expects that investor involvement will increase cash flows by about 10 percent and will reduce the standard deviation of cash flows by about 10 percent.

Here is a test of your intuition: Suppose you are the entrepreneur who is faced with these choices. Which one do you think is most attractive and why? How much negotiation room do you think there is for each? Don't be surprised if your intuition does not get you very far. You probably feel fairly confident that alternative (2) dominates alternative (1). But how much can you say about the relative values of alternatives (2), (3), and (4)?

To evaluate each alternative, we use a two-step process. First, we modify the simulation model in Table 11.2 to reflect the investor's proposed allocation of the Year 6 cash flows (the free cash balance plus continuing value) and rerun the simulation. For the active investor alternative, we use the simulated results to calculate the expected cash flow and standard deviation for the investor and for the entrepreneur. Second, we modify the assumptions in "Valuation Template 6" to reflect the terms of each alternative and then use the template to value the financial claims under each.

Table 12.2 contains a summary of the simulation results and valuations. Each column reflects one of the alternatives. Under the heading "Active investor," the expected cash flow is higher and the standard deviation is lower than that for the other alternatives. This reflects the investor's assumed effect on venture risk and return.

The "Investor allocation" panel shows the fractions of equity the investor would receive under each alternative, as well as the expected cash

TABLE **12.2**   **Comparative valuation of outside financing alternatives**

Market information	Passive investor (proportional)	Passive investor (CAPM)	Passive investor (subsidized)	Active investor
Risk-free rate	26.53%	26.53%	26.53%	26.53%
Market rate	97.38%	97.38%	97.38%	97.38%
Market risk premium	70.85%	70.85%	70.85%	70.85%
Market variance	13.50%	13.50%	13.50%	13.50%
Market standard deviation	36.74%	36.74%	36.74%	36.74%
Correlation	0.2	0.2	0.2	0.2
Project cash flows				
Years until harvest	6	6	6	6
Expected project cash flow	**$10,743**	**$10,743**	**$10,743**	**$11,817**
Project standard deviation of cash flows	**$5,527**	**$5,527**	**$5,527**	**$5,025**
Investor allocation				
Project beta (based on cost of project)	1.504	1.504	1.504	1.368
Fraction of investment that is notionally in project	0.294	0.294	0.294	0.256
Required percent of equity	75.00%	40.00%	30.00%	45.00%
Cash flow to investor				
Expected cash flow	$8,057	$4,297	$3,223	$5,318
Standard deviation of cash flow	$4,145	$2,211	$1,658	$2,261
Investor present value	**$5,104**	**$2,722**	**$2,268**	**$3,514**
Investor net present value	**$3,604**	**$1,222**	**$768**	**$2,014**
Cash flow to entrepreneur				
Entrepreneur's investment				
Expected project cash flow	$2,686	$6,446	$7,520	$6,500
Project standard deviation	$1,382	$3,316	$3,869	$2,764
Investment in market				
Expected market cash flow	$10,856	$10,856	$10,856	$10,856
Market standard deviation of cash flows	$2,021	$2,021	$2,021	$2,021
Expected portfolio cash flow	$13,542	$17,302	$18,376	$17,356
Portfolio standard deviation	$2,666	$4,214	$4,710	$3,736
CAPM market value estimate				
Portfolio present value	$7,201	$9,583	$10,264	$9,794
Market investment	$5,500	$5,500	$5,500	$5,500
Present value—project	**$1,701**	**$4,083**	**$4,764**	**$4,294**
Net present value—project	**1,201**	**3,583**	**4,264**	**3,794**
CAPM private value estimate—partial commitment				
Present value—portfolio	$6,639	$7,251	$7,346	$8,023
Market investment	$5,500	$5,500	$5,500	$5,500
Present value—project	**$1,139**	**$1,751**	**$1,846**	**$2,523**
Net present value—project	**$639**	**$1,251**	**$1,346**	**$2,023**

NOTE: *All monetary values in $ thousands.*

flow and standard deviation of cash flows. The last line is the NPV of the investor's investment, assuming that each is well diversified and (except for the subsidized investor) uses the CAPM to value its claim. For the subsidized investor, we assume that cost of capital is lower by 2 percent per year.

Based on the valuations in this panel, each alternative yields a positive NPV for the investor. The computed NPV is highest for the investor who is offering proportional sharing. Assuming that the investor is well diversified, the entrepreneur has considerable room for negotiation. However, if this investor is an individual and is not well diversified, then we cannot determine his actual PV. We assume that the other three investors all are well diversified. The computed NPVs suggest that each can still benefit even with a reduced ownership stake. The results suggest that the greatest potential for negotiation from among these three is with the active investor, who has an NPV of $2.014 million under the proposed terms. However, the NPV must also compensate for the investor's effort, which we have not factored into the calculations.

The "Cash flow to entrepreneur" panel shows the projected cash flow and standard deviation that the entrepreneur would receive under each alternative. We generated these results from the simulation trials based on the entrepreneur's investment of $500,000 in the venture. We assume that the balance of the entrepreneur's wealth, $5.5 million, is invested in a market index.

In the "CAPM private value estimate—partial commitment" panel, the PV of the entrepreneur's investment portfolio (including the venture and the market index) is always greater than the $6 million total investment. Thus, all four proposals are acceptable to the entrepreneur relative to not pursuing the opportunity. The maximum NPV is $2.023 million with the active investor (i.e., $2.523 million PV, less the $500,000 investment). As this is also the proposal where the investor seems to realize the greatest positive NPV, it appears that the best potential for improving the terms through negotiation is with the active investor.

12.7 A Recap of Contracting with Asymmetric Attitudes toward Risk

Thus far in the chapter, we have used the underdiversification reasoning from Chapter 11 to provide a conceptual framework for evaluating financing alternatives. The framework recognizes that entrepreneurs, as undiversified investors, should value projects at discount rates that can be substantially higher than the rates appropriate for well-diversified investors. The difference in attitudes toward risk gives rise to a significant opportunity for an entrepreneur to contract with investors in ways that reduce the overall required rate of return on the venture. Beyond this, we demonstrate that thoughtful design of contracts can enhance the value of projects and turn unacceptable projects into attractive ones.

Significant opportunities exist to extend the conceptual framework. For example, analysis in this chapter is limited to examination of contracts in which the entrepreneur and the investor hold identical claims. In most real settings, the investor holds a differentiated claim, such as preferred stock, and preserves a variety of rights and options. In addition, investments in many ventures are multistage, and the investor may retain an option to abandon. We postpone exploration of these real-world considerations to Chapter 13. For now we simply note that the framework developed here can be used to examine all of these considerations. Doing so can help to assess, for example, the optimal staging of capital infusions and design of financial contracts with embedded options.

We turn next to the issues we have deferred until now: the effects of information problems and incentive problems on financial contract design.

12.8   Information Problems, Incentive Problems, and Financial Contracting

Information and incentive problems are at the core of negotiations between entrepreneurs and investors. New venture markets are highly uncertain and subject to being influenced by unanticipated events. The parties involved may have different expectations about venture success and may have difficulty communicating their expectations. Outside parties often cannot know whether venture performance is due to luck or managerial capability and effort. We refer to such problems as information problems.

Information problems affect start-ups in many ways. For example, a prospective entrepreneur may have an idea with significant commercial value but be unable to protect it by patent or copyright. The entrepreneur cannot disclose the idea to prospective investors without risking its appropriation. How do entrepreneurs deal with such dilemmas? How, conversely, can investors determine the entrepreneur's true expectations?

In addition to information problems, incentive conflicts can arise between the investors and the entrepreneur and among different investors. An entrepreneur with a limited equity stake may not always act in the best interest of other shareholders. If outside financing is in the form of debt, the entrepreneur may want to take on more risk than creditors would like. How can incentive problems such as these be overcome?

Our first objective in the remainder of this chapter is to place information and incentive problems into an analytic framework, so that it is possible to think about solutions in a structured way. In Chapter 13, we extend our focus to the real-world challenges of designing value-enhancing relationships.

12.9   A Taxonomy of Information and Incentive Problems

A useful distinction exists between costs that arise before a contract is entered and those that arise afterward. Before the agreement, the fundamental problem is information; each party is unsure about what the other knows. After an agreement is reached, the problem is incentives. Of course, in designing the contract, the parties will try to deal with incentive concerns, but no contract can do so perfectly. A contract is sought in the first place because one party (or both) expects to make an investment in the venture and seeks to mitigate the adverse consequences of information and incentive problems.

There is no bright-line distinction between information and incentive problems. Information problems arise because the parties may not have correct incentives to reveal what they know, and incentive problems arise because the parties cannot costlessly acquire the information they need to evaluate performance.

Consider the notion of a perfect contract. A perfect contract anticipates and provides for every contingency. Its terms bind the parties, so that neither can try to take advantage of the other. The contract must contain sufficient detail so that a third party can fully enforce its provisions. A perfect contract is efficient in the sense that (1) each risk is allocated to the party who can bear it at least cost, and (2) collectively, the contract terms exhaust the possibilities for mutual gain.

New venture financial contracts are far from perfect. They often include extensive lists of representations and warranties and complex contingency structures. Such provisions are designed to deal with information and incentive problems. They tend to be complex but incomplete in that they do not address every contingency. Complexity arises from efforts to address information and incentive problems through contract terms.

Financial Contracting with Known Symmetrical Beliefs

If the entrepreneur and investor share expectations and know that they do, then even with uncertainty their contract can be simple. For a project without staged financing, the contract might reduce to a single statement regarding the fraction of harvest value the investor will receive. For a project with staged financing, the contract needs to describe the conditions under which follow-on investment will be made but can still be simple. Complexity arises because the parties either have asymmetric beliefs or do not know what the other party believes.

Precontractual Information Costs

Information costs arise before any sunk investment is made. They arise because the future is complex and uncertain, because the parties may have different information and expectations, and because each party has an incentive to distort his or her true information or beliefs. Oliver Williamson, who in 2009 received the Nobel Prize in Economics for his work on organizational choice and form, refers to these problems as bounded rationality, information asymmetry, and information impactedness.

Bounded rationality. The parties to a venture cannot anticipate every contingency the venture will face. Even if delineating the contingencies were possible, negotiating provisions to deal with each remote contingency would be too expensive to justify. Decision makers weigh the costs and benefits and rationally stop short of explicitly contracting over all contingencies. The idea that individuals have limited capacity to deal with complexity is referred to as bounded rationality.[2]

To illustrate, consider an entrepreneur who is seeking funding. Product development time may be short or long. Quality of the resulting product and consumer demand may be high or low. Rivals may be successful or unsuccessful in their efforts to compete. Catastrophic events (death of the entrepreneur, war, etc.) may intervene. The funding needs of the venture depend on all of these factors. In some scenarios the investor will be eager to provide funding but not in others. In some scenarios the entrepreneur would prefer to abandon the venture. If contracting costs were low, the parties could develop an elaborate list of contingencies and design a contract that would specify the response to each. Bounded rationality explains why entrepreneurs and investors do not try to do this.

Information asymmetry. Information asymmetry means one party has information that the other lacks and cannot easily acquire. Asymmetric information can prevent a bargain from being struck or cause risk and return to be allocated less efficiently than if information were shared.

The used-car market is a well-known example of how asymmetric information can disrupt a market.[3] Sellers have an information advantage in that each knows more about his car's quality than do prospective buyers. An owner of a high-quality used car would like to convey the quality information to buyers but cannot do so easily. Merely claiming that the car is a good one is not enough because all sellers can make similar claims. The result of information asymmetry is called adverse selection. Bad products drive good ones out of the market.

The adverse selection problem applies directly to the market for new venture financing. Most ventures do not have enough of a track record for investors to easily assess their merits. Entrepreneurs are likely to compete for funds by presenting optimistic projections and withholding negative information. To compensate, VCs and other investors sometimes (as we have discussed) use high hurdle rates to value the projected cash flows. Reliance on high hurdle rates, however, does not solve the adverse selection problem. Entrepreneurs with superior opportunities and realistic projections are confronted with undervaluation and may decide not to pursue them. Those with inferior ventures but who nonetheless can project rosy prospects remain in the market.

Information asymmetry can also be a problem for entrepreneurs. An entrepreneur usually cannot know why a prospective investor is interested in the venture. The investor may only be seeking to assess the venture as a competitive threat. Entrepreneurs claim that investors sometimes only get involved in a venture to keep it from reaching the market. This could happen if the investor was involved with another venture that targeted the same market.

Before concluding that you would not want to deal with either of these people, you should note that neither one may be trying to deliberately take unfair advantage. Many entrepreneurs are more confident than they should be. Many investors have experience with failed investments and are inundated with proposals from overoptimistic, would-be entrepreneurs.

Impacted information. The problem is not just that the information is held asymmetrically but also that each party has an incentive to distort what he or she knows. Consequently, each fears exploitation by the other and is reluctant to commit to the venture. Information is impacted when one party is uncertain about what the other knows and the parties cannot easily communicate what they know to each other. Impacted information raises the cost of market exchange and contracting because prospective trading partners fear being taken advantage of. To complete the exchange, one or both parties must expend resources to overcome real or perceived information disadvantages. For new ventures, the expenditures often take the form of due diligence investigations in advance of contracting or negotiating contractual contingencies that mitigate the value of information advantages.[4]

An Example: Adverse Selection in Capital Raising

Underinvestment occurs when a venture or public corporation has an attractive opportunity but lacks sufficient capital to pursue it and when investors are uncertain about the value of existing assets. In such cases, raising capital is excessively costly and good investments may be forgone. Public companies can mitigate this underinvestment problem by maintaining financial slack. However, absence of financial slack is a hallmark of new ventures. Consequently, the underinvestment problem can be more severe for new ventures than for public corporations.

Whose interests do managers serve?   Not all shareholders of public companies are the same. Among those who currently own the stock, some can be expected to sell in the near future, others to maintain their current investments over long periods, and still others to maintain their fractional ownership by purchasing new shares whenever the company issues new equity.

In a public corporation, it is unclear which of these shareholder groups' interests managers will serve. If they act in the interest of investors who try to maintain their fractional ownership, they will try to maximize the intrinsic value. If they act in the interest of short-run shareholders, though, they will avoid reducing short-run value, even if doing so would increase value in the long run. And if they act in the interest of buy-and-hold investors, they will try to issue shares when the market overvalues them. Doing so would benefit passive shareholders by taking advantage of new investors.

An early-stage entrepreneur is much like a passive investor who seeks to raise capital holding his own interest constant. The entrepreneur is raising money from outside investors, and doing so reduces her fractional ownership. Closer to harvesting, the entrepreneur (and other existing investors) may be more like an active investor who is concerned primarily with high near-term value. In either case, the entrepreneur has an incentive to raise capital when the venture is overvalued. Thus, at either point, new investors face an adverse selection problem—the risk of paying too much.

The underinvestment problem. Consider an entrepreneur's decision to seek new equity. The entrepreneur may need the money to finance a positive-NPV growth opportunity or may desire to capture a gain by selling overvalued shares. Consequently, when the entrepreneur seeks new equity, investors may regard the action as an indication that the entrepreneur thinks investors will overvalue the shares. The likely result is that the investor will demand a larger ownership stake in exchange for investing.

The investor's response is problematic for a venture that is not overvalued and needs capital to finance growth. The investor's reaction can cause the entrepreneur to forgo an opportunity that would be accepted if the venture could issue shares at a price that reflected intrinsic value. If the entrepreneur goes ahead anyway, some of the value of the opportunity will be transferred to the new investor instead of being retained by the entrepreneur.

An example. Table 12.3 concerns a venture in which an entrepreneur has already made a significant investment. Assets in place reflect the value of the entrepreneur's prior investment. The venture now has an opportunity to grow but requires $600,000 from a VC investor to do so. The values of the assets in place and the growth opportunity depend on which state of the world (good or bad) is realized. At Time 0, when financing is being sought, the entrepreneur already knows which state will occur; the VC investor knows only that the two states are equally likely. The VC will learn the true state at Time 1.

Suppose the entrepreneur tells the VC that he plans to pursue the opportunity no matter which state occurs. Doing so seems to make sense because the opportunity has a positive NPV in either state. The resulting value of the venture is $850,000 and the respective values of the entrepreneur's shares and the VC's shares are $250,000 and $600,000. Because the VC market is competitive, all of the NPV accrues to the entrepreneur. The VC pays $600,000 for new shares that are worth $600,000.

It turns out that this is not the best strategy for the entrepreneur. The values of the entrepreneur's shares and the VC's shares, conditional on which state occurs, reveal that the entrepreneur would be better off by not raising capital in the good state. The entrepreneur's shares will be worth $300,000 if the growth opportunity is passed up

TABLE 12.3 The new venture underinvestment problem

Assumptions

There are two equally likely states of nature: State 1 and State 2.
The entrepreneur learns the true state at Time 0.
The venture capital investor learns the true state at Time 1.

Asset values	State 1	State 2
Venture assets in place (thousands)	$a = \$300$	$a = \$100$
NPV of first-round outside financing (thousands)	$g = \$80$	$g = \$20$

The venture has no financial slack ($S = 0$).
The opportunity requires investment ($I = \$600$).
So the entrepreneur must raise equity from a VC ($E = \$600$).

Suppose the entrepreneur states at Time 0 that he is seeking outside financing and plans to undertake the expansion no matter which state occurs.

Then the value of the venture at Time 0, V', equals $250:

$\quad V' = (\$300 + \$100)/2 + (\$80 + \$20)/2 = \$250$

and the value of outside equity, E, equals $600.
Resulting total value, including the new investment, is $850.

The values of the entrepreneur's shares and VC's shares when the true state is realized are as follows.

If State 1 occurs, then total value of the venture, V, is $980 ($a + g + E$):

$\quad V^{\text{Ent.}} = V \times V'/(V' + E) = \$980 \times \$250/\$850 = \$288$
$\quad V^{\text{VC}} = V \times V'/(V' + E) = \$980 \times \$600/\$850 = \$692$

If State 2 occurs, then total value of the venture is $720:

$\quad V^{\text{Ent.}} = V \times V'/(V' + E) = \$720 \times \$250/\$850 = \$212$
$\quad V^{\text{VC}} = V \times V'/(V' + E) = \$720 \times \$600/\$850 = \$508$

The entrepreneur's shares and the venture capitalist's shares are correctly priced at the outset:

$\quad V' = (\$288 + \$212)/2 = \$250$
$\quad E = (\$692 + \$508)/2 = \$600$

In this case, the entrepreneur's decision to raise capital tells the VC nothing about what the entrepreneur knows the true state to be.

Raising capital in both states is not the best deal for the entrepreneur.

Payoff to the entrepreneur	Issue and invest ($E = \$600$)	Do not issue ($E = \$0$)
$V^{\text{Ent.}}$ in State 1	$288	$300
$V^{\text{Ent.}}$ in State 2	$212	$100

The entrepreneur is better off if he does not raise capital in State 1 (the good state) but does in State 2 (the bad state).

Equilibrium payoffs

But the VC will recognize that seeking financing signals that the entrepreneur knows that State 2 will occur. The VC will not invest $600 to receive value of only $508. Instead, the VC will demand a bigger fraction of the venture's equity in exchange for the $600 investment, such that the entrepreneur's shares are worth only $120 in State 2.

Payoff	Issue and invest ($E = \$600$)	Do not issue ($E = \$0$)
$V^{\text{Ent.}}$ in State 1	—	$300
$V^{\text{Ent.}}$ in State 2	$120	—

A growth opportunity worth $80 is passed up. The entrepreneur is worse off than had he been able to commit to always invest, $V'' = \$210$.

SOURCE: *Adapted from the corporate finance example of Myers and Majluf (1984).*

but only $288,000 if the investment is made. Further, the entrepreneur will want to go ahead with the growth opportunity even if he knows the bad state will occur because the value of the entrepreneur's shares will be $212,000 if the investment is made but only $100,000 if it is not.

The scenario described above is not an equilibrium. By investing in the bad state and not in the good, the entrepreneur is attempting to exploit an information advantage over the VC. If the VC goes along, she will be paying $600,000 for an asset that is worth only $508,000. To protect herself from opportunism, the VC must demand a larger ownership fraction, so that the $600,000 investment is actually worth $600,000. Because in the bad state the entire firm is only worth $720,000, the entrepreneur's share can only be worth $120,000 in the bad state.

Paradoxically, the entrepreneur ends up worse off than if he could commit to raise equity no matter what. Faced with the potential for opportunistic behavior, the VC reacts in a way that reduces the expected value of the entrepreneur's claim to $210,000 instead of $250,000. It follows that the entrepreneur would be willing to spend up to $40,000 on contractual or other mechanisms to overcome the problem.

Implications for new venture financing. Prospective investors in ventures with sunk investments, such as the past effort of the entrepreneur, are likely to be concerned that entrepreneurs will try to mislead them into overvaluation. They can be expected to respond in much the same way that investors in the capital market react to announcements of plans to issue equity—by discounting the value to compensate.

The entrepreneur and the investor need to find ways of overcoming investor concern about paying too much (the adverse selection problem). Common solutions include staging investments with abandonment options, allowing the investor to be directly involved with the venture, and other contracting provisions that mitigate information advantages. The investor can overcome concern that the entrepreneur may want to pursue a negative-NPV venture by ensuring that the entrepreneur's return is only high if the venture is a success.

Postcontractual Incentive Problems

Once a contract has been entered or a sunk investment has been made, incentives change. The parties may act in ways that are not consistent with their original intentions. Incentive problems arise when contracts are incomplete or when parties cannot monitor performance perfectly. Such problems are known as "moral hazard." Anticipating moral hazard is a first step toward finding ways to use deal structure to minimize the associated costs.

Health insurance is the classic example of moral hazard.[5] A person who is fully responsible for his or her medical bills makes value-maximizing tradeoffs in deciding whether to visit a doctor. But a person who is fully insured and does not regard the time spent on doctor visits as a cost will seek medical advice and treatment for every symptom or illness. The increased use of doctors as a result of health insurance is an example of moral hazard.

Financial contracts give rise to similar moral hazard problems. For example, once an investor commits to a venture and shares in the benefits of its success, an entrepreneur may devote less effort to achieving that success. It makes sense that the entrepreneur would devote less effort than if she were the exclusive beneficiary of her efforts. Replacing outside equity with debt financing changes the entrepreneur's incentives, but if the debt is risky, it does not eliminate the moral hazard.[6]

Specific investment.   Specific investments are investments that support a given activity or relationship but have little value in alternative use. Once these investments are made, they are, in effect, sunk. An example is an entrepreneur's investment in equipment that is particularly useful for making circuit boards that are customized to the needs of a specific customer.[7] Suppose the amortized quarterly economic cost of the equipment is $4,000 and the circuit board sales contract between the entrepreneur and the customer calls for the customer to pay $7,000 quarterly. For simplicity, we can assume that the variable cost of making the boards is zero. This means that the economic gain to the entrepreneur is $3,000 per quarter. The $3,000 gain is called an "economic rent." Economic rent is an *ex ante* concept and is measured as the excess of expected return over the opportunity cost of resources committed. In deciding whether to make the investment to produce the circuit boards, the entrepreneur commits the resources only if the economic rent is positive. Thus, the economic rent is what makes the NPV of the investment positive.

Now consider a scenario in which the resource commitment to manufacture the circuit boards has already been made. Economic rent is no longer relevant; instead, the concern is whether the return is sufficient to cover the alternative use value of the resources. Suppose the resources have a salvage value of $2,500 per quarter. The $7,000 quarterly revenue is more than sufficient to justify continuing to make circuit boards. The $4,500 difference between revenue and salvage value is called a "quasi rent." Quasi rent is an *ex post* concept. It measures the difference between revenue received and minimum revenue necessary to justify keeping the equipment in its current use.

Quasi rents exist because of sunk investments. Moral hazard problems are related to the existence of quasi rents. Because the entrepreneur will continue to supply circuit boards as long as the quarterly return is at least $2,500, the customer who is paying $7,000 has an incentive to threaten not to purchase unless the entrepreneur reduces the price. Such an attempt to appropriate the quasi rent is an example of moral hazard that arises after a specific investment is made.

This example shows that the parties to a new venture must be sensitive to the presence of specific investments. If the investment is not specific, competition can prevent appropriation. If it is, then the party investing in the specific asset faces the risk of appropriation, and the contract structure may need to address the risk.

Small numbers bargaining.   Market exchange works best when large numbers of buyers and sellers compete. The market for initial outside financing can be such a market.

It is easy to see how the presence of large numbers of potential investors facilitates exchange. Suppose an entrepreneur is concerned about losing control by "shopping an opportunity around" too early. By making an initial investment, the entrepreneur can advance the venture to a point where the merits will be apparent to prospective investors. Any investment the entrepreneur makes at this early stage is likely to be nonsalvageable when negotiations for financing begin. The entrepreneur must balance the risk of losing control against the risk of losing a return on a sunk investment.

With a large number of investors competing, the entrepreneur does not need to be concerned about making value-enhancing investments before agreeing to a contract. If the entrepreneur is right, competition among investors will result in terms that more than compensate for the sunk investment. The difficulty arises when the number of prospective investors is small; then the entrepreneur cannot rely on competition to give her an opportunity to recover sunk investment. In fact, sunk investment, while it may add value and help secure a first-mover advantage, invites appropriation by an investor.[8]

Having large numbers of competitors vying in the initial stage does not prevent opportunism in later-stage negotiations. Many ventures can evolve from large numbers to small numbers as the venture progresses. The winner of the first round may gain a first-mover advantage that

FIGURE **12.1**

Agency cost of outside equity

Adapted from Jensen and Meckling (1976).

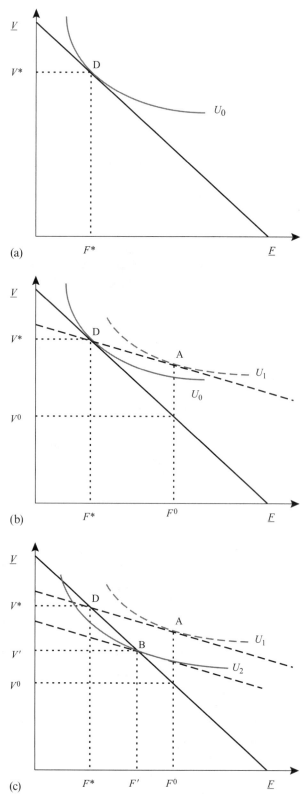

(a)

(b)

(c)

Line $\underline{VF}$ illustrates the feasible combinations of firm value, V, and perquisite consumption, F, attainable from a given level of investment. The slope of the constraint is -1. With the manager being 100% owner, the manager maximizes utility at point D, by choosing to consume perquisites of F^*, resulting in a firm value of V^*.

The former owner now owns only α% of the firm. If the outside investor values the firm at V^* and pays $(1 - \alpha) \times V^*$ for his or her share of the firm, the manager acts as if the dashed line (with a slope of $-\alpha$) is the new constraint for trading off firm value and perquisites, and maximizes utility at point A. Firm value declines to V^0 and the outside investor loses a fraction of the investment.

The outside investor values the firm at V', recognizing that the manager will increase perquisite consumption once some of the business is sold. The investor pays $(1 - \alpha) \times V'$ for his or her share of the firm. The manager acts as if the lower dashed line is the new constraint for trading off firm value and perquisites, and maximizes utility at point B. As expected, firm value declines to V'.

would make it difficult for rivals to compete in later-stage negotiations. It is not useful to characterize this practice as opportunistic, particularly if the pattern is characteristic of the market so that the ability to bargain more aggressively in later rounds is reflected in the terms for the initial investment.

Still, in new venture financing the potential for opportunism is large. To obtain initial financing, the entrepreneur may be asked to provide an abandonment option and possibly other rights, such as the right to acquire control or to terminate the entrepreneur. Why do venture financing contracts give so much control to investors, when it would appear that the potential for opportunism could be limited by using a more complex contract that might give similar rights but only under certain well-specified conditions? Apparently, entrepreneurs in such arrangements do not fear opportunism by investors—but why not? The answer is threefold: First, if the venture is successful, the entrepreneur can pursue other financing, even if the investor withdraws. Second, the investor needs to preserve a good working relationship with the entrepreneur. Third, any investor who wishes to be involved repeatedly in new ventures must avoid gaining a reputation for behaving opportunistically.

An Example: Moral Hazard in Organizations

An entrepreneur must decide how much effort and resources to commit to a venture and how much to commit to other activities. When the entrepreneur does not rely on outside capital, she bears the full costs and benefits of these choices. Involving investors, whether they hold equity or risky debt, weakens the link between individual effort and rewards. vThe resulting change in behavior is a moral hazard problem. It arises after the contract is entered.

Jensen and Meckling (1976) explore the effects of increasing outside ownership as a utility maximization problem. They look first at how the behavior of the entrepreneur (owner-manager) changes when outside equity is added. They extend the analysis to consider the choice between outside equity and outside debt. Figure 12.1 provides a graphical summary of part of their analysis.

Initially, the entrepreneur owns 100 percent of an all-equity firm. Figure 12.1a depicts the choices available to the entrepreneur. By applying all of her effort and resources to the venture, she can achieve maximum value of $\underline{V}$ in the figure; think of $\underline{V}$ as the present value of the entrepreneur's wealth, including human capital. Alternatively, she can allocate effort and resources to other activities (playing golf, etc.). If no effort is applied to the venture, it is worthless and the attained value of other activities is $\underline{F}$; Jensen and Meckling refer to F as "perquisite consumption." The line segment $\underline{VF}$ describes the entrepreneur's opportunity set. By definition, the value of perquisites consumed is measured in terms of opportunity cost of value forgone in the venture; thus, $\underline{VF}$ has a slope of -1. The entrepreneur's problem is to choose the effort level that corresponds to the entrepreneur's highest achievable utility. The indifference curve, U_0, reflects the tradeoff of satisfaction that the entrepreneur derives from increased V compared to increased F. Point D, the tangency between the opportunity set and U_0, is the point where the entrepreneur's utility is maximized. This point is associated with V^* and F^*.

Suppose that, to harvest a portion of her investment, the entrepreneur sells $(1 - \alpha)$ percent of her equity to an investor and retains α percent. Selling part of the equity changes the entrepreneur's decision calculus. Now, instead of being able to trade one dollar of value in the venture for one dollar of other activities, the entrepreneur can trade α percent of a dollar of venture value for one dollar of value from other activities. The entrepreneur's incentive to allocate effort to increasing the value of the venture has declined because some of the benefit of working hard accrues to the outside investor.

Figure 12.1b shows what happens if the investor fails to take account of the change in incentives. The investor pays $(1 - \alpha) \times V^*$ for $(1 - \alpha)$ percent of the venture. The change causes the opportunity set of the entrepreneur to become less steeply sloped. The slope changes from -1 to $-\alpha$; and, because the investor has paid a price based on V^*, the new opportunity set passes through V^*F^* (point D). The dashed line shows the new budget constraint. Because the entrepreneur's cost of allocating effort to other activities is now lower, the entrepreneur devotes less effort to the venture and more to other activities. The change is represented by point A, where the new indifference curve, U_1, is tangent to the entrepreneur's new opportunity set. The value of the venture is reduced to V^0, due to the entrepreneur's reduced effort. The investor pays $(1 - \alpha) \times V^*$ for shares worth only $(1 - \alpha) \times V^0$. The change of incentives is an agency cost of outside equity. This is a specific example of moral hazard.

Figure 12.1c illustrates the case in which the investor correctly anticipates the effect of the entrepreneur's changed incentives. By offering a price consistent with a valuation of V', the investor compensates for moral hazard. Point B is the point of tangency between the entrepreneur's opportunity set and indifference curve U_2, at the intersection of the entrepreneur's new opportunity set with $\underline{VF}$. If the tangency is above the intersection, then the price paid by the investor is too high and the

NPV of the investor's purchase is negative because of the overpayment. If it is below the intersection, then the entrepreneur loses value to the investor.

Suppose the entrepreneur is unusual and is not very interested in consuming perquisites. Demonstrating to prospective investors that she would not reduce effort as much as the typical entrepreneur could enable her to sell the interest in the venture for a higher price. But how can she credibly demonstrate that she is different from the others?

The Agency Cost of Debt—Distorting the Investment Decision

High-growth, high-risk ventures normally do not have much debt financing; but other ventures often do, and preferred stock claims issued to investors in new ventures can have similar effects. Debt financing creates its own kinds of agency problems. As long as the debt is riskless, debt financing does not create any incentive (or moral hazard) problem. But as the riskiness increases, the incentives of the equity holders (in our case, the entrepreneur) change. High default risk can cause an entrepreneur to underinvest in low-risk activities and/or overinvest in high-risk activities.

Suppose an entrepreneur must decide whether to invest in a warehouse and distribution operation to support expansion of his e-commerce business. Current financing includes high-risk debt. The entrepreneur is considering investing $100,000 in the expansion, and the project has a positive NPV. The entrepreneur may nonetheless decide against the investment, because some of the benefit of the investment accrues to the lender (by making the debt less risky), whereas the entrepreneur (who has the decision rights) would be making the investment. Equivalent to investing $100,000, the entrepreneur could be considering forgoing a large dividend or a large salary increase or bonus.

Overinvestment occurs under conditions that are somewhat similar. The venture is not doing well and default appears likely; the entrepreneur recognizes that liquidating is more valuable than continuing to operate. But if the entrepreneur liquidates, the proceeds will go first to the lender, and the entrepreneur gets nothing. Conversely, if the entrepreneur continues to operate until repayment is contractually required, there is a small chance of successful innovation. In the event of success, the venture can easily repay the loan and the entrepreneur keeps a large residual. Conversely, if the venture fails, the entrepreneur loses nothing. Because of the asymmetric payoff, even though the NPV is negative the entrepreneur will choose to go ahead. Overinvestment occurs when the entrepreneur is able to commit firm resources to high-risk activities where the cost of failure is borne largely by creditors but the reward of success accrues largely to the entrepreneur.

12.10   Essentials of Contract Design

The term "contract" is subject to varying interpretations. For our purpose, contracts span a spectrum. At one end, discrete contracts are those that contain very explicit provisions. The transactions are impersonal, self-contained exchanges, and performance is easily observable and measurable. The contracts are of short duration, and any contingencies are anticipated and provided for explicitly. MacNeil (1974) characterizes discrete contracts as "sharp in by clear agreement; sharp out by clear performance." At the other end of the spectrum are relational contracts. These are highly flexible, implicit contracts based on ongoing relationships between the parties. A relational contract is like a constitution that describes what the parties are trying to accomplish and how, in general terms, they aspire to share the benefits.

Discrete Contracting

Discrete contract terms are specific in content and duration. An example is a financial contract between an entrepreneur and a bank, where the venture requires occasional small infusions of cash. If the loan is collateralized, the contract is discrete. The bank does not need to accept the entrepreneur's sales projections or incur the expense of verifying the venture's financial performance, other than to make sure terms of the loan are met. The entrepreneur is not concerned that the lender will act opportunistically as long as it is clear that the venture can meet its debt obligations. If the lender does not renew the loan in spite of the entrepreneur's adequate collateral, the entrepreneur can turn to another lender.

Discrete contracting works best for simple exchanges, where the parties have similar expectations, objectives are easy to specify, and performance is easy to verify. If the parties have materially different expectations, it may be possible to design a more complex contract that is still discrete but circumvents the need to have similar expectations.

We established earlier that if expectations are held symmetrically and incentives are not a concern, then the better-diversified party should bear most of the risk of a new venture. The contractual solution will be different if beliefs are asymmetrically held; in such cases, deal terms may shift risk toward the better-informed or more optimistic party. Suppose, for example, that the entrepreneur is confident he can achieve $200,000 in monthly sales within 18 months. The investor is less optimistic and projects monthly sales of $100,000. A deal that provides for equity sharing can be based on the investor's projections but include a provision that if the entrepreneur's revenue expectation is met, he will receive a specified percentage increase in equity. Even though the diversified investor is better able to bear risk, the entrepreneur now accepts some of the risk to address the parties' different expectations.

Discrete contracting can also address incentive problems. Suppose an entrepreneur is concerned that a first-round investor may attempt to hold up the entrepreneur when second-round funding is needed. In the first round, the entrepreneur can rely on competition among investors, but afterward the selected investor may gain an information advantage over rivals and could exploit that position. Consistent with earlier discussion, the incentive problem arises because the entrepreneur will have made a specific investment in the venture that is appropriable by the investor. The concern can be addressed by discrete contracting: the parties can agree in advance on the terms and conditions under which the investor will provide second-round financing.

Discrete contracting, however, can also create incentive problems. It is usually difficult to state explicit conditions that do not distort incentives. If, for example, the entrepreneur's equity share is tied to sales in Month 18, then the entrepreneur may devote too much attention to sales and not enough to profitability. On balance, it is sometimes better to leave certain provisions general or unstated and to rely more on reputation.

Relational Contracting and Flexibility

Relational contracts rely more on implicit mechanisms such as damage to reputation for enforcement of an understanding.[9] The virtue of a relational contract is flexibility. Consider the alternatives of seeking financing from either a passive investor who has limited familiarity with the market served by a new enterprise or from a VC who is involved in the industry and would be an active participant in the venture's management. The passive investor is more likely to seek a discrete contract. Because of bounded rationality, the contract is likely to be designed around crude proxies for states of the world, such as revenue or profit targets that are only rough indicators of the likely success of the venture. Conditions for later-stage investment, allocations of ownership, and other factors may hinge on whether the venture meets those targets. Many unforeseen conditions could result in failure to meet the targets. The problem is exacerbated if the investor is passive and has no firsthand knowledge of why a performance target was or was not met.[10]

VC financing is likely to be more flexible. Because of industry expertise and active involvement, the VC often understands the reasons for hits and misses of performance targets. Essentially, the VC offers a flexible relational contract that provides continued funding as long as doing so is in its interest. Deal terms are likely to enable the VC to monitor the entrepreneur and even to restrict the entrepreneur's ability to act without VC consent. The net effect is that, if additional funds are needed, the VC is in a good position to evaluate whether to advance the funds.

VC deal structures reflect the idea of relational contracting, particularly with respect to commitments by the VC. The entrepreneur typically does not have a reputation for managing a business. The VC cannot know with certainty how much direct involvement will be required. The result is that the contracts are not explicit about the amount of oversight or monitoring the VC will provide.[11] Such contracts expose entrepreneurs to the risk of opportunism, which is mitigated by the reputation of the VC.

Ironically, an entrepreneur may regard passive financing as affording more "flexibility." A critical distinction exists, however, between the entrepreneur's discretion to make decisions about the direction of the venture and the flexibility of the venture to adapt to its environment. With passive financing, the entrepreneur may have a sense of greater discretion but for critical decisions be constrained by the rigid terms of the contract and inflexibility on the part of the investor. With active financing, there is likely to be more continuous oversight and a requirement of consensus before actions can be taken; however, because the investor is involved and informed, the venture is more capable of adapting to threats and opportunities.

Discrete contracts and flexible relational contracts are different responses to bounded rationality. Which response is better in any particular setting depends on the identities of the parties, the costs and benefits of flexibility, and the ability of the parties to agree on explicit terms.

Incomplete Contracts and Mechanisms for Resolving Information and Incentive Problems

Relational contracts do not specifically "solve" information and incentive problems. Because the contracts are incomplete, other mechanisms that address informational asymmetry and opportunism often accompany relational contracts. Among the mechanisms that are adopted to complement relational contracts are signaling, screening, bonding, and monitoring. Technically, the terms "signaling" and "screening" apply to mechanisms that address adverse selection (informational asymmetry), whereas "bonding" and "monitoring" apply to mechanisms that address moral hazard (opportunism).

Signaling.   It can be difficult for an investor to distinguish high-quality ventures (the "cherries") from the "lemons." The problem, of course, is that the entrepreneur's claims of success potential are costly or impossible to verify. Sometimes an entrepreneur can convey positive private information simply by showing the information to investors and leaving them to draw their own conclusions. But this is risky if an investor could decide to appropriate the opportunity.

Sometimes, providing the information is not feasible. How, for example, without elaborate documentation, can an entrepreneur establish that efforts to develop new voice-recognition software have progressed much more rapidly than expected? Conversely, how can a VC show that it is not involved with or considering any competing products that could influence its attitude toward the entrepreneur's product? The challenge is to do so in a way that is convincing, yet still preserves the value of the information.

One solution is for the holder of the information to use a signal. A signal is a credible demonstration that obviates the need to convey the information. Sometimes, deal terms can serve as credible signals. Suppose an investor is concerned that an entrepreneur's financial projections are overly optimistic. By proposing a contract that ties her return to performance targets, the entrepreneur "signals" her beliefs.[12] You may recognize that signaling is a potential way for the entrepreneur to address the adverse selection problem that we illustrated in Table 12.3.

Consider the following terms for a contract between an entrepreneur, Miles Stone, and a VC firm, Limited Deals, Ltd., concerning financing for a virtual amusement park venture. Upon signing the agreement, Limited is committed to finance the venture up to $4.0 million for one year, by which time specific benchmarks are to be met. If the benchmarks are met, Limited will invest an additional $2.0 million; if the venture fails to meet one or more benchmarks, Limited can decide not to invest in the second round. If Limited does not invest, then Miles has 60 days to find a new investor; if he is unable to do so, then Limited has the right to force liquidation. Miles retains ownership of the amusement park idea and the related copyrights and trademarks. If the other assets are sold, the proceeds are to be distributed in proportion to shares of invested capital. Finally, if Limited invests the second-round $2.0 million even though the venture does not meet the benchmarks, then Limited gains managerial control.

Willingness to abide by these terms signals several things about Miles. First, the benchmarks are based on his projections. By structuring the deal around them, Miles signals confidence that the projections are reasonable. Second, his willingness to relinquish control if performance expectations are not met signals confidence in his managerial skills. The arrangement also affects Miles's incentives to devote effort to the venture. By working harder, he helps assure that the benchmarks are met and that he maintains control. Thus, signaling also addresses moral hazard.[13]

Screening.   Screening is much like signaling, except that the party without the private information offers a menu of alternative terms such that the party with information reveals it through the act of choosing. In a new venture setting, offering entrepreneurs alternative types of financing can serve a screening function. Entrepreneurs with low expectations, for example, are likely to prefer financing that minimizes the investor's liquidation preference. Those who are uncertain of how the venture might perform are also likely to seek financing that reduces their own risk exposure. Thus, we see one reason that new venture deal structures normally require the entrepreneur to bear significant risk of both failure and success.

The identity of the actor is the main difference between a signal and a screen. The deal for financing the virtual amusement park, described earlier as a signal, could also be the result of a screening contract. If the entrepreneur (the party with private information) proposed the deal structure, then it appears that the entrepreneur is signaling. If, on the other hand, the investor (the party without private information) proposed the terms, then the investor would be trying to screen entrepreneurs based on confidence in their projections.

Bonding.   Posting a bond is one way to give credibility to a commitment not to engage in opportunistic behavior. A bond is a penalty that will be paid by the party who makes a promise in the event that the promise is broken. The fundamental element of a bond is that the party who posts it is made worse off if the commitment is violated. Thus, a bond provides an incentive to fulfill a commitment. The commitment can be explicit and specific (like agreeing to resign if the investor is not satisfied with the entrepreneur's effort) or implicit (like tying compensation to the attained level of sales).

Investors may not be concerned that an entrepreneur will not work hard but rather that he may not focus on the right activities and problems. For example, the entrepreneur may be more interested in working on technical problems than in managing a rapidly growing organization, or he may not recognize failure or may not be open to changing the focus of the venture. This can be an issue of adverse selection, but it is also possible that the untested entrepreneur is just as uncertain about his own capabilities and temperament as is the investor.

A bond can be provided in several different ways. Sometimes a set of specific contract provisions can function as a bond. Other alternatives include reliance on reputation and certification.

Using hostages to bond performance.   The economics literature recognizes a potentially important role for hostages to enforce performance.[14] The folklore version of hostage taking is a useful way to begin thinking about the economic role of bonding. Medieval kings used to guarantee peace by exchanging hostages. Each would voluntarily (or possibly not) exchange hostages with the other. The hostage was used as a bond to back up a promise not to attack the other; if one party reneged and started a war, the hostage was killed. An efficient hostage arrangement is one in which the hostage is very valuable to the hostage giver but not to the hostage taker. In medieval times, sons and daughters of the king made good hostages! Hence, royal marriages could help enforce treaties.

It sometimes is reasonable to think of the investments of the parties to a new venture as a mutual exchange of hostages. The entrepreneur invests specific human capital, the value of which depends on venture success. The investor contributes financial capital that is invested in project-specific assets. Because both parties are worse off if they are unable to work together, the relationship can rely to a greater degree on trust and promise than if the investment of one party is fully recoverable.

Using discrete contract provisions to bond performance.   The modern equivalent of exchanging hostages is to use explicit contract provisions to establish a bond. Suppose an entrepreneur seeks funding to begin commercialization. The entrepreneur has no experience in managing an organization but is hard working and devoted to the venture. Consequently, the entrepreneur wishes to continue as CEO. The investor likes the concept but is concerned that the entrepreneur may not be successful at commercialization. Neither party has a compelling information advantage concerning the entrepreneur's capabilities. The difficulty is that if the entrepreneur turns out to be an ineffective manager, then the venture is likely to fail, but the entrepreneur may still be resistant to making the changes needed to help assure survival.

The investor would like to select an experienced manager, but the entrepreneur does not want to relinquish control. A possible solution is for the entrepreneur to provide a bond. One way to do so is to establish performance benchmarks such that, if they are met, the entrepreneur retains control and, if not, control transfers to the investor. The bond can be achieved using warrants whereby the investor gains the ability to acquire additional voting shares, culminating in control if performance targets are not met. Or it can be achieved by giving the investor the right to terminate the entrepreneur as CEO if the targets are not met. The former approach shifts more financial risk to the entrepreneur. Hence, it can also help signal the entrepreneur's expectations.

In this example, the entrepreneur is protected against investor opportunism by establishing specific conditions under which the termination right can be exercised. However, as noted earlier, reliance on specific conditions is not ideal. Whether a particular condition, such as a sales target, is satisfied or not involves a random component that is beyond the control of the entrepreneur and is unrelated to the entrepreneur's abilities. Thus, the entrepreneur is not as protected as he would like. Moreover, explicit conditions are subject to manipulation in ways that are not in the parties' interests.

Using reputation to bond performance.

Rather than relying on explicit terms, the more successful relationships are likely to be based on trust. To see how reputation can be important, consider factors that would induce the parties to a venture to rely on mutual trust. In the economics literature, a party can be "trusted" when refraining from opportunistic behavior is the party's higher-valued course of action. The literature refers to trust in terms of reputation and defines "reputational capital" as a nonsalvageable, intangible asset that is most valuable in its current use. Because of its nonsalvageability, reputational capital functions as a bond. The owners of a reputable firm do not want to lose their sunk investments in reputational capital, as could result if the firm were to cheat by reneging on implicit long-term contracts.

Uncertainty is greater concerning the behavior of a new entrant to the VC industry or a first-time entrepreneur. If the VC firm or the entrepreneur has not made much of an investment in industry-specific nonsalvageable capital, then others cannot rely on reputation to enforce the contract. Thus, entrepreneurs and investors with significant industry-specific reputations can rely more heavily on promises and trust.

What happens in relationships where only one party has reputational capital? A VC with an established reputation, for example, might require that the contract contain explicit provisions regarding the entrepreneur's performance, whereas the first-time entrepreneur dealing with an established VC might settle for more generally worded promises without explicit enforcement mechanisms.[15]

Using certification to bond performance. There are indirect means of bonding performance as well. Consider a first-time entrepreneur who recognizes that if investors do not perceive the true potential of the venture, they will require too much ownership. Certification is a partial solution. With certification, rather than resorting to discrete terms, the party who lacks sufficient reputation can turn to a third party to certify some aspects of the financial projections.[16] For example, sales forecasts can be supported by tangible evidence that a significant customer is interested in buying the product. In effect, the entrepreneur is "borrowing" the reputation of one of its customers and using that reputation to enhance the credibility of projections.

Another area in which certification plays an important role is public issuance of equity. Although a firm can try to market its own securities, success is unlikely. The problem is the one illustrated in Table 12.3. Prospective investors will be concerned that the firm is trying to issue overvalued shares and react negatively to the issue announcement. To address this problem, the firm is likely to use the services of a reputable investment banker. An investment banker is an intermediary on whom investors can rely to effectively certify that the offer price is consistent with private information the investment banker has learned about the firm.

If the underwriter sets the issue price too high and the shares lose value after the issue, the underwriter will suffer reputational damage, especially if shareholders believe the decline is due to adverse information the underwriter should have learned.[17] Empirical evidence supports the certification role. When underwriters fail in their certification efforts, not only do they suffer losses of value but so do the issuing firms that relied on them for IPO certification.[18]

Monitoring. The other way opportunistic behavior is controlled is by monitoring. In lieu of bonding, the parties can rely on observation. Monitoring can be direct, as in the case of an investor who serves on the venture's board, or indirect, as in the case of requiring financial statements to be periodically audited by reputable accounting firms.

The relationships between VC firms and their portfolio companies involve elements of both bonding and monitoring. The deal structures frequently involve bonding arrangements such as termination rights or warrants, but the investors also closely monitor performance. Some monitoring involves formal triggers; for example, staging gives the investor specific, periodic opportunities to evaluate whether to continue investing. Use of debt covenants is another example of monitoring that employs a trigger. Debt covenants are contractual terms used by lenders to place restrictions on borrowers.

In a business setting, debt covenants may restrict the borrower from taking on additional debt or making capital investments beyond what originally was contemplated. They may also require the borrower to adhere to certain constraints with respect to various financial ratios and may limit the ability of the borrower to make distributions to other investors. Debt covenants protect the lender and provide a method of monitoring without requiring continual oversight. Such covenants lower the risk of the debt by protecting against unfavorable contingencies; as a result, they lower the interest rate.

If the lender's concern is that the entrepreneur may take on risks that do not benefit the lender, there are ways to alter the borrower's incentives by including debt covenants. One is to issue debt that is convertible at the lender's option to a predetermined number of shares of common stock. In that way the lender is positioned to benefit from the firm's performance if it is especially strong and the entrepreneur or firm manager has less incentive to take unwarranted risk. The conversion option thus aligns the interests of the entrepreneur more closely with those of the lender. It is common for high-risk new ventures to borrow using debt or preferred stock that is convertible.[19]

12.11 Organizational Choice

Organizational design concerns decisions regarding which functions the enterprise will outsource rather than perform in-house and the allocation of control rights within the enterprise. A start-up R&D firm, for example, may have to decide whether to build a facility to conduct pilot tests of a new drug, use a subcontractor to conduct the tests, or license the technology to another firm that will undertake testing and development. The right choice involves an array of considerations: protection of the venture's intellectual property, difficulty of communicating with a subcontractor or licensee, control over product quality, effects of the decision on ability to innovate in the future, and so on.[20]

Most goods are produced through a series of steps. Raw materials are used to produce inputs, which are assembled as intermediate goods, which are used to produce final goods, which are distributed and sold. Financing at each stage is an input. Although many e-commerce and service companies challenge aspects of this "value chain" model, the basic idea that final goods are produced through a series of sequential or simultaneous steps still holds. Every entrepreneur must decide which steps to outsource and which to integrate.

How can these basic organizational choices best be made? As a general proposition, the decisions are guided by the transactions costs of using markets compared to costs associated with performing the task internally.[21] Market exchange works best when transactions costs are small. Transactions costs include the costs of searching for trading partners, negotiating prices, and enforcing agreements. Market exchange is also more desirable when buyers and sellers have full information about product quality and availability of substitutes and complements, and when the numbers of buyers and sellers are large so that competitive pressures determine price.

When transactions costs of using markets are high or competition is imperfect, other organizational options may be preferred. Complete integration of an activity is one choice, but there are intermediate choices as well. The long-term discrete and relational contracts that we discussed earlier represent part of a continuum from spot-market exchange to complete integration. On this continuum, a relational contract is a significant shift away from reliance on discrete contracts and toward reliance on organizations. Joint ventures, franchising, and strategic alliances all are structures that can be thought of as relational contracts.[22]

Internal exchange also involves transactions costs. If costs of internal exchange are lower, then transactions-cost considerations favor internalizing. In such cases, internalizing transactions can lower the price, increase gross profit per unit, and increase the quantity of sales. One aspect of the difference between using markets and internal exchange is how residual decision rights are controlled.[23] Whether exchange occurs in a market or in an organization, the contractual structure is necessarily incomplete. Some contingencies will not be addressed with discrete terms. Responses to such contingencies depend on how residual decision rights are assigned. Efficient organization depends on efficiency of the allocation of rights to control asset dispositions that are not assigned by contract.

Control of residual decision rights is of obvious importance in the new venture context. Typically, both the entrepreneur and the investor must make specific investments if a venture is to succeed. Because the willingness of either party to make such an investment depends on how the investment will be treated in the event of unforeseen future developments, the interplay between explicit contract provisions and control of residual decision rights is an important consideration for choosing organizational form.

A distinguishing feature of organizations is that (in contrast to markets) decision making is hierarchical. In hierarchical organizations, entrepreneurs can be expected to devote some of their time to trying to influence the decision maker. Influence costs are an aspect of the transactions costs of coordinating activity within an organization.[24] Among other considerations, it makes sense to pursue ventures within organizations when influence costs are small relative to the benefits of hierarchical decision structure. For example, a venture that complements the other projects of the organization can be more efficiently pursued within the organization than can a venture that is in competition with other projects of the organization.

The VC practice of linking funding to involvement in the venture is a shift away from market exchange and toward an organizational form where ventures are funded internally. The VC financing process is more hierarchical than raising all funds in the market and is an example of adaptive sequential decision making by the VC. As the future unfolds, the VC investor can adapt financing commitments to unexpected changes in venture development.[25] Thus, one advantage of internal organization and relational contracts, as compared to discrete contracts, is that they facilitate adaptive sequential decision making.

The relational contracts between entrepreneurs and investors are consistent with the economic theory of organization. Where small numbers bargaining problems and opportunism can impede the effective use of markets or discrete contracts, long-term relationships enable the parties to use simpler contractual provisions than would be expected in discrete contracting. Hierarchical structure can go even further to help resolve some incentive conflicts. Potential gains from opportunism can be reduced because, within an organization, disputes can go to third parties for resolution. In the case of a venture that is pursued within a corporation, the management team responsible for providing financing has little reason to behave opportunistically. That team would not be able to capture the gain from opportunistic behavior as might an outside investor.

Hierarchical organization can also help overcome problems of im-

TABLE **12.4**   **The contracting framework**

| Behavioral assumptions | | | | |
Bounded rationality	Opportunism	Asset specificity	Implied contracting process	Comment
0	+	+	Planning	Without bounded rationality, complete contingent claims contracting is a feasible way to prevent opportunistic behavior.
+	0	+	Promise	Without opportunistic behavior, the parties can cooperate through a series of discrete transactions and rely on cooperation to work out the solutions to problems that arise in the future.
+	+	0	Competition	Without relationship-specific assets, there is no potential for opportunistic behavior.
+	+	+	Governance	When all three concerns are present, the parties may agree on a hierarchical mechanism of controlling the potential for opportunistic behavior.

SOURCE: *Adapted from Williamson (1987).*
NOTE: *+ = present to a significant degree; 0 = not present to a significant degree.*

pacted information. Keeping private information secret can be less valuable in an organization than in a market. Communication among parties can be more complete than in a market. Intellectual property is a good example of private information that may be easier to communicate within an organization than in a market. For example, divulging trade secrets within an organization involves less risk.

A framework for the choice of organizational form is summarized diagrammatically in Table 12.4.[26] The framework can be used to identify the organizational form that is most likely to be appropriate for a given kind of venture. As shown, organizational choices and the implied contracting process can be categorized into four different scenarios with respect to the presence or absence of problems of (1) bounded rationality, (2) opportunism, and (3) asset specificity. In each scenario, at least two of these problems are present. Generally speaking, if none is present or if only one is, discrete transactions can be an efficient way to organize the venture.

Additional aspects of large organizations go beyond the transactional issues. The rationale for reliance on governance often focuses on these other aspects. First, some hierarchical organizations, like pharmaceutical producers, undertake many projects simultaneously. For the employees, there is an element of risk pooling that contrasts sharply with the risk exposure of an entrepreneur. While an employee's earnings can be affected by successful innovation, the gains are not as skewed toward only rewarding success as they are for an entrepreneur. Second, the human and physical capital of hierarchical organizations tends to be less project specific than for independent ventures. Within a hierarchical organization, it can be relatively easy to reorganize the teams working on particular projects.[27]

In addition, development efforts may be capital intensive, and economies of scale may be achievable by using the capital on several related projects. Development of a single microwave tube used in satellite communication or radar navigation normally requires a small team of engineers plus a number of technical support personnel. The tubes undergo a variety of heat-treating, metallurgical, and testing processes. The entire development effort can require from two to four person-years to complete. Because the engineering properties of a microwave tube affect its performance characteristics (bandwidth, power, etc.), the same engineers, technicians, and equipment can be applied to producing a series of related tubes. Further, multiple teams of engineers can share the developing and testing equipment.

12.12 Summary

The chapter develops a conceptual framework for evaluating contractual features of new venture financing. The framework recognizes that entrepreneurs, as underdiversified investors, should value projects at discount rates that can be substantially higher than the rates appropriate for well-diversified investors. The chapter explores some of the opportunities that arise from regarding entrepreneurial investment in this way. The difference in attitudes toward risk gives rise to a significant opportunity for an entrepreneur to contract with outside investors in ways that reduce the overall required rate of return on the venture. Beyond this, the chapter demonstrates that thoughtful design of contracts between entrepreneurs and outside investors can enhance the value of projects and turn unacceptable projects into attractive ones over a broad range of expected rates of return.

Given the venture and the entrepreneurial team, the financial contract emerges as perhaps the single most important determinant of success or failure. A well-designed contract can contribute dramatically to the value of an idea and help allay the concerns of investors about the capabilities and commitment of an untested entrepreneur. A poorly designed contract, however, can just as easily prevent a good idea or product from reaching the market. Information and incentive problems arising from adverse selection and moral hazard are important determinants of financial contract terms and organizational structures.

Adverse selection arises when the parties enter a negotiation with asymmetric information and expectations. Informational asymmetry is an impediment to effective contracting between entrepreneurs and prospective investors, since each may be concerned that the other knows more and is trying to take advantage. Solutions to adverse selection include signaling and screening. A signal is a mechanism the party with positive information can use to distinguish him- or herself from those with negative information. A screen is a mechanism the parties without information can use to compel those with information to reveal whether the information is positive or negative. Screening and signaling are similar in that parties with negative information find that it is not economical to imitate those with positive information.

Moral hazard arises after an agreement is entered. If a sunk investment has been made and is specific to a relationship, a party to the agreement can attempt to appropriate the value of the investment. Techniques for controlling moral hazard problems include bonding and monitoring. Bonding involves making a commitment or investment such that the party who has the opportunity to appropriate would be worse off by exploiting the sunk investment than by not doing so. Monitoring can be used by one party to limit the ability of the other party to act opportunistically.

The bottom line in negotiations between investors and the entrepreneur is that all parties must expect to come out winners. Of course, each is trying to maximize the size of its own gain. But it is better to accept a smaller share, if doing so is expected to increase the amount of the party's gain. It is not unheard of, for example, for an investor to ask for less ownership than the entrepreneur is willing to offer. The investor may be concerned that if the venture does not meet the entrepreneur's expectations, the entrepreneur will become disillusioned and retreat from a venture that should be pursued or that without a larger share the entrepreneur will devote insufficient effort.

Organizational choice is an aspect of dealing with information problems. The basic choice of the entrepreneur is whether to organize an exchange by using a market-based contract or to integrate the transaction and perform it within the firm. If the entrepreneur decides on using a contractual structure, the choice becomes one of whether to organize the agreement with planning or promise, or to rely on competition to enforce performance. Choices about how to organize a transaction are not one-time, static choices. They are recurring choices, and the considerations vary with the maturity of the enterprise and the financing stage.

REVIEW QUESTIONS

1. In what sense is proportional sharing of ownership in a venture of a given size analogous to an entrepreneur independently pursuing a perfectly scalable venture?

2. Why, all else equal, would shifting nonmarket risk to a well-diversified investor increase the value of an opportunity?

3. Why, all else equal, would an entrepreneur do better by selling most of the equity in a new venture to a well-diversified investor than by retaining most of the equity?

4. If entrepreneurs discount the future cash flows of a venture at a higher rate than do diversified investors, why do entrepreneurs generally hold substantial equity interests in their ventures, and why are their claims usually riskier than the claims held by the investor?

5. Explain the difference between moral hazard and adverse selection. Why do these two pose contracting problems for new ventures?

6. What is the difference between an information problem and an incentive problem? How do these two problems relate to moral hazard and adverse selection?

7. What is the difference between a screen and a signal? How can screens and signals help to mitigate contracting problems?

8. What are the meanings of bonding and monitoring? What, from an economic standpoint, makes a bond effective?

9. What are some ways in which new venture deal structures can be designed to help signal the entrepreneur's true beliefs to an investor and/or better align the incentives of the entrepreneur with the interests of the investor?

10. How do bounded rationality, opportunism, and asset specificity influence the choice of organizational form?

NOTES

1. The spreadsheet for Table 12.1 is accessible on the book's companion website.

2. Williamson's (1975) discussion of bounded rationality in a contracting context draws on work by fellow Nobel Laureate Herbert Simon. Simon

first introduced the concept of bounded rationality in the context of employer-employee relations. See Simon (1957, 1961).

3. The example was developed by Akerlof (1970).

4. The cost of transacting increases whenever the importance of private information is high relative to the importance of common information. The parties may have different information, but neither may have a clear information advantage. They may even have the same information but be unaware that they do. In either case, an incentive exists to expend resources on information transfer.

5. See Arrow (1963).

6. For the effects of moral hazard problems on firm value and financing choices, see Jensen and Meckling (1976), Myers (1984), Darrough and Stoughton (1986), Harris and Raviv (1991), and Mello and Parsons (1992).

7. See Klein, Crawford, and Alchian (1978) for analysis of the risk of appropriation of sunk investments and the choice of organizational form.

8. Smith (1998) provides a comprehensive review of opportunism problems between entrepreneurs and VCs and discusses the implications for VC contracting.

9. For discussion and illustration of the distinction between discrete and relational contracting, see Joskow (1985, 1987).

10. Cornelli and Yosha (2003) offer a contractual approach for dealing with observability issues. Specifically, they consider the use of convertible debt in a relationship where the investor has an abandonment option. If straight debt is used, the entrepreneur may try to manipulate short-run performance to discourage the investor from abandoning the venture. If debt is convertible, they contend that the entrepreneur has less incentive to engage in this "window dressing."

11. Gorman and Sahlman (1989) report that venture capitalists regularly monitor their portfolio firms but are not normally involved in day-to-day management. Gifford (1997) provides an analysis of the optimal amount of monitoring effort from the perspective of the venture capitalist. Sapienza and Gupta (1994) report evidence of the determinants of frequency of VC interaction.

12. The signal also addresses a possible concern that, once the outside capital is committed, the entrepreneur may devote less time to the venture. Tying the entrepreneur's return to attainment of milestones can strengthen the entrepreneur's commitment of effort to the project. Chua and Woodward (1993) analyze the use of stock options to resolve differences in expectations and to align the interests of entrepreneurs and VC investors.

13. Fee (2002) examines motion picture financing arrangements to illustrate how contracting can mitigate incentive problems that arise when outside investors may not value the private benefits of control that accrue to the entrepreneur. While investors will want to monitor the filmmaker's decisions,

the presence of outside investors can dampen the entrepreneur's incentives to put effort into the film. Filmmakers (the entrepreneurs) choose between studio funds (losing control over the project) and independent financing (retaining control). In this setting, using independent motion picture financing is more common when a film requires a high level of creative effort and the filmmaker's specific investment in the film is high.

14. Discussion is drawn from work by Williamson (1983) on credible commitments and using hostages to support exchange and Cooter and Ulen (2008), p. 201.

15. For further discussion, see Ayers and Cramton (1994).

16. For evidence on certification, see James and Wier (1990). Thakor (1982) provides a model of third-party certification, and Millon and Thakor (1985) discuss the role of information-gathering agencies.

17. Booth and Smith (1986) provide a formal model of underwriter certification. Beatty and Ritter (1986) provide evidence of the reputational cost to underwriters of mispricing issues. Tinic (1988) examines evidence of litigation related to mispricing.

18. See Beatty, Bunsis, and Hand (1998).

19. See Berglof (1994) for an analysis of using convertible securities to allocate control rights to entrepreneurial ventures.

20. Hellman (2002) provides a model that predicts that an entrepreneurial company is more likely to be financed by a corporate investor if it complements the corporation's core business. The larger the opportunity for the corporate investor to control the strategy of the entrepreneurial firm, the more likely it is that the entrepreneur selects an independent venture capitalist.

21. Ronald Coase (1937) first espoused the idea that transactions costs of using markets can be substantial and that productive activity can sometimes be organized by firms to achieve the same productive efficiencies as market exchange. This shifted the focus of economic thinking to a view of the firm as a nexus of contracts and the choice of economic organization to be one of trying to minimize the effects of transactions costs. See also Coase (1960), Williamson (1975, 1985), and Klein, Crawford, and Alchian (1978).

22. Imperfect information is at the heart of the transactions costs identified above. Search costs arise because information is costly. Negotiation costs arise because each party spends resources to discover what the other party knows, to improve his or her own information, and to control incentive problems that may arise. Finally, enforcement costs arise whenever specifying and measuring performance is difficult.

23. Transactions-cost economics, as articulated by Coase and Williamson, has been criticized for its lack of specific attention to the costs of internal organization. Grossman and Hart (1986) and Hart and Moore (1988) account for the costs and benefits of different organizational forms on the basis of allocation of control rights.

24. Milgrom and Roberts (1992) identify influence costs as internal costs that are incurred by the participants in an organization to influence the decision maker.

25. The term "adaptive sequential decision making" was introduced by Williamson (1975), p. 40.

26. Williamson (1987) offers this framework for thinking about the nature of the contracting process (broadly defined) between the parties.

27. Alchian and Demsetz (1972) view team production, with the ability of a central decision maker to organize and restructure teams, as an important rationale for the organization of economic activity into firms.

References and Additional Reading

Akerlof, G. 1970. "The Market for Lemons: Quality Uncertainty and the Market Mechanism." *Quarterly Journal of Economics*8 4:488–500.

Alchian, A., and H. Demsetz. 1972. "Production, Information Costs and Economic Organization." *American Economic Review*6 2:777–95.

Arrow, K. 1963. "Uncertainty and the Welfare Economics of Medical Care." *American Economic Review*5 3:941–73.

Ayers, I., and P. Cramton. 1994. "Relational Investing and Agency Theory." *Cardozo Law Review*1 5:1033–66.

Beatty, R. P., H. Bunsis, and J. R. M. Hand. 1998. "Indirect Economic Penalties in SEC Investigations of Underwriters." *Journal of Financial Economics* 50:151–86.

Beatty, R. P., and J. Ritter. 1986. "Investment Banking, Reputation, and the Underpricing of Initial Public Offerings." *Journal of Financial Economics* 15:213–32.

Berglof, E. 1994. "A Control Theory of Venture Capital Finance." *Journal of Law, Economics, and Organization* 10:247–67.

Bernardo, A., and I. Welch. 2001. "On the Evolution of Overconfidence and Entrepreneurs." *Journal of Economics and Management Strategy* 10:301–30.

Bhide, A., and H. H. Stevenson. 1990. "Why Be Honest If Honesty Doesn't Pay." *Harvard Business Review* 68 (September–October): 121–29.

Bitler, M., T. Moskowitz, and A. Vissing-Jorgensen. 2005. "Testing Agency Theory with Entrepreneur Effort and Wealth." *Journal of Finance* 60 (2): 539–76.

Booth, J. R., and R. L. Smith. 1986. "Capital Raising, Underwriting, and the Certification Hypothesis." *Journal of Financial Economics* 15:261–81.

Brennan, M., and A. Kraus. 1987. "Efficient Financing under Asymmetric Information." *Journal of Finance* 42:1225–43.

Chua, J. H., and R. S. Woodward. 1993. "Splitting the Firm between the Entrepreneur and the Venture Capitalist with the Help of Stock Options." *Journal of Business Venturing* 8:43–58.

Coase, R. H. 1937. "The Nature of the Firm." *Economica* 4:386–405.

———. 1960. "The Problem of Social Cost." *Journal of Law and Economics* 3:1–44.

Cooter, R., and T. Ulen. 2008. *Law and Economics.* 5th ed. Upper Saddle River, NJ: Prentice-Hall.

Cornelli, F., and O. Yosha. 2003. "Stage Financing and the Role of Convertible Securities." *Review of Financial Studies*7 0:1–32.

Cumming, D. 2005. "Capital Structure in Venture Finance." *Journal of Corporate Finance*1 1:550–85.

———. 2008. "Contracts and Exits in Venture Capital Finance." *Review of Financial Studies*2 1:1947–82.

Cumming, D., and S. Johan. 2008. "Information Asymmetries, Agency Costs, and Venture Capital Exit Outcomes." *Venture Capital: An International Journal of Entrepreneurial Finance*1 0:197–231.

Darrough, M. N., and N. M. Stoughton. 1986. "Moral Hazard and Adverse Selection: The Question of Financial Structure." *Journal of Finance* 41:501–13.

Dessein, W. 2005. "Information and Control in Ventures and Alliances." *Journal of Finance* 60 (5): 2513–49.

Fee, C. E. 2002. "The Cost of Outside Equity Control: Evidence from Motion Picture Financing Decisions." *Journal of Business*7 5:681–711.

Gifford, S. 1997. "Limited Attention and the Role of the Venture Capitalist." *Journal of Business Venturing* 12:459–82.

Gompers, P. A. 1995. "Optimal Investment, Monitoring, and the Staging of Venture Capital." *Journal of Finance*5 0:1461–89.

Gompers, P. A., and J. Lerner. 1999. "Conflict of Interest in the Issuance of Public Securities: Evidence from Venture Capital." *Journal of Law and Economics*4 2:1–28.

Gorman, M., and W. A. Sahlman. 1989. "What Do Venture Capitalists Do?" *Journal of Business Venturing* 4:231–48.

Grossman, S., and O. Hart. 1986. "The Costs and Benefits of Ownership: A Theory of Vertical and Lateral Integration." *Journal of Political Economy* 94:691–719.

Harris, M., and A. Raviv. 1991. "The Theory of Capital Structure." *Journal of Finance* 46 (10): 297–355.

Hart, O., and J. Moore. 1988. "Incomplete Contracts and Renegotiation." *Econometrics* 56:755–86.

Hellman, T. A. 2002. "Theory of Corporate Venture Investing." *Journal of Financial Economics*6 4:285–314.

Krishnan, C. N. V., V. Ivanov, R. W. Masulis, and A. K. Singh. 2011. "Venture Capital Reputation and Post-IPO Performance." *Journal of Financial and Quantitative Analysis*, forthcoming.

James, C., and P. Wier. 1990. "Borrowing Relationships, Intermediation, and the Cost of Issuing Public Securities." *Journal of Financial Economics* 28:149–71.

Janney, J. J., and T. B. Folta. 2006. "Moderating Effects of Investor Experience on the Signaling Value of Private Equity Placements." *Journal of Business Venturing* 21 (1): 27–44.

Jensen, M. C., and W. H. Meckling. 1976. "Theory of the Firm: Managerial Behavior, Agency Costs, and Ownership Structure." *Journal of Financial Economics*3 :305–60.

Joskow, P. L. 1985. "Vertical Integration and Long-Term Contracts." *Journal of Law, Economics, and Organization* 1:33–80.

———. 1987. "Contract Duration and Transactions Specific Investment: Empirical Evidence from the Coal Market." *American Economic Review* 77: 168–83.

Kaplan, S. N., and P. Stromberg. 2000. "Venture Capitalists as Principals: Contracting, Screening, and Monitoring." *American Economic Review Papers and Proceedings*9 1:426–30.

———. 2002. "Characteristics, Contracts, and Actions: Evidence from Venture Capitalist Analyses." *Journal of Finance* 59 (5): 2177–2210.

———. 2003. "Financial Contracting Theory Meets the Real World: An Empirical Analysis of Venture Capital Contracts." *Review of Financial Studies* 70:281–316.

Klein, B., R. G. Crawford, and A. A. Alchian. 1978. "Vertical Integration, Appropriable Rents, and the Competitive Contracting Process." *Journal of Law and Economics* 21:297–326.

Klein, B., and K. Leffler. 1981. "The Role of Market Forces in Assuring Contractual Performance." *Journal of Political Economy*8 9:615–41.

Landier, A., and D. Thesmar. 2009. "Financial Contracting with Optimistic Entrepreneurs." *Review of Financial Studies* 22 (1): 117–50.

Leland, H. E., and D. H. Pyle. 1977. "Informational Asymmetries, Financial Structure, and Financial Intermediation." *Journal of Finance* 32:371–87.

Lu, Q., P. Hwang, and C. K. Wang. 2006. "Agency Risk Control through Reprisal." *Journal of Business Venturing* 21 (3): 369.

MacNeil, I. 1974. "The Many Futures of Contract." *University of Southern California Law Review*4 7:691–816.

Mello, A. S., and J. E. Parsons. 1992. "Measuring the Agency Cost of Debt." *Journal of Finance* 47:1887–1904.

Milgrom, P., and J. Roberts. 1992. *Economics, Organization, and Management.* Englewood Cliffs, NJ: Prentice-Hall.

Millon, M. H., and A. V. Thakor. 1985. "Moral Hazard and Information Sharing: A Model of Financial Information Gathering Agencies." *Journal of Finance* 40:1403–22.

Myers, S. C. 1984. "The Capital Structure Puzzle." *Journal of Finance* 39: 575–92.

Myers, S. C., and N. S. Majluf. 1984. "Corporate Financing and Investment Decisions When Firms Have Information That Investors Do Not Have." *Journal of Financial Economics*1 3:187–221.

Prasad, D., G. Burton, and G. Vozikis. 2000. "Signaling Value to Business Angels: The Proportion of the Entrepreneur's Net Worth Invested in a New Venture as a Decision Signal." *Venture Capital*2 :167–82.

Ravid, S. A., and M. Spiegel. 1997. "Optimal Financial Contracts for a Start-Up with Unlimited Operating Discretion." *Journal of Financial and Quantitative Analysis*3 2:269–85.

Ross, S. A. 1977. "The Determinants of Financial Structure: The Incentive Signaling Approach." *Bell Journal of Economics* 8:23–40.

Sapienza, H. J., and A. K. Gupta. 1994. "Impact of Agency Risks and Task Uncertainty in Venture Capitalist–CEO Interaction." *Academy of Management Journal*3 7:1618–32.

Simon, H. 1957. *Models of Man.* New York: John Wiley & Sons.

———. 1961. *Administrative Behavior.* 2nd ed. New York: Macmillan.

Smith, C. W., and J. B. Warner. 1979. "On Financial Contracting: An Analysis of Bond Covenants." *Journal of Financial Economics* 7:117–61.

Smith, D. G. 1998. "Venture Capital Contracting in the Information Age." *Journal of Small and Emerging Business Law*2 :133–74.

Spence, A. M. 1973. *Market Signaling: Information Transfer in Hiring and Related Processes.* Cambridge, MA: Harvard University Press.

Thakor, A. V. 1982. "An Exploration of Competitive Signaling Equilibria with 'Third Party' Information Production: The Case of Debt Insurance." *Journal of Finance* 37:717–39.

Tinic, S. M. 1988. "Anatomy of Initial Public Offerings of Common Stock." *Journal of Finance*4 3:789–822.

Williamson, O. 1975. *Markets and Hierarchies.* New York: Free Press.

———. 1983. "Credible Commitments: Using Hostages to Support Exchange." *American Economic Review*7 3:519–40.

———. 1985. *The Economic Institutions of Capitalism.* New York: Free Press.

CHAPTER 13

VALUE CREATION AND CONTRACT DESIGN

> My ventures are not in one bottom trusted, nor in one place; nor is my whole estate upon the fortune of this present year; therefore, my merchandise makes me not sad.
>
> William Shakespeare, *Merchant of Venice*

Contract terms can enhance value by helping to overcome information asymmetries and by aligning incentives. They can also add value through the structure of real options that comprise the venture. Because the effects are complex, comparing deal structures can be challenging. In this chapter, we use the valuation methodology developed in earlier chapters to examine how contract design affects value. Risk allocation, reward allocation, information signaling, and incentive alignment all are elements of contract design that can affect value.

Imagine that you are an angel investor and that an entrepreneur has approached you for financing. Her venture will need substantial capital before harvesting is feasible. You have several concerns. First, the entrepreneur's projections seem too optimistic. Second, the entrepreneur may not be an effective manager. Third, competing ventures are under way, and one of them may capture the opportunity before the entrepreneur's venture comes to fruition. Finally, the entrepreneur will not be motivated unless she can expect to retain significant control and a large fraction of ownership. Here we focus on designing financial contracts to deal with these complex yet common issues.

Contracting choices build on the fact that investors and entrepreneurs are likely to have different attitudes toward risk and different expectations about performance. We extend the discussion from earlier chapters by considering staging and real options. Staging has great potential to help mitigate the full range of information and incentive concerns. A well-planned staging strategy can create tremendous value, especially for venture opportunities that succeed, and can help the entrepreneur realize a larger share of the value. Toward the end of the chapter, we discuss the use of standard venture finance contracting provisions designed to address information and incentive problems. As usual, we adopt the convention of maximizing value for the entrepreneur.

13.1 Staged Investment: The Venture Capital Method

Recall that under the VC method, the cash flows of a success scenario are discounted at a hurdle rate greater than cost of capital. Because the probability of failure declines as a venture achieves its milestones, the hurdle rates are lower for investments made at later stages.

Consider a venture that needs $700,000 of capital per year for five years, beginning at Time 0. Table 13.1 summarizes the essential information about the venture. The entrepreneur's business plan includes a projection of negative earnings during the first few years, followed by rapid growth. The venture is projected to generate no free cash flow during the first five years. By the end of Year 5, the plan shows earnings (EBIAT) of $2.5 million. The entrepreneur projects a public offering of equity at the end of Year 5. Because (we have determined that) the typical earnings multiple of comparable public companies is 15, we project that in the success scenario continuing value as of Year 5 will be $37.5 million.

The table shows hurdle rates for investments made each year. The rates are roughly consistent with the VC method rates an investor might use. They begin at 50 percent for Time 0 investment and decline by 5 percent per year. Recall that a hurdle rate of 50 percent means that, for an investment at Time 0, success-scenario cash flows must return 50 percent annually; for an investment at Year 3, success-scenario cash flows must return 35 percent annually.

We use this example to see how, based on the VC method, staging affects the allocation of ownership. To establish a baseline, we first determine the allocation under single-stage investment.

Single-Stage Investment

Suppose that the entrepreneur would like to raise enough cash at Time 0 to cover projected cash needs for the entire five years. In Table 13.1, capital raised at Time 0 but not needed until later is invested at a risk-free rate of 4 percent until it is needed. On that basis, the entrepreneur seeks $3.241 million of equity at Time 0. The cash balance portion of the "Cash flow information" panel demonstrates that this is sufficient to yield the required $700,000 of cash per year.

⊤TABLE **13.1**   **Valuation Template 7: VC method—Single-stage investment**

			Year			
	0	1	2	3	4	5
Income statement information						
Earnings before interest and after tax		($500,000)	($200,000)	$400,000	$1,400,000	$2,500,000
Cash flow information						
External funds required to support operations	$700,000	$700,000	$700,000	$700,000	$700,000	$0
Equity capital raised	$3,240,927					
Beginning cash balance	$3,240,927	$2,642,564	$2,020,267	$1,373,077	$700,000	$0
Uses of cash	$700,000	$700,000	$700,000	$700,000	$700,000	$0
Cash invested in marketable securities	$2,540,927	$1,942,564	$1,320,267	$673,077	$0	$0
Return on invested cash	$101,637	$77,703	$52,811	$26,923	$0	$0
Ending cash balance	$2,642,564	$2,020,267	$1,373,077	$700,000	$0	$0
Investor valuation and ownership allocation						
Investor hurdle rate	50.00%	45.00%	40.00%	35.00%	30.00%	25.00%
Continuing value earnings multiplier						15
Continuing value of venture						$37,500,000
Required future value of investment						$24,610,789
Ownership share required						65.63%

NOTE: *Shaded cells are inputs that can be changed.*

Our objective is to determine the fraction of equity an investor would require in exchange for an investment of $3.241 million at Time 0. Two equivalent approaches are possible. The normal approach from corporate finance is to discount projected continuing value by 50 percent per year and compare this (post-money) PV to the amount invested. The easier approach when we consider staging, however, is to find the future value of the investment as of Year 5 and compare it to projected continuing value. We use the second approach in Table 13.1. The $3.241 million investment earning 50 percent annually must generate a Year 5 cash return of $24.611 million in the success scenario. Because the continuing value of the entire venture is $37.5 million, the investor would require 65.63 percent of the equity.

If the entrepreneur cares about control and about holding a majority stake of the equity, she will not find this financing arrangement attractive. However, because we do not know the entrepreneur's cost of capital, we cannot use Table 13.1 to value her financial claim.

TABLE **13.2** Valuation Template 8: VC method—Multistage investment

			Year			
	0	1	2	3	4	5
Income statement information						
Earnings before interest and after tax	($500,000)	($200,000)	$400,000	$1,400,000	$2,500,000	
Cash flow information						
External funds required	$700,000	$700,000	$700,000	$700,000	$700,000	$0
Equity capital raised	$1,373,077		$1,373,077		$700,000	
Beginning cash balance	$1,373,077	$700,000	$1,373,077	$700,000	$700,000	$0
Uses of cash	$700,000	$700,000	$700,000	$700,000	$700,000	$0
Cash in marketable securities	$673,077	$0	$673,077	$0	$0	$0
Return on invested cash	$26,923	$0	$26,923	$0	$0	$0
Ending cash balance	$700,000	$0	$700,000	$0	$0	$0
Investor valuation and ownership allocation						
Investor hurdle rate	50.00%	45.00%	40.00%	35.00%	30.00%	25.00%
Continuing value multiplier						15
Continuing value of venture						$37,500,000

Investor's required future value and equity share	Required beginning share	Required ending share	Value
Third stage	2.43%	2.43%	$910,000
Second stage	10.30%	10.05%	$3,767,723
First stage	31.77%	27.80%	$10,426,803
Ownership required		40.28%	$15,104,527

NOTE: *Shaded cells are inputs that can be changed.*

Multistage Investment

Suppose that instead of investing only at Time 0, the investor proposes to contribute the capital in stages. Table 13.2 illustrates a staging alternative in which capital is invested at Time 0 and in Years 2 and 4. Because some of the capital contributed at Time 0 can be invested at the risk-free rate until it is needed in Year 1, the amount required for the first two years is $1.373 million. A like amount is needed at the end of Year 2, and an investment of $700,000 is required at the end of Year 4. In aggregate, the investor's three infusions total $3.446 million. However, because the investor can also earn the risk-free rate, the Time 0 equivalent is the same $3.241 million as in the nonstaged scenario (if the venture is successful).

To find the investor's required ownership interest under the staging scenario, we must evaluate each stage separately. Working from the last to the first, we begin with the $700,000 third-stage investment in Year 4. According to the hurdle rates in the table, the investor seeks a return of 30 percent for that investment. Thus, the Year 5 future value of the third-stage investment must be $910,000. Given the total continuing value of $37.5 million, the investor requires 2.43 percent of the equity in exchange for the third-stage investment.

We determine the required percentage of ending ownership for the second-stage investment in a similar manner. The desired return on the $1.373 million investment is 40 percent per year for three years, resulting in a Year 5 value of $3.768 million. This corresponds to 10.05 percent of continuing value. By the same reasoning, the required ownership percentage for the first stage is 27.80 percent. Collectively, the investor requires a 40.28 percent interest for the three stages. Thus, with staging, the entrepreneur can retain control and majority ownership.

Why Does Staging Reduce the Outside Ownership Share?

Comparing Tables 13.1 and 13.2, according to the VC method, staging reduces the investor's ownership and apparently benefits the entrepreneur. To understand why, you must know why the hurdle rates decline at later stages. How is the investor's commitment different in Table 13.2 from that in Table 13.1? For a single-stage investment, the commitment is absolute. Even if, during the five years, it becomes clear that the project is destined to fail, the investor's capital is irrevocably committed. In the event of liquidation, because (we have assumed that) the investment is in the form of common stock, the investor would recover only a 65.63 percent share of liquidation value. The balance would go to the entrepreneur.

There is no economic difference between the Table 13.1 scenario and an alternative in which investment is staged as in Table 13.2 but with the commitment to invest made irrevocably at Time 0. Because the commitment is made at Time 0, the investment must be evaluated as if it were made at Time 0. The 50 percent hurdle rate would apply to all investments. It follows that the lower hurdle rates in Table 13.2 arise because some of the uncertainty about venture performance is resolved before the decision to invest in later stages is made. The later-stage investments occur only if the venture continues to be attractive.

Because staging shifts additional risk to the entrepreneur, it is not clear which of the two scenarios is a better deal for her. In Table 13.2, the entrepreneur can expect to retain control if the "success" scenario is realized but bears more risk that either financing will not be available or the investor will require a larger fraction of equity in a scenario that is not as good. The VC method provides no guidance to the entrepreneur for comparing these alternatives. Later in the chapter, we evaluate the entrepreneur's choice. We cannot do so with only the limited information that the VC method uses. The entrepreneur cannot choose between the scenarios in Tables 13.1 and 13.2 simply by comparing the fraction of equity retained in the success scenario.

Determining the Required Ownership Percentage When Follow-On Investment Is Expected

Investors who invest during one round often anticipate that the venture will seek additional financing in subsequent rounds. Because additional rounds increase the number of shares outstanding, an investor who bases his decision on continuing value must take future financing rounds into account. Table 13.2 demonstrates how, under the VC method, anticipated future financing affects the fraction of equity an investor requires at each stage.

Beginning with the third stage, because no subsequent rounds are anticipated, the required ownership share is 2.43 percent. A second-round investor who estimates continuing value of $37.5 million anticipates a third round of financing in exchange for 2.43 percent of the equity. Before the third round, the combined shares of the entrepreneur and investor represent 97.57 percent of ending (Year 5) equity. Because they own 100 percent of the outstanding equity at the time of the invest-ment, a second-round investor who wishes to end up with 10.05 percent of equity at harvest must seek a larger fraction at the time of invest-ment. Equation (13.1) shows how you can determine the required fraction of equity when future rounds are anticipated.

$$\text{Fraction of Equity Required} = \frac{\text{Ending Fraction of Equity Required}}{(1 - \text{Sum of Fractions Required in Future Rounds})} \quad (13.1)$$

Using this equation, the investor's required share in the second round is 10.30 percent:

$$\text{Fraction of Equity Required} = \frac{10.05\%}{(1 - 2.43\%)} = 10.30\%$$

Similarly, the investor's required share in the first round is 31.77 percent:

$$\text{Fraction of Equity Required} = \frac{27.80\%}{(1 - 2.43\% - 10.05\%)} = 31.77\%$$

This method for determining the investor's required ownership fraction when additional rounds of financing are expected is recursive, the same for other valuation methods discussed later in the chapter.

How the Capitalization of a Venture Relates to the Stage of Financing

Normally, investors expect the capitalization of a venture to increase at each round. If it does not, or even if the increase is small, they may become concerned about the venture's prospects. Table 13.2 demonstrates the basis for such concerns. In the first stage, the investors contribute $1.373 million in exchange for 31.77 percent of the equity. This implies that they are capitalizing the venture at $4.322 million (i.e., the post-money valuation).

$4.322 million = $1.373 million / 31.77 percent

Because, under the success scenario, the second-stage investor contributes $1.373 million for 10.30 percent of outstanding equity, the second-stage capitalization is $13.330 million, a substantial gain over the first stage. Similarly, the third-stage investor is expected to contribute $700,000 for 2.43 percent of equity, an implied capitalization of $28.807 million.

These increases occur because the venture is progressing according to the success scenario. The gain is due partly to reduced uncertainty and partly to increasing proximity of exit. Even if the uncertainty were not reduced, capitalization would increase merely due to proximity of a harvest opportunity. If implied capitalization decreases from one round to the next or does not increase very much, it follows that the venture is not performing according to the success scenario.

Limitations of the Venture Capital Method

The VC method is easy to use but has two major limitations. First, it provides no analytical way to determine the appropriate hurdle rates. The rates are based only on rules of thumb and experience. Second, it does little to help an entrepreneur decide whether to proceed with a venture or compare financing alternatives. The first limitation can be addressed by incorporating risk into the analysis and focusing on expected cash flows. The second requires explicit valuation of the entrepreneur's financial claims. Hence, we return to CAPM-based valuation.

13.2   Staged Investment: CAPM Valuation with Discrete Scenarios

This section and the next include core material on structuring contracts that include real options. Because the analysis of staged financing quickly becomes involved, we present only a basic example.

Consider a venture that, according to the entrepreneur's business plan, requires cash infusions from an investor totaling $3.5 million. The entrepreneur needs $2 million now and an additional $1.5 in one year. At the current risk-free rate of 4.0 percent, the infusions have a PV of $3.442 million. The entrepreneur will work for the venture without salary. Her opportunity cost of forgone employment is $100,000 per year on a present-valued basis. The entrepreneur proposes to develop a navigation system that will be attractive to private aircraft owners. If the venture is successful, pilots will be able to download detailed three-dimensional map and navigation information from the Internet and use the information with a GPS-enhanced PDA for real-time navigation. The system would provide important flight plan and terrain information as well as information about runway and weather conditions at airports. The parties agree that the venture is not expected to generate any free cash flow before harvest. The entrepreneur expects that the venture can be harvested in three years.

Single-Stage Venture Capital Method Valuation

The projections in panel (a) of Table 13.3 reflect the entrepreneur's belief that the venture can generate sales from two different customer groups: OEM aircraft avionics suppliers and aircraft owners. The VC method success scenario assumes that both groups adopt the new product. The entrepreneur estimates that the venture will have a total harvest value of $35 million under the success scenario. Believing that the historical average annual return to limited partners of VC funds has been around 18 percent, the entrepreneur proposes to offer a VC investor 20 percent of the equity in exchange for the $3.442 million investment. Discounting the projected harvest value by 18 percent for three years yields a value of more than $21.302 million. The offer of 20 percent seems to the entrepreneur to be more than sufficient to compensate the LPs and provide a return to the VC. The entrepreneur's VC method analysis is summarized in panel (a) of Table 13.4.

As shown in panel (b) of Table 13.3, the VC investor disagrees for several reasons. First, the investor thinks four years is a more realistic estimate of time until harvest. Second, the investor believes that

TABLE **13.3**   **Financial model based on business plan**

Panel (a)—Entrepreneur's assumptions	Conditional cash flows	Scenario probabilities	Round 1	Round 2
Harvest value forecast				
Success with both groups	$35,000,000	40%	$14,000,000	$21,538,462
Success with first group	$15,000,000	25%	$3,750,000	$5,769,231
Failure	$0	35%		$0
Expected cash flow at harvest			**$17,750,000**	**$27,307,692**
Standard deviation of cash flows			**$15,204,851**	**$9,730,085**
Investment				
Burn rate per year			$2,000,000	$3,000,000
Years			1	0.5
Total investment	$3,500,000			
Present value of unconditional total investment	$3,442,308			
Present value of expected investment	$2,937,500			

Panel (b)—Investor's assumptions	Conditional cash flows	Scenario probabilities	Round 1	Round 2
Harvest value forecast				
Success with both groups	$28,000,000	32%	$8,960,000	$17,230,769
Success with first group	$13,500,000	20%	$2,700,000	$5,192,308
Failure	$0	48%		$0
Expected cash flow at harvest			**$11,660,000**	**$22,423,077**
Standard deviation of cash flows			**$12,303,430**	**$7,054,312**
Investment				
Burn rate per year			$1,800,000	$2,500,000
Years			1.25	1
Total investment	$4,750,000			
Present value of unconditional total investment	$4,630,391			
Present value of expected investment	$3,487,803			

NOTE: *Shaded cells are inputs that can be changed.*

the $35 million harvest value is too optimistic by about 20 percent; he also believes that the entrepreneur's success probabilities are optimistic. Third, the investor recognizes that the projected harvest value depends on being successful with both groups of customers, just a 32 percent probability outcome by his estimation. Fourth, based on projected burn rates, the investor believes that the venture will ultimately require infusions totaling $4.75 million, $2.25 million immediately and another $2.5 million in 15 months (1.25 years). These contributions have a PV of $4.630 million. The investor's assumptions are shown in panel (b) of Table 13.3. Recognizing that the business plan reflects only complete success and considering the early stage of development, the investor be-

⊤ TABLE **13.4**   **Valuation Template 9: VC method—single-round financing**

Panel (a)—Entrepreneur's assumptions

3	Number of years until your projected harvest date
$35,000,000	Harvest-date value of the venture assuming success
18.00%	*Annual hurdle rate:* Customary discount rates for seed to start-up ventures are 50–100% per year. Discount rates are lower for more established ventures, declining gradually to rates of 20–30% for expansion-stage financing. The discount rate for turnaround financing is comparable to that of a start-up.
$21,302,081	Post-money valuation of the venture
$3,442,308	Amount of financing required
16.16%	**Fraction of harvest-date equity needed to justify the financing.**

Panel (b)—Investor's assumptions

4	Number of years until your projected harvest date
$28,000,000	Harvest-date value of the venture assuming success
40.00%	*Annual hurdle rate:* Customary discount rates for seed to start-up ventures are 50–100% per year. Discount rates are lower for more established ventures, declining gradually to rates of 20–30% for expansion-stage financing. The discount rate for turnaround financing is comparable to that of a start-up.
$7,288,630	Post-money valuation of the venture
$4,630,391	Amount of financing required
63.53%	**Fraction of harvest-date equity needed to justify the financing.**

NOTE: *Shaded cells are inputs that can be changed.*

lieves that his success-scenario projection of $28 million ($35 million reduced by 20 percent) should be discounted at a VC-method hurdle rate of 40 percent for four years. The resulting value is $7.289 million. Consequently, as shown in panel (b) of Table 13.4, the investor would require at least 63.5 percent of the equity in exchange for committing the $4.630 million.

Identifying the Real and Financial Options

Given the disparity between their projections, it may seem that the parties should give up on trying to reach a deal. However, by staging the investment they may be able to reach agreement. Rather than using the VC method (with its ambiguity about appropriate hurdle rates), we use the CAPM-based valuation approach.

Suppose the parties recognize that three outcomes reasonably describe the range of plausible scenarios. In addition to complete success, the venture might succeed only in marketing to aircraft OEMs, or it might fail entirely. Development and marketing of the navigation software can be staged easily. The software is unlikely to be successful with aircraft owners unless it can first be sold to OEMs. If market-

FIGURE **13.1**

Staged investment model of aircraft navigation software venture

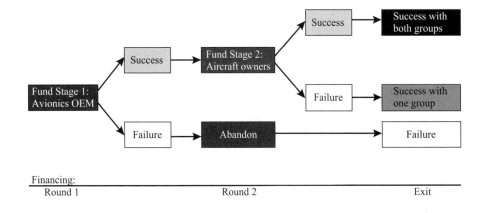

Financing:

| Round 1 | Round 2 | Exit |

ing to OEMs is successful, the venture can initiate marketing to aircraft owners.

Figure 13.1 illustrates the interplay between the investor's financial options and the real options of the staged venture. The investor's initial financial commitment (Round 1) enables the entrepreneur to pursue the OEM market (Stage 1). If those efforts are sufficiently successful, the investor will fund the next stage (Round 2), marketing the software to aircraft owners; if Stage 1 is not successful, the venture will be abandoned. If Round 2 financing is provided, the harvest value depends on whether the venture is a complete success or succeeds only with OEMs.

Of course, Figure 13.1 simplifies the actual decision and range of outcomes. At each stage in the figure, there are only two outcomes, success and failure, and the next round of investment depends only on which of the two occurs. The discrete scenario valuation approach is simplified here by using the knife-edged assumption that failure at Stage 1 means that no subsequent investment occurs and that success at Stage 1 results in investment in Stage 2.

The figure is a representation of the parties' understanding. For example, the investor expects that it will be valuable to invest in Round 2 if the entrepreneur is successful in Stage 1. However, there is no specific definition of success in the figure that the entrepreneur could use as a milestone for triggering the next financing round. Nor is there any indication of how the ownership claims might be reallocated. We return to contracting issues below.

Specifying Key Assumptions

The staging structure in Figure 13.1 requires that the parties estimate the expected harvest value associated with each scenario, the probability of each scenario, and the investment assumption for each financing round. In panel (a) of Table 13.3, we set out the entrepreneur's assumptions. Based on those assumptions, we compute the expected harvest cash flow and standard deviation of cash flows at each investment round. The expected cash flow and standard deviation by round will become inputs to the valuation. Panel (a) also shows the entrepreneur's burn-rate assumption for each stage and the entrepreneur's expectation of the duration of the stage.

Panel (b) shows the same information based on the beliefs of the VC investor. As is typical, the investor is less optimistic about the harvest values and the probabilities of various levels of success. In contrast to the entrepreneur, the investor expects harvesting to take longer and cash investments to be higher.

CAPM-Based Valuation with Irrevocable Commitment to Invest

To establish a baseline we can use to assess how staging affects value, it is useful to begin with a valuation where the investor's entire commitment is made at the beginning. Thus, under the entrepreneur's assumptions from Table 13.3, the investor would commit all $3.442 million at Time 0 (the PV of the $3.5 million commitment). The entrepreneur would use the money to achieve as much success as possible. This unconditional valuation is the same as if the venture were not staged and can be calculated using approaches developed earlier.

In Table 13.5, we compute the value from the perspective of the VC as a well-diversified investor who also seeks a return on effort. The table combines parts of other valuation templates we have seen in earlier chapters. The first panel (numbered "1") shows assumptions about the market and the VC's contract with limited partners. We assume that the VC seeks a management fee of 2.5 percent based on the value of the investment as well as a carried interest of 20 percent of the return to the fund. We implement the contract provisions in a simplified way, by adjusting the harvest-date cash flow down by 20 percent (deducting the carried interest) and then adding the annual fee (as a percentage) to the discount rate that is used to compute PV.

Based on the entrepreneur's harvest cash flow assumptions (in the second panel), the venture has a PV of $10.257 million to a well-diversified investor, as shown in the third panel. The investor's more pessimistic assumptions imply a PV of $5.844 million, roughly half the value that the entrepreneur's assumptions yield.

In the fourth panel, we use the valuations to impute cost of capital. The entrepreneur's assumptions yield a cost of capital of 20.06 percent

TABLE **13.5** **DCF valuation of unstaged investment**

	Entrepreneur's assumptions	Investor's assumptions
1. Market and contract data		
Annual risk-free rate	4.0%	4.0%
Annual market rate	10.0%	10.0%
Standard deviation of market	20.0%	20.0%
General partner's annual fee	2.5%	2.5%
General partner's carried interest	20.0%	20.0%
Correlation of venture with market	0.25	0.25
2. Single-stage investment and timing		
Total investment committed	$3,442,308	$4,630,391
Years to harvest	3.00	4.00
3. Investor valuation of harvest cash flows		
Expected harvest value	$17,750,000	$11,660,000
Standard deviation of harvest cash flows	$15,204,851	$12,303,430
Value of venture at time of investment	**$10,257,406**	**$5,843,845**
4. Investor's required rate of return		
Annualized VC cost of capital	20.06%	18.85%
INVESTOR OWNERSHIP REQUIREMENT		
5. Ownership requirement		
Round 1 investment	$3,442,308	$4,630,391
Value at Round 1	$10,257,406	$5,843,845
Share of incremental value required	**33.56%**	**79.24%**
VALUATION OF ENTREPRENEUR'S INTEREST IN VENTURE		
6. Entrepreneur's wealth		
Entrepreneur's wealth in market	$1,700,000	$1,600,000
7. Valuation of harvest cash flows		
Venture (entrepreneur's financial claim)		
Expected harvest value	$11,793,235	$2,421,159
Standard deviation of venture cash flows	$10,102,219	$2,554,765
Market		
Expected harvest value	$2,262,700	$2,342,560
Standard deviation of market cash flows	$588,897	$640,000
Portfolio		
Expected portfolio value	$14,055,935	$4,763,719
Standard deviation of portfolio cash flows	$10,265,291	$2,784,591
Value of entrepreneur's portfolio	**$7,065,242**	**$2,321,104**
Value to investment in market	**$1,700,000**	**$1,600,000**
Value of entrepreneur's interest in venture	**$5,365,242**	**$721,104**
8. Entrepreneur's required rate of return		
Annualized portfolio cost of capital	25.77%	19.69%
Annualized venture cost of capital	30.02%	35.36%

NOTE: *Shaded cells are inputs.*

for the VC investor, about 1.20 percent higher than the 18.85 percent imputed cost of capital under the investor's assumptions. Because we imputed the cost of capital based on the gross harvest cash flow, the management fee and carried interest are built into the imputed cost of capital. Accordingly, this is the relevant cost of capital for the entrepreneur to consider in seeking capital from the VC fund.

As shown in the fifth panel, based on the entrepreneur's valuation, the investor would need 33.56 percent of the equity in exchange for the $3.442 million commitment. Under the investor's assumptions, the investor would require 79.24 percent of the equity in exchange for the $4.630 million commitment.

In the sixth panel, as we did in Chapter 11, we estimate the amount of wealth the entrepreneur can invest in the market. We assume that the entrepreneur has total wealth of $2.0 million and will commit $100,000 per year (present valued) in forgone salary to the venture. For a three-year commitment, this leaves $1.7 million invested in the market.

In the seventh panel, as in Chapter 11, we compute the entrepreneur's expected portfolio harvest cash flows and risk. The $1.7 million market investment has grown to $2.263 million, and the entrepreneur's share of the venture (66.44 percent) is expected to yield $11.793 million, for a total expected harvest-date portfolio value of $14.056 million. With the assumed level of risk, in PV terms, the entrepreneur's portfolio is worth $7.065 million today. Subtracting the market investment of $1.7 million means that the investor's interest in the venture is worth $5.365 million, or an NPV of $5.065 million after the entrepreneur's human capital investment of $300,000. Under the investor's assumptions, the entrepreneur's 20.76 percent venture interest would be worth only $0.721 million, or an NPV of $0.321 million, given the higher $400,000 investment in human capital (for four years instead of three).

In the final panel of the figure, we impute the entrepreneur's required return for investing in the venture, which, because of underdiversification, is much higher than that of the investor, shown in the fourth panel. Under the entrepreneur's assumptions, the underdiversification premium is about 10 percent (30 percent, versus 20 for the investor). With the investor's assumptions, the premium increases to 16.5 percent, in part because the longer time commitment reduces the entrepreneur's diversification.

Valuing the Staged Venture at Each Investment Round

When investment is staged, the investor's claims and those of the entrepreneur can be adjusted at each investment round. The value of staging

TABLE **13.6**   **DCF valuation of staged investment**

1. Market and contract data	Entrepreneur's assumptions	Investor's assumptions
Annual risk-free rate	4.0%	4.0%
Annual market rate	10.0%	10.0%
Standard deviation of market	20.0%	20.0%
General partner's annual fee	2.5%	2.5%
General partner's carried interest	20.0%	20.0%
Correlation of venture with market	0.25	0.25
Time from first investment to harvest (years)	3.00	4.00
2. Staged investment timing and burn rates		
Round 1—Aircraft OEM		
Burn rate per year	$2,000,000	$1,800,000
Years to complete	1.00	1.25
Round 2—Aircraft Owners		
Probability of Stage 1 success	65%	52%
Burn rate per year	$3,000,000	$2,500,000
Years to complete	0.50	1.00
3. Valuation of harvest cash flows		
Round 2		
Expected harvest value	$27,307,692	$22,423,077
Standard deviation of harvest cash flows	$9,730,085	$7,054,312
Value to investor at time of investment	**$18,481,990**	**$14,421,393**
Round 1		
Expected harvest value	$17,750,000	$11,660,000
Standard deviation of harvest cash flows	$15,204,851	$12,303,430
Value of Round 1 at time of investment	**$10,257,406**	**$5,843,845**
4. Investor's implicit cost of capital at each round		
Round 1	20.06%	18.85%
Round 2	21.55%	17.41%

NOTE: *Shaded cells are inputs*

derives primarily from reductions of uncertainty about the likelihood of subsequent success. The changes in value that occur as the venture evolves affect the compensation the investor must receive for investing. In Table 13.6, we compute values that correspond to each round. The values reflect the assumptions in Table 13.3. While actual results will certainly be different, the valuations in Table 13.6 are the best estimates the parties can make at the time of the initial investment decision.

The first two panels summarize previously discussed assumptions. Valuations at each round are computed in the third panel. These valuations are based on the entrepreneur's or investor's beliefs as to the expected harvest cash flow and the standard deviation of harvest cash flows at each round. The values are for a well-diversified investor after providing for the VC's management fee and carried interest. The Round 1 valuations (and implicit cost-of-capital estimates, in the fourth panel) are the same as in the unstaged valuation in Table 13.5.

Comparing the Round 1 and Round 2 results, you can see the benefit of staging. Based on the entrepreneur's beliefs, the Round 2 value is $18.482 million, an 80.2 percent increase over the Round 1 value. Most of the increase in value arises because of the option to make the Round 2 investment only if Stage 1 is successful. Thus, staging does two things: it reduces the expected investment and it results in additional investment only when prior success warrants it. Parallel results obtain when considering the investor's assumptions in the final column.

Determining the Investor's Required Ownership Share

The valuation results can be used to determine the minimum equity the investor would need at each stage. We focus on minimums to maintain consistency with our general approach of assigning positive NPV to the entrepreneur. Thus, in Table 13.7, we compute the zero-NPV (after fees and carried interest) ownership percentages of the VC investor.[1] Consider the results based on the entrepreneur's assumptions. We use backward induction to establish the minimum equity allocations that will trigger exercise of the financing option. Beginning with Round 2, assuming the venture has been successful in the first stage, the venture will require $1.5 million to fund Stage 2. Because the venture is worth $18.482 million at the time of the Round 2 decision, in exchange for investing $1.5 million the VC investor would need to realize 8.12 percent of the expected harvest value at that time to achieve an NPV of zero.

TABLE **13.7**   **Valuation-based contracting model of ownership shares**

Ownership requirement	Entrepreneur's assumptions	Investor's assumptions
Investor's Round 2 investment	$1,500,000	$2,500,000
Venture value at Round 2	$18,481,990	$14,421,393
Incremental equity required	**8.12%**	**17.34%**
Investor's value from Round 1	$3,603,638	$5,552,531
Investor's value required with investing	$5,103,638	$8,052,531
Investor's required ownership after investing	**27.61%**	**55.84%**
Investor's Round 1 investment	$2,000,000	$2,250,000
Venture value at Round 1	$10,257,406	$5,843,845
Investor's required ownership after investing	**19.50%**	**38.50%**
Required percentage increases in investor's shares if new shares are issued		
Round 2—new shares to investor (percent of shares owned)	57.50%	101.95%

Concerns about Ownership Dilution

As we saw with the VC method example earlier, the new Round 2 investment reduces the percentage ownership held by prior investors and the entrepreneur. In the current example, however, to maintain a zero NPV for the investor at each round, we employ a structure where the early-round investor's claims are not diluted by later-round financings. The "Investor's required ownership after investing" percentages in Table 13.7 are the percentages that result in no dilution of the investor's existing equity claims. Thus, for example, using the entrepreneur's assumptions and further assuming that the venture is successful in Stage 1, the entrepreneur expects the venture to be worth $18.482 million at the time of the Round 2 financing. At this point, the investor's 19.50 percent of harvest value from Round 1 is worth $3.604 million. This would represent a positive NPV for the investor. However, the NPV is offset by what the entrepreneur believes is a 35 percent probability that the venture will fail in Stage 1 and be worth zero.

The table provides a way to find the investor's required zero-NPV ownership stake in Round 2, without diluting the Round 1 investment. The required ownership stake is computed by adding the new investment to the $3.604 million value of the original 19.50 percent interest. To avoid diluting the initial ownership, the investor would require a total of 27.61 percent of harvest value in exchange for investing in both rounds.

If the entrepreneur's beliefs are correct and accepted by the investor and the venture is successful in the first stage, so that the Round 2 investment is made, the investor would end up with 27.61 percent of the equity after his Round 2 investment. This compares with the 33.56 percent we found the investor would need if the investment were not staged. Under the investor's assumptions, the investor's required ownership would decrease to 55.84 percent if the investment is staged, compared to 79.24 percent if it is not.

13.3 Valuation-Based Contracting Model

Designing the Investment Agreement

The challenge facing the parties to this venture is to design an investment agreement that enables the investor to realize the intended share of harvest value depending on which scenario is achieved and on whether the entrepreneur's expectations or the investor's prove to be more accurate. The agreement should also allow for the possibility that different parties may invest in some of the later stages.

We can begin, arbitrarily, with the ownership percentages implied by the entrepreneur's beliefs. One way to prevent dilution of the investor's Round 1 ownership, if the same investor provides both rounds, is to simply give the investor additional new shares at Round 2 so that the intended new ownership percentage is realized. The calculations in the last panel of Table 13.7 show the percentage increase in the investor's shares that would be required to accomplish this. Hence, for example, for the investor's stake to increase from 19.50 percent after Round 1 to 27.61 percent after Round 2, the investor would need a 57.50 percent increase in shares owned.

To illustrate the dilution that could result from raising capital from a new investor, consider the Round 2 investment under the entrepreneur's assumptions. A new investor would not be concerned about dilution of the Round 1 investor's interest. Thus, the valuations in Table 13.7 imply that a new Round 2 diversified investor would require 8.12 percent of Round 2 post-money equity, which is equivalent to 8.83 percent of pre-money value.[2] The 8.83 percent increase in equity would dilute the Round 1 investor's interest from 18.50 percent to 17.78 percent. Total investor equity after Round 2 would then be 25.90 percent, instead of the (*ex ante*) zero-NPV share of 27.61 percent.[3] The reduction in the Round 1 investor's share would effectively transfer wealth to the entrepreneur.

Dealing with Ownership Dilution

The VC method seems to suggest that it is possible to neutralize the potential wealth transfer by anticipating the dilutive effects of subsequent rounds. However, this approach does not work. If the investor's initial equity is selected to produce a zero NPV in the event of complete success, then the percentage will be too low if later-round investments are not made.

An easy way to prevent dilution of early-round investments is to maintain the total number of shares outstanding and compensate later-round investors by transferring equity from the entrepreneur. In that way, for example, the Round 1 investor's share of harvest value does not depend on which of the scenarios is achieved. Alternatively, the investor's interest could be protected with antidilution rights that maintain the value of the investor's ownership without significant additional investment.

Dealing with Parties' Differing Beliefs

Now, consider the differences in the parties' assumptions. Some differences can be addressed, whereas others cannot. For example, the parties differ mainly in how likely they think it is that the venture will fail. Because, in our example, failure is determined in the first round, staging is the only way to mitigate this issue. By staging, the parties reduce the fraction of equity and amount of capital exchanged at the point when their beliefs are most disparate.

In this example, after Round 1 the parties' assessments of relative probabilities of different scenarios are identical. You can see this from the data in Table 13.3. If the venture is successful in the OEM market, both the entrepreneur and investor believe that the probability of success in the aircraft owner market is about 62 percent. The remaining differences relate to the amounts of cash that will be required, time to harvest, and amount of harvest cash flow. The parties can use contingent claims contracts to address these differences. If, for example, the first stage takes less time than the investor expects, the investor could agree to give warrants to the entrepreneur to reallocate ownership based on the realized lower amount of Round 1 investment relative to what the investor had anticipated. Alternatively, the contract could be based on the entrepreneur's assumptions, with the investor receiving warrants. After Stage 1, the parties' expectations may converge and warrant structures may no longer be important.

Valuing the Entrepreneur's Claim

We still do not know the value of the entrepreneur's claim. Based on the investor's ownership percentages in Table 13.7, the entrepreneur would hold the remaining equity and would be committed to seeing the venture through to harvest unless it is abandoned earlier. Under the entrepreneur's assumptions, the entrepreneur would have 72.39 percent ownership in the event of Round 2 investment and 80.50 percent without it. These ownership structures are substantial improvements over single-stage investment, where the entrepreneur had only a 66 percent share. In Table 13.8, the entrepreneur's conditional ownership percentages are used to compute the entrepreneur's expected harvest cash flow and standard deviation. Under the entrepreneur's assumptions, the expected harvest cash flow is $12.848 million. Under the investor's assumptions, it is $5.149 million.

Table 13.9 shows the computed value of the entrepreneur's claim, taking account of the entrepreneur's total wealth and commitment to the venture. If the investor accepts the entrepreneur's projections as correct, the entrepreneur's claim is worth $5.826 million dollars, an NPV of $5.526 million after the human capital commitment. This is a fairly modest improvement over the $5.065 million NPV under the single-stage approach in Table 13.5. The investor's assumptions yield a much greater gain for the entrepreneur. Moreover, as noted earlier, this improvement in value does not include the value to the entrepreneur of the intangible benefits of self-employment. Depending on how confident the entrepreneur is of her assumptions, the true expected value of the entrepreneur's interest likely lies between the two extremes.

TABLE **13.8**   **Risk and return of entrepreneur's financial claim**

Based on entrepreneur's projections

Ownership by round	Investor's share	Entrepreneur's share		
Round 2	27.61%	72.39%		
Round 1	19.50%	80.50%		
Harvest value forecast	Venture conditional cash flows	Scenario probabilities	Entrepreneur's conditional cash flows	Probability weighted cash flows
Success with OEMs	$35,000,000	40%	$25,335,059	$10,134,024
Success with both groups	$15,000,000	25%	$10,857,883	$2,714,471
Failure	$0	35%	$0	$0
Expected cash flow of entrepreneur's claim			**$12,848,494**	
Standard deviation of entrepreneur's claim			**$11,006,166**	

Based on investor's projections

Ownership by round	Investor's share	Entrepreneur's share		
Round 2	55.84%	44.16%		
Round 1	38.50%	61.50%		
Harvest value forecast	Venture conditional cash flows	Scenario probabilities	Entrepreneur's conditional cash flows	Probability weighted cash flows
Success with OEMs	$28,000,000	32%	$12,365,527	$3,956,969
Success with both groups	$13,500,000	20%	$5,961,951	$1,192,390
Failure	$0	48%	$0	$0
Expected cash flow of entrepreneur's claim			**$5,149,359**	
Standard deviation of entrepreneur's claim			**$5,433,515**	

TABLE **13.9**   **Valuation of entrepreneur's interest in venture**

Market data and entrepreneur's wealth	Entrepreneur's assumptions	Investor's assumptions
Annual risk-free rate	4.0%	4.0%
Annual market rate	10.0%	10.0%
Standard deviation of market	20.0%	20.0%
Correlation of venture with market	0.25	0.25
Time from first investment to harvest (years)	3.00	4.00
Entrepreneur's wealth in market	$1,700,000	$1,600,000
Timing of staged investments		
Round 1—Aircraft OEM		
Years to complete	1.00	1.25
Round 2—Aircraft owners		
Years to complete	0.50	1.00
Valuation of harvest cash flows		
Venture (entrepreneur's financial claim)		
Expected harvest value	$12,848,494	$5,149,359
Standard deviation of venture cash flows	$11,006,166	$5,433,515
Market		
Expected harvest value	$2,262,700	$2,342,560
Standard deviation of market cash flows	$588,897	$640,000
Portfolio		
Expected portfolio value	$15,111,194	$7,491,919
Standard deviation of portfolio cash flows	$11,167,956	$5,627,735
Value of entrepreneur's portfolio	**$7,525,846**	**$2,865,420**
Value to investment in market	**$1,700,000**	**$1,600,000**
Value of entrepreneur's interest in venture	**$5,825,846**	**$1,265,420**

NOTE: *Shaded cells are inputs.*

13.4   Negotiating to Increase Value, Signal Beliefs, and Align Incentives

In Table 13.9, the difference in value to the entrepreneur between the entrepreneur's valuation and the investor's is substantial. Both parties have an interest in moving closer to agreement about value. They can pursue this objective in a variety of ways. We established in Chapter 12 that because of their differences in risk tolerance, all else equal, value could be increased by shifting risk to the investor—in the extreme case, selling out to the investor and staying on as an employee.

Suppose, in an effort to increase the investor's valuation, the entrepreneur were to propose that the investor buy her out and hire her back at a salary equal to her opportunity cost. If the entrepreneur's proposal did not change the investor's expectations about performance, this would result in a higher return for the entrepreneur. It could also be expected to reinforce the assumptions underlying the investor's valuation. First, with all of the value being extracted by the entrepreneur, the investor might interpret the entrepreneur's willingness to sell as a negative signal. Second, the investor might be concerned that, because the entrepreneur has nothing at stake, she will not work as hard. Dealing effectively with these information and incentive problems is an important aspect of new venture financial contracting, and an important reason that entrepreneurs bear much of the risk even though it is easier for the investor to do so. Tying the entrepreneur's return to performance helps preserve the entrepreneur's incentives and can signal the entrepreneur's expectations, making it possible to negotiate a shift in the contract terms to better reflect the entrepreneur's projections. Retaining a material fraction of equity, as well as the use of warrants linked to milestones, earn-outs, and other devices, all can help to overcome the initial difference in assessment.

S 13.5   Using Simulation to Design Financial Contracts

Analyzing discrete scenarios is not a very convenient or accurate way in which to value deal structures. Furthermore, limiting the analysis to a small number of scenarios is likely to undervalue embedded real options. Options are most valuable when results are either very good or very bad, but extreme outcomes are usually ignored in discrete scenario analysis. Simulation affords an expedient and insightful way of comparing alternatives.[4]

The value of any venture depends on how the deal is structured, and specific contract alternatives can only be assessed in the context of the venture. The process parallels our discussion from Chapter 5 but with additional specificity.

Step 1: Model the venture and the deal. Build a financial model that reflects the structure of the venture and any important real options. A model is simply a set of mathematical expressions that converts operating and financial assumptions into a forecast of project cash flows. If a financial contract allows for abandonment if revenue is low or expansion if revenue is high, then the model must incorporate those options. To be used for valuation, the model must be structured to yield the cash flows that would be committed or received by investors and the entrepreneur.

Step 2: Specify the assumptions and uncertainties, including terms for exercising the options. The assumptions include such factors as how rapidly sales are expected to grow and how profitable sales are expected to be, the structure of ownership claims that control cash flow allocation, and so on. In addition to specifying expected performance, it is necessary to make assumptions about the uncertainty of key financial variables, such as sales and profitability. For any real options, it is necessary to make specific assumptions about the conditions under which each option would be exercised.

If each party can have different expectations about cash flows, different sets of assumptions can be used to reflect the different expectations. Specific assumptions may depend on the signaling and bonding aspects of the proposed financial contract.

Step 3: Run the simulation. Based on the assumptions, you can run the simulation model to generate expected cash flows and standard deviations for investors and the entrepreneur. You should also be able to derive estimates of incremental cash flows and uncertainty conditional on the exercise of any embedded options.

Step 4: Value the expected cash flows. Use the valuation models to evaluate the financial claims and conditional investment decisions. If the investor is well diversified, evaluate the investment based on the CAPM. If the entrepreneur is poorly diversified, evaluate the financial claim based on the total risk of the entrepreneur's portfolio.

Step 5: Search for the option-exercise criteria that result in the highest value. Consider the problem of contract design from the perspective of the entrepreneur. For options where the investor has the control rights, the entrepreneur would like to predict the investor's exercise decision and understand the implications for the value of the entrepreneur's claim. In addition, the entrepreneur would like to determine optimal exercise decisions for options where she has control rights. Evaluate the exercise decisions by experimenting with a range of possible exercise choices.

Step 6: Search for the allocation of claims that results in the highest value. By changing assumptions in the model, you can search for the allocation of ownership claims that yields the highest value to the entrepreneur.

In the remainder of this section, we illustrate the approach and discuss its use to evaluate contract alternatives.

Developing the Financial Model of the Venture and Specifying the Assumptions

To illustrate the use of simulation for designing a financial contract, we use a financial model based on a decision tree. The model provides for some of the uncertainty about the venture's probable success to be resolved by the second year. It includes a real option where the investor can decide, at that point, whether to make a second-stage investment. The investment would expand the capacity of the venture. For simplicity, we assume the parties have symmetrical beliefs. Alternatively, we could run separate simulation models for each party and use the results as a foundation for negotiating.

The model we use for this illustration is quite simple. Table 13.10 shows the results from one simulated trial. The model is designed to generate forecasts of the cash flows that the investor and entrepreneur will commit and receive. Because we addressed financial modeling in detail in earlier chapters, we abbreviate description of the financial aspects of the model here.

The model is driven (in the first panel) by a forecast of market potential that is subject to uncertainty. Much of the uncertainty is resolved by the end of the second year, so that if potential revenue is high at that point, it probably will continue to be high. The venture's capacity to supply the market depends on the total amount invested (in the second panel). Time 0 investment is $2.5 million, which includes $500,000 of the entrepreneur's human capital. The investor has an option to expand the capacity of the venture at the end of Year 2 by investing an additional $5 million. The investor will want to make the second-round investment only if market potential is expected to be high. The precise conditions under which the investor would want to exercise this expansion option depend on the venture's profitability, its other cash needs, and the financial claim that the investor would gain by exercising the option.

In the table, we must evaluate the venture in light of the terms of a specific deal. Accordingly, we assume that in the first round the investor commits $2 million in exchange for 10 percent of the equity and the entrepreneur commits $500,000 as the value of human capital. In the second round, if the option is exercised the investor receives new shares sufficient to increase total equity by 30 percent. Because of dilution, this would make the investor's total stake 37 percent. We assume that the investor exercises the option if Year 2 revenue is at least $15 million. We selected this exercise-decision criterion after we evaluated several alternatives to see what would work best for the investor. Also, for the purpose of evaluating alternative contracts, we assume arbitrarily

TABLE **13.10**   New venture simulation with conditional second-stage investment

	Year					
	0	1	2	3	4	5
Market potential (thousands of units)		101.16	204.80	435.20	606.92	833.88
Price (dollars)		$100	$100	$100	$100	$100
Potential revenue		$10,116	$20,480	$43,520	$60,692	$83,388
Total investment						
Investment	**$2,500**		**$5,000**			
Cumulative investment	$2,500	$2,500	$7,500	$7,500	$7,500	$7,500
Total income						
Sales revenue		$10,116	$20,480	$43,520	$60,692	$83,388
Cost of sales		$8,092	$16,384	$34,816	$48,553	$66,710
Gross profit		$2,023	$4,096	$8,704	$12,138	$16,678
Operating expenses		$1,809	$2,638	$4,482	$5,855	$7,671
Interest expense		$72	$479	$1,471	$2,335	$2,753
Interest income		$0	$0	$0	$0	$0
Net profit		$214	$1,458	$4,222	$6,283	$9,007
Total cash flow						
Beginning cash		$0	$0	$0	$0	$0
Operating cash flow		$214	$1,458	$4,222	$6,283	$9,007
NWC required		$1,012	$5,182	$11,520	$8,586	$11,348
Free cash		($798)	($3,725)	($7,298)	($2,303)	($2,341)
Borrowing		$798	$3,725	$7,298	$2,303	$2,341
Repay loan		$0	$0	$0	$0	$0
Ending free cash		$0	$0	$0	$0	$0
Loan balance	$0	$798	$4,522	$11,820	$14,123	$16,464
Total ending value						
Continuing value						$72,052
Plus: free cash						$0
Less: loan balance						$16,464
Value						**$55,588**
Total investment						
Investor's first-stage investment						$2,000
Investor's second-stage investment						$5,000
Entrepreneur's first-stage investment						$500
Total equity share and return						
Investor's share in first stage	10.00%					
Investor's share in second stage	30.00%					
Investor's total share	**37.00%**					**$20,568**
Entrepreneur's total share	**63.00%**					**$35,020**

that the investor will not participate unless the investor's NPV is at least $1 million (rather than setting it to zero as we usually do). Thus, the entrepreneur searches for deal terms that maximize value subject to a constraint that the investor's claim be worth at least $1 million.

The deal terms and investment levels are advantageous for the entrepreneur. We settled on them only after some experimentation. The assumptions, including investment levels and exercise decision, appear in the investment line of the table. You can evaluate alternative terms and exercise decisions by modifying these cells. You can design more complicated allocations by making other simple modifications, for example, to allow for the possibility that bonding and monitoring aspects of contract terms affect revenue and profitability expectations.

In the model, the cash flows available to the parties depend on net profit and annual free cash flow. We compute net profit as operating profit, plus interest income on surplus cash, minus interest expense on any borrowing needed to fund the operation. We assume that a liquidity event occurs at the end of Year 5. Value at that point is computed by capitalizing Year 5 earnings, adding the free cash balance and deducting any outstanding debt. The parties allocate total ending value according to their relative shares. For simplicity, we assume that the venture pays no taxes.

Using Simulation to Estimate Expected Cash Flows and Risk

Simulating Table 13.10 generates forecasts of expected cash flows and cash flow risk for both parties. The investor is interested in two questions. First, assuming that the investor makes the initial investment, under what conditions would it make sense to make the second-stage investment? Second, is the NPV of the investor's interest high enough to justify making the first-stage investment? The entrepreneur would like to know the condition under which the investor would make the second-stage investment. Given that condition, the entrepreneur would like to know the value of her financial claim. Because the entrepreneur's commitment is irrevocable, the entrepreneur has no decision to make at the end of the second year and needs to try to design an agreement in which the investor's decision would also work to the benefit of the entrepreneur.

To assess the investor's option-exercise decision, Table 13.11 is a version of Table 13.10 that is modified to isolate the incremental cash flows from exercising the option. It includes (1) a projection where the second-stage investment is assumed to be zero regardless of potential revenue and earnings and (2) the incremental revenue and earnings, together with cash flow returns to the investor and entrepreneur, measured as the difference between the projection from the model in Table 13.10 and the model with no second-stage investment. The table shows the results of one random trial, an example in which the option to make the second-stage investment is made.

When the condition for exercise is satisfied, the investor commits an additional $5 million in Year 2 and receives an increased interest in the

TABLE **13.11**   New venture simulation: Incremental effects of conditional second-stage investment

		Year				
	0	1	2	3	4	5
Potential revenue		$9,365	$19,531	$41,088	$54,199	$64,717
Total investment						
Investment	**$2,500**		**$5,000**			
Total income						
Sales revenue		$9,365	$19,531	$41,088	$54,199	$64,717
Net profit		$124	$1,344	$3,931	$5,504	$6,766
Total ending value						
Value						$43,184
Total equity share and return						
Investor's total share	**37.00%**					**$15,978**
Entrepreneur's total share	**63.00%**					**$27,206**
Investment—no second stage						
Investment	$2,500		$0			
Income—no second stage						
Sales revenue		$9,365	$19,531	$30,000	$30,000	$30,000
Net profit		$124	$1,344	$2,600	$2,600	$2,600
Ending value—no second stage						
Value						$22,285
Equity share and return—no second stage						
Investor's total share	**10.00%**					**$2,229**
Entrepreneur's share	**90.00%**					**$20,057**
Incremental investment—second stage						
Investment	$0		$5,000			
Incremental income—second stage						
Sales revenue		$0	$0	$11,088	$24,199	$34,717
Net profit		$0	$0	$1,331	$2,904	$4,166
Incremental ending value—second stage						
Value						$20,898
Incremental equity share and return—second stage						
Investor's incremental share	**27.00%**					**$13,749**
Entrepreneur's incremental share	**−27.00%**					**$7,149**

venture's cash flow. Table 13.11 presents a summary version of the three parts of the spreadsheet for one trial.[5] The "Total income" panel shows the cash returns to the parties if the investor makes the second-stage investment whenever the exercise condition is satisfied. The "Income— no second stage" panel shows cash returns for the same trial, assuming no second-stage investment is made. The "Incremental income—second stage" panel shows the incremental cash returns due to the option-exercise decision. We use the results from these three panels to evaluate the conditions under which it would be rational to make the investment, to test whether the investor's incentive is aligned with the interest of the entrepreneur, and to evaluate the financial interests of both parties.

To assess the deal structure, we ran 1,000 iterations of the model in Table 13.11. *Venture*.SIM includes a decision tree simulator that can be used to compile statistics for only the iterations that satisfy a stated condition. In this case, we collected results for five variables: For all 1,000 iterations, we collected data on the investor's total share of cash flows, the entrepreneur's total share, and the investor's second-stage investment. Then, looking only at the iterations where the second-stage investment occurs, we collected data on the investor's incremental share and the entrepreneur's incremental share. We will use these results to value the option.

The following table summarizes the simulation results:

Variable	Mean	Standard deviation	Number of cases where condition is satisfied
Investor's second-stage investment	−$2,475	$2,501	1,000
Investor's total share	$9,112	$8,483	1,000
Entrepreneur's total share	$19,505	$10,842	1,000
Investor's incremental share	$14,312	$4,187	495
Entrepreneur's incremental share	$7,824	$5,429	495

SOURCE: *Results generated by Venture.SIM decision tree simulation routine. To see the output table, please refer to the version of this table on the companion website.*

The table shows the expected second-stage investment of the investor together with the means and standard deviations of cash flows for the parties from all 1,000 iterations of the financial model. In addition, it shows the expected incremental cash flows and standard deviations computed over the 495 iterations where the condition for making the second-stage investment—Year 2 revenue is at least $15 million—is satisfied.

The Value of the Second-Stage Investment to the Investor

We now can evaluate the various decisions to invest. We follow the conventional approach of evaluating the conditional decisions first. Accordingly, Table 13.12 concerns the investor's decision to invest in the second stage. A minimum condition for investing is that the investor's NPV for exercising be positive at the time of the decision. To as-

TABLE **13.12**   **Valuing the second-stage option claims by discounting the conditional cash flows**

Market information		Year 2	Year 5
Risk-free rate of interest		0.00%	12.49%
Market rate of return		0.00%	40.49%
Market risk premium		0.00%	28.01%
Market standard deviation		0.00%	34.64%
Correlation between venture and market		0	0.2
Investor interest and value— *conditional second-stage investment only*			
Cash flows			
Expected cash flow	$0	($5,000)	$14,312
Standard deviation	$0	$0	$4,187
Present value of option cash flows (Year 2)		($5,000)	$12,121
NPV of option to invest in second stage (Year 2)	$7,121		
NPV of interest in venture (Year 2)	**$0**		
Entrepreneur interest and value—Year 2 value			
Entrepreneur's wealth	$2,000		
Cash flows of investment in venture			
Expected cash flow		($300)	$7,824
Standard deviation		$0	$5,429
Cash flows of investment in market			
Expected cash flow		($1,700)	$2,388
Standard deviation		$0	$589
Portfolio cash flows			
Expected cash flow		($2,000)	$10,212
Standard deviation		$0	$5,577
Value of entrepreneur's investments—CAPM based			
Present value of portfolio	$5,071		
Present value of investment in market	$1,700		
Present value of interest in venture	$3,371		
NPV of interest in venture (Year 2)	**$3,071**		

sess this, we use the "Investor interest and value" panel of the spreadsheet to compute the value of the investor's incremental cash flow as of the end of the second year. We compute discount rates and market risk over the three-year holding period from Year 2 to Year 5. For the investor, the Year 2 value of the expected $14.312 million incremental cash flow in Year 5 is $12.121 million. This value is based on the CAPM and on the assumption, shown in the "Market information" panel of Table 13.12, that the correlation between incremental venture cash flows and the market is 0.2. The resulting (Year 2) NPV of the $5 million investment is $7.121 million.

We can see from the table that exercising the expansion option whenever Year 2 market potential is at least $15 million is beneficial for the investor. It may be that the trigger value of $15 million is too high, however, so that additional opportunities to add value are overlooked. Or it may be too low, so that the investment is sometimes made even though the expected value is negative. To determine the optimal critical value, we would need to run the simulation model several more times, trying different critical values for exercising the second-stage investment option.

How the Investor's Decision Affects Value to the Entrepreneur

Ideally, the entrepreneur would like to design the contract so that the investor would want to make the second-stage investment only when doing so is beneficial to the entrepreneur as well. To help design deal terms, the "Entrepreneur interest and value" panel of Table 13.12 includes evaluation of the NPV of the entrepreneur's incremental cash flows over the iterations where the investor makes the second-stage investment. Because total risk matters, this value depends on the entrepreneur's other assets. The entrepreneur expects to have $1.7 million invested in a market index at the decision point. The value of the committed three years of human capital investment is $300,000.

In the table, we compute the CAPM-based value in light of the total risk of the entrepreneur's portfolio. The NPV of the entrepreneur's incremental human capital investment is $3.071 million. Thus, the entrepreneur would regard the assumed deal terms as positive. To determine whether this is the best choice, we would need to test other assumptions.

The Value of the Investor's Interest in the Venture

Now that we have valued the option for both parties, we need to back up one step and determine whether the overall deal is sufficiently attractive for the investor. Then we need to determine whether undertaking the venture is worth the entrepreneur's commitment. The "Investor interest and value" panel of Table 13.13 contains the evaluation of the investor's total financial claims. The calculations assume that the second-stage investment is made whenever the trigger value is reached. For the investor, the Time 0 NPV of the deal is $1.5 million; this includes the PV of the $9.112 million expected cash flow in Year 5 and the PV of the negative $2.475 million expected second-stage investment in Year 2.

TABLE **13.13**   **Valuing financial claims by discounting all expected cash flows**

Market information		Year 2	Year 5
Risk-free rate of interest		8.16%	21.67%
Market rate of return		25.44%	76.23%
Market risk premium		17.28%	54.57%
Market standard deviation		28.28%	44.72%
Correlation between venture and market	0	0.2	
Investor interest and value			
Cash flows			
Expected cash flow	($2,000)	($2,475)	$9,112
Standard deviation	$0	$2,501	$8,483
Present value of first-stage interest	$3,500	($2,288)	$5,788
NPV of option to invest in second stage			
NPV of interest in venture	**$1,500**		
Entrepreneur interest and value			
Entrepreneur's wealth	$2,000		
Cash flows of investment in venture			
Expected cash flow	($500)		$19,505
Standard deviation	$0		$10,842
Cash flows of investment in market			
Expected cash flow	($1,500)		$2,644
Standard deviation	$0		$671
Portfolio cash flows			
Expected cash flow	($2,000)		$22,149
Standard deviation	$0		$10,996
Value of entrepreneur's investments—CAPM			
Present value of portfolio		$7,177	
Present value of investment in market		$1,500	
Present value of interest in venture		$5,677	
NPV of interest in venture	**$5,177**		

The Value of the Entrepreneur's Interest in the Venture

For the entrepreneur, the "Entrepreneur interest and value" panel of Table 13.13 shows that the NPV of the entrepreneur's interest in the venture is $5.177 million. Thus, the venture is acceptable to both.

The valuation in Table 13.13 is based on one set of assumptions about when the second-stage investment option would be exercised and one allocation of ownership claims. To determine whether the exercise decision is the highest-valued one for the investor or whether some other assignment of ownership claims would be better for the entrepreneur, we must repeat the simulation and valuation steps using different assumptions.

13.6   Information, Incentives, and Contract Choice

In this section, we discuss ways of applying financial modeling and simulation to other contracting issues. We consider four broad classes of issues: types of claims, number of contracting parties, contracting to resolve information problems, and contracting to align incentives. Our treatment here is conceptual but can be integrated with the structural models.

Valuing Different Types of Financial Claims

In the preceding example of an avionics navigation venture, the portfolios of claims of the parties were different. In exchange for the first-stage investment, the investor received common stock plus a call option on additional shares, with an exercise price of $5 million. For someone to buy a call, someone else must write (sell) it. In that example, because the second-stage investment would increase shares outstanding, both parties effectively were involved in writing the call. In that analysis, we did not attempt to value the equity of the venture or to determine the value per share; instead, we valued the complete distribution of cash flows each party would expect to receive, given their deal. This approach, of valuing the entire distribution of cash flows, can be applied to any contracting structure the parties may consider. The following are examples.

Debt financing.   Straight debt can be incorporated easily in a financial model. In fact, in the previous example we did provide for temporary debt financing. However, we made an arbitrary assumption about the interest rate. We did not derive the rate from the risk characteristics of the cash flows, nor did we analyze whether the rate was higher than necessary to attract the funding.

Consistent with the example, if competition generates a competitive interest rate, then the entrepreneur does not need to value the financial interest of a creditor. All that is necessary is to model and value the residual cash flows of the entrepreneur in a way similar to that shown in the previous illustration. On the other hand, if the entrepreneur has to negotiate debt-financing terms bilaterally with a single prospective lender, there may be good reason to estimate the NPV of the creditor's financial claim—for example, to design terms that would work to the parties' mutual benefit.

The model of the venture can be structured to incorporate default states and generate the corresponding cash flows to the creditor. Thus, simulation of the debt contract can be used to estimate the series of periodic expected cash flows and standard deviations of cash flows. The expected cash flows and their standard deviations are inputs to the valuation.

Personal guarantees.   Until now, we have assumed that the worst possible outcome for the entrepreneur is a return of −100 percent. However, when debt is used in new ventures, it is common for the entrepreneur to personally guarantee the obligation or to pledge collateral. In that case, if the venture fails and the liquidation value of the assets is below the venture's financial liabilities, the entrepreneur may personally have a negative cash flow at liquidation. The issue we address here is how the prospect of a negative cash flow can be treated in the valuation.

A reasonable approach to valuing claims that involve personal guarantees is to consider the amount of the guarantee as part of the entrepreneur's investment in the venture. In nondefault states, the guarantee portion of the investment earns a return that is appropriate for the nature of the assets that are committed by the guarantee; this might be the riskless rate on a debt instrument, the return on the market, and so on. In nondefault states, the return on the guarantee assets is part of the entrepreneur's total return for investing in the venture. In default states, the return on the guarantee is divided between the entrepreneur and the creditor per the contract.

You can then value the entrepreneur's interest in the venture in the usual way. Any assets not committed to the venture are treated as a second asset of the entrepreneur's portfolio.

Convertible securities.   Often, the investor's financial claim is a hybrid, such as convertible preferred stock or convertible debt. Valuing convertible securities is not fundamentally different from what we have already discussed. The simulation analysis must be based on a financial model that anticipates the conditions under which conversion is expected to occur. This is similar to simulating when a real option is likely to be exercised.

Preferred shares and debt give the investor priority in the event of liquidation. They may also generate dividend or interest payments or accrue rights to dividends or interest that are to be paid at exit. The model must incorporate the dividend or interest provisions in the cash flow allocations. With these modifications, the valuation methodology is the same as in the previous example. Each claim is valued on the basis of expected cash flows, standard deviation, and the estimated correlation with the market.

Warrants. Warrants are long-term call options whereby exercising the option increases the number of shares outstanding. Warrants can be issued as a sweetener for a loan or equity investment or to the entrepreneur. Warrants issued to an entrepreneur are usually subject to the condition that a specific performance target be achieved or exceeded. Warrants can also be issued to other parties, such as employees, as compensation that is tied to performance.

In the previous example, the first-stage investor effectively had received warrants that could be exercised by making a substantial investment in the venture in the second round. Thus, we already have demonstrated how to use simulation to value financial claims involving warrants.

Ratchets or antidilution rights. A ratchet is a right to receive future shares in the event that value per share is lower in a subsequent round of financing. If value declines, the investor's average cost per share is reduced by issuing additional shares for a nominal price. One difficulty in evaluating a ratchet is that the modeling must include an estimate of the variable that can precipitate exercise. If exercise depends on share price in a subsequent round, exercising the ratchet would increase shares outstanding without adding to value. Consequently, the share price in the round depends on whether the ratchet would be exercised. Share price and exercise of the ratchet provision are simultaneous outcomes; the model needs to incorporate the simultaneity.

Abandonment. Suppose an investor has committed to making a second-round investment on the condition that a certain milestone is achieved; otherwise, the investor can abandon the venture. If the investor does abandon, suppose that the venture will be liquidated before the planned harvest date. From the investor's perspective, this looks similar to the expansion option example.

For the entrepreneur, if abandonment shuts the venture down early, then the entrepreneur's commitment of human capital is different from the example. Specifically, the entrepreneur may receive a positive or negative cash flow at the time of abandonment. Rather than attempting to value cash flows at different times, our suggestion is to simplify the valuation by using the risk-free rate to shift all cash flows to the same period.

Control rights, termination rights, and other rights. New venture deals commonly allocate some control rights separately from ownership share. For example, an investor may have the right to appoint some of the directors or to terminate the entrepreneur if performance targets are not met. The entrepreneur may have an employment contract or a right to sell out if she is terminated. An investor may have a right to limit future financings or a first right of refusal on such financings. Both parties may have registration rights in the event of a public offering, and the investor may have rights that can compel a liquidity event of some type.

Sometimes these rights can be valued formally through their effects on the cash flows of the financial claim; other times, value is subjective. If it is subjective and if the right is conditional, then a reasonable approach to valuation is for the party to assign a value to the right and to add the expected value to the NPV of the financial claim. Suppose the entrepreneur values having control at $50,000 (i.e., the amount the entrepreneur would be willing to pay in order to have control), and the investor values control at $80,000. Suppose, further, that in 40 percent of the random scenarios, the entrepreneur is expected to retain control. Under this approach, the entrepreneur's NPV would be increased by $20,000 (40 percent times $50,000) and the investor's would be increased by $48,000 (60 percent of $80,000).

Increasing the Number of Contracting Parties

Many new ventures involve three or more parties. The nature of involvement can be explicit or implicit and can be direct or indirect. In this subsection, we identify and consider the implications for valuation.

Direct explicit involvement of a third party. Suppose a venture is seeking funds for a second round. A new investor is interested in providing the financing; alternatively, the existing investor could provide the financing. In such a case, the interests of existing parties may diverge. The entrepreneur may want to bring in a new investor to reduce the existing investor's control, or the new investor may be a strategic partner who, for example, can aid with distribution of the venture's product. The existing investor may want to retain a larger ownership share or may regard the prospective investor as a competitor. In addition, both current parties may be concerned about the valuation and how the shares will be allocated to the new investor.

To evaluate the alternatives, you would need to model the venture, including the allocations of cash flows to all three parties. Using the model, you can experiment with the conditions under which the investment would be made by a new investor or by the existing investor.

Direct implicit involvement.   Often, the existing parties are considering terms that could affect the conditions under which a subsequent party would invest. There are many such aspects of negotiation. The most obvious is a ratchet, but other provisions, such as conversion rights or the right to force registration of the shares, can also affect the decisions of future investors.

To assess the impact of such provisions, you can design the model to anticipate a subsequent round. By running a simulation, you can examine the effects of the provision on the likely terms of subsequent investment and assess how the provision affects claim values.

A right to invest in a subsequent round at a prespecified price can also be evaluated as possibly affecting an investment by a third party. In the previous example, we assumed that if the investor did not make the second-stage investment, then no investment would be made; we valued the financial claims accordingly. An alternative assumption is that if the option is not exercised, then some other investor might contribute the needed capital. The first-stage investor could also forgo exercising the option but still be willing to negotiate a second-stage investment.

Indirect involvement.   A VC fund is a good example of indirect involvement. The cash flows received by the fund are allocated between the general partner and the limited partners according to their agreement. The general partner must be concerned with the returns to both. By modeling the venture, including the terms for allocating cash flows between the general and the limited partners, you can consider how financing terms would affect the parties to the partnership.

Contracting to Resolve Information and Incentive Problems

The parties to a venture may disagree about many aspects of the potential for success. They may disagree about when certain milestones are likely to be achieved or about the achievable level of sales or profitability in the event of success. There may also be concerns about incentive incompatibilities. Many contract provisions can mitigate information asymmetry and align incentives. Because provisions can have both effects, we cover them together.

If the parties disagree about the prospects of a venture, they cannot be expected to use the same assumptions and possibly not even the same financial model. In general, a negotiation is most likely to be successful if each party attempts to recognize the concerns of the other and to seek financing terms that mitigate the effects of information asymmetries and incentive problems.

Actual deal structures demonstrate that information and incentive problems are at the core of new venture deal structure. Our analysis, in earlier chapters, leads to the conclusion that if the parties have symmetrical expectations, then the highest-valued contract is one in which most of the risk is borne by the well-diversified investor. Although some aspects of new venture contracting go a long way in this direction, in most cases the entrepreneur continues to bear a large fraction of the total risk. This fact underscores the importance of information and incentive problems.

We have already discussed these problems to a degree. Our objective here is to highlight a few examples and to relate them to financial modeling and valuation.

Debt financing. Expected cash flows to the entrepreneur are usually higher if outside financing is in the form of debt, but the entrepreneur's risk is also higher. Substituting outside debt for outside equity shifts risk to the entrepreneur. Because the entrepreneur is concerned with total risk, increased reliance on outside debt is likely to reduce value.

Why, then, would it ever make sense for an entrepreneur to seek debt financing? The most compelling reason is that with debt, the investor (creditor) and the entrepreneur can have widely divergent expectations about the venture. An entrepreneur may legitimately be optimistic about the potential but be unable to convince prospective equity investors. Consequently, an equity investor would demand more equity than the entrepreneur would think necessary. If the failure scenarios are more symmetrically perceived, then the entrepreneur may be better off with debt, even if the risk of the entrepreneur's claim increases as a result. Straight debt also obviates the parties' need to reach agreement about the entire distribution of potential cash returns.

Debt maturity can signal the entrepreneur's beliefs about when she expects to reach a milestone. Suppose, for example, the entrepreneur anticipates having a marketable product in two years but seeks financing for five. The entrepreneur's proposed repayment schedule might be based on her view that it will take five years to generate cash flows sufficient to repay the debt.

However, the entrepreneur's proposal undermines the credibility of her claim that it will take two years to reach the market. If she is correct, then refinancing in two years should be possible at lower interest cost. Consequently, her proposed five-year term suggests that she is not confident. You can expect the creditor to respond by demanding a higher rate of interest. An entrepreneur who truly expects to reach the market in two years can do better by selecting shorter-term financing. In general, shortening the term moves repayment ahead of full resolution of uncertainty. The investor does not need to make a complete assessment of development timing, because in two years there will be an opportunity to reassess.

If the entrepreneur believes the investor is overly pessimistic, then the entrepreneur's financial model alone will not generate results that lead to the highest value for the entrepreneur. The model cannot be used to generate financing alternatives that will be equally acceptable to the investor. Instead, the entrepreneur must seek financing choices that are achievable in light of the investor's beliefs. The entrepreneur can then evaluate those alternatives in the context of a model that reflects the entrepreneur's beliefs. Also, if the terms affect the expectations of either party, then the model assumptions must be made conditional on the deal terms being evaluated.

Earn-ups and earn-outs.   An earn-up is a financial arrangement in which an acquirer of a venture provides financial incentives to the entrepreneur to encourage strong future performance. The earn-up addresses moral hazard issues. An earn-out is a financial arrangement in which the investor or acquirer provides for the entrepreneur to receive additional future payments, usually based on the venture's future earnings. This type of arrangement addresses adverse selection.

Protecting the entrepreneur.   An investor can demonstrate good faith in a variety of ways. The simplest is through the investor's reputation of dealing fairly with entrepreneurs. The advantage of reputation is that it mitigates the need to envision an array of contingencies against which the entrepreneur seeks protection. An alternative to reputation is to specify conditions under which control of key decisions resides with the entrepreneur. If, for example, the entrepreneur is concerned about a hold-up when financing is needed, the investor can agree to give the entrepreneur a call option on additional funds, where the entrepreneur's right to exercise the call is tied to achievement of a milestone.

13.7   Summary

The primary focus of this chapter is on demonstrating how staging a venture can create value and providing the tools for valuing staged investments. We first demonstrate use of the VC method in a staged investment context. While the method is helpful, focus on the success scenario is more problematic when an investment is staged than when it is not. We turn then to using the CAPM and value expected cash flows. The example we use is a fairly simple two-stage opportunity, as the analysis becomes complex quickly. Among other things, we illustrate how staging can help to overcome a difference in expectations between the entrepreneur and the investor.

The focus of the remainder of the chapter is on an examination of how standard new venture contract terms and practices help to contribute to value by addressing information and incentive problems. Contract terms enhance value when they overcome information asymmetries and align incentives. Using valuation methods developed earlier in the book, including the VC method and the CAPM-based DCF method, we illustrate how value is created by adding milestones to a contract and embedding real options in the deal structure. In particular, by staging investments the entrepreneur can retain control and majority ownership of the venture.

Financial modeling techniques presented here allow the entrepreneur to assess how the required ownership percentage changes when follow-on investment is expected. By employing more sophisticated modeling approaches, the parties are better able to understand the interplay between the investor's financial options and the real options of the staged venture and to address concerns such as ownership dilution.

The starting point for the analysis assumes that the investors and entrepreneurs have differing beliefs about the capabilities of the entrepreneur and the likely success of the venture. We use scenario analysis and simulation to more accurately reflect the inherent uncertainty surrounding the venture. The financial modeling approach can be applied to a myriad of related contracting issues, such as the impact of various types of financial claims on value (debt, equity, convertible securities, personal guarantees, warrants, ratchets, etc.); how changing the number of contracting parties affects value; and how debt financing, earn-outs, and similar provisions can help mitigate incentive and information issues and thereby increase value.

REVIEW QUESTIONS

1. In the context of the VC method, describe how to address dilution to correctly determine the amount of ownership an investor would require for a staged investment. Refer to Tables 13.1 and 13.2.

2. How does staging of new venture investments create value for the entrepreneur? What about for the investor?

3. What is the likely impact of staging on the level of risk facing the entrepreneur?

4. Why might an investor in an early financing round want to anticipate the need for additional financing rounds even in cases where the entrepreneur and investor agree on the terms for investing?

5. Explain how an entrepreneur can use staging of investment to both signal the entrepreneur's beliefs and better align the entrepreneur's incentives with the interest of investors.

6. Why is simulation preferred over scenario analysis for valuing real options embedded in new ventures?

7. Describe the ideal "trigger" for modeling the value of an embedded real option.

8. How can you model the impact on value of the personal guarantee given by entrepreneurs when they raise new venture debt?

9. How can the entrepreneur use debt terms to signal confidence in the venture?

10. Describe the process of valuing the entrepreneur's ownership interest in a two-stage investment. Refer to Tables 13.10 through 13.13.

NOTES

1. The zero-NPV increase in ownership is not necessarily the same as the minimum ownership change necessary to cause the investor to exercise the option to invest. To determine the necessary ownership change requires comparing the value of the ownership claim with exercise to an explicit assumption of the value without exercise. That analysis depends on what would happen if the option were not exercised. Not exercising could mean, for example, that

the real option to go to the next stage could not be exercised. In this example, if the venture is successful in the prior stage but the investor does not invest in the next round, we effectively assume that another investor provides the funds on the same terms but in a way that does not dilute the existing investor's claim. The assumption assigns all positive NPV to the entrepreneur.

2. This is calculated as [new investment/(post-money value − new investment)].

3. The diluted total investor holdings percentage is calculated as (new investment percentage of post-money value + diluted percentage of Round 1 investment).

4. To fully understand the discussion in this section, you should download the Excel files of the tables from the companion website and examine them as you read.

5. The hidden rows and cell formulas can be studied in the Excel file, which is available on the companion website.

REFERENCES AND ADDITIONAL READING

Berger, P. G., E. Ofek, and I. Swary. 1996. "Investor Valuation of the Abandonment Option." *Journal of Financial Economics* 42:257–87.

Bernardo, A., and I. Welch. 2001. "On the Evolution of Overconfidence and Entrepreneurs." *Journal of Economics and Management Strategy* 10:301–30.

Bhide, A., and H. H. Stevenson. 1990. "Why Be Honest If Honesty Doesn't Pay." *Harvard Business Review* 68 (September–October): 121–29.

Brennan, M., and A. Kraus. 1987. "Efficient Financing under Asymmetric Information." *Journal of Finance* 42:1225–43.

Chua, J. H., and R. S. Woodward. 1993. "Splitting the Firm between the Entrepreneur and the Venture Capitalist with the Help of Stock Options." *Journal of Business Venturing* 8:43–58.

Cornelli, F., and O. Yosha. 2003. "Stage Financing and the Role of Convertible Securities." *Review of Financial Studies* 7 0:1–32.

Cumming, D. 2005. "Capital Structure in Venture Finance." *Journal of Corporate Finance* 1 1:550–85.

Gompers, P. 1995. "Optimal Investment, Monitoring, and the Staging of Venture Capital." *Journal of Finance* 5 0:1461–89.

Kaplan, S. N., and P. Stromberg. 2002. "Characteristics, Contracts, and Actions: Evidence from Venture Capitalist Analyses." *Journal of Finance* 59:2177–2210.

———. 2003. "Financial Contracting Theory Meets the Real World: An Empirical Analysis of Venture Capital Contracts." *Review of Financial Studies* 7 0:281–316.

Landier, A., and D. Thesmar. 2009. "Financial Contracting with Optimistic Entrepreneurs." *Review of Financial Studies* 2 2:117–50.

Ravid, S. A., and M. Spiegel. 1997. "Optimal Financial Contracts for a Start-Up with Unlimited Operating Discretion." *Journal of Financial and Quantitative Analysis* 3 2:269–85.

Sahlman, W. 1987. "Note on Financial Contracting: Deals." Harvard Business School Press Teaching Note 9-288-014. Boston: Harvard Business School Press.

Stevenson, H. 1988. "Deal Structure." Harvard Business School Press Teaching Note 9-384-186. Boston: Harvard Business School Press.

14

CHOICE OF FINANCING

Money often costs too much.

Ralph Waldo Emerson

The menu of financing sources for start-ups and privately owned businesses is extensive and constantly evolving. We cannot provide a comprehensive and timely survey of the menu in a single chapter. Instead, our objective is to emphasize decision making with regard to the choice of financing and to provide a framework for evaluating alternatives. In Chapter 2, we introduced many of the financing sources that are commonly used by ventures as they develop and grow. Now, with a better understanding of a venture's financing needs and how financing choices can affect valuation, we revisit the topic with the objective of matching these considerations to financing sources. You may find it helpful to refer back to the descriptive information in Chapter 2 as you consider the issues related to choice of financing.

14.1 Financing Alternatives

Figure 14.1 lists 25 sources of business and venture financing. A comprehensive list would be much longer. Why are there so many alternatives? Part of the answer is that the providers have different objectives, capabilities, and constraints. Some, like banks, seek low-involvement, low-risk investments, usually of short to moderate duration; others, like angel investors, seek high-risk, high-involvement investments of moderate to long duration. In some cases, financing is linked to operational aspects of the business, such as production or sales. The providers of

FIGURE **14.1**

Selected financing sources for new ventures

- Angel investors
- Asset-based lending
- Capital leasing (venture leasing)
- Commercial bank lending (various forms)
- Corporate entrepreneurship
- Customer financing
- Direct public offering
- Economic development program financing
- Employee-provided financing
- Equity private placement
- Export/import bank financing
- Factoring
- Franchising
- Friends and family
- Public debt issue
- Registered initial public offering
- Research and development limited partnerships
- Relational investing or strategic partnering
- Royalty financing
- Self
- Small Business Administration financing
- Small Business Investment Company financing
- Term loan
- Vendor financing
- Venture capital

various financing sources seek to reduce risk and protect the value of their investments in diverse ways. Some, like venture capitalists, engage in active monitoring to protect their investments; others, like factoring companies and secured lenders, rely heavily on collateral.

The second part of the answer is that businesses have financing needs that change over time and over circumstances. Financing needs may be small or large, immediate or in the future, temporary or permanent. An established business may be able to offer considerable security, whereas an early-stage venture may require the investor to bear substantial risk. Businesses also differ in their tax exposures, management capabilities, needs for flexibility, and numerous other dimensions that bear on the financing choice. Most financing alternatives are market-based responses to demand for financing within the context of tax and regulatory concerns. Others are the result of public policies that promote and subsidize new ventures and small businesses.

Although the list in Figure 14.1 may seem daunting, the choices are manageable once the list is narrowed to sources that are appropriate for the specific venture and situation. In the balance of the chapter, we develop a systematic approach to matching the venture's financing needs with the most appropriate financing sources.

14.2 The Objective and Basic Principles of the Financing Decision

When evaluating financing choices, we start with the presumption that the entrepreneur seeks to maximize the NPV of his stake in the venture. Other considerations, such as a desire to maintain control and the need for an active investor, can be introduced as factors that argue for or against a funding source or affect the specific terms of the deal.

Basic Considerations That Affect Financing Choices

Several principles affect the choice of financing. First, we have seen that if prospective investors agree with the entrepreneur about the venture's prospects, external financing is preferred to financing by the entrepreneur. Outside investors are generally capable of more fully diversifying risk. Consequently, they can justify lower expected returns for a given level of total risk. All else equal, for a successful venture, greater reliance on outside financing can increase the value of the entrepreneur's ownership stake. An offsetting consideration is the cost associated with managing relations with external providers of financing. Investors expect periodic reporting and access to information. In addition, external financing is likely to affect the entrepreneur's ability to control future decisions.

Second, if the entrepreneur and investor have symmetric expectations about the venture's future, financing that shifts risk to the investor increases the value of the entrepreneur's financial claim. Well-diversified investors need not be compensated for bearing nonmarket risk. All else equal, the entrepreneur can benefit by using equity for as much outside financing as possible.

More realistically, the parties are unlikely to agree about the prospects for the venture. Information and incentive concerns limit the entrepreneur's ability to raise outside equity. Certain types of financing can mitigate this problem. For example, if investors' evaluations take account of the entrepreneur's willingness to retain a significant residual equity interest, then value-maximizing financing choices must strike a balance between reducing the entrepreneur's exposure to risk and signaling confidence in the venture. Fundamentally, this is an issue of credibility. Similarly, financing that does not maintain the entrepreneur's incentive to commit substantial effort to the venture is unlikely to result in maximum value for the entrepreneur.

Other Considerations That Affect Financing Choices

A number of other issues bear on the desirability of a particular financing choice. Some providers of financing perform advisory, monitoring, or other functions that can enhance value. However, the actual worth of such tasks varies. For some ventures, they may be critical to success. For others, monitoring and advisory functions that are tied to financing may be of little value or may even be counterproductive.

Taxes can also affect the financing choice. Not all organizations generate taxable income, and the applicable tax rate depends in part on organizational form. For example, tax rates and other aspects of taxation differ for C corporations, S corporations, and proprietorships. Also, the tax treatment of debt differs from that of equity. Debt is not attractive for many new ventures, partly because if they are not generating taxable income, they may not be able to benefit from the tax deductibility of interest payments.

Financing that is subsidized through agencies such as the SBA may carry lower financing costs for the venture. However, these savings must be weighed against restrictions imposed by the agencies and against the additional time required to complete the financing transaction.

Finally, maximum value for the entrepreneur normally is not achieved by raising all of the anticipated financing needs at one time. The riskiness of successful ventures declines over time, and staging can produce higher expected value for the entrepreneur, especially if the stages are associated with milestones that resolve uncertainty and lower financing costs.

The effects of these considerations on the value of the entrepreneur's claim are complex and sometimes counterintuitive. A sensible approach to making the financing decision is to model the venture and study the effects of alternatives on the value of the entrepreneur's claim. More often than not, the realistically available choices are limited to a few. But even if the entrepreneur has few options, he will want to evaluate such variables as the amount of the funding, the form of the commitment the investor plans to make (e.g., debt versus equity, passive versus active commitment), and the effects of restrictions the investor imposes on future actions (through restrictive covenants or by other means).

14.3   An Overview of the Financing Decision Process

Four critical questions link financial needs to choice of financing:

1. Is there an immediate (urgent) need for financing?
2. Is the need for near-term financing large?
3. Is the need for near-term financing permanent?
4. How does the need for financing in the near term relate to the cumulative need for financing?

These questions divide the financial need into three periods: immediate, near-term, and cumulative. The distinction between immediate and near-term needs is based on the time required for negotiation. If financing needs are immediate, there is no time to negotiate over terms that are tied to performance; instead, the venture must rely on its existing relationships, assets, and operations. Alternatively, the entrepreneur may offer personal assets or guarantees to secure funding quickly.

Near-term financing needs are those required over an intermediate term, such as progressing from one milestone to the next. The choices for near-term funding should not be constrained by immediate cash needs. Cumulative financing needs connect near-term and ultimate financing needs. Cumulative needs may be more or less than near-term needs, but cumulative needs affect future rounds of financing, which in turn influence the near-term decision. For example, if the cumulative need is expected to remain high, it may be appropriate to meet near-term needs with a permanent source of financing.

To introduce a structured approach to making the financing choice, Figure 14.2 is a diagrammatic representation of the primary aspects of the decision-making process related to the choice. There are other, more subtle aspects of the decision, such as the cumulative need, that the figure does not capture.

The three panels of Figure 14.2 are based on the stage of venture development at the time when the choice is being made. Panels (a), (b), and (c) are, respectively, for ventures at the seed/start-up stage, the early-growth stage, and the late/expansion stage. Earlier in the book we described these stages in the context of venture development. The information in the figure includes several defining characteristics of each stage.

After identifying the development stage, we turn to the question of the immediacy of the financing need and then to the size of the need. Immediacy can severely limit the venture's options. For example, if the

FIGURE **14.2**
**The financing
decision process**

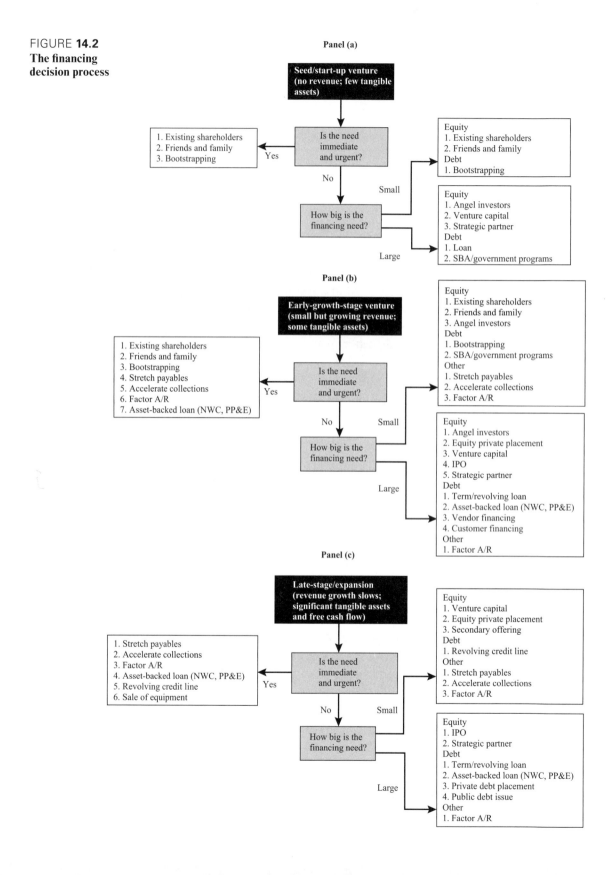

need facing a seed-stage venture is urgent, the entrepreneur will normally be limited to raising capital by liquidating other assets, borrowing on other assets, raising additional capital from existing investors, or raising it from friends and family. A growth-stage venture that is in need of immediate financing has a few additional options. Because it is operating, it may be able to defer payment of payables, factor its accounts receivable, or take steps to accelerate collection of receivables. It may also be able to borrow using tangible assets as collateral (where the lender is not relying on the merits of the venture).

If financing needs are not immediate, the entrepreneur has time to arrange financing from third-party sources that is based more directly on the merits of the venture. As we discussed in Chapter 2, for small investments, such as $50,000 for a seed- or start-up-stage venture, there still are no outside sources because investors will normally expect the entrepreneur to provide financing at that level. If the need is larger, such as in the $250,000 range, and the venture is appropriate in terms of risk and potential return, angel investing could be feasible. For still larger amounts, such as $1 million or more for research and development, venture capital could be an option. If the start-up involves acquisition of tangible assets, various debt-style options could be available. Similar considerations affect the feasible menu of options for later-stage ventures, such as during rapid growth.

Figure 14.2 is not a comprehensive picture of all of the factors that affect the financing choice. The previous section and the discussion that follows highlight additional factors relevant to the decision. For now, we focus on the stage of the venture and the timing and size of the financing need.

14.4 First Step: Assess the Current Stage and Condition of the Venture

A realistic menu of financing alternatives depends on the current condition of the venture. Considerations include the stage of development, the value of outside advice, the asset base, organizational structure, track record, the level and stability of earnings and cash flow, and existing financing, among others.

The Stage of Development

Stage of development is a natural place to begin consideration of financing choices for any venture.[1] Many capital providers prefer to fund ventures at a specific point in their life cycle. Because they usually have some flexibility, what follows are general guidelines rather than rigid rules. Our discussion is focused on the venture's financial and operational characteristics as they relate to financing choices.

Seed and start-up stage.   For seed- and start-up-stage ventures, typically characterized by no revenue and few tangible assets, the dominant form of financing is equity, beginning with the founder's own funds. These ventures may be conducting research or developing a prototype product, and there may be considerable risk about the viability of the concept or idea. Sources of equity for smaller ventures include the entrepreneur, family and friends, and business angels. Larger ventures might approach business angels or be candidates for VC firms.

Exceptions to the "equity only" proviso for start-up ventures are, for the most part, limited to bootstrap debt financing and government-backed loans. Bootstrap sources of debt include credit cards, second mortgages, and loans secured by the entrepreneur's personal guarantees or assets.[2] Start-up financing can also come through loans from, or guaranteed by, government agencies.[3] In addition, there are entities that operate somewhat like venture capital firms but with the ability to access public loan guarantee programs such as certain SBA programs to make combined equity and debt investments.[4]

Start-up ventures with few tangible assets that are not yet generating revenue are typically not candidates for debt financing.[5] Such a venture would be unable to make interest payments on the debt, except with cash from subsequent financing. The lack of collateral presents an additional impediment. Moreover, the venture cannot realize the potential tax benefit of interest deductibility.

For a start-up venture that is facing a high degree of uncertainty, debt financing also puts the entrepreneur and the lender in antagonistic positions. If the amount of debt is significant, the entrepreneur has an incentive to gamble on high-risk strategies, recognizing that the rewards of success will be realized by shareholders while the cost of failure will be borne by the creditor. Because creditors recognize this agency conflict, they seek provisions in the form of debt covenants that restrict how the funds can be used and help ensure that the debt is repaid even if the venture fails.[6] By requiring such covenants, a creditor may actually increase the likelihood of failure.

Early-growth stage.   Sources of capital to finance a venture's early growth are more numerous than those for a start-up. Early-growth-stage ventures typically have small but rapidly growing revenue and some tangible assets but no profit or operating cash flow. They may also have a significant investment in net working capital. For these firms, growth capital can be debt or equity. The choice depends on numerous factors, including the size of the need, the venture's expected growth, estimates of profitability, and the amount of risk.

For small equity needs, existing shareholders, including friends and family and angel investors, may provide follow-on financing. For larger amounts, angels and VC firms may be approached. Many VC firms are more interested in providing growth financing than start-up funds. With a proven product, there may be interest from corporate investors or strategic partners as equity investors. Depending on the amount, equity can also be sold through private placement, subject to the legal and regulatory requirements discussed in Chapter 2. Finally, if capital needs are very large and market conditions are conducive, even early-stage companies may be able to raise equity capital by means of an IPO.

Growth ventures may also have access to a wider range of debt financing options. Suppliers and customers both may be willing to provide loans to a new venture if it means more business for them or if they want the product badly enough.[7] Government-guaranteed loans are generally available for expansion financing. Traditional bank loans—either term or revolving lines of credit—are feasible if assets are available as collateral or if cash flows are sufficient to allow repayment.

Finally, growth-stage ventures may have access to additional funding sources that are tied to their operations. Cash flow can be increased temporarily by stretching accounts payable and accelerating collections. Doing so, however, can harm relationships with suppliers and customers, as it can suggest to them that the venture is having financial difficulties. Accounts receivable can also be sold or "factored" to raise cash, either infrequently as needed or on a regular basis. For some business models, factoring can be a significant source of funds and can have the added benefit of outsourcing the responsibility for collection of payment.

Late-stage/expansion.   These are mature firms with significant assets and positive operating cash flow. Revenues may still be growing but at a slower rate than in the growth stage. With operating cash flow and slower growth, the venture's need for external financing should be moderating. Companies seeking expansion capital actually have a smaller menu of options than ventures at earlier stages because of the larger size of their funding needs. The availability of operating cash flow for interest and principal payments makes debt funding more likely for late-stage companies.

Smaller amounts of equity (relative to the size of the firm) may come from VCs or through private placement. However, because of the lower risk associated with late-stage ventures, these may prove to be expensive sources. Large equity needs would likely be met through an IPO or possibly a strategic partner. Firms that are already public and seek to continue growth can also sell additional shares through a seasoned offering.

For an established firm, a revolving line of credit may be the best choice for meeting small and irregular borrowing needs. For larger levels of financing, a late-stage firm has access to a wide range of commercial banking products, including term and asset-backed loans. Finally, selling bonds—either publicly or privately—can be a desirable way for a late-stage venture to raise large amounts of debt at relatively low cost. Profitability at this stage would also make debt desirable because of the interest deduction.

With established operations, small financing needs may be met by stretching payables or accelerating collections, but this is not a viable long-term funding strategy. Factoring, however, could be an important component of financing strategy. Depending on the nature of the venture, the amounts raised by factoring may be small or large.

Development Stage and the Financing Option for High-Risk Ventures

Many people believe that VC funds and angel investors are close substitutes for each other and that either VC or angel investment could be an appropriate funding source for any high-risk, high-growth venture. In reality, while there is some overlap, the targets for angel investment are considerably different from those for VC. Table 14.1 shows recent data on angel investing from the Center for Venture Research and on VC investing from the National Venture Capital Association (NVCA). Although the angel investment statistics are estimates based on unclear methodology, they suggest that in recent years the angel capital market has been similar to the VC market in terms of total dollars invested. That, however, is where the similarity ends. On average, angel investors fund about 14 times as many deals per year as VC funds. The average deal size for angel investors is about $440,000, compared to about $6.9 million for VC. Even for seed- and start-up-stage investments, VC deal sizes average $3.0 million, which is much larger than angel deals.

The statistics in Table 14.1 also show that seed and start-up investing is not the primary focus of venture capital. Such deals are a small fraction of the total deals in any year and an even smaller fraction in terms

TABLE **14.1**   Comparison of angel investor and venture capital/private equity investment styles

Angel investors

Year	Total investment (billions)	Ventures receiving funding	Average investment size	Seed and start-up	Number of active investors	Percent of opportunities funded
2002	$15.7	36,000	$436,111	47.0%	200,000	7.10
2003	$18.1	42,000	$430,952	52.0%	220,000	10.30
2004	$22.5	48,000	$468,750	na	225,000	18.50
2005	$23.1	49,500	$466,667	55.0%	227,000	23.00
2006	$25.6	51,000	$501,961	46.0%	234,000	20.10
2007	$26.0	57,120	$455,182	39.0%	258,200	14.00
2008	$19.2	55,480	$346,071	45.0%	260,500	10.00
Average	$21.5	48,443	$443,671	47.3%	232,100	14.7

SOURCE: *Center for Venture Research, www.unh.edu/cvr (various reports).*

VC funds

Year	Total investment (billions)	Ventures receiving funding	Average investment size	Seed/start-up investment (millions)	Number seed/ start-up	Average seed/ start-up investment	Seed and start-up	Expansion stage
2002	$21.0	3,125	$6,712,640	$324.4	179	$1,812,291	1.5%	56.3%
2003	$19.1	2,967	$6,437,479	$335.1	208	$1,611,058	1.8%	50.1%
2004	$22.0	3,148	$6,978,399	$458.0	221	$2,072,398	2.1%	41.6%
2005	$23.0	3,208	$7,159,289	$912.4	250	$3,649,600	4.0%	37.3%
2006	$26.3	3,746	$7,024,826	$1,233.5	379	$3,254,617	4.7%	43.0%
2007	$30.5	4,027	$7,578,346	$1,429.7	484	$2,953,926	4.7%	37.0%
2008	$28.0	3,985	$7,024,341	$1,623.9	493	$3,293,915	5.8%	37.1%
2009	$17.7	2,795	$6,325,581	$1,650.2	312	$5,289,103	9.3%	31.0%
Average	$23.4	3,375	$6,905,113	$995.9	316	$2,992,113	4.2%	41.7%

SOURCE: *2010 National Venture Capital Association Yearbook, prepared by Thomson Reuters, available at http://www.nvca.org/index.php ?option=com_content&view=article&id=257&Itemid=103.*

of percent of funds invested. Whereas seed and start-up investments account for almost half of angel-investor investment dollars, they account for only about 4 percent of VC. Venture capital is much more focused on expansion-stage financing, and buyout funds are heavily focused on late-stage financing.

The Value of Outside Advice

An important consideration in the choice of financing is whether the venture can benefit from active involvement of an investor.[8] Investors in new ventures can be passive or active to varying degrees. Active involvement may be limited to monitoring the operation and serving on the board. Or it may be as extensive as stepping in as CEO for a period to help get the venture on track, make key strategic and tactical decisions, and help build the management team. In most cases, the active investor's return comes mainly through ownership in the venture.

For the entrepreneur, the decision to include an active outside investor depends on the cost of the investor's involvement, which usually takes the form of a larger ownership stake. This cost needs to be compared to the expected value added by the investor. Angel investors are generally the most active outside investors, though some are passive.[9] Those who are active often seek to leverage their experience from a previous venture into another that has related product-market overlap. If the entrepreneur is a technical visionary, an angel investor may contribute the managerial expertise required for execution of the business plan. If the entrepreneur is able to implement the vision without significant outside involvement, then active angel investors may not be the best choice.

Venture capitalists are generally less involved but are still considered active investors. They may assist with financing and hiring and often serve on boards, but for the most part they are focused on monitoring the investment for their limited partners. The cost of any monitoring services ultimately must be borne by the entrepreneur in the form of reduced ownership share. There are several reasons why it might be worthwhile for the entrepreneur to incur the cost of subjecting the venture to monitoring.[10] One pragmatic reason is that monitoring is a precondition of getting outside capital from an angel or VC firm and that alternatives that do not involve monitoring are not usually available to early-stage high-risk ventures.

Monitoring adds value for at least two reasons. First, the entrepreneur's willingness to accept monitoring can help overcome investor concern that the entrepreneur will try to take advantage of the financing relationship for personal gain. Second, a monitoring relationship can enhance the flexibility and adaptability of the venture. Flexibility to use available financing to change the focus or direction of a venture may not be very important if the assets of the venture and the entrepreneur's human capital are specific to a particular activity. New ventures with assets that are less specific, however, may benefit from the ability to react rapidly to new information.

Suppose, for example, that product development efforts are lagging behind business plan projections. How should investors respond? At one extreme, it may be increasingly evident that development efforts are unlikely to succeed, in which case the venture should be abandoned. At the other extreme, perhaps the delay is due to a lack of resources, and the venture is likely to be very successful if additional funds were available. In the latter case, increasing the financial commitment is appropriate. A passive investor may be unable to distinguish between these two very different scenarios, whereas an active investor who closely monitors the venture may discern the reasons for delay and be able to make a well-informed choice between abandonment and new investment.

It is important to recognize that flexibility and survival are different and that survival is not the goal. Flexibility includes the ability to close a venture down. It also includes the ability to change focus or alter the resource commitment. The ability to abandon a losing venture quickly can benefit both the investor and the entrepreneur. Early abandonment reduces the investor's financial commitment and enables the entrepreneur to redeploy human capital to other activities. Because it mitigates downside risk, including the option to abandon a losing venture quickly can increase the entrepreneur's ownership stake in the event that the venture is a success. The need for and usefulness of flexibility depend on the extent to which value hinges on being able to make timely decisions about exercising, retaining, and abandoning real options. Generally, as the importance of relying on financing sources that provide flexibility declines, the venture increasingly is able to raise capital from sources that entail less active monitoring.

The Asset Base

Although borrowing is usually not the preferred financing for an early-stage venture, debt may sometimes be a viable choice. Even a high-risk venture with no track record and an unproven entrepreneur can attract debt financing if assets are available to secure the loan. If the assets are of sufficient value in alternative use to repay the loan, the entrepreneur may not even need to convince the financing source of the merits of the venture.

Secured or collateralized lending is one way an entrepreneur can assuage investor concerns about adverse selection and moral hazard. Any entrepreneur willing to collateralize a loan is unlikely to use the borrowed money to speculate on a high-risk opportunity.[11] In addition, because failure would likely result in losing the collateral to the lender, a highly leveraged capital structure still would not induce the entrepreneur to opportunistically increase risk.[12] A personal guarantee by the entrepreneur serves the same function as asset-based collateral.[13]

One advantage of secured lending is that collateral facilitates enforcing loan covenants and reaching agreement on ways of dealing with financial distress.[14] These advantages to the lender translate into lower borrowing costs, because they commit the entrepreneur to dealing reasonably with future adversity and because they signal confidence. An offsetting concern is that a secured lender has little interest in the success of the venture. For an entrepreneur who desires active outside involvement, secured lending is unlikely to come with much useful advice, other than on ways to ensure that the loan is repaid in a timely manner.[15]

Aside from collateral and personal guarantees, the primary means that lenders have of ensuring that their loans are repaid is to condition the loan on the borrower's willingness to be bound by covenants. Covenants are intended to protect the value of the assets used to secure the loan and to help the lender recognize quickly that a venture is having difficulty. Covenants can be advantageous to an entrepreneur who is confident about the future but can deprive a high-risk start-up of important flexibility.

Loan covenants are not immutable. If it is in the lender's interest to do so, covenants can be renegotiated. In fact, renegotiation of covenants is common for privately placed loans.[16] When a venture faces a high level of uncertainty, however, future developments can result in conflicts of interest between the entrepreneur and the lender. Suppose, for example, that revenue and income are not growing as rapidly as projected. A secured lender, who will not share in the success if the venture turns around, may be unwilling to renegotiate the loan and may seize the collateral, even if doing so threatens the venture's survival.

14.5   Second Step: Assess the Nature of the Venture's Financing Needs

Stage of development, value of outside advice, and asset base are not the only factors that bear on the financing choice. In this section, we consider the nature of the financing need.

The Influence of Immediate Financing Needs

If a venture faces an immediate funding need, many sources are foreclosed. Generally, government-supported financing sources cannot react quickly to financing needs; their approval processes usually have multiple steps and involve many parties. Most SBA-guaranteed loans, for example, have a two-step approval process that requires extensive paperwork that the entrepreneur must complete.[17] In addition, subsidized lending programs may have waiting lists or may base lending decisions on political objectives.[18]

If financial needs are immediate, most equity funding sources are precluded, unless the entrepreneur has an established relationship with the investor. Venture capital firms and angel investor groups have lengthy due diligence and approval processes. The same is true of corporate venture funds. If immediate financing appears to be available from one of these sources, the entrepreneur should be skeptical. Such funding is likely to come only from investors without established reputations, and some "would be" angels or VC firms will act as if they can invest quickly but may not be able to do so. Moreover, if the funds really are available, the terms and conditions may be so onerous that they threaten the existence of the venture or the value of the entrepreneur's interest in it.

An IPO takes several months to complete and is not feasible if the need is pressing. Even more expedient methods of raising equity, such as direct public offerings or private placements, are unlikely prospects if needs are urgent. Selling a patent or other intellectual property asset to raise immediate cash and then agreeing to pay royalties or lease payments is probably not realistic unless the asset is generating revenue. And even then, such asset sales can take time.

The most realistic sources of immediate financing are those for which little or no negotiation or approval process is required or for which financing is preapproved. Early-stage/start-up ventures face the most limited set of options for raising immediate cash. Such firms typically have few tangible assets and no payables to stretch or collections to accelerate. The only realistic alternatives are the personal resources of the entrepreneur, friends and family, and possibly existing shareholders.[19] Investments from family and friends are based not on the merits of the venture per se but on the strength of the personal relationship with the entrepreneur. Early-stage ventures can approach prospective customers or potential suppliers for funds, but it is unlikely that a suitable agreement can be reached on short notice since such relationships are not sufficiently strong at that point. The last and often only resort is for the entrepreneur to bootstrap the venture using personal assets and resources. Running credit cards up to their limits and tapping into home equity credit lines are two ways in which the entrepreneur might obtain needed funds quickly.

The Influence of Near-Term Financing Needs

Financing available from immediate sources can be used to satisfy near-term or long-term needs. However, financing raised in a crisis usually is expensive. Forgoing trade credit discounts—by stretching payables, for example—can have an effective interest cost of more than 40 percent. Factoring accounts receivable often is even more expensive, particularly if the venture has developed its own credit management capabilities. Consequently, sources of immediate financing are often not desirable for ongoing financing.

Some near-term financing choices may limit flexibility. For example, if financing requires collateral, then the collateral cannot be sold and is unavailable to secure subsequent borrowing. Stretching payables may affect relations with suppliers and make it difficult to ramp up production quickly.

Another consideration is the present condition and expected future prospects of the venture. Financing is less expensive when the venture is strong financially or its future looks very bright.

More alternatives are available for near-term financing than for immediate financing. Three primary factors influence the venture's choice of near-term financing. First, the choice depends on the amount the venture is seeking. For small amounts, likely sources include the SBA, economic development agencies, banks, and private placements of equity with a few individuals or a group of angel investors. For larger amounts, private placements of debt with institutional lenders, VC investors, and strategic partners gain importance. If required financing is very large, the entrepreneur could consider a registered public offering of debt or equity.

Second, the choice of near-term financing depends on the permanency of the need. If the need for financing is permanent or long term, it usually does not make sense to use financing sources that are short term in nature. Conversely, short-term needs are generally best financed with short-term sources. The transactions costs of short-term financing usually are lower than those of long-term financing, because providers of short-term funds do not need to conduct due diligence investigations that are as extensive as those conducted by providers of long-term funds.

Short-term financing is generally debt financing that is secured by business assets of easily ascertainable value (such as accounts receivable or inventory). Alternatively, short-term financing can be generated by selling business assets (such as by factoring accounts receivable) or by leasing (rather than owning) the venture's assets. Because the value of the security is clear to the provider of funds, such transactions are comparatively easy to arrange. For a venture with long-term needs, however, repeatedly incurring the smaller transactions costs of short-term financing can accumulate to more than the cost of one round of long-term financing.

Depending on the form of financing and industry conventions, the effective interest cost of short-term financing can be more or less than that of long-term financing. As noted, the cost of using vendor financing can be very high. In contrast, formal short-term loans can have very low interest rates. Shorter-term loans usually face less risk of default, and inflation-related risk is also reduced.[20] With vendor financing, the effective rates tend to be high partly because the entrepreneur can unilaterally decide to borrow by postponing payment for purchases. In contrast, a short-term loan is made only after the lender is satisfied with the risk exposure. An entrepreneur may prefer vendor financing if the need is very short term, because reliance on vendor financing requires little advance planning, the loan can be used to deal with surprises, and it can be repaid as soon as cash becomes available. Clearly, however, high-interest-rate short-term sources are not attractive for long-term needs.

The third reason to match the source of financing to the permanency of the need is that, except for passive equity financing, long-term financing usually comes with more constraints on future decisions. Providers of long-term funds—both debt and equity—may restrict future borrowing, limit the scope of venture activities, demand control over certain kinds of decisions, and require more access to information about the venture. Sometimes the terms of a long-term financing arrangement can impede a venture's ability to raise additional capital. A ratchet provision, for example, can make it impossible for a firm that has performed below expectations to raise more equity without first restructuring the existing claims. In summary, long-term financing can significantly limit flexibility, whereas such limitations can be minimized if financing is short term.

Finally, addressing short-term needs with long-term financing can reduce expected cash flows and increase the riskiness of cash flows. Long-term financing, while potentially providing a liquidity cushion, can cause the venture to incur interest expenses on unnecessary borrowing. Conversely, the cost of short-term financing can be volatile, and, if the financing is used to acquire long-term assets, it may increase the uncertainty of cash flows or even threaten venture survival.[21]

Equity and long-term debt are the obvious sources for meeting long-term needs of large and established firms. Table 14.2 shows estimates of the relative cost of IPO versus debt by issue size. The issue cost percentages clearly favor debt issues, and the difference would be even greater if we were to include underpricing as a cost of issuing equity.[22] Offsetting the lower cost of debt issues are two important factors: first, the costs of debt issues are recurring whereas equity is a

TABLE **14.2**   **Initial public offering and bond issue cost
by issue size**

Issue size (proceeds in $ millions)	Total direct cost (% of proceeds)	
	IPOs	Debt
2.0–9.99	17.0	4.4
10.0–19.99	11.6	2.8
20.0–39.99	9.7	2.4
40.0–59.99	8.7	1.3
60.0–79.99	8.2	2.3
80.0–99.99	7.9	2.2
100.0–199.99	7.1	2.3
200.0–499.99	6.5	2.2
500.0 and up	5.7	1.6

SOURCE: *I. Lee, S. Lochhead, J. Ritter, and Q. Zhao, "The Cost of Raising Capital,"* Journal of Financial Research *19 (1996): 59–74, table 1.*

NOTE: *The cost of a public offering includes three components: the spread between the offer price and net proceeds to the issuer, issue costs borne directly by the issuing firm, and underpricing. This table provides estimates of the first two components (excluding underpricing) for different types and sizes of issues.*

source of permanent financing; and second, compared to equity issues, debt issues limit flexibility.

The Influence of Cumulative Financing Needs

The third factor affecting any financing decision is cumulative needs. If the entrepreneur expects that the venture will soon begin to generate positive cash flow sufficient to fund growth, then he can make near-term financing choices with little regard to their potential effect on the availability or cost of future financing. In such a case, it is little sacrifice to accept provisions that limit the venture's ability to raise additional capital. The important scenarios, however, are the extremes. How should near-term financing be arranged if the entrepreneur's cumulative needs may be substantially higher or substantially lower than the venture's ability to generate free cash flow?

If cumulative needs are expected to be higher than present needs, current financing must not seriously impede the ability to raise capital later. Options to make additional investments at pre-agreed prices, first rights of refusal to provide financing, and financing arrangements that include other options and rights can be costly for the new venture. If such terms are accepted, their effects may be offset by other provisions, such as call options on the financing or buyout options that enable the venture to restore flexibility, such as by paying off the existing investors or lenders.

If the entrepreneur expects future needs to be lower than near-term needs, the arrangements should enable the venture to pay off the financing with little or no penalty as cash becomes available. Call options and buyout rights are useful under these conditions, as well as when the venture is expected to grow rapidly.

14.6 Financing Choices and Organizational Structure

Some financing choices are linked to organizational structure.[23] For example, financing by a strategic partner may commit the venture to use the partner's marketing and distribution capabilities, offer its product only under the partner's brand, or commit to a course of action that will eventually transfer control to the partner. In a similar fashion, pursuing a new venture within a corporation or university can limit the entrepreneur's ability to realize much of the gain.

Franchising is another example of connecting organizational structure to financing. In some industries, entrepreneurs use franchising as a means of financing rapid growth. In such a case, the franchisor also is committing to an organizational structure that involves dealing with a large number of more or less independent business operators (franchisees) whose objectives and interests only partly overlap with those of the franchisor. For the venture to rely instead on debt and equity financing also involves an organizational choice, that of substituting employees for franchisees. The interests of employees may be even less well aligned than those of franchisees.

How is an entrepreneur to select between strategic partnering and a financing relationship that does not restrict product-market choices or between franchising and a financing relationship that does not depend on a network of franchisees? Again, these choices involve cost-benefit comparisons. We use strategic partnering and franchising to illustrate the considerations that bear on the choice.

The Relationship between Financing and Strategic Partnering

Strategic partnering can enable the entrepreneur to take advantage of an investment in resources that the partner has already made. If that investment would otherwise be idle or less productively employed, then strategic partnering can reduce the incremental real resource commitment to the venture. The benefits of the saving can accrue to both parties. In some strategic partnering relationships, the partner is willing to take on more risk than would an outside investor. The entrepreneur may benefit by negotiating financial claims that are of lower risk than otherwise would be possible. Suppose the partner agrees to license the technology of the venture in exchange for a royalty and will bear the cost and risk of manufacturing, marketing, and distributing the product. In addition to the shift in risk, such an arrangement also may add value by enabling the entrepreneur to focus on product development. Corporate venturing can have many of the same effects.

Some of the disadvantages of strategic partnering arrangements relate to conflicts of interest. A strategic partner may have other products that are substitutes for the entrepreneur's product. If so, the entrepreneur runs a risk that the partner is investing in order to protect the market for its existing product. Alternatively, the partner may have limited capability to distribute the product but be unwilling to license distribution to competitors because of complementarities between the entrepreneur's product and the partner's other products.[24]

It appears that established corporations have difficulty promoting entrepreneurial activity within the organization because managerial approaches commonly used in large organizations tend to inhibit entrepreneurship.[25] Strategic partnering can overcome some of the organizational difficulties, but concerns remain about conflicts of interest.[26]

The Relationship between Financing and Franchising

Franchising is both a means of implementing rapid growth and an organizational form with decentralized decision making. Rapid growth is possible because decentralized organizations that do not require extensive monitoring are relatively easy to expand and because franchisees contribute to financing their own operations. It is most likely to be an appropriate means of financing expansion in cases where there are distinct advantages to decentralized organizational form and where incentives of franchisees and the franchisor can be aligned. The difference between a franchise operation and a company-owned operation is that the franchisee is the residual claimant on the success of the operation and makes an investment that would be lost if the franchisee were terminated. Residual claimant status, combined with the sanction of termination, aligns the franchisee's incentives with the interests of the franchisor.[27] Franchising is advantageous when centralized management cannot serve market demand as effectively as management that is closer to the market.[28] Accordingly, franchise operations are likely to be more effective than company-owned operations in specific types of markets. Franchising is more likely when the prospect of repeat business and the franchisee's reputation in the local market discourage the franchisee from depreciating the quality of the franchisor's product. Franchising is also more likely when knowledge of local market demand is important and when centralized oversight is difficult.[29]

A concern of prospective franchisors is whether the franchise form of organization is as robust as alternative forms in which financing and organizational form are more separate. Empirical studies find little evidence that franchise organizations have different survival rates than other forms.[30] These studies find that high rates of franchise creation are offset by high failure rates and that exits are more likely for the less well established franchisors. However, another study demonstrates that termination of the franchise form of organization is a planned-for event, which suggests that failure rates of different organizational forms have different interpretations.[31] The study concludes that ongoing operations of franchise organizations are most effectively governed by a contract structure that is relational but that discrete terms are more effective for franchise initiation and termination. Thus, franchise contracts tend to include discrete terms related to initiation and termination but are less specific about describing ongoing relationships.

14.7 How Financial Distress Affects Financing Choices

The financial condition of a venture affects its financing opportunities. A profitable business with a steady cash flow can arrange financing more easily than one that is struggling. For many new ventures, however, at some stages of development, struggling to meet financing needs is normal. The term "financial distress" means more than simply that a venture is in need of cash to fund its operations. A distressed firm is one that is fundamentally disappointing investors. If the investors are creditors, a distressed firm may have violated important debt covenants or have defaulted on its repayment obligations or be about to do so. For equity-financed ventures, financial distress can mean that the venture is so short of cash that it is unable to carry out its business plan. The cash shortage can be symptomatic of missed milestones or other disappointing performance. Such a firm may be compelled to terminate or significantly scale back operations and may be at risk of losing key employees.

Why Turnaround Financing Is Different

Financing distressed firms is different from financing high-risk start-ups for two reasons. First, distress means that the entrepreneur has already failed to achieve a level of success consistent with projections. That failure can undermine the entrepreneur's credibility. Although it is common to search for external causes of underperformance, the evidence suggests that the usual causes are fundamental failures of management.[32] A venture may get into trouble because of strategic issues, management issues, or financial planning and control problems. Strategic issues include such problems as misperceiving the market opportunity or selecting the wrong organizational design. Management issues include lack of critical skills, excessive turnover, and similar deficiencies. Inadequate financial planning and controls can contribute to unanticipated cash shortages, poor pricing decisions, lack of control over costs, and similar problems.

Although any new venture may encounter problems such as these, a financially distressed venture has already faced them. Given that the venture has failed in fundamental dimensions, why should investors assume that projections in a revised plan are achievable or that the entrepreneur is capable of managing the operation? In all likelihood, they will not make such assumptions and instead will start a race for the lifeboats. Without investor support, the venture is almost certain to fail.

In the United States, an entrepreneur who has encountered trouble can take advantage of a legal presumption that the cause of financial distress, if not completely external, is curable. A Chapter 11 bankruptcy offers a window of protection against creditors' demands for repayment of their loans. The underlying concept is that, if a venture is fundamentally viable, then creditors, as a group, are better off remaining on board. The statute gives the entrepreneur time to try to achieve a reorganization plan that creditors find acceptable.

This leads to the second reason why financing of distressed firms is different. The financial structures of most firms are based on a premise that the venture will be successful.[33] Creditors, including trade creditors and even employees, expect that they will be paid. When a venture gets into trouble, the orientations of creditors change.

Secured creditors begin to look more intently at the value of collateral as a source of repayment. They worry that, if the entrepreneur is allowed to continue to operate the business, the collateral may depreciate. They may press for liquidation as a means of repayment. Suppliers to distressed firms no longer assume that they will eventually be paid for merchandise they sell on credit; they may demand cash payment.

Employees may assume that their jobs are at risk and try to protect themselves by seeking new employment. Even customers may become concerned and stop purchasing. After all, what good is a product guarantee from a venture that may be out of business in a few weeks?

Turning around a distressed firm can be more difficult than raising initial financing for a risky venture. This is because the original financing is already in place and the threat of financial distress creates conflicts among the stakeholders. In the United States, once a company declares bankruptcy, individual creditors can no longer attach the company's assets. Instead, the assets become part of a common pool, and they are not dispersed unless the creditors reach an understanding about how the various debts will be settled. For example, the creditors as a group might conclude that the assets should be liquidated and the creditors paid out of the proceeds, or they might decide to refinance the failing company.

The rationale for bankruptcy protection is to prevent creditors from participating in a defensive frenzy that destroys the value of the remaining assets. On the other hand, if it appears that the venture's going-concern value is greater than its liquidation value, then existing investors may be more willing than new investors to commit resources.

The objective in turnaround financing is to devise a new financial structure such that each party expects to be better off by maintaining or increasing its investment than by collecting the liquidation value of its financial claims. Financial restructuring can involve significant changes in the financial claims held by different investors. Claims of creditors, for example, may be exchanged for common stock or for securities convertible to common. In general, restructuring must achieve three results: it must reduce the cash needs of the venture for servicing existing debt; it must reallocate the going-concern value to creditors and away from the entrepreneur and other equity investors; and it must provide a means of raising enough cash to restart the venture.

Even if it is apparent that going-concern value exceeds liquidation value, financial restructuring is not easy. The bankruptcy laws are more complicated than merely implementing a simple formula. Different parties, for example, may dispute the going-concern value. Creditors, in general, have incentives to argue that the going-concern value is low, whereas the entrepreneur has an incentive to argue that it is high. Furthermore, the bankruptcy laws do not require that investors unanimously accept a restructuring proposal. Consequently, groups of investors may attempt to form coalitions to allocate claims in a way that works to their benefit and to the detriment of others. Finally, the process takes place in the context of employee concerns about job security and wages, supplier concerns about the future of the enterprise, and customer concerns about the venture's ability to continue to supply products of acceptable quality.

The Influence of Financial Distress Costs on Choice of Financing

We have identified risk allocation, information problems, incentive problems, taxes, and a variety of other considerations that affect choice of financing. The prospect of financial distress and the resulting costs should also be a consideration.[34] For some kinds of ventures, the real costs of financial distress are small. Business assets, though they may be specialized to a particular use or geographic location, are readily marketable, and success or failure of the venture does not depend on the special knowledge or skills of employees. In such cases, financial distress can result in little more than a reallocation of ownership claims and may not materially affect the revenue or profit stream of the venture. Financing for such a venture can be guided primarily by risk allocation and tax considerations.

For other kinds of ventures, even the rumor of financial distress can have important real consequences. Key employees, who would be difficult to replace, may resign. Customers may switch to alternative suppliers to avoid the possible consequences of dealing with a firm that might fail. Managers who anticipate failure may engage in excessive risk taking or may depreciate the assets of the venture. When the costs of financial distress are large, financing choices should be based, in part, on the value of avoiding financial distress. Among other things, this could imply raising a higher level of capital at the outset and using a financial structure that limits the risk of defaulting or violating debt covenants.[35]

14.8 How Reputations and Relationships Affect Financing Choices

Reputations and relationships with providers of financing affect the availability of financing for a new venture. Reputation, in the context of financing, is an intangible capital asset that can lose value if the entrepreneur takes advantage of a financing source. An entrepreneur who develops a reputation for treating investors fairly, however, and who values that reputation is unlikely to take advantage of investors after the financing commitments have been made. Reputation thus operates like a performance bond on the actions of the entrepreneur. Investors who might otherwise be concerned about opportunism may be willing to base financing decisions in part on the entrepreneur's desire to avoid damage to his reputation. For example, a lender may advance funds without requiring extensive collateral if the lender believes that the entrepreneur's concern with reputational damage is sufficient to discourage excessive risk taking.

Unfortunately, most new ventures are unable to rely on reputation. Although the essential element of reputation is a concern that opportunistic behavior today will impair ability to raise capital in the future, the value of an entrepreneur's reputation is difficult to assess. Commonly, investors assess reputation on the basis of track record. Investors can easily perceive that a venture that has been around for a significant time and has been involved in raising capital repeatedly is likely to continue to need financing; such a venture is unlikely to try to engage in opportunism toward investors. However, an entrepreneur with a venture on the verge of failure may not place much weight on the venture's ability to secure financing in the future. Survival in the short run is of more immediate concern than damage to reputation.

In addition to reputation, evidence suggests that providers of financing rely, to some extent, on having an established relationship with the entrepreneur. Banks, for example, are more likely to make loans to customers with whom they have relationships.[36] Through a long-term relationship, a lender can develop private information about an entrepreneur that provides a basis for lending, information that is similar to reputation. The lender may learn that the venture is not as risky as it might appear or that the entrepreneur is concerned about ability to raise capital in the future.

Using data collected in a survey of small firms by the SBA, Petersen and Rajan (1994) find that the primary benefit of building relationships with institutional creditors is that the availability of financing increases. It appears, however, that the relationship has only a small effect on the cost of the financing. Hence, the primary benefit comes in the form of availability of funds (and other financial services) rather than the price of funds.[37]

The same study documents that small firms organized as corporations are more likely to borrow than are firms organized as proprietorships and partnerships. Twenty-eight percent of corporations and 45 percent of noncorporations have no institutional borrowing. This is partly a size effect: corporations are much larger, on average, than are sole proprietorships and partnerships. For firms that do borrow, the sources of borrowed funds vary with firm size. Based on book value of assets, the smallest 10 percent of firms borrow about 50 percent of their debt from banks and 27 percent from firm owners and families. The fraction borrowed from personal sources (owners and family) declines to 10 percent and the fraction from banks increases to 62 percent for the largest 10 percent of firms. Small firms also tend to concentrate their borrowing in one lender. The smallest 10 percent of firms that have a bank as their primary lender secure, on average, 95 percent of their loans from that bank. On average, the smallest firms tend to have just over one lender, while the largest firms have about three lenders.

14.9 Avoiding Missteps and Dealing with Market Downturns

It is important for the entrepreneur to recognize that market conditions can change quickly and to factor the risk into the financing decision. The last decade has seen two dramatic downturns in financial markets, both of which had significant impacts on the availability and cost of financing.

During the late 1990s, in the midst of the dot-com bubble, equity markets, in particular the technology-heavy NASDAQ, soared in the United States. IPO valuations reached extremely high levels that in the view of some investors were disconnected from financial fundamentals. Ventures with no track record, no profits, and in some cases no revenue were able to go public and raise millions of dollars at high valuations. It is not surprising that, in such an environment, many high-tech ventures set their sights on an IPO.

Capital market investor perceptions can change very quickly, and when markets decline, opportunities to raise capital via public offering may evaporate. The NASDAQ index peaked on March 10, 2000; by the end of the year, it had fallen 55 percent and the IPO market was almost dead.[38] When markets decline significantly, many companies withdraw planned offerings.[39] In that environment, a company that persists in efforts to issue shares publicly raises questions in the minds of prospective investors. The net result is that a company that proceeds with an offering may be compelled to accept a price that is much lower than anticipated. One that had planned a public offering but decides not to go ahead may find that because of the delay and other market changes, raising capital from other sources has also become more difficult and more urgent.[40]

The financial crisis of 2007–8 caused an economic downturn widely viewed as the worst since the Great Depression. Rooted in the housing bubble and subprime mortgage meltdown, the crisis had a dramatic impact on both equity and debt markets. In the six months from September 2008 to March 2009, the Dow Jones Industrial index fell 43 percent. IPO volume dropped from 162 transactions in 2007 to 21 in 2008.[41] As the crisis unfolded, sources of debt financing disappeared and short-term interest rates jumped. Firms that previously had access to cheap and plentiful credit found they were unable to borrow as banks and other lending institutions tightened lending standards.

When markets are in turmoil, deciding where to search for funds requires the entrepreneur to have a sense of what can go wrong and an awareness of the implications. A public offering might seem attractive, but if the market declines before the offering is completed, the venture may end up short of cash and in an adverse bargaining position, needing to complete a deal with someone quickly. In pursuing an IPO, it makes sense to begin the process far enough in advance that a canceled offering would not result in financial hardship. Borrowing arrangements should be negotiated and managed to ensure sufficient liquidity in market and economic downturns.

The Investor's Perspective on Timing

Both parties have some motivation to complete deals quickly. A deal can fail for no other reason than that negotiations have been so protracted that one party or the other has concluded that trying to work together in the future will be more trouble than it is worth. There are other risks associated with delay. Because the venture and the environment are in a state of continual change, delay can result in circumstances sufficient to justify modifications in the deal structure or require additional due diligence.

In spite of these considerations, an investor also has, to some extent, an incentive to delay finalizing the deal. Usually while negotiations are proceeding, the entrepreneur's ability to pursue alternative financing sources is limited. The investor, for example, may reasonably demand a standstill agreement from the entrepreneur as a condition for initiating any serious due-diligence effort. During this period, the venture continues to consume resources and its ability to arrange alternative financing diminishes. Unless the parties have agreed to a mechanism for solving the short-run cash flow needs of the venture in case of a failed negotiation, the investor's negotiating ability increases as the cash balance of the entrepreneur decreases. Sometimes, for high-risk ventures, the investor can treat the deal as a free option. By waiting to invest, the investor can gain more information about the likelihood of venture success. The combination of these factors can be of great advantage to the investor. The entrepreneur needs to recognize that investors sometimes have incentives to delay completing a deal and try to protect against opportunism. At the same time, the entrepreneur needs to recognize that financing decisions require time to complete and that delay is not necessarily opportunistic.

Financing after a Marketwide Downturn in Valuations

When financing of a nonpublic venture is staged, the expectation is that the valuation will increase with each succeeding round. Normally, valuations rise as uncertainty is resolved favorably and as the anticipated harvest date approaches. "Down-round financing" is the term used to describe a financing round that occurs at a valuation lower than the preceding round. A down round can happen either because the venture has failed to achieve the projections reflected in the prior valuation or because, even though the projections may have been achieved, valuations have declined marketwide. The former problem is an aspect of financial distress due to the venture's own shortcomings. The latter, rather than being a symptom of distress, can be a cause of distress. Down rounds were common after the dot-com bubble burst in 2000; they were attributable both to market conditions and to the realization that many funded firms would never achieve the lofty projections that pervaded the tech bubble.

The difficulty associated with a marketwide decline in valuation arises if the existing deal structure impedes negotiating a new round at a lower valuation. If, for example, in an earlier round, the parties have negotiated antidilution rights for the initial investor, it can be impossible for the entrepreneur to negotiate new financing from another investor unless the earlier investor agrees to modify or not enforce the dilution protection. Negotiation of the new round, instead of being bilateral, becomes trilateral and may be very difficult to consummate. This type of negotiation has many of the same problems as a bankruptcy restructuring but without the benefit of using bankruptcy laws to constrain the scope of the negotiation.

One way to limit the potential problems of down-round financing is to avoid complex deal structures in early financing rounds. An early-round investor who does not have dilution protection will necessarily invest at a lower valuation than if her claim is enhanced with a variety of sweeteners. The low initial valuation does two things: first, it reduces the probability that the next round will be a down round; and second, with straight equity, the investor has less ability to impede negotiation of the next round.

Going Private as a Response to Declining Market Valuations

When the Internet bubble burst, it became necessary for many public technology companies (which had potential but were short of cash) to restructure in order to raise the additional financing. Public stockholders, however, cannot generally negotiate effectively with creditors and others who have claims on company assets. The solution selected by many was for private investors to reacquire the public shares and return the companies to private status. For that purpose, buyout financing to take public companies private has been a significant focus of private equity activity in recent years.

14.10 Summary

Although the menu of financing sources is extensive, the alternatives that are realistically available to any new venture or small business constitute a much shorter list. A number of factors influence which financing sources are appropriate for a new venture or small business.

- A venture's financing choice is affected by its financial condition and stage of development, which in turn, are related to the completeness of the management team, the value of outside advisors and consultants, the risk/reward profile of the venture, its tax status, and its ability to use assets as collateral and to service debt.

- A venture's financial need includes considerations such as urgency of the need, size of near-term need, permanency of need, and size of the cumulative financing need.

- Product-market and organizational considerations include the importance of rapid growth as an element of product-market strategy; the nature of relationships with suppliers, customers, and others; and the costs and benefits of centralized control.

- The track record, reputation, and relationships of the venture and the entrepreneur bear on the basis for making investments in the venture and on conditions for investing.

- Existing financing relationships affect the ability to raise capital in important ways, particularly if the new investment would alter the values of existing claims.

In the chapter, we examine a number of financing alternatives from the perspective of matching the venture's stage, funding needs, and current financial condition with the capabilities of investors. Although the discussion is qualitative, it is based on the principle of value maximization. Debt financing, for example, may be available at a lower cost than equity financing; however, financing with debt instead of outside equity adds risk to the entrepreneur's financial claim, and the entrepreneur is usually less able to bear risk than is a diversified investor.

The approach we suggest for analyzing financing choices is one that incorporates insights from previous chapters. The parties involved in a venture differ in their ability to bear risk, have different information, and possess potentially conflicting incentives. Because the simulation and valuation tools from earlier chapters are designed to address these considerations, they can be used to evaluate financing alternatives.

REVIEW QUESTIONS

1. Discuss how you would expect the financing choices of the following firms to differ, and explain the reasons for the differences.
   (a) An early-stage R&D venture, compared to an established venture that is generating revenue.
   (b) A venture with revenues that are growing very rapidly, compared to a venture with revenues that are growing at the inflation rate.
   (c) A venture that is highly profitable and growing, compared to a venture that is growing at a similar rate but has not yet achieved profitability.
   (d) A venture that is organized as a C corporation, compared to one that is organized as an S corporation.
   (e) A venture that is being undertaken by an entrepreneur who has a significant track record of new venture successes, compared to a venture that is being undertaken by an entrepreneur with no previous new venture experience.
   (f) A venture that requires large investment in tangible assets, compared to one whose assets are all intangible.

2. What are the advantages and disadvantages of the following financing choices?
   (a) A strategic partner
   (b) Factoring of accounts receivable
   (c) Venture capital
   (d) Franchising
   (e) Postponing payment of accounts payable
   (f) A secured loan
   (g) Direct public offering
   (h) Initial public offering

3. How do the following considerations affect the choice of financing?
   (a) Expected growth is high, but growth prospects are highly uncertain.
   (b) Venture reputation is important to customers and suppliers.
   (c) Employees needed by the venture are not highly skilled or particularly specialized.
   (d) The venture's financing needs are volatile and unpredictable.

4. How can advice from an outside investor affect the value of the venture? What types of ventures will benefit most from outside investor advice?

5. What considerations enter into the financing decisions of ventures that are facing financial distress?

NOTES

1. Berger and Udell (1998) present a framework for small business finance in the context of the venture's stage of growth. Gregory et al. (2005) empirically evaluate the framework and find partial support. Cassar (2004) finds that size is an important factor in how new businesses are financed.

2. In a 1989 survey of 100 of *Inc.* magazine's 500 fastest-growing private companies in the United States, Bhide (1992), p. 110, reports that "more than 80% of these companies were financed through the founders' personal savings, credit cards, second mortgages." Van Auken and Neeley (1996) find that bootstrap sources accounted for 35 percent of start-up capital in a sample of 78 firms. Stouder and Kirchhoff (2004), using data from the Panel Study of Entrepreneurial Dynamics, report that more than half of the founders surveyed relied on personal debt to finance their ventures. Credit cards were the most common source (28.3 percent), followed by personal bank loans (23 percent). Robb and Robinson (2009), p. 3, use data on 5,000 firms from the Kauffman Firm Survey and report that external debt financing—primarily through owner-backed bank loans and business credit cards—is the primary source of financing during a firm's first year.

3. In addition to the SBA, the Farmers Home Administration, the Department of Commerce, the Department of Energy, the Department of Housing and Urban Development, and the Department of the Interior all offer loans or loan-guarantee programs. Other state and federal government financing sources include state business and industrial development corporations, the Export-Import Bank, and the Small Business Innovation Research Program.

4. SBICs and MESBICs generally invest their own money, along with borrowed funds covered by SBA loan guarantees. Business development companies (BDCs) are consortial arrangements that raise funds from sources that promote economic development. Investments that can generate steady streams of cash flow are most appropriate for these sources.

5. Bougheas (2004) models the small firm decision of R&D financing and finds that having a high ratio of intangible assets to total assets and high overall riskiness of investments explains the inability to raise debt externally. The model also attributes the observed cross-country differences in R&D financing to varying levels of monitoring by banks.

6. Berlin and Mester (1993) find that use of covenants increases with moral hazard.

7. Huyghebaert, Van de Gucht, and Van Hulle (2007) find that entrepreneurs prefer trade credit over bank debt, even if it is more expensive. They argue that suppliers are more willing to negotiate with borrowers in the event of default, rather than compelling them to liquidate. Fisman and Love (2003) study the relationship between trade credit and industry growth.

8. Inderst and Mueller (2009) model the impact of active investor involvement on new venture growth. They observe that involvement by active investors can create a competitive advantage over rivals. The advantage comes through better and faster information conveyance, quicker shutdown of less promising ventures, and faster growth of ventures with better prospects.

9. Wetzel (1994) describes active angel investors. Barry (1994) notes that many angels are looking for passive investments with high potential returns. In a field study, Freear, Sohl, and Wetzel (1994) document the heterogeneity of involvement by angel investors. Prowse (1998) notes that angels often work in groups. Current examples are the Breakfast Club in the Boston area and the Band of Angels in Silicon Valley. Chemmanur and Chen (2006) model the choice between angel and VC financing.

10. Bettignies and Brander (2007) model the entrepreneur's choice between bank and VC financing. Their model implies that VCs cannot survive purely as financial intermediaries and that VC funding will be most attractive to entrepreneurs who value the skill set or industry knowledge provided by the VC. Ueda (2004) compares bank and VC investment decision making and monitoring. See also Winton and Yerramilli (2008).

11. Stiglitz and Weiss (1981) note that for a given level of collateral, the interest rate quoted by a lender gives rise to adverse selection. Only those borrowers who regard the interest rate as advantageous will apply for loans, and higher interest rates attract riskier borrowers. Bester (1985), Chan and Kanatas (1985), and Besanko and Thakor (1987) show that lenders can use the signaling value of collateral as a self-selection and incentive mechanism to address the adverse selection problem.

12. For analysis of secured debt and moral hazard, see Boot and Thakor (1994) and Stulz and Johnson (1985).

13. Avery, Bostic, and Samolyk (1998) find evidence that personal guarantees are more important to small business financing than is collateral.

14. See Gorton and Kahn (2000).

15. Cornelli and Yosha (2003) study the role of convertible securities in new ventures with staged financing. They suggest that with straight debt, the entrepreneur may have an incentive to "window dress" to attract the next round of financing. Financing with convertible securities reduces the entrepreneur's incentive to engage in such actions because the lender shares in equity returns.

16. Kwan and Carleton (2010) report that in a sample of privately placed loans by corporations, a large fraction were renegotiated. In fact, one reason for a firm to place a large loan privately is that, compared to public debt, privately placed debt adds the flexibility of being able to renegotiate covenants. See also Boot, Gopalan, and Thakor (2006).

17. The SBA has taken steps to expedite certain kinds of loan approvals. Its LowDoc loan program promises a response within two weeks and streamlines the application process. Approval is based more on experience with the borrower, credit history, and collateral than on the perceived merits of the venture. FA$TRAK is another SBA program with streamlined documentation.

18. Some states have established economic development investment programs where assets of the state retirement fund can be used to fund "economic development" investments in new and ongoing ventures.

19. Ou and Haynes (2006) find that younger firms, especially those needing immediate financing, are most likely to rely on internal equity.

20. Ortiz-Molina and Penas (2008) examine maturities of credit lines to small businesses. They find that shorter loan maturities serve to mitigate the problems associated with borrower risk and asymmetric information.

21. Illustrating the risk of using short-term financing to cover long-term needs, at the height of the 2008 financial crisis the "TED spread," that is, the difference between the three-month T-bill rate and three-month LIBOR rate for loans between banks, exceeded 300 basis points, more than 10 times its long-term average. In addition, many sources of short-term borrowing dried up completely.

22. The cost of a public offering has three components: the spread between the offer price and net proceeds to the issuer (which constitutes the underwriter's fee), issue costs borne directly by the issuing firm, and underpricing. For equity issues, in addition to the fee and expenses, it is standard practice for the underwriter to set the offering price 10–15 percent below what the market price is expected to be at the time of the offering. If the underpricing is considered to be part of the issue cost, then the total cost of an IPO could be in the 15–30 percent range, depending on issue size. The costs for debt issues are considerably lower than for IPOs at all offering sizes. However, most debt issues are made by established companies that can easily demonstrate their ability to repay. In such cases, investors value the debt almost entirely based on repayment terms stated in the debt contract. The underwriter

does not need to devote much effort to due diligence, and investors do not need to devote much effort to valuation. A risky venture that wanted to do a public debt offering would face a much higher issue cost.

23. Cassar (2004), p. 278, reports no link between organizational structure and leverage, but does find that both outside and bank finances appeared to increase as a result of the firm being incorporated.

24. See Hellmann (2002) concerning the effects of conflicts of interest arising in corporate venturing. He suggests that VC firms are less prone to such risks.

25. See Sathe (2003) and Fast and Pratt (1989).

26. Zahra (1995) finds that entrepreneurial activity increases following management LBOs. The finding is consistent with the view that corporate structures and practices discourage entrepreneurship.

27. Based on a study of franchise contracts, Lafontaine (1993) concludes that the contracts are designed to align the incentives of the parties.

28. Norton (1988) finds that franchising arises in organizations where separation of management from risk bearing is inefficient.

29. Brickley and Dark (1987) study organizations that have both franchise and company-owned outlets and find that franchising is more likely where centralized monitoring and control are difficult.

30. See Bates (1998) and Lafontaine and Shaw (1998).

31. See Leblebici and Shalley (1996).

32. See Timmons and Spinelli (2008) for elaboration of the causes of new venture failure.

33. Pindado, Rodrigues, and de la Torre (2006) find that for nondistressed firms, the amount of long-term debt is related to both tax shields and insolvency costs. These relationships do not hold for distressed firms. They conclude that equity issues and renegotiation with creditors are used by distressed firms to reduce leverage.

34. See Chung and Smith (1987) and Titman and Wessels (1988).

35. Wruck (1990) notes that financial distress can create an opportunity to make changes to management and governance. To an extent the costs of distress, such as investors jockeying for position, can be avoided by relying on strip financing, where outside investors hold equity claims as well as debt.

36. See Cole (1998) as well as Berger and Udell (1995).

37. Hanley and Crook (2005) find that follow-on loans are actually more expensive. They attribute this to a relatively fixed base of tangible assets, which means that less collateral is available to secure subsequent loans.

38. From 987 IPOs raising $192 billion in 1999–2000, the number of deals and funds raised fell to 191 and $71 billion, respectively, in 2001–2 (http://www .ipovitalsigns.com/Content/Going Public by Year since 1970.htm; accessed January 27, 2010).

39. In the fourth quarter of 2001, the number of withdrawn IPOs (87) exceeded the number of companies that went public (54) (http://valuationpros.com/ipo_2000.html; accessed January 27, 2010).

40. Dunbar and Foerster (2008) find that only 9 percent of firms that withdraw their IPOs return for a successful offering.

41. J. R. Ritter, "Some Factoids about the 2009 IPO Market" (http://bear.warrington.ufl.edu/RITTER/IPOs2009Factoids.pdf; accessed January 27, 2010).

REFERENCES AND ADDITIONAL READING

Avery, R. B., R. W. Bostic, and K. A. Samolyk. 1998. "The Role of Personal Wealth in Small Business Finance." *Journal of Banking and Finance* 22:1019–61.

Barry, C. B. 1994. "New Directions in Research on Venture Capital Finance." *Financial Management* 23:3–15.

Bates, T. 1998. "Survival Patterns among Newcomers to Franchising." *Journal of Business Venturing* 13:113–30.

Berger, A. N., and G. F. Udell. 1995. "Relationship Lending and Lines of Credit in Small Firm Finance." *Journal of Business* 68 (3): 351–82.

———. 1998. "The Economics of Small Business Finance: The Role of Private Equity and Debt Markets in the Financial Growth Cycle." *Journal of Banking and Finance* 22 (6–8): 613–73.

Berlin, M., and L. J. Mester. 1993. "Debt Covenants and Renegotiation." *Journal of Financial Intermediation* 2 (2): 95–133.

Besanko, D., and A. Thakor. 1987. "Competitive Equilibrium in the Credit Market under Asymmetric Information." *Journal of Economic Theory* 42:167–82.

Bester, H. 1985. "Screening vs. Rationing in Credit Markets with Imperfect Information." *American Economic Review* 75:850–55.

Bettignies, J., and J. Brander. 2007. "Financing Entrepreneurship: Bank Finance versus Venture Capital." *Journal of Business Venturing* 2 2:808–32.

Bhide, A. 1992. "Bootstrap Finance: The Art of Start-Ups." *Harvard Business Review* 70 (6): 109–17.

Boot, A. W. A., R. Gopalan, and A. V. Thakor. 2006. "The Entrepreneur's Choice between Private and Public Ownership." *Journal of Finance* 61:803–36.

Boot, A. W. A., and A. V. Thakor. 1994. "Moral Hazard and Secured Lending in an Infinitely Repeated Credit Market Game." *International Economic Review* 35 (4): 899–920.

Bougheas, S. 2004. "Internal vs. External Financing of R&D." *Small Business Economics* 22 (1): 11–17.

Brickley, J. A., and F. H. Dark. 1987. "The Choice of Organizational Form: The Case of Franchising." *Journal of Financial Economics* 18 (2): 401–20.

Cassar, G. 2004. "The Financing of Business Start-Ups." *Journal of Business Venturing* 19 (2): 261–83.

Chan, Y. S., and G. Kanatas. 1985. "Asymmetric Valuation and the Role of Collateral in Loan Agreements." *Journal of Money Credit and Banking* 17 (1): 85–95.

Chemmanur, T. J., and Z. Chen. 2006. "Venture Capitalists versus Angels: The Dynamics of Private Firm Financing Contracts." Working paper. Available at http://papers.ssrn.com/sol3/papers.cfm?abstract_id=342721.

Chung, K. S., and R. L. Smith. 1987. "Product Quality, Nonsalvageable Capital Investment and the Cost of Financial Leverage." In *Modern Finance and Industrial Economics: Papers in Honor of J. Fred Weston*, ed. T. E. Copeland, 146–67. New York: Blackwell.

Cole, R. A. 1998. "The Importance of Relationships to the Availability of Credit." *Journal of Banking and Finance* 22 (6–8): 959–77.

Cornelli, F., and O. Yosha. 2003. "Stage Financing and the Role of Convertible Debt." *Review of Economic Studies* 70 (242): 1–32.

Dunbar, C. G., and S. R. Foerster. 2008. "Second Time Lucky? Withdrawn IPOs That Return to the Market." *Journal of Financial Economics* 87 (3): 610–35.

Fast, N. D., and S. E. Pratt. 1989. "Individual Entrepreneurship and the Large Corporation." In *Frontiers of Entrepreneurship Research*, 443–50. Wellesley, MA: Babson College. Available at http://www3.babson.edu/ESHIP/outreach-events/fer.cfm.

Fisman, R., and I. Love. 2003. "Trade Credit, Financial Intermediary Development, and Industry Growth." *Journal of Finance*5 8:353–74.

Freear, J., J. Sohl, and W. Wetzel Jr. 1994. "Angels and Non-Angels: Are There Differences?" *Journal of Business Venturing* 9 (2): 109–23.

Gorton, G., and J. Kahn. 2000. "The Design of Bank Loan Contracts, Collateral, and Renegotiation." *Review of Financial Studies* 13 (2): 331–64.

Gregory, B. T., M. W. Rutherford, S. Oswald, and L. Gardiner. 2005. "An Empirical Investigation of the Growth Cycle Theory of Small Firm Financing." *Journal of Small Business Management* 43 (4): 382–92.

Hanley, A., and J. Crook. 2005. "The Higher Cost of Follow-Up Loans." *Small Business Economics* 24 (1): 29–38.

Hellmann, T. 2002. "A Theory of Strategic Venture Investing." *Journal of Financial Economics* 64 (2): 285–314.

Huyghebaert, N., L. Van de Gucht, and C. Van Hulle. 2007. "The Choice between Bank Debt and Trade Credit in Business Start-Ups." *Small Business Economics*2 9:435–52.

Inderst, R., and H. M. Mueller. 2009. "Early-Stage Financing and Firm Growth in New Industries." *Journal of Financial Economics* 93 (2): 276–91.

Kwan, S. H., and W. T. Carleton. 2010. "Financial Contracting and the Choice between Private Placement and Publicly Offered Bonds." *Journal of Money Credit and Banking* 42:907–29.

Lafontaine, F. 1993. "Contractual Arrangements as Signaling Devices: Evidence from Franchising." *Journal of Law, Economics, and Organization* 9:256–89.

Lafontaine, F., and K. L. Shaw. 1998. "Franchising Growth and Franchisor Entry and Exit in the U.S. Market: Myth and Reality." *Journal of Business Venturing* 13 (2): 95–112.

Leblebici, H., and C. E. Shalley. 1996. "The Organization of Relational Contracts: The Allocation of Rights in Franchising." *Journal of Business Venturing* 11 (5): 403–18.

Norton, S. 1988. "An Empirical Look at Franchising as an Organizational Form." *Journal of Business* 61 (2): 197–218.

Ortiz-Molina, H., and M. F. Penas. 2008. "Lending to Small Businesses: The Role of Loan Maturity in Addressing Information Problems." *Small Business Economics* 30 (4): 361–83.

Ou, C., and G. W. Haynes. 2006. "Acquisition of Additional Equity Capital by Small Firms—Findings from the National Survey of Small Business Finances." *Small Business Economics* 27 (2–3): 157–68.

Petersen, M. A., and R. G. Rajan. 1994. "The Benefits of Lending Relationships: Evidence from Small Business Data." *Journal of Finance* 49 (1): 3–37.

Pindado, J., L. Rodrigues, and C. de la Torre. 2006. "How Does Financial Distress Affect Small Firms' Financial Structure?" *Small Business Economics* 26 (4): 377–91.

Prowse, S. 1998. "Angel Investors and the Market for Angel Investments." *Journal of Banking and Finance* 22 (6–8): 785–92.

Robb, A., and D. T. Robinson. 2009. "The Capital Structure Decisions of New Firms." Working paper. Available at http://ssrn.com/abstract=1345895.

Sathe, V. 2003. *Corporate Entrepreneurship.* Cambridge: Cambridge University Press.

Stiglitz, J., and A. Weiss. 1981. "Credit Rationing in Markets with Imperfect Information." *American Economic Review* 71 (3): 393–410.

Stouder, M., and B. Kirchhoff. 2004. "Funding the First Year of Business." In *Handbook of Entrepreneurial Dynamics*, ed. W. Gartner, K. Shaver, N. Carter, and P. Reynolds, 352–71. Thousand Oaks, CA: Sage.

Stulz, R., and H. Johnson. 1985. "An Analysis of Secured Debt." *Journal of Financial Economics* 14 (4): 501–22.

Timmons, J., and S. Spinelli. 2008. *New Venture Creation: Entrepreneurship for the 21st Century.* 8th ed. Chicago: Irwin.

Titman, S., and R. Wessels. 1988. "The Determinants of Capital Structure Choice." *Journal of Finance* 43 (1): 1–20.

Ueda, M. 2004. "Banks versus Venture Capital: Project Evaluation, Screening, and Expropriation." *Journal of Finance* 5 9:601–21.

Van Auken, H. E., and L. Neeley. 1996. "Evidence of Bootstrap Financing among Small Start-Up Firms." *Journal of Entrepreneurial and Small Business Finance* 5 (3): 235–49.

Wetzel, W. E. 1994. "Venture Capital." In *Portable MBA in Entrepreneurship,* ed. W. D. Bygrave, 172–94. New York: John Wiley & Sons.

Winton, A., and V. Yerramilli. 2008. "Entrepreneurial Finance: Banks versus Venture Capital." *Journal of Financial Economics* 8 8:51–79.

Wruck, K. H. 1990. "Financial Distress, Reorganization, and Organizational Efficiency." *Journal of Financial Economics* 27 (2): 419–44.

Zahra, S. A. 1995. "Corporate Entrepreneurship and Financial Performance: The Case of Management Leveraged Buyouts." *Journal of Business Venturing* 10 (3): 225–47.

HARVESTING AND BEYOND

CHAPTER **15**

HARVESTING

Money never starts an idea; it is the idea that starts the money.

W. J. Cameron

Harvesting is the final stage of the entrepreneurial investment process. It also is a critical component of initial investment decisions. Investors evaluate opportunities based on the expectation of a liquidity event that enables them to realize a return and allows them to shift attention to other projects. To estimate value when they make the investment decision, investors must make assumptions about how and when the investment will be harvested and the return they will realize.

Harvesting is also of direct importance to entrepreneurs, but the issues may be different. Some entrepreneurs are like investors in their desire to harvest and move on to other endeavors. Others view the venture as a lifetime commitment and seek to earn returns through the continuing free cash flow of the venture or through partial liquidation of their holdings. Both types should be seeking to realize a return that compensates for the opportunity cost of investing their capital and effort.

In this chapter, we examine the more important harvesting alternatives. As with financing, there is a menu, and it includes some of the same possibilities. For any given venture at any given time, the harvesting alternatives realistically available are limited. Accordingly, much of the chapter concerns the factors that bear on the decision of how and when to harvest.

Going public and the private sale of the venture to another firm (i.e., acquisition) are the harvesting alternatives that normally receive the most attention in business plans. Other important alternatives include a management buyout (MBO), sale of the business to employees or other members of the team, and continuing to operate the venture. We begin by surveying the alternatives and conclude by examining the factors that affect the harvesting choice.

15.1 Going Public

When a venture goes public, an ongoing market is created for its common stock. An IPO is usually a primary market transaction. The issuing firm raises capital by selling new shares to investors. The IPO is really only the first step in the process of harvesting by going public. By placing freely tradable shares in the hands of investors, the IPO initiates the public market for the shares and allows the investors in the stock market to establish a value for the equity. The public market is predominantly a "secondary market." A secondary market transaction is one where market participants transact with each other. Thus, secondary market transactions transfer ownership among investors; they do not generate new funds for the firm that originally issued the shares.

A venture that has already gone public can raise additional capital by issuing new shares in a subsequent primary offering. Such an offering is called a "seasoned offering," meaning that the issuer's shares have already gone through a "seasoning" period of trading in the market. A seasoned offering is not the same thing as a secondary offering unless the shares that are sold in the offering are not newly issued. In a secondary offering, the shares that are sold were issued previously and are being resold in a formal public offering. Sellers may include venture capitalists and other early-stage investors, the entrepreneur, and others who acquired shares from the firm.

Market value (or market capitalization) is the share price times the number of shares outstanding. It is based on the price that equates secondary market demand with secondary market supply. Except for primary market transactions and first-time public sales of shares by entrepreneurs and others who invested before the IPO, secondary market supply (the "float") is fixed. With supply fixed, fluctuations in market value result from changes in demand. Such value changes reflect changes either in expectations about the future free cash flows or in the rate of return required by investors.

Equity investors can harvest their investments in public companies in four ways:

1. *Secondary sale as part of the IPO.* Existing investors, including the entrepreneur and the VC, can harvest a portion of their investment by selling some of the shares they own in the IPO.[1]

2. *Sales in the secondary market.* Once the public market has been established, the investors can sell small amounts of shares from time to time directly into the public market.[2]

3. *Seasoned offerings of secondary shares.* They can sell larger quantities in a secondary public offering after the IPO.

4. *Private placements of secondary shares.* They can use the public market value to benchmark the price and make a private sale to another investor, the entrepreneur, or the company.[3]

The IPO Process

The IPO process described here is a general cash offering, which is the process used most often in the United States. A rights offering process, which is more common in some other countries, is discussed below.

Selecting the underwriter.   The management team that is considering a public offering normally begins by selecting an investment banker or team (syndicate) of investment bankers to underwrite the offering. The selection process, sometimes referred to as a "bake-off" or "beauty contest," can include multiple contestants. The selected underwriter is responsible for advising the issuer, distributing the shares, and underwriting the risk of market price fluctuations during the offering. A broader notion of the term is that the underwriter also makes explicit and implicit representations about share value.[4]

The choice of investment banker involves matching underwriter capabilities with the issuer's specific interests and objectives. Investment bankers have different capabilities and different technologies for carrying out the offerings. Some, for example, focus on institutional brokerage clients, whereas others focus on retail. This focus affects the kinds of investors with whom the underwriter is likely to place the stock. Some investment bankers have established reputations and expertise for handling offerings in particular industries. Some have more limited capabilities but may be able to underwrite small issues at lower cost. These different capabilities explain why the issuer may select a lead and co-lead underwriter and may go further by using a syndicate of underwriters to help market the offering.

Other considerations may affect the issuer's choice of underwriter. If the issue is to be large, is the underwriter capable of organizing the syndicate needed to complete a large offering quickly? If secondary-market liquidity is important, how strong is the market-making operation of the investment banker? In some cases, one or more investment bankers may already have identified the venture as a prospect for public offering and may have initiated a relationship. Sometimes VC investors draw upon their relationships with investment bankers as prospective underwriters. The investment banker may even have a VC operation that has invested in the venture at an earlier stage.[5]

It may seem that an issuer could use competitive bidding to select the underwriter; that is, the issuer could select the investment banker who bid the lowest fee for underwriting the issue. However, current practice is for the issuer to negotiate IPO fees and other terms bilaterally with the prospective underwriter. Competitive bidding is used in the United States primarily for low-risk debt offerings of regulated firms.[6] It is not, however, an effective way to select an IPO underwriter. Providing multiple underwriters with information to enable them to bid effectively is not practical, and new information and market fluctuations during the process of preparing to market the offering make negotiating specific offer terms infeasible. This is less true of low-risk debt issues, where negotiating the underwriting spread may be all that is needed.[7]

Due diligence and issue pricing.   The underwriter is an intermediary between the issuer and public market investors. The issuer is a well-informed seller of shares. As we discussed in Chapter 12, the issuer may be motivated by the desire to raise capital for investment opportunities or by a perception that the market will overvalue the shares. The seller may also want to establish a public market value for the venture. The value can be used as a basis for future transactions, or the public market can enable existing investors to harvest their investments. Public market investors, by comparison, are uninformed about the issuer. They run the risk of being exploited by issuers who expect that the market will overvalue the shares.

Serving as intermediary in such transactions is a challenge. Investors who are uninformed and concerned about paying too much are likely to be conservative in their valuations. Their concerns about overpaying discourage prospective issuers. One of the underwriter's responsibilities is to mitigate the effects of the information disparity. In part, the underwriter does this by preparing a prospectus that describes some of the issuer's operating history, the market, the management team, and how offer proceeds will be used. The underwriter verifies the information in the prospectus through an elaborate due-diligence process. The objective of due diligence is to help ensure that the underwriter discovers any material adverse information about the issuer.[8]

The underwriter, however, cannot disclose all of the relevant information in the prospectus. For example, some information is strategically sensitive. Still, the information must factor into the underwriter's

FIGURE **15.1**
The IPO issue pricing process for a firm commitment underwriting

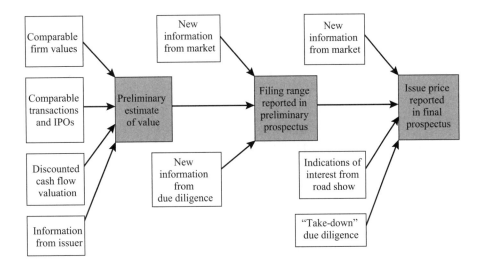

decision about pricing the issue. As a result, due diligence is sometimes sufficient to discourage private firms with negative information from issuing shares via public offering. Such firms, if they need equity capital, are more likely to negotiate private transactions.

The other way in which the underwriter addresses the information disparity is by establishing the offer price. Information contained in the IPO prospectus is never sufficient to enable investors to arrive at an accurate valuation. Some relevant information is too commercially sensitive to publish. Moreover, issuers and underwriters uniformly refrain from making forecasts during the offering process.[9] Based on information acquired in due diligence, the underwriter (in consultation with the issuer) establishes a price for the offering.

The actual process of pricing an issue is more protracted. Figure 15.1 illustrates the process in the United States.[10] The underwriter first establishes a "filing range" of prices at which the offering is likely to be made and publishes the filing range and other information in a preliminary prospectus. At that point, the underwriter and the issuer normally begin a series of "road show" presentations to brokers and institutional investors. During the road show, the underwriter collects information on demand, in the form of nonbinding indications of interest. This process is referred to as "bookbuilding" (building an order book). The final issue price is determined in light of information from the due-diligence process, indications of interest, and new information that arises between the time of the preliminary prospectus and the offer date.[11]

The offer price represents an opinion about the value of the issue relative to the contemporaneous market values of other companies. Even though prospectus information is incomplete, many investors rely on the issue price as a conservative estimate of what the shares are worth. On average, their reliance is justified, because, as documented below, the immediate aftermarket price of most IPOs in the United States is above the issue price.[12]

Underwriter and Venture Capitalist Certification and Issue Pricing

Why are investors able to rely on the offer price of an issue as a representation of value? The financial economics literature suggests that one function of the underwriter is to certify the offer price.[13] An underwriter with an established reputation uses that reputation to certify that the offer price is consistent with information the underwriter could reasonably be expected to discover through due diligence and consistent with prevailing market values. The underwriter's fee includes an (implicit) premium for using its reputation to certify the issue price. If the issue is overpriced, the underwriter's reputation is harmed and its ability to charge a premium for future offerings is reduced.[14]

A similar argument is that if an issue is overpriced, the underwriter may bear the cost of defending itself in litigation brought by investors who purchased shares in the IPO. This is a version of the certification hypothesis, as underwriters must charge premiums to offset the expected cost of litigation.[15]

VC firms also appear to contribute to the certification and monitoring of companies that go public. VCs and other early investors are usually precluded from selling their positions in or shortly after the IPO. "Lockup" agreements with the underwriter typically prevent selling for 180 days. VC investors normally retain ownership in their portfolio companies for at least one year after the companies go public.[16] During the period while the VC is still invested, it has an incentive to continue to monitor the company. Thus, the VC can provide an important monitoring function that works to the benefit of public market investors. In addition, there is evidence that, in the United States, companies with VC backing are less underpriced than other companies.[17] The finding suggests that VC firms contribute to certification, enabling companies to issue shares at prices closer to market value.

An Illustration—Underwriter Selection, Issue Pricing, and Distribution

To illustrate the mechanics underlying the IPO process, consider one recent IPO we will call XYZ Company. The issuer entertained proposals from no less than 15 leading investment bankers, each of whom prepared a preliminary estimate of value. The offer prices inferred from those presentations ranged from $12 to $38 per share. At the end of the process, two investment banks were selected as co-lead underwriters. One had indicated a preliminary valuation of $31 to $36 per share. The other had indicated $16 to $24. Two months later, a preliminary prospectus was circulated, indicating a filing range of $20 to $23. In the interim, the overall market had declined somewhat, and the overall level of IPO activity had fallen. During the road show, it became apparent that demand for the shares was not as high as had been hoped. The IPO took place about one month after the preliminary prospectus was circulated. The shares were offered at $20, the bottom of the range, and the total size of the offering was reduced in response to information from the road show. Immediately following the IPO, the closing price in the aftermarket was $21, up 5 percent from the issue price. Subsequently, the market for the shares languished, with the stock price remaining below the issue price.

The IPO of eToys, which debuted during the so-called Internet bubble, provides a counterexample with substantially more underpricing. Goldman Sachs was selected as lead underwriter. The preliminary prospectus indicated a filing range of $10 to $12 per share. In response to indications of strong demand and overall gains for Internet stocks, the offering was priced at $20. The stock closed on the first day of trading at $80 per share, a gain of 300 percent, and gave eToys a market capitalization of $7.8 billion. The company went bankrupt in 2001 and its remaining assets were purchased by KB Toys for $5 million. Shareholders from before the IPO and others filed a lawsuit against Goldman Sachs, alleging that Goldman underpriced the offering for its own purposes. These stakeholders argued that if the issue had been priced closer to market, eToys would have had enough cash to avoid bankruptcy.

The cost of initial public offerings.   Going public is expensive. The costs associated with an IPO include the fee charged by the underwriter, the out-of-pocket costs of the issuer, and the effective cost of underpricing. Underpricing is normally measured as the difference between the issue price and the first aftermarket closing price. Historically, in the United States, underpricing has averaged about 16 percent of gross issue proceeds (20 percent during the 1990s, when a number of high-tech IPOs were significantly underpriced).[18] Underpricing tends to be greater for smaller and riskier issues. In Chapter 14, we presented information on typical out-of-pocket costs and underwriter fees. The evidence suggests that those costs range from 6 to about 17 percent of gross proceeds and that the percentage is inversely related to issue size.

Why are IPOs so expensive, and why do both fees and underpricing tend to be larger percentages of proceeds for smaller issues? One reason is that there are significant fixed costs associated with underwriting a new issue. Much of the cost of preparing the prospectus, for example, is fixed. The presence of fixed costs contributes to the negative relationship between issue size and the fee percentage. Furthermore, due-diligence costs depend on how fully the issuer hopes to price the offering. The closer to expected market value the price is set, the harder the underwriter must work to discover information that could adversely affect value and the more likely a price decline after the offering is to result in litigation.[19] Also, the more fully the offering is priced, the more direct costs the underwriter will have to incur to market the issue. For a small offering, it may be less expensive to underprice more and save some of the costs of due diligence and marketing.[20]

Another way to think about why IPOs are underpriced is to recognize that prospective investors include investors who are informed about demand for the issue and those who are uninformed.[21] If, on average, issues were priced correctly relative to market demand after the offering, then informed investors (who are better able to assess value) would not participate in overvalued offerings. So informed investors would buy only the undervalued shares, and uninformed investors would get 100 percent of the overvalued shares but a smaller fraction of the undervalued shares. Thus, when issue pricing is correct on average but too high or too low in each individual case, the result is losses for uninformed investors. These expected losses would cause the uninformed investors to withdraw from the IPO market. If it is important to keep them in, then an underwriter must set offer prices low enough, on average, so that uninformed investors end up with fair rates of return.

The winner's curse problem seems to suggest that issuers would fare better by using an auction process to sell their shares. That way, the private knowledge of informed investors could influence the offer price. However, auctions still reward investors for concealing their private knowledge about value, do not eliminate underpricing, and diminish the ability of the market to rely on representations of value by the underwriter. As an alternative to auction, underwriters can use their ability to allocate IPO shares to reward investors for revealing their private knowledge or even to encourage investors to produce information about value.[22]

Methods of valuation and pricing. Underwriters develop their own procedures when establishing offer prices. As a common first step, the underwriter estimates enterprise value on a pre-money basis (before the

IPO proceeds but reflecting the value of opportunities). That valuation may be based on market values of comparables, the prices of other recent IPOs or other transactions, or the present value of projected cash flows. Normally, an underwriter uses several approaches and, based on the results, makes an assessment of value. Next, the underwriter deducts the value of debt financing. Equity value is divided by the existing number of shares to arrive at an estimate of market value per share. The underwriter determines the number of shares to be offered and price per share based on the estimate of existing value per share.

Suppose an issuer hopes to raise $20 million in net proceeds. The underwriter estimates that the market value of equity is $10 per share. From this, the underwriter might deduct $1.50 of desired underpricing, and the underwriter fee might be estimated at 10 percent of gross proceeds. Thus, the venture would issue shares priced at $8.50 and would net $7.65 per share. Given the target of $20 million, the venture would need to issue 2.614 million shares. Using this information, the underwriter might specify a filing range of $7.50 to $9.50 and report the filing range in the preliminary prospectus, along with the fact that the company plans to issue about 2.614 million shares, to net $20 million. If, at the time of the offering, the market has improved, the underwriter is likely to select an offering price near the top of the range and may issue more shares, depending on how the issuer would like to respond to the change in the market.

In some cases, it can make sense for the issuer to agree to overallotment and Greenshoe options. An overallotment option allows the underwriter to offer additional shares, anticipating that some investors may not honor their commitment to buy or may "flip" their shares to make a quick profit, which would depress the price. A Greenshoe option (named after the first company to make use of them) allows the underwriter to issue additional shares if demand turns out to be higher than anticipated. In the United States, both options can vary in size up to 15 percent of the original number of shares offered. The options usually occur together but may be exercised together or separately. These features allow the underwriter to affect the supply of shares, thereby providing more latitude to affect the aftermarket price.

The cost of harvesting by going public. The high percentage cost of an IPO does not translate to a high percentage cost of harvesting. To see why, consider a venture that seeks to raise $30 million via an IPO. Prior to the offering, the venture's investment banker estimates the pre-money valuation to be $120 million. The offering is expected to make the post-money valuation $150 million.

To assess the cost of the IPO, suppose the offering is structured to achieve a target aftermarket value per share of $30.00. This means that after the IPO, there should be 5 million shares outstanding. Consistent with normal practice, the underwriter builds in underpricing of 15 percent, compared to the estimated aftermarket value. Thus, the IPO is priced at $25.50 per share. In addition, the underwriter's fee is 12 percent of gross proceeds. So the issuer nets $22.44 per share (0.88 × $25.50). To achieve net proceeds of $30 million, the firm plans to issue 1.337 million shares ($30 million/$22.44). Existing shareholders (the entrepreneur, VC investors, and others) retain the balance of 3.663 million shares.

There are several ways to measure the cost of the IPO. Total cost per share issued is $7.56 ($30.00 − $22.44). This is 29.6 percent of gross proceeds, or 25.2 percent of expected aftermarket value of the issued shares. In dollars, the cost is $10.1 million ($7.56 per share times the number of shares issued).

Alternatively, cost can be measured by recognizing that if the issue could have been done at $30, with no issue cost, the firm would only have needed to issue 1 million shares; existing shareholders could have retained 4 million. The 337,000 fewer shares they retain, valued at $30, yields a total cost of $10.1 million.

Although the percentage cost is substantial, the market value of the venture after the IPO is expected to be $150 million. If the $10.1 million is viewed as the cost of harvesting the pre-money value of $120 million, it amounts to 8.4 percent.[23] The percentage cost would be even lower if the venture's pre-money value were higher compared to the size of the offering.

Therefore, do not be misled into thinking that the high percentage issue cost is the same as the percentage cost of harvesting. The dollar cost is the same, but the percentage cost may be much lower. It is best to think about the cost of harvesting via going public in dollar terms. If raising new financing is a secondary concern, it could make sense to select the offer size that is expected to minimize the dollar cost of the offering.

Other approaches to public offering. The approach we have described is a firm commitment general cash offering. The term "firm commitment" means that the underwriter commits to buying all of the shares the issuer plans to offer, at the net price in the prospectus. The underwriter's compensation is realized by reselling at a higher price. The difference between the gross price and the net price is the underwriter's fee.[24]

There are other ways to issue equity. An offering can be done on a best-efforts basis. In a best-efforts offering, the investment banker acts more like an agent of the issuer and does not guarantee net proceeds. You might expect that issuers would select best-efforts offerings when they wish to raise capital but do not have specific concerns about the amount that is actually raised. However, the best-efforts approach also suggests that the issuer is concerned about achieving a high price and that the issuer and the underwriter may disagree about the value of the shares.[25] By proceeding on a best-efforts basis, the underwriter provides distribution services but does not certify the price. The evidence on best-efforts offerings is not very positive; generally, it appears that issuers could have achieved more success with a general cash offering.[26]

The term "general cash offering" signifies that the shares are sold to the investing public in exchange for cash. In contrast, a "rights offering" is offered only to existing shareholders, in exchange for cash and warrants. Rights offerings are more common outside the United States and are mandatory in some countries.[27]

In a rights offering, the issuer raises equity by issuing warrants to existing shareholders. The warrants are call options that enable the shareholders to purchase new shares at a fixed price for a specified period. Shareholders who do not wish to exercise the rights can sell the warrants to others. Assuming that each new share requires one warrant, the effective price of a new share is the exercise price of the warrant plus the market value of the warrant.

The issuing firm receives the exercise price, and existing shareholders receive the market value of the warrants. A public market for the shares is created by first allowing the warrants to trade and then allowing the shares to trade.

The strongest argument for the rights offering approach is that the issuer and the underwriter do not need to predict the market price or establish an offer price. Because the effective price of newly issued shares is determined by trading in the market, existing shareholders do not lose if the exercise price of the warrants is below market. Similarly, new investors do not need to worry that the issue price is set above market value.[28]

An argument against rights offerings is that the approach limits the certification function of the underwriter to warranting the accuracy and completeness of the prospectus. Because the underwriter does not establish an issue price, information in the prospectus gains importance. However, as mentioned earlier, it is unlikely that all information relevant to value can be included in the prospectus. In the United States, issuing firms are free to select either a general cash offering or a rights offering. The fact that rights offerings are rare is evidence that, for most

US issuers, the price certification function contributes more to expected proceeds than concern with mispricing takes away.[29]

OpenIPO—A Test of Efficiency of Current Practice

General cash offerings involve intentional underpricing, such that the aftermarket price is expected to be above the issue price. This indicates that, at the issue price, there is more demand for the shares than there are shares available. Underwriters respond to excess demand by rationing the shares in ways that appear to favor preferred customers, such as those who are willing to buy even when an issue seems overpriced, who refrain from "flipping" the shares to make a quick profit, or who may be sources of future business ("spinning").

There are two extreme views of underpricing. On the one hand, it may be seen as an efficient aspect of the offering process that contributes to the certification efficacy of the underwriter and reduces costs of due diligence and marketing. Or, on the other hand, it may be seen as an unnecessarily good deal for the underwriter's preferred customers.

As an alternative, several companies have gone public using an auction method. This approach, made highly visible by Google in 2004, is known in the United States as an OpenIPO and represents a test of the efficiency of current practice. The rationale for the auction method is that it can reduce underpricing and the practices of flipping and spinning.

W. R. Hambrecht and Company, a split-off from the investment banking firm Hambrecht and Quist, is the originator of the OpenIPO process. Under this process, shares are offered via direct submission of bids to the Hambrecht Internet site. Hambrecht initiates the process by distributing a preliminary prospectus over the Internet. The prospectus indicates the number of shares being offered and the filing range. The auction opens when the registration statement for the issue is filed with the SEC, and it remains open until the SEC allows the offering to "go effective," normally a period of 6 to 10 weeks. Bidders submit the prices and quantities they are willing to buy. When the offering goes effective, demand information is matched with the quantity of shares available and the market-clearing price is found. Orders may be filled at or below the market-clearing price, but in the United States, because of SEC regulations, all bidders whose orders are accepted pay the same price, even if they bid higher.

The OpenIPO is modeled after an auction process developed by Nobel Prize–winning economist William Vickery. As of this writing, 36 offerings have been completed. The first was Ravenswood Winery in

1999. The auction price for that IPO was determined to be $10.50, and in the subsequent month the stock continued to trade in the $10.50 to $11 range. It appears that the process eliminated underpricing for this issue.

In contrast, Google's controversial IPO in August 2004 did not eliminate underpricing. In late July 2004, Google publicized its target price range of $108 to $135. Just before the auction, it lowered the range to $85 to $95. Several analysts had suggested that the earlier range was too high. The IPO price was $85 and the first public price after the auction was $100, an 11 percent increase over the midpoint of the range and almost 18 percent above the issue price.

What are some possible explanations for the mispricing of the auction process? One is that individual investors, who are supposed to be the primary participants in this auction, may lack sufficient information to appropriately price the security. Another is that because the offer price is determined by an auction, the underwriter is less able to certify value. A third is that, while the general principles of the auction are followed, the underwriter may still decide to fill orders at a price below the market-clearing price in order to include some preferred investors who have submitted low bids. In this case, there is still rationing and underpricing is likely relative to the first aftermarket price.

In a study of Japanese IPOs during a period when both an auction method and bookbuilding were available to issuers, bookbuilding was the clear winner. The concern is that the auction method gives rise to an adverse selection or "lemons" problem and that bookbuilding solves the problem. The bookbuilding process supposedly reveals adverse information so that only firms with something to hide will try to use an auction. Availability of bookbuilding can reduce auctions or eliminate them altogether, which is what happened in Japan and other places.[30]

It remains to be seen whether the OpenIPO process is as effective in raising capital as the traditional approach. So far, the market test suggests that while this approach has appealed to some issuing firms, the number is limited and the concept does not have much momentum.

Harvesting in the IPO

The IPO is only the beginning of the harvesting process. The entrepreneur, VCs, and or other early investors do not normally sell shares during the IPO. Historically, the lead VC investors, for example, sell in only about 27 percent of the IPOs where they hold shares.[31] When they do sell, they typically sell only about 20 percent of their holdings.

There are three reasons for an investor, such as a VC, to refrain from selling during the IPO of a portfolio company. First, investors are likely to perceive insider selling as a negative signal (though not when the VC is facing expiration of the fund). A second reason to refrain from selling is that the investor expects to continue to add significant value to the venture. The investor would want to hold the shares until the ability to add value fell below what the investor could achieve by focusing on other ventures. The third reason is that shares sold in the IPO are likely to be underpriced. By waiting, the investor can usually obtain a higher price.[32]

Harvesting after the IPO

Typically, even if an early investor does not sell in the IPO, the investor's shares will be registered along with those sold by the issuing firm. Registered shares are freely tradable in the aftermarket and can be sold. The main limitation is that existing shareholders normally have agreed with the underwriter to refrain from trading, usually for 180 days after the IPO.

This "lockup period" serves at least two functions: First, it removes the need for an underwriter, who normally supports the market during an offering, to purchase shares that are being sold into the market at the same time by existing shareholders. Second, it allows enough time to pass so that the sellers cannot easily be accused of trading on the basis of information that should have been disclosed in the prospectus.

Rule 144 sales.   In the United States, shares that are not registered can still be sold into the market, but SEC Rule 144 limits the rate at which the sales can occur. An investor who owns unregistered shares but is not a control person (such as an officer, director, or large block holder) can periodically sell small amounts of unregistered shares. After one year of ownership, any remaining restricted shares become freely tradable. If the investor is a control person, the shares remain restricted and subject to the gradual liquidation process. One consideration behind Rule 144 is a concern that rapid sale into the public market could depress share prices.[33] Gradual sale gives the market time to absorb the shares and reduces concerns about opportunistic selling.

Seasoned offerings that include secondary sales.   Sometimes existing investors are eager to liquidate; in such cases, gradual sale may not be attractive. The alternatives are to arrange a large private transaction or to participate in a seasoned offering. Companies sometimes use seasoned offerings to lower the overall cost of raising equity or to enable investors to harvest. The issuer may undertake a small IPO to establish a market price and then follow a few months later with a seasoned equity offering (SEO).

It is more common for existing shareholders to participate by selling in the SEO than in the IPO. Normally, the underwriter's fee for an SEO is less than the fee for an IPO. In addition, SEOs are priced very close to the prevailing market price at the time of the offering. When an SEO is announced, the market price of the stock drops by about 3 percent on average, far less than the 16 percent average underpricing of IPOs.[34]

15.2 Acquisition

When investment in a venture is harvested by acquisition or merger with another company, the transaction can take any of several forms. The acquirer can purchase the equity of the venture for cash or exchange it for shares of the acquiring company. Alternatively, the acquirer can purchase all or some of the venture's assets for cash or stock. The choice is affected by a variety of considerations.

Purchasing the Equity of the Venture for Cash

By purchasing the equity, the buyer acquires ownership of the assets of the venture and assumes the liabilities.[35] The parties enter a stock purchase agreement that sets out the terms and describes the assets and liabilities.

The acquirer normally undertakes some level of due diligence to verify its assessment of value. In addition, sellers are normally expected to provide representations and warranties that go to issues of value. For example, the sellers may warrant that the accounts receivable balance the purchaser will acquire was prepared in a manner consistent with Generally Accepted Accounting Principles (GAAP); that the venture is the legal owner of any intellectual property being transferred; and that the sellers are unaware of any existing or prospective litigation against the venture. The actual list is likely to be much more comprehensive.

To an extent, due-diligence efforts and representations and warranties are substitutes. A seller may be hesitant to open its records to the review of a prospective buyer. This is understandable because, if the transaction is not consummated, the buyer could have gained access to confidential information about the seller. In addition, if the venture is small, the cost of extensive due diligence can exceed the expected benefit. In such cases, the parties may place greater weight on representations and warranties. If the seller can credibly guarantee the representations and warranties, then the potential for litigation after the acquisition can substitute for more due diligence.

If extensive due diligence is not practical and the seller is not able to credibly warrant the assets being acquired and liabilities being assumed, then the transaction price is likely to be reduced. Thus, due diligence, representations and warranties, and the transaction price are interdependent.

From the perspective of an investor, such as a VC firm, sale of equity for cash is likely to be the preferred form of transaction. However, it may be the most difficult form on which to agree. It may also be unattractive to the entrepreneur. For the investor, selling for cash facilitates harvesting; cash is easily distributed to limited partners. In addition, because most institutional limited partners are not taxed on their earnings, receiving cash does not give rise to adverse tax consequences.

An entrepreneur who is selling equity in a venture may have a different perspective. If the sale involves a gain, the entrepreneur and members of the management team may be exposed to a significant immediate tax liability. On a more qualitative level, selling for cash has an aspect of finality to it that may not be to the entrepreneur's liking.

For the purchaser, acquiring equity for cash involves the most risk. By acquiring shares and paying cash, the acquirer is giving up a safe asset and acquiring one that is risky. Furthermore, if the acquirer must borrow the cash, then leverage increases. The increase in risk is not particularly important in itself; but adding leverage can deprive the acquirer of financial slack that could be used for other opportunities.

Purchasing the Assets of the Venture for Cash

Transferring only the essential assets of the venture to the buyer can reduce the buyer's risk. In an asset purchase, the seller continues to be responsible for the venture's liabilities. Because the buyer does not assume direct liability, the cash price will be higher than for an equity purchase. The seller can use the extra cash to pay off the liabilities.

Automobile dealerships, for example, are often transferred using asset purchase agreements. The buyer acquires the facility, the vehicle inventory, and other essential business assets but does not assume liability for the loan the seller used to finance the inventory. Vehicle inventories are normally financed with "flooring" loans secured through specific claims against individual vehicles in the dealership inventory. When a vehicle is sold, the dealer is supposed to repay the loan amount associated with that vehicle. When new inventory arrives, the dealer can borrow more, based on the specific vehicles received. If a dealer sells vehicles without repaying the loan, a purchaser who assumes the obligation can be liable for the repayment. Instead of verifying that the inventory securing the loan is still on the dealer's lot, the purchaser simply buys the inventory (possibly arranging new financing) and leaves the seller to repay the loan.

For similar reasons, a purchaser may decide to acquire only those assets that are central to future operations. The accounts receivable balance is an example. Rather than trying to verify the quality and status of receivables, it could be easier not to purchase them.

Exchanging Equity or Assets of the Venture for Equity of the Acquirer

Some transactions are structured as exchanges of the acquirer's stock for either the stock or assets of the venture. Exchanges of stock for assets are difficult because the seller is left with the liabilities and may not have the liquidity to service the debt. Accordingly, we focus on exchanges of stock for stock. In such exchanges, uncertainty about value exists on both sides. Not only must the buyer conduct due diligence on the venture, but sellers must also value the shares they will receive. The problem is particularly difficult if the acquirer is not a public company. In such cases, there are no public stock prices and no SEC reporting requirements or analyst reports to facilitate agreement. Instead, both parties must rely on due-diligence investigations and the representations and warranties of the other party.

A further issue, if the acquirer is not public, is that the exchange does not directly accomplish the likely objective of investors in the venture, which is to harvest their investments. For VCs and similar investors, exchange of nonpublic shares for other nonpublic shares is helpful only if the resulting entity is better able to undertake a public offering in the future or if the acquirer is willing to purchase the holdings of the investor for cash, even though the entrepreneur and members of the management team may receive shares.

If the acquirer is an entity with publicly traded stock, the exchange is easier, as the shares have an established market value. Furthermore, investors who receive registered shares may be able to liquidate the shares shortly after the transaction is completed. If the shares are not registered, liquidating under the provisions of Rule 144 can take longer, but the path to harvesting is clear.

Exchanges of stock for stock have some advantages over cash transactions. An acquirer who wants to expand rapidly may be able to consummate acquisitions more easily by using stock than by arranging financing for each transaction. Another advantage is that, to the extent the share values move together, exchanging shares can address the moving target problem that arises when using cash for shares. Consequently, abrupt changes in the market are less likely to disrupt the transaction. Finally, in some cases exchanging shares enables the seller to postpone recognizing a capital gain, which adds value to the exchange.

After the Acquisition

In some transactions, the acquirer would like to retain members of the venture's management team. Employment agreements protect the acquirer from loss of value resulting from resignations by team members. The acquirer may also seek to align the incentives of team members with the interests of the acquirer. Approaches include asking the team members to accept restricted shares of the acquirer (so their ability to trade and defeat incentive alignment is limited), compensating team members with equity claims or options on the acquiring firm, or offering incentive pay.

The acquirer may also be concerned that once the venture is sold, team members will decide to reenter the market as competitors. Accordingly, sellers are sometimes asked to accept noncompete agreements or earn-ups as a condition of the transaction.

Agreeing to Disagree

When the sellers are more optimistic about the venture than is the acquirer, reaching agreement on fixed terms of exchange is difficult. The parties can try to address the difference by devoting resources to due diligence or by strengthening representations and warranties. Conceivably, the additional effort will lead to valuations that are more consistent.

The parties also can use an earn-out provision to make the acquisition price contingent on its future performance. The compensation can be adjusted whether or not the seller remains with the venture. If the seller is no longer with the venture, contractual compensation can be adjusted based on performance. If the seller has stayed on as an employee, then the employee's bonuses can be tied to firm performance.

Valuing Private Transactions

How much is a venture worth in a private transaction? The answer depends on a myriad of factors, but the overriding considerations are its value in the next best alternative use and costs of the transaction. We consider the transactions costs first, followed by opportunity cost.

Costs of the transaction.   The cost of raising capital in the public market can be substantial. Public issue costs are related to due diligence, marketing, supporting the offer price, and expected cost of litigation (for issues that experience significant losses of value after the offering). The costs of private transactions are of a similar nature but less directly observable. For a private transaction, we usually know only the net proceeds the sellers receive; hence, there is no convenient measure of transactions costs.

We can gain perspective on the transactions costs of private sales by examining the pricing of private equity sold by companies that have public equity outstanding. One study of equity private placements that includes data for a sample of small public companies finds that, on average, shares of private transactions are priced 20.1 percent below the contemporaneous public market value. Discounts are larger for smaller firms, when small amounts of proceeds are raised, and when a placement is large relative to firm size. Discounts are also larger when uncertainty about value is high, such as when a firm is involved in development of a speculative product or is threatened with financial distress.[36] Assuming that private value is similar to public market value, these discounts are estimates of the purchaser's due-diligence cost. Private transaction prices may also reflect a discount for illiquidity; however, illiquidity discounts generally are small.[37] Comparing these results with the total issue cost for IPOs, including underpricing, shows that the average transactions costs for private sales are somewhat lower.

Opportunity cost.   The value of a venture to an acquirer depends on its stand-alone value, plus the value of any synergistic gains, less transactions costs. For a private venture that is acquired by a public firm, value can also be created by transfer of ownership from underdiversified investors to the capital market.

Whether sellers can capture any of the synergistic gains or the gains from movement to a public market, depends on comparison of opportunities. If the venture is unique and multiple public acquirers are competing to acquire it, then sellers should realize most of the full public market value, including synergies, less the buyer's transactions costs. Conversely, if there is only one prospective buyer and there are no good private market alternatives, and if other ventures would be similarly attractive to the buyer and would substitute for each other, the buyer should be able to capture most of the value that is created. These are the extremes. In other cases, the gains are likely to be shared on the basis of availability of substitute buyers and sellers.

Thus, a reasonable approach to valuation is to estimate public market value assuming gains are captured by the seller and estimate stand-alone private market value. These are the bounds on value before subtracting the buyer's transactions costs. The value can be estimated by considering how the parties are likely to share the gains.

Noncash transactions.   How should the entrepreneur and other sellers value their claims if the venture is sold for claims other than cash? Clearly, if freely tradable stock is received, then except for tax considerations there is little difference between receiving stock and receiving cash. However, the stock is often restricted from trading for a significant period. Sometimes, the restriction is designed to align the entrepreneur's incentives with the acquirer's interests. Restricting resale is also a way of making sure the entrepreneur's gain is related to the acquirer's subsequent performance (including the acquirer's interest in the venture).

Stock that is not freely tradable leaves the entrepreneur with a financial position that is still underdiversified. This form of compensation is less valuable than if the entrepreneur were to receive cash or tradable shares. The methods developed in earlier chapters can be used to assess the impact of trading restrictions on value. For a diversified investor, such as a VC firm, it is reasonable to value the shares as if they were tradable.

Illustration: Estimating the Cost of Private Transactions

It is possible, using comparable public firms or other data, to estimate the value of a venture as if it were public. Assuming that the acquirer is public and values the acquisition on the basis of comparables, the acquisition price can be estimated by deducting the expected discount to reflect the cost of the private transaction:

$$\text{Acquisition Price} = \text{Public Company Market Value} \\ - \text{Private Transaction Discount}$$

TABLE **15.1** **Private placement discounts compared to equity market value**

Variable	Mean discount	Variable	Mean discount
Proceeds (millions)		Market value of equity (millions)	
≤$1.0	43.7%	≤$10.0	34.6%
$1.0–$5.0	33.1%	$10.0–$25.0	35.6%
$5.0–$10.0	15.1%	$25.0–$75.0	17.2%
$10.0–$20.0	10.1%	>$75.0	7.6%
>$20.0	0.2%	Single investor	
Book-to-market equity ratio		Yes	11.7%
≤0.1	31.3%	No	23.3%
0.1–0.4	25.0%	Speculative product	
0.4–0.7	21.9%	Yes	32.2%
0.7–1.0	5.0%	No	14.7%
1.0	3.3%	Financial distress	
		Yes	34.8%
		No	16.5%

SOURCE: *Hertzel and Smith (1993).*
NOTE: *Although the study uses data from private placements of public companies, the findings capture many of the qualitative considerations that are likely to affect the costs an acquirer would incur in acquiring a private venture.*

Table 15.1 summarizes some of the statistical evidence of private transaction discounts.

Consider a biotechnology venture that has begun to generate revenues but is not yet profitable and for which there is significant potential that the firm will ultimately lose out to rivals. The venture has book assets of $5 million and no debt. Based on comparable public firms, its market value is around $20 million.

Given the market value estimate, the "Proceeds" data in Table 15.1 suggest an acquisition price of about $18 million (a discount of 10.1 percent). The "Book-to-market equity ratio" of .25 suggests an acquisition price of $15 million (a discount of 25 percent). The "Market value of equity" estimate of $20 million suggests an acquisition price of about $13 million (a discount of 35.6 percent). The average discount for single-investor transactions is 11.7 percent, suggesting an acquisition price of about $17.5 million. The average discount for speculative products is 32.2 percent, suggesting an acquisition price of about $13.5 million.

Although some of these estimates are likely to be more accurate than others, a simple equal-weighted average suggests an acquisition price of $15.4 million, a discount of about 23 percent. Based on this estimate, the entrepreneur can begin to consider the relative merits of private acquisition or public offering.

Going Public by Reverse Merger

The distinction between merger and IPO is not as sharp as might at first appear. Reverse merger is an alternative way for a private company to become public. In a reverse merger, an existing public company nominally acquires the shares of the private company and possibly then changes its name to that of the private company. The public company is usually nothing more than a shell—often a remnant of an unsuccessful public company whose only remaining value is that its shares are publicly traded, making it a target for a firm that wants to establish a public market but does not need to use an IPO to raise capital.

The notional acquirer (the public company shell) does not need to have any resources to accomplish the acquisition. Rather, the owners of the private company simply exchange their shares for shares of the public company.

Reverse merger does not require an underwriter, avoids the cost of an IPO, and can be accomplished relatively quickly. By one estimate, the cash cost of a reverse merger can be $100,000 to $300,000 (depending on whether the reporting company is listed or not and on the percentage of shares that are sold to the private investors). As there is no certification of value, however, the aftermarket capitalization may be less than if the company were to go public via IPO. Because such companies tend to have little liquidity, lack of analyst following, and few active market makers, the valuation may remain low for a sustained period.

Whether, in individual cases, reverse merger makes sense depends on the firm's circumstances. By creating a public market for company shares, reverse merger enables existing investors to eventually harvest their investments, creates a medium of exchange that can be used in other M&A (merger and acquisition) transactions, and may enable the formerly private firm to use market-based incentive compensation more effectively. However, because it does not generate immediate capital and may result in lower valuation, reverse merger is not suitable for near-term capital raising and may not be ideal for near-term harvesting when the firm is large enough and mature enough for an IPO or a true acquisition.

Examples of Reverse Mergers with Public Shells

- Siebert Financial Corporation, a holding company for Muriel Siebert and Co., Inc., engages in discount brokerage, investment banking, and trading on its own account. Muriel Siebert, the first woman to purchase a seat on the New York Stock Exchange (NYSE), transformed Siebert Financial into a public company by reverse merging into a defunct furniture company, J. Michaels, Inc.

- In 1970, Ted Turner (founder of Turner Broadcasting) acquired once publicly traded Rice Broadcasting (WJRJ-TV) in Atlanta. He merged the billboard company he inherited from his father into Rice Broadcasting. Turner was then in a position to tap the public capital markets.

- In 1999, seeking to "awaken the giant within," motivational speaker Tony Robbins reverse merged his company, Dreamlife, into a medical company shell, GHS, Inc. The company, which was subsequently renamed EOS International, Inc., launched a website in February 2000 devoted to personal and professional improvement. The then public venture failed and became the corporate shell in the next round. In July 2001, EOS acquired the outstanding stock of nonpublic Discovery Toys, Inc. After the transaction, former holders of Discovery Toys stock held a majority of the voting shares of EOS.

- Allied Waste Industries, Blockbuster Video, Occidental Petroleum, and Waste Management all became public through reverse mergers

15.3 Management Buyout

Harvesting opportunities are critical to VCs and other outside investors. They may be less important to the entrepreneur and key members of the management team. Recognizing that harvesting is a source of potential conflict, the parties normally negotiate harvesting options at the time of the initial investment. The investor may negotiate the right to demand registration of shares, which could be tantamount to compelling the venture to go public. Short of the ability to force a public offering, the investor may have the right to insist on being bought out by the entrepreneur on terms related to the value of the venture.

A management buyout (MBO) proposal can be a response to investor insistence on exercising demand registration rights or rights that could trigger an acquisition. Suppose investors wish to sell and have located a buyer. The prospective acquirer wishes to retain the management team but purchase their existing equity. Members of the management team, however, value their status as equity holders; perhaps they believe the venture has more potential than is reflected in the transaction terms under consideration. One response is to counter with a proposal to buy out the investors' equity interest.

MBOs are usually financed with debt. The investors' equity is valued and borrowing is arranged so that the venture, the entrepreneur, or other members of the management team can repurchase the investors' shares. Regardless of how the transaction is implemented, the venture normally ends up with a capital structure that is more highly leveraged than before the MBO. An MBO is feasible only if the venture is reasonably successful. Value must be high enough to justify the price the investors receive. In the case of a leveraged transaction, the venture must be capable of generating enough cash flow to service the debt.

Valuing MBO Transactions

The advantage of an MBO is that the buyer (the management team) already knows almost everything there is to know about the venture. Because due diligence is not necessary, the transactions cost can be low. If outside debt is used, the buyers must be able to demonstrate that repayment is likely or must have collateral to secure the loan. However, because the lender only needs to assess repayment potential and not overall value, even that aspect of the transaction can be low cost compared to a public offering of equity.

Offsetting the cost saving, the entrepreneur and members of the team continue to be underdiversified. This makes MBO transactions paradoxical. Investors, who are well diversified, are selling to management team members, who are not as well diversified. Saving of transactions costs is one factor that can help explain such transactions. Others include differences in expectations about future performance and the subjective value that team members place on continuing to own and manage the venture. Generally, the rationale for an MBO is stronger if management expects that capital market investors will recognize and accept its assessment of value within a short period, thereby enabling a public offering.

15.4 Employee Stock Ownership Plans

In many private businesses, the entrepreneur has little desire to harvest in any formal sense. Instead, the entrepreneur's objective is to realize a return through the stream of free cash flows the enterprise produces. The need for liquidity is low if the venture has no outside investor who is pressing for a liquidity event. In some cases, enterprises such as these are family businesses, where family members expect that, over time, management will pass from one family member to another. In other cases, there may be no specific line of succession.

Even family businesses with no outside investors, however, need liquidity from time to time. The most obvious liquidity need is associated with estate management. When an owner dies, the estate is obligated to pay taxes based on the gain in market value of the venture over many years and not on current earnings or cash flows. The tax liability can be large even though no cash flow is available for paying taxes. Businesses with positive earnings and cash flow can sometimes satisfy the tax liability by borrowing. But what if the venture's earnings and cash flow are too limited to support the level of borrowing that is needed?

A related problem may arise when, following the death of the owner, venture shares are distributed to heirs. What if some or all of the heirs are uninterested in the business or the heirs have significant disagreements about direction? These problems are difficult to solve without some means of introducing liquidity.

Another problem can arise if the entrepreneur wishes to tie employee compensation to venture performance as a way of aligning incentives or wants to use employee ownership as a way to lower cash compensation. Paying bonuses might help align incentives, but bonuses can cause employees to focus excessively on short-run performance and ignore long-run value creation. Similarly, reducing cash compensation in the present requires that the firm offer employees higher compensation in the future based on their present contributions of effort.

Employee stock ownership plans (ESOPs) are used widely in public corporations to allocate ownership to employees for a variety of purposes. The ESOP, however, was originally conceived as a means of providing liquidity to owners of private businesses, in lieu of alternatives such as public offering or acquisition. ESOPs can also be used in private businesses to help align incentives or to enable employees to defer some of their compensation.

The ESOP Process

The ESOP of a private business creates liquidity by establishing an internal market for its shares. It does so by providing a mechanism that enables employees to invest their retirement funds in equity of the business and to liquidate their investments at retirement or upon a change of employment. ESOPs can be leveraged or unleveraged. A leveraged ESOP is more complex and provides liquidity for the business more quickly than does an unleveraged ESOP.[38]

Figure 15.2 illustrates the structural elements of a leveraged ESOP. Panel (a) describes ESOP formation. The process begins when the company establishes an ESOP trust. The trust is responsible for administering all of the share transactions and for assuring that the transactions are based on fair valuations. In a leveraged ESOP, the trust acquires ownership of enough shares to meet the expected needs of the company retirement plan for several years. If the company is publicly traded, the trust can purchase the shares in the market or directly from specific stockholders. For a private company, the trust purchases shares from one or more of the existing owners. So, for example, the owner who is facing retirement may want to sell his shares to the ESOP trust, which would convert the owner's estate to cash or liquid assets.

To ensure that employees receive equitable treatment, the company or the trust normally arranges for an outside party, such as a valuation consultant, appraiser, or accountant, to value the equity. Based on the valuation, the ESOP trust agrees to purchase an appropriate number of shares from the entrepreneur or an investor who wants to harvest. To pay for the shares acquired in a leveraged ESOP, the trust arranges for a bank loan. The loan is a primary obligation of the trust and is secured by the shares the trust acquires. In addition, the bank loan is normally guaranteed by the company, which commits to make annual retirement contributions of cash to the trust on behalf of its employees.

Initiation of the leveraged ESOP is the primary liquidity event for the entrepreneur. The bank loan is used to purchase the entrepreneur's shares. From that point forward, the entrepreneur is not directly involved in ESOP transactions. The same structure can be used to deal with liquidity issues arising among different owners. An investor who desires liquidity, be it a VC firm or a family member who disagrees with the direction of the company, can be bought out via a leveraged ESOP.[39] The main difference between a leveraged ESOP and one that is unleveraged is that, in the latter, the trust purchases shares from the existing owner(s) as needed, over a period of several years. One consideration in the choice between leveraged and unleveraged is how the existing owner (the entrepreneur or founder, for example) expects the value of shares to change over time: if they are expected to increase significantly in value, an unleveraged ESOP may be preferred.

Panel (b) of the figure illustrates how annual retirement contributions are funded. The amount of contribution is determined by the company's retirement plan and is a function of total compensation to employees who are plan members. The company transfers the required funds to

Panel (a): ESOP initiation

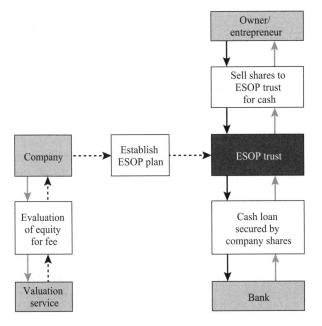

FIGURE **15.2**
**Structure of a private
leveraged ESOP**
Black arrows designate flow
of shares; grey arrows designate
flow of cash; dashed arrows are
other flows.

Panel (b): Annual retirement contribution funding

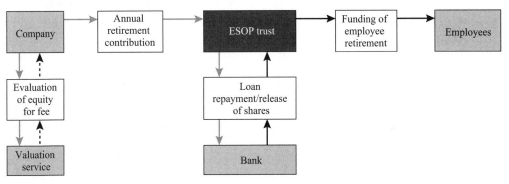

Panel (c): Share redemption at employee retirement

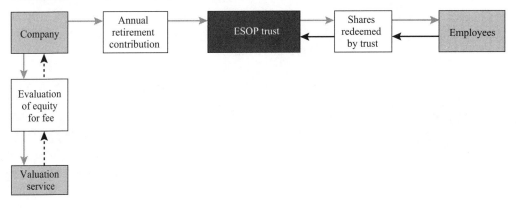

the trust, based on a new valuation of company equity. The money the company pays is used by the trust to pay interest and a portion of the principal of the bank loan. Based on the repayment, the bank releases its claim to some of the securities. The trust then is free to assign appropriate numbers of shares to the retirement accounts of the employees. This process of valuation, funds transfer, and loan repayment continues each year until the loan is repaid.

Because there is no market for company shares, employees must have a means of converting their equity into cash. As shown in panel (c), this is accomplished by allowing employees to sell shares back to the ESOP trust at their estimated value at time of retirement (or resignation). Thus, in any given year, the cash retirement contribution of the employer goes partly to repay the loan and partly to repurchase shares from retiring employees.

Valuation Considerations

Although the ESOP provides liquidity needed for certain critical transactions, the company remains private. The entrepreneur's underdiversified position can be improved by liquidating some of the holdings and reinvesting the proceeds. The values at which shares are purchased and transferred to the ESOP and to employees usually reflect discounts from public market value. Discounts are appropriate because employees are relying on a valuation estimate rather than a verifiable market transaction and because an employee's retirement savings is underdiversified. Even if the company is public, employee investments of retirement funds in company stock are normally made at discounts to reflect underdiversification.

On the positive side, it is argued that giving employees equity interests aligns their incentives, which enhances the value of the organization. On technical grounds, it does not appear that a small ownership interest can do much to align incentives. The cost to an individual employee of shirking and free riding is spread over all shareholders and is negligible for an employee who is deciding how hard to work. Nevertheless, stock ownership may give rise to feelings of esprit de corps and result in more effective teams.

15.5   Roll-Up IPO

A company that is too small to go public by itself may be able to do so by combining with others to create an organization that is large enough

FIGURE **15.3**
Roll-Up IPO

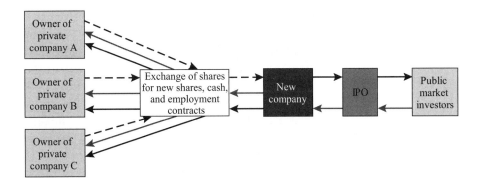

to make efficient use of the public offering process. A roll-up IPO is a device that enables this to occur. Figure 15.3 illustrates the process. Normally, a roll-up combines several smaller firms that are similar in orientation and have track records of profitable operation. The owner of each firm exchanges existing shares for shares of the new company. Each seller may also receive cash and frequently enters an employment contract that ties her to the new company for several years.

The new company goes to the capital market with an IPO based on the consolidated financial statements of the rolled-up companies. The new company may operate essentially as a portfolio of the smaller companies, or some centralization may be sought. Funds from the IPO provide any cash that is distributed to owners of the rolled-up companies, and the IPO leads to a public market, in which shares of the new company can eventually be sold. Usually, trading by sellers of the rolled-up companies is restricted for several months by the lockup provisions of the IPO and may be restricted for longer by terms of the roll-up agreement.

Valuation Considerations

Although most roll-up IPOs advertise the benefits and synergies the new company hopes to achieve, many of those benefits could have been realized through mechanisms short of consolidation. For example, the individual firms could have entered into reciprocal referral arrangements or consolidated their accounting operations without a formal merger. Thus, the driving force in a roll-up is not synergies but the value that may be created by transition from private, undiversified ownership to public ownership. Detracting from this is any loss of operational efficiency that may result from conversion of entrepreneurs to employees of a larger corporation.

The concept of a roll-up is not new. Companies in the 1960s and early 1970s are sometimes criticized in finance textbooks for having played a "price/earnings multiple game." A public company with a high P/E ratio would acquire smaller private companies in the same industry, paying a substantially lower price relative to earnings. The hope was that the earnings of the targets would be capitalized by the market at the P/E ratio of the acquirer. The criticism is that it should not be possible to create value by simply transferring earnings from one company to another. Thus, the P/E multiple of the consolidated firm should be a weighted average of the individual firm P/E multiples. The criticism is correct when both firms are already public; combining their earnings, without creating synergies, does not create value. If the target is private, however, then value is created by enabling the owner to achieve diversification.

15.6 The Harvesting Decision

Going public is generally perceived to be the harvesting alternative that yields the highest valuation. Whether to operate as a publicly or privately owned firm, however, is a multifaceted decision. Because public ownership involves publicly traded shares, the owners have more liquidity. Also, public market investors can diversify easily; hence market value depends on systematic risk. The gain associated with transferring ownership to diversified investors argues in favor of harvesting by going public or merging with a public firm. However, public ownership also involves more public scrutiny and restrictions on corporate governance.

Decisions regarding how and when to harvest are complex. Not only does the menu of choices include alternatives that are substantially different from each other and difficult to compare, but harvest timing also involves a choice between exercising an option or waiting. In the following discussion, we review factors that bear on the decision.

Company Size

Public offering is more cost effective for large firms than for small ones. Many of the costs are fixed, and some of the benefits of being public depend on the firm's ability to achieve a reasonable volume of trading activity in the market. A small firm can achieve liquidity for its investors if it is acquired by a public company. Acquisitions also involve significant fixed costs, but private contracting provides more ways to limit the costs. The parties can, for example, structure the transaction so that the seller's return depends on how the acquired firm performs after the acquisition. This is more difficult to achieve for a public sale of equity. However, because the entrepreneur usually cannot begin selling her shares until a few months after the offering, aftermarket performance can affect the return.

The Value of a Public Market for the Shares

Going public subjects a firm to periodic reporting requirements and the need to commit resources to maintaining relations with investors. The public market, however, provides a continuous measure of value that facilitates the firm's use of its shares as a medium of exchange. A public market for the stock also facilitates using shares for incentive compensation and means that the company's managers are subject to the discipline of the market.

Another benefit of going public is that the process may raise consumer and investor awareness of the company's products and enhance the company's image. Public offering can also have strategic significance. Because public offering is expensive and because the offering prospectus commits the firm to a fairly specific course of action, going public is a way to credibly commit the firm. The commitment can be attractive to customers and suppliers and can discourage rivals.

Going public also gives investors flexibility over harvest timing. In a private transaction, the ownership interests of the entrepreneur and early investors are bought out. If the company is public, the entrepreneur can sell shares according to a schedule that potentially is more attractive. Gradual sale of shares is both an opportunity and a necessity. In some cases, even if the entrepreneur would like to liquidate quickly, going public can delay liquidation because of lockup provisions and regulatory restrictions on selling.

Synergies

An important benefit of going public is the transition from private, underdiversified ownership to public ownership. Opportunities to create additional value by selling to a company that can make complementary use of the firm's resources and capabilities is not directly achievable via public offering. Generally, if synergistic benefits are significant, the harvesting choice is likely to be influenced by the owner's ability to capture as much of the gain as possible. A private firm that should be merged with an existing public firm might, for example, go public as a way of establishing a public market value as a floor on the acquisition price.

Track Record and Ease of Valuation

Going public at a reasonable valuation is not always possible. The most important factor affecting a venture's ability to go public is its record of accomplishment at the time of the offering. A venture with a solid operating history of steady revenue and earnings growth and predictable future growth is relatively easy for public market investors to evaluate. A less well established venture that is at an early stage of development is hard for investors to value. For such a venture, small deviations from expected performance and small changes in the market or in competitive conditions can trigger precipitous changes in market value. The more difficult it is for public market investors to evaluate a company and the more they must rely on the investment banker's reputation rather than specific information, the stronger is the case for private sale. In a private transaction, commercially sensitive information can be shared and the buyer may be particularly well suited to evaluate the company.

Timing

An IPO cannot be completed quickly. From the time that a venture decides on public offering until the offering occurs, market conditions can change dramatically and drastically affect the market values of early-stage companies. Particularly for going public, timing is a factor that is closely related to track record. During expansionary periods, it is relatively easy to convince investors of a venture's need to raise capital. However, if market values have declined and other firms have postponed or canceled their offerings, a company that proceeds with an offering is regarded with skepticism by investors. During such periods, it may be advantageous to wait, or if waiting is not possible, a private market transaction may be warranted. The venture should be better able to communicate the reasons for its decision to a private acquirer than to the market at large and to better structure the deal.

Ownership and Control

The various harvesting alternatives have different implications for control. In an acquisition (except for reverse merger), the entrepreneur is almost certain to lose control to the acquirer. In a public sale, the entrepreneur may be able to maintain control, even if the entrepreneur's investment is significantly reduced. Dual class ownership, where the entrepreneur's shares have superior voting rights, is increasingly common. However, public firms are subject to the Sarbanes-Oxley Act of 2002, which sets standards related to company management and governance and for the accounting firms that provide audits of public companies.

Even if public market investors have very limited control, they can exert influence over the venture by making some courses of action more expensive and time consuming than they otherwise would be. Private ownership by the entrepreneur is a way to preserve a high level of control with minimum outside intervention, but it comes at the cost of continuing underdiversification.

Taxes

For some investors, such as pension funds, tax considerations have little influence on the choice of harvesting alternatives. For the entrepreneur, however, the tax implications of harvesting are likely to be important. It is difficult to generalize about the tax advantages of the alternatives. An ESOP can yield a tax deferral, but whether it does so depends on a variety of factors that are beyond the scope of this book. Private sale in an acquisition may or may not generate an immediate tax obligation. Going public provides the entrepreneur with a tax-timing option, inasmuch as shares can be sold during periods when the tax consequences would be most favorable for the entrepreneur.

Transactions Costs

Generally, private market transactions are less costly and have lower fixed-cost components than going public. Consequently, transactions costs and firm size are related. Small firms are more likely to remain private or be harvested in a private transaction than are large firms. The main exception is that if small firms can be consolidated without significant loss of operational efficiency, then a public offering may be possible.

15.7 Venture Capital Harvesting and the "Internet Bubble"

Figure 15.4 shows daily closing values of the Morgan Stanley High-Tech Stock Index over the years from 1995 through 2005. From the end of

FIGURE **15.4**
Morgan Stanley High-Technology Stock Index, 1995–2005

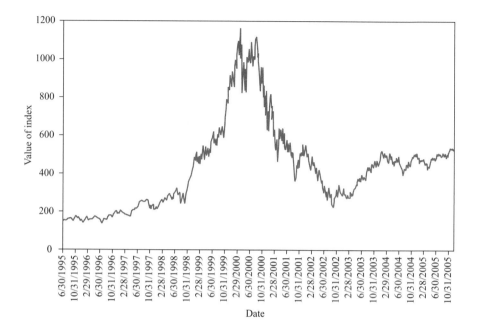

1997 through mid-March 2000, the value of the index increased by a factor of more than four. By mid-April 2002, the index had lost about two-thirds of its value. Over this period, broader indexes, such as the S&P 500 and the NASDAQ Index, followed a similar but less severe pattern.[40] This rise in market valuations, followed by a precipitous decline, has been referred to as the "Internet bubble," suggesting that market valuations during the period were irrationally exuberant.

In earlier chapters, we have discussed how the booming market of the late 1990s affected new capital commitments of VC and the market for new venture financing. Here we address two further questions. First, can we necessarily infer from a pattern such as the one in Figure 15.4 that stock market valuations are driven by irrationality? Second, what are the implications of stock market declines for harvesting investments in new ventures?

Investor Irrationality

At the pinnacle of the dot-com boom, market valuations of high-technology firms were extremely high compared with conventional indicators of value. Microsoft, the firm with the highest market capitalization of any firm, was selling for 23 times annual sales and $17,000 per employee, whereas General Electric, with the second-highest market capitalization, was selling for only 4 times annual sales and $1,300 per employee. Amazon.com, with only 2,000 employees (compared to 293,000 at General Electric), was not profitable yet was selling for 37 times annual sales and $11,000 per employee.

Could any forecast of performance based on rational economic theory justify such extreme valuations? Perhaps the answer is yes. Based on the disparate multiples above, you might think selling Amazon and Microsoft and buying GE would be a good idea. But in the subsequent 10 years (through the end of 2009), GE's stock price declined by about 70 percent, Microsoft's declined by about 12 percent, and Amazon's increased by about 85 percent. Apparently, the April 2000 optimism about Amazon was not entirely unwarranted. In early 2000, the high valuations of Internet businesses were based on a belief that the Internet would displace conventional means of marketing and distributing. People were referring to that transformation as "from bricks to clicks," implying that many of the marketing- and distribution-related tangible assets of established businesses were becoming liabilities and that new economy businesses that were not saddled with large investments in bricks and mortar might be the winners in the economic transformation.

That view, even today, is not necessarily wrong and certainly helps to explain why Amazon has done so well compared to its direct competitors in book sales such as Borders and Barnes & Noble. In fact, the gyrations in market valuations can be rationalized by the long-standing theory that market value is the present value of expected future cash flows, but where investors' assessments were changing dramatically as to the probability that commercial and retail markets would be transformed to Internet-based models. If the Internet were to quickly replace traditional marketing and distribution, companies like Amazon.com, which were building market share and had developed effective websites, could conceivably become very profitable. If the Internet transformation was slower than expected or if the Internet became simply another path to consumers, then early movers (with only websites) could easily fail.

The "Internet bubble" is only the latest of a number of historical episodes in which capital markets have been confronted with the potential for major transformations. The computer-hard-drive boom, the telecommunications boom, and the biotechnology boom are other recent examples where new technologies with the potential to transform the economy in major ways led to the rise of market prices in the face of potential transformation and their subsequent decline when that transformation either did not take place or happened more slowly or less dramatically than anticipated.

Only if investors were chronically overoptimistic could we conclude that market valuations are irrational; however, there are not enough market experiments on which to base such a definitive conclusion. In each of these periods, the stocks of the innovator companies are essentially call options on the transformational technology. Just as with other options, when the transformation does not materialize or is slow to materialize, the riskiest stocks are likely to end up "out of the money" and worthless. These same stocks, however, are the ones that would produce the greatest returns if the transformation did materialize. Hence, more often than not, we should expect to see stock-price patterns that look like the "Internet bubble," but occasionally we should find that even the high valuations prove to be much too conservative.

Economic transformation is always a matter of degree. Averaged over the five years from late 1997 to late 2002, stocks such as Qualcomm, Amazon, Dell, Apple, and Microsoft generated positive returns, while some notable blue-chip stocks, including Campbell Soup, Ford, Eastman Kodak, Boeing, and Gillette, posted striking losses. This evidence suggests that some gains in the tech sector were legitimate and created long-term value for investors.

In one fundamental way, it does appear that valuations during the "Internet bubble" were influenced by irrationality. During the period, many VC-backed companies went public at very early stages, including prerevenue. Those IPOs, which enabled VC investors to harvest quickly, were driven by the desire of public market investors to participate in VC investing related to the Internet and did not make much sense at a fundamental level. Underwriters may have anticipated this sentiment, as the IPOs during this period tended to be substantially underpriced relative to their first aftermarket values.[41]

Public market investment in very early stage ventures is difficult to justify on economic grounds. Normally, such firms need financing from sources that can stage financial commitments and respond quickly and correctly to new developments. The public equity market lacks the needed flexibility and access to private information about company successes or failures. As we discussed in Chapter 14, for an early-stage company, going public can reduce flexibility and contribute to ultimate failure. It appears from the low level of IPO activity in recent years that public market investors may now have learned this lesson.

Public Market Valuation and Harvesting Choices

Figure 15.5 shows that IPO activity by VC-backed firms correlates with market valuations. Activity is high when market valuations are high and have been rising. Activity declines when market values decline. Following the market crash beginning in 2007, VC-backed IPO activity

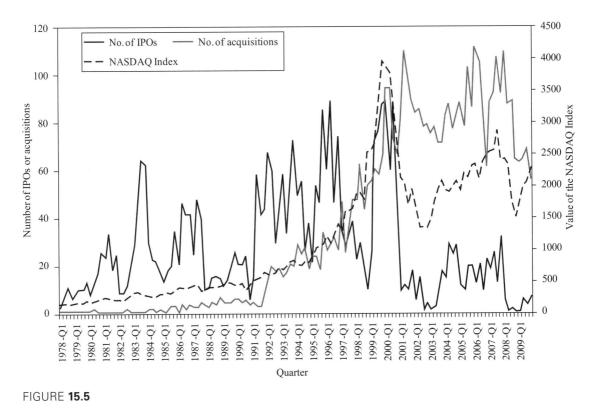

FIGURE **15.5**
Numbers of exits of venture-backed firms via IPO and merger and the NASDAQ Index by quarter (1978–2009)
SOURCE: Ball, Chiu, and Smith (2010).

declined to zero and remained at or near zero for several quarters. Systematic fluctuations in IPO activity may be another indication of irrationality in market valuations. If market values are a random walk, why should IPO activity decline when valuations decline? To a degree, systematic changes in IPO activity can be traced to the backward-looking valuation practice of investment banks and the way in which issuers and underwriters respond to changes in market prices after the IPO filing range has been published. Generally, if market values rise substantially after the preliminary prospectus is issued, the IPO goes forward but with an upward adjustment of the offer price. However, if market values decline, IPOs tend to be canceled. This asymmetric practice means that IPO activity will tend to increase when market values rise and decrease when market values fall. When market value changes correspond to positive or negative economic news or changes in real interest rates, the asymmetry may imply that the issuing firm's need for capital changes depending on the state of the economy. If market values decline, perhaps the opportunities underlying the firm's need to raise capital have also declined in value, leading to cancellation of the IPO.

What about firms, though, that go public mainly to enable investors to exit? It is apparent from Figure 10.2 that marketwide average P/E ratios do not follow a random pattern; rather, P/E ratios appear to be mean reverting. If so, investors who are not under pressure to exit and believe company earnings are not sensitive to economywide changes may be better off trying to time IPOs to occur when P/E ratios are high.

As we discussed earlier, if declining market values cause firms not to issue, then a firm that goes forward with an IPO is likely to be viewed with skepticism by investors. What does this imply for firms with good prospects for success that want to facilitate harvesting? The answer is that IPO is only one exit strategy available to investors. Merger and acquisition (M&A) is another. In fact, in recent years, despite the decline in the IPO market, M&A has remained a popular liquidation strategy. Figure 15.5 also shows M&A exits by year by VC-backed firms. The advantage of M&A, when IPO activity is low, is that a single investor may be better able to understand the basis for the seller's optimism about the firm or may be able to agree to a contract, such as an earn-out, that ties the seller's return to actual performance. Even during periods of high IPO activity, M&A activity has also been high. Over the time span from 2000 through 2009, mergers outnumbered IPOs in all but three quarters.

What are the determinants of the choice to use IPO versus merger as an exit strategy? A recent large-scale study of exit choices for 7,082 US venture-capital-backed private companies over the 29-year period from 1978 through 2006 addresses this question.[42] The findings show that IPOs are selected during periods when marketwide demand for growth capital is high, adverse selection costs of equity issues are low, and the value of protecting private information is low. The evidence also shows that the fixed costs for IPOs are higher than for acquisition. There is little support for the hypothesis that IPO issuers can "time the market" to go public when the market is overheated.[43]

15.8 Summary

Harvesting is an essential aspect of entrepreneurial finance. Harvesting strategies are considered when investment decisions are made and are factored into the valuation of financial claims and often provided for explicitly in deal structures.

Frequently, the business plan of a new venture envisions an IPO within a few years after the first significant outside investment; but going public is only one of several alternatives. For many kinds of ventures, it is an unlikely possibility. Other alternatives include private acquisition; management buyout; creation of an ESOP to provide liquidity to a venture where harvesting of the entire investment is not an objective; and indirect approaches to public offering, such as reverse merger and roll-up IPO. The costs and benefits of the alternatives differ markedly. Going public requires an IPO, which is usually expensive as a percentage of proceeds received. Harvesting by going public, however, normally involves selling a small percentage of the venture's outstanding shares; therefore IPO costs can be a small percentage of firm value. Furthermore, existing investors in the venture normally do not sell significant fractions of their shareholdings during the IPO. The actual cost of harvesting by going public depends on the process that is used by investors to sell their shares. Developing a public market for company shares has some distinct benefits that can influence the choice of harvesting alternatives.

Private acquisitions also can be expensive. However, acquisition may enable the selling shareholders to realize some of the gains arising from synergies with the acquirer. MBOs, ESOPs, and roll-ups all have distinct advantages and disadvantages. The correct choice in any instance depends on factors such as transactions costs, firm size, track record, timing, tax implications, and regulatory oversight.

REVIEW QUESTIONS

1. Identify at least four methods by which investors in a new venture can harvest their investment in a new venture. Describe the costs and benefits of each, and provide a framework for how you would analyze the choice by identifying the key factors you would consider when evaluating which method of harvesting to use.

2. What services does an underwriter provide for a company that employs the underwriter to facilitate going public? What factors influence an issuing firm's choice of underwriter?

3. Describe the process of going public using an IPO, starting with underwriter selection and proceeding through the various stages that lead to determination of an issue price.

4. From the perspective of the entrepreneur, what are the pros and cons of an IPO as opposed to private sale of the venture to a public company in exchange for stock or cash?

5. Discuss the reasons why periodic valuation is important when ownership of a private company is transferred to employees via an ESOP. What factors do you think would lead an entrepreneur (whose shares an ESOP is purchasing) to favor a leveraged ESOP over an unleveraged ESOP?

6. Explain what underpricing is and review the various explanations for why it might occur. How does underpricing figure into the cost of going public?

7. How does a firm commitment offering differ from a best-efforts offering? A rights offering? How does an OpenIPO differ from a traditional bookbuilt IPO?

8. How does Rule 144 restrict the ability of shareholders to liquidate their positions? Why might such restrictions be important to VC investors? Describe conceptually how you would attempt to value a venture in a private transaction. What discount would you apply for illiquidity?

9. How do the VC's objectives influence the harvesting decision of the entrepreneur?

10. Explain why harvesting is an important consideration when the initial decision to invest in a venture is made. How might harvesting be factored into the deal structure and the valuation? Provide examples.

Notes

1. In this case, the IPO combines a primary market transaction to raise capital for the firm and a secondary offering by existing investors.

2. SEC Rule 144 governs the rates at which such sales can occur in the United States.

3. Private transactions of unregistered shares in the United States are subject to SEC Rule 144A.

4. Smith (1992) discusses the history of thought related to underwriting.

5. From the narrow perspective of a single transaction, integration of the investment banker into VC seems to create a conflict of interest, as the banker might be motivated to overprice offerings where it also is a VC investor. Gompers and Lerner (1999) examine this possibility but find no evidence that such issues are priced differently from others. Apparently, the investment banker's interest in maintaining reputation is sufficient to overcome the concern.

6. Certain regulated firms in the United States are sometimes required by state or federal laws to use competitive bidding. Competitive bidding is rarely used when it is not required and then only for low-risk debt issues.

7. Smith (1987) analyzes the relative costs of competitive and negotiated underwriting of public utility debt issues.

8. Due diligence for IPOs in the United States normally takes several weeks. The final stage occurs just before the offering. This final "take-down" due diligence is usually a request by the underwriter, asking that the issuer disclose any new information that could materially affect value. At this stage, the venture's accounting firm issues a "cold comfort letter," stating whether it is aware of any material changes in the business. Such information could affect pricing.

9. The concern is that if, for any reason, the forecast is not achieved, investors may claim that they relied on the forecasts and may seek compensation for any resulting loss. Legislative changes in 1995 supported by the SEC are intended to encourage issuers to make fuller disclosure and to include "forward looking statements" or forecasts in the prospectus. For the most part, the new legislation has only been used to protect issuers and underwriters against liability for inadvertently making such statements. See the Private Securities Litigation Reform Act of 1995.

10. The price formation process varies across countries. In Japan, the pricing of JASDAQ IPOs is more transparent than in the United States. The transparency facilitates analysis of important issues in the IPO literature, such as why offer prices only partially adjust to public information and adjust more fully to negative information and why adjustments are related to initial returns once the issue is public. Evidence from Kutsuna, Smith, and Smith (2009) indicates that early price information conveys the underwriter's commitment to compensate investors for acquiring and/or disclosing information. Offer prices reflect pre-IPO market values of public companies and implicit agreements between underwriters and issuers that originate well before the offering.

11. The actual offering may be priced inside the filing range or above or below it. Hanley (1993) documents that offer prices only partially adjust for differences between anticipated demand (as reflected by the filing range) and actual demand. In Japan, underadjustment of offer prices is substantially reversed in the aftermarket during the first year (see Kutsuna, Smith, and Smith [2009]).

12. Studies of IPOs in other countries also generally find evidence of underpricing.

13. Booth and Smith (1986) formally develop the hypothesis that investment bankers certify the prices of the issues they underwrite.

14. Benveniste and Spindt (1989) make a similar argument. Beatty and Ritter (1986) provide evidence that underwriters who frequently underprice too much or too little tend to lose market share. Hansen and Torregrosa (1992) contend that, in addition to certification, the underwriter monitors the firms it brings public.

15. See Tinic (1988).

16. This finding is reported by Barry et al. (1990). Also see Brav and Gompers (2003), who find that lockup provisions serve as a commitment device to alleviate moral hazard problems. Arthurs et al. (2009) observe that a longer lockup period can provide certification and may substitute for VC and/ or prestigious underwriter backing.

17. See Megginson and Weiss (1991).

18. For additional evidence on underpricing, see Ritter (1987) and Ljungqvist (2006).

19. Choe, Masulis, and Nanda (1993) find that the percentage underpricing is lower during periods of economic expansion. They interpret the finding as evidence that expected costs of adverse selection are lower when the economy is growing. During such periods, firms are more likely to be motivated to issue because of the need to raise capital for opportunities. Loughran and Ritter (2004) show how the levels of underpricing have changed over time and conclude that the reasons for the underpricing vary depending on the environment.

20. Ruud (1993) offers an alternative view. She notes that market-value declines at the time of the IPO are not observable, owing to the market-stabilization activities of the underwriter. By extending the window over which returns are studied, she finds that overpricing takes longer to be reflected in stock prices, whereas underpricing is observable immediately. Benveniste, Busaba, and Wilhelm (1996), on the other hand, point out that price stabilization is one way the underwriter can bond (guarantee) the valuation.

21. See Rock (1986).

22. The literature related to this view is extensive, beginning with Benveniste and Spindt (1989). For more recent treatments that include reviews of the literature, see Sherman (2000) and Kerins, Kutsuna, and Smith (2007).

23. This does not include costs investors would incur by selling shares in the secondary market or in a seasoned offering. Such costs are considerably smaller than the cost of an IPO.

24. Sometimes underwriters also receive warrant compensation. Reasons for using warrants are complex. Barry, Muscarella, and Vetsuypens (1991) contend that warrants enable underwriters to circumvent legal limitations on compensation. Dunbar (1995) suggests that issuers select between warrant and cash compensation to minimize issue cost. Ng and Smith (1996) also argue for issue cost reductions and suggest that warrant compensation is a way in which underwriters who lack established reputations can certify new issues. They find empirical support for all three reasons.

25. Consistent with this view, Bower (1989) suggests that high-quality firms (undervalued firms) select firm commitment, but low-quality firms (overvalued firms) select best efforts because the effective cost of certification is too great.

Booth, J. R., and R. L. Smith. 1986. "Capital Raising, Underwriting, and the Certification Hypothesis." *Journal of Financial Economics* 15:261–81.

Bower, N. L. 1989. "Firm Value and the Choice of Offering Method in Initial Public Offerings." *Journal of Finance* 44:647–62.

Brav, A., and P. Gompers. 2003. "The Role of Lockups in Initial Public Offerings." *Review of Financial Studies* 1 6:1–29.

Carter, R., and S. Manaster. 1990. "Initial Public Offerings and Underwriter Reputation." *Journal of Finance* 45:1045–67.

Choe, H., R. W. Masulis, and V. Nanda. 1993. "Common Stock Offerings across the Business Cycle." *Journal of Empirical Finance* 1 (1993): 3–31.

Cronqvist, H., and M. Nilsson. 2005. "The Choice between Rights Offerings and Private Equity Placements." *Journal of Financial Economics* 78: 375–407.

Cumming, Douglas. 2008. "Contracts and Exits in Venture Capital Finance." *Review of Financial Studies* 2 1:1947–82.

Dunbar, C. G. 1995. "The Use of Warrants as Underwriter Compensation in Initial Public Offerings." *Journal of Financial Economics* 38:59–78.

Fernando, C., V. Gatchev, and P. Spindt. 2005. "Wanna Dance? How Firms and Underwrtiers Choose Each Other." *Journal of Finance* 6 0:2437–69.

Gompers, P. 1996. "Grandstanding in the Venture Capital Industry." *Journal of Financial Economics* 42:133–56.

Gompers, P., and J. Lerner. 1999. "Conflict of Interest in the Issuance of Public Securities: Evidence from Venture Capital." *Journal of Law and Economics* 42:1–28.

Hanley, K. W. 1993. "The Underpricing of Initial Public Offerings and the Partial Adjustment Phenomenon." *Journal of Financial Economics* 34:231–50.

Hansen, R. S. 1988. "The Demise of the Rights Issue." *Review of Financial Studies* 1:289–301.

Hansen, R. S., and P. Torregrosa. 1992. "Underwriter Compensation and Corporate Monitoring." *Journal of Finance* 47:1537–55.

Hellmann, T. 2006. "IPOs, Acquisitions and the Use of Convertible Securities in Venture Capital." *Journal of Financial Economics* 8 1:649–79.

Hertzel, M. G., and R. L. Smith. 1993. "Market Discounts and Shareholder Gains for Placing Equity Privately." *Journal of Finance* 48:459–85.

Jovanovic, B., and B. Szentes. 2007. "IPO Underpricing: Auction vs. Book Building." Working paper, New York University.

Kerins, F., K. Kutsuna, and R. Smith. 2007. "Why Are IPOs Underpriced? Evidence from Japan's Hybrid Auction-Method Offerings." *Journal of Financial Economics* 8 5:637–66.

Kutsuna, K., J. K. Smith, and R. L. Smith. 2009. "Public Information, IPO Price Formation, and Long-Run Returns: Japanese Evidence." *Journal of Finance* 6 4:505–46.

Kutsuna, K., and R. L. Smith. 2004. "Why Does Book Building Drive Out Auction Methods of IPO Issuance? Evidence from Japan." *Review of Financial Studies* 17:1129–66.

Lin, T., and R. L. Smith. 1998. "Insider Reputation and Selling Decisions: The Unwinding of Venture Capital Investments during Equity IPOs." *Journal of Corporate Finance* 4:241–63.

Ljungqvist, A. 2006. "IPO Underpricing." In *Handbook of Corporate Finance: Empirical Corporate Finance*, ed. B. E. Eckbo, vol. 1, ch. 7. Amsterdam: Elsevier/North Holland.

Ljungqvist, A., and W. J. Wilhelm. 2003. "IPO Pricing in the Dot-Com Bubble." *Journal of Finance* 5 8:723–52.

Loughran, T., and J. R. Ritter. 2004. "Why Has IPO Underpricing Changed over Time?" *Financial Management* (Autumn): 1–38.

Lowry, M. 2003. "Why Does IPO Volume Fluctuate So Much?" *Journal of Financial Economics* 6 7:3–40.

Megginson, W., and K. Weiss. 1991. "Venture Capitalist Certification in Initial Public Offerings." *Journal of Finance* 46:879–903.

Mikkelson, W. H., and M. H. Partch. 1985. "Stock Price Effects and Costs of Secondary Distributions." *Journal of Financial Economics* 14:165–94.

Ng, C. K., and R. L. Smith. 1996. "Determinants of Contract Choice: The Use of Warrants to Compensate Underwriters of Seasoned Equity Offerings." *Journal of Finance* 51:363–83.

Ofek, E., and M. Richardson. 2003. "DotCom Mania: The Rise and Fall of Internet Stock Prices." *Journal of Finance* 58:1113–38.

Ritter, J. R. 1987. "The Costs of Going Public." *Journal of Financial Economics* 19:269–81.

Rock, K. 1986. "Why New Issues Are Underpriced." *Journal of Financial Economics* 15:187–212.

Ruud, J. S. 1993. "Underwriter Price Support and the IPO Underpricing Puzzle." *Journal of Financial Economics* 34:135–51.

Sherman, A. 1992. "The Pricing of Best Efforts New Issues." *Journal of Finance* 42:781–90.

———. 2000. "IPOs and Long Term Relationships: An Advantage of Book Building." *Review of Financial Studies* 13:697–714.

Silber, W. L. 1991. "Discounts on Restricted Stock: The Impact of Illiquidity on Stock Prices." *Financial Analysts Journal* 47:60–64.

Smith, C. W. 1977. "Alternative Methods of Capital Raising: Rights versus Underwritten Offerings." *Journal of Financial Economics* 5:273–307.

———. 1986. "Investment Banking and the Capital Acquisition Process." *Journal of Financial Economics* 15:3–29.

Smith, R. L. 1987. "The Choice of Issuance Procedure and the Cost of Competitive and Negotiated Underwriting: An Examination of the Impact of Rule 50." *Journal of Finance* 42:703–20.

————. 1992. "Underwriting of New Issues." In *The New Palgrave Dictionary of Money and Finance*, ed. P. Newman, M. Milgate, and J. Eatwell, 722–24. New York: Macmillan.

Tinic, S. 1988. "Anatomy of Initial Public Offerings of Common Stock." *Journal of Finance* 43:789–822.

Weston, J. F., K. S. Chung, and J. A. Siu. 1998. *Takeovers, Restructuring, and Corporate Governance*. Upper Saddle River, NJ: Pearson/Prentice-Hall.

Wruck, K. H. 1989. "Equity Ownership Concentration and Firm Value: Evidence from Private Equity Financings." *Journal of Financial Economics* 23:3–28.

CHAPTER 16

THE FUTURE OF ENTREPRENEURIAL FINANCE: A GLOBAL PERSPECTIVE

Adaptive efficiency . . . is concerned with the kinds of rules that shape the way an economy evolves through time. It is also concerned with the willingness of society to acquire knowledge and learning, to induce innovation, to undertake risk and creative activity of all sorts, as well as to resolve problems and bottlenecks of the society through time.

Douglas C. North, *Institutions, Institutional Change, and Economic Performance*

In this final chapter, we highlight the essential concepts and tools that have emerged from the study of entrepreneurial finance. We also identify areas where more data and research would provide clearer understanding of unresolved issues. We then study public policy and how it can impact entrepreneurial activity. We consider such questions as: Why has entrepreneurship thrived in some countries and regions of the world and not in others? Can other countries and other regions be effective in imitating the success formula? We conclude with a discussion of the future of entrepreneurial finance.

As a field of study, entrepreneurial finance builds on the concepts and methodology of finance and economics. In particular, we have stressed principles of finance, investments, valuation, and contracts, all in the context of new ventures. The concepts and methodology are helpful not only to prospective entrepreneurs but also to those who supply funds to entrepreneurs—angel investors, VCs, lenders, employees, friends of the entrepreneur, trading partners, universities, and government agencies.

The study of entrepreneurial finance is not limited to new ventures or even to small or privately owned businesses. A great deal of entrepreneurial activity is carried out by corporations, social entrepreneurs, and faculty members working in universities. We have discussed how financing problems vary depending on the source of financing and how they vary over the life of the venture. Thus, we address the financial aspects of a venture up to the point where the teachings of corporate finance can be applied directly.

In much of our analysis, we stress the importance of incentive and information problems that face participants in the market for entrepreneurial finance. Efforts to address these problems give rise to key features of the market, including staging of investments, terms of financial contracts, the role of reputation, trade practices, and valuation approaches. Entrepreneurs and investors who understand the financial determinants of new venture organizational and contractual structure, including the incentive and information structure, can more effectively design their own contracts to reflect deal-specific issues and to increase the value of an opportunity.

16.1 Completing the Circle

In the Preface to the book, we identified eight fundamental differences between entrepreneurial finance and corporate finance. We now return to that list for a final review.

Entrepreneurial Investment and Financing Decisions Are Interdependent

The decisions entrepreneurs and investors make concerning allocation of outside and inside ownership have important implications for the venture and for the values of its financial claims. You now have the tools to evaluate their interdependence and design financial contracts that deal with it effectively.

In corporate finance, we usually assume that a firm makes its investment decisions without regard to choice of financing. This is strictly justified only if corporate investors care only about nondiversifiable risk. Although the assumption is a reasonable approximation for a publicly held corporation, it is not appropriate for a new venture.

An entrepreneur is often compelled to choose between being underdiversified or not pursuing the venture. Underdiversification exposes the entrepreneur to risk that is specific to the venture. Opportunity-cost reasoning implies that an entrepreneur who must either be underdiversified or forgo the venture should require compensation for bearing venture-specific risk. As well-diversified investors do not care about venture-specific risk, the entrepreneur's required rate of return should be higher than that of an investor who can diversify.

When an entrepreneur participates in a venture along with an investor who can diversify, the parties place different values on the same financial claims, even if they agree about the expected cash flows and risk. The diversified investor values the claims more highly. It follows that the value of an opportunity depends on how the financial claims allocate risk and expected return. All else equal, allocating more non-market risk to diversified investors increases the value of an opportunity. Thus, effective use of financial contracts to allocate risk can enhance project value and even change negative-NPV opportunities into positive-NPV opportunities.

Investment Value Depends on the Entrepreneur's Ability to Diversify

For the entrepreneur, ability to diversify increases the value of a new venture opportunity. You have the tools to estimate the entrepreneur's wealth and to value an opportunity in light of the entrepreneur's diversification.

Even if no investor is involved, the entrepreneur's ability to diversify affects value. The entrepreneur's required rate of return for investing in a venture depends on the fraction of total wealth the entrepreneur must commit. The larger the fraction that is committed, the higher the entrepreneur's required rate of return.

Total wealth includes more than just financial wealth; it also includes the present value of human capital. Methods illustrated in this book can be used to estimate the entrepreneur's total wealth and the fraction that is invested in a venture. Project value also depends on how the risk of the investment in the venture relates to the risk of the entrepreneur's other investments. You can value an opportunity when the entrepreneur's other wealth is invested in a market index portfolio, another risky investment, or a riskless asset.

Because more wealth enables an entrepreneur to achieve greater diversification, the same venture is more valuable to an entrepreneur who is wealthier. It follows that reducing investment in the venture can also enhance its value to the entrepreneur. Pursuing an opportunity on a smaller scale, bringing in an investor, or finding ways of reducing the duration of the entrepreneur's commitment can reduce the size of the entrepreneur's investment. The methods you have learned allow you to evaluate the effects of such changes on the value of the entrepreneur's interest in the venture.

Investors Supply More than Money to the Ventures in Which They Invest

Active involvement by investors can add value to a venture. Understanding the contributions of active investors enables the entrepreneur to better evaluate financing alternatives.

New ventures raise capital from myriad sources. Some provide only financial capital; others provide both capital and managerial skills. Angel investors and strategic partners are often involved in managerial aspects of the enterprise. VC firms are involved at critical junctures and continuously monitor their investments. Investors such as these seek returns on both their financial and human capital investments. An important theme of the book has been to illustrate how managerial and monitoring efforts affect investment and financing choices and the structure of financial claims.

Investors who are actively involved can add value by changing both expected returns and risk. You can use the tools and techniques you have learned to study how financial sources impact expected return and risk and how different types of investors are likely to affect the values of the parties' financial claims.

Financial Contracts and Other Devices Can Address Information Problems

Information problems present a significant obstacle to raising outside financing. Entrepreneurs are often overly optimistic and presume that their venture ideas will be successful; consequently, investors often severely discount the entrepreneur's projections. The business plan, financial contracting, and devices such as signals, reputation, and certification can help overcome such problems

In the new venture environment, both parties can have trouble credibly communicating their beliefs to each other. The communication difficulties not only impede raising capital but can also result in two types of mistakes: investing in ventures that should be forgone and failing to invest in those that should be pursued.

The parties to a new venture financial contract can use contractual provisions to signal their beliefs to each other. An entrepreneur, for example, can lend credibility to projections that otherwise would seem optimistic by tying ownership interest or other compensation to future attained performance and by using milestones that enable some of the investment to be postponed until some important uncertainty is resolved.

Well-chosen contract provisions help convey the beliefs of the parties. Reducing information asymmetry results in better decisions about when to pursue a venture and when to forgo it. However, contract terms sometimes also shift additional risk to the entrepreneur, a factor that works against the risk-allocation benefits of contracting with a diversified investor. Alternative ways of signaling can be compared and contract structures can be designed that are advantageous for both parties.

An investor's assessment of the value of an opportunity depends on more than the financial contract terms. The business plan can also signal the entrepreneur's capabilities and commitment to the venture. By supporting and documenting the assumptions behind the financial projections in the plan, an entrepreneur can narrow the information gap between the parties. By identifying critical milestones and assessing the financing needs for moving from one to the next, the parties can limit the investor's financial commitment. Doing so enables the entrepreneur to preserve a larger ownership stake in the venture.

An advantage of thinking about information problems in this way is that it focuses attention on how to design contracts that are advantageous to both parties. Dealing with information problems is an ongoing concern. Information asymmetry affects subsequent financing arrangements, even through the harvesting stage. Throughout the process, financial contracting, signaling, certification, and other devices can be used to deal with informational concerns.

New Venture Financial Contracts Can Align Incentives

Understanding the tradeoff between risk allocation and incentive alignment contributes to design of organizational structures and financial contracts that optimally address the tradeoffs. Well-structured contracts anticipate and provide for incentive conflicts that may arise as the venture progresses.

The direct effect of transferring risk to a diversified investor is to increase the value of the opportunity. However, risk allocation also affects incentives. An entrepreneur whose reward is not tied sufficiently to success may not be motivated to work toward that success. Additionally, the incentives of investors can sometimes be in conflict with the entrepreneur's interests. A creditor, for example, may emphasize safety, even to the detriment of overall value. Providers of financing sometimes have options to increase the total amount of financing or to call for repayment. They often have the option to force a sale of the venture or a public offering and may have the option to terminate the entrepreneur.

Real Options Are an Important Source of Value for New Ventures

Decision trees and game trees are particularly useful for describing the real options that are embedded in new ventures. Simulation, scenario analysis, and other approaches are useful for assessing the uncertainties that are pervasive in entrepreneurial ventures and for evaluating the real options embedded in alternative organizational structures, financial contracts, and strategic choices.

In many settings, investment opportunities are treated as one-time decisions. The decision is made at the beginning, as if there were no opportunity to abandon the project, expand it, or change direction. This approach, however, does not reflect the nature of new venture opportunities that can be structured as portfolios of real options. The real-option portfolios provide opportunities to expand the venture, abandon it, and change direction, among others. Existing investors may also have options to contribute additional funds in exchange for additional ownership, terminate the entrepreneur, and make various other choices.

The real-option structures of new ventures are complex, and the options are interdependent. Exercising one option can preclude exercising others or change the values of others. In addition, the conditions that support using standard option pricing model approaches to valuation are not satisfied.

Because a venture is a portfolio of real options, riskiness can change dramatically over time. As the venture progresses from one milestone to the next, risk is likely to decline. A decision tree is useful for modeling the real-option structure of a venture. Financial modeling and forecasting can be used to project the cash flows, assess uncertainty, and value complex financial claims under different assumptions about exercising or abandoning the options.

Harvesting Is Critical to the Investment Decision

Understanding the costs and benefits of harvesting alternatives is key to maximizing the value of the investment decision for the entrepreneur and for investors.

The analysis of new venture harvesting contrasts sharply with corporate investment decisions, where capital market investors are not specifically concerned about how the corporation will harvest its investments. In contrast, the parties to a venture may have different interests and incentives when it comes to harvesting. Solutions can be designed, such as formation of an ESOP, which enable each party to pursue his or her own objectives.

We have reviewed the main harvesting alternatives that are available to a venture and the primary factors that influence the choice. We have reviewed evidence on the costs of various harvesting methods, including IPO and private acquisition.

An IPO is only the first step in harvesting an investment in a venture that has gone public. The IPO establishes the public market for the venture's securities, the market in which investors will ultimately sell their ownership interests.

The investment decision depends on making assumptions about likely harvest value. This harvest value can be incorporated into the valuation at the time when the investment decision is made. Doing so helps enable the parties to agree on the fraction of equity an investor would need to receive in exchange for making an investment.

Organizational and Financing Choices Can Be Compared Based on Their Effects on Value

Because there is a difference between value to the entrepreneur and value to a well-diversified investor, the ability to evaluate financial claims from both perspectives allows the parties to design financial contracts that allocate value in the optimal way. Financial contract structures can be developed to allocate value in ways that reflect the realities of the market for new venture financing. If the market is very competitive, the entrepreneur can capture most of the value. Conversely, if many similar entrepreneurs are competing for scarce financing or the skills of a few active investors, then investors may capture most of the value.

16.2   Breaking New Ground

Entrepreneurial finance is a new and growing field in financial economics. Recent academic research has focused on providing a better understanding of institutions and practices. Considerably less research focuses on tools for improving decision making and for adding value to new ventures. The underlying motivation of this book is to emphasize the latter type of research by drawing on the fundamentals of financial economic theory to generate applications for the practice of entrepreneurial finance. The following are a few areas in which theoretical and empirical advances have the potential to contribute significantly to our understanding of the field.

How Can Portfolio Theory Best Be Adapted to Evaluate High-Risk Opportunities with Significant Probabilities of Failure?

In the evaluation of new venture opportunities, we have relied on the principle of risk aversion. We have assumed that a mean/variance approach to evaluating return and risk (such as the Capital Asset Pricing Model) is a reasonable representation of how risk aversion maps into value. We demonstrated, however, that the mean/variance framework tends to undervalue opportunities that are highly risky and have long investment horizons. No simple solution to this problem occurs to us, particularly because value to the entrepreneur depends on how risk relates to the entrepreneur's other holdings.

What Is the Opportunity Cost of Capital for High-Risk, Long-Term Investments?

The standard approach to valuing investment opportunities assumes that the investor can leverage the market portfolio to achieve comparable systematic risk. We employ this opportunity-cost concept to value investments in new ventures. For high-risk, long-term projects, however, risk levels can exceed practical limitations on the ability of investors to leverage the market. New research may suggest a better alternative for estimating the opportunity cost.

What Is the Best Way to Value Investment Opportunities Involving Portfolios of Complex and Interdependent Real Options?

We employ decision trees to describe real- and financial-option structures. We use simulation and scenario analysis to describe how uncertainty changes over time and with different organizational, product-market, and financial strategies. We value uncertain cash flows using discount rates that reflect risk aversion. In contrast to standard option pricing approaches, we do not attempt to estimate "risk-neutral probabilities" that can enable cash flows to be valued at the risk-free rate. We have not used valuation approaches based on option pricing theory because the no-arbitrage assumptions that support those approaches are not satisfied for new ventures. Also, new venture option structures are too complex and interdependent to value as if the options were independent. The result of applying the mean/variance assumptions to investment portfolios of real options is unclear. Likewise, we do not use the tracking portfolio approach as a "fix" that could enable use of standard option pricing methods, because commonly used tracking portfolios tend to materially understate risk and therefore the value of the option. More practical and consistent methods of valuing structures of interdependent real options are needed.

What Is the Best Way to Estimate the Uncertain Cash Flows of a New Venture and the Correlation of Those Cash Flows with the Market?

Required rates of return and standard deviations of holding-period returns are determined simultaneously. The risk-adjusted discount rate approach of corporate finance finesses simultaneity by valuing cash flows at discount rates that are inferred from market data. When total risk affects value, however, as it does for the entrepreneur, data on other firms are useful only if both total risk and systematic risk are comparable. We provide some evidence that should make reliance on market data more feasible, although that evidence is from a period that may not be representative. Although data on public companies are readily available, early-stage ventures are likely to be riskier and less diversified.

To avoid both the simultaneity problem and the need to rely on comparable firm data, we have adopted the certainty equivalence approach to value new venture cash flows. The CEQ approach is sensitive to assumptions about the total risk of venture cash flows and the correlation between venture cash flows and the market. Users of this approach would benefit from new data and evidence that could be used in estimating the risk of an investment and its expected cash flows.

What Is the Best Approach for Valuing Multiple-Period Cash Flows for an Underdiversified Investor?

In corporate finance, the present values of cash flows in different periods are additive. This facilitates valuation of investments that generate cash flows in multiple periods. The intertemporal correlations only matter if they are correlated with the market. The discount rate applied to each cash flow accounts for correlation with the market. By contrast, the intertemporal correlation of cash flows does matter for an underdiversified investor. Currently, we have no easy way in which to address the effect of intertemporal correlation on value to an underdiversified investor. We have addressed the problem by simulating the risk and return of a single-period project where risk of the single-period cash flow depends on the time series correlation of cash flows. A tractable and intuitive alternative would be of significant practical value.

What Kinds of Investment Opportunities Are Most Effectively Pursued by Individual Entrepreneurs and What Kinds Are Most Effectively Pursued by Corporations?

Corporations owned by diversified investors have a cost-of-capital advantage over individuals. However, experience shows that large organizations have difficulty managing entrepreneurial ventures. Little is known about how the tradeoff is resolved in individual cases or what types of organizational and incentive-structure changes are more likely to be successful in generating innovations within large corporations. A common concern is that employee researchers will work for the firm until they discover an attractive idea and then leave to pursue the venture individually. Such behavior discourages firms from investing in research. More research on this topic could generate insights regarding the organization of entrepreneurial activity and enhance the ability of corporations to undertake entrepreneurial ventures.[1]

Is VC Firm Success a Result of Persistence or Luck?

There is evidence that VC firms that have funds that do well for the limited partners are more likely than other firms to be successful in their subsequent funds. The correlation of success from one fund to the next seems to suggest that the VC firm has superior skill. An alternative view, however, is that early success is perceived by entrepreneurs and investors as an indication of skill and that entrepreneurs and investors seek out VC firms with positive track records. The result is that the firm has better deal flow and an easier time raising investment capital than do others; so even if the firm has no special skill, it should be expected to do better than others. There is some evidence to suggest that this sorting effect is an important factor in persistence but also some inferential evidence of skill.[2]

There is a related question as to why, if a VC firm is able to produce superior performance, it does not raise its fees and carried interest to the point where the expected return to limited partners of its funds is normal for the industry. The explanation is likely to lie in issues related to reputation formation and maintenance or to the benefits the firm derives from its lower search cost for deals and investors.

How Do Financial Wealth and the Opportunity Cost of Human Capital Affect an Individual's Decision to Undertake a High-Risk Entrepreneurial Venture?

We expect the decision to pursue a venture to be a decreasing function of the fraction of total wealth the entrepreneur must commit. However, we do not know much about how individuals assess the opportunity cost of the time they must devote. Research could generate insights into which types of individuals choose to become entrepreneurs and how variations in the required commitment of human capital affect their decisions.

What Social and Economic Institutions Foster Entrepreneurial Activity and Can Communities Proactively Develop Such Institutions?

Entrepreneurship is thriving in some countries and regions, largely because of institutional environments that encourage individual risk taking and innovation. However, it is not clear that a one-size-fits-all approach to public policy will be successful for countries and regions at different stages of economic growth and with different institutional constraints. Hence, more research on the complex and endogenous relationships among entrepreneurship, economic growth, and public policy is likely to continue to produce benefits for policy makers and others who have an interest in promoting growth and entrepreneurial activity and in understanding the causal relationships.

How Will a Decrease in the Rate of Innovation Affect the Allocation of Resources Devoted to Entrepreneurial Activity?

In the last decade, the rate of technological progress in such areas as the Internet, computer software, medicine, and telecommunications has generated a growing stream of investment opportunities. Many entrepreneurs and investors in these new ventures have become wealthy quickly. Many companies that received early financing have made rapid transitions to the public capital markets.

What will be the effect on institutions such as VC firms and angel investor groups of a decline in the rate of technological progress and a change in industry orientation toward new venture activity? Will the same kinds of institutions function as well if the focus of entrepreneurial activity changes substantially? Can existing institutions efficiently downsize when the flow of investment opportunities slows? Alternatively, will institutions continue to search for opportunities even if expected investment returns are low?

Related questions are how entrepreneurial activity varies with the business cycle and whether public policy that encourages entrepreneurship can be effective in reducing the private and social costs of recession? During a recession, entrepreneurship may increase as individuals without jobs decide to start their own businesses. It is not clear, however, that this type of entrepreneurial activity has a significant potential to generate growth by creating jobs for others. Nevertheless, there are examples of companies that were started during recessions that have had a significant impact on the economy (e.g., CNN, Trader Joe's, FedEx, Hyatt). Untangling the complex relationships between public policy, entrepreneurship, economic growth, and technological change is a challenging and multifaceted research area.

16.3 Public Policy and Entrepreneurial Activity: An International Comparison

Policy makers around the globe have an intense interest in finding ways to facilitate and encourage innovation and entrepreneurial activity. By most accounts, the United States generates more high-growth start-up businesses than any other country in the world. Understanding the causes of this extraordinary amount of entrepreneurial activity may have economic payoffs for other countries. On the other hand, there may be significant cultural, social, and economic costs of policies that are conducive to entrepreneurial activity, including costs of bankruptcy and litigation.

Although entrepreneurial activity can contribute to growth, it can also be symptomatic of a lack of opportunity in conventional areas. Individuals tend to move into entrepreneurship when their opportunity cost is low relative to the value of entrepreneurial effort. Moreover, as pointed out early in the book (see Figure 1.3), entrepreneurship that arises out of necessity is different from entrepreneurship that arises out of new opportunities.

Some countries, such as the United States and the United Kingdom, have been extremely successful at incubating and nurturing high-growth firms. Others have been successful in more limited ways by developing institutions that encourage growth in specific sectors, such as

FIGURE **16.1**

Early-stage entrepreneurial activity and GDP per capita, 2008

SOURCE: Estimates based on data from the Global Entrepreneurship Monitor (GEM) project (2009); available at http://www.gemconsortium.org.

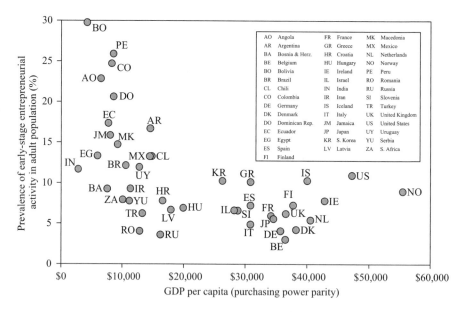

basic manufacturing. Those institutions provide less support for service and R&D-intensive industries.

Figure 16.1 illustrates the worldwide variation in early-stage entrepreneurial involvement. The data are compiled by the Global Entrepreneurship Monitor (GEM) project. It appears from the figure that countries in similar parts of the world, which may share similar institutions and culture, tend to cluster together. The figure also illustrates the importance of understanding the source of entrepreneurial activities. The more agrarian economies exhibit high levels of entrepreneurial involvement, whereas industrialized economies with many large employers and factory jobs exhibit less involvement. In some Latin American and Asian economies, entrepreneurial involvement is high because of limited employment opportunities.

Necessity-based entrepreneurship may be symptomatic of infrastructure problems—it may be high when institutions that support the financing of entrepreneurship are weak, when policies impede business entry and expansion, and when research is not supported and intellectual property rights are not well protected. Hence, policies that focus on finding solutions to these problems can be useful.

In connection with the importance of creating institutions that encourage R&D, Figure 16.2 shows a cross-country comparison of expenditures on R&D as a percent of GDP. Countries such as Denmark, Finland, Korea, and Germany have high levels of R&D (both by business and by nonbusiness entities including universities and governments) and are among the world's wealthier countries in terms of GDP per capita. Countries shown in the figure differ in terms of how research is funded and where it is conducted. The top four all have high percentages of research conducted by businesses (often by large corporations), even though such private research efforts are encouraged by government. Those toward the low end of total expenditures tend to have little private sector research but still report fairly high levels of funding from nonbusiness sources such as governments and universities.

A useful typology for thinking about entrepreneurial activity and economic growth and development derives from Porter's (1990) work on competitive advantage of nations. Porter, Sachs, and McArthur (2002) classify countries into three broad types: factor-driven economies, efficiency-driven economies, and innovation-driven economies. GEM uses these distinctions in its research and includes in the first category countries such as Bolivia, Egypt, India, and Iran, which derive much of their wealth from primary extractive sectors (including mining, agriculture, oil, etc.). In these countries, entrepreneurs find ways to develop industries around natural resources. As the industrial sector develops, institutions emerge to support economies of scale and to increase

FIGURE **16.2**
Gross expenditures on R&D, 2006

SOURCE: OECD in Figures 2009; available at http://www.oecd.org/document/44/0,3343,en_21571361_33915056_34004076_1_1_1_1,00.html.

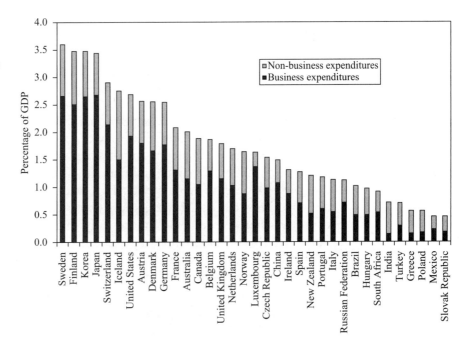

FIGURE **16.3**

Entrepreneurship and the BRIC countries

"BRIC," an acronym coined by Goldman Sachs in its research, refers to the fast-growing developing economies of Brazil, Russia, India, and China. The growth rates of these countries are projected by Goldman to be so rapid that by 2050 the combined economies of the BRIC countries could eclipse the combined economies of what are now the richest countries of the world.* The four BRIC countries currently account for more than a quarter of the world's land area and more than 40 percent of the world's population.

According to a paper published in 2005, Mexico and South Korea are the only other countries comparable to the BRICs in terms of growth potential, but their economies are excluded from the group because they are considered more developed.† As an indicator of their increasing prominence in the world, the leaders of the BRIC countries held their first summit in Russia in 2009 and discussed financial institution reform and how developing countries, such as the nations of BRIC, could be more involved in global affairs.‡

Entrepreneurship in the BRIC countries is key to their success. A recent study provides insights into the differences in approach to entrepreneurship of the two most populous countries of BRIC, India and China. Khanna (2007) documents that entrepreneurship in both countries is thriving, but under very different conditions. He compares their approaches to entrepreneurship in terms of access to capital, freedom, reliability of information, government involvement, and infrastructure. The study surveys the varied landscapes for large-, medium-, and small-scale ventures, ranging from rural health care initiatives to Bollywood. Khanna's findings are summarized below.

- In China, the government is often the entrepreneur and initiative for change and innovation is often top-down. In contrast, in India, the government is not nearly as prominent compared to the pri-

---

*   Goldman Sachs, Global Economics Paper No. 99 (2003).
†   Goldman Sachs, Global Economics Paper No. 134 (2005). When Mexico and South Korea are included, the acronym becomes BRIMCK.
‡   T. Halpin, "Brazil, Russia, India and China Form Bloc to Challenge US Dominance," *London Times* (June 17, 2009); available at http://www.timesonline.co.uk/tol/news/worltl/us_and_americas/article6514737.ece.

---

productivity throughout the supply chain. Much of the entrepreneurship in resource-based economies is necessity based.

Entrepreneurs in efficiency-driven economies generally find new opportunities that create small and medium-size manufacturing firms and find ways to increase productivity. This category of economies includes, among others, Brazil, Mexico, and Russia, three of the so-called BRIC countries that are described more fully in Figure 16.3. As economies move into this development stage, reliance on necessity-based entrepreneurship is reduced and institutions tend to reflect policies that encourage opportunity-based entrepreneurship.

As economies mature, they generate more wealth per capita, the emphasis of economic activity shifts from the manufacturing to the service sector, and the economies support substantial innovation. Entrepreneurs vate sector, and entrepreneurship is more endogenously determined by individuals and firms. The command-economy approach of China can result in faster growth in sectors on which government decides to focus, but at the risk of missing opportunities or making wrong choices. The market approach of India can be better at identifying opportunities, but prospective entrepreneurs may have more difficulty arranging funding.

- China is much more open to foreign direct investment, much of it coming from former Chinese residents who live abroad. In contrast, India has not embraced foreign investment to the same degree and engages in more protectionist behavior. Lack of openness to foreign direct investment, while designed to preserve opportunities for residents of the country and build domestic businesses, exacerbates the challenges of raising capital to fund new venture opportunities. The few who can tap the capital markets are likely to benefit, even if they are not ideally suited to launch and grow the opportunities.

- Information on the economy and business entities is unreliable in China. Unreliable information hampers the ability to raise capital and to contract generally. Analysts are not independent; rather, they are state owned or controlled, as are companies on which the analysts issue reports. Moreover, market information generated by impartial, objective observers is scarce in China—the most valuable information comes from *guanxi*, a term referring loosely to a "relationship." The *guanxi* networks are important because they are the primary conduits of reliable information.

- In contrast, public information in India is plentiful and more generally reliable. Real-time stock market data on all publicly traded companies is good, in part as a result of competition between the National Stock Exchange (NSE) and the Bombay Stock Exchange (BSE). While fraud and errors do occur, India has embraced competition and market forces, whereas China has relied on government control of the stock exchanges.

SOURCES: Khanna (2007); Martha Legace, "Interview with Tarun Khanna (January 28, 2008)," *Working Knowledge*, Harvard Publishing; available at http://hbswk.hbs.edu/item/5766.html.

in innovation-driven economies are, as Schumpeter (1934) referred to them, "agents of creative destruction." Countries in this category include Japan, the United Kingdom, the United States, Norway, the Netherlands, Italy, and Israel (GEM [2009]).

This taxonomy of stages of economic development is useful as establishing a context for examining the relative successes of countries' policies for promoting entrepreneurship. The GEM project surveys entrepreneurs to ask them how many employees they expect to hire within five years' time. The prevalence of high-growth firms is important because early-stage, high-growth firms contribute a disproportionate share of the jobs created by new firms.[3] Figure 16.4 compares how active various countries' populations are in pursuing "high-growth expectation" entrepreneurship.

FIGURE **16.4**

Early-stage high-growth entrepreneurship (prevalence rate in the adult population)

SOURCE: Based on data from the Global Entrepreneurship Monitor (GEM) project (2009); available at http://www.gemconsortium.org.

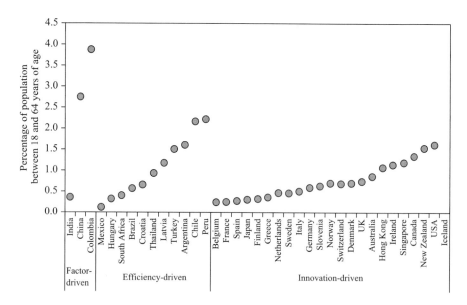

To provide context, the figure groups countries into Porter's three economic development categories. For example, China ranks high in prevalence of entrepreneurship compared to India, Peru ranks high relative to Mexico, and Hong Kong and Singapore rank high relative to France and Japan. While there are, of course, measurement errors and reporting distortions associated with survey methods and self-reported forecasts, the results illustrate the differences across countries in the level of optimism regarding growth prospects for new ventures and suggest that policy and institutions can affect this optimism.

Caveats about the Objectives of Public Policy

Whether, on net, entrepreneurship fosters economic growth is an open question. Unquestionably, entrepreneurial opportunities and infrastructure supportive of entrepreneurship can soften an economic downturn, energize a stagnant economy, and enable resources to flow quickly into new opportunities. Thus, for example, research has demonstrated a short-run relationship between entrepreneurial involvement and subsequent economic growth.[4] However, there may be opportunity costs associated with entrepreneurship. A climate supportive of entrepreneurship may entail changes in social mores (such as a tolerance of bankruptcy or increased litigation) with long-run consequences that a country may not wish to incur. It is also possible that policies aimed at fostering entrepreneurship may interfere with labor market dynamics and the smooth operation and growth of established businesses. As yet, there is no definitive understanding of the tradeoffs.

Moreover, public policy discussions would benefit from a clear definition of the goals of policy and the type of entrepreneurship that is desired. As we have noted, entrepreneurship means different things in different contexts. In a general sense, it can arise within existing organizations, both large and small, or from individual initiative. Entrepreneurial activity can be highly innovative and disruptive of existing business models; but it can also be imitative of existing business models, leading perhaps to more self-employment but not necessarily to economic growth or net job growth. Entrepreneurship can arise out of necessity (if there are no good alternative employment opportunities) or it can be opportunity driven. While these ways of thinking about entrepreneurship are not mutually exclusive, it is nonetheless imperative for policy makers to have a clear idea about the type of entrepreneurship they would like to promote.

As a corollary, there is also a useful distinction between public policy directed toward small and medium-size enterprises (SMEs) and public policy directed at encouraging innovation through entrepreneurship. While the two policies may overlap, they are not the same: SME policy is directed specifically at supporting SMEs and self-employment, whereas entrepreneurship policy is much broader.[5]

With these caveats in mind, in the discussion below we identify some key features that are linked empirically with high-impact entrepreneurial activity. We use the United States and some other countries to illustrate how these features can be employed to encourage entrepreneurship.

The Role of Institutional Structure in Stimulating Entrepreneurial Activity

The "institutional structure" of an economy is a general term for the mix of financial markets, institutions, regulations, and contracts that characterize the economy. Institutional structures vary across countries and as countries develop.[6]

The following attributes of an institutional structure are likely to stimulate new venture activity:[7]

- The institutional structure facilitates assessment of risks and rewards.
- The institutional structure limits exposure to risk and increases expected rewards.

- The institutional structure both facilitates and limits risk taking by the entrepreneur.
- The institutional structure includes patient investors with minimal need for liquidity.
- The tax structure favors capital investment.
- The institutional structure facilitates diversification and pooling of risk.
- The institutional structure provides easy access to public capital markets.
- Investment decisions are predominantly market driven.

The institutional structure facilitates assessment of risks and rewards.   The decision to pursue or invest in a venture depends on the ability to assess risks and potential rewards. Entrepreneurs and investors are more likely to be successful in settings that are conducive to producing high-quality information upon which to base their assessments. This includes sources of information on market size and market characteristics as well as on production and distribution costs.

In an information-rich environment, it generally is possible to assess market responses to new products quickly and comprehensively. In many countries, however, market information is very costly, difficult to obtain, or inaccurate, making risks and potential rewards difficult to assess.

For many high-technology fields, as well as other fields such as motion picture production and publishing, the United States is on the frontier of economic activity. Within the United States, activity is clustered in small geographic areas (Silicon Valley; Route 128; Austin, Texas; the Research Triangle in North Carolina; etc.). International examples of regional clusters include Ottawa, Canada; Seoul, South Korea; and Tel Aviv, Israel. Newly emerging clusters in Sweden and Denmark are built around technology-based industries. These regions have access to skilled human capital, legal and technical services, universities, and financial resources such as VC firms that provide finance appropriate for their sectors.

Clustering facilitates information flow among industry participants and helps each to do a more effective job of assessing market potential and competitive actions and reactions; in this way, clustering improves the accuracy of risk-reward assessments. The economic benefits of clustering, however, tend to arise organically and are not easy to nurture or replicate by deliberate action in other regions.

The United States has another important advantage that is relevant to many ventures. It is a large market, with good data on the characteristics of potential consumers, even down to small geographic areas like zip codes or census tracts. As a result, information on market responses to product introductions can be assessed quickly. With the rise of the Internet, the ability to process customer acceptance data quickly is becoming increasingly important, and the competitive advantage of US entrepreneurs may be diminishing.

The institutional structure limits exposure to risk and increases expected rewards. An important way in which institutional structure can limit risk and increase rewards is by establishing and enforcing property rights. Property rights are established both formally (through the legal system of patents, copyrights, and trademarks) and informally (through credible commitment, bonding, and reputation). The US structure fares well on both fronts. Formal legal property rights are relatively easy to establish and enforce. Good information flows promote reliance on reputation as a means of enforcing property rights.

The institutional structure both facilitates and limits risk taking by the entrepreneur. A society that insulates entrepreneurs against some of the consequences of adverse outcomes facilitates risk taking. The US institutional structure achieves insulation through several channels. First, US bankruptcy laws enable entrepreneurs to avoid destitution if their ventures fail. The entrepreneur's assets are protected, up to a point, from the claims of creditors. Entrepreneurs are also precluded from entering contracts that could indenture them to lenders and from using pension fund assets or rights to social security payments to secure obligations.

It is sometimes argued that US bankruptcy laws encourage entrepreneurs and others to take excessive risks. Examples of abuses of the bankruptcy laws are numerous. However, an important effect of the laws is on risk *allocation*. Risk that otherwise would be borne by the entrepreneur is borne instead by others (including creditors, customers, suppliers, and employees). Our analysis of the relative differences in risk tolerance between the entrepreneur and well-diversified investors leads to the implication that, as long as the effect of bankruptcy laws is purely on risk allocation, the laws are socially beneficial. This is because bankruptcy laws allow risk to be transferred to others who can bear it more easily.

Compared to many countries, business failure or bankruptcy in the United States carries relatively little social or financial stigma. Individuals who have failed at one venture are nonetheless often able to attract support for subsequent ventures. Attitudes toward failure carry over to the corporate level. In the United States, we expect pharmaceutical producers to fail in many of their development efforts and oil drillers to fail in many of their explorations. Consumer products firms occasionally market things that no one wants to buy.

The institutional structure not only facilitates taking risk but also limits the extent of the risk the entrepreneur must take. Financing and development activities accelerate discovery of the likelihood of failure and allow the parties to abandon the project quickly. This aspect of US institutional structure can be imitated in other countries by using similar contract terms. However, while the contracts directly limit financial investment, limitations on human capital investment are only indirectly related to the contract.

When an entrepreneur makes the calculation of how much human capital to invest in a venture, the entrepreneur must consider the opportunity cost of the time it will take to determine whether the venture is going to succeed or fail. Beyond this, if the venture fails or the entrepreneur is terminated, the entrepreneur must find new employment. Thus, the total commitment of human capital depends on how quickly the entrepreneur can find new employment and on how adversely the entrepreneur's earnings would be affected by failure.

In the United States, labor markets are fluid, workers are mobile, and midcareer moves are common. Consequently, the costs associated with human capital investment are lower than in economies such as Japan, where midcareer moves are difficult.

The institutional structure includes patient investors with minimal needs for liquidity. Most private money invested in entrepreneurial activity in the United States comes from either public corporations for R&D activities or institutional investors such as pension plans and endowments. Normally, these financial institutions can manage their liquidity needs from other sources, such as the dividends and interest on their other investments; and large corporations can manage liquidity needs with operating cash flows. Consequently, these investors are able to commit significant amounts of funds to new ventures quickly, without interfering with their other activities. They can also maintain investments for years without realizing any significant cash flow.

A prominent feature of the US market, with its mature VC sector, is that pension funds, endowments, and other institutions are able to invest in early-stage ventures. As described early in the book, US rules for institutional investing have had a positive influence on the growth of the VC sector and hence on generating funds for new ventures. Under ERISA, the "prudent investor" standard enables pension funds to make high-risk investments, including investments in VC.

Countries that lack significant private retirement savings programs or large endowment funds also do not have resources to support illiquid investments in new ventures. For funding of new ventures, equity has significant advantages; in particular, many ventures that are capable of rapid growth are unlikely to generate positive cash flows needed to service debt in the near term. They also typically need flexible forms of financing; flexibility allows managers to reinvest cash in the business rather than paying off debt contracts.

Pension funds have become the largest source of VC funding in the United States, United Kingdom, Ireland, and Denmark, all of which have capitalized pension funds and rules that facilitate investing in VC.[8] This type of pension regulation contrasts sharply with that of many countries, which either do not have capitalized pension funding or have prohibitions against investing in VC. In many industrialized countries, banks are the primary source of new venture financing.[9] Banks are primarily lenders, as opposed to equity investors.[10] Reliance on debt reduces the funding available to ventures that do not generate regular cash flow.

Another advantage of equity financing for new ventures is that often it is tied in with managerial and technical expertise. Most entrepreneurs are not versatile enough to come up with a good idea *and* implement it *and* manage it to maturity. In the United States, angel investors, VC firms, and other equity participants provide managerial expertise, industry knowledge, advice, contacts, and other types of support. This type of participatory financing is rare in most other countries. Active angel investor communities are not common outside of the United States and the United Kingdom. In many countries, VC firms are staffed with individuals from the commercial banking sector, who often continue to think in terms of collateral for loan repayment and do not have entrepreneurial experience.

The tax structure favors capital investment.   Tax structure affects investment in new ventures in several ways. In countries where the primary tax is based on income (not revenue or value added), for example, an entrepreneur who attempts a new venture but fails may pay no income tax. The entrepreneur's living expenses, in effect, are subsidized, compared to a system where the primary tax is on sales or value added.

Because the entrepreneur's expenditures include a large component for taxes, entrepreneurial activity in countries that emphasize value-added or revenue-based taxes is discouraged.

The differential between individual tax rates on capital gains and ordinary income can also create incentives to invest. This differential, combined with the benefit of being able to defer realization of gains, encourages investing in equity that does not generate cash flows. The entrepreneur is better off taking a larger equity stake or stock options and drawing a smaller salary.[11]

There are other ways in which the income tax structure in the United States encourages early-stage ventures to raise capital in the form of equity instead of debt. A venture that generates no taxable income cannot take advantage of the deductibility of interest payments. The net effect is that for some ventures, equity can be a less expensive form of financing on a risk-adjusted basis.

Finally, many VCs believe that the differential between capital gains and ordinary income tax is an important determinant of incentives to invest in new companies. The tax structure encourages individuals to save through tax-deferred programs such as pension funds. However, the net effect of the capital gains tax structure on VC investment is not clear. Although tax deferral makes the pension fund indifferent between dividend income and capital gains, the more important effect may be that pension funds are patient investors that do not need to invest in assets that can be liquidated easily.

International differences in tax treatment of entrepreneurs' incomes may play a role in new venture creation and success. In the United States, wealth accumulated through stock and stock option ownership is taxed as a capital gain when the securities are sold. In many European countries, including Germany and France, options are taxed as income, when granted, even though the holder may not be able to exercise the options for several years and may be short of cash to pay the taxes. Stock options often represent a large part of the financial incentive for entrepreneurs and other managers of start-up companies.

The institutional structure facilitates diversification and pooling of risk.
Ability to diversify lowers required rates of return. Wealth that is insulated from bankruptcy, rapid assessment of venture potential, and efficient labor markets all enhance the entrepreneur's ability to diversify. VC funds and public corporations represent investors that are well diversified. Even angel investors have begun to organize in ways that facilitate diversification; furthermore, most angels devote small fractions

of their total wealth to venture investments and can diversify with the remainder.

Differences across countries in firm ownership structure affect ability to diversify, take risks, and reward risk taking. State ownership is more extensive in continental Europe than in the United States or the United Kingdom. Family ownership and cooperatives/mutual organizations are also more prevalent on the continent. These differences are consistent with less reliance on private investment and equity funding. The differences may partly explain the lower levels of entrepreneurial activity. For example, many important innovations in Germany have originated from large companies such as BMW and BASF, rather than from start-up firms. The same is true for Japan, where a few dominant firms are responsible for the majority of significant innovations.

The institutional structure provides easy access to public capital markets. Well-functioning capital markets are essential to many areas of new venture investment. They enable investors to diversify, which lowers the cost of outside capital; they also enable entrepreneurs to diversify more fully, thereby lowering the entrepreneur's required return for investing in the venture. Larger, more liquid markets make it easier for an investor to profit from investing in information. Well-functioning markets provide for monitoring and means of incenting and disciplining managers. The markets also provide exit mechanisms for entrepreneurs and investors.

The market value of a financial asset is reduced by the present value of expected future transactions costs related to trading and monitoring, including costs of evaluating opportunities. Thus, public equity is less valuable if the costs of secondary market transactions are high, and private equity is less valuable if the cost of gaining access to public capital markets is high. Well-functioning capital markets have low transactions costs for raising capital and for secondary market trading.

The United States has developed significant disclosure requirements that facilitate trading of securities. Requirements for the firm to disclose information reduce duplicative search efforts and ensure that the least-cost producer of information will provide it. Requirements to disclose can move the market closer to optimal information production. Thus, capital markets that make efficient assignments of responsibility to produce information tend to have lower transactions costs.

Well-functioning capital markets promote entrepreneurial activity in other ways. Information and certification functions enable companies to transition to public ownership at earlier stages than would be possible otherwise. If ventures go public at earlier stages, entrepreneurs are able to harvest more quickly. Hastening liquidity reduces the adverse effect of the entrepreneur's higher required rate of return. Investors can liquidate their positions more quickly and are able to redeploy their human capital more efficiently. They can make larger but shorter-term commitments of human capital to the ventures in which they invest.

The US capital market includes the NYSE, several smaller exchanges, and the dealer or over-the-counter (OTC) market. Although the NYSE is the largest equity stock exchange in the world, most small companies go public on the OTC. In the United States, the OTC market hosts public trading of some of the most remarkable entrepreneurial successes of the century, including Microsoft, Intel, and others.[12]

Other countries have launched similar markets and exchanges in the last four decades.[13] These include new OTC markets in countries with established exchanges and entirely new exchanges in the so-called "emerging market countries.[14] Efforts to develop new markets and exchanges have not been particularly successful, however; the mere existence of the market is not enough if transactions costs of using the market are high and trading volume is low, as is often the case.

Partly in response to the problems experienced by the secondary markets in other countries, VCs around the world, most notably from Israel, have opted to bring companies to the US capital market for their IPOs. Doing so commits the companies to the information requirements of the US market and gives the issuer better access to US underwriters and accounting firms.

Investment decisions are predominantly market driven. Institutional structures that foster entrepreneurial activity reward entrepreneurs and investors for good decisions as to which projects to pursue, when to abandon, and when to harvest. In this context, government programs that promote entrepreneurial activity can be constructive or destructive. Subsidy programs that lower the cost of funds for investors may foster entrepreneurial activity. They are more likely to do so if the profit motive still guides fund allocation decisions and if those directly involved in investment allocation must compete for the subsidized funds in ways that preserve some benefit for the entrepreneur.

The main arguments for more proactive government involvement are that private processes fail to achieve certain social objectives and that some individuals or groups need protection from potential abuses. However, private mechanisms can promote and capitalize on positive externalities that may be related to public policy goals. Silicon Valley, for example, emerged as a private structure to capitalize on high-technology opportunities; it was not the result of any government program to nurture high technology in that region. Other industry clusters are likewise predominantly private market responses to opportunities.[15]

Public policy efforts to protect individuals from abuses can stimulate or impede entrepreneurship. Policies that lower information costs for investors and are not excessively burdensome are likely to be beneficial. Policies that restrain the contracting choices between the general and limited partners of a VC fund are more likely to impede investment than to ensure that all the parties are compensated fairly.

16.4   The Future of Entrepreneurial Finance

Much of what we have discussed concerns entrepreneurial finance as it is today. There is great potential for dramatic change, however, and for improving upon current approaches to making entrepreneurial and investment decisions related to new ventures. Thirty years ago, the market for VC investing barely existed. Twenty years from now, the market is likely to be very different from what it is today. Ten years ago, the Internet was a major focus of new venture investment, and 10 years before that it was biotechnology. Currently, the clean-tech sector (wind, solar, electric vehicles) is a focus of VC investing. No one can know what the focus will be 10 years hence. Here are a few thoughts and conjectures about the future of entrepreneurial finance.

Methods of Selecting New Venture Investment Opportunities Will Improve

Financing of entrepreneurial ventures occurred long before VC firms existed as an organizational form and long before entrepreneurial finance existed as a field of study. The field is young but is evolving rapidly, as academic research grows and innovations occur in the private sector. As these contributions increase, methods for selecting investment opportunities are certain to improve.

Both investors and entrepreneurs will develop better methods for deciding whether to pursue opportunities.   Both parties will likely pay more systematic attention to the opportunity costs of investing resources in a new venture and to the merits of the opportunity. Improvements in the technology for evaluating entrepreneurial investments are certain to continue.

The most successful investors will be those who can most accurately value and beneficially structure promising new ventures. This suggests increased competition not only in screening opportunities but also in valuing and structuring deals. Although these qualities have always been integral to smart investing, the market increasingly reflects the use of more sophisticated valuation tools. These tools include valuing real options and recognizing the value of strategic commitment. Modern valuation tools, including simulation, offer promising ways to reflect uncertainty in valuation.

In addition to tools aimed at improving the *ex ante* aspects of deal making, there is competition in postdeal development as well. Most investors, such as VCs and angels, devote considerable time to working with their investments. In the future, we expect that VCs will compete more intensely to improve portfolio company performance. Financial instruments will be designed to facilitate transactions by lowering the monitoring and enforcement costs that impede efficient investment.

Data available for assessing potential rewards and risks will improve.   Corresponding to improvements in valuation technology, availability of data that are relevant to selecting and valuing opportunities will improve. All asset pricing models and methods have information requirements. For example, the CAPM normally requires an estimate of beta and the market risk premium. When the model was introduced, its users had to devote effort to estimating both pieces of information. Now it is possible to retrieve estimates of equity betas of public companies from dozens of sources and to retrieve estimates of the market risk premium from several sources. If an approach to asset valuation is useful, companies that specialize in providing financial information will begin to generate the information that complements the valuation approach.

Better ways to structure deals will be developed.   The value of a new venture investment opportunity is sensitive to how the deal is structured—how it is staged, the flexibility options that are retained or excluded, the amount of financing provided, how risk is shared, and so on. We have a fundamental understanding of how such factors affect value, but designing value-enhancing deal structures is hard work, and the value of the effort depends on the quality of the valuation technology and information used. As the models and information sources improve, so will the quality of the deal structures.

Changes in the Set of Investment Opportunities Threaten Existing Institutions

The rate and nature of entrepreneurial opportunities are certain to change over time. Some changes will significantly threaten the viability of existing organizations and institutions, including the current division of entrepreneurial activity among individuals, corporations, universities, VC firms, angel investors, strategic partners, and others.

The rate of technological progress will change. Technological progress does not occur at a constant rate. Economies go through periods when investment opportunities are plentiful and periods when they are severely lacking. Based on Schumpeter's view of dynamic economics, a healthy economy is constantly "disrupted" by technological innovation.[16] The upswing in a cycle of economic activity starts when a set of innovations is adopted and becomes generally used. After a period of rising adoption, innovation and related entrepreneurial activity begin to decline. Historical examples include innovations in water power, iron, and textiles (late eighteenth century); steam, railroads, and steel (mid-nineteenth century); electricity, chemicals, merchandising, and internal combustion (early twentieth century); and petrochemicals, electronics, and aviation (mid- to late twentieth century). During expansionary periods, it seems that almost anyone who has money to invest can expect to profit; during slow periods, only the strongest competitors survive. Marginal competitors, faced with unacceptably low returns, tend to exit.

The latest wave in new venture activity and investment peaked in 2000. E-commerce, telecommunications, and computer software industries were booming, attracting high levels of interest in the public capital market. As the rate of entrepreneurial activity slowed, the importance of making good entrepreneurial investment decisions increased. In the current environment, firms need to reassess their existing human capital allocations. Even if good investment prospects diminish, it may be appropriate to increase the allocation of resources to investment selection and evaluation. It may become appropriate to maintain existing investments for a longer period so that harvesting can occur when the venture has a successful history backing it.

The direction of technological progress will change. Not only will the aggregate level of technological progress change, but so will the focus of technological activity. The current institutional structure in the

United States suits the kinds of new venture that emerge in the high-technology sectors. The next technological shock may require an entirely new structure and set of institutions.

In the past, some innovations have occurred in the corporate sector. In contrast, some of the more recent innovations were hatched in college dormitories and were easier to pursue by new entities unencumbered by the baggage of established physical distribution and retailing structures. There is no reason to assume that the progression over the last century represents a trend toward innovation being concentrated in this particular way. The next wave could be one for which the large corporate structure is essential.

The frontier for new opportunities will be global. Despite differences that exist across countries, the capital markets of the world are growing together. At a more basic level, corporations are diversifying internationally. Even an investor who only holds securities of US firms has a significant international risk exposure. Entrepreneurs increasingly can select between their local institutions for funding and those that exist in other countries. As the constraining effects of local financial structures are removed, the local financing environment becomes less limiting in terms of when and where technological progress occurs. Other factors, such as education, wage rates, natural resources, and distribution capabilities, gain importance as determinants of the nexus of activity. The result is that technological progress is likely to be less constrained by political boundaries or local financial market conditions.

Clustering of entrepreneurial activity will persist. Clustering is not driven by artificial or political constraints; it is an endogenous response to the advantages of agglomeration. Globalization of capital markets for new venture financing will not diminish the economic advantages of clustering. This fact has significant implications for policy makers responsible for deciding whether and how to invest resources in promoting economic development and entrepreneurship.

It is useful to recount what experience and economics have taught us about building infrastructure to facilitate growth. First, developing markets, including entrepreneurial markets, require a range and coordination of talents. Clustering makes coordination of activity less costly to accomplish. Michael Porter and others point out that close working relationships with suppliers spark innovation and that proximity to rivals enhances effective competition. Such clustering results in more efficient and quicker transfer of technical knowledge and skills.[17] In entrepreneurial markets, participants require financing and hands-on managerial help. An entrepreneur decides to locate near VCs and angel investors to reduce the cost of personal contact with the VC, rivals, and prospective partners and employees. Proximity allows the entrepreneur more frequent monitoring and arguably higher-quality managerial advice.[18]

Agglomeration economies that arise from clusters suggest that a community may develop a comparative advantage as an entrepreneurial location if it attracts a broad spectrum of specialized firms and individuals, including VCs, input suppliers, technically trained workers, accountants, lawyers, consultants, and so on. Typically, entrepreneurial groups locate near research universities that supply a stream of talented individuals with innovative ideas and connections to facilities such as computer and research labs.

As there are scale economies associated with clusters, it is likely that only a few communities will be successful in capturing them. Success depends on building a competitive advantage that is sustainable. Strategic efforts to transplant or mimic the product-market orientations of existing clusters of new venture activity (such as Silicon Valley) that do not leverage existing strengths seem poorly conceived.

Changes in the Competitive Climate Are a Threat to Existing Institutions

Separate from changes in opportunities to pursue and invest in new ventures, the competitive environment will change in ways that threaten existing institutions.

Competition among investors will intensify. As demand for opportunities to invest in new ventures grows, competitors will have access to better information and analytical capabilities. Competitors who can easily identify prospects and rapidly and accurately evaluate them are likely to win the contests to select and invest profitably in new ventures. As a result of such competition, superior ability to identify and evaluate opportunities will become valuable. Nonetheless, such an advantage is likely to be small and easily lost to competition. New ventures are often highly technical in nature. Providers of financing compete to build the technical skills needed to assess the viability of the concepts. The nature of VC firms reflects this; VC firms frequently specialize in particular industries and develop complementary human capital.

Innovations in financial instruments and contractual provisions are likely to continue and will be applied more systematically to the market for new venture finance. Competition will require both entrepreneurs and investors to develop good working knowledge of how these devices can add value to deals, as well as the risks they may pose.

Competition among investors will be increasingly global.   US venture capital firms are developing funds that focus on entrepreneurial activity in specific foreign countries. Moreover, foreign investors are significant investors in US venture capital funds. Some countries, such as the United Kingdom and Israel, have already achieved success with new venture financing capabilities that parallel those of the United States. Other countries are pursuing similar objectives. There is little to deter any VC firm from locating in one country, raising capital in another, and investing and deploying some of its human capital in a third.

The rate at which capital flows to new opportunities will increase. There is broad-based capital market recognition of the economic advantages of diversification. Individual investors increasingly are moving away from direct selection of investments and are delegating stock selection and bond selection to portfolio managers. The result is that an increasing share of investment capital is under professional management in mutual and pension funds. Furthermore, investors less frequently allow professional asset managers to engage in stock selection. In recent years, index funds have grown significantly in comparison to actively managed funds. The force driving these changes is recognition that stock selection is expensive, yet it usually accomplishes little more than random selection. Although there will always be a role for some investors to devote resources to investment valuation, most investors are better off accepting the market return.

One aspect of investment management that is lagging is asset allocation across classes of assets. For the most part, asset allocation decisions are made either by individuals, as they decide how much to invest in equity funds versus debt funds, or by pension fund managers, as they select allocations across different kinds of asset managers. Reallocating investment funds across different asset classes is relatively difficult. Indexing across (as opposed to within) asset classes, except for debt and equity, is not feasible. This is especially true for new asset classes (small-capitalization firms, international equities, emerging market equities, real estate securities, VC, and other alternative investments) that continue to be identified.

New competitive structures will emerge.   Historically, public corporations and universities have been unable to develop structures that sufficiently reward innovation within the organization. As a result, entrepreneurs have tended to create independent new ventures to develop their ideas. For the most part, the new venture finance industry exists because of this unsolved problem. The differential between required rates of return for diversified and underdiversified investors provides significant incentive for public corporations and universities to work on possible solutions. Although we do not know that a comprehensive solution is achievable, it is likely that improvements will occur. As they do, corporations and universities will likely displace individual entrepreneurs to an increasing degree.

What Will Be the Drivers of Success?

For dealing with the uncertain future of entrepreneurial finance, the drivers of success fall into two categories: short-run and long-run. The drivers are the same for entrepreneurs as they are for investors.

Entrepreneurs and investors for whom success is likely in the short run will use the best available methods and information to decide which ventures to pursue and how to structure the deals. These entrepreneurs and investors will be able to add the most value to the ventures they pursue. They will form the best teams and deal most effectively with suppliers and customers.

Entrepreneurs and investors for whom success is likely in the long run will develop organizational structures that are agile and can react quickly to changing environments and opportunities. They will perceive changes in the environment and distinguish between transformative or disruptive changes and transitory fluctuations. Finally, they will have an orientation to the future. They will abandon practices that are ill suited for the future and replace them with plans that should be effective in the new environment.

NOTES

1. For a perspective on the puzzle of why start-ups are observed when investors have lower required rates of return than entrepreneurs, see Bankman and Gilson (1999).

2. See Kaplan and Schoar (2005), Smith, Pedace, and Sathe (2010), and Sorensen (2007).

3. See Autio (2007).

4. See Global Entrepreneurship Monitor (GEM) Global Report, various years. Available online at www.gemconsortium.org.

5. See Henrekson and Stenkula (2009) and Kreft and Sobel (2005).

6. As Levine (1997) documents, economists have different opinions regarding the importance of the financial structure to economic growth. Schumpeter (1912) contends that well-functioning banks spur technological innovation by identifying and funding the entrepreneurs with the best chances of implementing innovative products and production processes. In contrast, Joan Robinson (1952) states that "where enterprise leads finance follows" (p. 86). The reasoning is that economic growth development creates demand for financial institutions that facilitate growth. Levine reviews the literature. His findings indicate that many types of studies (cross-country studies, case studies, industry- and firm-level analyses) document "extensive periods when financial development crucially affects the speed and pattern of economic development" (p. 689).

7. Milhaupt (1997) identifies five "traits of the active venture capital market" that correspond with our list of structural attributes: existence of large and independent sources of funding, liquidity, highly developed incentive structures, labor mobility, and risk tolerance.

8. In the United States, United Kingdom, Ireland, and Denmark, 1994 pension funds investment as a percentage of total VC funding represented 47 percent, 30 percent, 36 percent, and 32 percent, respectively. See O'Shea (1996). Also see Mayer, Schoors, and Yafeh (2002) for updated information on Germany, Israel, Japan, and the United Kingdom. Aside from the United Kingdom, where 49 percent of VC investment comes from pension funds, the other three countries had negligible contributions from pension funds.

9. In Mediterranean countries, for example, firms often borrow from state-owned industrial finance agencies, which in turn borrow from state banks. In Germany and most northern European countries, state-sponsored industrial finance is used less, and corporate debt largely consists of long-term bank credits. Compared to the United States and United Kingdom, the magnitude of the bank credit is larger and the terms of the debt contracts are longer.

10. In some countries, notably Japan and Germany, banks are the most important large shareholders. Banks in these countries have powerful positions as active monitors through their presence on boards and their votes in shareholder meetings.

11. Gains from investing in VC funds are currently treated in the United States as capital gains, as has been the carried interest portion of the gain that is retained by the general partner of the VC fund. Recently, the United States has focused attention on taxation of the carried interest of VC funds, private equity funds, and hedge funds. Legislation passed by the House of Representatives in May 2010 would substantially increase taxation of carried interest, treating 75 percent of it as ordinary income and 25 percent as capital gains. The bill stalled in the US Senate, however, and as of this writing, carried in-

terest is still taxed as capital gains. As evidence of the importance of the tax environment for fostering entrepreneurship, a number of fund managers have begun to relocate to Switzerland and other countries where the expected future tax treatment is more favorable. A similar migration is occurring away from the United Kingdom, for similar reasons.

12. The US OTC market includes NASDAQ, which is a highly active segment of the OTC market. Firms traded on NASDAQ often have many market makers and may have greater liquidity than some firms traded on the NYSE.

13. Jeng and Wells (2000) examine the factors that influence VC fundraising internationally. They find that the strength of the IPO market is an important determinant of VC commitments. See also Black and Gilson (1998).

14. A number of European countries have created new OTC markets, including Brussels-based EASDAQ, London's AIM, France's Nouveau Marche, Frankfurt's Neuer Markt, Belgium's Euro NM, and Amsterdam's NMAX (see Martin [1997]).

15. As an example of public intervention, Lerner (1999) finds that award recipients of the US government's Small Business Innovation Research programs contribute to certification of firm quality, but there also appear to be distortions resulting from the award process.

16. See Schumpeter (1912).

17. See Porter (1990).

18. As Dennis Weatherstone, former CEO of J. P. Morgan, once quipped, "Financial centers would not exist without lunch." This insight is equally applicable to entrepreneurial centers.

REFERENCES AND ADDITIONAL READING

Autio, E. 2007. 2007 Global Report on High-Growth Entrepreneurship. Global Entrepreneurship Monitor Project. Available at www.gemconsortium.org.

Bankman, J., and R. J. Gilson. 1999. "Why Start-Ups?" *Stanford Law Review* 51:289–308.

Black, B., and R. Gilson. 1998. "Venture Capital and the Structure of Capital Markets: Banks versus Stock Markets." *Journal of Financial Economics* 47:243–77.

Bonini, S., and S. A. Aktuccar. 2009. "The Macro and Political Determinants of Venture Capital Investments around the World." Working paper. Available at http://papers.ssrn.com/sol3/papers.cfm?abstract_id=945312.

Bottazzi, L., and M. Da Rin. 2005. "Financing Entrepreneurial Firms in Europe: Facts, Issues and Research Agenda." In *Venture Capital, Entrepreneurship, and Public Policy*, ed. V. Kanniainen and C. Keuschnigg, 3–32. Boston: MIT Press.

Gilson, R. 2003. "Engineering a Venture Capital Market: Lessons from the American Experience." *Stanford Law Review* 55 (4): 1067–1103.

Global Entrepreneurship Monitor (GEM). 2009. 2008 Executive Report, Niels Bosma, Zoltan J. Acs, Erkko Autio, Alicia Coduras, Jonathan Levie, eds. Global Entrepreneurship Research Consortium (GERA). Available at http://www.gemconsortium.org.

Gompers, P., and J. Lerner. 2001. "The Venture Capital Revolution." *Journal of Economic Perspectives* 15:145–68.

Henrekson, M., and M. Stenkula. 2009. "Entrepreneurship and Public Policy." IFN Working Paper No. 804. Available at http://papers.ssrn.com/sol3/papers.cfm?abstract_id=1458980.

Jeng, L., and P. C. Wells. 2000. "The Determinants of Venture Capital Funding: Evidence across Countries." *Journal of Corporate Finance* 6:241–89.

Kaplan, S., and A. Schoar. 2005. "Private Equity Performance: Returns, Persistence and Capital Flows." *Journal of Finance* 6 0:1791–1823.

Khanna, T. 2007. *Billions of Entrepreneurs: How China and India Are Reshaping Their Futures—and Yours*. Boston: Harvard Business Publishing.

Kreft, S., and R. Sobel. 2005. "Public Policy, Entrepreneurship, and Economic Freedom." *Cato Journal* 2 5:595–616.

Lerner, J. 1999. "The Government as Venture Capitalist: The Long-Run Effects of the SBIR Program." *Journal of Business* 72:285–318.

———. 2004. "When Bureaucrats Meet Entrepreneurs: The Design of Effective 'Public Venture Capital' Programs." In *Public Policy and the Economics of Entrepreneurship*, ed. D. Holtz-Eakin and H. S. Rosen, 1–22. Boston: MIT Press.

Levine, R. 1997. "Financial Development and Economic Growth: Views and Agenda." *Journal of Economic Literature* 35:688–726.

Martin, J. 1997. "Financing the Entrepreneurial Enterprise—the UK and Continental Europe." Paper presented at NYU Conference on Small Business Finance, May 23, 1997, New York.

Mayer, C., K. J. L. Schoors, and Y. Yafeh. 2002. "Sources of Funds and Investment Activities of Venture Capital Funds: Evidence from Germany, Israel, Japan and the UK." Oxford University working paper. Available at http://papers.ssrn.com/sol3/papers.cfm?abstract_id=308279.

Milhaupt, C. J. 1997. "The Market for Innovation in the United States and Japan: Venture Capital and the Comparative Corporate Governance Debate." *Northwestern University Law Review* 9 1:865–98.

North, D. C. 1990. *Institutions, Institutional Change and Economic Performance*. New York: Cambridge University Press.

O'Shea, M. 1996. "Venture Capital in OECD Countries." Paper no. 63 in *Financial Market Trends*, Financial Affairs Division of OECD. Bern: OECD.

Porter, M. E. 1990. *The Competitive Advantage of Nations*. New York: Macmillan.

Porter, M. E., J. J. Sachs, and J. McArthur. 2002. "Executive Summary: Competitiveness and Stages of Economic Development." In *The Global Competitiveness Report, 2001–02*, ed. M. E. Porter, J. D. Sachs, P. K. Cornelius, J. W. McArthur, and K. Schwab, 16–25. New York: Oxford University Press.

Robinson, J. 1952. "The Generalization of the General Theory." In *The Rate of Interest, and Other Essays*, 67–142. London: Macmillan.

Schumpeter, J. A. 1912. *Theorie der Wirtschaftlichen Entwicklung*. Leipzig: Dunker & Humblot. Translated as *The Theory of Economic Development* by Redvers Opie. Cambridge, MA: Harvard University Press, 1934.

Smith, R., R. Pedace, and V. Sathe. 2010. "Venture Capital: Performance, Persistence, and Reputation." Working paper, University of California, Riverside. Available at http://papers.ssrn.com/sol3/papers.cfm?abstract_id=1432858.

Sorensen, M. 2007. "How Smart Is Smart Money? A Two-Sided Matching Model of Venture Capital." *Journal of Finance*6 2:2725–62.

INDEX

Boldface terms are defined in the glossary on the text's website.

695